Hermann Hesse
Pilgrim of Crisis

By the same author

Divided: A Novel

The Lyrical Novel: Studies in Hermann Hesse, André Gide, and Virginia Woolf

Hermann Hesse

Pilgrim of Crisis

A Biography

by Ralph Freedman

Pantheon Books
New York

Copyright © 1978 by Ralph Freedman

All rights reserved under International and Pan-American Copyright Conventions. Published in the United States by Pantheon Books, a division of Random House, Inc., New York, and simultaneously in Canada by Random House of Canada Limited, Toronto.

Library of Congress Cataloging in Publication Data

Freedman, Ralph. 1920–
  Hermann Hesse: Pilgrim of Crisis.
  Includes bibliographical references and index.
  1. Hesse, Hermann, 1877–1962—Biography.   2. Authors,
German—20th century—Biography.
PT2617.E85Z6955   838'.9'1209[B]   78–51795
ISBN O–394–41981–2

Grateful acknowledgment is made to the following for permission to reprint previously published material:

Jonathan Cape Ltd. and the Estate of Hermann Hesse: Excerpts from *Autobiographical Writings* by Hermann Hesse, trans. by Denver Lindley; and *Klingsor's Last Summer* by Hermann Hesse, trans. by Richard and Clara Winston.

Farrar, Straus & Giroux, Inc.: Excerpts from *Autobiographical Writings* by Hermann Hesse, edited and with an introduction by Theodore Ziolkowski, trans. by Denver Lindley. Trans. Copyright © 1971, 1972 by Farrar, Straus & Giroux, Inc. Excerpts from *Crisis* by Hermann Hesse, trans. by Ralph Mannheim. Trans. Copyright © 1975 by Farrar, Straus & Giroux, Inc. Excerpts from *Klingsor's Last Summer* by Hermann Hesse, trans. by Richard and Clara Winston. Trans. Copyright © 1970 by Farrar, Straus & Giroux, Inc.

Princeton University Press: Excerpts from C.G. Jung, *Letters*, edited by Gerhard Adler and Aniela Jaffe, trans. by R.F.C. Hull, Bollingen Series, XCV, *Vol. 1*, 1906–1950. Copyright © 1971, 1973 by Princeton University Press.

Deutsches Literaturarchiv, Schiller National Museum, Marbach, West Germany: Excerpts from *Hermann Hesse: Neue deutsche Bücher. Bonniers Literrära Magasin (1935–1936)*, edited by Bernhard Zeller. 1965.

Fretz und Wasmuth, Zurich, Switzerland: Excerpts from *Hermann Hesse–Romain Rolland: Briefe,* 1954.

Gundert Verlag: Excerpts from *Marie Hesse*, edited by Adele Gundert, 1953.

Suhrkamp Verlag, Frankfurt, West Germany: Excerpts from *Briefe*, 2, Auflage, 1965. Excerpts from *Gesammelte Briefe*, edited by Volker Michels and Heiner Hesse, Vol. 1, 1973. Excerpts from *Gesammelte Werke*, Werkausgabe Edition, Vols. VI and X, 1970. Excerpts from *Kindheit und Jugend vor 1900*, edited by Ninon Hesse, 1966. Excerpts from *Materialien zum "Glasperlenspiel,"* Vols. I and II, 1973, 1974. Excerpts from *Materialien zum "Steppenwolf,"* 1972. Excerpts from *Piktors Verwandlungen*, 1976. Also unpublished manuscripts on deposit in Deutsches Literaturarchiv, Schiller National Museum, Marbach, West Germany, Copyright © Suhrkamp Verlag, Frankfurt.

Grateful acknowledgment is made to the following for the use of illustrations:

Buchhandlung, J. J. Heckenhauer. Antiquariat. Tübingen, West Germany
Das Basler Missionshaus, Basel, Switzerland
Schiller National Museum, Marbach, West Germany
Suhrkamp Verlag, Frankfurt, West Germany

Manufactured in the United States of America

FIRST EDITION

For my children and stepchildren
Molly, John, Jonathan
Stephen, and Mark,
who grew as this book grew;
and in memory of
Ruth,
who had just begun

He was transformed. And because this time he had achieved the correct, eternal transformation, because he had now became a whole from a half, he could, from this hour on, transform himself as much as ever he wanted. Constantly the magic stream of becoming flowed through his blood, eternally he took part in Creation rising new each hour.

He became deer, he became fish, he became man and snake, cloud and bird. In each incarnation, however, he was wholly himself, was a pair, contained moon and sun, contained male and female in himself, flowed as a double river through all the lands and stood as a twin star in the sky.

—From "Piktor's Metamorphoses"

Contents

List of Illustrations

xi

Acknowledgments

During the years I worked on this book, I received generous help from all sides. My research was greatly facilitated by the staff of the Deutsche Literaturarchiv, Schiller National Museum, Marbach, West Germany. First and foremost, therefore, I want to thank Professor Bernhard Zeller and his helpful assistants, as well as the former curator of the Hesse Collection, Dr. Walther Migge. I am especially grateful to Heiner Hesse for easing access to previously unpublished material and for many long and important conversations. Similarly, I want to thank Volker and Ursula Michels, who kept me in touch with the flow of Hesse material they have edited and published, and with whom I was able to broaden my views through lengthy discussions.

This is also the time to salute Fred Haines, creator of the film *Steppenwolf*, with whom I worked during several productive months.

Throughout this biography, I have referred as much as possible to available translations. Unpublished texts were especially translated for this volume. As my notes show, all material I knew to be unpublished when this book went to press is cited, without specific footnotes, from the collection of Hesse's correspondence on deposit at Deutsches Literaturarchiv. It is quoted by permission both of the director, Professor Zeller, and of the Suhrkamp Verlag, Frankfort, West Germany, which holds the copyright. Some of the unpublished letters have since appeared in Volume II of *Kindheit und Jugend vor 1900* (*Childhood and Youth Before 1900*), edited by Gerhard Kirchhoff. Similarly, further letters cited as unpublished will appear in the forthcoming second and third volumes of *Gesammelte Briefe* (*Collected Letters*), edited by Heiner Hesse and Volker Michels.

Among my friends and colleagues at Princeton, I want to acknowledge with pleasure those valuable hours of talk with Theodore Ziolkowski, as well as his writings, from which I learned a great deal, especially about Hesse's reception in America. I also wish to express appreciation for the fine help I received from William McGuire. And warm thanks to Robert Fagles for his encouraging way of removing bureaucratic obstacles where they arose.

Last but not least, I owe a debt of gratitude to my editor, James Peck, and his assistant, Jeffrey Faude, for many months of caring.

My thanks, then, are manifold but the responsibility is my own for this life of Hermann Hesse, a pilgrim of crisis.

—Ralph Freedman
Princeton, New Jersey
August 1978

Hermann Hesse
Pilgrim of Crisis

PROLOGUE
A Perspective

I

Never since his youth had Klein been left so starkly and solitarily to
his emotions. Never had he been exposed so utterly to alien surroundings, been so naked beneath the sharp, inexorable sunlight of fate. He
had always been busy with something, with something other than himself. . . . Now he was suddenly suspended naked in space, confronting
sun and moon alone, and he felt that the air was icy and rarefied.

—From "Klein and Wagner"

DISCLOSURE IS ALWAYS intriguing, and literature is no exception.
The masks artists have created for themselves have been persistently
raised to allow the curious and the morbid a glimpse at the man underneath—his face at times anguished, at times quite bland. On the surface,
this temptation to know more than meets the eye is easily explained. We
all love gossip, and biography is gossip sublime. Yet nearly eight decades
of psychoanalytic thinking have sharpened our perceptions. We look for
truths about works of art not only in the texts themselves but also in the
personal dynamics of the men and women who produced them—in their
hidden deformities, in the suffering that lies behind their work; and often
we believe that these are truths greater than those we have deciphered in
the texts.

Such psychic probing, of course, has not gone unchallenged. Our
curiosity about writers' lives may eventually be satisfied, but in the end
we are tempted to ask whether the satisfaction was worth the candle. The
practice, until recently most prevalent among critics, of denying altogether the relevance of an author's life to his works may well have been
motivated, in part, by a delicate response to just this sort of inquiry, an
attempt to cover up nakedness, just as Noah's sons, walking backward,
covered the nakedness of their father. Today, a new romanticism has
again placed a premium on nakedness, but the problems it has raised
remain largely unsolved.

3

Clearly, we would not indulge our wish to know more about an author if he had not written books and stories that are, in some sense, important. We must therefore examine how our knowledge of a writer, our empathy, our identification with him, clarifies his books for us; how the love and suffering in a man's work are illuminated by the love and suffering in his life. The problems involved are both obvious and manifold, and they are demonstrated with exceptional clarity in the life and work of Hermann Hesse—that remote yet public artist whose reputation grew from the confines of his native Swabia and Switzerland to embrace not only the entire German-speaking world but also Japan and, particularly after his death, the United States.

Reshaping personal feelings and encounters into artifacts is, of course, the task and craft of artists. But in Hesse, far more than in most modern writers, this process can be illuminated in quite an extraordinary and incomparable way.[1] Hesse's struggle for a sense of self led him to write relentlessly about even the most mundane experiences of his life, as if each were unformed material waiting to be fashioned, through the power of the written word, into a work of art.

Through Hesse's incessant writing—formally in his fiction and poetry, informally in his innumerable letters and diaries—the line between his conscious and unconscious experience was artistically drawn. He acted and wrote as though everything in his daily life had to be brought into a circle of tension, where an unceasing quest for form was at the heart of his sustained effort to hold his life together. Although this is also true of other artists, in Hesse the immediacies of his life are incessantly, and at times almost unreflectively, transformed and molded through the word.

Throughout his life, Hesse sought to maintain this remarkably fluid boundary between life and art, daily routine and creativity, sanity and psychological crisis, through his studiously pursued role as an artist. In view of this extraordinary confidence in the healing power of art, it is indeed surprising that he neither wrote a full-length autobiography nor published long sequences from his diaries or journals. In fact, what he did do was to construct in his published and unpublished writings a single "creative autobiography," which this book seeks to capture.

For these reasons, the relation between Hesse as an individual and the persona he projects in his books is both simpler and more complex than might be anticipated—simpler because many of the biographical analogies are so striking that it is seductively easy to discern their relevance to his novels and stories; more complex because we may be so dazzled by these biographical analogies that we ignore their transformation. Nor can we stop with Hesse's novels, stories, and poems. The letters and other personal documents in themselves comprise a new work with constantly shifting personae. This is especially true of such important published collections as Ninon Hesse's documents about Hesse's childhood or the exchanges with Thomas Mann, Karl Kerenyi, R. J. Humm, and his publisher Peter Suhrkamp. Each time the editor has been forced, by the sheer volume of Hesse's oddly impersonal revelations, to mold his material into narrative form. This is particularly true of the rich first volume of Hesse's collected letters, which creates episodes of an impressive story by the sheer force of its content.

Such biographical material, then, is as much a part of Hesse's art as his narratives are representative of episodes in his life. Always these events, which extend from a visit to an eye clinic to his father's death, are reshaped in the telling to project a certain image or pose. Hesse's stories—like the dreams he collected in special notebooks—are told from both conscious and unconscious experience and therefore reveal and conceal events, encounters, and feelings from himself, his friends, his public. The way Hesse lived and wrote about his life, constantly aware of his conflicting impulses as part of the tension of his art, made this revelation and concealment permeate all his writings. If such is the predicament of the modern artist, it has rarely been so evident as in the life and work of this man.

Each of the many episodes in Hesse's long history has therefore been a subject of debate. Beginning with the romanticism with which he has been charged and praised since his first biographer, Hugo Ball, so described him during the twenties, to questions about his marriages and his friendships with men, which seemed to supersede and contradict them, to the volatile problem of his politics—all these matters remain unclear because following the impulse of his antithetical mind, Hesse both disclosed and obscured these issues and their implications for his work.

These many different aspects of Hesse's consciousness, insofar as we can reconstruct them from his testimonies, are fashioned by his conviction that, like Jean Jacques Rousseau, he embodied those divisions of his age which have left their mark on our culture. They demonstrate most lucidly Hesse's profoundly moral concern that arose from this insistent and pervasive reconstruction of himself. Having begun as an autodidact as a child, Hesse always remained a teacher. He made himself into an example for his readers, just as Rousseau, by no means a stranger to the art of disclosure and concealment, had presented himself in his *Confessions*. With its "pole" and "counterpole," Hesse's work became an ongoing act of instruction even as it took the shape of a continuous novel. In this close interrelation of personal, moral, and artistic concerns lies the value, as well as the great difficulty, of Hermann Hesse's achievement.

II

Hesse had striven to be an artist from childhood on and had absorbed his personal life into his work. In a manner unique among writers, he wove his immediate experiences into his books to portray many of the dilemmas and historic crises of his time. If one element of this biographical reconstruction of his work is to trace many of Hesse's daily encounters in his official writings, another is to show how he saw, experienced, and ultimately endured the social and political life around him. It was this finely tuned interaction between his psychological conflict and historical events that was to make him a poet of crisis.

Crisis in the poet's eye found its resonance in the minds and hearts of his readers. Hesse's life—with its many private and public relationships, its politics, its book reviewing, its theories and fiction—became a mirror in which entire generations since the beginning of the century have seen themselves reflected. In this manner, Hesse, so often dismissed as inconsequential, could become again and again a cult figure for many who believed he pointed the way to solutions neither novels nor poems ordinarily attempt, to lead them, in some biblical way, out of the crises in which they were caught.[2] No dynamic constitutes a more crucial dimension in any portrait of Hermann Hesse and the great, almost disproportionate influence he wielded over several generations.[3]

Crisis showed itself in the world around Hermann Hesse from his earliest childhood. The Hesses were missionaries, and the very terms of their vocation made it necessary for them to live in two worlds and several faiths at once while still maintaining their own convictions. Crisis also existed in Hesse's personal life. When he was just six years old, he was sent away to live in the mission school in Basel because he was too unmanageable at home. All of these are matters that might produce a sense of crisis, but they are also incidents that arose from a peculiar social and cultural admixture—a missionary family, pietism, and a blend of puritanism, sentimentality, and evangelical fervor. In a most impersonal way, crisis also existed in the historical context within which Hesse grew up. There were not yet any world wars to contend with, but his young years coincided with the first two decades of the new German Empire formed by Bismarck in 1871. As one of the consequences for the Hesses, the border between German Württemberg, where they mostly lived, and Switzerland, which was their other home, became more of a barrier; and an alien, militant industrialism began to invade their lives. These early crises are nothing compared to the upheavals of the twentieth century, both in Hesse's personal life and in the world around him, but they do document the interaction between his personal and historical perceptions later conveyed to his readers.

Both responding to crises and being responded to by his readers, Hesse rode the crests of several waves of enthusiasm for his work at specific points: at the beginning of the century, when he was only twenty-seven; toward the end of the First World War, when he had turned forty; after the Second World War; and finally, mostly after his death, in the United States. All of these are moments of psychological, social, and cultural crisis. This coincidence with recurrent phases of Hesse's popularity may explain why this withdrawn man, this mountain climber and restless traveler, could have evoked such a variety of responses in such different settings.

Each point was not only an important moment in Western history— the beginning or end of a war, industrial or economic crisis, social insecurity or public unrest—but also a turning point, a change of direction in the world and in the readers' response to it. When Hesse's first successful novel, *Peter Camenzind*, appeared in 1904, his fame rested not only on the beautiful evocations of the Bernese landscape or on the long conversations about art, but also on his ability to express a sense of hidden danger. The simple life away from the corrupt cities was threatened, and this fear affected not just Hermann Hesse but also an entire generation of readers. When a few years later *Beneath the Wheel* added immeasurably to his reputation by exposing the impersonal "wheel" of established education crushing youth, he once again pointed to a crisis in private and public life. Hesse's Peter was not simply a young artist, just as his schoolboys were not merely unhappy children in a secondary boarding school; rather, they all embodied a "counter-culture" determined to fend off the encroachments of technology and the impersonal state.

The next important turn came at the end of the Great War, when Hesse's *Demian* was published anonymously. The book addressed itself to readers born around the turn of the century who now, at the threshold of adulthood, were facing the aftereffects of a long, lost war. At this juncture, the crisis was both historical and psychological. *Demian* dealt with the war's end and with the resulting shift in personal and public values; but it also dealt with the sexual fears and fantasies of young adults at the brink of maturity. These were the conditions both of the hero, Emil Sinclair, who at first was also the declared author, and of the saviors like Demian who wisely led him out of his despair.

One reason for Hesse's success with *Demian* can be ascribed to his dual impulse: his ability to both criticize the war and empathize with those who were its victims. What made this novel so effective for German audiences at the time was Hesse's sense that war was a terrible disaster, coupled with his feeling of intimacy not only with those who had fought and died in it but also with those who, although too young to have been soldiers, had suffered a crisis of values nonetheless. Hesse counseled a spiritual renewal without the cant of the political factions of the left and right then dominating the political scene. He also countered the teaching of the schools and the ideals of commerce and business his readers associated with their parents. His early success had been the creation of a new language based on the mystique of the individual self. Now he could write in his introduction to *Demian*: "I only wished to live out fully what sought to break out of me. Why was that so hard?" This idea of *Verinnerlichung*—or internalization—fashioned a bond between Hesse and his readers.

A third wave naturally followed the Second World War, less typical than the others because it affected mostly those older German readers whose imaginations had been captured in their youth by *Demian* and *Narcissus and Goldmund*. When *The Glass Bead Game*, first published in Switzerland in 1943, came to the attention of a broad German public after the war's end in 1945, it at first left a deep impression. With its network of learned references, musicology, and philosophy, this novel opened the door to an academic vogue, particularly inasmuch as the book made a point of turning away from direct political involvement. Furthermore, in the midst of the post-war crisis of 1946, Hesse received the Nobel Prize for Literature, a sign that at least cultural wounds were being bound, since this important prize was given to a German writer who had been neither an emigrant nor a Nazi.

During the first years after the end of the war, Hesse took every opportunity to state his political position. In fact, his commitment as a writer began to turn from imaginative to political writing. His various essays, however, could not conceal that for many young readers of 1946 and 1947, Hesse was the author of their parents' generation. He was, many of them felt, too deeply implicated in the romantic values of the past, which they now sought to repudiate. During the fifties, young Germans in particular stopped reading Hesse, and he was treated with an increasing measure of distrust by younger writers like Günter Grass and Heinrich Böll, who saw in his *Verinnerlichung* an unfortunate legacy of the past. Only quite recently has there been a slight revival of Hesse in Germany, but he is still far from regaining the appreciation he once enjoyed in the German-speaking world.

III

A fourth wave of enthusiam for Hermann Hesse occurred in America during the sixties, opening the door to a far wider international reputation than he had previously enjoyed.[4] Again, the immediate occasion of this wholly unanticipated revival was a crisis—or rather, a premonition of crisis—introduced by the discontent of the late fifties and enlarged to almost incredible proportions at the time of the political and social frustrations of the Johnson and Nixon years. Until that time, Hesse had lain fallow; even the Nobel Prize he received in 1946 did not stimulate trade in his works, and by the early fifties most of his books were being remaindered. At that time, Hesse came to the attention of the American public almost by accident—a suggestion by Henry Miller to his followers that the small novel *Siddhartha*, beautifully translated by Hilda Rosner and published at Miller's suggestion in 1951, pointed out a new mystical way that fulfilled many of the expectations of the time. Miller was eminently correct in his perception: especially after it appeared in paperback in 1957, *Siddhartha* began to be read more widely than it had ever been read in the original during its thirty years of existence.

The crucial book for America, however—equal in force to *Peter Camenzind*, *Beneath the Wheel*, and *Demian* during the German crises earlier in the century—was *Steppenwolf*. Its almost mythical rise in the mind of the American counter-culture beginning in the late fifties marked the origins and contours of the Hesse phenomenon in the United States. The roots of this revival can be traced to the publication, in 1956, of Colin Wilson's *The Outsider*, which projected an image of Hesse as the symbolic figure of the age that had just produced Jack Kerouac's *On the Road*.[5] The notion of being "outside the system," of creating a new "subterranean" culture, was paradoxically associated with Hesse, who for his own countrymen is very much a part of the German literary tradition. It is nonetheless clear that the symbolically urban, underground novel *Steppenwolf* suitably reflected the attitudes of those who read it. In the late fifties and early sixties, the so-called Beat Generation in and around San Francisco first took up that novel. By 1963, when the Vietnam War began to take on serious dimensions, *Steppenwolf* became a bible for all. In a now classic essay, Timothy Leary described the novel as a psychedelic journey; and while this view of Hesse's book represented only one aspect of the vogue he had created, it was an important one.[6]

Leary's article, "Hermann Hesse: Poet of the Interior Journey," followed, in the main, Hesse's actual course in the book, since that novel clearly pointed in the direction of the Way Within. But by associating it with the drug culture, which he traced to the twenties as well as to his own time, Leary and his collaborator, Ralph Metzner, highlighted a particular solution—that of the heightened sensibility seeking to establish its own distinct universe in response to a corrupt and menacing external "reality." Psychologically, this perception was not wholly out of tune with the way Hesse thought. Like others of his age, he still believed that in the interior life of the imagination there exist reservoirs of power that allow men and women to overcome a threatening and oppressive world. It was therefore easy to identify that stress on the *artistic* imagination with an interior psychedelic journey as an important dimension of Hesse's significance.

American interest in Hesse did not remain limited to Timothy Leary and his coterie. Waves of enthusiasm radiated from the East to the West, from the Midwest to the South; from junior and senior high school students to those in colleges and universities and people in all walks of life. Approval of Hesse had never been this extensive in Central Europe, where he had been essentially read as a middle-class writer in *Gymnasiums* and universities and by members of the white-collar professions. But the young readers on a continent where he thought he would never be understood responded to his uncanny knowledge of what it means to be young and especially what it means to want both acceptance and approval by authority and the freedom to protest its injustice. Hesse's wide acclaim was possible in part because translation blurred the distinct upper-middle-class flavor of his original language; but the main reason his acclaim took on such unexpectedly great proportions was that Hesse was being read in an entirely new way. The counter-culture that came to appreciate him so volubly in America—and soon in South America, England, and France as well—detached him from his Central European milieu and created an almost entirely different Hermann Hesse.[7]

Hesse's famous dictum that he could never be appreciated by more than "ten people" in the United States has often been held up as one of those wild misapprehensions even great men can suffer. Like Rainer Maria Rilke, Hesse thought of America as a technological inferno without a soul, and he feared that Germany and Switzerland might soon follow its example. Hesse may not have been far wrong about his assessment of the "real" Hesse's chances in the United States, for a new, ahistorical Hesse was being constructed by his readers. In Germany, Hesse's following—which often viewed itself as part of a counter-culture—was drawn to different books than was his American audience, and its image of Hesse himself was also quite different. In the German-speaking world, Hesse had often been seen as an outdoor author: *Peter Camenzind* led the way, but the important Swabian stories, the novellas of *Knulp*, and even the mythology of *Demian* were concerned with a polemic between nature and spirit, and a corrosive civilization. Where he was not dismissed as the usual German romantic author of sensitive "family novels," Hesse was viewed as a guide for the young whose interior salvation was more often than not identified with a return to nature. In the novels of the twenties, this polemic was sharpened: nature was replaced by art and eventually by a spiritual regeneration that had been provided by his Indian and Chinese researches.

In America, by contrast, Hesse was seen far more radically as the writer of man's interior, psychological life, and as a mystic of the East. His involvement in psychoanalysis, clearly known in Germany but perhaps of less significance there at the time, was made into a central issue, and the symbolic world he reconstructed served the readers of the most varying levels of sophistication—from young people who had adopted a "hippie" way of life to conventional students in secondary schools and universities. It was a peculiarity of this generation that a writer could be meaningful only if he were stripped of both his artistic disguises and his connections with a specific time and place. For these readers, Hesse's stories were not fiction in the ordinary sense but texts for instruction and meditation. Although he had served as a mentor for his many European admirers during his lifetime; although he had been flooded with letters and with young people who, on foot and on bicycles, had come to his retreat in Montagnola to seek his advice, he had remained, for the most part, a human sage and teacher. In his American incarnation, however, he became a myth—a mixture of Jesus and Buddha in no way tied to contemporary time schedules or geography.

In this ahistorical role, Hesse enjoyed posthumously an explosion of acclaim considerably greater than anything he had enjoyed during his lifetime. His books glut newsstands even today; commercial interests have moved in with T-shirts displaying motifs from his novels; and his stories have been reduced to comic-book form and other expressions of the mass culture Hesse so despised. A night club in San Francisco and a rock group have been named after *Steppenwolf*, and *Siddhartha* has been used to advertise many establishments from cafés to boutiques. These commercial interests could avail themselves of the Hesse phenomenon in America as they never could have in Europe because the class base of his acclaim is wider in the United States. Still, this success has so far not extended into areas where one would have most expected it: television and film.

Two movie versions of Hesse's books have thus far been attempted by international companies but with an eye on the American market. *Siddhartha* was filmed by Conrad Rooke; *Steppenwolf* was written and directed by Fred Haines. Both were commercial failures, even though Hesse's popularity was at its zenith at the time. The reasons (despite some excellent acting, beautiful photography, and sensitive handling of character) may well lie in the peculiar nature of Hesse's appeal, which had re-created and constructed a *phenomenon* of the imagination. Not only were his novels pretexts for self-exploration (and seldom taken seriously as fiction), but their very nature precluded dramatization. For as texts of instruction and edification, they were not suitable for visual representation. The figures that enacted the various changes of the hero's psyche were so clearly dreamlike and allegorical that the partially realistic setting contradicted the anticipated dreams. There was no real India in *Siddhartha*; there was no real Basel and Zurich of the twenties in *Steppenwolf*. There was only a dream and a sermon spoken by a mythical persona, Hermann Hesse.

The recent decline of Hesse's popularity, at least on the two coasts of America, can be traced to a number of causes. The Vietnam War has been over since 1975; economic hardship has made job security more important than visions of self-consciousness detached from mundane pursuits and directed toward individual freedom; and the drug culture no longer requires validation from Hermann Hesse. But a further share of this decline is quite probably due to just the kind of demythification of Hesse's persona, and of the interior universe he has created, that has become more and more prevalent in recent years. Factual material has poured from the presses; *College Outline* series has treated him as though he were any other writer taught in the schoolroom.[8] In fact, the entire business of uncovering the myth of Hermann Hesse—that Sage of the Interior Journey—may have been counter-productive.

A very private public poet, elevated to a universal Master Teacher whose symbolic explorations of the self were above place and time, now stood exposed as a writer who had labored in Germany and Switzerland from 1877 to 1962; who had wives, worries, and a career to think about; who was, in short, stripped of his mythical garb. Possibly Hesse, the actual writer, will survive this demythification and be read like any other major author of our difficult century; but from Hesse's myth the disguises have been removed, and his image must be reconsidered. To this end, too, this book has been dedicated.

IV

A biographical interpretation of Hermann Hesse, and the myth projected about him, reveals a common denominator which his enthusiasts shared through the various decades of his intermittent acclaim. This synoptic view reveals that the common denominator has been an awareness and a mirroring of social crisis in the individual psyche and of the poet in his audience.

The reciprocal tension in which Hesse's self-detailed documentations relate to his works explains his success in reflecting his own personal crises in the crises of his time, which eventually encompassed the crises of his entire culture. It was in this sense that he could give so much to so many even as he often withdrew personally. During his long, difficult life, and that slow, quiet death, Hesse gave sustenance and guidance to too many to be ignored. If he is not always acknowledged as a literary master, or if questions can be raised about the depth and complexity of his style, he nonetheless remains enormously significant to the social historians of our age. Hermann Hesse continues to be a force of considerable magnitude as he reflects the uncertainties and betrayals of our history from the late nineteenth century to the present—a poet of crisis who achieved his identity as a pilgrim into the inner life.

1

Childhood
and Its Discontents

I

I walked, shivering, among the ruins of the world of my youth, over
broken thoughts and distorted dreams, with twitching limbs, and whatever my eyes fell upon turned into dust and ceased to live. . . . I was
avoided. Soon I was surrounded by an enormous void, a windless
quiet. I had no one close to me, no loved ones, no community; and my
life rose up within me and I was shaken with disgust. As though each
measure were filled to overflowing, as though each altar had been
desecrated and each sweetness turned into ugliness, as though each
height had been conquered. . . .

THIS SHARPLY ETCHED portrait of isolation and guilt, written at
the age of twenty, was Hermann Hesse's interior landscape as a boy and
young man. It is a grim picture drawn in his first book of prose, *One
Hour Behind Midnight*, a motley collection of vignettes and prose poems,
partly picturesque and heavily symbolic, partly sweetened with sentiment.
From its pages unfolds a sense of unworthiness, of degradation, of a
gloomy awareness of the passage of life. The prose poem's title, however,
"Incipit Vita Nova," suggests a counterpoint, a new life emerging from
such isolation and despair. "New stars arise in the firmament, new eyes
within ourselves," Hesse wrote in a later passage. Still, beneath the
sentimental crust of a young man's self-important words lies a sharply
focused picture of inner darkness.

When we look at the places which have marked Hermann Hesse's
childhood, at the photographs and letters of his father and mother, his
sisters and brothers, his grandfather and uncles, it is difficult to believe
in the reality of this despair. Born on July 2, 1877, in the small Swabian
town of Calw on the River Nagold, Hesse grew up in a large and
sprawling but deeply interdependent family of pious Protestants that at
first glance would seem to have provided the underpinnings of a secure
personal existence. Both his parents were devout Pietists. His maternal
grandfather had been a missionary for the Pietist faith in India and his

15

father and mother had both worked there. Moreover, their lives were controlled and protected by a benign organization, the Pietist mission in Basel, in which both his grandfather and father were prominent. There was no lack of daily bread. And the two places where he grew up—provincial Calw embedded among the ridges of the Black Forest mountains, and the stolid, brown-tinted city of Basel—provided modest but firm roots in the middle class. No apparent quicksands anywhere. Bible teaching and earnest entreaties may have seemed burdensome, but there was also tenderness and a sense of community, of family.

Yet this life was punctuated by cries of anguish at night, by defiances in the face of frequent altercations, by withdrawals and impotent weeping. In the midst of apparent warmth, the family responded to a recurring sense of crisis stubbornly perpetuated by their second child, Hermann. Where did it begin? With the wide-eyed child that looks out of the voluminous photo albums kept by the family? With Dr. Gundert, his overpowering maternal grandfather with his white beard and enormous white sideburns, with the stern voice and the humorous twinkle in his eye? Or with Johannes, the thin, ascetic-looking father and his incessant headaches? Or with Marie, his mother, whose almost severe mask—an impassive broad face framed by her black bonnet—was contradicted by her warm, lively eyes? Her lips were thin as if drawn into her mouth. Her bust seemed to be enclosed by armor. Yet as Dr. Gundert's humorous eyes contradicted his severity, so his daughter's eyes radiated feelings that contrasted visibly with the mask of her face.

One can begin to search for these contradictions in the family itself, for they were all moved by conflicting impulses. They seemed replete with personal ambition, yet they placed themselves at the service of an intractable though deeply emotional religion that, in turn, was part of their unique regional culture. For life in Swabia—at that time the kingdom of Württemberg—with its small picturesque towns and centers of literature and art, had been deeply marked by its Protestantism, which was different from the Lutheranism of the north. Living almost in an enclave in the Catholic south, many Swabian Protestants remained Nonconformists, and Pietism, a strict but highly personal religion, was allowed to grow roots in their region. It was a religion based on personal faith and piety, but it was also formed by a highly puritanical strain. Having emerged in the seventeenth century following the Thirty Years' War in response to the increasing orthodoxy of official Lutheranism, Pietism presented a more evangelical Luther. Hesse's biographer of the 1920s, Hugo Ball, who, though Catholic himself, was deeply involved in the cultural ambience of Swabian Pietism, described it accurately and with feeling:

The Pietists have rediscovered the mystically steeped Luther who had been almost forgotten in the midst of religious strife and princely Enlightenment. People who want to be or become Brothers or Saints, are guided by an enthusiasm which, however childish its external forms may be, is in league with eternity. In the Baltics and in Swabia this movement that sought awakening [in an evangelical way] bore the most profound and very often the most ascetic features.[1]

On the one hand, then, this movement took Luther's confrontation with the devil seriously: it exhorted to ascetic discipline and service and expressed the usual abhorrence of sensual indulgence and sin. On the other hand, it also insisted on taking literally the immediate closeness between God and man's consciousness and conscience. Feeling and sentiment were elevated above ritual and intellect. In moving in both of these directions at once, Pietist thought deepened the opposition between authority and self while paradoxically bringing them together. And since Hermann Hesse's family was composed of Pietist theologians, the conflicts that occurred in their daily lives were seen as mirroring those embedded in the precepts by which they sought to live.

Sentiment and severity went hand in hand in Dr. Hermann Gundert, the patriarch and guiding spirit of the family, who did much to shape Hesse's youth.[2] Young Hermann Hesse remembered him as a man of grandeur, both stern and kind, molded by selfless service. Gundert had pioneered for his religion as others in that age of the white man's burden had conquered new markets and land. Born in Stuttgart in 1814, educated as a theologian and linguist, he responded at twenty-one to a request by a Nonconformist English missionary, originally a manufacturer of false teeth, named A. Norris Grove, to accompany him to India as the tutor of his sons. They set out from Liverpool in 1835—a small party of Protestant dissenters from various countries—to take their faith to the Hindus and Moslems of India. They arrived in the summer of 1836 to begin their work.

Young Dr. Gundert's first two years as a missionary reflect many of the vagaries of religious politics of the time. After arriving in Madras, Grove decided to remain, but he sent out Gundert to make contact with some German missionaries who worked some distance away. Conflict ensued—Gundert wanted to join the German brothers but Grove would not release him—but after two years, following the death of the head of the German mission, he was allowed to take charge of that group. Gundert accepted happily, especially since he had just spent two depressing years of misery and isolation. He hoped for better times at the promised new post, but before he could assume it, he had to marry.

To fulfill the requirement, Hermann Gundert chose Julie Dubois, a French-Swiss woman who had been part of their original group and was a devoted worker in the children's wing of the mission. She was not much to look at, young Dr. Gundert confessed in one of his letters home, but endowed with great capacity for hard work. She was "short, slender, and nimble." "The hotter it is the better she works." A strict Calvinist, she was later described by her granddaughter as someone who belonged more in the seventeenth than in the nineteenth century. Filled with a burning desire to "save souls," she loathed housework ("In Heaven no one cooks and cleans any longer!") and labored indefatigably at her missionary tasks. She also never quite learned German, her husband's language (her daughter was to correspond with her only in French or English), although, paradoxically, she acquired the local Indian dialects better than "learned Mrs. Grove."[3]

Hermann Gundert and Julie Dubois were married when they were twenty-four and twenty-nine respectively. Courtship and wedding were part of a public service. Letters and notes quoted by Ninon Hesse, their grandson's third wife, tell a pathetic story of the beginning of their relationship, entered into without inclination. For the bride, the decision to marry had been as much an act of service as it had been for her suitor. She felt deeply inferior to him and merely promised to serve him well. They were quickly married at the Groves' house, then set out for the new post, traveling by ox cart, teaching and preaching on the way. When they reached their destination Gundert was not satisfied. His post had in the meantime been turned into an English operation, while he wanted to preach his own Swiss-Swabian Pietism. The Gunderts continued on to Malabar, changing their base of support from Grove and his English Nonconformists. After some negotiations they were accepted by the Mission Institute in Basel. In its service, decades went by; with time out for ill health, their arduous life in India lasted twenty-two years.

For Hesse's mother, Marie, born in Malabar in October 1842, the key to childhood was emotional hardship, a condition that rarely changed even in her adult years. In her autobiography she characterized herself as sad: "A joyous, red-cheeked child that would capture all hearts at once with its laughter and baby talk I was not; rather, I was a weak, nervous, easily agitated, gloomy, pale thing with burning dark eyes." And again: "A happy child I was not. . . . Already in my tenderest youth I was tortured by nameless fears, woke up at night screaming loudly out of gruesome dreams and then lay listening, trembling, to the howling of the jackals."[4] The third of four children born in quick succession during the first few years of the Gunderts' marriage, she was to have less than four years in the shelter of her home. In 1846 the family hurried back to Europe because of her mother's illness and, when her parents went back to India after a few months, they decided to follow the usual practice of missionaries and leave their children behind. Hesse's mother, then, found herself abandoned at a very early age. The whole episode of her departure from her native India when she was barely three to the moment of her separation from her family is told in touching detail in the autobiographical sketch her eldest daughter published after her death. All four children—including her two older brothers and her younger sister—made the arduous trips through the Red Sea and the Mediterranean in a tiny cabin with bad food. But the greatest moment of anguish came ten days before Marie's fourth birthday, on October 8, 1846, when her parents left her in a home near Basel.

Actually, most of the time the stay in the Basel home for missionary children evoked rather tender memories, but the moment of separation was etched out with bitter clarity: "I can still see how I stood weeping in the courtyard and tried to hold on to my mother by force, hanging on to the edge of her shawl. I was pulled away and carried into the nursery. . . . My entire inner life was outraged. I felt as though the whole world had conspired against me. . . ."[5] She accepted the best toys of a new friend who hardly shed a tear when in a tantrum Marie destroyed them all in her pain. She remained in the private Basel home for eight years, soon enjoying the kindness of her foster father and being generally happy there. As she grew older, Marie reported in her autobiography, her innocence was shattered by a young teacher named Lotte who introduced the girls in her charge to that world of secret love affairs, deceit, and violence that the poet Hermann Hesse was later to designate the "world of darkness." But the peace was wholly shattered in 1854 when, at age twelve, she was forced to make a further move. She was sent to a strict religious boarding school for girls in Swabian Korntal, closer to Stuttgart where her brothers had been boarded with their grandparents in order to obtain a secondary education.

Marie's diaries show how deeply at war she was within herself between her strict upbringing, with its ideal of service, and her own highly emotional nature. The mere fact that she put down so many of her intimate thoughts in detailed journals suggests not only a religious need for self-examination but also an artistic need to shape her feelings in words. Yet this very activity created a rift between herself and both her proxy and her actual parents. It suggested a turn toward the unaccepted, which had already been signaled by the undermining influence of that wayward teacher, Fräulein Lotte, during Marie's last few years in Basel.

In the school in Korntal, Marie Gundert aggravated her rebellious posture. Again she had been removed by fiat from a home she had loved —her foster family in Basel—and she felt deeply bereft. In her anguish she allowed herself to be comforted by an older girl who understood her and for whom she soon conceived a passionate love. But Olga, that seventeen-year-old friend, was caught having secret communications with a pupil in the boys' wing of their school, and by the severe standards of that religious institution she was marked as a sinner. In order to make her pay for her transgression, no one was allowed to communicate with her. But Marie refused this injunction; her fierce loyalty toward her friend got her house arrest (she simply continued to befriend her), a form of punishment that only served to intensify her anger. Olga left the school, but Marie and her friends continued to daydream of "freedom." Her brothers in Stuttgart smuggled "forbidden" poetry to her (including even love poems by Friedrich Schiller). Although well-meaning teachers and conservative schoolmates tried to influence Marie to relent, she did not weaken in her opposition to the school and the narrow strictures that she felt surrounded her.

The message was not lost on Dr. Gundert in India. To guard his daughter against future "frivolities," her father removed her from the school—causing yet another separation—and, after allowing her a brief stay with her former foster parents near Basel, sent her to live with the Jacquets, a French Calvinist family living in a village near the Swiss town of Neuchâtel. The account of this episode has been preserved in Marie's autobiography and suggests a difficult life; Ninon Hesse indicates that the strain was severe and some of Marie's remarks support this contention. She had been a schoolgirl, someone unaccustomed to housework and small children. In her new job she was surrounded by her employers' children, who clamored for affection. Difficult or not, Marie was overjoyed when in 1857 (at age fifteen) she heard at last from her parents that she was to join them once more in India. Momentarily, at least, her life could begin anew.

The prospect of a very different kind of life, however, opened up unexpectedly at sea. After the land transfer from Alexandria the party of missionaries boarded the steamer *Bombay* in the Red Sea that would take them the rest of the way to India. On board Marie met an Englishman named John Barns who, she felt instantly, was the man destined for her. Their intimacy, fraught with emotion, soon assumed far greater significance than a mere shipboard romance, and Barns sent a letter ahead asking Dr. Gundert for his daughter's hand. The degree of passion generated by these two people may be gauged by Marie's description of their final farewell as she was getting ready to climb into the boat that would take her ashore while John remained behind to continue the journey to his destination, Karachi. "John took both my hands into his," she wrote, "and looked steadily into my eyes. So we stood for a moment, without a word, without tears, hand in hand, eye to eye, heart to heart."[6] She departed, soon to be met by a cool and distant father. A secular man, Barns was beyond consideration.

Is this where Hermann Hesse's anguish began? On a deeper level than theology, the contradictions in the mother may foreshadow those in the son. Marie met her father's severity with a submissiveness that at first concealed but eventually overcame her rebellious instincts. She waited for word from her lover for many weeks while plunging into the women's work at the mission. She felt bitterness toward her father, to be sure— also perhaps toward her erstwhile lover, who, it appeared to her, had maintained absolute silence. Years later Marie discovered that there had been some letters that had never reached her and that for a while at least he had saved and prepared for a possible household. He remained a bachelor.

In her autobiography, Marie Hesse declared that she had forsaken her lover, and all her other refractory attitudes, on a specific date that she associated with a specific conversion. It happened, so she wrote, on February 24, 1858, when, under the influence of a missionary she ad-mired, she experienced an illumination that led to a decision to accept the ways of God and service to her parents.[7] It was a conscious choice. The missionary's purpose had become her own. When, one year later, in 1859, Dr. Gundert was forced to return to Europe because of ill health he was able to leave a devoted daughter behind to assist her mother in the missionary tasks, until they, too, went back when they received the news that their husband and father had to stay permanently at home. In 1860 the Basel mission entrusted Dr. Gundert with the direction of its publishing house, the Calwer Verlagsverein. It was in this way that the family found its way to the small town on the River Nagold. The two youngest sons, who had spent most of their childhood in the mission's Boys' House in Basel, were able to join the family, and at last, for the first time, the Gunderts could be all united under one roof. It was a new phase in all their lives, but one that was to be equally filled with pressures.

Dr. Gundert was overburdened at once. Besides directing the publica-tion of books and pamphlets for missionaries in the field, he was also required to spend part of his time compiling a dictionary of the Malay-alam language for missionaries' use. Marie worked hard, helping her mother with housework and her father in his study. Then, in 1861, she met a young missionary, Charles Isenberg, who was barely twenty-one, and gradually a courtship developed, which this time was encouraged by her parents. He was of their faith; in fact, Charles had gone to the boys' school at Kornthal near which Marie had spent those painful years. Although he was a British subject, he had been raised in Germany and shared with the Gundert family the tradition of service in India. His father had also worked in that distant part of the world and returned home to die during their courtship. It is difficult to tell from the effusive language in Marie's autobiographical notes whether she loved him in the usual sentimental sense, but self-indulgent romantic love was clearly irrelevant to the relationship of these two people who set out together to serve their religion. She waited for him for three years while he completed his training in England. Soon he was sent overseas and his fiancée followed him. In 1865, at the age of twenty-three, she married him in India, where her mother had married her father, and like her mother she traveled to her first mission in an ox cart to work and to teach.

Four difficult years followed during which Marie served, waiting for her husband while he was on his many journeys, moving with him when he was transferred from place to place, doing women's chores, bearing his children. Three pregnancies—one child who died in infancy and two boys, Theodor and Karl, who lived—marked these Indian years. Then, suddenly, Charles became seriously ill. Beginning with fever and dysentery, the illness seemed to invade his entire body. He began to cough up blood and grew constantly weaker. An English doctor signed a death warrant—"Lung, liver & Co." was his verdict, and another physician simply advised that Charles's life was now in God's hands. There was only one thing to do: to take the dying man home. Just before they were able to leave a violent storm swept through their corrugated iron cottage, sending streams of water to inundate the floor. As quickly as slow steamboats could take them, they were on their way back to Germany, barely managing to reach a hospital in Stuttgart before Charles died. Marie gave a moving account of their last hours together as she prayed with him and wiped the perspiration from the dying man's brow.[8] Whatever she may have felt when they first met, their marriage, tempered by those years in India, had brought them together. Now, in 1870, she was left with two little boys, one four, the other just one year old. Again she helped her parents in Calw. She gave English lessons. She produced translations and even rewrote books about martyred missionaries in Asia and Africa. She played the piano. She prayed. The dark shadow of illness and isolation that had fallen over both generations of missionaries had settled upon her, and, barely twenty-eight, she had become severe, middle-aged.

The early life of Johannes, Hermann Hesse's father, was hard in a different way. He had been born in 1847, five years before Hesse's mother. His father, Carl Hermann Hesse, was a country doctor in

Weissenstein, Estonia, then, as now, part of Russia, where he served a German community. Pietist by religion, German in origin and language, though Russian by citizenship, he served his district tolerably well, yet without the rigor that characterized the Gunderts. He was more easygoing than the missionaries from the south, more lighthearted, but in his way just as tyrannical. Dr. Hesse produced many children and used up two wives in the process. His first wife, Jenny Lass, had six children, including Hesse's father. She died as she was about to give birth to her last. Lina Müller, the twenty-one-year-old daughter of his brother-in-law, bore him two and died delivering the second. His third wife, Adele von Berg, bore only one child and lived almost to the time of his death. She died in 1891 at the age of seventy, five years before the patriarch followed her at ninety-four. If the Gunderts' temperament was marked by self-denial, Hesse's dealings with his wives suggests at least a measure of self-indulgence.

Severity versus indulgence: were these the alternatives that described Hermann Hesse's division? Old Dr. Hermann Hesse grieved profusely for both his wives, yet his mourning was soon followed by the celebration of another marriage. When his young wife Lina, whom he adored, expressed her fear of an oncoming death while lying in childbirth, he said simply: "Dear heart, Lina, go." When she demurred, saying "I have no joy. I am so happy with you and want to stay," he replied: "Dear heart. Jesus requires only obedience, nothing else. You will find Joy only where He dwells."[9] Years later, himself a man in his sixties, his grandson Hermann commented upon this scene to his sister. Citing from a letter he had just received (in 1944) from someone who knew the old man well in those days, he reported: "At first glance it must have sounded almost loveless when he sat at the deathbed of his second wife, his beloved Lina, and responded to her . . . words that alas she must die by saying abruptly: 'Dear heart, Lina, go!'. Truly, a living affirmation of the divine will!"[10]

Along with this precept, Hesse cited his correspondent in fine detail both on the grandfather's love of life and his rather tyrannical high spirits. The first story was about the young man who wooed his wife at a picnic. He had suggested a race, then proposed to the girl, breathlessly, at the goalpost—and was accepted. The second, of the older man, translated that sense of physical power into actual domination. Even the author of the letter had suggested something about the dictatorial power the old man exercised over his little town. The correspondent's father, an old friend of Dr. Hesse's, had been in the process of building a new house for his growing family. Again and again the doctor had walked by the construction site to give it his approval. But when it became evident that the new house was being built higher than the older surrounding buildings, the old man became outraged. Although the family had been at first very pleased with the plans, the doctor insisted that they be cancelled, accusing his friend and neighbor of the sin of pride. His influence was so great that the plans were changed and the new building was completed at the usual height.

Ninon Hesse, who commented at some length about her husband's grandfather, wrote many decades later that old Dr. Hesse was more of a Christian than a doctor; he believed more in the healing power of the spirit than in the physician's art. [11] He was praised and decorated by his townsmen, yet he was a "splendid but sometimes also rather arrogant man." At least this was the judgment of his grandson's correspondent, writing during the following century.

Though Johannes Hesse's mother, Jenny, was his father's first wife, he grew up considering his father's third wife as his mother, for Dr. Hesse married her when Johannes was only nine. Adele Hesse was a rather settled person who provided her new family with some stability. But as he was growing into puberty Johannes became too difficult to keep at home. In the child, as in the adult, there was enough anxiety, defiance, suffering—even anger— to make life with him difficult. His father sent him to the Estonian capital of Reval to attend a religious high school and arranged for him to live in the home of his lifelong friend Baron Ferdinand von Stackelberg, who himself had two sons. Henceforth Johannes came home only on holidays. Exile and isolation were perhaps as well known to Johannes Hesse as to his son.

For Hesse's father, during his formative years, alienation was made into an ideal of service. In his son's life the crucial decision as an adolescent, which eventually put him on his own feet, had been his decision to become a writer. In Johannes's life the analogous decision was to serve the Pietist faith. On March 12, 1865, when he was almost eighteen, Johannes Hesse wrote to the Basel mission and informed them that he was possessed of a longing "to serve with practical deeds the Lord to whom I felt and still feel bound with all the bonds of gratitude." The words that follow could equally well have been written by his son: "My longing went out to a corporate community in which my 'I' might disappear—for this self has long since become too powerful. I hope for an education that might reestablish the proper relationship to my self and my life."[12] He wanted to become a missionary.

By July Johannes heard from the Evangelical Mission Organization that he had been accepted, and he set out for Basel later that month. For the next three years he studied at the mission, then spent another year as assistant to the director, Inspector Hans Josenhans, who became one of his most admired teachers. Indeed, sixteen years later he was to write a loving biography of Josenhans, a small brochure portraying his teacher's life along with that of his institution. In August 1869, when he was just twenty-two, Johannes was ordained in the small Swabian town of Heilbronn. He preached for a few Sundays with great success, since he had already developed that flowery, didactic prose that was to survive in his writings. Then he went to India to become the missionary he had been trained to be, but he lasted less than four years. In March 1873 he was on his way back to Basel. The climate had done him in.

It was at this juncture that the lives of the Gunderts and the Hesses crossed. After a few months in Basel, Johannes Hesse was sent to Calw as Gundert's assistant to help him edit the mission's magazine. Whether the work or the presence of the thirty-one-year-old widow Marie Isenberg with her two young sons was decisive in the selection of the bachelor of twenty-six remains speculative, but it is probable that his eligibility had a great deal to do with the appointment. Even the way Johannes was recommended by a mutual friend who wrote directly to Marie is suggestive: "He is very gifted, enormously attractive in his manners. I believe you [Marie] will take great pleasure in him: I still have to hear a single stupid word, so nobody can get to him easily. . . . Especially nice for his conversations with your father is the fact that he enjoys languages and conducts etymological studies."[13] Marie's response was more muted. Relating Johannes's arrival to the same friend, she wrote: "So much to tell. Hardly had I mailed my last letter to you a week ago when our new boarder (Johannes Hesse who has been expected as father's assistant) arrived unexpectedly." She then proceeded to describe her future husband as being in a poor state—he had a bad cold and possibly the flu—but she also wrote: "Your description was very good. One must respect and love him, that fine, pious, intellectual man." But there was always a sad aspect of him, too, "as though he had been made for a better world."[14] Johannes Hesse had arrived on December 4, 1873. On November 22, 1874, he and Marie Isenberg were married.

Hermann Hesse, second child of his mother's second marriage, was born into these two histories and into the temperaments they had shaped. His mother lived through many years of struggle, which always ended in her abnegation. Before she had met Johannes, she had felt compelled to refuse the opportunity to study medicine in India in order to serve as a physician in the women's mission houses because of her two children. In remarrying, moreover, she undertook additional obligations. Although she often smiled, sang, and played music, Marie remained deeply true to the terms of her conversion after the debacle of John Barns. Subservient to her own father, who devoured women in his own way as old

Dr. Hesse had devoured them in his, she tried to extend the same un-questioning support to her husband. Their early years contained pleasant times, even moments of joy. At one time they traveled as far north as distant Estonia to visit old Dr. Hesse, taking the little girl Adele with them. The old man loved to play with her and especially impressed Marie with his indomitable spirit. But soon the years closed in on them. Marie kept on watching her *Herzensjohnny* studying Hebrew at dawn across the breakfast table. Locked into the routine of religious small-town life, she bore a continuing succession of children.

There were six. After Adele in 1875 came Hermann in 1877. In quick order there followed Paul in 1878, Gertrud in 1879, Marulla in 1880, and Johannes in 1882. Paul and Gertrud died in infancy. The other four Marie brought up with intermittent help from her husband. Nine pregnancies—six living children, including the Isenberg sons—and laboring for her father and husband had put her painfully acquired abnegation to the test of a very hard life. From it emerged a woman of very deep feeling, given to anguish and finally physical illness that led to her death, aged far beyond her years, in 1902. Self-indulgent and often ineffectual, though judicious and competent as an administrator and teacher, Johannes Hesse outlived his wife by fourteen years. Cared for in his old age by his daughter Marulla, he lived to see the fame of his son Hermann and to be reconciled with him after many years of tension. When he died at sixty-nine, blind and in pain, he, too, had become a patriarch.

Both parents, then, seemed burdened, though they bore these burdens in very different ways. Whatever they endured, however, their children sensed. Hermann especially felt a strain in his childhood that mingled with his recollections of closeness and warmth and lent them a distinct coloration. In fact, his conscious memories, which recur in his poems, stories, and novels, focus on that world of light and mutual affection, tempered only by a stern morality, that drew the contours of the early world he cherished. Yet a harsher reality appears, for example, in Marie's memoirs and letters as well as in the documents selected and published by Ninon Hesse: a reality composed of intermittent crises. Both these worlds existed side by side, but their concurrent impact on Hesse's life before the age of eighteen could not have been easy. He was suspended, it seemed, between one kind of home—a place of contentment, accept-ance, and warmth—and another kind split by worry and fear that often rejected him in his need.

In Hesse's childhood memories, a recurring image is that of being alone in the dark, wanting to return to the circle of light where his family seemed to live. Hesse acknowledged this divided image of home in

Demian, that classic of childhood and adolescence, when he named his first chapter "Two Worlds." One was the world of light—home and parents as he liked to remember them. The other was the world of dark, of outsiders and of hostile yet alluring powers lurking beyond the circle of light from which he felt expelled. Beneath the connotations gained from Hesse's psychoanalysis, of which *Demian* had been the result, there remains a strong, literal image of two contrasting, yet interdependent worlds, worlds that provided an ambience for his childhood that ultimately extended to his entire life. In the first he felt accepted and good. In the second he felt evil, an outcast. The first world stood for security; the second meant expulsion. The first world came to be that of the spirit; the second world remained that of the senses. It was between these two worlds that Hesse's life was suspended and his difficult childhood began.

II

It was a clear blue day on top of the mountain. Below stretched the forests and meadows leading down to the valley and the brown and red clusters of villages and towns. Tiny spires sparkled in the sunlight. The boulders and rocks of the old ruin loomed, gross and enormous in the eyes of a three-year-old boy. He first clung to his mother's light coat, then clutched his father's large hand. The warm sun of early spring left bright blotches on the stark gray rocks. Huge arms and legs seemed to be all around him, people with binoculars walking up to the parapet. "Look!" he heard, and all of a sudden he felt himself being gripped under the armpits and swung high above the wall of the lookout. Yet the strong hands of his young uncle seemed peculiarly shaky and insecure as the child stared into the vast expanse below. The tiny houses, the white strips of road, the band of rivers—they all seemed to congeal into a large threatening mass. Behind him he heard the hum of voices, the Sunday tourists, the laughter of children. But all he could really sense was the depth below, the abyss. All that connected him with life seemed to be in the precarious hands of his uncle. Fear seized him. He became dizzy. The gulf below seemed to draw him down, to rise and swallow him. He began to tremble, and only then, after what seemed an endless moment, did he feel himself swung back to where firm ground was within sight. The warmth of his mother's arms finally enclosed him, but tears welled up uncontrollably. They hurried the child home. He was convulsed with weeping and did not stop trembling until he felt safe in his bed.

This is the first scene in his life that Hermann Hesse remembered with any clarity. "From then on," he wrote in the words of Hermann Lauscher, the hero of his autobiographical first novel, "this abyss oppressed me often in dreams of anxiety and I would moan in my dreams and wake up crying."[15]

This was the beginning of a contradictory life—filled equally with a fear of abysses, of losing contact with father and mother, and with a sense of great comfort, of almost idyllic warmth. On the one hand, his fears crystallized into fears of being expelled, of not being "forgiven" for minor sins and indiscretions. He found himself constantly waiting for his father's relenting voice, for his mother's good-night kiss. On the other hand, his childhood, as he portrayed it in his many autobiographical writings, appeared as a beautiful idyll that had passed from view. The memory of his mother's black hair and brown eyes mingled, in his mind, with the rustling of the wind in the chestnut trees and the sight of the bluebells spread over the large meadow next to his father's house. He remembered the towers and the bridges across the river, intermingled with the sound of the folk songs sung in his native dialect to convey a feeling of "happiness and homesickness alike."[16] These are early memories, to be sure, but they are images of an Eden in Hesse's life to which he always returned. However disturbing the events of his childhood and adolescence, they were always counterbalanced by this memory of love, of comfort, even of acceptance.

Hesse's continuous memories really begin in Basel, where his family moved in 1881 when he was four. After several years of service under the aegis of Dr. Gundert, Johannes Hesse was transferred to the Mission Institute to teach church doctrine and history. It is questionable how much he welcomed the move, but there is no doubt that his wife was delighted. She sensed a breath of fresh air and enjoyed the easier atmosphere of the city, the opportunity to escape from the constraints of a small town and most likely also from the pressures exerted by her father, who ruled in Calw. In the larger city of Basel they had more freedom. Their house was more spacious and afforded more room for the children. It was a farmhouse situated at the edge of the city, just where the open country began, with an ample backyard next to a huge expanse of green meadowland in which the children could play. Sharing the good and bad fortunes of the other families of the mission, Marie Hesse felt less isolated and alone. "One loves more," she wrote. "One prays more." It was "a warmer, more active life than in narrow Calw."[17]

At first, the child Hermann Hesse enjoyed life in Basel, too. He recalled later how the old Alsatian railroad separated their street from the city, which looked toward them with its towers and roofs beyond the wide ancient gate. The sight of the trains close by belongs among his earliest impressions.[18] And he recalled playing Indians and chasing butterflies in the large meadow near their house. But there was also always the world of darkness. He had violent temper tantrums and seemed incorrigible. At an early age he constantly had the sense of sinning, and even his carefully selected memories, which appear in his autobiographical books, mention all kinds of transgressions which his father would punish and for which he had to ask forgiveness of his mother: a stolen fruit, a lie, a fit of temper. These incidents extended from his preschool and early school years into his later childhood and adolescence. But always there remained a counterpoint: the music he shared especially with his mother, sudden bursts of kindness to his younger sister and brothers, the warmth of his feeling for his older sister Adele.

Still, the attitude his parents expressed in various letters, and therefore surely communicated to the child, was that they were facing a difficult problem. Even in his early years they thought of Hermann as the child they could not manage.[19] After a few months at the mission nursery school, his behavior temporarily improved. He was fond of the principal, Parson Pfisterer, who was to remain his mentor—deep into the troubled years of his adolescence. The parson seemed to temper his sternness with a good deal of human warmth, which the child was never sure of in his father. For a while it seemed as if a new plateau had been reached. The family spent July 1883 on vacation in the mountains of the Swiss Jura, and his mother reported that Hermann seemed happy, healthy, and tanned. Again, by the end of the month he became concerned whether they would get back to Basel in time for the beginning of school, for he was to enter first grade.

The adult writer's image of life as a pendulum movement between opposite poles is reflected in his ambivalence as a child, his sense of being constantly tossed back and forth between the impulse of love, and his need for acceptance, and anxious withdrawal or anger. His parents' responses, even when he was barely six, mirrored the same divided spirit. On November 5, 1883, Marie Hesse wrote to her parents in Calw: "Our Hermann now attends Sunday School in the Boys' House (with Frau Pfisterer at the mission) at his own request. Thank God, he is now much better mannered and more tractable." But nine days later, on November 14, Johannes wrote his parents-in-law that he was considering the possibility of sending Hermann to an institution or foster home, "however degrading this may be for us." "We are too nervous," he continues, "too weak for him, and our entire domestic life is not sufficiently disciplined and regular." At the same time, however, he recognized his son's talent, his close observations of nature ("the moon and the clouds"), his improvisations on the harmonium, his drawings, his singing, and his ability never to be at a loss for a rhyme.[20]

The parents struggled with their problem child for two more months, but by January 1884 the recalcitrant first grader was sent for several months to live at the Boys' House of the Mission School. It was not an outrageous decision. Hermann's own uncles had been brought up there at one time or another, for it was common practice for the families of missionaries to leave their young children behind at the Boys' House when they went abroad. Still, Hermann's family was not in Africa or India but only a short distance away in the same town, and the child was not unaware of this difference. Although he liked the Pfisterers and many of the children, he also felt set apart from home.

At six and a half years of age, then, Hermann Hesse spent his week-days and nights at the school. When he came home on Sundays, he appeared calmer and a little depressed, but he seemed pleased with the greetings of his brother Hans and to be with his parents and sisters. Sundays were usually long days for the children, stretching out endlessly between church and bedtime, but to Hermann, during these months of his exile, they seemed only too short. Soon after church they would sit down to their noon dinner. If the weather was fine that spring, they would play outdoors. Then it would be evening again, and he would have to leave. But basically, by adult standards, he was now better behaved, and in June his parents took him home again to see how it would work out. At first they seemed very satisfied. His perceptive mother thought the experiment had been a success, although she also recognized the threat of depression. "With Hermännle," she wrote in her diary later that fall, "whose education had cost us so much pain and trouble, things are decidedly better. From January 21 until June 5 he lived in the Boys' House and spent only Sundays with us. He kept a stiff upper lip there, but came home pale, thin, and depressed. The aftereffect was definitely good and wholesome. He is much more tractable now. . . ."[21]

Soon, however, the old problems reappeared: tears, fits of temper, taciturn withdrawals. Both parents sought solace from the Gunderts in Calw and unburdened themselves to them in letters, seeking guidance on the question of his removal. But old Gundert counseled vehemently against sending Hermann away: "It is wrong of you to say you can't affect him. God who gave him to you surely did not leave you without the means of influencing him." Contradictions in Hermann's behavior seemed to match the contradictions in his family's perceptions of him. Dr. Gundert wrote this letter in September—the very month during which Marie had expressed her satisfaction at Hermann's progress. He prefaced his remarks with the assurance that he "pitied" them for their difficulties with the child, who was at other times perfectly well behaved.[22]

These difficulties were reinforced by an event later in September 1884 that did not involve Hermann Hesse directly but provided him with a model, and created for him a new alternative of service—the service of art. His much older half brother Theodor Isenberg, then two years out of high school and apprenticed with a pharmacist, disappeared in September. A telegram brought the news. Johannes Hesse went to the station to meet the eighteen-year-old boy, but the child never arrived. For three days and two dark nights, as Marie Hesse put it in her diary, they did not know where he was. Then, three days later, he arrived, thin, pale, disturbed, and asked only to be allowed to sleep. He had gone to Munich, presented himself to a music director there, who, according to his fond mother, "recognized his talent" and encouraged him. Now he demanded his parents' permission to devote himself fully to music and to leave the pharmacy. A compromise was reached: Theodor promised to return to his apprenticeship for another year to complete his examination in return for his parents' permission to devote himself fully to music after that.

It was a mild incident and Theodor followed it up by entering the conservatory in Stuttgart in the fall of 1885. But his insistence on his mission as an artist made a deep impression on young Hermann, who came to connect art with rebellion, with the need to express what lies within regardless of the consequences. That year, 1884, was also the year he began to write. His grandfather, not as impressed as his parents had hoped, wrote them rather peremptorily after his first reading of Hermann's poetry that he thought more highly of his good resolutions than of his verse, which seemed to him almost unnatural for a child of his age. "One can see he is already full of stuff that he has sucked in from everywhere."[23] But some sense of purpose began to appear in Hermann Hesse's life. He started violin lessons.

If music played a large role in Hesse's family, poetry was almost equally important, since language and its sounds claimed such a large share of their lives as missionaries in foreign lands, as preachers, and as lovers of chorales and hymns at home. Johannes Hesse's art was contained in his preaching: his direct and powerful sermons, which exerted such a wide appeal, and his various tracts for the use of missionaries abroad, which showed both sensibility and craftsmanship. Especially during the time in Basel, when Hermann Hesse was still small, his father Johannes wrote many tracts about a wondrous Orient where the word of

God was to be spread. Most of them were illustrated and all of them introduced the kinds of characters missionaries were likely to meet. In 1880, for example, Johannes Hesse published a tract called "Jamunabai's Wandering, or a Look at a Widow's Life in India." In 1885 his "Sermons to the Heathens in India" contained all the rich exhortative language that later molded the style of his son.[24] Marie Hesse, moreover, wrote actual verse. Along with translations of religious tracts and martyred missionaries' lives, she composed many poems—about saints and missionaries and their subjects ("pious heathens") as well as on family occasions both joyful and sad. The language of her verse was unsophisticated, full of sentimentality, yet pure in its simple piety. When her mother, Julie Dubois Gundert, died in September, 1885, she wrote:

> From us she's departed in silence
> From this world of fear and of pain
> Our mother who here on earth
> Never forgot being friend to all.
> . . . .
> Returned home from alien lands
> From battle to the peaceful home
> Relieved of all torment of suffering
> Which she has tasted here.

Alien lands—both the foreign shores of the tropics from which she had returned to find rest and peace, and the earth itself upon which Julie Dubois Gundert had now turned her back:

> Sitting at the Savior's feet
> Already here her heritage was lovely.
> Oh how she will greet Him there
> Blissfully upon Zion's heights.

Whether Marie expressed her own personality in these lines or mainly followed a conventional pattern, the simplicity of her verse underscores her decision, taken in India many years ago, to devote herself entirely to the prospect of sitting at her Savior's feet where she had now placed her mother. Most independent life had been drained from this poem, yet a sense of language, a talent for the music of verse, had survived. For her son, especially at this receptive early age when he imitated his mother above anyone else, it fixed a sense of sounds and rhythms conforming to easily discernible, conventional patterns. Images and rhythms mirror simple articles of faith. But this eulogy in verse brought more light to bear on his mother's grief, and her ideal of service, than on the image of that strange grandmother with whom he was never comfortable, with whose French he had never been at home.

Family events, like Julie Gundert's funeral, and small eruptions and crises were soon overshadowed by a crucial change in their lives that also brought with it a significant turn in Hesse's life as a future artist. They had to leave Basel. In February 1886 the committee of the mission decided that Johannes Hesse should return to Calw and begin to take over the burdens of office at the publishing house. His father-in-law was then seventy-two years old and would soon have to retire. Leaving Basel was very difficult for Marie Hesse but impossible to avoid, since her father had also requested their return. "Basel," she wrote in her diary, "with its lively stimulating activities, the delightful circle of friends at the mission, our sunny, homey lodgings, our dear neighborhood, will be very hard to leave. On the other side, Papa draws me to him."

In July the family moved back to the small Swabian town, and Marie Hesse tried to adjust to the old life in the familiar, narrower surroundings. At first, being again close to her father seemed to compensate for what she had lost in leaving Basel: "Papa is here who replaces everything for me." But bad times with Hermann began to occur again more frequently and the question of what to do with him had to be constantly reopened. Marie felt more and more oppressed by the relentless monotony of the life to which she had returned. She felt circumscribed and controlled not only by her father but also by an aunt, Henriette Ensslin, Dr. Gundert's cousin, who had assisted him in the office and had run his household after his wife's death. Characteristically, Marie interpreted her unhappiness as a healing force. "If I think of our home in Basel," she wrote in her diary, "the freedom, the social life, our free and easy life as a family, I feel hemmed in here. . . ." But at once she thought of it as spiritually wholesome: "But it's better this way for one's inner growth." And she turned to her husband for support: "How deeply I sense only now what I have in Johannes, what we are for each other, how we understand each other, how we are one."[25]

These words foreshadow her son's future rhetoric, just as the poems Marie wrote and the music she played became part of his life. But it was not only her rhetoric that seemed to anticipate his, nor even the poems and journals and translation she fitted into her crowded days; it was also her oddly strained sense of moral purpose. Like her son, she felt a great need for freedom, a need that had been painfully suppressed when she was sixteen years old, and an equally genuine, almost triumphant need for a superior will—her father's, her husband's, her God's.

Meanwhile, the house was crowded and narrow. Her husband was tense, her children querulous. Their new beginning in Calw was by no means idyllic.

III

The next four years molded a vision in Hermann Hesse's mind that formed his identity as a writer and man. Calw was a small, old-world town stretching along the banks of the Nagold like a wide band thickened at the center. Its crooked alleys converged upon the oblong town square and its traditional well. As its houses gradually detached themselves from the thick clusters around the river bridge, they seemed to trail off gradually among the foothills of the Black Forest mountains. Deep snow clogged the streets in winter. Spring rains washed the pavements on which the children played. The seasons passed with the regular monotony Marie Hesse had deplored in her diary.

Hermann Hesse blended in well with these surroundings, and was to become in a true sense a regional writer. Although he constantly strove to be more than that, and in large measure succeeded, the general region in which he grew up—centered in the two focal points of Swiss Basel and Swabian Calw—flavored all his writings and provided his cultural milieu well into the twentieth century. He was neither German nor Swiss: he was both. His home comprised a large region, stretching from Heilbronn and the Black Forest in the north across the border into Switzerland, culminating majestically in the St. Gotthard Pass in the south. This enlarged regional homeland, crossing political boundaries, was a richly bedecked, colorful world: it included Lake Constance and the birthplace of the Rhine; it also contained many cities and towns on both sides of the line—Stuttgart and Tübingen in German Württemberg; Swiss cities like Basel, Zurich, and Bern. For Hesse the area always remained a single country where variants of the same German dialects were spoken and where religion and architecture were similar. He was to picture this world throughout his life, but as times changed he reflected these changes as well, since the unified world was severely strained by the growth of an industrialized Germany and its drift toward war.

During the period when Hesse grew up, the Pietist religion of his family was still an important faith among Protestants of the region. Its mixture of emotionality, sternness, and simple faith permitted an approach to religion that allowed these men and women to flourish independently. For just that reason, the Pietist tradition, like so many others that had emerged in a romantic, preindustrial Germany, was entering its decline. As the presence of the all-German Empire under Prussian leadership made itself felt, formerly independent states like Württemberg found that their cultural autonomy was being gradually eroded. People like the Hesses and Gunderts were confronting a rapidly changing world. The atmosphere became charged with political slogans and military enthusiasms. The consolidation of a united Germany directed from the north divided the region and made the Swiss border more of a barrier than it had been. Because their religion had placed them under the control of the Mission Institute in Basel, the Gunderts and Hesses did not fully take part in this change, though eventually they also began to move toward a more specifically German identity. Marie was admittedly vague about nationalities, but she noted events at the Hohenzollern court as loyally as the wife of an English clergyman might have noted the comings and goings at Buckingham Palace. Still, the Swiss regions south of Lake Constance were not foreign territory. Hermann did not change his citizenship from Swiss to German (or rather from Basel to Württemberg) until the age of fifteen when he wanted to qualify for the State Theological Seminary at Maulbronn. Yet, as industrialization grew, as a more impersonal technological spirit descended from the north, life changed noticeably. Around them, the religious fabric was becoming gradually threadbare, though their own spirit survived. This spirit Hermann Hesse carried with him as a son of Pietist missionaries, applying to the secular, industrial culture the same zeal for conversion that his parents had displayed in bringing Christianity to India. To expose modern society, its technology that split men from their roots, was to become the underlying motif of his life and work.

Hesse was to write often about that Swabian region, which during his early years as a writer he made famous under the assumed name of *Gerbersau*. Swabia's small towns and green valleys always remained the most precious memories of his childhood and adolescence, and he was as much at home in the Black Forest mountains as he was in the large city of Stuttgart. Although the region that connected it with Switzerland was in some ways a unity, it also had its very distinctive characteristics and its particular intellectual and cultural tradition. Hugo Ball, linking the region closest to Pietism, pointed out its literary and artistic wealth most succinctly: "One must not underestimate Swabian Pietism. Schelling and Hegel, Mörike and Hölderlin . . . are unthinkable without it. And the seminaries of Maulbronn, Blaubeuren, and Urach are linked with the oldest German recollections."

The philosophers Friedrich Wilhelm Schelling and Georg Friedich Hegel were both steeped in that Swabian world of the early nineteenth century, and Hesse's indebtedness to them in his later life has often been documented. His tendency to see events as mental experience, which was later reinforced by his readings in Indian and Chinese philosophy, and especially his bent for dialectical thinking, in which opposites are discerned and reconciled, were obviously molded by these philosophers. The poets Mörike and Hölderlin, of course, were closer to his own métier.

Eduard Mörike was a native Swabian poet. Born in Ludwigsburg in 1804, he was first a parson, then a teacher, but essentially became one of the last romantic lyricists of the nineteenth century. He wrote well-modulated, intense poems, rhythmically musical and reflecting the colors and images of nature with accuracy. His novel *Painter Nolten* is a classic. Again it is easy to see a connection between him and the young poet Hermann Hesse, who was born two years after his death. His nature imagery, his musical tone, his romantic sentimentality, and his interest in painters and painting all fitted into Hesse's own repertoire from his early work on. Similarly, the poet Friedrich Hölderlin was also part of that Swabian ambience. Born in 1770, he wrote brilliant verse and prose, highly prophetic and abstract, until he went insane in the early 1800s. Though he lived on until 1843, when he died in Tübingen, his sane life ended in 1803—but not before he had written some of the most important lyric poems in the German language. It was a source of awe and inspiration for Hesse during his brief stay in the seminary at Maulbronn, where he was to learn the practice of being a minister, that one of his revered predecessors in that school had been Friedrich Hölderlin.

It seems strange, however, that among the various cultural strains that fashioned Hesse's early years, it was particularly this Swabian-Swiss culture and the conflicts it engendered, that was most decisive. His family was steeped at least as much in thoughts about India, for India after all was the fabric that had once held their lives together. It would therefore seem that India would also supply a dominant conflict, that from childhood on Hesse would have been faced with a missionary's opposition between a faraway culture and his own Christianity. There is, however, little evidence of that motif in Hesse's life—at least not until middle age. In his autobiographical sketches written during the early twenties—"Childhood of the Magician" (1923) and "Life Story Briefly Told" (1925)—the Indian roots are exposed, but casually, with hindsight. He acknowledged the East as a place that had been familiar to him since childhood, as a world where "his parents and grandparents had been at home."[26] Especially, in the opening passages of "The Childhood of the Magician" he devoted a long section to Indian artifacts and to the memories of his grandfather and mother. It turned out to be a magical, distant world, but it was a world Hesse had perceived in middle age while wrestling with his Indian legend, *Siddhartha*. Even that memory, gathered so late, was colored in retrospect by a marked contrast between the India of his maternal family and, despite Johannes Hesse's long list of titles on Indian missionary work, the more occidental world of his father.

A telling passage from "The Childhood of the Magician" describes the Indian inheritance of the Hesse family through the person of Dr. Hermann Gundert and his relationship with his daughter as recalled by Hermann Hesse thirty-five years later:

> This man, my mother's father, was hidden in a forest of mysteries, just as his face was hidden in the white forest of his beard; from his eyes there flowed sorrow for the world and there also flowed blithe wisdom, as the case might be, lonely wisdom and divine roguishness; people from many lands knew him, visited and honored him, talked to him in English, French, Indian, Italian, Malayalam and went off after long conversations leaving no clue to their identity, perhaps his friends, perhaps his emissaries, perhaps his servants, his agents. From him, this unfathomable one, I knew, came the secret that surrounded my mother, the secret, age-old mystery, and she, too, had been in India for a long time, she too could speak and sing in Malayalam and Kanarese, she exchanged phrases and maxims with her aged father in strange, magical tones. And at times she possessed, like him, the stranger's smile, the smile of wisdom.

Whether or not by design, this magical vision of the distant Orient (with its silent yet musical secrets) is contrasted with the clear, rational, German-speaking world of his father:

> My father was different. He stood alone, belonging neither to the world of the idols and of my grandfather nor to the workaday world of the city. He stood to one side, lonely, a sufferer and a seeker, learned and kindly, without falseness and full of zeal in the service of truth, but far removed from that noble and tender but unmistakable smile—he had no trace of mystery. The kindness never forsook him, nor his cleverness, but he never appeared in the magic cloud that surrounded my grandfather, his face never dissolved in that childlikeness and godlikeness whose interplay at times looked like sadness, at times like delicate mockery, at times like the silent, inward-looking mask of God.

And, finally, his father did not speak to his mother in Indian languages, "but spoke English and a pure, clear, beautiful German faintly colored with a Baltic accent."

These passages were written at a time when the mature writer sought to refurbish the image of his father, yet the underlying conflict of his life, which was surely present during those first years in Calw, is apparent even among these Indian memories in his family. The very positive appearance of his father—straight and direct—is still questioned in the face of magic clouds, mysterious languages, and inward-looking masks of God associated with his grandfather and mother. He knew that his roots "reached deeper into [his] mother's soil, into the dark-eyed and mysterious," but he strove to emulate his father "with zeal, all too much zeal." His mother, he concluded, was full of magic, his father was not; "He could not sing."[27]

On all levels, then, Hermann Hesse's world as a child was divided. Even the contrast between the reality of the Swiss-Swabian landscape and the Orient of the family's memory and imagination appeared split into the more personal categories of paternal and maternal landscapes. It reinforced the child's sense that, wherever he may be placed, he would always be pulled somewhere else. When they were in Calw, they looked toward Basel; when they were in Basel, they looked toward Calw. And while they were living in Swabia or Switzerland, the family's memories and commitments lay on the other side of the globe, in another culture, which he had never experienced. There remained, then, always another division, a distant place to be made into another grail.

If in his childhood India was connected with his mother and grandfather and the German cultural world with his father, this very split in his perspective suggests how deeply enmeshed he was in conflicts of allegiance between his parents. Although at more guarded moments he created pictures of a harmonious family life, the facts of his anguished childhood reinforce his ambivalent feelings toward his parents, whom he viewed in opposite corners of his life. Especially crucial was the image of his father, which, despite later efforts to reverse his judgment, remained tarnished by his failure to support his son.

Hesse's first encounter with mental illness or hysteria, at the age of twelve, it appears, came to him through his father, who suffered a severe depression during the summer of 1889. The tension in which they all lived, in cramped quarters under constant pressure of work, must have been too much for him. They still shared old Dr. Gundert's house, which also contained the offices of the Calwer Verlagsverein. There was just not enough room, and lack of space was added to all the other tensions. They began to look for a home of their own, but before they could move, Johannes Hesse suffered his collapse. From the end of July until the middle of August he was treated in a hospital in Bern for severe symptoms of compulsive weeping and melancholia. At this point, Marie Hesse took one of her decisive actions, this time to rescue her "Johnny," as she was to take action later to rescue her son. After placing a final stamp of approval on a new house, which she surveyed with her eldest daughter and confidante Adele, she rushed to her husband's bedside in Bern. The children stayed behind. Hermann was very depressed by his father's illness, a fact that, Dr. Gundert noted, "made us all feel good."[28] Evidently, the family had not expected him to show any concern. The parents returned on August 12. Johannes Hesse seemed reasonably cured, although attacks of melancholia, weeping, and headaches continued to pursue him. Mental illness was to become a lasting motif in Hermann Hesse's life, in himself and others close to him, but his father's collapse first brought it home to him consciously.

Conflicts, traumas, moments of hysteria, blending with the normal life of a small town schoolboy, may well have produced those difficult alternations of mood and those strange phases of acquiescence followed by violent defiance. They may have also helped in preparing the unconscious ground from which Hesse's decision to become a writer had grown. His gifts had been present for his family to appreciate since he was a preschooler in Basel, when his father had praised his ability to compose images and rhymes; and though his grandfather had been impatient with the derivative scribblings of the seven-year-old, the writing of verse and of lofty prose had been his favorite pastime since childhood. But now it had also become a decision of psychological import; Hesse's inchoate awareness of himself as a possible artist coincided with his growing rejection of his family's values.

The near success of his half brother Theodor had been an example. He had admired his brother for his courage to defy the values of his family of theologians, missionaries, ministers, and teachers, to whom the life of a tradesman, or an artisan even, would have been preferable to that of the artist. Unfortunately, Theodor failed. Just after the Hesses moved into their new house, in 1889, he appeared with the news that he had been engaged as a tenor by the German opera house in Groningen; but only a few months later, in February 1890, this incipient career was over. He had evidently been found wanting, and so Theodor reentered the trade of pharmacy, which he followed for the rest of his life. Seeing his brother almost succeed, then fail, underlined Hermann Hesse's sense of the frailty of his desired vocation. But it also strengthened his own resolve to succeed.

In 1889–90, as he approached the age of thirteen, the idea that he wanted to become a writer had taken root in Hesse's mind. It became for him blurred with his need for release, for freedom. And he stubbornly clung to it. At the same time he was going through puberty. In the brief autobiographical sketches and stories Hesse wrote later in his life he hinted almost whimsically at his underground existence as an adolescent, how he knew his way among cow pastures and chicken coops and artisan workshops. He dwelt lovingly on the story of how a cheerful neighbor named Frau Anna introduced him to at least the sight of her body, and he spent a great deal of time daydreaming, inventing wild stories and practical jokes, and being alternately recalcitrant and withdrawn. But he had been imbued with a sense of his mission, as his father had been when he applied to the Mission Institute in Basel. It may have been motivated in part by defiance, by the desire to enact the role of the artist defying the conventions and restrictions of small-town and family life, but it was also a positive mission. He loved poetry and literature in general—the only subjects in which he excelled at school. He loved music and language, color and sound. Still, his resolve to follow the "poet's trade" (which, he made clear, could not be learned like that of pharmacists and carpenters) widened the schism between him and his family. Long-dormant anxieties and antagonisms came back to the surface.

Whatever the immediate cause, four years after the family's return from Basel, in February 1890, Hermann Hesse was finally sent away from home. To be sure, there were also good academic reasons for the decision. The thirteen-year-old had to prepare himself for statewide competitive examinations the following year in order to become eligible for the free education the state of Württemberg provided for its Protestant clergy. If he was to follow the examples of his grandfather and his half brother Karl Isenberg and enter the Theological Seminary at Maulbronn, this examination had to be passed. And for Johannes Hesse's first son, missionary service was almost a predestined career.

Deeper reasons for the change never lagged far behind. Hermann continued to be a "problem." The cycle of transgression, punishment, forgiveness, and tears was part of the Hesses' daily life. Hermann stole figs and was punished. Hermann started a fire. Hermann was ill; he had to be kept from physical activity; he was not allowed to go skating and was therefore morose. Hermann had a tantrum. Many of these incidents, which Hesse later recorded in his memoirs and fiction, took place during these last two years in Calw. Marie Hesse was constantly aware of his emotional frailty. When they had to find a school for him, they chose the small Latin School in Göppingen in preference to a larger more institutional school in nearby Kornthal, because, as Marie confided to her daughter Adele, individual attention was particularly important for an "abnormal boy like our Hermann." "God give," wrote the dubious mother as she was preparing his blankets and shirts, "that Hermann will discipline himself and improve in diligence and manners."[29]

On February 1, 1890, Marie Hesse accompanied her son to the town of Göppingen and enrolled him in the school.[30] From all indications, this first phase of Hesse's school life away from home was not a total disaster. He liked the widow in whose house he boarded. He got on well with roommates and classmates, beginning to develop that genius for friendship that was to save him throughout his difficult life. He was good at Latin. He admired their principal, old Rector Otto Bauer, for his sense of humor and humanity. He even accepted, with amusement, the silly exercise the aging clergyman set for his Latin class—to translate Friedrich Schiller's play *Wallenstein* into Latin. In a letter written only a few weeks after his arrival, he happily admonished his little brother Hans to behave well so that he too might be allowed to go to Göppingen. There were some complaints—the landlady was too strict, although Hermann enjoyed browsing in her library—and Marie Hesse records in her diary various minor mishaps and illnesses. Toward the end of the year, more severe discomfort, illness, headaches, and homesickness appeared. Still, most of the year passed without those traumatic scenes he had created at home. He was a good student. He had a sense of achievement. Perhaps the main drawback of this episode was that it ended too soon.

In July 1891, Hermann Hesse traveled to Stuttgart, in the company of his mother, and for two seemingly endless days he took the examinations for the seminary. He had dreaded them, but he passed. The next few weeks were filled with the comings and goings of the busy Hesse home, for summer was always the season for visitors to call and stay with them—relatives from the Baltic, visiting scholars, a boy from England. Hermann went on walking tours, paid farewell visits to his friends, roamed once more in his hometown and the surrounding fields along the familiar alleys and footpaths. Then, in September, Marie Hesse took her son to the Protestant Theological Seminary in Maulbronn where he was to begin his career as a clergyman, theologian, and missionary.

Maulbronn was a sinister place—old, dark, and forbidding, though set in a beautiful countryside of open fields bordered by mountains. The seminary's medieval structure was separated from the nearby village by a wall and a moat. Before it had been taken over by the Protestant regents of Württemberg in the sixteenth century it had been run by Cistercian monks, and the buildings still showed traces of their sparse life. In the church adjoining the school a starkly carved wooden figure of Christ rose high in the midst of the nave, facing the scarred pews. Dark corridors swept by cold drafts led to the schoolrooms beyond and to the large dormitory rooms upstairs.

For all this austerity, however, the building possessed an imposing beauty. Having gradually evolved through many centuries, they piled different styles not ungraciously upon one another: rounded Romanesque archways, late Gothic ceilings, high narrow windows of early Gothic style. Nearby was a carefully cultivated garden. A well-wrought fountain stood in one of the cloisters. Hesse's first impressions were mostly positive. He praised the countryside, the nearby lake, and the view from a hilltop not far from the school. And he had an approving word for

Maulbronn itself: "The dignified monastery with its ancient cloisters
offers a lovely view. Especially beautiful is the old church. . . ." He also
liked many of the boys and was to keep up his friendship with several
of them throughout his life. In his large dormitory room, named Hellas,
he took a prominent part in fierce conversations and only occasional
quarrels. He was even elected the representative of his roommates. Although he disliked athletics, and found the music class useless, he continued to enjoy studying Latin. In a long letter home, written on October
4, just two weeks after his arrival, he was full of enthusiasm about his
success. It contains almost idyllic descriptions of his schedule and his
menus, details about his new companions, and culminates in a description of gatherings on a hilltop near the school, where he and his friends
would sing and talk. Sometimes, he wrote, he would go there alone to
prepare himself to recite poems in German, Latin, and Greek, since the
view and open air would be more inspiring than the dark atmosphere
surrounding the desk in the monastery. For this reason, he concluded
irrelevantly, "You need never fear that this young novice may become a
monk. The tonsure doesn't suit a German."[31]

These early enthusiasms were by no means dimmed in subsequent
letters. Hesse was neither despised nor even unpopular. In one of his
letters he reported a fistfight with another boy, but he seems to have
been none the worse for it. His glasses broke. He was always short of
money. He began to collect books. And he enjoyed food packages from
home. Even the Christmas holidays back in Calw were uneventful. He
was cheerful and relaxed, and went back to school reasonably content.
The only event a nervous Marie Hesse found disturbing was the part he
played in a bad fire that occurred during the night of January 19.
Perhaps recalling his adventure of the year before, when he had started
a fire, and some peculiar anxieties about matches as a young child, she
seemed to be afraid that hidden fears might have been brought back to
the surface. Hermann took a very active role in fighting the fire, and
reported it in almost obsessive detail in letters reflecting a noticeable
strain. But soon his life became normal again and in February his letters
were chatty and full of cheerful news.

Nevertheless, within a few months the fourteen-year-old boy was to
run away from the school. Many reasons emerge from Hesse's writings,
for he often returned to this period of his life, especially in *Beneath the
Wheel*, the novel he wrote thirteen years later as a thinly disguised account of the affair. He had become obsessed with the evils of formal
education, with the "wheel" of an unfeeling system that crushes any
sensitive child. It was a pertinent vision. In the fiction of the early years

of this century—of the time, in 1905, when *Beneath the Wheel* became a popular success—official education was often described as tyrannical, and its effect on young minds was viewed as a pervasive condition: children victimized by pompous and often cruel teachers who had nothing useful to teach them. This vision of arbitrary teachers—which the mature Hesse contrasted with images of natural leaders or guides nurturing true knowledge—Maulbronn made concrete as an institution in which the adolescent Hesse had to participate. Despite his apparent acquiescence, this turned out to be a difficult undertaking, for his beginning manhood was not to be confined within a rigidly ordered system. The novice, as he had warned his parents, would never be a monk.

The desire for openness was faintly sensed in a religious garb even at the moment when it first assumed shape in Hesse's adolescent mind. In fact, throughout his life, his rejection of restrictive teachers indifferent to individual sensibilities had all the earmarks of a personal religion in which they were evil demons. For the fourteen-year-old who had just decided to become a "poet," this recognition was a revelation: doors would be opened to allow privacy of feeling, individual sensibility, personal freedom. If his mother as a disappointed and hurt young girl allowed herself to be "converted" to an acceptance of her restrictive religion, her son moved in the opposite direction: at a time when he saw himself hemmed in by authority he tried to escape it, fearing that he might be crushed, and put his faith in his personal revelation.

Dimly, self-consciously, he underwent this growth toward becoming a man, a process always involving for Hesse the danger of dissolution and despair. In *Beneath the Wheel*, written at the age of twenty-eight, this drama is enacted by two characters, one representing Hesse's despairing state of mind at the time, the other representing the way he would have liked to have acted. One hero, Hans Giebenrath, falls ill and commits suicide. The other hero, the "poet" Hermann Heilner whose surname roughly translates as "healer," runs away successfully. In the work of the adult Hermann Hesse about this worst crisis of his childhood, the illness, the despair, the suicidal fantasies of the adolescent are all gathered up in one character; the desire for real freedom from authority is gathered in the other, who turns out to be an idealized image of himself.

This split between two characters reflects the discrepancy between the ideal poet he wanted to be and the actual boy and his escape and breakdown, for which there was little warning. The lost boy trying to find himself while being misunderstood by his teachers, his illness and thoughts of suicide, are portrayed in the features of Giebenrath, who felt caught and crushed. This tone, not present in his letters to his family, is sounded accurately and realistically in the novel. It was illuminated in a Latin class in which Giebenrath fell ill:

> "Giebenrath," shouted the professor. "Are you asleep?"
> The student slowly opened his eyes and fixed them on the teacher with astonishment, and shook his head.
> "You were asleep! Or can you tell me what sentence we're on. Well?"
> Hans pointed his finger at the page. He knew very well where they were.
> "Won't you get up, maybe?" the professor asked with a sneer. Hans got up.
> "What are you doing? Look at me!"
> He looked at the professor. But the teacher did not like the way he looked and shook his head, puzzled.
> "Are you unwell, Giebenrath?"
> "No, Herr Professor."
> "Please sit down and see me in my room after class."

Hans Giebenrath's condition was one of physical illness and despair. Voices around him echoed in his head. Benches, lectern, and blackboard; the huge wooden compass and square on the wall; everything was still in its place, yet he felt curiously detached. His classmates seemed to eye him curiously and insolently. He was terrified.[32]

In Maulbronn, Hesse recalled, "I learned the Hebrew alphabet and was just about to comprehend the *Dagesh forte implicitum* when storms broke over me from within which caused my flight from the monastery school. . . ."[33] Hesse's escape was not Heilner's idealized rejection of authority but Giebenrath's suicide. The crisis that developed during those months in Maulbronn brought to a head all his earlier hatreds and fears. It was quite remarkable that in his letters home, even in his dealings with most of his classmates, he could suppress so much of that hatred, but it underscores the existence of conflicting impulses functioning side by side. Heilner accompanied Giebenrath; hatred cohabited with desire to please; fears of intellectual suffocation existed side by side with his first serious writings (he even finished a play). But the dark fears won out in the end. For the real Maulbronn was only part of the prison; the inferno Hermann Hesse entered in the monastery school—guarded by dark hallways and thick prison-like walls—was the labyrinth of himself. It was not only the school but a whole life he did not want, a whole future that threatened him. The anxiety of his early childhood in Basel had returned. Maulbronn was the Boys' House at the mission. Once more he reached out toward the "light."

At recess, in pouring rain, as he crossed the wide square between the church and the school buildings without a raincoat, his books for the next class under his arm, he did not seem like a runaway poised for a breakout. But suddenly he disappeared. Just as he was about to turn back into the building, just as he was waving to his friends, he turned and walked away. He went across a bridge and onto a road. The rain seemed to thicken and he was soon wet to his skin. For a while he walked between railroad tracks, stumbling over rails and ties, then on dirt roads. He crossed fields, avoiding houses. He grew hungry, but he had no money for food. It was a cold night in early March, and when darkness came he had no place to turn. He hid in a haystack and spent a long wet night, shivering, feeling drenched and lost. The next day, after twenty-four hours of roaming, he found himself looking into the severe face of a gendarme who took him to the nearest station house.

This crisis in Hermann Hesse's life was matched by an equivalent crisis at home. Suddenly, the ghosts of the past, the agonies of Basel barely laid to rest, returned to pursue them. Marie Hesse noted the events meticulously in her diary. She had just been through a hard night, because her younger daughter Marulla had come down with a fever and a sore throat. The doctor feared diphtheria. And Hans was under confinement at his school. When late in the afternoon she heard the mailman at the door loudly announcing the arrival of a telegram, she first thought that this had to be an announcement of old Dr. Hesse's death, at last, in his Baltic village. But it was from Maulbronn and contained the news that Hermann had been missing since two o'clock. Terror ensued. Adele rushed the message to her father. Telegrams were exchanged with equally upset authorities at the school. The night Hermann spent drenched in a haystack was even worse for his mother. Marie lay down next to her sick daughter, holding her feverish hand. But what she felt that night was not just a mother's anxiety. "At first I was afraid," she wrote, "that Hermann had fallen into some particular sin or disgrace, that a dreadfully evil act had preceded his escape . . . and so I felt most grateful when finally the feeling seized me that he was in God's merciful hand, perhaps already wholly with Him, redeemed, dead, perhaps drowned in one of the lakes he admired so much. . . ." And she added: "Any misfortune, any mere falling into the hand of God would seem more bearable than Hermann's falling into sin and shame." Darkness, then, was not only outside. It was also within the gates. The next day, when the news of Hermann's discovery came, his mother's relief again expressed itself in a judgment. It was clear, she wrote, from the headmaster's letter that "*Weltschmerz* and mental confusion had been responsible, but no planned evil."[34]

This escapade was decisive for Hermann Hesse's immediate future, for it ushered in several years of trauma, but it also led to his liberation from the imprisonment of the monastery school and from the clergy for which he had been destined. Although his actual punishment at the school was not very severe (he received only a few hours of solitary confinement), the authorities now viewed him in a different light. He was allowed to continue his classes and to take examinations, but his removal from the school by the end of the year was strongly recommended. As time went on, his teachers began to regard his behavior as mentally confused, even disturbed. For a time he hung on. Partly at home, partly at school, trying to serve out the year, he fell victim to frequent illnesses and accidents. Even the letters from his schoolmates to his parents became alarming, and early in May it became evident that Hermann could no longer function.

On May 7, 1892, Marie Hesse traveled to Maulbronn to pick up her son, and three days later took him to the small spa of Bad Boll where a Protestant clergyman named Christoph Blumhardt had made a small reputation treating mental disorders by exorcising the Devil. Blumhardt was a colleague of Hesse's father and grandfather, and so it was expected that the child would receive special care. But the deep melancholia that closed in around him after his unsuccessful escape still held him in its grip.

Life at Bad Boll was not uniformly unpleasant. Hesse played billiards and checkers to the sound of Beethoven sonatas. He also had considerable freedom of movement and was able to take up old relationships, for Göppingen, where he had gone to school, was not far away. He received permission to hike there to visit old Rector Bauer of the Latin School, his former landlady, Frau Schaible, and his former school friends. He was also able to visit Cannstatt, which was not too far away, and to spend time with his half brother Theodor Isenberg, who lived there. Indeed, in Theo's house he met a girl named Eugenie Kolb with whom he proceeded to fall in love. She was twenty-two years old—seven years his senior—but vivacious and friendly. She and her mother provided at least the idea of a "home" away from the institution to which he had been exiled.

The deceptive ease of Bad Boll, which made Hesse's meeting with Eugenie possible, was contradicted by the puritanical preacher Blumhardt. For Hesse, his violent sermons on Sundays were disturbing and painful. Hence, when his declaration of love (as an antidote to hell fire and thunder) was gently but firmly rejected by Eugenie, he was seized by despair. Six weeks of prayers to drive out the Devil, combined with an abortive attempt to be loved, were more than the depressed child could endure. He bought a gun and tried to use it on himself.

Blumhardt was livid with rage. Marie Hesse received his angry letter on the morning of June 21. She left immediately, wiring her brother David Gundert to board her train in Stuttgart. Blumhardt was waiting for them in nearby Göppingen, spilling over with reprimands. He demanded that the child be confined to an insane asylum at once. Prayers having proved to be of no avail, the only alternative was bedlam. Luckily, the physician they were referred to opposed the idea. He suggested that they look for other possibilities before committing anyone so young. But the doctor also felt that the illness was very deeply rooted, since it had such a long history.

Accompanied by her brother, Marie next traveled to Bad Boll to see Hermann. She met him the next day, a withdrawn child imprisoned in a small room of a local restaurant. Meanwhile, Blumhardt continued to rage. The language of his hell-fire sermons intruded into his judgment of the boy, whom he no longer regarded as being ill but as being possessed by evil spirits. He preached to her about the bad upbringing the boy had received and how the Hesses were now harvesting the fruits of their neglect.[35]

Finally the decision was made to take Hermann to Stetten, a place for retarded and epileptic children. But it was by no means certain that he would be accepted. Instead, Blumhardt suggested that they simply arrive and throw themselves at the mercy of the director, Parson Gottlieb Schall. For this ordeal Marie needed the support of her family. David Gundert, who had temporarily returned home, was summoned once more. Marie's eldest son, Theodor Isenberg, was asked to join her. And together they took Hermann to the castle that housed the unfortunate children. When they arrived in the courtyard, he shouted in anguish: "Do you want to lock me up in a prison? I'd rather jump into that well over there." But after a long talk with the mild-mannered parson, who had agreed to accept him, he was persuaded to stay. Marie Hesse returned home that night "wholly exhausted, crushed in body and soul, as if after a long hard illness."

On the surface, Hermann Hesse adapted rather well to life at the institution. Indeed, he usually conformed to institutional pressures—in Basel, at Maulbronn, even in Bad Boll—up to a point. During the time he spent in Stetten in Parson Schall's care he was employed in light gardening (a pastime he was to enjoy all his life) and in tutoring some of his retarded fellow inmates. Only his later letters to his parents suggest the anger and violence he kept suppressed—at a time, toward the end of his stay, when he demanded to be let out. He knew, of course, that he was in an institution for the mentally disturbed, but he was encouraged to continue his Latin and other studies. Nor was he wholly confined. He was

soon allowed to visit friends, picking up again those acquaintances he
had made and renewed in Bad Boll. He also picked up the thread of the
hoped-for love with Eugenie Kolb, and even sent her a volume of poems
written in her honor. But this time the girl was careful to guard against
a repetition of the last disastrous declaration. On July 20, one month
after the attempted suicide, she wrote him:

> I beg you fervently, dear Herr Hesse, *forget* what you have gone through
> and above all take care of your health. Remember, and believe me, when
> I say to you: The first love is *never, never* the *right one*—even if a
> disappointment in matters of the heart is bitter—it was still best for
> you . . . not to have found a response to your love. . . .[36]

In the end she concludes that she would gladly be his friend, his "blood
brother," and asked him over for the following Saturday when Theodor
would also be free. At first, Hesse accepted this offer of friendship and
indeed wrote home a week later proposing that he be permitted to attend
the *Gymnasium* in Cannstatt after his recovery to be near the Kolbs since
Eugenie and her mother had become "mother and sister" to him. When
later in the year he did enter the Cannstatt school, he felt a lack of contact with her that again proved to be a source of crisis. At the moment,
however, the continuing warmth with which he was received, the excursions in the countryside, the caring of the inspector (who spoke to him
often, encouraged him in his Latin and gardening, and had him to tea)
suited him well. Progress appeared to be extraordinarily rapid for a boy
who had been delivered to the institution in a state of severe depression
only a month earlier. Superintendent Schall sensitively observed that
Hermann was like an egg without a shell, yet he was most optimistic
about his complete recovery.

In August, Johannes Hesse took his son home, and the picture
darkened again at once. Home was where he most wanted to be as he
sought substitutes for home (with the Kolbs, for instance) in his various
places of exile. But the moment he returned it seemed to him forbidding
and hostile. Life was continuing with the usual gentle confusion at the
Hesses' home in Calw. There was the usual coming and going of visitors
and overnight guests; there were the children's illnesses and demands.
Yet Hermann refused to take part in most of the family's undertakings.
He did not go on walks, or talk much to his family, or take the medicine
the doctor had prescribed for him. When the *Gymnasium* in the town of
Reutlingen refused to accept him because of his record, his tantrums
and angry withdrawals increased. Two weeks after his return, Johannes
Hesse wrote to Parson Schall, asking him to take the boy back, and on

August 22 he traveled to Stetten to deliver his son, who was to remain there for six more weeks.

The brief time at home in the late summer was perhaps the hardest time of Hesse's difficult childhood and adolescence, for he felt confirmed in his belief that he had been condemned to permanent exile. While first at Stetten he had been so docile that Parson Schall was amazed and a little defensive when he was told about his behavior in Calw. When he was returned, his anger increased, but his true feelings were revealed more fully in his letters to his family than in his overt manner at the institution. He felt caught. Aware of having been branded mentally ill, he wrote an angry statement to his parents:

> If you could look now into my innermost soul, into that black cavern where only one point of light glows and burns hellishly, you would wish for and grant me my death. Livy is lying open before me: I'm supposed to work on it and can hardly do it. I'd love to throw all of Livy into the fire, including dictionaries, and with it that whole insane asylum, Boll, Calw, present and past, and fling myself after them. . . .
>
> . . . In Boll, I first learned how to laugh, then how to weep. In Stetten I learned something too: how to curse. I know, first of all, how to curse myself and Stetten, then (to curse) all my relatives, the heated dream and illusion of world and God, happiness and misery. When you write to me again, don't appeal to your Christ. He's being touted about enough in this place. "Christ and Love. God and Salvation" etc., etc. is displayed everywhere in this place which is so full of hatred and hostility. I believe that if the spirit of the departed "Christ," of the Jew Jesus, could see what he had wrought, he would weep. I am a man, as much as Jesus was, and see the difference between ideal and life as much as he. But I'm not as tough as that Jew.[37]

Hermann Hesse felt betrayed, especially by his father. Earlier, when he was needed at the time of Maulbronn, he had been absent, and now, when he was needed even more, he exiled him to a place where the only music was a sleepy organ and the nasal voices of the retarded singing a children's song. Johannes Hesse tried to explain himself, assuring him that everything possible would be done for him the moment he was well, but he could not mollify his son. "Dear Sir," wrote the fifteen-year-old on September 14, "Since you show yourself so conspicuously ready for sacrifice, may I perhaps ask for 7 marks or immediately for a revolver?"[38]

Hermann's anger did not remain without effect. Toward the end of September the Hesses wrote to their old friend at the Basel Mission School, Parson Pfisterer, and begged him to take their son for a while. His superintendant at Stetten, Parson Schall, warmly endorsed the idea, and the Pfisterers extended their welcome. On October 4, the day before he set out on his journey to Switzerland, Parson Schall delivered his final diagnosis in a letter to Hermann's uncle David Gundert:

> I spoke this morning with Dr. Habermaas (the physician). He agrees that we should let Hermann go to Basel. It is his opinion that Parson Pfisterer's influence will surely be favorable. The prognosis of primary insanity he is not yet willing to make. These may be the symptoms of initial stages of such an illness, but he does not want to judge this with certainty. That would indeed be, as Herr Hesse put it, a verdict of death. Let us hope to God that matters will not be that bad.
>
> Tomorrow I will therefore put Hermann on the train that will arrive in Stuttgart at 6:40. . . .[39]

Hermann traveled directly to Stuttgart, without stopping at home, where his mother lay ill with a gastric fever; and he was warmly received in Basel, where he greeted his old mentor with *"Grüss Gott, Papa!"* and then made himself at home. He soon moved into the old Boys' House, where he had lived as a small child. Parson Pfisterer functioned as a "father" who understood him at last. He was active in his behalf, for he managed to persuade Johannes Hesse to try one more time to place the boy in a regular educational setting to enable him to pass the examination that would assure his reduction of military service to one year. He was precisely one school year away from obtaining this exemption, which imperial Germany permitted to those subjects who were sufficiently well placed on the social ladder to obtain a secondary education. Since Hesse had just changed his citizenship from Swiss to German in order to benefit from the free schooling at Maulbronn, the danger of serving three years had become acute. For all these reasons, and upon Parson Pfisterer's prodding, Johannes Hesse managed to enroll his son in a *Gymnasium* in Cannstatt, the town not far from Bad Boll where Hermann had once wanted to move to be near Eugenie Kolb. On November 4, just a month after his arrival, he left Basel, the Boys' House, and the Pfisterers behind to start yet another new life in a different setting, to try his hand at formal education one more time.

Cannstatt was to be the scene of the last of that series of episodes that beset Hermann Hesse during his childhood. Parson Pfisterer had recommended that a single room be secured for him. Johannes Hesse was not able to achieve it (the room he found had to be shared with three other boys), but Hermann managed it quite easily, obtaining an attic room across the street in the home of a rather anxious widow, Frau Montigel. Herr Geiger, the proctor, in whose house he boarded, was a simple, easy-going man, though his letters to the Hesses were full of complaints and constant requests for money. For a short while, Hermann appears to have fallen into his usual institutional acquiescence. He visited old friends, even went on walking tours as far away as Stuttgart, and, except for falling through the ice in an attempt to skate before the proper time, his first two months in his new surroundings were fairly uneventful. He was even agreeable while he was home during the Christmas holidays. But he was seized by disappointments—caused especially by the absence of Eugenie Kolb's love in the place where he had hoped to find it, which confirmed his sense of failure. By January 20 a new crisis had broken out.

A long, disturbing letter, rambling, full of dire forebodings, arrived at the Hesse home and shattered their peace:

> And your "God," too. He may exist, He may even be the way you think He is, but He does not interest me. Don't think you can influence me in this way.
>
> By the way, I pity you; for, thinking of me in sorrow and pity are the most unpleasant thoughts and the most worthless ones. I sit here in Cannstatt and live and learn, what is there to worry and pity about? If you think I am sad about this last year, about disappointments, about the painful loss of love; if you think I am tormented by remorse about suicide, you are mistaken! That my ideals of world and love and art and life and knowledge, etc., have been exploded, I'm not particularly sad about that. For all these dreams, the desire to be loved, etc., were unnecessary and senseless.

If everything had failed—parents, family, religion, and even the abortive affection of his older "beloved" Eugenie—there was nothing for it but to turn to renewed thoughts of suicide. With the grandstand play of the adolescent, yet with a serious sense of grievance as well, Hermann Hesse sounded his note of warning, his shout for help, in a long second letter scribbled that evening. He had an "attack" (of anger and depression) as he had not experienced since Basel. There he sat, reading the gentle lyrical verse of the poet Eichendorff, when all of a sudden the "old devil" feeling swept over him again: all the heartache, the pain of lost love, the memories of his experiences at Boll. He gathered some books at random and went to Stuttgart to sell them and to buy a revolver with the proceeds. "And now here I sit and before me . . . lies that rusty thing."

> I have conquered myself this time, or I was a coward! I don't know but my head is full of rage and noise, and I'd like to know someone to whom I could say: Help me!
>
> Now you'll immediately serve me up Jesus and God, but I don't know them; still I'd like to say to someone: Help, help me!
>
> But there'd have to be someone who'd understand me and who would have the power to put me into a different world.

He tried everything, including playing his violin, but nothing worked. "So it goes with everything," the letter concluded. "Whether you scold me or are saddened by me, whether you laugh at me, reprimand me or weep; I always remain the same unhappy fool and in the end—who knows? True, for the moment I stayed my hand with the weapon—but what for?"[40] The same self-pitying awareness of inevitable doom was to accompany many of the writings of the adult Hermann Hesse. At this moment, however, it mostly frightened his mother.

Marie Hesse tells in her diary, with severe understatement, how she responded to this letter. She rushed at once to Hermann's side and found him "very ill, angry, unhappy." Proctor Geiger, who was supposed to look after him, had evidently noticed nothing. She took a room next to Hermann's and tried to calm him. On the evening of her arrival, a Saturday, she followed Hermann's wish and paid calls to the director of the school and his teacher (who praised him) in a heavy snowstorm. The next day was Sunday. After a sleepless, ice-cold night in the unheated room she had to face her raging and screaming son. Later, at the station, Hermann was quieter and more accessible, but they were interrupted by some acquaintances and so could not talk. "I was sick in body and soul," wrote Marie, "got a bad catarrh and felt so powerless against that evil power. . . . Father [old Gundert] feels with us and prays often for Hermann. . . . Only God can help us."[41]

This episode was soon superseded by other moments of pain and despair and threatened suicides, but a fresh element—an expressed need for independence—began to assert itself. For Cannstatt, a middle-sized town not far from the city of Stuttgart, offered Hesse the first real opportunity, after months of boarding schools and institutions, to cut loose and act on his own. His letters to his family speak of headaches and illness. Herr Geiger's more and more incensed letters tell a story of bad company, drinking, and late nights. Hermann did little work at school and spent a great deal of time with various men—some of them good friends, including even a young teacher with whom he was to correspond for years, and some newly found and robust drinking companions whom he quickly converted into his satanic tempters.

Cannstatt had seemed like a very different place earlier in the year when he had hoped to live close to Eugenie Kolb and to enjoy his love for her, but this changed atmosphere had its own rewards. Hesse could give in to his need to break through the shell of himself, to overcome his withdrawals—his shyness as well as his depressions—with the help of beer, wine, and the companionship of other young men. As a result, he was constantly in debt, selling books and school supplies to get cash, being treated by his older, more loose-living companions.

Attempted escape and suicide were now followed by drinking and smoking, by clandestine visits to Stuttgart (disguised by faked telegrams sent to his proctor), by sanctimonious promises to Herr Geiger and to his parents, which were immediately broken. But the episodes became worse. An overwrought Geiger wrote at length about Hesse's friendship with a man in his twenties whom he met secretly in Stuttgart and who supplied him with loans and treats. Yet at the same time Hermann still wanted to be accepted at home. He appealed to his family with tales of headaches, dizzy spells, and fever. He appealed to them for money. But he also felt that he had been abandoned and now turned toward the world of "dark." He clearly enjoyed that world—and the self-loathing it inspired.

In April 1893, his grandfather Gundert lay dying, and Hermann was summoned home for the funeral which took place on April 25.[42] He returned quickly to Cannstatt and by early May his father was again chastising him for his dissolute life. He was home again briefly in early June, but left after a day. Still, he was able to take his examinations, despite all the losses of school time and the drinking bouts, and managed to pass. For a brief time the Hesses even considered the possibility that Hermann continue for another three years to obtain a final degree that would qualify him for the university. But that dream had to be abandoned. It was to become one of the painful burdens for Hesse during his younger years that he had been unable to achieve this aim.

The reason for this failure was Hesse's continuing inability to accept a coherent education. It took no more than a month after his return to the school in the fall for his "moral insanity" (as Parson Schall eventually diagnosed his illness) to manifest itself. Complaining of incessant head-aches, unable to keep up with his work, he begged to be taken home. On October 15, 1893, Marie Hesse was on the road again to pick up her son. His acquiescence in an accepted way of life was now at an end. Within days of his return home, his father had placed him as a bookseller's apprentice in the nearby town of Esslingen. Another arrangement was made: contracts were signed committing the bookseller to apprentice the boy for the usual three years. But within three days another urgent letter arrived at the Hesse home. He had vanished. Eventually he was found in Stuttgart, where he had gone to see his mother's relatives. This time it was his father who brought him home.

The face that the sixteen-year-old Hermann Hesse turned to the world was that of an outcast, from a family in which, paradoxically, he was a constant object of worried love and concern. Whether he was actually ill—the "primary madness" or "moral insanity"—is difficult to ascertain, since diagnostic terms in that age, a decade before Freud, were as vague as the treatment was medieval. Hesse's life as a boy was clearly torn by his doubts in his family's religion, by his sense of exile and loss, by his sense of his father's failure: a young man's life that seemed to dissipate itself in impulsive gestures. He reached toward home, toward the love of women—his mother; his sister; his first love, Eugenie Kolb—and toward the friendship of men of his own generation. But the authority of older men, of the men who created and sustained the society that exacted demands from him, he could not meet. His crises had taught him that theological seminaries, mental institutions, restrictive proctors and teachers could be met in only one of two ways: one either acquiesced or escaped. He tried both. But in Esslingen he did not have the patience to acquiesce, to wait and endure. He ran away. And now the family had no plans for their son, except to keep him at home and employ him as best they could.

IV

When Hermann Hesse returned to his home as an invalid at the age of sixteen, he found it greatly changed. His grandfather was gone. The family had moved back into the old quarters that housed the Calwer Verlagsverein, for Johannes Hesse was now in full charge of the publishing company and was even tenser and busier than he had been when he was working for old Dr. Gundert. Impatient, preoccupied with conferences and travel, he appeared anxious and irritated. Hermann withdrew. He tended the garden and read eagerly in his grandfather's library —a storehouse of books from various parts of the world: eighteenth and nineteenth century German poets, dramatists, and novelists; Western and Indian philosophers and mystics. Among them, the late eighteenth century German novelist Jean Paul Richter—a humorous, sentimental writer relying on dialect in a large number of his books—appeared to him particularly meaningful (he was able to read through the entire collected works). He also rediscovered Goethe and the romantic poet Novalis, both opening a new form of perception to him.

This time of intermittent leisure became for Hesse the beginning of a new education, of self-education. Concentrating only in subjects that interested him, he tended his adolescent self-consciousness as a writer like a plant in his family's garden. At the same time his relationship with his father continued to deteriorate. He started to work for him in his office, but the strain was unbearable. It became a continuous series of abrasive encounters—the father irritated by his son's unserious attitude toward his life and work; the son angered by his father's refusal to acknowledge his artistic temperament. An interchange of demands made by the son, rejected by the father, began to take the place of ordinary dialogue. Heatedly, in letters (through they lived in the same house), Hermann demanded and Johannes refused an allowance sufficient for him to strike out on his own as a free-lance writer. It was a divisive time for them all, and the family simply did not have confidence in Hermann's ability to function by himself. Their prejudice against any unconventional way of making a living surely played a part, but more than a year of Hermann's explosive behavior did not make them confident that he would manage as an independent writer.

Instead of allowing their son to leave home with an allowance to try his luck, his parents cast about for a solid, regular, undemanding occupation. By June 1894 he had sufficiently recovered, and regular work outside the house seemed best suited to defuse the anger that flared up at home. They came up with an apprenticeship in a completely different world from any of those to which he had been accustomed. They found a place in a small factory manufacturing tower clocks. Its neat brick buildings and smokestack were arranged near a bend of a long street that ran alongside the Nagold, almost at the end of town. The new master was Heinrich Perrot, a square-jawed, slow-moving man to whom Hesse gave a name and a place in the novel of his old age, *The Glass Bead Game*. At first, as usual, the change was surprisingly positive. Hesse was pleased to think of himself as a mechanic, a workman, a *Techniker*. In fact, proudly or ironically, he signed some of his letters "H. Hesse. Mechanic." In the beginning at least it led him to think of his job as an enrichment of his experience, as an adventure. It did not deflect him from his desire to be ultimately a writer and poet.[43]

Hesse's new life was extraordinarily regular. His mother was pleased to see him leaving "for business" in the morning and coming home at the usual hour when the day was done. And from all indications—there are scattered references to this episode in various autobiographical essays and a more extensive description in *Beneath the Wheel*—he was by no means unhappy filing metal and tightening bolts. In many ways, this agreeable manner can be attributed to Hesse's style, for he usually accommodated himself to a new situation until regrets, bitterness, and, ultimately, rebellion set in. But clearly his life of filing gears, bent over the vise, took up only the surface of his thoughts. Another life took place mostly on paper, in poems written at night, in letters to his many friends—former schoolmates in Cannstatt and Maulbronn and even to a young teacher, Ernst Kapff. These letters often turned into learned disquisitions about literature, philosophy, and art, advanced with the declamatory seriousness of a very young man who had just discovered the possibilities of learning. More and more his life during his off-hours came to resemble his ideas of a writer's life: from his rather pompous but lively correspondence, to walking tours, to poems hastily scribbled and sent to a friend before the ink had dried.

Yet Hesse continued to be uncertain about a career in which he could earn a living. By the summer of 1895, the novelty of being a laborer had worn off and the question of earning his daily bread in a more congenial occupation had to be faced anew. Harebrained schemes occurred to him, only to be discarded. At one point he thought of becoming a farmer and emigrate to Brazil. He also thought of forays to other places, including India, and in preparation spent part of the summer of 1895 trying to learn English with his sister Adele. Gradually, his situation was threatening to become acute again. Discontent with his work manifested itself more and more in headaches and tense brooding. By September it had become ominous, and therefore yet another contract was torn up. A forbearing Heinrich Perrot certified that young Hesse had learned the rudiments of his trade (having served less than half his apprenticeship) and wished him luck.[44] Once more Hesse was free.

The new freedom, however, was different from the freedoms into which he had escaped before. He now knew he wanted to live in books, that he wanted to be a poet and a writer. He also sensed that he was now able to act on his decision by himself. Two weeks after quitting the machine shop he noticed an advertisement in a Stuttgart newspaper: "Heckenhauer's Bookshop" in Tübingen was seeking an apprentice. Three days later he applied and was accepted. The change that had begun in Maulbronn was now complete. His sense of himself as a writer, his awareness of where and what he wanted to be, finally had led him in the right direction. He could leave home without straining to return. He had found his own source of "light."

In Tübingen, at barely eighteen, Hesse began to find his way out of the labyrinth. When the train curved through the Black Forest valley and he saw the towers of the university below, he knew he had made a new beginning. Doors were open—or at least that was how he felt as he dragged his suitcases onto the station platform. On the other side of the doors of that railroad station was the expanse of mountains and forests. There was the river not far away, and beyond the bridge lay the alleys and towers of the town. It was not home. It was no school and no institution. It was his own.

2

The First New Life: *From Bookseller to Author*

I

Oct. 17, 1895
—just arrived in Tübingen

Dear Mother: My best congratulations on your birthday. I'm stopping for a moment at Marulla's and can write only very briefly. More on Sunday. Arrived well after a very cold trip and was received in a *very* friendly way. Room, etc. all very lovely. Haven't been to see Herr S. yet. Many best regards.
(I'm writing in haste, at Marulla's, with very bad ink.)

Your grateful Hermann

THIS IS HOW young Hermann Hesse began his new life, reflecting it intensely in the mirrors of the old—of that home and family he had struggled so hard to embrace and to leave. Even as he set out on his own, he was able to touch base with his sister, who was then staying in Tübingen.[1] But especially striking is the voluminous correspondence with his parents, which began at once and which, in Hesse's paradoxical way, became his route to himself.

That Thursday in October when Hermann Hesse arrived in Tübingen he became "Hermann Lauscher"—"Hermann Listener"—the central figure in his first full-length novel, which was to portray his years at the turn of the century. He was his own persona, Hermann, his own listening ear absorbing the sounds around him, recording the talk of people. Throughout his life, his eye, too, caught movements, light, sights, persons and turned them in the mirrors of his past and of his dreams.

The bookseller's apprentice was also the writer who practiced his craft in his letters. These voluminous epistles sought to draw a full picture of his life in Tübingen: the wonders of his arrival, his adjustment, his daily routine. All minutiae were projected with the voice and authority of a story teller, a journalistic raconteur, a lecturer to be heard by his family and his various friends. Details were precise, often colorful. They included close descriptions of the town, of his room, of his landlady and new acquaintances and of his day-to-day doings. They also draw a vivid picture of his early days as an apprentice in Heckenhauer's Bookstore.

That encounter was contained in a long second letter written to his mother the same Thursday of his arrival. He had felt slightly oppressed when he opened the narrow door to the bookshop facing the Stiftskirche (the seminary church) and had looked around the piles of books and the slow-moving clerks and the student customers browsing among piles of volumes. Then he was shown into the inner office, and it is this scene that he described vividly to his mother. His new boss, Herr Carl August Sonnewald, was a tall blond man with an imperial mustache hanging down the sides of his mouth. Looking somber in his black morning coat, he glanced up only briefly when the new apprentice—thin, close-cropped, with a pinched face—approached him hesitantly. "You want to enter our firm?" Hermann nodded and was about to say his farewells until morning when his employer rose, led him wordlessly to a stand-up desk that had been readied for him, and put him to work making out inventory slips and gluing the backs of damaged books. Only at 7:30 in the evening, at regular closing time, was he allowed to find his way back to his room on the ground floor of Herrenberger Strasse 28 at the edge of town to finish unpacking.

The apprentice's workday stretched out in twelve endless hours—from half past seven in the morning until the same time at night—with only an hour and a half for lunch. Still, the early letters suggested the same open-eyed pleasure that Hesse had shown each time upon beginning his new lives: in Maulbronn, in Cannstatt, at the factory in Calw. He was determined to accept, even to like, as much as he saw, yet to appear discriminating and instructive as well. He was unable to contain his correspondence. All his seeing and hearing had to be reflected in the mirror of that invisible audience in Calw. If he wrote in his first quick note on Thursday that he would write at length the following Sunday, that resolution was impatiently discarded. Not only did he report at length on his first hours at work that very same evening, he also began a marathon epistle the next day that took him through Friday and Saturday.

It was clearly staging for an audience, characterized by the delight in teaching and preaching that was one of Johannes Hesse's legacies. He passed somber judgments, as though his parents had never been away from Calw: he liked the town of Tübingen with its crooked alleys and its medieval-romantic spirit, even if it was a bit smelly and dirty. The castle, which he could see from his room, was splendid and the view from its height breathtaking. His landlady fitted in with the atmosphere of the town. Frau Leopold was a deacon's widow—as loquacious as she was maternal. She stuffed him with food of the choicest kind, pampering him at the price of making him listen endlessly to torrents of words. He had a hard time getting away from the table as he was filled up with stories about people and places in Frau Deacon's long life. Yet Hesse also felt strangely touched by that mixture of lives from Calw, Basel, the Baltic—all places from his own life—and of those missionaries and their various friends with their illnesses, deaths, betrothals, and travels. And as Frau Deacon turned to herself—her own childhood, marriage, and widowhood—he felt drawn to her while feeling strangely restless, as though he were held to that place at her lunch table against his will.

He was being taken care of in that small bourgeois world, being mothered tenaciously. Frau Deacon put a fresh bottle of apple cider in his room, then mysteriously apologized, and inundated him at night with sausage, salad, tea, rolls, and other goodies—even when he refused —talking all the time. In his moralizing way, the young chronicler allowed that he did not mind her talk, because she never indulged in vicious gossip, which, in turn, permitted him to enjoy her food. All these reflections were projected through an already distinctly literary turn of mind. Frau Deacon appeared to him like a character out of Dickens. Indeed, the food, the talk, the mothering acted as stage props in an imaginative performance in which he was the lead actor and the audience alike.

And then there was the assumption that each event in Hesse's life would be of great interest to his readers. His room on a bare ground floor was no different from any other room he had occupied away from home —in Göppingen or Cannstatt—yet he described it in the minutest detail and even drew a floor plan: the stage on which he moved, the furniture of his mind. It contained bed, nightstand, desk, and a "beautifully painted ceiling." These fond descriptions of middle-class decor prefigure many others like them in his stories and novels and form significant motifs in the work of his middle age like *Demian* and *Steppenwolf*. The sense of living on a stage, moreover, joined the ambivalent movement away from home and back toward it as one of the major impulses of his life and art. He was equally perceiver and perceived. At this point, in October 1896, the young writer on the verge of writing rehearsed his future by projecting it on a stage for the benefit of his captive audiences in Calw.

Although his prose was still tinged with the usual touch of self-pity, Hesse nonetheless managed to portray a fairly positive picture of his work. His duties became part of the action on that stage on which he saw himself perpetually observed. His work he pronounced to be "interesting." He had to organize all incoming merchandise, check the cash register in the morning, examine secondhand books for missing pages, ship periodicals, and occasionally run special errands that could not be entrusted to the regular messengers. Although the shop was a large place with spacious rooms, it was constantly cluttered with books and browsers. In addition, Heckenhauer's ran its own bindery in the cellar. Two large extensions in the back housed extensive stocks, mostly books on theology, law (which he learnedly called *ius*), and philology. He commented on the relative paucity of stock in medicine texts and the even greater poverty of books on music and art.

For years these letters continued, but the unusually lengthy and frequent early epistles from Tübingen were the most detailed and self-conscious: narrative and didactic, they easily adopted the tone of the entertainment literature of Hesse's time. He had done up his world for display and he treated the men for whom he worked like characters in a drama he had written for his family in Calw. The main staff consisted of six regular employees in addition to the apprentice Hesse and two messenger boys. They were the proprietor, August Sonnewald; the office manager, Heinrich Hermes; and four additional variously difficult men named Straubing, Schmidt, Kapp, and Klett. His superiors at the office were men he had to respect for their "education and knowledge," especially Herr Hermes, the life of the shop. These judgments were often contradicted later on and are barometers of Hesse's moods at the time. Still, a picture emerges of his place of work and its denizens that portrays not only Hesse's own features but the texture of his daily life.

Herr Sonnewald, the boss, represented the greatest problem. "When he speaks he just hisses—I have enormous respect for him." He worked in his heated office wearing hat and coat. Money was everything to him, or at least so Hesse felt. Herr Sonnewald, he observed, so much loved the physical possession of money that he even loved the *word*. He would use such phrases as "little money" or "much money" instead of "cheap" or "expensive." Indeed, his alert employee, who was never known to disdain money himself, discovered that the word "money" appeared in practically every one of his sentences. In addition, he spoke in a "very Swabian" dialect despite his "high education" and he would use such barnyard terms as "Saukerl" and "Rindvieh" when he spoke of bad customers or any loss of money. In fact, Hesse reported, the loss of even the pettiest sum would result in a plaintive, whining tone of voice that lasted all day.

But there was always the counterpoint. Something in Herr Sonnewald both repelled and frightened him. Perhaps sometime in the future, he wrote at one point, he might get used to his strange manners and get to like him better. "But he is a sufferer," wrote the eighteen-year-old in a manner that foreshadowed the older Hesse, "and it is in my nature not to be angry at people for whom one must feel pity." Each time his temper flared up, Herr Sonnewald had to sneeze and cough violently—as though he had to pay for his anger. At once, Hermann felt sorry for him. He even saw that this man of business sense and temper was also a man of high moral character with a strong sense of ethics, even though his morality was not grounded in religious convictions. This fact seemed to surprise Hesse: his boss's probity was not connected with piety, "at least not in any superficial sense." Something like a free-thinking spirit was abroad in their office and shop. But whether to please his parents or to satisfy his own needs, the young chronicler turned into a preacher as he contrasted his suffering, temper-burdened, money-conscious, yet secularly ethical boss with his less burdened associates. There was no question that Hesse's hero of the establishment was the office manager, Herr Heinrich Hermes.

He was the *hero*—as the name suggests, Hesse instructed his parents— "fat and comfortable," the pride of the firm. A man of affairs with a quick eye, he spoke several languages fluently and easily managed to keep ten things in mind at once. He handled the salesmen, advertising, all special and legal correspondence, and at the same time he could talk sensibly to printers and bookbinders. Occasionally, he contributed to journals, presided over a club or two, and even dabbled in politics. Most significant for Hesse, however, was his sense of humor. It was important to him that Herr Hermes could set the whole office into roars of laughter. Being the lowliest apprentice, Hesse felt excluded from these conversations, but he happily joined the laughter at Herr Hermes's jokes. For the stout office manager had a fine glance for the artistic and, above all, the humorous aspects of life.

These assessments delivered by the beginning apprentice to his family and friends indicate both a pose and a succinct perception of the men with whom he worked. While he expressed some disapproval and fear of his associates, Hesse actually managed to convey a generally favorable picture of his work. Words like *laconic, close-mouthed, angry, unapproachable* figured prominently in his various accounts, and his fellow employees were measured largely by the degree to which they showed an open or accepting appearance. Humor was therefore important. Equally important, on the negative side, was Hesse's sense of being excluded from most conversations. Still, the tone in his early letters resounded with a sense of success, with the feeling that he had arrived at last, that he was now functioning on his own, and that he had attained a place from which he could moralize and instruct. He conveyed a sense of happy superiority. He may have expressed some fear of men like Sonnewald, but he also judged them, as he judged practically everyone in the voluminous letters he wrote throughout his life.

The pendulum movement from positive to negative attitudes toward his colleagues corresponded to a similar ambivalence about his duties. His work was monotonous. Glued to his stand-up desk all day long, he wrote laboriously in his crabbed script—mostly invoices. But when his mother responded with sympathy for the "unending monotony" of his work, he insisted he liked it and brought up all kinds of small tasks that gave him more status and afforded some unexpected variety. His English —that very small amount he had learned the previous summer from Adele—now came in handy since in handling English books he was at least able to decipher the titles. Occasionally, he was asked to do errands; only when the mission could not be entrusted to one of the messenger boys (like going to the post office or bank) would he be allowed to go. Sometimes he was sent to the library in the Tübingen Castle. This errand he enjoyed especially, for it allowed him to take a pleasant walk, to do his job in an extensive and well-appointed library, and then to stroll back.

This was the tenor of Hermann Hesse's prose during the early months of his new life in Tübingen. He was on *good terms* with his superiors; he *liked* his work. But he was also *exhausted* from his duties and the long hours and *beaten* by those headaches and bouts of insomnia that plagued him all his life. It is sometimes difficult to tell whether he was boasting or complaining. He probably meant to do both. He was *worn out* on Saturdays, not only because they occurred at the end of a long week of twelve-hour days, but also because on Saturdays all the large shipments arrived from the publishing centers of Stuttgart and Leipzig. The day would be spent in back-breaking labor, sorting, cataloging, and pricing the new shipments. Hard as it all was, he would look back on these early months of his apprenticeship *with a smile*. One had to watch out for errors or dreadful things might happen. Even the smallest mistake in ordering could cost the firm large sums of money. But good things could happen when one was alert. Thus continued his contradictory moods.

One positive result of his growing involvement in his trade was that he was able to apply his experience to his future development as a writer just as he had used the months working with his father in Calw as an opportunity to browse in his grandfather's library and to prepare himself for his ultimate profession. At this point he began to take many of the catalogues home with him to study them after hours. He especially favored the Leipzig catalogues because they were "good for literature," but he also enjoyed working with periodicals, including popular family and women's magazines, because they were useful in getting to know the "reading public." Publishers' catalogues especially helped by giving him useful literary statistics such as the sales of Zola's novels. Still, as he explored the mysteries of the mails, cash, order blanks, and catalogues, he felt tired. Fatigue was the main burden of his work and troubled him more than annoyances and humiliations. The cross had to be borne and his work ground on, twelve hours a day, six days a week.

Intermingled with these unending stories of the office were also vignettes and impressions of Tübingen. He disliked the poor quarter of the town, the muddy alleys he had to pass on his way to work. In a letter written on October 23, less than a week after his arrival, he described walking to work at dawn. He saw the sun rising and flooding the steeples and houses along the hillsides with brilliant red, while the town below lay buried in white mist. When he turned in the opposite direction another beautiful view offered itself: the hunchbacked ancient town with its castle and church. But as he approached it, a different, sinister aspect revealed itself. The nearby alleys were narrow and dark, covered with mud and manure after the autumn rains. The filth seemed indescribable, and when Hesse got stuck in the slimy mud more than ankle deep and, startled, tried to pull out, an old man shouted to him from a doorway in the grossest dialect: "Go on, Herr, go to it. Don't shirk the dirt." Hesse was horrified and described the townspeople as a dreadful breed, gross and dirty and usually full of wine. Since he had to pass through "their" worst alleys to get to work, he at least indulged in moral indignation. He regarded them with derision and pity: the drunken men; the slovenly, skinny women; the filthy, insolent children. "Still," ended his description, "it seems to be a healthy breed." For even in these self-conscious letters he never once shed those contraditions that he was to dwell upon as a middle-aged man. The beauty of Tübingen at dawn was at once counterpointed by its filth. The dirty slum dwellers were also a "healthy breed."

Hermann Hesse's accounts of his life after hours were equally afflicted by contradictions. Having heard of the informative lunches with Frau Deacon, the nourishing suppers, the profitable readings, the family also heard of heavy fatigue. "Supper of herring and potatoes." "Dead tired." On the floor above his room lived a fiend, Herr Christaller, who soon developed into the devil threatening Hesse's paradise. His nerves were constantly jangled by the lusty, loud man in his heavy boots. He was an orientalist who whistled, sang, and recited Hebrew and Arabic words even as late as ten o'clock. The whole issue of sleep and insomnia—the bane of both Johannes's and Hermann's lives—with its constant complaints of headaches and fatigue became focused in the behavior of that man upstairs, and Hesse's letters on the subject became almost hysterical. Whenever Herr Christaller whistled, he would respond by whistling from his bed or he would strike up his violin, which he enjoyed playing in those days but which he carefully put away at the stroke of ten to avoid disturbing his neighbors. Now, to spite an indifferent Herr Christaller, he would deliberately play at one o'clock in the morning. For weeks the man's noises and the sound of his heavy boots overhead continued to be a source of agony, and Hesse told his parents that he would live to see that inconsiderate "Arab" either in the seminary (where he hoped he would move) or in Africa, "where he could be thought of painlessly among lions and cannibals." In the end the first of his two wishes came true: Christaller went to live in the Tübingen seminary.

Everything was fraught with doubt and anxiety, yet along with his fear and loneliness, Hesse gradually developed some social life. On Sunday he often visited his aunt, who had a pleasant flat just out of town where he would enjoy music. More important was his introduction to the home of Fräulein von Reutern, an acquaintance of his parents who also loved music and befriended the sons and daughters of her friends in an open house she held most Sunday afternoons. A vivid account of Hesse's first visit to her place reflects the same contradictions that marked all his experiences. The affair had begun on a solemn and formal note. The chronicler had found himself perched gingerly on the edge of a chair. It was during the afternoon coffee hour and he sat at the well-appointed table with several young people. Intimidated, he carefully spaced his bites of cake with precise, measured movements. The atmosphere was tense and he was momentarily relieved when one of the girls giggled and broke the spell. After a while they rose to play music. Hesse had brought his violin, yet even as he performed, he felt he had blundered by asking for the title of a piece of music he held in his hand. All afternoon he sought a way to make amends. They sang hymns together, but they soon lost tunes and words and ended up in fits of coughing, Finally, they played a game that allowed Hesse to redeem himself after his error: it involved guessing lines of poems—at which he naturally excelled. Before they left they were served fruit, and Hesse again displayed his awkwardness by dropping a heavy iron nutcracker on a delicate plate. Despite the clattering noise, the earlier mistake, the awkwardness, the tension, he knew he would be asked again. His debut at Fräulein von Reutern's had not been wholly unsuccessful.

More problematic were Hesse's relationships with his contemporaries, former friends who, unlike himself, had gone to Tübingen as full high school graduates and were now students at the university or the theological seminary. There is no question that they presented a problem that began to disturb him soon after his arrival. For example, he mentioned an old roommate, Gotthilf Ehninger, with whom he had lived five years earlier in Frau Schaible's place in Göppingen. At the time he had admired his scholastic prowess (he had placed nineteenth in the state boards), but now Hesse was more ironic. Visiting him at the seminary where Ehninger was a student, he still found him to be the slightly odd boy with small pig's eyes, fat cheeks, and large, prominent ears. On the other hand, his marks for another friend, Ludwig Geiger of Cannstatt, were higher. A prospective insurance expert, Geiger was about to leave for Göttingen, where a new department had been organized to deal precisely with insurance matters. Although he liked and even admired Geiger, and was very sad to see him leave (he liked him better now than during their earlier years in Cannstatt), he also had to distance himself critically. "Too bad he has so little polish," he wrote his parents. "He has not been able to shed that awkward, pedantic manner." Judging his more successful friends was his way of coping with his difficult situation.

The early letters from Tübingen abound with these and similar references to young men his parents had known as schoolboys and who were now students of medicine, theology, or law, and he always managed to sound just a bit patronizing. "Siegnitz is about to study medicine here. A gifted man." But as time went on his old school friends removed themselves more and more. Occasionally he drank wine with them in a pub, and this would give him a chance to boast to his parents—they belonged to a "harmless, non-combatant fraternity" and were mostly seminary students—by making a point of being accepted, but he felt the widening distance between them. They were too busy with their studying and carousing, he reported with a touch of pique, and so could not visit him too often. As he became more and more unable to accept their infrequent invitations on weekdays because of the early hour he had to start work in the morning, the gap between them widened even more.

Occasionally he had some contacts with the faculty. Hesse's main entrée to that society was through a friend of his father's, the theologian Professor Theodor Haering, who also knew his mother and old Dr. Gundert, and who taught Protestant theology at the seminary during that winter semester 1895–96 when Hermann Hesse arrived. For years he had been on the board of directors of the Calwer Verlagsverein and had often been a guest at the Hesses. In consequence, the Haerings were extremely cordial. Hesse was promptly invited to lunch—a sumptuous, elegant meal, which he fitted into his busy weekday schedule. He also enjoyed errands in other professors' homes. For example, he reported in great detail on his visit to the home of Professor von Martisch, also a theologian, who lived in a luxurious home. Hesse arrived on his errand just as some well-known faculty members had gathered in conversation. They included him briefly, but although he felt pleased and proud, he also immediately raised questions about them. "I want to get to know this caste," he announced, and then proceeded to lecture. There were about a hundred professors and lecturers at Tübingen and they were always bickering. "What is true, genuine, noble?" he asked rhetorically. He was pleased that exertion and fatigue had not dimmed his eyes for greatness, even though he sensed shadows and mourning everywhere. These moods anticipate the theme underlying his early writings—the poems he was soon to begin and the prose poems and diary passages that partly at least stemmed from these lonely early months. He wrote in one of his letters of this time:

> Is it really true . . . that our time is fully permeated with sickness—that everything and everyone enters this world with a rotten core, destined to go under? Why is it that, in our time, talent and genius enter this world wrapped in a filthy veil that hides their greatness? Why can we no longer find in the artist, the sage, the poet that flowering, laughing courage that can heal any sickness?

Hesse's critique of academic life became a critique of his time. While these remarks reveal some of his longings at a time he felt isolated and alone, they were also a form of bravado, a way of populating his empty world.

Another way of filling the void was reading, about which he reported learnedly, especially in letters to his father. Hugo Ball, whose biography was inspired by Hesse himself, viewed the years in Tübingen as a time of Goethe studies, and this assertion is generally confirmed by Hesse's correspondence. Other literature, and other poets, were also studied, but, as Hesse said in one of his more pretentious pronouncements, "learning and judgment" came more easily when he was occupied with Goethe. On Sunday mornings he read chapters from the Bible and he studied Virgil after supper, but on each of these occasions he followed suit with one or two chapters from Goethe's *Wilhelm Meister*. This novel became an important guide for Hesse, for it contains many of the stylistic and thematic ingredients for his own work: the veneer of a Mozartian plot, the motif of wandering; the themes of literature, theater, and art; but above all the coincidence between the novel's form and the main character's life. Later he expanded his readings in Goethe, but during the early months *Wilhelm Meister* provided the young autodidact's basic course of study just as he was on the verge of writing on his own.

It took more than reading, however, to set Hesse on his course. He needed a friend. Soon after settling down to his lonely life in Tübingen he found, at least in part, some of the support he needed. A letter from his former Cannstatt teacher Dr. Ernst Kapff was forwarded to him from home, and it opened up—for a brief spell at least—a new avenue of communication. Kapff was a writer of historical novellas as well as a teacher, and his approval meant a great deal to Hesse, who was delighted that his former mentor approved of his decision to become a bookseller in Tübingen. He also needed to think of him as a model. Kapff's novellas, he wrote, were "full of color and life." He produced "little but what he does is good." And Hesse felt sure that his friend would become a well-known writer—a prediction that was not fulfilled, since Kapff died in 1944 as a retired schoolteacher and never achieved literary recognition. But while his influence was intermittent, at this time it seemed clear that Kapff's example was needed to fortify Hesse's own decision to write seriously himself.[2]

A major obstacle was anxiety, that onerous weight that in one form or another burdened Hesse throughout his life. Saturday nights were "magical" because they would be followed by Sundays: hence *keine Angst*—no fear. As it was to happen for the many years to come, these anxieties expressed themselves in headaches and insomnia. They continued to be with him as the exciting early weeks in Tübingen began to spread out into late autumn and winter. Heavy snow began to fall early in December, covering town and country with its monotonous white before turning brown and slushy in the miserable alleys. Nor did the approach of Christmas cheer him up. On the contrary, it intensified his misery. "My mood isn't festive. I have a cold and a sore under my right arm which is very painful with all the moving about in the store." He debated whether he should come home for the holidays, because he would have only the two Christmas days off and the trip was long (in the end he went). Even work on the Christmas display did not revive his spirits: it only confirmed his malaise because he felt burdened by the unusually heavy work. Gilt-edged picture books and various luxury editions had to be carefully arranged, only to be packed away again when the season was over. Although Hesse approved of some of the Christmas merchandise—the classics, religious books, and generally "good literature"—he did not want to see those books displace, in their fancy gift editions, the scholarly and scientific texts that were Heckenhauer's principal fare. But all these feelings merely concealed his depression. He wished, he wrote in his exhaustion, that one Christmas could hold good for three years.

If one were to search for the basis of Hesse's unhappiness during his first year at work, one would probably find it in the role of the outsider, which he had forced himself to play since his childhood and which was to become one of the most recurrent themes in his books. His psychological inability to graduate from high school had closed the university to him, yet when he had finally felt compelled to choose a congenial trade he settled down as a bookseller in a university town. Tübingen was a natural place for him to go, as it had been for Grandfather Gundert, for his half brother Karl Isenberg, and for most other prominent members of his family. But they all had been students. Hermann Hesse had run away from another bookseller, in Esslingen, barely a year and a half earlier, yet Esslingen would have been far less difficult. Hesse suffered from his self-imposed isolation in the very place where this isolation was bound to be most painful. He decorated his room with the likenesses of Nietzsche and Chopin cut out of magazines and publishers' catalogues and, to produce a student atmosphere, displayed a symmetrical arrangement of tobacco pipes above his bed. He copied his former friends' smoking and drinking habits as much as this was possible in his confining life, and he often imitated their dress. His reading, too, can be seen in this context. Although Hesse had always been an autodidact, the systematic pursuit of learning suggests, at least in part, the outsider's attempt to reflect the intellectual world around him. For he was able to observe Tübingen's academic world only from a distance—as a messenger delivering books to professors' houses or as an occasional drinking companion of his former schoolmates. As a merchant's apprentice he could never be part of that world.

If Hesse had not come to Tübingen, if he had remained a self-taught writer who made his living as a bookseller in an ordinary small town, he might not have felt as defensive about his trade. But since even his former school friends thought of him as a "merchant," his literary ambitions took on considerably greater importance. In a long letter to his half brother Karl Isenberg, written at the height of his pre-Christmas doldrums early in December 1895, he made clear that the main point of his daily work lay in its value to him as a prospective writer. Indicating that the details of his daily routine were too boring—"there is no lack of annoyance, headaches, and similar pleasures"—to be of interest to his brother, he went on to say that he had become a bookseller with a specific purpose in mind from which he did not want to be deflected. Lecturing about "the history of European literature" and his own "reactionary literary tastes," he sought to demonstrate that he was no ordinary apprentice to a trade, but rather that his future was that of a poet. He was determined not to repeat the fate suffered by their brother Theodor, whose dreams of becoming an opera singer—an artist—had collapsed.

In the midst of these reflections Christmas came and went. It turned out to be not unpleasant at all. Christmas Eve he had dinner at the Haerings, then took the early morning train to Calw. The two days at home, if the hurried notes written on the return journey are any indication, appeared to have been pleasant as well as renewing, and Hesse was pleased to distribute his mother's gifts to his aunt and Fräulein von Reutern. New Year's Day he spent again at the Haerings. He was invited for the afternoon and evening with several students. The food was excellent: tea, cake, and cigars in the afternoon followed by two kinds of fish, pudding, and wine later at night. But the social situation was difficult. His companions were medical students who, he thought, "lacked luster." He felt slightly ill and could not drink his wine because he had a headache. When they decided to recite poems as a party game, he should have been pleased—and indeed he did well reciting some verses from the work of his favorite poet, Eduard Mörike—but he did not really join in the spirit of the evening. He was silent most of the time: inhibited, depressed, an alien.

As Hesse's life in Tübingen stretched into spring, he felt more and more isolated and consequently spent more and more time reading and reporting on his reading to his father. He worked on the *Iliad* as well as on a work on Greek mythology by the painter Friedrich Preller. He also read Nietzsche's *Ecce Homo*, along with Goethe's *Wilhelm Meister* and *Faust*, with Horace and Hesiod.[3] In a remarkably clear-sighted letter written on March 29, 1896, Hesse gave voice to the underlying purpose of his disquisitions to his family.

> Very little happens to me. Business is always the same, and when I write to you about my beloved books, of my thoughts, and my reading, it always seems to me as though this could be only of secondary and even tertiary importance to you, with the exception of Papa. Goethe once told Lavater that he wrote his loved ones from his travels almost every day without any particular purpose—just to tell them each day that he loved them. I hope you can gather that from my lectures about Goethe and Homer; if I don't say it explicitly I say it between the lines, and what is said between the lines is always more important.

As the year went on, Hesse's letters became gradually standardized. The monotony of his work, and its anxieties, still formed part of their message. He expected to be initiated into the mysteries of bookkeeping later in the summer. Sometimes he was too idle, then again too swamped. Criticism of his handwriting became acute, and Hesse took an expensive correspondence course in penmanship after which his lettering improved for a while. Some of his views of his colleagues, again expressed in terms of smiles and frowns, began to shift. Herr Hermes no longer impressed him all that much, and Herr Sonnewald spoke to him only when he found an error. Occasionally Hesse was still sent on errands to faculty homes, but

not as often as he liked. The days became longer and he enjoyed the sunshine. At noon he still liked to stroll in the castle gardens.

In late spring Marie Hesse became ill—the beginning of the long
illness that ended in her premature death six years later—and children
and father exchanged worried notes.[4] But her sickness did not prevent
Hesse from hesitating again—just as he had done at Christmas—before
agreeing to come home during the Easter holidays. Even as he agreed,
his stated reason was not his wish to see his family but the fact that
Frau Deacon was celebrating her niece's confirmation and needed his
room for the weekend. Still, it was again unexpectedly pleasant to be
home and he found his mother considerably improved.

Summer weather buoyed his spirits but did not dampen his zeal for
learning—and for delivering himself of learned disquisitions. Having just
completed a reading of Lessing's *Laocoön*, he drew, in a rather elegant
discussion, a comparison between Goethe's generous classicism in *Tasso*
and Lessing's purity of genres. These lectures were, of course, principally
for Papa, but he also wrote to Karl Isenberg commenting lengthily on
his favorite thinkers, Goethe and Nietzsche, and his favorite subject,
aesthetics. While the sun raised his spirits, it also depressed him, since he
was cooped up in the office so much of the time. In May he complained
a great deal of headaches and catarrhs, and although Herr Christaller,
the scourge of his sleepless nights, had left, the nights remained wakeful
and difficult. He missed the open land and tall forests around Calw. He
was homesick, he told his mother, and, with misery all around him, he
longed to be in their garden at home. Summer weather in Tübingen, in
Frau Deacon's house, was not always unpleasant. On hot June nights he
might sit in a bower in front of her place, snug and cool, protected by
heavy leaves while tossing firework candles at unsuspecting passersby.
And when nights were too warm for sleeping, he often tried to spend
them in bars, singing and drinking beer.

Hesse's official social life continued unchanged. He faithfully visited
his aunt, occasionally was asked to the Haerings, and still enjoyed the
delicate Sunday afternoon musicales and coffee hours in the home of
Fräulein von Reutern. But he began to withdraw, for when later in the
summer he considered going less often, he added grandly and neurasthen-
ically: "Everything is too much for me." Another new house, however,
had by then opened itself to him: the home of a Fräulein Ohler, where
he felt under less strain. As all these trivia filled his long letters home,
the one truly important item remained omitted. What he did not yet say
was that he was writing—poems, prose poems, reminiscences, vignettes
—indeed, that in his loneliness he was writing a great deal.

II

"Hermann Listener" had begun his work as a writer soon after his arrival in Tübingen. The subterranean images he was to describe so vividly in his books impressed themselves upon him with great richness and urgency. The void of his loneliness had to be filled, and the young chronicler filled it with figures of his fantasy and dream, with the shadows of his past, and inhabitants of his present. He had justified his reading in these terms to his parents at the end of March. Early in April he wrote Kapff that he had been solitary for three months "including Sundays." Although this claim was most exaggerated (it corresponded to similar, equally false claims throughout his life) in a sense it was not off the mark. Sunday dinners at his aunt, occasional invitations to the Haerings, or even an evening or two in a bar with a former school friend did not really fill his life. Neither friendship nor love had entered his closed universe of shop and books: both still had to be manufactured by his imagination. But his talent saved him. For the difference between any poor, depressed apprentice alone in a strange town and the storyteller Hermann Hesse was precisely that these seemingly empty months could be fashioned into poems and stories. His life in Tübingen, and the memories of his childhood, became the subjects and impetus of his work.

During that autumn of his arrival, when he was initiated into the mysteries of the bookselling trade and wrote about it voluminously to his family, Hesse also began work on his childhood reminiscences. If proof were needed that he was lonely, his activities during those early months supply it amply. Working twelve hours a day, writing huge letters, reading Virgil, Homer, and Goethe, and reporting on these readings to his father, he still found time to begin thinking of his novel and to write many poems and prose poems. But it was not just that he had a great deal of time to fill. Rather, Hesse's work habits as a lonely eighteen-year-old were not substantially different from those of the middle-aged writer. He always alternated intensive work on a novel or story with long barren periods of recovery, depression, or other diversions. Still, for a young man finding his way in strange surroundings, his readings, letters, and writings were quite remarkable. As it would happen for the rest of his life, these were precisely the activities he always chose as antidotes for his depressions.

The pastiches and vignettes Hesse wrote at the time, based on reminiscences garnered from various notebooks and journals, provide a fresh dimension of his inner life. They represent a person quite different from the young man who appears in his correspondence and in the recollections of those who knew him during those early years. Intermingling nostalgic idylls with passages portraying intense anxiety, they present loving descriptions of nature and childhood counterpointed by fear in the usual *chiar'oscuro* of Hesse's perceptions. Like the "picture albums" he was fond of writing later in life, indeed like most of his novels, they displayed his paradoxical world to his inner eye in distinct imagistic scenes, each drawing a picture of positive warmth, and the glory of bright colors, or of dark shades suggesting fear of sin or punishment.

The first scene of this sequence describes an anxiety: the hysterical moment we have already witnessed when the little boy was held above an abyss. Subsequent images turn to tender evocations of nature and parents and home. The field near their house in Basel, which Hesse described lyrically in many poems and stories—that sea of bluebells and goldenrod—was reproduced with great tenderness. This meadow, where he played cowboys and Indians with his friends, must have seemed to the preschooler like an Eden from which he was literally expelled: to the Boys' House of the mission and later altogether, when they had to move back to Calw. Throughout these passages Hesse already displayed his gift of combining sharp observation with lyrical prose. The bluebells and butterflies of his meadow and the railroad nearby appear crystal clear to the reader's inner eye, yet the language is cast in a musical as well as colorful prose.

During these early years Hesse had already developed that painter's eye he was to perfect in his forties. Trees, houses, woods, and country roads illuminated by the sun or reflected in ponds appear vividly, along with the people who populated his childhood. The most touching images are provided by two scenes, one in which he sat with his father on a church wall overlooking the valley below, the other in which he walked behind his parents on a summer evening. In the first scene the father appeared idealized, as in a dream, with his black beard and hair, "his strong, noble nose, the dark curls in the neck, and, at the same time, his large eye turned toward me, the entire head resting, firmly and with dignity, upon the blue background of the summer sky." The image of walking behind his parents was even more affecting:

> Yet another image may belong to the same summer, which I recall without context yet which is astonishingly clear and faithfully imprinted upon my mind. I see the full tall spare figure of my father walking toward the setting sun, upright, head bent backward, holding his felt hat in his left hand. My mother leant gently against him as they walked, smaller and stronger, a white shawl about her shoulders. Between their two dark heads, barely separated, glowed the blood-red sun. The contours of their

figures were drawn firmly in luminous golden lines; on both sides of the road lay rich, ripe cornfields.[5]

And he added that he could think of no *picture* more alive and unforgettable than the view of trotting behind his parents that summer night.

The image is suggestive, especially because of the time when it was written. That scene depicts his early life as he deliberately nurtured it in his memory while dealing with Herr Sonnewald or mending damaged books: the luminosity of home to which he felt drawn even as he felt expelled or sought to escape it. Home, then, was father and mother, bluebells and butterflies, the sights and sounds of nature. Clearly these scenes were edited for a work of fiction. Hesse did not have to distinguish between Basel and Calw or to include the time he spent in the mission house. But he remained faithful to the double life that plagued him. He recalled leaning against his mother's knee as she told him fairy tales, he remembered images of anxiety, darkening and contracting as the child got closer to being able to express himself articulately. Along with the pleasant childhood imagery, recollections were drawn from deeper and more troubled levels of his mind, evoking the fears that fed on his feelings of guilt.

Many of these incidents were later incorporated into Hesse's books. Although the specific incidents vary, the pattern remains similar: images of fear; lies judged by a stern but eventually forgiving father; and a general anxiety that alludes to the part of his childhood that had been spent in mental illness and institutions. Indeed, Hesse's fears as a child had mounted to the point where they truly disturbed him, and it is significant that, however disguised they may be, they are recalled during his lonely months in Tübingen. For example, he remembered walking with two half-grown girls as a very small boy and overheard how they titillated themselves with a horror tale about a mythical bell named Barbara that had emerged from black magic and crime. When an actual church bell began to peal, the child was practically destroyed by dread. At other times he designated special places where ghosts and goblins lived and people trespassed at their peril. When he refused to fetch his father's slippers from one of these places, and lied about it, he was punished for lying. This "night" side of his childhood grew darker as he grew older, and the eighteen-year-old apprentice and aspiring writer collected each of these moments with care. Parental punishments at home were followed by impersonal punishments at school. Yet each of these recollections was always balanced by a tale of tenderness and light. The last scene in this picture album of his childhood portrayed a touching reconciliation with his father. Unruly and angry, Hermann had been one of the ruffians in the neighborhood. A window was smashed and the angry neighbor had accused Hermann. Evidently it had been an accident. Refusing to confess his guilt, he found that his father was adamant in demanding that his son take responsibility for his action. But Hesse had not lied: he had broken the window but he had not done so on purpose, and his father finally accepted his explanation. At that time, Hesse recalled, he was nine years old. There was a positive note, even in his remembrance, a sense of being supported by his father's confidence and his mother's faith. That July, on his birthday, he was given the violin that he enjoyed playing for many years.

On this note the childhood sequence ended, written at a time when he felt confined at work. Years later it was inserted in his novel *Hermann Lauscher*, but at the time he composed it in Tübingen it was his first sustained effort in the painful task of becoming a writer. It was summertime, yet his own life remained largely confined to twelve hours, six days in office and store. In August he was able to get away briefly to visit Ernst Kapff in Cannstatt. They went sightseeing together, looking at the ancient Roman castle, and afterwards had a pleasantly long lunch in his apartment. They stayed together until late afternoon, talking of literature and religion over wine and coffee, until it was time for him to catch his train back to Tübingen. It was a brief break in his deadly routine, yet even at work matters did not seem to be as uniformly dismal as he sometimes felt. Herr Sonnewald, who suffered from a lung ailment, seemed better and there was less pressure. Herr Hermes was "very friendly," trying to draw him into his society—a temptation he resisted because, so he wrote his religious parents, he was disgusted by the superficial culture and "blasé godlessness" of his circle. But more and more it became evident that his colleagues thought of him as a desirable companion. They began to invite him to their club, from which apprentices were usually excluded. In fact, when he received a printed invitation to an outing of the Swabian Clerks' Club he reveled in the glory of their acceptance. Yet when Grandfather Hesse in the Baltic finally died that November, he turned the event against himself. In a condolence letter to his father he recalled his grandfather's kindness to him during the bad days at Maulbronn and took the occasion to reassess his own guilt and sin. These expressions of guilt to his parents were poses, of course, but there is no reason to believe that they were not also genuinely felt. Hesse was too much the son of his Pietist parents not to feel constantly caught by their disapprovals. Visiting home at Christmas again that year despite the usual hesitations, he continued to rely on the support and comfort of his parents, on their approval and disapproval.

In January 1897 Hesse experienced a crisis that was to remain with him periodically for more than twenty years: the threat of army service. For him it turned into an especially severe crisis, because the army represented to him that institutionalized authority, the regimentation of private life, that he had loathed at school, hated at work, and had even found at home. It was a relief to have his father's help in gathering the necessary papers, then in mid-January he presented himself to the recruiting station. Fortunately his bad eyesight saved him, but for weeks he was suspended "between fear and hope."

In the midst of these anxieties, Hesse's writing progressed well. While he went to open houses at the Haerings, worried about Herr Sonnewald's health and Herr Hermes's morals, he wrote volumes of poetry and even saw his work published. Not until August, however, did he mention his progress to his parents. The Viennese journal *Deutsches Dichterheim* had responded to his work. He had sent in two of his poems merely as "literary exercises" in the hope of getting some encouragement and criticism, but the gruff editor returned the far more encouraging notice: "Both contributions will appear in print. It is clear that you create with love and hard work."

Hesse's aesthetic "theories" and his lopsided social life had issued in a harvest of poetry that led to his new beginning. The poems were about beauty and loneliness, illness and death; they mirrored the landscapes around Calw with sunlight in the trees and told of soldiers dancing their last waltzes. Young girls were addressed as "departed darlings." Images evoking voids and abysses alternated with brilliant colors at dusk.

> O pure wondrous vision
> When, composed of crimson and gold,
> You spread in peace, serious, benign
> You luminous late heavenly blue.

And the counterpoint:

> You remind us of a blue sea
> Upon which happiness is anchored
> For blissful rest. From the oar falls
> The final drop of earthly pain
> as all life is absorbed into the crystalline blue of eternity.[6]

While he was composing these unfortunate verses, Hesse, at nineteen, also self-consciously reflected the relationship of his craft to other arts— music, which he then practiced, as well as painting. Again it was a pre-occupation that lasted throughout his life, but at this point it was a particularly self-conscious awakening. Eager disquisitions filled long letters to his parents, his sisters, and his half brother Karl. With Chopin's portrait on his wall, with his music in his ear, he sought to reproduce in words the master's *Grande Valse*:

> A dance by Chopin noisily spreads in the hall
> A wild untamed dance[7]

Despite their sentimentality, their technical flaws, and their naiveté, more and more of these poems found their way into print. Stirred by this recognition as he stood at his desk or waited for the doorbell to ring in the shop for a customer to enter, he filled pages and pages with his crabbed Gothic script. The poems that were to be published as *Romantic Songs* were followed by prose poems and further autobiographical vignettes later that year. Hesse began to emerge from his cocoon.

Although he felt as isolated from his contemporaries in 1897 as he had upon his arrival almost two years earlier, his self-confidence was buoyed by his successes and allowed him to seize an opportunity that summer that changed his fortunes. He discovered a group of students whom he could join as an equal. It was a propitious moment. They were outsiders themselves, and while they were studying such subjects as medicine and law, they had literary ambitions. Hesse immortalized that group in a long story he later included in *Hermann Lauscher*: they were a "Club of Outsiders—Of Irredeemable Misfits," a *petit cénacle* of intellectual iconoclasts. These aspiring artists and self-styled aestheticians who had remained on the fringes of their own student society remained good friends of Hesse's for years. At the time there were three—Ludwig Finckh, Carlo Hamelehle, and Oskar Rupp. Later they were joined by two more students, and the six of them worked hard, and ambitiously, to establish the kind of literary circle that was much in vogue at the time. Hesse's closest friend in the group was undoubtedly Ludwig Finckh, nicknamed "Ugel," a law student who later switched to medicine and ended up as a minor novelist. Indeed, Finckh became one of his most intimate companions during the prewar years of Hesse's success, and their relationship buckled only under the strain of the war, when Finckh became its jingoist supporter and Hesse its hesitant opponent. At this earlier point in their lives, however, their friendship was a mutual discovery.

In September 1897 Hesse first mentioned Finckh to his parents, and from then on hardly a letter was written that did not devote a sentence or paragraph to him as well as to others in his new circle of friends. "This man Finckh," he wrote, "is a student of jurisprudence, a gifted, rather well-to-do but in a strange way very modest and lovable man. His interests are literary but he is mostly devoted to art and owns a number of our best moderns from Munich and Berlin." He also wrote poems and sketches imbued "with enormous tenderness." Hesse's descriptions of his visits to Finckh's home in nearby Reutlingen show how deeply impressed he was by the quiet wealth of that world and how proud he was to have been accepted. He and his friend would sit in the garden under the falling leaves where they would be served coffee. Then they would look at his various collections of pictures—both originals and reproductions—or talk about literature and art. They would share a late afternoon meal and after some wine or beer in the evening eat a late supper before Hesse would return to Tübingen. He felt comfortable with Finckh's parents and with his twenty-three-year-old sister. The family was quietly at ease and accustomed to guests. "I succeeded in not falling in love with the daughter," added the chronicler, "so that my relations with the family would not become complicated." Their home would remain open to him as a source of renewal.

The group was most active during 1897–98. They met once a week over beer from half past seven to eleven o'clock at night, but these regular meetings were supplemented by many informal gatherings. They were a motley crew of very proper young men: Finckh with his round face and lorgnette, his hair brushed high, looked like the sensitive "politician" he was; Hesse with his close-cropped hair and sharply etched nose and rimless glasses looked serious and intense. The entire group gives the impression not of students or aesthetes but of earnest young businessmen congregating to consider weighty issues of profit or loss. Hesse described Rupp as a silent man, questioning each statement by implication; Hamelehle, on the other hand, constantly raised unanswerable questions, while Hesse and Finckh tried to answer them both. This new life absorbed more and more of Hesse's energies, and his letters home became less frequent. Rupp, Finckh, and Hamelehle took up most of his evenings and Sundays. When he did not visit Finckh in Reutlingen he went on an excursion with Rupp, sightseeing or visiting family or friends. The feeling of being accepted in a circle of like-minded friends, even of being able to function as one of their leaders, compensated richly for the long hours at the store and his persistent headaches.

But as the year wore on difficulties began to reappear. His friends went home for long periods of time—at Easter, during the summer months, and at Christmas—while he was glued to his bookshop twelve hours a day, six days a week, pleased to get a couple of days off now and then. Already at Easter 1898 he felt ill at ease because neither Finckh nor Hamelehle returned immediately after the holidays. In fact, Finckh decided to move more and more permanently to his parents' home in nearby Reutlingen. At the same time their circle was enlarged by two new members, both of whom Hesse liked—a candidate in theology named Schöning and a student named Otto Erich Faber. They took turns meeting in each other's rooms. In early April, for example, when it was Hesse's turn to be the host, they had a furious argument about theology and art in the course of which candidate Schöning bounced so hard on the sofa that it gave in, while a tipsy Finckh knocked on their door at half past ten, greeted by their raucous debate.

Friendship developed for Hermann Hesse during 1897 and '98, but Eros still had a long way to go. That part of his life developed gradually as an underlying theme during a year in which his writing was beginning to earn him a measure of success and his personal life had been given a fresh direction by his friends. Clearly there had been other loves—his passion for Eugenie Kolb had almost cost him his life—but the first overt instance since Hesse's arrival in Tübingen and the beginning of his independent life occurred ephemerally and, typically, by mail. In September 1897 he told his parents that the next issue of *Deutsches Dichterheim* would contain a "small Chopin poem" by him and that in October a new publication in Wismar would print two more of his songs. The Chopin piece was picked up in November by a young North German writer named Helene Voigt, who, for a few brief months, was to enliven Hesse's fantasies. She had read *Grande Valse* and had liked it so well that she had taken the trouble to track down his address through *Deutsches Dichterheim*, which had printed the poem. Thereupon she addressed these effusive words to its author:

> What did I want to say? O what does one say when someone wants to stir a string within us with a few words, a string that continues to resound for a long, long time. Constantly one must turn one's head and listen to the long secretive sound. The mood is too fine to be touched by one's hands. . . .

And the intense response came at once:

> My cordial thanks for your letter, my dear honored lady.
>
> I was sitting in a friend's place, angry, worried, and tired from work. My friend, a dear artist who shall be nameless, played on an old plain fiddle. And just then I thought of you, that is, of the few whom I would like to count among my listeners and friends . . . At that moment your letter was brought to me and greeted me like an old friend and did me good. . . . I am so little used to friendship and friendliness.[8]

They were almost of the same age—Helene Voigt was born in 1875—but otherwise a gulf divided them. Her roots were in the land, for she had grown up as the fifth of nine children on a large estate on the Baltic coast of Schleswig-Holstein. After a childhood and adolescence of horses, harvests, and fields, she had just become successful as a writer: her book of country tales was about to be published. She and Hesse never met. They had planned to get together on the occasion of Helene's trip to Italy and Southern Germany, but their meeting never worked out, probably because she had just fallen in love with the young publisher Eugen Diederichs. Despite the emotionally charged language of her letter, her approach to Hesse most likely had been professional rather than personal. Still, their correspondence during the first few months had strong emotional overtones. As early as March 1, 1898, however, Helene informed Hesse that she had become a bride ("laughing and weeping at the same time")—her tone suggesting that she was at least aware of the possibility that she might be writing to a disappointed suitor. Hesse's response showed that she had not been mistaken. Although he extended his warmest congratulations and expressed his hope for a continuation of their fine friendship, the tone of his letter showed that he was affected.[9] In fact, the day after her wedding he could not suppress a brief reference to it in a note to his parents. In a single sentence set off as a paragraph he wrote: "June 4 was the wedding day of Helene Voigt, the friend I knew only from a distance." While this report, in its brevity and apparent detachment, underlined his disappointment, his need for friendship continued to be real.

The wings of that friendship had been borne by Hesse's poems. Finally, with his own money, he brought out a sizable collection, called *Romantic Songs*, with E. Pierson in Dresden. Dated 1899, the book actually appeared in the autumn of 1898, little noticed yet nonetheless his first published work. Friends like Ernst Kapff and Helene praised his book, but he suffered a great shock when his mother strongly disapproved. As we know, Marie Hesse had written some verse herself: naively, full of sentiment, yet with great piety. Somehow the "romantic" poems produced by her son appeared to her self-indulgent and secular, perhaps even impious, vaguely sinful, and disturbed. She did not conceal her attitude and Hesse answered her strongly early in December to dispel her concern for his state of mind. He tried to convince his mother not to see his poems entirely as a personal confession, that while in editing he could not make his selections on the basis of how revealing his poems were, his main aim was nonetheless to develop a form, to bear witness to an aesthetic and personal creed. They were *romantic* songs. He assured his mother of his trust in her and made clear that he understood her maternal concern. Despite the conciliatory, even submissive, tone of this letter, Marie Hesse's response to his first published work created a gulf between them that was not to be bridged during the two and a half years that remained of his mother's life.

All this activity produced a change: Helene and her new husband Eugen Diederichs assumed great, if passing, importance in Hesse's life. In the elation of seeing his poems in print, Hesse forged on from verse to prose poetry, fairy tales, and further vignettes, which he collected under the title *One Hour Behind Midnight*, the hour of timeless art beyond the threshold of the last hour of time. A poem in *Romantic Songs* of the same title had already sounded that theme:

> One hour behind midnight
> Where only forest and late moon
> And no other human soul's awake
> Stands wide and broad the marble castle
> Inhabited only by me and my dreams.[10]

The prose poems developing this theme were vague imitations of Maurice Maeterlinck and others of that late-romantic generation whom Hesse had read in translation. They mirrored ponds and lakes, revealed symbolic diadems, showed pastoral princes and princesses in stylized conversations, and also evoked terror and despair. They reflected an underlying current in a life that was still occupied with visits to the Haerings or mild contretemps with Herr Sonnewald. The book was to be mildly approved by no less an authority than the famous poet Rainer Maria Rilke, who added, however, that it was "on the *verge* of art."[11]

Before Rilke could review the volume it first had to be published, and for this reason it became the focus of a brief triangular relationship between Hesse and the Diederichs. As a parting gesture to her epistolary friend Helene had asked her husband, an ambitious publisher who was to build his firm into an important house, to bring out the seven delicate prose pieces of *One Hour Behind Midnight*. Diederichs admired his young wife—her beauty as well as her talent—and to please her agreed to publish the book. His business sense warned him clearly against becoming overcommitted, and so he printed a bare minimum of six hundred copies. To compensate for the precious content and the obscurity of the author, he designed the book decoratively and used special print. But it sold very poorly. Hesse withdrew the book even before the edition had been exhausted and did not allow it to be reissued until 1948. His correspondence with both Diederichs lasted a while longer. He frantically tried to keep his ties with the firm intact by constantly proposing projects and sending manuscripts, only to be politely rejected. A friendship of sorts continued with Helene two years longer, though it became less and less coherent as her life first as a wife, then as a mother, claimed her more and more. Yet some contact remained—Hesse rarely broke off a relationship—but it became very tenuous. When, near death, the eighty-two-year-old Helene Voigt-Diederichs wrote her last letter to Hesse in 1957, she noted that during the sixty years that had passed since their first exchange they had written each other some thirty letters.[12] Eros had indeed come to him, but it was still a correspondence course.

If *One Hour Behind Midnight* revealed his fantasies and dreams, the bulk of his next book, *Hermann Lauscher*, was based on recollections of his actual life in Tübingen. The childhood sequences, which were inserted much later, had been among the first products of his literary activity in the first year of his apprenticeship, but, with a retrospective vision, the most vivid account of his Tübingen life in fiction was also composed after the fact—after he had moved to Basel in 1900. The unity of this "novel" was provided by the creation of a persona, Hermann Lauscher, a poet who, he imagined, had recently died, and whose literary estate he now pretended to publish. In maintaining this curious parallelism between protagonist and author, its elaborate games with names and pseudonyms, and its themes of death and suicide, Hesse's *Lauscher* foreshadows the experimental novel he wrote at the age of fifty, *Steppenwolf*. Moreover, through the double game, which Hesse developed far more skillfully two years after the Tübingen experience when he wrote the book, the reader obtains a very clear picture of his life in the university town. In the longings it expresses, in the language it uses, in its humorous and its morbid episodes, *Lauscher* supplements the extensive letters he exchanged with his family and friends.

Perhaps most revealing of Hesse's mood at the time is the inserted novella "November Night: Remembrances from Tübingen," which forms the core of the book. Written with deliberate irony in the manner of romantic models like Jean Paul Richter, this story draws a very contrived picture of student life. Here Hesse actually names his fictional double, Hermann Lauscher, who is in all respects like Hesse except that instead of being a bookseller he is a poet. Still deeply self-conscious about his status as a tradesman (it took him a whole year to reveal his true occupation to Helene Voigt) he required a mask that elevated him to a character of fiction superior to the students he could not equal: a freewheeling, footloose poet. But as a poet he used his ear and eye to perceive the sounds and sights around him more sharply than others, to perceive the atmosphere of the university town and its hidden tensions beneath the coldly observed exterior of town, castle, and church. Like Klingsor, that intoxicated painter of Hesse's middle years, he recreated the world and the people in it and remolded them into a landscape representing his inner life.

The story is instructive both in its atmosphere and in its plot. Its outlines were borrowed from life: an actual suicide by a desperate student.

But the way Hesse developed that unhappy incident from painstakingly detailed descriptions of student life suggests yet another dimension. The students' jargon, their drinking, their humor deprecating the weak, in effect created the denouement. As Lauscher and his friends sit together in the basement wineshop arguing about theology and history, their talk echoes a ruthless gaiety that drowns out their ideas. Despite his profession as a maker of language and a conveyor of thought, Lauscher is accepted by his raucous companions and even recognized as a leader. With bravado he makes himself instantly a center of the group, demands glasses and wine, drinks quickly, lights his thin cigars—"black, poisonous snakes"—and reveals an underlying power to control his admirers. It was Hesse's own wish dream about his relationship with the students, only partially realized by his membership in the *petit cénacle*. But this dramatic image of himself in the seat of power is at once confronted by its opposite. The outsider—a student named Elenderle (derived from "miserable")—is indeed the other side of Hesse's contradictory perception of himself: unsure, hesitant, drinking too much too fast to fortify himself against the derision he expects. As a counterpoint to Lauscher's bravado, this sad young man was probably closer to his own self image than his swashbuckling protagonist. It is most suggestive of Hesse's state of mind that both these figures end in suicide. Lauscher's suicide had formed the occasion for the book—Hesse pretended that he was merely publishing Lauscher's collected papers—and hence the reader knows in advance how that poet had ended. But the point of this novella is also the discovery of Elenderle's corpse. As Lauscher and his friend find his body on the steps near the old bridge, one alter ego discovers the other: a pistol nearby (the pistol Hesse had bought as a schoolboy and never used) becomes the stage prop that binds them together.[13]

This episode, however, cannot be understood only in psychological terms, for Hesse's intentions were also self-consciously aesthetic. Clearly all those readings and subsequent lectures, mostly about abstract questions of aesthetics and literature, had not passed him by, nor were those heated arguments with his friends of the *cénacle* without repercussions. Constantly he raised questions about the role of unconscious experience in relation to artistic form, developed numerous variations on the theme of romanticism and classicism and linked them with moral and theological questions. The names Goethe, Lessing, and others were always on his lips. As *One Hour Behind Midnight* had been modeled on Maeterlinck's highly esoteric prose poetry, so the episodes in *Herman Lauscher*, as they began to develop in Tübingen, suggest imitations of romantic writers whose mastery he acknowledged.

Hesse's work with Goethe and Nietzsche, on which he reported to his parents, to Karl Isenberg, and to friends like Ernst Kapff, now gave way to a new interest in romantic poetry and fiction that was to remain a live issue for Hesse for the next sixty-five years. Late in August he mentioned that he had begun to study two romantic writers. One was Wilhelm Heinrich Wackenroder, a figure not too well known outside the realm of specialized scholars of romanticism, but a spirit most congenial to Hesse. Wackenroder, with his better-known friend Ludwig Tieck, had wandered through many parts of Germany in search of treasures of medieval architecture, after which the two friends had delivered themselves of a small piece of prose called *Outpourings from the Heart of an Art-Loving Friar*, an elevated "tour book" through the remnants of the Middle Ages in the nineteenth century. Scholars consider this small book a landmark of German romanticism, but it is also not suprising to see the eighteen-year-old apprentice bookseller Hermann Hesse identifying with this pilgrim among art treasures of a bygone age. The other spirit with whom he began to work closely is better known: Novalis, a pen name for Friedrich von Hardenberg, a young poet at the turn of the nineteenth century, whose religious and mystical hymns and allegorical prose appealed particularly to Hesse at this stage of his life.

Although Hesse wrote learnedly about many important figures of Germany's romantic age—writers of prose like Joseph Freiherr von Eichendorff and E. T. A. Hoffmann; poets, dramatists, and critics like Ludwig Tieck and the brothers August Wilhelm and Friedrich Schlegel; or theologians like Friedrich Schleiermacher—he was especially engaged by Novalis. He wrote about him so effusively that Marie Hesse began to fear that the poet's "Catholic temperament" might subvert her son, and Hermann had to convince her that despite his medieval and mystical themes, Novalis was a Protestant—in fact, a Pietist's son. At this time, of course, Hesse also wrote the prose poetry of *One Hour Behind Midnight* and revised some of the poems destined for *Romantic Songs*—both beginning to show traces of his deep involvement in reading Novalis, whom, with Wackenroder, he called the most lovable poet of recent times. At the same time, he reread romantic narratives like Jean Paul's then famous humorous novels, often written in his native Franconian dialect, as well as the tales of Eichendorff and Hoffmann, who had built occult and unexpected happenings into ostensibly realistic settings. These contrasting techniques had become more than just object lessons or lectures to his family based on his readings. They conformed well to the contours of Hesse's own mind and were consciously applied to the writings then under way. His first attempts in *Lauscher* attest to their effectiveness.

Meanwhile at least one decisive change occurred in Hesse's life. On October 2, 1898, precisely three years after his arrival, Herr Sonnewald

certified that he had finished his apprenticeship and invited him to remain with the firm as a regular employee. Hesse accepted, at least for a
year, and found that in most ways life in office and store did not change.
A new man, expert in secondhand books, had joined the firm, and although Hesse claimed he did not dislike him, he must have felt some
discomfort since that was precisely his own favorite branch of his trade.
On the other hand, he was genuinely pleased with a new neighbor who
moved in that month. He turned out to be a musician with whom Hesse
could share the pleasure of playing the violin. He also liked Hesse's books
and engaged him in long conversations about aesthetics. Naturally, Hesse
was worried that there would soon be problems, for he thought that
having a true friend next door would be too much to ask—but for the
moment he was satisfied. This was particularly important because the
petit cénacle he had counted on so much was beginning to break up.

The gradual decline of the group made itself felt more and more
strongly as the year 1898 moved into late fall and winter. Not only had
Finckh moved to his parents' home in Reutlingen and was seldom with
them, but the others, too, had become more and more preoccupied. Only
Hesse's life remained almost unchanged. In November he wrote home
that he rarely saw his friends. Headaches and depressions returned,
although he tried to reassure his mother that they seldom bothered him
and that his intensive reading did not make him sick. These feelings were
not helped by reports that both his parents suffered several bouts of
illness that fall. He became morose and withdrawn, and with this renewal
of his sense of isolation 1899 did not augur well.

This constant alternation of elation and depression, isolation and
conviviality, or, later in Hesse's life, of stasis and motion, made of each
summit a plunge and of each plunge a summit. In March he joyfully
recounted a trip to Munich. And, having weathered fresh worries about
the army in June, he was able to make an important decision. He gave
notice at Heckenhauer's. On July 7 he told his parents of that important
step: he was leaving his job on August 1 and was planning a vacation
before coming home. "[The] medicine men advise strongly against Calw
in August," he wrote with an affectation of student jargon, "and want
to put me on top of an alp." Since Finckh was taking a cure in the spa
of Kirchheim-on-Teck he decided to join him and his other friends of
the *cénacle* in August before coming to Calw in September. But time
became much shorter than he thought, because a new opportunity presented itself: a position in W. Reich's bookstore in Basel that promised
to be lucrative and interesting, replacing the difficult university ambience
with that of a well-appointed cosmopolitan store. The vacation in Kirchheim, however, took place and lasted ten days. It became both an emo-

tional and a literary occasion: Eros appeared once more and this time was slightly more palpable.

In another story incorporated in *Hermann Lauscher*, Hesse described his poet's infatuation with a beautiful maiden named Lulu. The lady in question was actually Julie Hellmann, niece of the innkeeper at the Krone in Kirchheim where the friends had their rooms. How real this relationship was, how much of it was even personal is open to question. To some extent Hesse simply shared in the general appreciation of her by their entire group. He certainly shared her attentions with Finckh. Julie was one year older than Hesse, slender, graceful, and much put upon, as well as protected, by her uncle and aunt. But in the "Lulu" chapter of *Lauscher* Hesse made of her a grand lady:

> If you have never been filled with rapture at the sight of a beautiful woman's portrait and had the sudden sense of Beauty stepping out of that picture's landscape alive, then you can have no inkling of how the brothers of the cénacle felt at this moment. All three men rose and thrice they bowed. "Beautiful dear lady," said the poet.[14]

The story is particularly engaging because Hesse sought to pay tribute to their dying *cénacle* by recreating that episode as a fairy tale dedicated to E. T. A. Hoffmann. Finckh, Hamelehle, and Hesse, who were actual guests in the Krone, became magical figures in a realistic setting. Their names were only thinly disguised: using Finckh's nickname, Hesse called him Ludwig Ugel; Carlo Hamelehle became candidate Karl Hamelt; while Hesse, of course, was Lauscher. Later in the week they were joined by two other members of their old *cénacle*, Oskar Rupp and Erich Faber, who were similarly absorbed into that enchanted world.

In the story that was to become the memorial to their friendship, Hesse was bent on putting all his recent reading and romantic theorizing into practice. The realistic frame was retained: the spa, the five friends, the Krone and its owners and niece. At the same time different levels of reality were projected. Falling asleep after too much wine on a hot August morning, Karl Hamelt has a dream in which Lulu-Julie is foreshadowed as the Dream Princess Lilia. Another dual figure—part magical, part real—appears to them when they arrive at the lodgings. He turns out to be a philosopher named Drehdichum (or Turnaround) who teases and inspires them with pretentiously intellectual talk, but who also represents Hesse's philosophical point of view. He instructs the brothers of the *cénacle* that memory and feeling must be superior to science and knowledge as he miraculously appears out of nowhere blowing tobacco smoke and speaking of a dreamworld. He also encourages the enchantment surrounding the "Beautiful Lulu." A sage-magician who will appear again and again in Hesse's books, Drehdichum connects the two levels of reality—that of the real world and that of symbolic dream—which are telescoped in the story. He is the fairy king in mortal dress from the world Hamelt had envisaged in his dream: the world in which Lulu-Julie had been Lilia.

The old philosopher-magician and the young waitress-princess are focal points in a story that is both magical and real. After "Lulu" has been feted and the old man has had his say, the latter disappears in a cloud of smoke curling from his own pipe to leave the stage to her. A painful scene between the niece and her aunt who tries to keep her charge away from those noisy young men is evidently drawn from life and contrasts with the magical disappearance. But the talk among the friends shows what they had learned as they explore the reasons behind the magic. "Our friend Lauscher," Karl Hamelt says, "just told us how poets must draw from the unconscious. . . ."[15] The function of "Lulu" as a barmaid and as Princess Lilia becomes clear: she exists in an unconscious as well as conscious universe; indeed, the entire Kirchheim episode assumes meaning in both of these dimensions at once. In a final scene, in which Lauscher and Ugel flee into a dreamland to pick flowers for Lulu, both these levels are brought together. The girl Lulu-Julie is turned back into Lilia—the lily—of the opening dream.

The story was so easily transformed from life that it reverberated beyond its fictional frame. The day after leaving Kirchheim for Calw, Hesse wrote a long letter to Julie Hellmann, addressing her as his "Lulu girl" and telling her how sad he felt that he now had to recall her beautiful image rather than being able to see it palpably before him.[16] But even this letter, and several letters to follow, do not show conclusively that the enchanted week had been based on a personal rather than a collective and symbolic experience. Julie—whom Finckh similarly celebrated in a story called "Magic Enchantment"—may have existed only as a highly literary figure in a symbolist universe; she may have had her place "one hour behind midnight," as Helene Voigt had had her epistolary existence one year before. The love letters Hesse sent to Julie from Calw and Basel during the next few months were flowery and sometimes urgent, but it is striking how much they remain essentially nostalgic. They seemed to focus almost entirely on that particular "enchanted" vacation and the final gathering of the *cénacle*.[17] Still, Hesse remained in touch with her, however tenuously, for life, as was to become his usual habit. In 1946, when he received the Nobel Prize, the sixty-nine-year-old writer was expected by seventy-year-old Fräulein Julie Hellmann in her small house in the Swabian village of Möckmühl. Most of this episode, written by Finckh (himself over seventy) and published in the *Schwä-bische Merkur* turns on Julie's intense anticipation. At last the great man arrived and they all shared coffee and cake. They were pleased to be together (especially since Hesse and Finckh had been estranged for years) and to relive that episode of their youth. But Finckh's com-ment is especially instructive: he wanted to see "Lulu again in Möckmühl" and to remember her and Hesse and to read in his own story "Magic Enchantment" about their magic week.[18] But for Hesse at the time this story was primarily a literary étude, a study in reality and magic, which according to a letter to Eugen Diederichs in August 1900 he very much wanted to publish as his testimonial to romantic art in a modern age.[19]

With this note Hesse had turned his back on the places of his appren-ticeship. After a brief stay in Calw he moved to Basel, where he began his new job. He had returned to the place where he had lived as a small child, but he had done so as a man poised on the edge of achievement.

III

Basel had to be both old and new. It could not help but remain the place of his childhood and the home of his family's religious institution. Yet as Hesse gave himself up to the city as a new experience, it came to represent less a homecoming than a fresh beginning. As he wrote many years later, everything was waiting for him in that city of his childhood. He had arrived with the works of Nietzsche and a framed reproduction of Arnold Böcklin's "Island of the Dead" in his luggage. That other city of the mission house and the Spalenthor still existed, but having published his work, having taught himself Goethe, Nietzsche, and the romantic poets during four years of compulsive reading, he was entering Basel as a new cultural home.[20]

Hesse's first letters were full of enthusiasm. His spirits were high. His work was most pleasant. Actually the store was smaller than Hecken-hauer's: there were five regular employees and one apprentice, but Hesse thought it a fine business, new and well established. Two days after his arrival, on September 17, he reported on his new boss, Herr Reich, as a very agreeable man, and his first reaction to him was certainly different from that mixture of rejection and fear he had conveyed after his first meeting with Herr Sonnewald four years earlier. His routine, however, was quite similar to the tasks he had done in Tübingen: shipping, receiv-ing journals, handling mail and petty cash, and shelving books. Soon he felt the burden of monotony again: his predecessor had let many things slide and it was hard for him to catch up. He had to learn French in Basel and this was a burden he found as cumbersome as had been his earlier attempts to learn English.

Complaining was always part of Hesse's repertoire, and these early reports were no exception after the first flush of enthusiasm had waned. His new position continued to please him. It was not a university bookstore like Heckenhauer's and served a wider public interested broadly in literature and the arts rather than in buying mostly scientific or theological texts. Still, the wider interests of his customers were too much taken up by current productions for his taste. He regretted that the establishment was rigidly divided into its three separate wings—current literature, the secondhand section with its treasures of old volumes, and the publishing house—for Hesse disliked being tied to selling only contemporary books. This sense of being locked into only one phase of the business and "not even the most attractive part," which he expressed to his parents at the time, is sustained by his remarks in the sketch "Life Story Briefly Told," which he wrote as a man in his forties. Then he claimed that at first he had experienced the "almost intoxicating joy" of swimming in the most modern literature, but that he soon came to feel that "the life of the spirit is made possible [only] by that constant reference to what is past, to history, to the ancient and primeval."[21] Eventually he was to leave Reich's to work, briefly, in a store devoted exclusively to secondhand books.

In contrast to his early months in Tübingen, however, life in the office did not command Hesse's main interest. He was training himself to become a writer, and his increase in salary—he had more than doubled his income—made it possible for him to expand. He was able to live better, to meet interesting people, and finally to travel. His personal well-being was served more lavishly than had been possible in Frau Deacon's house. His room was pleasant and tastefully decorated. Food was excellent and plentiful. Again, of course, there was a drawback. His regular company at table consisted of three Frenchmen, only one of whom could speak German; and while Hesse liked the opportunity to work on his French, he was also chagrined by the lack of communication.

The most remarkable turn in his fortunes was provided by the society that, thanks to his parents' connections, he was able to enter. His main contact was Dr. Rudolf Wackernagel, archivist and city historian. Johannes Hesse had befriended him and his brother Jakob, a professor of linguistics, when they lived in Basel during the eighties. Through them and their family and academic connections Hesse gained entry to a circle of artists and professors, many of whom were to become famous. They included the historian Karl Joel and the art historian Heinrich Wölfflin, both of whom taught at the University of Basel. Through them, and the atmosphere they generated, Hesse's interests began to tilt toward a new appreciation of history and art in place of his earlier literary and philosophical speculations.

It is always difficult to separate Hesse's self-conscious statements about himself from his actual life, but the fact remains that painting and art history became meaningful to him in Basel as never before. Years later he identified that fall of 1899 as the time when he first experienced "a serious vital relationship with the graphic arts."[22] Already a week after his arrival he proclaimed his new interest. On his way to the Rudolf Wackernagels for his first dinner he slipped into the art museum for a quick initial glance and discovered that a whole room was now reserved for his favorite artist, Arnold Böcklin, which contained twelve canvasses. "You know," he wrote, "how I have always adored Böcklin, even before I had seen any of his work in the original." This visit was indeed a landmark, forming the beginning of his serious involvement with the art of painting that molded his personal and artistic attitudes for the remainder of his life.

Hesse's discovery of painting had immediate intellectual implications. He identified his new interest with the figure of the famous art historian Jakob Burkhardt, who had died in 1897 two years before his arrival, and whose presence still dominated the cultural atmosphere in Basel. The circles around the Wackernagels were "completely saturated by the influence of Jakob Burkhardt." In a lengthy reminiscence written for the Zurich journal *Weltwoche* in 1951 Hesse told how everything around him on his arrival in Basel was steeped in the spirit of Burkhardt, who for decades had functioned as "the *arbiter elegantiarum*" of all matters cultural. He felt surrounded by people "whose reading, travels, whose thinking, whose conception of history and whose conversation had been affected by nothing as strongly as by Jakob Burkhardt."[23] Being nothing if not impressionable, Hesse must have found all this learned talk focused on the author of *The Renaissance in Italy* most productive, supplementing his love for Böcklin and enhancing his lifelong infatuation with painting and architecture. But he also knew that he was still too much involved in his interests in philosophy and Nietzsche to be fully open to Burkhardt. Actually, despite many assertions to the contrary, Hesse rarely applied Burkhardt's teaching to his work directly. A significant exception is the character of Father Jakobus in *The Glass Bead Game*, that Goethean magnum opus of his old age, where he conveys Burkhardt's philosophy of history rather than his specific judgments of art. Still, among the paintings and buildings of Basel, and especially among his new friends, Burkhardt remained an influential spirit coloring all their lives.

As Hesse's life in Basel settled into its new routine, his family and friends were again treated to lively descriptions of his activities. His first comments on the Wackernagels were enthusiastic—and they were largely to remain so despite Hesse's fluctuations. He found the city archivist Rudolf Wackernagel a most pleasant, forthcoming man who spoke a fine, educated German and opened the doors to his house wide. Hesse's life away from these grand houses, however, was not always satisfactory. Living in the *pension* with his French companions was not altogether to his liking. They were theologians, yet Hesse found their religious fervor wanting: too little theology and too much savoir faire. He also sometimes attended services in a French Calvinist church and was pleased to be able to understand about one-third of what was going on. Otherwise there was only the office, and neither his French companions nor his current literature in the store were enough to assuage his restlessness. The Wackernagels remained his base—"how dear and valuable their house has already become for me"—and gave him a social circle in which to function, but the rest of his private life was taken up by nostalgic walks in Basel in the autumn sun, with almost daily visits to his Böcklin canvasses in the art museum, and with writing—letters, journals, essays, and vignettes that would soon make up that account of his Tübingen years, *Hermann Lauscher*. Yet all this was not enough: good food and plenty of milk in the company of French theologians were still not quite the fare he could be content with.

By late October he had found a change: both friendship and attempted love came his way. At one of the *soirées* at the Wackernagels he met two young architects, an artist named Hans Drach and a brilliant young Rhinelander, Heinrich Jennen. They struck up a friendship and in October they moved together into a three-room apartment. "My new flat is pretty," he wrote his parents, "and has the attraction of splendid company." Jennen was to win first prize for plans for an addition to the ancient Gothic town hall. He was a genius, Hesse told his parents, who "is designing the new Town Hall splendidly in Gothic style." But what Hesse enjoyed most was the camaraderie with men of his own age who replaced the *cénacle* of the previous year. His friends would drop in with interesting stories, look at his books and borrow a few, while he would be allowed to see their drawings and designs. Gradually he observed how their overall plans emerged and so experienced vicariously the excitement of shaping that he associated with the pictorial arts. Three busy artists were working together in that pleasant flat: though each was different, they shared their common tasks as creators.

If during the Tübingen years the ideal had been provided by the student society he could not enter, Hesse now found his model among artists. The artistic temperament, as he was to write again and again, became an essential ingredient of his life and work, and the artist of whatever medium (painter, musician, or poet) became an ideal embodiment of human vision and creativity. Artists were also associated with freedom from social restriction, a state he thought essential to creation. It is therefore not surprising that in his first enthusiastic letter to his parents about Heinrich Jennen he pictured him as a true artist, "a person of genius and moods, frequently idle when he is not in the right frame of mind, then again working with enormous energy and perseverence." In his reminiscences of Basel in 1951 Hesse recalled that Jennen was "a young man overflowing with the pleasure of life who introduced me, the loner and ascetic, into many pleasures and comforts of material life." They had "orgies" with wine and asparague in nearby Alsatian villages and made the rounds of the bars and inns of the town. Hesse may not have been altogether a loner and ascetic (he needed to wear that mask all his life) but he was clearly attracted by the artistic and freewheeling spirit of that brilliant young architect with whom he moved into a flat alone just after New Year's 1900. But shadows soon appeared. Early in January he wrote Helene Voigt-Diederichs that working was not easy: "I am sitting at an enormous drafting table, almost too high for writing; everything is covered by paper, drawing instruments, carbon, cigars, etc. For since a short time ago I have been living with a friend, the architect Jennen, who has completed designing the Archives here and is now about to make his name with his Gothic design of the Town Hall." Although a dear person, and a genius in his work, he was "absolutely unliterary and only sensually artistic." He treated Hesse like a fragile child who is difficult to understand. "This is no place for writing. Our rooms are suitable only for talking and drinking, but absolutely not for working pen in hand." He would move in the spring.[24]

By March, when he decided to move, Hesse found that his friendship with Heinrich Jennen had become a cause for alarm to his parents. "My dears," he began a letter home written on March 10, 1900, "Thank you for Mama's letter. . . . Some of the things in the letter I could not understand and others I did not want to understand." And he added: "That I am moving away from that Monster Jennen at the end of March will fill you with pleasure." Jennen's "monstrosity" of course was not a true judgment, but Hesse's phrase was a device to allay his parents' concern with irony. It all seemed like a repetition of his mother's worries about Hermann in Cannstatt, when he had been lured into drinking and gambling by an "older man in Stuttgart." A deception seemed desirable to reassure his mother: "Since Mama believes that [Jennen] is dangerous or may rob you of my interest in you, I may report that since moving in with him on the first of the year I spent one Sunday and three evenings with him and otherwise never exchanged more than three words with him." He still defended his friend: "By the way, much to my regret. For he is not only a great artist but also a very fine person."[25] The figure of Heinrich Jennen illuminates Hesse's view of the artist as the sensuous creator, the tempter, the foil and opposite of the respectable bourgeois or the ascetic saint. Although to parents—and to society at large—he had to be denied, his type always existed as a half-hidden, subterranean figure until Hesse's old age.

Hesse's daytime life during that same fall and winter continued to be bright. Although in writing home every Sunday he mentioned the usual sleeplessness, indigestion, and headaches, he enjoyed his widening social life. By the end of October he had been introduced through the Wackernagels to the family of Parson Laroche. Frau Laroche received him warmly and reminisced about the Hesses' stay in Basel during the 1880s, recalling precise details of the farewell visit paid her by Marie Hesse and her then small daughter Adele. Hesse was to make of this connection an emotional episode that was channeled from his life into his work. As Hugo Ball first "revealed" in 1927, and as Hesse has confirmed, her daughter Elizabeth became the "Beatrice" of his Basel days and appeared in this form in the *Basel Diary 1900* in *Hermann Lauscher* on which he was then at work.[26] In various ways, then, Hesse's life developed on an eminently ordinary plane. On Sundays he roamed the fields near the city. At one time he started to ride back to town in a horse-drawn omnibus that was so slow and rattled so badly that he jumped off at a convenient point and made his way back on foot. At least part of himself was involved in rediscovering that world of his early childhood outside the gates of Basel, with its fields, its slow cows, and its bright, mild air.

In this atmosphere Hesse's life continued in an even rhythm, at least at first glance. Friend Finckh visited in November and they had a pleasant time together. Later that month he resisted his family's urging to attend their silver wedding anniversary. The proximity of Christmas made the trip inadvisable, he argued, for he had to conserve his energies for the holiday rush. He added, however, that he could not make it at Christmas either because of the enormous amount of work to be done at the store between the holidays and New Year. Withdrawal, however, was not sufficient protection. His younger brother Hans had a very difficult time at school and was sorely beset by a sadistic teacher. His father was also in poor health and Hermann suggested that he hire some help in the publishing house. At the same time he continued to be happy in his social life. With the help of the Wackernagels he was introduced to the head of the Basel art gallery. He also continued to enjoy their parties. In fact, his schedule sounded like that of a debutante: a formal dinner on Monday, an evening party at the "enormously rich" Wackernagel-Merians on Wednesday—a party he found exceptionally pleasant—and so on through the week. Hesse discovered that he could make his mark with the ladies, since he was less "buttoned up" than the local young men. He felt at home, surrounded by art and by pleasant, intelligent people. Social relationships outside the Wackernagel circle were still difficult: while the archivist's and the professor's houses became homes for him, other natives of Basel were stiff and forbidding.

In spite of his busy life, Hesse's writing progressed well. In November he was able to offer a rather anemic essay on neoromanticism to Eugen Diederichs while he was also working on his *Lauscher* manuscript, then still called *Swabian Stories*. Christmas found him ill with fatigue, home-sickness, and headaches, but also buoyed by the sense of being socially accepted. As usual, both these feelings emerge from his letters: on the one hand, his heart was heavy and he felt isolated and alone; on the other, he delighted in an invitation to spend Christmas Eve at the Wacker-nagels. He mentioned this event at length in letters to his family as well as to Helene, describing the warmth of their home, where he could find a "haven" from his loneliness, and the "merry band of small children." He was on good terms with them and they even roughhoused together. This sense of being accepted by prominent people contributed perhaps more to the building of his self-confidence as a writer than any other single event during his Basel years.

In January 1900, just after Hesse had begun to room with Jennen, news from home became more ominous. His half brother Karl had suffered a nervous breakdown. Significantly, however, Hesse maintained his distance from the family crisis. He was full of sympathy and, from the perspective of a young man of twenty-four who had been through all that, full of feeling, yet he also remained peculiarly aloof: "With horror I heard of Karl's mishap. . . . I beg you to send me news of Karl and I intend to write him soon. Is he in a medical hospital or in a special clinic? I can well imagine his condition. I for one regained my strength in the days of my breakdown from my fear and rebellion against such a situation." Then, exclaiming, "Enough of these things!" he talked about Herr Reich's return after a two-month absence ("He looks so unwell that he will probably soon go away again to recuperate") and about an evening at the Laroches, who sent regards to Mama and Adele. He involved himself in his brother's fate precisely as he retreated from it, and although he eventually sent him a letter to cheer him up, he remained detached.

During these early months of the year, Hesse's life, too, was torn by uncertainties, and it therefore stands to reason that he tried to keep his distance from his family's troubles. Finckh paid another visit in February. At a house concert at the Wackernagels he heard Beethoven's *Kreutzer* Sonata played by Elizabeth Laroche and a Herr Dr. Bernoulli—the first time the name of Hesse's future wife cropped up. But he still roomed with Heinrich Jennen, feeling by then miserable and tense. His angry letter to his parents about that subject had been written on March 10. Four days later he sent a very different letter—depressed, tired, "in need of being taken care of." Still, despite all these upward and downward curves of his moods, a line of development emerges: Hesse was gradually gaining a sense of himself. A judgment made in January on the occasion of Karl's breakdown contained the truth of his condition: "My own existence here is a continuing progress towards health." It may have been callous, but in establishing this contrast with his half brother he was also setting himself apart from the danger of psychological dissolution he knew so well.

Hesse's growth in Basel, in the midst of pain, occurred during that first year and a half until, through crisis and buoyant success, he had made a place for himself as a writer. *Hermann Lauscher*, which developed scenes from his life in Tübingen from the perspective of Basel, gradually reached completion. At the same time he was writing a diary, *Basel Diary 1900*, which was incorporated into the book some years later and which portrayed graphically his constant conflict between elation and attraction to death. In these pages, Hesse's muse, Elizabeth Laroche, becomes the "Fever Muse," combining Fever, Insomnia, and Love in a single figure. In a journal that reads like prose poetry, Hesse dedicated to his Fever Muse images that transformed his sexual fantasies into precise poetic figures: in touch with history, with the history of art, with musical form.

> How your hand knows to caress. I feel in your touch the entire history of this hand, the entire culture of nobility in its form and gesture, as it had been wrought by the painters of early Florence. . . .[27]

These and similar lines may be as precious as Hesse's tended to be at that time, but they express that sense of culture, of Burkhardt's vision of the connection between history and art, that lingered from those many evenings spent with his Basel friends. But anguish and death also remained prominent themes. His "oppressed soul," wracked by insomnia, "wrestled without weapons . . . with all the cunning and cruelty of despair." During these hours of "wakeful anguish" all the "dams and boundaries" he had drawn for his inner life were demolished. Through these images Hesse was able to reach his subterranean existence and eventually make it public. They also helped him overcome his fears and to mature. Insomnia, illness, the desire for death that he portrayed in his "Basel Diary," fused with a daily life of growing confidence in his ability to succeed as a writer.

IV

As he explored his inner recesses in his published and unpublished work, Hermann Hesse was also very much involved in the practicalities of his career. Although he was naturally aware of Eugen Diederich's loss from the poor sales of *One Hour Behind Midnight*, he constantly belabored him and Helene with new projects, partly to make up for those losses, partly because he wanted a chance to rebuild that important connection. Meanwhile he had left Jennen's lodgings and taken a room in another part of town. While the place was calmer, his life was still unsettled until he turned it in a fresh direction.

Hesse had loved nature all his life. As a child he had roamed in the fields and on the small roads around Calw, and even his earliest work showed him to be a master at sensitive descriptions of landscapes. Now he quite consciously turned to nature. During those later months in Basel—through the late spring and summer of that year—he began to spend his Sundays in the country and to note his feelings and impressions not only in letters and journals but also in his fiction, which he was then beginning to write intensively. It also reflected his activities. In May he joined the Reich family and his colleagues on a trip in the nearby countryside. Usually alone though sometimes accompanied by a friend, he explored the Bernese Plateau to Lake Lucerne and sometimes even as far south as the St. Gotthard Pass. Inconvenient interruptions did not really deflect him. Hans Hesse moved to Basel to work in the mission house because he could no longer bear the pressure at school. While Hesse saw him occasionally, his brother's arrival did not interfere with the summer's activities. Induction into the German army was becoming an ever more serious threat to his peace of mind. After traveling to the border town of Loerrach to present himself, he was again deferred because of his eyesight and this time he was placed in the reserve unit likely to be called only in the gravest emergencies. Relieved from this anxiety, he was able to welcome a summer of explorations. In late August he went to Vitznau on Lake Lucerne where he enjoyed the sunshine, fished, and spent long hours floating on the lake in his boat, his fishing tackle at his side, while he watched the sky and the butterflies.

His new orientation turned him from art back to nature. It was a sign of his growing maturity because it allowed him to look back upon the small town where he had grown up and upon the fields, lakes, and woods that had marked his childhood and adolescence and where he was still quite naturally at home. Yet it was also a pose. In Vitznau he was not just a dreaming poet under the open sky living off meager but nourishing food purchased at isolated farms. He was also a young man on vacation who was staying at the Hotel Alpenrose with a friend, who made satiric comments about the other guests, and who generally behaved exactly as would be expected of a young man on vacation. The idylls on the lake were put to literary use: the identical scene of floating idly in his boat found its way into a letter to Frau Mathilde Wackernagel-Burkhardt, the city archivist's wife who had become something of a mother to him; it also appeared in letters home. Indeed, these scenes of boating and hiking on and near Lake Lucerne recurred in *Lauscher*, then being completed, and were to be inserted in his next novel, *Peter Camenzind*. Like Eros in Kirchheim, like the symbolic Fever Muse in Basel, they were not only genuine expressions of his moods but also literary études.

In October Hesse wrote again to Eugen Diederichs (but in vain, as it turned out) that *Hermann Lauscher* was almost finished. He continued to travel. After visiting Bern in November he resumed his forays into the open country—to Alsatian and Swiss regions around Basel—enjoying mountain streams and strenuous hikes with a welcome sense of isolation and relief. And while Hans, who had some trouble adjusting to life in the city, took some of his attention, Hesse's life remained basically steeped in his enjoyment of paintings, music, and especially of natural landscape. When on New Year's Eve 1901 Hesse appraised his life in a letter home, his judgment was not altogether wrong. He had been away for two Christmas seasons, he wrote, but he felt he had grown by ten years. He did not put it precisely in these terms, but he was deeply aware of how far he had come. He had arrived in Basel on the brink of awakening, a dependent, uncertain member of the *petit cénacle*, a bookseller's apprentice who had completed his service only the year before. Now he felt he had obtained a new sense of achievement not just in his trade but also in his chosen vocation.

The ups and downs of Hesse's life naturally did not allow him to rest long on his summit of self-valuation. Reich's bookstore agreed to bring out his *Hermann Lauscher* after Diederichs had definitely turned it down, and it appeared early in 1901 under the elaborate title *Posthumous Writings and Poems of Hermann Lauscher*, so far without the "Lulu" story and the "Basel Diary." Yet Hesse was depressed. He felt full-time work in the store, and the pressures it generated, interfered more and more with his literary activities, and he began to negotiate with a second-hand firm, Wettenwyl's, for a change in positions that might make his life easier. Late in December he had mentioned to Helene Voigt that he wanted to leave Reich's business in February. By the end of January the deal was concluded. He would earn only 100 francs a month (which would reduce his salary almost to the level of his income at Hecken-hauer's), and the business would be more old-fashioned, but he would have a great deal of free time and he would finally be able to devote all his working time to his favorite branch of the trade, secondhand books.

Emotional pressures played an important part in the move. Hesse was eager to leave Reich's, as though he had a premonition of illness. This possibility also emerged in a note to his family in January during which Hesse signaled his intention to return to Calw. Whether there was con-sternation at the other end is difficult to tell, but he was offered em-ployment at the Calwer Verlagsverein helping his father. In his reply Hesse insisted that while he could not commit his mind in this way, he would be glad to help reorganize their file of journals. There were many fluctuations, although the plan to live in Calw for a while before taking on his new employment was decided upon in March. At the same time Hesse was planning a long journey to Italy, which he took that spring.

This pendulum movement between the desire to come home and the desire to strike out into the world was most noticeable at this time in the spring and summer of 1901. While he toyed with a move to Calw he also made preparations for the first of his great journeys to Italy. With his headaches and insomnia he wanted to come home. With his tough artistic ambition he went south. The journey had been carefully prepared. He had taken Italian lessons for several months—no small feat for a man who disliked learning foreign languages—and indeed Italian became the only foreign language in which, finally, he could manage. And he loved the art treasures and buildings, the bright Italian sun, and the combination of comfort and footloose life his journey allowed him. He was not the usual sight-seeing tourist, not even a parsimonious traveler eking out each additional week by saving expenses. Rather, he saw him-self as a cultural tourist, a vagabond of the soul wandering through a new land admiring its nature and art. He loved St. Francis of Assisi and soon wrote a small book about him. He admired the paintings and architecture of Italy in the spirit of Jakob Burkhardt. As his letters and postcards arrived in the homes of his parents, brothers, sisters, and friends, it became clear that for Hesse this journey had again become a measure of his own education as an artist—a way of perceiving and a way of learning.

No details were left unobserved, few details remained unreported. In Milan he drove past the Duomo in the moonlight. The next day he spent hours on the train observing the tremendous surf as he rode by the shore. The apricots were blossoming, the trees were turning green, the air was mild. In Florence he stayed in a high-ceilinged room, beautiful, looking out on a piazza, "a princely location opposite the Palazzo Vecchio and the Uffizi." "Here Savonarola was burned in 1498 and it still bears the greatness of those days." "All of Italian life attracts me; add to that the impression of the ocean, the fullness of history and art." Beneath the lecturing tone familiar since Hesse's first letters from Tübingen, his readers could discern the strong emphasis on visual perceptions through which he sought to convey that compound of history, nature, and art that to him had become the core of his Italian experience. That same spring in Florence, Hesse portrayed the images he had perceived on a walk just outside the city, which he later published in his *Picture Book:*

> Do you know springtime in Florence? When the roses begin to blossom on the Viale? When up the gentle hills flows the tender red of the blooming fruit trees? When primroses and yellow daffodils gaily cover the meadows bedecked with gold?
>
> Oh, it is wholly beautiful. Those days when black cypresses sway in the first warm air. Those hot noon hours in April when the stone walls along the mountain trails begin to glow gently and the first warm siesta beckons on sun-baked rocks. How the earth stretches and glistens; how the distant mountains reach toward us, ever more blue, ever more longingly, until your entire heart is filled with a sweet, feverish wanderlust. . . .[28]

Hesse was to return to Italy again and again during the ensuing years, and these journeys, like his travels in Germany and Switzerland, became like the albums of photographs and picture postcards he liked to assemble. Nature arrayed itself for him in a series of images.

Inspired by these images, Hesse turned to his new novel, *Peter Camenzind*, which eventually became the source of his first success. The seeds of the novel had been sown that spring. The winds of Vitznau and Lake Lucerne, the hours of idling in the boat, had first been incorporated in *Lauscher* but were now made part of the perceptions of Peter Camenzind, a more involved character who viewed them as part of his psychological conflict. During that summer in Calw, between his return from Italy and his move back to Basel and the job at Wattenwyl's, this story began to take shape as he sat in his old room or even while he talked to his ailing mother on the veranda on hot summer evenings.

Daily routine engulfed him again as he returned to Basel and began to take up his trade one more time. He preferred Wattenwyl's old-fashioned store to the brisk trade at Reich's, as he sat in a shop crowded with old books and took care of a few select and knowledgeable customers. This greater leisure was worth the loss in income, which was largely made up by honoraria and royalties Hesse now earned with his writings. It was not always easy. In November he was about to ask his family for money but was saved when an unexpected sum for an anthology of poetry came in. It was Hesse's last important step before he was entirely free to venture into the life of that free-wheeling poet, Lauscher, whom he had created for himself some time before.

Hesse's spirits, while still being occasionally drawn to that dark side of drinking and depressions, remained generally high. Although his mother's illness grew more severe and his brother Hans threw in the towel and returned to Calw, Hesse did not allow himself to be affected by the trials of his family. This insulation from their world, which became ever more striking in 1901–02, was remarkable. Marie Hesse's illness became constantly graver. A bone disease had given way to a very painful, terminal kidney condition. Yet Hesse drank, wrote, and traveled feverishly. By early 1902 he had completed another book of poems, which he dedicated to his mother. To his pleasure, it was accepted by the publisher Grote in Berlin for the prestigious series of "New German Lyricists." He was getting constantly closer to having "arrived." But despite his growing success in the world and his troubles at home, he did not go near his family even that Christmas. Rather, he took a trip to the Odenwald farther north where he visited the editor of the "German Lyricists" series, Pastor Ernst Knodt. He deplored the absence of snow there and promptly took another trip to the Swiss ski resort of Grindelwald in February. Maintaining his distance from dangers to his psychic health, he followed a singleminded course to his goal: to establish himself as an independent writer.

V

Life was opening its doors to Hermann Hesse just as Marie Hesse underwent a long and difficult illness. Not even sixty (she would have celebrated her sixtieth birthday that following October), she spent her last year in pain. Her son Hermann, to whom she had devoted years of anxiety, was full of feeling and remembrance, but except for letters he kept aloof. He rejoiced when he heard his mother had a "good day," but being constantly caught in his headaches and insomnia, constantly on the move on his outings and journeys, he was unable to get closer to her suffering. It seemed as though he would dissolve if he allowed her agony to touch him, and he was determined to maintain himself—to preserve the taut core of his being that created his art— even as his language turned languid and soft. Toward the end of his mother's life, after his return from the Swiss resort, his letters to his father became dense with mutual concern, yet his distance remained. A few days before Marie Hesse's death Hermann was able to wish that she would soon be released from her torment. The feeling was clearly right— her pain had become unbearable and continuous—but it was wrapped in a letter full of newsy items and self-concern. He could not engage himself in his mother's death, just as for the past two years, since her rejection of his poetry, he could not fully engage himself in her life.

When death finally came to Marie Hesse on April 24, 1902, he was as prepared for the shock as he remained distant from its effect. He did not attend his mother's funeral in Calw, a day's journey from Basel. On April 25 he wrote on a postcard:

> My dears: I was already in my traveling clothes when Papa's two postcards arrived at the same time. After hard thoughts I decided to remain here.

He was not saying why he was not coming home, but his motive became clearer during the following days. Joining his family at that time would have drawn Hesse into a vortex he feared most, that palpable awareness of loss from which he tried to protect himself all his life. In his response to the family he sought to make up for this fear by expressing the grief he shared with them:

> Despite the great pain I am nonetheless glad of our dear mother's final release. In my thoughts I stand with you by her graveside and hold your hands.

He had not been able to bring himself to hold their hands at the actual graveside but held them instead in his thoughts: "May all these days be sacred and turn into our blessings." In the conclusion of this revealing postcard he sought to provide relief by promising a future presence: "That I'm not coming Papa has already forgiven me for in advance. Should some time from now, when the present emotion-laden time is over, you find my visit agreeable, I will come with pleasure." But in a letter immediately following, Hesse became quite explicit. On April 30 he wrote to the family:

> As sad as I am not to have been present at the funeral of our dear Mama, it was still perhaps better for me as well as for you than if I had come. I was and still am very depressed; still, I suffered less during the days since the 24th than during the weeks preceding it. Since the news of her death I have been too numbed and fatigued to sense anything more than a dull pain. In addition I wished so strongly for Mama's release during recent weeks that, despite all our mourning, I also feel glad of her blessed, gentle return home. Also ever since I have had the feeling not to have lost her but to be in her spiritual presence, beneficently and consolingly.[29]

The crucial words explaining his absence remain that "it was better for me as well as for you." In his depression, Hesse feared the risk of exposing himself to psychological damage. All the evidence of the time indicates that he was determined to succeed in overcoming his depressions and to insulate himself from dangers that might draw him back—including family disasters. His feeling for his mother, and his isolation from her, he expressed with simple honesty in a tender poem he wrote upon her death, which Adele later reprinted in her book about Marie Hesse:

> I had so much to tell you.
> Too long was I in foreign lands,
> But still in all those days,
> It was you who understood me most.[30]

From that person who "understood me most," who responded most strongly to each of his contradictory impulses, he finally had to withdraw because he felt threatened by a loss that could have also entailed a loss of himself. For up to the end he felt that his own health and that of his dying mother were intertwined.

Without his mother, Hesse's life continued to reflect the same contradictions, though his father became less commanding and Hermann Hesse soon assumed direction of the family. He would always be torn by conflict between being "derailed" and being an established artist. It neatly bridged the gap between the artist's need to give in to his impulses and social acceptability. His next novel, *Peter Camenzind*, was to be the first in a long line of books to dramatize this conflict and to make it attractive. In preserving his sense of self from the danger of disintegration in the face of his mother's death, he had allowed himself to portray these conflicts with some detachment.

Fortunes continued to improve for Hesse in 1902. He began to be published more and more widely. Magazines and newspapers picked up his numerous travel sketches and poems, and his new book of poetry was flatteringly advertised and introduced. He gained a new sense of purpose. Hesse's contradictions, of course, remained, and he headed for a fresh crisis, which could not, in the end, be staved off. But he also looked upon his career as a writer with great seriousness and was able at last to defer some of his desires and fears to the necessities of that career. Although breakdowns still threatened, they left Hesse's creative strength undiminished. The bookseller's apprentice had matured and had become an author.

3

The Second New Life:
The Author and
His Household

I

Thus I saw between me and my distant goal nothing but abysses yawn-
ing; everything was uncertain, everything devoid of value, only one
thing remained constant: that I intended to become a poet, whether
that turned out to be easy or hard, ridiculous or creditable.

THESE SENTENCES, written in "Life Story Briefly Told" when
Hermann Hesse was forty-eight, were actually about the decision of his
youth—the single decision that remained constant in the midst of all
his hesitations and uncertainties. He had made it as a boy of thirteen; as
a man of exactly twice that age he was to reach his goal. The last year
in Basel became the year of Hesse's success, even as, ironically, it was
the year of his mother's death and of his personal failure.

The remainder of 1902 following the upheaval of Marie Hesse's dying
was under the aegis of her suffering and "release" and of her son's
multiple ailments. In early May he told a friend that his "present condition" was bad. "Out of habit and an inner reticence I show my suffering
to no one; many of my acquaintances whom I see every day don't even
know of my loss. Thus I wear day after day a torturous mask; I live and
talk with people just as before only to be overwhelmed by my pain
during the unguarded hours of the night."[1] He had been either ill or
traveling all winter and spring—a further excuse not to come home for
several more months following the loss of his mother. At Whitsun, when
he might have gotten some time off, Hesse again decided that it did not
pay to go to Calw. He compensated for these constant, if inadvertent,
rejections of his family with fervent assurances that he would write home
more and more often to make sure there would be no hiatus in their
relationship. He also indulged in poetic evocations. He did not have to
look for his mother in her grave, he wrote, as she would always be in

his heart. And when he received a copy of their father's funeral oration, he described at length, and without the slightest hypocrisy, how intensely it had moved him.

Guilt and mourning went hand in hand, but they were necessary because Hesse had reacted instinctively to protect himself and his health. Even at this early age, he felt constantly threatened by ailments both mental and physical. His various aches and pains, which ran as a theme through the remainder of his long life, were genuine enough, and if they were often interlaced with hypochondria, this, too, was part of his personal burden. Since emotional illnesses had been much in evidence during Hesse's life, it would be strange if his tensions and anxieties had not made themselves felt in physical symptoms as well. But there were more solid reasons for some of his agonies. His eyestrain, which became his principal torture, first made itself felt seriously in 1902. Although his eyes had always been vulnerable (broken glasses at school were a catastrophe), the muscular eye problem that was responsible for many of his headaches was clearly diagnosed only now. He assured his family that he had "really bad" pains only rarely, but even as he enjoyed the outdoors, and his hikes and walks, he again and again referred to his eyes and the agonies they caused him.

Hesse's attempt to become an artistic *persona* was accompanied by many efforts to look the part, but he also tried, with great expenditure of mental energy, to bolster the outward trappings of an artistic life with actual accomplishment. His next novel, *Peter Camenzind*, however, moved ahead too slowly for him. Actually he was very busy: he had his job at the bookstore and was writing a great many poems and brief essays, which were beginning to gain wide acceptance. Still, the weight of that unfinished book lay heavily on his conscience during that spring and summer of 1902, exacerbating his sense of depression. That spring Hesse stopped attending the weekly musicales at the Wackernagels and no longer called at the Laroches—his two adopted homes during the past two years. Whatever relationship there had been with Elizabeth Laroche, whom he undoubtedly liked in 1900, it did not survive this year of great difficulty. As the summer went on, Hesse isolated himself more and more. Mourning, guilt, pain, and the sense of facing a writer's block appeared to hem him in from all sides. A crisis was once more upon him.

By early August Hesse evidently had had enough. He announced an impending trip to Calw because he "could no longer bear to be alone on long evenings." It still took him some weeks before he managed to tear himself away, but when he finally made the short journey home, he remained deep into the fall. The length of his stay in Calw at a time when he still had a job in Basel suggests that he was going through a difficult period. By October, however, he seemed to improve. He began to mend fences and to think of his writing. In a long letter to Dr. Rudolf Wackernagel-Burkhardt he apologized for having been absent from his house and also mentioned the new novel he was working on. "For almost a year now I've been working on a novel," he wrote, "which, if it continues at the present rate may perhaps be done in ten or twelve years."[2] In the meantime he tried to recapture some sense of energy and health by hiking in the vicinity of Calw. As he did so, that region of his childhood and adolescence once more cast its spell and, with its fields and forests, furnished images and scenes for his later work. When Hesse returned to Basel late in October, after an absence of almost twelve weeks, he was able to write Adele that Calw had been a renewing experience.

At the time Hesse returned to Basel he still lived in those picturesque rooms facing the noisy traffic on the cobbled street. He was also still conscious of his loneliness. But he was strong enough to move to new rooms and generally accommodate himself to his chosen life as an aspiring young artist in Basel. For the present he found the job at the bookstore and its routine soothing. Although his eyes continued to ache, his depression gradually lifted. Perhaps one of the reasons for his change in spirits was an improvement in his social life; greater professional success was another. He had met a new friend, he told his sister in November, a "very young Basler painter" named Rudolf Löw, and this took the edge off his loneliness. Since leaving Jennen's rooms earlier that year, Hesse had missed that bond of male friendship with someone whose temperament corresponded to his own. Evidently his withdrawal from that "monster" had not been as complete, emotionally, as he had pretended to his mother at the time. He missed being close to a *Künstlernatur* —an artistic sensibility. It was crucial to his survival. This new contact with the outside world restored some of that ambience for him, and Hesse appeared once more on the verge of a new phase of work.

At Christmas, Hesse went north again, as he had done the previous year, to see Pastor Ernst Knodt in the Odenwald.[3] As those mountains were north of the Black Forest, close to the River Main, Hesse had to traverse his home country, but he evidently bypassed Calw once more. If he had gone in quest of comfort, it had clearly helped. When he got back to Basel he felt sufficiently buoyed to write some poems and even added a few paragraphs to his novel. Gradually a new spirit began to lift him out of that mood of mourning. *Hermann Lauscher*, which had come out the year before, had begun to receive much favorable attention, which raised Hesse's spirits even further. Now, a year later, his second book of poetry since *Romantic Songs*—simply titled *Gedichte*, or *Poems*—was brought out in the prestigious series "New German Lyricists" under Knodt's direction and Hesse's mail was happily enlarged by more and more accolades.

One rich dividend of these latest bevies of approving letters was the beginning of Hesse's first sustained relationship with an important writer of his generation. Stefan Zweig, who was to be known especially in the twenties and thirties as an influential German-Jewish novelist and essayist, responded so favorably to *Poems* that early in 1903 he wrote Hesse challenging him in effect to begin a regular correspondence. A copy of Zweig's latest collection of poems, *Silver Strings*, accompanied the letter. Hesse took up the challenge, and an interesting correspondence ensued. Although they were roughly of the same age (Zweig was four years younger than Hesse), they were of very different temperaments—Zweig was a far more analytic writer even then, while Hesse, especially during those early years of their correspondence, was still imbued with the Pietist spirit of his past and its vibrant emotionality. They continued to write each other for many years and, after meeting at last in 1905, intermittently maintained a long relationship until Zweig's suicide in 1942.

Hesse's first letter to Zweig is an interesting example of the pose he liked to strike in those days and provides an insight, however oblique, into the way he lived—and liked to see himself living—during those last years in Basel. He began, characteristically, by presenting himself as a *persona* rather different from the actual *person*. His life, he wrote his new correspondent, was not really stable enough for long-range contacts with people, nor did he possess a mind for literary correspondence. Then, following this disclaimer, he proceeded to write in great detail about his personal life: how his eyes had kept him from reading and writing for months, yet how he usually enjoyed books, romanticism, poetry, and his own writing. He professed not to be interested in love affairs or such matters for "my heart actually never belonged to people but always to nature and books." It was clearly a staged letter and he (with a faint resemblance to the "young chronicler" of the early Tübingen days) was the performing soliloquist.

In the course of his letter Hesse confirmed the substance of his note of apology to Rudolf Wackernagel: he had retired from society for the past year. But, he added in his letter to Zweig, he was not really a misanthropist. He rather enjoyed "children, peasants, seamen" and was always ready for a good drinking bout in a sailors' dive. Hesse was surprisingly frank about his bread-winning trade. While his days were still spent working in a secondhand bookstore, he wrote, he liked to spend his weekends and the rest of his free time roaming the mountains and valleys near the city.[4] While this was not an accurate picture of his life, it remained "fictionally true"—as many of his letters throughout his life presented a true image, yet retouched and disguised to convey Hesse's state of mind indirectly, often anticipating its reflection in stories or novels. It was nonetheless an auspicious beginning. At this point in the lives of both young men this epistolary meeting was a symbolic encounter meaningful in many unexpected ways. For Hesse, it entailed the sense that he was becoming known, that he was being courted, that his opinions were requested and valued. With this kind of approval, and his newly released ambitions, his first "real" novel began to take shape.

II

My first novel written in Basel during the early years of this century. . . . Stems from that mythical era, long before the great wars and revolutions of our time . . . of which you may have heard our parents and grandparents speak. Still, it does not exude contentment and satiety, for it is the work and confession of a young man. . . .[5]

Hesse wrote these words fifty years after the fact, recalling *Peter Camenzind*, the novel with which he had ushered in the new century. It was also his first novel transmuting his personal traumas into the mind and world of a fictional character more removed from himself than the *personae* of *One Hour Behind Midnight* and *Hermann Lauscher*. Although the new hero, Peter Camenzind, bears many of his own features and goes through episodes that reflect events in his life, Hesse was to find a fitting narrative formula through which the character of his protagonist could be developed as a more distant relative of the author than had been the case in the past.

From a practical point of view the key to Hesse's success in *Camenzind* had been his previous book, *Hermann Lauscher*, which had received pleasing notices. Among the admirers of his youthful novel and poems was Paul Ilg, a Swiss writer who sent a copy of the book to the well-known publisher Samuel Fischer in Berlin with his strong recommendation. It seems odd and yet, in retrospect, a sign of the times that so perceptive a businessman as Fischer saw not only literary but also commercial possibilities in this young Basel writer. He was not to be disappointed. As soon as Hesse heard from an editor at Fischer's publishing house that his previous little book had been "pleasing" and that they hoped he would send them anything further he might have under way, he was electrified. "It was the first literary acknowledgement and encouragement of my life," he wrote years later, somewhat inaccurately; but the remainder of the statement was undoubtedly true: "I had started *Camenzind* and Fischer's invitation spurred me on. I finished it. It was accepted at once. I had arrived."[6]

Actually, Hesse's response in a letter to Fischer on February 2, 1903, was rather coy. He wrote that he had indeed been working for a while "on a little story" and that he would send it to them as soon as possible. He also intimated that he did not write very much and only following a very personal need. Since he had set for himself the goal of becoming a writer at the age of thirteen, this was a rather startling disclaimer. In fact, he went to work furiously at once. When Fischer first wrote, the book was still in its early stages (we may recall that he had predicted ten to twelve years of composition in his letter to Wackernagel), but he finished it during February and March, although at that time he still worked at Wattenwyl's secondhand bookstore. Even if we take into account the possibility that he might have done some of this writing on the job, it was still a remarkable achievement, especially since Fischer's response was both immediate and enthusiastic. After a trip to Italy in early April, he was able to send out the complete manuscript on May 9, and by May 18 it had already been read and accepted.[7]

A flowery letter from the publishers congratulated Hesse upon his achievement, thanking him, "in time for Whitsun," for his "wonderful work." In fact, the new novel had all the virtues of the previous book, which had caught the attention of Fischer and his associates. It conveyed an intimate sense of nature; it presented rural episodes and social commentary about Bohemia and city life in a philosophical spirit; and it brought all these elements together in a highly poetic language and mood, rich in imagery and sentiment. At the same time, the new book provided a fresh substance and style of its own. Interwoven with the fine feeling for natural landscapes is a varied cast of characters and a coherent plot. All of Hesse's days of rowing and fishing in mountain lakes, of hiking along hilly trails and walking aimlessly in the streets of his city were contained in this small volume.

Peter Camenzind was the first of several sparks that were to ignite Hesse's audiences throughout his career and to begin vogues or cults. His reputation waxed and waned during his life, but it was always punctuated by these points of mysterious confluence of psychological and social crises endured by his readers with his own insights. At this first occurrence of the peculiar Hesse phenomenon, the flare-up of enthusiasm (which, as his biographer Hugo Ball put it accurately, carried his name at once all over Germany)[8] allowed him to take a very special message to his readers at a crucial point in their lives. Ball saw this book as Hesse's farewell to both depressions and bookishness: "If 'Lauscher' was the echo of his bibliophilic studies, 'Camenzind' represents a step into life, into another difficult medium." No longer was there any pietism or parental home with its maxims and prohibitions. "Here *pura natura* reigns supreme."[9]

Hesse's turn to nature served him well in developing his new style while allowing him to remain within an established context. As he saw it, he had written about the *Künstlernatur* he considered essential to his identity, about an artistic sensibility nurtured by the cultural changes of his time, which demanded new forms. Hesse's hero was not just the artist, as in Thomas Mann's contemporaneous "Tonio Kröger." He was also that young person sensitive to change and fearful of the claustro-phobic norms of an indifferent society. The values enshrined in *Peter Camenzind* were more popular than Mann's. They appealed not only to artists and those who saw in them the heroes of their time, but to young people whose counter-culture of nature, sainthood, and dream had been created precisely in response to the pressures of the new age that began to close in on them in the empire of Wilhelm II.

Even in sensing the appeal of his new novel, Hesse was aware of its dual message; to the young people who were roughly of his own genera-tion, and to the generations of his older brothers and his parents, who were soon to become the backbone of his support. As an old man in 1951, responding to a letter of inquiry by some French *lycée* students who were writing their main school essay on *Peter Camenzind*, he ad-mitted the relevance of the Youth Movement of that time for the appeal of his new novel even as he strongly repudiated the connection:

> [Peter Camenzind] loves (nature) . . . with the passion and devotion of an artist. . . . [His] place is nevertheless not among the wanderers of the youth movement and the youth communes . . . who either play their guitars at campfires or spend their nights in argument. . . . He will not go the way of the many but obstinately his own way . . . mirroring nature and world in his own soul and experiencing them in new pictures. . . . He is the lonely king of a dream empire which he himself has created.[10]

This statement suggests that *Peter Camenzind* faced the very issues the cultural revolutionists of the Youth Movement—the *Wandervögel*, or *Free German Youth*—had raised at the turn of the century, and that Hesse knew it. The new social forms and styles to a very buttoned-up age appeared revolutionary enough, and these were clearly the forms that were also reflected in *Peter Camenzind*. Young men in open shirts and shorts and middle-class women in rough dresses and work clothes went on communal hikes in which the sexes often intermingled. They lived in camps and communes, played guitars, and read to one another at campfires. But this life-style (usually combined with a perfectly normal middle-class routine in business offices, universities, and schools) was intended as a re-creation of the past rather than as a signal for involvement in any class conflicts. Their discontents were those of middle- and upper-class people between eighteen and thirty, usually urban, longing for nature, spiritual regeneration, and brave suffering knights.

Hesse's affinity with these readers at the time of *Camenzind* and his disclaimer are revealing both of the sources of his success as well as some of the problems that dogged him for the rest of his life. If he disapproved of the Youth Movement, he did so mostly because he disliked any organized form of living that might threaten the integrity of the individual life. He did not, however, disapprove of the return to nature or the quest for ideals or the romance of the simple life. Nor did Hesse fail to understand them when, for just these reasons, many of these young readers supported the war in 1914 and died in it in great numbers.

In Hesse's contradictory way, this potential conflict was intertwined with another. Some of the very epithets about the Youth Movement that he used much later in response to a request for information, were clearly meant to reflect his feelings at the time: they asserted what Peter Camenzind was *not*. It must be remembered, however, that these faintly condescending references to campfires and guitars were not just descriptive but were part of the standard vocabulary. Hesse, then as later, knew only too well that most people did not take those young hikers in their funny costumes very seriously, and, while appreciating their values, he also sought to gain some distance for himself. This desire to disguise his closeness to those nearest to him was no mere hypocrisy. Since his young audience reached considerably farther than the Youth Movement itself, his references to it can be taken in a larger sense, as symptomatic of Hesse's identification with the language of the established culture along with that of its opponents. It was part of his perennial need to be accepted even while courting those who broke away.

In addressing the young and sharing their doubts and fears, Hesse also reached toward their elders. The very approach of the new novel, and some of the issues he raised in it, dredged up problems everyone shared: the danger of dissociation from the roots of human life, from nature, from the rural village or small town in the face of the growing city. Young people drew one lesson from this apparent danger: old values must be restored wherever possible in a new spirit. But older people were also concerned with the danger to their culture involved in the rapid urbanization of their age and the threat of domination by a faceless state. Only they looked at it more passively, nostalgically. Hesse seduced them with his style, which clearly echoed that "old world." His form and language were reminiscent of writers of the preindustrial age, most notably of the famous Swiss storyteller Gottfried Keller, who reproduced idylls of small towns and villages in the middle of the nineteenth century. In form and style, in its sentimental veneer, even in its language and traditional narrative frame, Hesse's first important novel conformed in most of its detail to the highly realistic yet also poetic and implicitly didactic fiction that was then in fashion.

Here Hesse's own description in 1951 is a guide. While Peter Camenzind will "obstinately go his own way," it is a very special route—that of "mirroring nature and world in his own soul and experiencing them in new pictures." Projecting the world within was to be a mark of Hesse's mysticism for the rest of his life. It had grown out of his reading of Novalis in Tübingen and Basel and, more recently, from his studies of Nietzsche, a philosopher who viewed man's relations with the world in terms of dual yet indubitably inner impulses of passion and order. Peter Camenzind found his own way in an interior landscape. That favorite figure of the turn of the century, the sensitive young artist, could thus be cast in the role of a cultural heretic. Form and plot were steeped in a carefully drawn, highly realistic yet poetic world reminiscent of Keller and his latter-day imitators, which enabled the book to be accepted as conventional fiction.

Peter Camenzind first appeared in S. Fischer's journal *Die Neue Rundschau* in installments during the summer of 1903. Anticipating its hoped-for success, Hesse decided to leave the bookstore and to start seriously his career as a free-lance writer. Even in "Life Story Briefly Told" a note of satisfaction remained in his voice:

> Thus, amid so many storms and sacrifices, my goal had now finally been reached: however impossible it may have appeared, I had become a poet and had, it would seem, won the long, stubborn battle with the world. . . . Now for the first time I realized in what dreadful isolation, asceticism, and danger I had lived year after year: the warm breeze of recognition did me good and I began to be a contented man.[11]

Contentment did not last long. Hesse at once added a new and disturbing theme to his life, if not his work. Having made clear to friends and family for years that he was too much of a loner to be suited for marriage, he embarked on the venture of taking a wife.

The name Bernoulli had been a muted yet persistent motif since Hesse's arrival in Basel three years earlier. A young Herr Bernoulli had played duets with Elizabeth Laroche even during Hesse's first weeks in the city. Two years later his social life extended to the local community of artists among whom he met two sisters, Maria and Mathilde Bernoulli, who together operated an artistic photography studio in an old part of town. After knowing them and their circle for a time, Hesse began to court Maria, a brooding woman of thirty-five (to his twenty-six) whose talents as a photographer were enriched by her great gifts for music, and who appeared to provide that *Künstlernatur*, or artistic temperament, that he thought he needed. Earlier, Maria and her circle had already furnished the backdrop for the artistic city crowd in *Peter Camenzind* from which his hero had to extricate himself. When now, after the completion of the work, its author reentered their circle after months of withdrawal, his relations with Maria seemed to bring with them the echoes of its involvement in his work.

Because he had built his novel as a biography—a novel of education of the "artist as a young man"—it is instructive to view *Peter Camenzind* as an index of this time in Hesse's life and as a barometer of his actions on the threshold of his full artistic commitment. He was evidently also preparing himself internally for marriage and weighing it against his independence and personal friendships. Although time sequences were reshuffled, most of the incidents reflect Hesse's own history during the past two years of his restless life.

Even more significant than the parallels are the differences, the complex, upside down relationship this novel bears to Hesse's personal life. Peter Camenzind was indeed Hermann Hesse. Unlike his predecessor, Hermann Lauscher, however, he wore a completely reshaped mask. Hesse had designed a character who was outwardly almost his opposite, but the inner life was Hesse's alone. If Hugo Ball was able to describe Peter as a robust, outgoing farm boy from the Bernese mountains, he was merely following the author's stage directions.

Similarly, the other *dramatis personae*—parents, women, friends in the art world—were for the most part costumed to suit the stage on which they performed. In their confrontation with the protagonist they reflected in carefully altered ways Hesse's actual relations. Hesse retained, for example, the opposition of the hero's provincial origins to the city in which he made his way, but Calw in the Black Forest was transformed into the mythical village of Nimikon in the mountains and plateaus beyond Bern. The child of Swabian missionaries had become a boy raised on a small farm, yet, like the real Hermann Hesse, this farm lad was educated in a Latin school in a very middle-class way. Flora and fauna on the farm and in the parents' garden were solemnly celebrated with images drawn from both places. By contrast, when this child of nature left for "the city," a vaguely described Zurich and a very real

Basel, with undefined shadows of Paris and Berlin in the background, were established as suitable counterpoints.

Relations of place were matched with similar portrayals and distortions in the family. Hesse may have projected an awareness of his own bilateral relations with his parents, often shutting out his many siblings, when he made Peter an only child. A similar balance between outer disguise and inner truth appeared in Peter's perceptions of his parents. Like Hermann, the young hero from Nimikon was close to his mother and found his father taxing, but the parents themselves bore only a distant resemblance to the actual Hesses. Still, if the mother is described as large and physically stronger than the father, though endowed with Marie's lively dark eyes, and the father (though ostensibly a peasant) as short and slight, it reflects on Hesse's perceptions of his parents' relationship to one another symbolically. Similarly, if we read that Peter's father was in love with wine (reversing the theological image) and even passed this legacy on to his son, we can perceive a similar link between the generations in the legacy of headaches and anxieties that passed between them.

Parallels and inversions shaped structure and plot. Peter was propelled from his native soil by two events that changed him profoundly. The first, not surprisingly, was the death of his mother, though the way the death was described in the novel is surprising indeed. Her demise in the book came quickly, without preparation, the way events usually occur in Hesse's fiction. One day Peter discovered that she lay ill and dying, although at first he did not realize how serious it was. But early one morning on a hot summer day when he woke up to get some fresh water from the vat in the kitchen, he heard moans as he passed his parents' bedroom. Hermann, the author, may have been emotionally unable to attend his mother's funeral, but Peter, the character of fiction, sat by her bedside as she died. When she finally closed her eyes for the last time, he bent over and kissed "for the first time in my life the cool, withered mouth of my mother." Hermann had recalled kissing Marie's cool, withered mouth when he last visited her before her death. In this fictional version, moreover, it was the father rather than the son who was remiss. The elder Camenzind had slept through the episode in the next bed and woke up when it was over. After a while, "the old man" followed Peter to his room and cursed him for not waking him. The following pages are filled with funeral preparations that Hermann had carefully avoided.[12]

The other force that sent Peter from his village was ambition. He had received a scholarship to attend the university in Zurich. In sending his hero from his natural idyll in the Bernese Oberland to the corrupt metropolis to become a university student, Hesse once more turned to that subterranean theme that had plagued him in Tübingen and had informed *Hermann Lauscher*. But here that academic image remained a superficial gesture. Student life hardly figured in the novel, for it was already replaced by the community of artists and by the bread-winning trade of free-lance journalism he was about to undertake. Clearly, however, the student status still remained significant at this juncture for his hero's external mask.

Even before his mother's death, Peter Camenzind's life had been marked by an adolescent adoration for a girl who became a symbol of his awakening, a mark of his beginning manhood. She was called Rösi Girtanner, the beautiful daughter of the local lawyer. Rösi was an image of that early idealizing love that leads to self-awareness, whereas most of the other women throughout the book actively functioned as "educators" who brought "sense knowledge" to their "pupil" in his ascent toward maturity. They did this symbolically rather than literally, for in the story they either rejected Peter or were rejected by him. In Zurich, for example, he fell intensely in love with an older painter, Erminia Aglietti, whose minutely described pale features resembled many Italian beauties Hesse had seen in life and on canvas but whose age, maturity, maternal caring, and ambivalent attitude toward her craft suggest a good deal of Maria Bernoulli. Like Goethe's suicidal young lover Werther, who is frequently invoked in the book, Peter soon discovered that she was tragically in love, but not with him. In the meantime, however, she had awakened in him an awareness of his potential sensuality necessary for his future as a poet.

A similarly inadvertent "tutor" was a scantily fictionalized Elisabeth Laroche. When Peter became a free-lance journalist in Basel, where creator Hermann knew the social scene only too well, his new love focused quite naturally on an idealized, piano-playing "Elisabeth" who appeared on that stage along with faithful reproductions of the Wackernagels and all the others whom Hesse had avoided during that year. Although she and Peter shared a great deal, talking about Italy and art, "Elisabeth" did in the novel what she had done in life: she married another. And Peter, like Hermann, continued to frequent her house and preserved his adoration as best he could. In the meantime, "Elisabeth" had become yet another image, a way station in the hero's progress of learning.

Finally, closer to the end of the novel, a third type emerged. Disgusted with academia, journalism, and cities, Peter twice sought refuge in the artist's Mecca, Italy. On both journeys he found pure distillations of his dreams, but it was on the second that he met a rotund embodiment of sentimental femininity, his landlady, the vegetable vendor Signora Annunziata Nardini, who, as a widow of thirty-four and of enormous proportions, fell warmly and givingly in love with the young hero. Although Peter could not reciprocate this affection, she, too, taught him something of the sensual life—though combined with self-sacrifice and the adoration of saints—because she was presented as an embodiment of simple, naturally pious, if also somewhat ridiculous, love.

Hesse's novels from this book onward were always constructed on the principle of point and counterpoint. In this novel, built, as it is, on the model of biography and sensual education, these musical antipodes are also identified with the two sexes. In a more abstract way, this occurs in practically all of Hesse's important books, especially in those of his forties like *Demian* and *Steppenwolf*; here it emerges in palpably sensual terms.[13] At each stage of Peter's progress of learning (which is also always an ascent toward an ideal), each woman "tutor" is matched by a male counterpoint. Even at the time of Rösi, Peter was involved with two schoolmates—one brown-haired older boy whom he adored from afar, one lighthearted blond boy who betrayed him—and the process is deepened in the later phases of the novel. Remarkably, while the description of his love for women remains lofty and general, expressing itself mostly in evocations and conversations, similar episodes with male friends tend to be dramatic and concrete.

In the main episodes in Zurich, Erminia's counterpoint was Richard, who actually functioned as the novel's central love. Peter had been drawn to this beautiful and clever young man at once and was immediately jealous of all his relations with others, especially with women. But it was only after his rejection by Erminia (evidently a symbolic way station that had to be passed) that the liaison with Richard became close. In the company of this friend, Peter underwent some of the most intense moments in the book. Their friendship was marked by play surprisingly frank in its sexual allusiveness—as, for example, when swimming in a mountain stream they were surprised by tourists and, hiding in a watery cave, teased them by popping out now and then, naked and wet, to laugh at their shocked, philistine faces. Peter also served as Richard's guide through Italy, and they traveled together while he introduced his friend to the lore of his ideal, Saint Francis of Assisi. When at the end of his university studies Richard finally had to leave, their farewell was particularly intense. In his grief at their separation, Peter clambered back on the railroad car moments before the train pulled out of the station, and they embraced and kissed. Like all abortive loves, there even was a tragic end: Richard died two weeks later, drowning in a mountain stream, and Peter was disconsolate. No such encounters, involving real touch and feeling, exist in the episodes with the women.

The male friendship to correspond to the love of "Elisabeth" in Basel is the most intriguing, for it introduced yet another theme that occupied Hesse at the time—sainthood. This love radiated outward from Peter's depression and self-imposed loneliness and from his drinking and self-loathing as he felt more and more trapped by the trade and politics of journalism. The antibody for all that was the love of Saint Francis of Assisi. Author Hesse published a biography of the great saint (along with a biography of Boccaccio) only one year later, in 1904, but in *Peter Camenzind* he gave him a fictional role. Having found no satisfaction in the world of commerce after a year in Paris Peter settled again in Basel and after continuing his visits to the grand house of "Elisabeth" for a while, he picked up, as a counterpoint, a carpenter and his family. The relationship with that carpenter, his thin, overworked, and somewhat acerbic wife, and his three children (one of them dying at the start of their acquaintance), was in itself peculiar. But the denouement, which triggered both the tragic and the positive resolution of the novel, was provided by the crippled brother of the carpenter's wife.

Boppi, condemned to death from the start, was described with loving care (including his beautiful childlike hands) with all his infirmities. He was utterly helpless. His mother, like Peter's, had died, but, unlike Peter, he was unable to function by himself. In this conclusion, the hero acted like Saint Francis. He gave himself to his charge, renting an apartment for the two of them and even acquiring a poodle for his crippled friend. In devoting himself entirely to Boppi, Peter achieved a semblance of married life in which he found contentment and happiness. His depressions began to leave him and he was beginning to work again. Moreover, he retained the parallel to "Elisabeth," who, at the cripple's request, consented to appear before him with all her distant elegance and feminine saintliness. When Boppi died, it became clear that this death represented yet another great loss, another great love gone from the hero's life.

In the concluding phase of the book, Peter returned to Nimikon, to "nature," to the Alpine village of his childhood, where his origins had been encapsulated by myth, to take care of his father, who was now eighty years old. Unless biographical analogies deceive entirely, this return from the city (which Hesse was able to achieve at last in the fall of 1902 when he went to Calw) reflects his move toward a reconciliation with his father. In the open-ended conclusion of the novel, the child of nature, having passed through sainthood, and having lost all his loves through death, now considered renewing the link with his father by taking over management of the pub they had shared—in a mutual embrace of the god of wine whom Hesse had celebrated in imagery redolent with sexual feeling in this strangest of simple tales. It is no wonder that no less an expert of unconscious longing than Sigmund Freud praised *Peter Camenzind* as one of his favorite readings.

III

Hesse's first novel had clearly emerged from his recent past, but it also prefigured the conflicts into which he now entered. February and March 1903 had been filled with feverish writing until the work was almost done. Early in April he joined some of his artist friends on a spur-of-the-moment trip to Italy. One of the painters in their circle, a woman who was moving to Italy, invited some friends to accompany her to Florence over Easter. At first Hesse had decided not to go, but he allowed himself to be persuaded by Maria Bernoulli. It was a departure for more than just Italy.

Hesse's account of this adventure in a letter to his family in Calw was extremely detailed. Referring to his companion as off-handedly as possible, he told them that he did not think of going "until on the last day Fräulein Bernoulli, another artist, caught fire and persuaded me to go along." They started in a great hurry. Hesse had just time to change his clothes and stuff some shirts into a suitcase and they were off. The train left at six that evening. Riding third-class for lack of money, they sat through the night upright on wooden benches until they got to Milan in the morning. After sightseeing and a night spent in the city, they left for the final lap to Florence the next day. He found a beautiful, inexpensive room for Maria and her friend in a sixteenth century palazzo. They took in sightseeing and heard a great deal of music: organ recitals and concerts. Hesse still suffered from eyestrain and so did not accompany the women on their visits to art galleries. Instead, he roamed in the alleys and squares of the city and enjoyed bars and cheap restaurants, which kept him in touch with ordinary people as well as with good wine and food.[14]

In the spring, while *Peter Camenzind* was awaiting the judgment of Samuel Fischer, and later when it was being prepared for publication in installments, the relationship with Maria Bernoulli became steadily closer. Twenty years later, after their divorce, Hesse occasionally referred to his pursuit of a marriage that at the same time he resisted, but the conflict was evident from his correspondence even then. Early in June, when the success of his book became a real possibility, Hesse's involvement grew even more intense. Yet he also argued with his friends, his father, even with his potential father-in-law, who were all concerned about this decision. In one of his letters, Hesse related how he had withdrawn from women for years and was almost a Puritan, but how he had finally acquired a girl, a "delightful, petite, black-haired, wild sweetheart of a girl." Books and writing paper were gathering dust, for all of his time now belonged to his girl. There was no word about the fact that this "girl" was in her thirties; rather, the image he created in these letters was of a passionate "little girl who reaches only up to my beard and yet can kiss so powerfully that I almost suffocate."[15]

At first, Hesse presented them only as lovers with no future commitments. "Marriage, of course, is out of the question. I have no talent for that sort of thing." But he was also moved: this "sweet wild love stirs me deeply . . . and takes me closer to the roots of life."[16] Wisdom, art, and literature were meaningless by comparison. But the friend to whom these confessions were addressed was skeptical. Hesse had to backtrack in a later letter, and Maria ceased to be a wild thing in love. Instead, he now indicated that she was a woman equal to himself in education, experience, and intelligence, "in every respect an independent, capable person." They had been good friends for some time, while she had secretly loved him, and only recently had they become romantically involved.[17]

Gradually, however, the idea of marriage emerged more clearly. In a letter to his father in June, Hesse suggested this possibility and for the first time also allowed that there would be difficulties. He found it impossible to decide this matter, Hesse wrote, because he was still too poor (the sales of *Camenzind* were to change all that) but more importantly because he had "a certain horror of marriage." After the contract with Fischer had been signed he became more definite. For the moment, he told his father on June 24, his life would remain unchanged. Still secretive, he "divulged" that a "famous publisher" had given him a favorable five-year contract but that the extent of his independence would be determined by the volume of his sales.[18] In his letter to his skeptical friend in October he cited his future father-in-law's objections, which showed that potential success was not quite enough. That he loved his daughter, old Fritz Bernoulli would find quite understandable, Hesse told his correspondent, but an engagement or marriage to his daughter without Hesse's being sure of his daily bread was unacceptable. (His friend, he suggested, held precisely the reverse point of view: marriage was morally right; it was loving her that he considered sinful.)[19] But despite objections from father-in-law and friends, they became engaged at Whitsun that year.

To the objective eye, the new bride was not a fiery beauty. She was short, and though pleasingly dark-haired and possibly passionate in her love, she appeared in photographs even at relaxed moments as tense and contained. She seemed to exude an aura of suffering, even of foreboding, with her square head and her brooding eyes. Yet there was also a startled look about her, soft gestures that betrayed the musical sensibility that Hesse had first perceived in her. A famous passage in the fairy tale "Iris," written to her as a farewell and dedicated to "Mia," as Hesse was to call her later, presents a rather clear image of what he felt about her in 1903. It was written sixteen years later, after three children and storms of illness and suffering, but the clarity distilled by his psychoanalysis of the previous years remains preciously distinct: "She was older than he might have wished his wife to be. She was peculiar in her ways and it would be difficult to live with her and at the same time to pursue one's goals." She was not very strong and healthy and enjoyed best "just living among flowers and music." But "sometimes she was so tender and sensitive that anything that approached her from outside pained her and caused her to weep." In this highly poetic way Hesse tried to account for his feelings with some clarity. He ended on a painfully admiring note: "Then again she radiated light, still and fine in her solitary happiness, and whoever saw her in this way knew how difficult it would be to give anything to this strange, beautiful woman, and to mean anything to her."[20]

Maria Bernoulli was not the conventional bride who often appears in Hesse's books. Rather, she was on the verge of middle age, turned into herself, yet leaning on him for support. The question why Hesse decided on this marriage invites many answers, but one was undoubtedly connected with the death of his mother. Maria was almost a decade older than Hesse—a fact that obsessed him from the start—and their friendship turned into love precisely one year after his mother's death and his own failure, for which he tried to account, partly, in *Peter Camenzind*. There were even some parallels in their appearances—the broad face, the dark hair, the contained body—and in their love for music and flowers. They had the same name. These parallels, of course, are too close to have been overlooked. Even Hugo Ball, whose work was authorized by Hesse, suggested some of these connections, and no psychoanalytic researches are required to perceive them.[21] Still, marriage, which at once attracted and repelled Hesse, involved considerations in its own terms. It required a need to discover a home, to re-create for himself what had been only ambiguously his during those childhood years in Basel and Calw.

But there were also more mundane considerations. The liaison was most desirable: Maria's family was an old house of Basel patricians. Bernoulli-Strasse near the university was named after her family, and Maria counted an amazing number of mathematicians among her fore-bears who had calculated their way through the eighteenth century. To be connected with the Bernoullis was to be well connected indeed, and clearly Hesse was aware of it. Some such knowledge may also have impelled Maria's father to oppose the marriage. When the question came up, Hesse was still penniless and, in the view of a protective father, such a man was likely to take advantage of a distinguished liaison. Actually, however, Herr Bernoulli continued his aloofness even after his son-in-law became moneyed and famous. An odd unease always pervaded their relationship, as though the older man subtly discerned Hesse's secret misgivings.

By the end of the summer Hesse knew *Camenzind* would do reason-ably well, and they made plans for their wedding the next year. After leaving Wattenwyl's secondhand bookstore, he decided to go home to Calw and work on his new novel while getting ready for their marriage. A Peter Camenzind retiring to Nimikon, he prepared to return to the Black Forest. Unlike his hero, however, he had obtained the ballast of a fiancée whom he decided to take home in September to visit his family. It is another quirk in this strange courtship that in the midst of all these arguments and indecisions he had never revealed his plans, or even the existence of his intended, to his confidante Adele. As late as September 4 he finally wrote his sister about her in announcing their arrival: "For I am bringing Fräulein Bernoulli along to whom I am secretly engaged." He admitted that "father knows a little," but that above all he wanted to show his girl to his family. Yet he felt impelled to add: "No one must know except you, Marulla, and father" (he left out Hans). His bride-to-be would be able to stay only three or four days, although he intended to remain with them at least to the end of the month.

Actually, Hesse moved to Calw for an even more extended period, but Maria's brief visit in September took place and went off rather well. Hesse's reluctance about his plans also showed itself in another way: he was extremely self-conscious about his fiancée's appearance. "Don't be startled," he begged his sister, and "tell father not to be either." "I beg you to be loving to my girl (who is also much older than you and I), and I believe you will like each other." The meeting turned out to be rather tentative and shy, but they got along, and the bond between the families was finally established.

Early in October, having moved from Basel, Hesse settled in Calw for a longer stay to begin his new novel *Beneath the Wheel* about his

Maulbronn experience and to immerse himself in other work that flooded in on him from all sides. The prodigal son had returned, and for almost a year he was to live in Calw. The importance of this time cannot be overestimated. While more and more harbingers appeared of *Camenzind*'s impending success, Hesse buried himself in his childhood and adolescence. He returned to school in his imagination and, splitting himself into two *personae*, he reenacted the implications of the escape from the seminary that had ushered in the most painful years of his life. This novel, if anything, was to be even more successful than the previous book, and in attacking the pedagogy of the time it trespassed on even holier ground.

The value of Hesse's extended return at this juncture of his life, however, went deeper. It allowed him to enrich Peter Camenzind's vision as he literally returned to his home ground. A new body of work was nourished in Calw that eventually established him as one of the foremost writers of his generation. For in getting back in touch with his home in the Black Forest, he began to write short stories and novellas (they eventually filled several volumes) that turned his romantic perceptions of "self and world" into pictures of his region that were drawn minutely, in sharply penciled strokes, with the care and realism and poetry of a Gottfried Keller.

Calw was rechristened "Gerbersau" and its inhabitants—its schoolmasters, fools, spinsters, and lovers—came to life as a personal mythology. These stories were written in the style of the day—slightly sugary and sentimental but also realistic, didactic—infused with an imagery that distilled vivid impressions of a natural landscape, like a house or a face, and illuminated them as psychological visions. Hesse's memories of his childhood were deeply rooted, despite his agonies, but they could not have been as sharply etched as he portrayed them in the stories of the next three years if he had not returned home for such an extended stay, living in the town and wandering and climbing the mountains of the Black Forest.

It may seem strange, however, though by no means surprising, that at the very moment he committed himself to marriage, Hesse removed himself from his bride and went home to seek isolation. Early in 1904, *Peter Camenzind* actually appeared, and by then it had become an anticlimax. His friends sent comments, sometimes critical but usually approving, as each installment appeared. At the same time, he was aware that in withdrawing from Basel so abruptly he had been both impolitic and rude to those who had opened their houses to him during his lonely years in the city. He told one friend that while he was pleased to be home (his childhood home—"very very beautiful"), he eventually wanted to live in the vicinity of Basel, though in the country, "if I ever marry."[22] But though he claimed that the panoramas of the Rhine and the Alps were vital to him, he remained in Calw throughout the remainder of his courtship.

An apologetic letter to Dr. Rudolf Wackernagel expressed Hesse's feelings at the time most succinctly. He claimed he had recently avoided his house, which had been always open to him, because of "my peculiar personality," which made him antisocial now and then. Basically, however, he felt that an inner change had come over him. He had dropped his social façade and had eventually left Basel altogether to write the novel that his former benefactor would soon be able to read.[23] In fact, *Beneath the Wheel*, which grew alongside the stories, was completed quickly. That spring, a finished version was already printed in installments in the *Neue Zürcher Zeitung*. Fischer, however, did not publish it in book form until 1906.

IV

The months of spring and summer before Hesse's wedding were consumed by work, by travel, and by days at home in Calw fishing and hiking. Hesse had spent Easter in Munich where he was beginning to make himself known, and where Samuel Fischer introduced him to Thomas Mann. Early in 1904, however, he was not yet moneyed (the installments had brought him 400 marks plus an advance of 300 marks for the first edition of the bound book—even in those days not an enormous sum) and he was content with a simple rural life, mending his fishing tackle and hoping for good weather. He began, despite eyestrain, those small tasks that were to be his bread and butter for the rest of his life: book reviewing and feuilletons. He also published those two small biographies of Boccaccio and Saint Francis of Assisi that had been the direct result of his Italian journeys.

In the meantime, Hesse felt himself being drawn deeper and deeper into marriage. In June, he told his cousin Paul Gundert that his wedding was impending. "My bride, as you know, is the older sister in the [photography firm] Studio Bernoulli with whom I was in Florence and Genoa last year."[24] In the meantime, he remained in Calw working on his biographies and rewriting *Beneath the Wheel*. He felt he needed to tone down language that might possibly prove offensive to the pedagogic establishment and to eliminate some "salty" passages. While Hesse was buried in his work, he became more and more uneasy, but, as so often in his life, work to the limits of his capacity became the antidote to his threatening depression. By removing himself from his bride, who was both cause and symptom of his anxieties, he hoped to weather the storm. While he barricaded himself behind his writing, he continued his conversations about the future in his correspondence. A letter to Helene Voigt-Diederichs during that summer draws a clear picture of his uneasiness. He told her he was now leaving his childhood behind just as in his fiction he was giving up abstract speculations for concrete, everyday life. He was about to become a proper citizen and husband as he had become a realist in his art. There was no mistaking the anxious note.[25]

The day of the wedding, however, kept moving inexorably closer, and Hesse was unable or unwilling to draw back. Indeed, his very hesitation seemed well suited to his state of mind. His combination of escape into nature and bourgeois stability had been the core of his initial success. Now the new status of *Hausherr* would be informed by a similar dialectic. The cliché that the increasingly successful author Hermann Hesse would henceforth try to lead the life of a contented, middle-class citizen did not really hold true. The relationship of Hermann and Maria Hesse, even in its early, relatively easy years, was never conventional. Marriage to Maria Bernoulli may have been advantageous, but her own needs were not to be those of a successful author's wife. Rather, she at once viewed their alliance as that of kindred Rousseauistic spirits—Hesse also cited Ruskin, Morris, and Tolstoy—leaving the city to recapture rural simplicity. Since this view conformed at least with one side of Hesse's own credo, he had to take the consequences.

During the summer Hesse spent in Calw, Maria combed the region for a home that would suit them—one that would be both rural and beautiful. At first she searched around Basel, but after they paid a visit together to the writer Emil Strauss (who was to become their friend and distant neighbor), they decided to look more closely at possibilities around Lake Constance. After concentrating her search on the small villages of that area, Maria finally discovered a suitable farmhouse in the isolated hamlet of Gaienhofen on the Lower Lake. In his later reminiscences Hesse indicated that her discovery occurred after their marriage, but his letters of the time show that the couple were already installed in their new home just two or three days after the wedding.[26] Hence, the episode of Maria's house hunting while Hermann remained in Calw must have occurred before, not after, the ceremony. This discrepancy may be only the result of faulty memory (all of these reminiscences were written during and after the 1920s), or they may represent an edited version of what went on.

The wedding took place in Basel on August 2, 1904. It was, as Hesse told Stefan Zweig a short time later, a "wedding on the double."[27] While the "old man" was out of town Hesse took his daughter to the registry office where they were married in a civil ceremony. Soon after they went off to Gaienhofen to move into their farmhouse. One half was still used by the farmer as a shed and storage place, but they were able to rent the dwelling part. They arrived so quickly that they were still without the furniture they were bringing from Basel, and for days they lived without tables and chairs until gradually they could set up housekeeping.

The new ménage began outdoors. Hesse transformed the sparse ground around the house into a garden that he intended to plant in the spring. Inside, both he and his new wife painted and decorated. The rough beams in the upstairs bedroom and the long narrow second floor, which Hesse turned into his study, were painted a deep red. Downstairs, they left panels of natural pine unpainted and cleaned up the old green tiles on the large stove that was to warm their kitchen in the winter. There were no indoor facilities nor was there even indoor water, and the new husband was kept busy carrying pails of water from the well, along with doing many other chores around house and yard. Yet it was a graceful place, overlooking the lake on one side while hugging close to the small village square on the other. When they turned away from their view of sky and water and the Swiss villages across the lake, they faced the well and the small church whose bell sounded sonorously each Sunday morning.

Their location, like the life they had chosen, was extraordinarily isolated. No railroad line brought the world to them. There were no stores, not even a butcher's or baker's shop. As Hesse wrote to various friends, including Stefan Zweig and the poet Alexander von Bernus, in September, the best way to put in provisions was to row across the lake to the Swiss village of Steckhorn and to return by way of the customs inspector. He soon learned the tariffs for his various purchases by heart (but he also liked to do a bit of smuggling) and hoped to supplement his fare with fishing.[28]

The beauty of their new home was overwhelming. They had majestic views from their living room and study, and they were surrounded by wooded hillsides. There was an abundance of fruit and wine. Hesse recalled this phase of their life together with some (though not unmixed) pleasure, from the rough beams and the green-tiled oven to their first pet, the beautiful cat Gattamelata:

> In this house I lived for three years. Our first son was born there and it was the place where many of my stories and poems were written. . . . It was unique . . . the first refuge of my new marriage, the first real workshop of my profession. Here for the first time I felt truly settled, but also sometimes imprisoned, hemmed in. Here, for the first time, I

gave in to the pretty dream of creating something like a homeland in a place of my own choosing.

This description was written in 1931, in a memoir "Upon Moving Into a New House" that gives an excellent account of the various phases of Hesse's life from the retrospect of age fifty-four. Here he suggests both his positive dream and his doubts, his pleasure in consolidating the workshop of his profession as a writer and his sense of being "sometimes imprisoned, hemmed in." For eight years, in two houses in Gaienhofen, Hesse "attempted to lead a natural, industrious life close to the soil."[29]

The dream was disturbed almost at once. They had been married in August, but by October Maria became ill—the first of many ailments, which undermined their life together from the start. It was "not very dangerous but painful," wrote the new husband as she returned to Basel to be under her doctor's care.[30] Hesse stayed behind, working and keeping house. "Everything is still the same with Maria," he reported to Adele in November, "no improvement yet; she sends all of you her warmest regards." Her stay in Basel lasted almost until Christmas, and during that time Hesse's life was divided between visits to her in Basel and isolated days living alone in their Gaienhofen home. When she returned on December 17, he felt that because of her recent illness and convalescence he was in no position to invite his family. In a Christmas letter to Johannes he expressed his sadness at not yet being able to show him house and village, but he affixed a hopeful note: "In the large pleasant living room burns the powerful tiled oven and we can see the lake through the windows. Now the *Hausfrau* is home again, not yet fully recovered but cheerful and dear." He mentioned how often he thought of his mother, now that he presided over a home of his own. Toward the end of the letter, however, his father might have detected a not so hopeful counterpoint: "Our married life—since Maria has been ill and gone for such a long time—has not yet found any firm, accustomed *habitus,* but we'll find our way."

Hesse's feelings about marriage were tested even more profoundly by the news that his favorite sister Adele was engaged to be married. It was a meaningful test, because he valued his sister's capacities very highly and she had chosen a not too distinguished rural clergyman, a cousin of theirs, Hermann Gundert. His hesitancy about her step was, of course, expressed *sotto voce*, contained as it was in his letter of congratulations, but his doubts were noticeable beneath the surface, a harbinger of their future relationship in which his brother-in-law and cousin Hermann always remained a distant and neglected third. Now, on the threshold of his sister's marriage, Hesse wistfully tried to recapture their old intimacy and to communicate his awareness of her loss of independence. Cousin Hermann was a good and upright man, but Brother Hermann could not say more. He was "immensely happy" for his sister. "I hoped to see you enter a happy new life, with new hopes and plans." He intimated, however, that it had not quite turned out the way he had expected: "Now it happened in a way I had not foreseen." What happy life with new hopes and plans *had* Hesse foreseen for his sister? He did not say, but he surely felt that her lively mind would be circumscribed.

Strangely, among these various disappointments, his great personal and financial success, which also happened at this time, should have given Hesse a great lift, yet it failed to do so. He was happy about earning money, to be sure, but he also felt imposed upon. Demands were made on him that seemed not wholly unlike those made on him by his marriage. His independence was being chipped away. In fact, loss of freedom became almost an obsession. That he described his fame largely in negative terms can be only partly explained by false modesty. He consciously linked fame and marriage. "Many things have happened to me," he wrote a friend. "I'm married, etc., and unfortunately along with my past lack of funds, a large part of my beautiful freedom also went overboard." "Except for money, Peter's exaggerated successes haven't really pleased me. I've become . . . fashionable and that I never wanted to be. . . ."[31] The pendulum movement between need and fear of confinement colored both letters and books. His pose was evident when, planning a trip to Munich after New Year's, he refused an invitation to Freiherr von Burnus's house on the grounds that with his "gypsy instincts" he "hardly fitted in an elegant home."[32] A new set of terms settled into Hesse's vocabulary: he was a gypsy, a wandering minstrel, a footloose wanderer, a hermit. This pose formed a neat contrast to the theme of marriage and home. The bird was caught in its cage, the gypsy in his comfortable prison.

This theme of the wanderer, and its opposite, the newly settled husband, occupied Hesse almost at once. That first winter became a time for regrets. It was the beginning of his "clandestine" writings—as Hugo Ball called them in his biography—which described Hesse's agony as a writer who had begun along the path of fashion, security, and family life, but who felt profoundly guilty about his decision and nostalgic for his earlier independence. If (as Ball suggested) he wrote officially acceptable novels to sustain him as a recognized author, he also led a subterranean life, roaming the countryside and feeling profound misgivings about his settled state, which he portrayed in some of the vignettes published in *Picture Book* in 1926.[33] In one of these sketches, written in 1904 about this first winter in Gaienhofen, entitled pertinently, "In the Land of the

Philistines," Hesse expressed his sense of his loss of freedom in bitter language as he looked out at the lake:

> It has been dark for hours. Across the lake I can see the villages along the range of hills with their red windows, each of them separated from me by rain, clouds, storm, and darkness. . . .

The sharp and exhilarating weather outside contrasted sharply with the world within:

> The stove, long since extinguished, still warms me a little. The cat sleeps in the oven, occasionally wakes up for a few moments and begins to purr. Along the walls, with a thousand wide and narrow spines, stand my books. And as often as I step to the window and wipe the moist window panes, I see, beyond on the other side of the lake, the villages on hills with their softly glowing windows, each of remembrance. . . .

The books led Hesse to speculate upon his newly found security, for they had always meant home to him, ever since he first arrived in Tübingen in 1895. Now almost ten years later they were at last "on firm and solid boards" and were no longer scattered everywhere on sofa and floor. Comfort reigned:

> The large stove can burn as long as I want it; I don't have to count my logs and scrimp and save. There is even a small keg of wine in the cellar, with a friendly tap, and always enough tobacco in the old tin box.

"I'm well off, very well off," he continued, and explained that even his cat was getting fat.

His musings soon became specific. With the onset of winter and the storms brewing over the lake he was forced to store his boat and oars. Rage now seized him at his comfortable life. "Then my heart hurts within my body, for it knows I'm no longer a solitary, a wanderer, and I would gladly give away my little bit of home and comfort for an old hat and pack to salute the world once more and to carry my homesickness across the water and the land." Awake in the house while Maria was asleep he heard how "the wind pounded so urgently against the window," "the clouds flew so . . . greedily through the night" that he took his hat and stick and walked outside. He involuntarily fell into his hiking steps, sensing "as if all my youth were breaking upon me with all its freedom and power" and were lifting him up and taking him far away. Yet after an hour he reached a crossroads. Would he go on into that land "garbed by the night like a fairyland"? He stood "laughing at myself, thinking of my wife and my house." He also remembered that in storming out of his house he had forgotten to extinguish the lamp in his study. That lamp, as he turned back, reflected the counterpoint of his need to be a vagabond again: it "now shone on, as long as the oil would last, shedding its light upon the yellow pages of my old book, over desk and walls, and through the windowpanes out into the sleeping village."[34]

At that time Hesse was no more firmly committed to vagabondage and the life of a hermit than he had been to family life and home. He may have suppressed the essays in *Picture Book* until their publication in 1926, but they did not really say more than was reflected in his pose during his Gaienhofen years. Still, few personal documents are more revealing than this lyrical sketch. Simplicity, a rustic family life, even economic security were at once undercut by his contradictory wish to become a vagabond. The conflict was real, but it was also absorbed into his literary *persona*, since being a hermit and footloose and close to the earth were also fashionable literary attitudes. As the success of *Peter Camenzind* shows, the "child of nature" was a popular figure, and by settling down to a bourgeois life (even with Rousseauistic overtones) Hesse might have disappointed part of his natural audience. Yet these contrasting feelings went deeper. This was after all a time in Hesse's life when his longed-for success had finally been achieved, a solid marriage had been contracted, and his literary production was at its peak.

By creating the trappings of outward success and respectability (even in a rural retreat), Hesse expressed one part of himself. Yet as he met that need for stability and social acceptance he undercut the needs that had determined his anger in his youth at a home that had both attracted and rejected him. In many ways at this point in his career, Hesse began to play the role of André Gide's protagonist Michel in *The Immoralist*, which had been published in 1902 and owed as much to Nietzsche in literature as Hesse owed him in his life. For like the fictional Michel, Hesse searched for personal freedom to express himself even at his own expense.

During the next few years, the more restless Hesse became in his inner life the more he sought outwardly to display conventional attitudes. Having acquired a wife, he soon also acquired a son. The months from early in 1905 until December, when his first child, Bruno, was born, were fraught with difficulties. By spring, Maria, just pregnant, was again under her doctor's care, and Hesse found himself again going back and forth between Basel and Lake Constance.

There were, of course, better times as well. In May, friend Finckh, his old companion of the *petit cénacle*, came to Gaienhofen to stay permanently—to establish a practice as a doctor and to write. If Ball's account is any indication, the two men soon banded together to form their "clandestine" brotherhood that kept Hesse afloat in a world of interviews and royalties, and allowed him to bear his wife's frequent indispositions and needs during her pregnancy. They fished and rowed and wandered in the countryside—a welcome counterpoint to Maria's increasingly sedentary life.

In a letter to his father on July 3, 1905, the day after Hermann's birthday, he placed these elements side by side. On the one hand, he told Johannes of Maria's ailment: "The heat is very strong, but I bear it well, and am even glad because it is the best medicine for Maria's sciatica and rheumatism." On the other hand, Hesse reported with pleasure that his birthday celebration the day before had been the most sumptuous occasion in his life. He had been awakened at six in the morning by a five-piece brass band, blowing hymns and dance tunes. Since no musicians lived in Gaienhofen, they had to be brought in from another village two hours away by horse and buggy. The entire population of Gaienhofen assembled in the village square around the well and greeted him with cheers when he appeared in the door. Finckh arrived at seven and Hesse was shown to a table laden with birthday gifts, its centerpiece being twenty-four bottles of wine contributed by a friend in Frankfurt. When the Hesses and Finckh decided to celebrate the day with a trip on the lake, they found their boat had been decorated with garlands, reeds, and flowers by girls from the orphanage in the nearby castle.

Other items in the letter also suggest that for the moment Hesse's life had begun to simmer down, although it is difficult to say whether he considered carrying eighty-five to a hundred liters of water from well to garden each day a burden or simply part of his busy life in the country. Hesse's account of this chore is bracketed with a boast that he had grown many fine pumpkins and sunflowers, but the boast was also self-deprecating, because he added that not much else succeeded on their small plot of land. Maria wrote a postscript to this letter to her father-in-law in which she mentioned her husband's travel plans.

Gardening, work on the house, writing, and wandering in the countryside with his friends occupied Hesse throughout the summer. He still worked on revisions of *Beneath the Wheel* and composed many of the short stories that contributed so much to his success during the early 1900s. He also began to experience the mixture of disgust and flattery he always felt when contemplating those streams of visitors who beset him in most places where he lived. That summer, large numbers of guests passed through Gaienhofen—from Switzerland, from Swabia, from Frankfurt, Munich, and Vienna. At this time, Stefan Zweig visited Hesse after three years of correspondence. According to a story Hesse often told, Zweig hit his head on the low beams of the ceiling as he entered the upstairs study and was so stunned by the blow that he had to lie down for fifteen minutes to recover. Whatever they talked about after that, there is no question that Zweig had a very sensitive understanding of Hesse, although their work shows little affinity.

In 1923, in an article that led up to an appreciation of *Siddhartha*, Stefan Zweig gave an uncanny picture of Hesse's literary role in those early days of solidity. The prewar Hesse was seen as a writer whose popularity had been one of general, broad complacency, warmhearted even to the point of reaching a family audience. Zweig still remembered many of the musical verses in Hesse's early poetry by heart, sounds that had magically touched him. True, Hesse's language did not contribute anything new to a lyrical idiom, as the work of poets like Rilke or the young Hugo von Hofmannsthal had done, but they still reflected the old German romantic forest, "the hunting horns of Eichendorff . . . Mörike's shawm." Hesse's sudden fame was based on the purity of his longing for that romantic past. He was also, Zweig suggested, a peculiarly German writer in those days, echoing a spirit of "German sentiment, a gentle verve of sensibility, a cautious muting of the passions." Stefan Zweig used musical terms to indicate Hesse's way with words: the Italian *brio* for verve and a word based on *sordino* for the muting of the passions. In fact, he caught the predominantly sentimental spirit of Hesse's prewar language in prose and verse whose words reflected musical variations of tone while its images created pictures.[35]

By the end of 1905 and early in 1906, Hesse put the final touches to his revisions of *Beneath the Wheel*. Though this novel was Hesse's reckoning with the past, it echoed a vogue of similar novels and stories that were then popular in Germany—novels about sensitive pupils crushed by educational tyranny in public *lycées* and private as well as military boarding schools. It is no coincidence that Heinrich Mann's *Professor Unrath* (more familiar as the famous film *The Blue Angel*) first appeared in 1905. In his fine study, *Hermann Hesse: Mind and Art*, Mark Boulby pointed out long ago that during these early years from the *fin de siècle* to the First World War, an extremely popular literature of protest against the educational establishment had grown up in Germany.[36] Hesse's neighbor and friend Emil Strauss, whose residence on Lake Constance had led to the Hesses' move to Gaienhofen, had published a novel about the subject, *Freund Hein* (translatable as *Friend Death*) in 1902, which had become a bestseller by the time Hesse had settled back in Calw to write the first draft of *Beneath the Wheel*. Hesse could fit his personal protest, and the memory of his pain at the Maulbronn experience, into a current fashion. Once again he was able to combine his

1. Paternal grandfather, Dr. Carl Hermann Hesse

2. Maternal grandfather, Dr. Hermann Gundert

3. *(right)* Hesse Family, 1889. *From left to right:* Hermann, Father, Marulla, Mother, Adele, Hans

4. *(below, left)* Hesse's mother, Marie Hesse

5. *(below, right)* Hermann Hesse and his sister Adele, 1880s

6. Hesse's father, Johannes Hesse, Calw, 1903

7. Hesse Family, 1899. *From left to right:* Marulla, Hans, Mother, Hermann, Father, Adele

8. Hesse's first wife, Maria, ca. 1912

9. Friends in Basel, early 1900s. *In the center:* Maria *(left)* and sister Mathilde Bernoulli (Hesse's future wife and sister-in-law)

10. Hesse's and Maria's sons Bruno and Heiner, with Martin in crib, Gaienhofen, 1911

11. Sisters Adele and Marulla, early 1900s

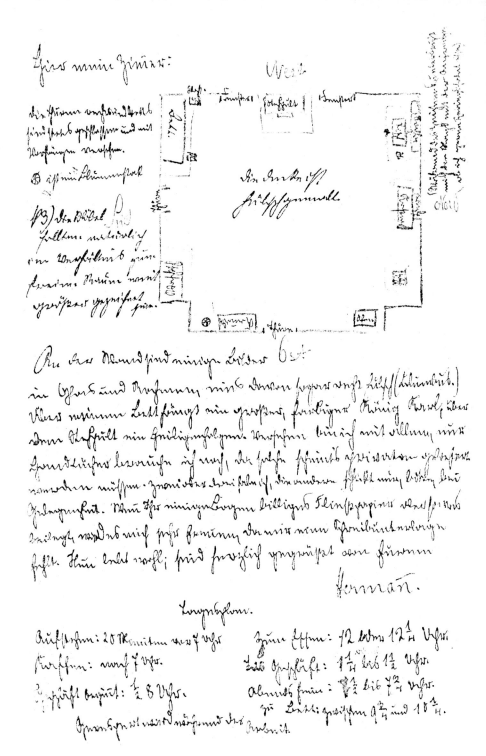

12. Excerpt from letter to family in October 1895, with daily schedule and a floor plan of his room

13. Calwer Verlagsverein, publishing house and Hesse's early home in Calw

14. (below) Herr Hermes (left) and Herr Sonnewald at Heckenhauer's Bookstore in Tübingen

15. *(above, left)* Basel Mission where Johannes Hesse taught, and Hesse lived and went to school as a young boy *(Photo by F. Zimmer)*

16. *(center)* Hesse with Emanuel von Bodman, Gaienhofen, 1907

17. *(below)* Italian journey. With Monsignore, Montefalco, 1906

18. With friend, composer Othmar Schoeck, Pisa, Italy, 1911

19. With Othmar Schoeck, Chiavari, Italy, 1911

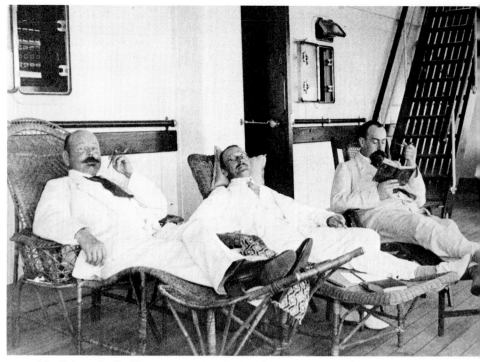

20. Trip to India. Hesse *(center)* and Hans Sturzenegger *(right)*, September 1911

21. Palembang

22. Palembang, view from hotel

23. On board ship. Hesse and Sturzenegger, second row

24. Hermann Hesse, 1911

critique of the "system" with a language composed of finely wrought pictures in the manner of earlier local colorists like Gottfried Keller.

Beneath the Wheel, like the other works that cemented his fame as a popular writer, was critical of current affairs while retaining a poetic veneer and a fine sense of nostalgia. As he recast his experience as a boy, projected it into two *personae*—an escapee and a suicide—then mellowed the material in subsequent revisions, he achieved at last that gentle balance of critique and attractive lyricism that ensured his success. In his final version, he followed not just external demands but also his own need to be fundamentally accepted even as he took a critical stance. The two impulses of his life—for "home" and for its rejection—created yet another productive tension in the final version of his book.

As time went on, Hesse not only gathered a large reading public but also caught the attention of his peers. Although he was always to remain reluctant to join the literary establishment (the *Betrieb*, or "system," as he called it deprecatingly), he was eager to consolidate his reputation as a literary figure. A self-styled wanderer, he was also a sharp bargainer with publishers. He knew when to accept and when to reject an invitation to lecture. He knew when to be a hermit and an outsider, but he also knew how to comport himself as a successful professional man.

4

The Idyll Unraveled

I

And sometimes, when the black depths are silent, we can do even more.
We can then be gods for moments, stretch out a commanding hand
and create things which were not there before and which, when they
are created, continue to live without us. Out of sounds, words, and
other frail and worthless things we can construct playthings—songs and
poems full of meaning, consolation, and goodness, more beautiful
and enduring than the grim sport of fortune and destiny.

—From *Gertrud*

BRUNO HESSE, born December 9, 1905, ushered in a new era in his
father's life. The cage seemed shut—at least for a while—and Hesse
knew it. Still, at first the child's presence neither smoothed nor sharpened
Hesse's conflicts.

Illness, however, remained a symbolic theme for Hesse, the counterpoint of "normalcy," the figurative mole that dug beneath the well-kept
gardens of his life. It undermined his settled routine, yet paradoxically,
opened gates to freedom. His eyes hurt in January, while Maria had a
bad tooth problem. At the same time he was by no means inactive. In
March, after working hard on several stories, he spent a few weeks in
Northern Italy, drinking wine and climbing several steep mountainsides.
In April he attended Adele's wedding (Maria had to remain home with
the baby), which he took as an occasion for a more extensive trip through
his native Swabia. He went to Munich in May.

Hesse's growing connection with several writers and artists in Munich,
and especially his increased involvement with editors and contributors
of the humor magazine *Simplizissimus*, opened up important new dimensions in his professional life. This satiric periodical, while sometimes
saucy and occasionally even gamy (its editor, the writer Ludwig Thoma,
once had to spend six weeks in prison for obscenity), was nevertheless
part of a literary establishment, and it was an honor to be drawn into its
circle of contributors. For many years, until and beyond the outbreak of
the First World War, Hesse remained a frequent contributor.

In the spring of that year, 1906, between his trips to Swabia and Munich, Hesse received a visit from Ludwig Thoma with the proposition that he join in a new biweekly periodical to be called *South Germany*. Combing the region around Lake Constance, Thoma picked up a number of successful literary people, including Emil Strauss, Hesse, and Finckh, whose novel *Rosendoktor* had just earned him a *succès d'estime*. Thoma, Hesse, and Strauss went on a walking tour together, climbing a small mountain, and drinking many mugs of homemade wine. The result, which Thoma related to Conrad Haussmann (his and later also Hesse's attorney and friend), was the decision to found the periodical, which was to encompass the entire south German cultural region. "We want to gather up everything (and everyone) knowledgeable about southern Germany: in politics, literature, art, and scholarship," Thoma told Haussmann. It was to be positive in spirit and liberal in thought, preserving the spirit of the revolution of 1848, and defending it against Prussia —those "Germanized Slavs" of Berlin. The journal was to become a cultural instrument of liberalism, and, in a strange way, it reflected Hesse's own impulses. For seven years, beginning in 1907, under the revised title *März* (or *March*, to commemorate the revolution of March 1848), Hesse contributed to its pages as a cultural liberal, while at the same time he assured his conservative father that he was "only" the literary editor. Eventually, the magazine—like *Simplizissimus*—was to support the Great War, after which Hesse withdrew in consternation. At this time, however, journal and contributor appeared perfectly well matched in a liberalism that in the end turned toward accepted values. In any event, the decision Hesse made in 1906 to join both *Simplizissimus* and *März* reflected his own dual positions: it assigned him a liberal place in a respectable context.[1]

Hesse's way of dealing with the palpable constraints of a new son, as well as a wife, was to use his family as a base from which to move. He retained his subterranean freedom as much as possible, often using his greater income to function for wife and child in his place. In June he was back in Bavaria while he sent them and their maid to Maria's relatives in Switzerland. He had intended to stop in Munich to see his business friends and his eye doctor, but he abandoned the idea when he found his publisher ill and the hotels crowded. Instead, he spent three relaxed weeks with a friend, the painter Theodor Rumelin, and his wife, who made a living building canals in the village of Wartenberg. A little later, toward the end of his stay, he returned to Munich after all and had a very good time with his *Simplizissimus* friends, especially the brothers Paul and Reinhold Geheeb, with whom he began a lifelong friendship. He also saw his painter friends and discussed the progress of their forthcoming periodical with Ludwig Thoma. By July he and his family were reunited back home. Two hot summer months on Lake Constance followed with sun-bathing, swimming, and work on his stories. Yet the feeling of being drawn into a steadily narrowing trap manifested itself again. Writing to his own father about Maria's family, he mentioned old Herr Bernoulli, then eighty-one years of age, whose health had improved lately. But he turned especially to his mother-in-law's state of mind, an emotional disturbance that clearly threatened him. Only by traveling, by being outdoors with friends, by establishing his many personal relationships with painters and musicians, did he find a door that allowed him to "escape."

In 1906 Hesse was undoubtedly ready for his first encounter with that strange underground figure Gusto or Gustav Gräser who played a part in various natural health endeavors centered around Ascona in Switzerland's Italian-speaking canton of Ticino where Hesse was to spend the greater part of his life. Gräser had wandered all over Germany and Switzerland and at one point also touched Gaienhofen where he made an impression on Hesse. He had all the appearance of a "guru" wearing Indian garb who acted out the opposition to established society that Hesse mostly implied. His appearance in Hesse's life during that summer of 1906, just as he felt compelled to fall back into his family routine, must have been electrifying. As his friend Finckh tells it, Hesse caught fire when he saw four strange-looking creatures with "long hair, sandals, and bare legs" walk through the village, and followed them at once to their settlement in Ascona.

Both the timing and even the destination of Hesse's journey south is open to question, but he did travel to Ticino later that year partly to revive his energies in the southern landscape he loved, partly because beginning at this time he felt a need to use the autumn months for cures of his physical and psychic ailments. Indeed, if the cursory reference to him in the description of the Ascona sanatorium is correct, he may also have been there to "dry out." In any event, he journeyed south later that summer and returned much later tanned but irritated.[2]

The sanatorium for which Hesse headed had been founded, among others, by Gustav Gräser's older brother Karl and he himself had once been part of its inner circle. That there might have been some affinity between Hesse and Gustav Gräser seems possible. Gräser was two years younger than Hesse, middle class, from a German minority in Hungary as Hesse's father had been from the Baltics. Like Hesse, he had left school early and for a while had been quite successful as a sculptor and painter. But in 1900, when Hesse was poised for success, Gräser had destroyed his work, disposed of his possessions, and had actually become the footloose pilgrim Hesse always wanted to be. Even as he at first joined the commune on Monte Verità as the younger brother of one of the founders, he was unable to fit into the group, soon was cast out, and began a wholly footloose, itinerant existence. It is therefore not certain whether Hesse met him in 1906, since he and his family lived separately in a nearby cave or wandered about the countryside. With his soothsaying wife and her many children, he was a more radical apostle of peace and the natural life, and it is in this function as a subterranean "guru" that he seems to have crossed Hesse's path on several crucial occasions.

The following year continued to reflect the contradictions in Hesse's life, because precisely as he widened his travels and spent more and more time by himself and with his friends, and followed his needs for "cures" by journeying south, he began to make elaborate plans for building a house. In a letter to his family in Calw written on January 17, he explained at length what they had decided about their building plans and the lot they had chosen. It was a beautiful location with a wide view of the lake on two sides, three minutes from their village. The first floor of the building would be constructed in brick, the upper floors with shingles. In his letter to Johannes, Hesse elaborated these plans even more fully, discussing the location of bedrooms, the placement of windows in relation to the front door, and similar details. More revealing than these plans was their proposed method of financing the project. The total estimate of the cost, at the beginning, was set at 20,000 marks, of which the major portion was to be advanced by his father-in-law. "Father Bernoulli will advance us the cost of the building without interest so that we might regard the house as a prematurely received portion of our inheritance." Another trap had been set, quite of Hesse's own doing, and he would refer to it explicitly, and regretfully, in later years.

The new house, as it grew during 1907, was designed to please him. Its ample space for gardening was to give him much pleasure, since gardening was his hobby and he enjoyed the many fruit trees. A lovely veranda graced the lakeside and, upstairs, there would be a large balcony, a study with a built-in library and a huge stove, which, it turned out, seldom worked.[3] At the same time, even as plans for the house matured and the workmen arrived to break ground for it, Hesse was in constant motion. In January, Ludwig Finckh got married and Hesse traveled north to Tübingen to attend the wedding, taking this opportunity to look in on family and friends in the Black Forest. Perhaps inspired by Hesse, Hugo Ball named Finckh the symbolic counterpart to Hesse's home-owning, home-building way of life.[4] Actually, Finckh, too, acquired a house with guests and garden in Gaienhofen, and he, too, got married to live a similar dual existence—except that, just as he was returning to Lake Constance with his new wife, his house burnt down. Hesse met the new couple on the road before they had reached Gaienhofen, gave them emergency shelter and then collected money, most successfully, to replace their loss. Even as everything was rebuilt in Finckh's life, however, he remained at least one part of Hesse's alter ego of that time, the self driven by a need to shed permanent bonds.[5]

Hesse's own descriptions of his relationship with Finckh during those early Gaienhofen years bear out Ball's account: his vicarious delight in Finckh's menagerie of donkey, Saint Bernard, cat, trout, chickens, ducks, and goat; their days of climbing and fishing and sunbathing at the lake "bronzed like Indians." Distinctive of this period in both their lives is, of course, the reversal in their relationship. When they first knew one another in Tübingen they had met as the young bookseller's apprentice and the far more elevated student of law (later of medicine) who shared literary ambitions. But when they lived side by side in Gaienhofen, Finckh was a doctor and a minor author while Hesse was famous. This made intimacy easier, for Hesse could accept their friendship man to man, yet could reserve vast areas of personal and professional life that Finckh could not enter.

Hesse's horizon, however, expanded far beyond Finckh—to friends in Munich and to a circle of painters and musicians who had settled near them in Gaienhofen. Some of these friendships Maria Hesse could share, but others were exclusively Hermann's. In addition, the composer Othmar Schoeck, the conductors Volkmar Andreae and Fritz Brun, or the soprano Ilona Durigo—all lifelong friends of Hesse's—would frequently visit from Switzerland. Maria's musical passion allowed her to enjoy these friends a good part of the time, although they retained (with the obvious exception of Ilona) a distinctly masculine coloration.

If Hesse had returned home to Gaienhofen after his trip to Finckh's wedding early in 1907, he was not there long. In the spring of that year he seriously undertook a "cure" in the sanatorium for the natural treatment of nervous disorders in Monte Verità near Ascona. A photograph taken in April 1907 shows him with a group of unconventionally dressed and coiffured men and women on the steps of the building against the backdrop of majestic mountains. Hesse was to report to his father about the benefits to the body of direct exposure to sun and air after his return, but in a reminiscence published in *März* during the following year, his own "cure" of exposure and meditation was considerably more drastic. Entitled "In the Rocks: Notes of a 'Natural Man,'" it drew a detailed picture of agony as he allowed himself to be burned by the sun, drenched by rain, his skin torn by thorns as he moved about the mountains and woods with his naked body exposed to the elements. Freezing on the bare ground of his hut, his body covered only by a thin blanket, this "natural man" underwent a draconian cure.[6] Whether this passage indicates that he was also under Gräser's tutelage or whether this regimen was imposed on him by the sanatorium is unclear.

It is probable, however, that these experiences were connected in some way and form part of Hesse's precarious inner life. For it was during the year this "cure" occurred that Hesse aimed most for respectability. He was successful, he was earning money, he was a contributor to distinguished journals, he was building a house. Yet he entered into a state of emotional crisis that made him reach out for any cure, however unconventional, and to indulge in activities he did not like to see publicly mentioned. In his letter to Johannes Hesse in May he made the whole experience respectable by giving his father instructions about the healthful use of the elements, but in July he told a friend, on the occasion of his own thirtieth birthday, that he had gone through an emotional hell: "The thirtieth year in which I now am has brought me a violent crisis, at first physically—sickness, cure, and gradual recovery—but then also within." Following this declaration, Hesse referred to the kind of renunciation that had been part of his recent regimen. A young man, he wrote, who had until then been giving himself gladly to the sensual life and now managed without any delicacies and wine, cigars and coffee, did not want to be forced into that condition, "but wants to construct a suitable philosophy." With this task of finding the appropriate ideological reasons for self-deprivation he claimed to have been occupied for months.[7]

"Brown like a Hindu," Hesse faced another summer of work and the task of building his house. Both were chores and had their annoyances. Construction dragged on longer than expected. Costs rose higher than had been originally estimated. Hesse told friends and family not to visit soon, because they were in the midst of confusion. Nevertheless, he found time to travel. The impending appearance of *März* necessitated several welcome trips to Munich, but he also managed to do a great deal of work between his various journeys.

Meanwhile, Hesse was writing many of those stories that were to become pillars of his reputation. Nourished by his return to his home ground during the previous year, Hesse created his own version of Keller's famous book of tales, *Folk of Seldwyla*, with "Gerbersau" as his corresponding stage name for Calw. Even in these stories of childhood, amorous encounters, and tragic as well as humorous scenes, a sharp eye could detect their author's longing for escape combined with an equal longing for stability buried under the veneer of happy wanderlust. Also evident is the sense of pressure from uncontrollable circumstances to which the helpless individual falls victim. In one of these stories, "The Marble Saw," for example, Hesse projected his own indecisive wooing into the mind of a girl who commits suicide when faced with a choice between the author's *persona* and the more solid, middle-class fiancé to whom she was promised. In most of these stories, which combine a sense of fate with local color, a dramatic turn usually focuses on this kind of duality to create tragic and in many instances comic effects.

The first large selection of these stories appeared as *Diesseits (On this Side of the Line)* in 1907; the second a year later as *Neighbors*. More were to follow, and each was a fine success, both commercially and critically. But his most significant book, the one that cast the divided nature in his art and in his personal life into the sharpest relief, was the novel *Gertrud*. It was his major achievement of 1907 and formed the last and most substantial work of the time in Basel and Gaienhofen.

An early version of the book had been written during 1905–06 while Hesse was revising *Beneath the Wheel*. As in his first two novels, *Hermann Lauscher* and *Peter Camenzind,* he portrayed the artist as an outsider in conflict with the bourgeois world. The decor had shifted. Lauscher, the poet, and Camenzind, the child of nature turned poet in a world of painters, had now given way to two musicians. As he had done in *Beneath the Wheel*, Hesse again split his own *persona* in two—in this instance the composer Muoth who functioned as the objective third-person self and the first-person narrator and the performer Kuhn. The theme of the artist as a sick man, which had communicated itself to Hesse's generation by way of Rimbaud and his successors, if not of Freud, and was treated at about the same time in Thomas Mann's "Little Herr Friedemann," became the primary theme of the novel.

The incident that triggered the novel's plot was a near fatal accident. Kuhn was crippled as a schoolboy while sledding with more daring than expertise to impress a stimulating girl named Liddy. Having been goaded to this foolhardy action by that lively representative of society, Kuhn remained the lame outsider. The sham reward of acceptance had merely concealed an inevitable rejection. But the accident merely allowed Kuhn to take stock and begin his interior journey. He met the great Gertrud, the priestess-mistress-mother who was to turn up again and again in Hesse's books, and fell in love with her. This mother of artists (in the early version of 1905–06 she was actually a painter) subsequently fell in love with Kuhn's alter ego, the composer Muoth, who had been Kuhn's teacher and friend and remained his benefactor. But in time their positions reversed. After a hair-raising marriage and separation, Muoth committed suicide—just like Giebenrath in the previous book or the girl in the "Marble Saw" when she was faced with the choice between her artist lover and her bourgeois fiancé.

These two characters can be seen as complementary parts of a single *persona*. One part, represented by Kuhn, was physically crippled but had made his peace with society; the other part, Muoth, underwent the dramatic denouement that Hesse, in a real Wagnerian spirit, always reserved for the artists who were his ideals. In a separate, not quite convincingly motivated plot, Kuhn saved his mother from a grasping maiden lady, then eventually returned to his former love, Gertrud, the widow of his departed friend, and served her silently for the rest of his life.

Hesse's own features are clearly discernible, along with the places where he lived. Most of the elements appear to be reflections of his own difficult life. He portrayed an agonized marriage to a musical, sensitive woman; he used the idea of being crippled at an early age, of being stamped an outsider; and he perceived a struggle with his father and mother and finally a suggestive fantasy of saving his mother from distress. In fact, the ease with which Hesse passed from the love triangle of the two friends with Gertrud, to the involvement with the mother, and finally to the involvement with Gertrud herself suggests, symbolically, that all four major participants had been conceived as one.

Pervasive throughout this interesting if two-dimensional novel is also the familiar struggle between sense and spirit, the night and light sides of the soul. Gertrud herself often rises to remarkable heights, and, unlike most of Hesse's women, she sometimes appears as a real person, however idealized. With her fine musical sensitivity and her role as a mother of artists she suggests many of Maria Hesse's traits. She also acts, however, as that goddess-idol and universal source of inspiration encountered so often in Hesse's books. At this time of supposed stability Hesse wrote a novel about music that suggests highly fluid, unstable motifs. The artist's search for fulfillment could take place only after the crippling of one part of himself and the suicide of the other. His integration occurs, however, through the symbolic Gertrud, a stabilizing image of the mother.

Gertrud, while written during the time Hesse's new house was being built in 1907, was not to appear for another two and a half years, but the stories and his two major novels (*Camenzind* and *Beneath the Wheel*) were enough to fortify Hesse's reputation, to keep his small family clothed and fed, and to allow him his life either in the garden or on the road. Though they contributed to his acceptance by the established literary journals and authorities of the day, they were only part of his literary life. His actual state of mind was reflected in different work.

If the theme of the outsider is treated as part of the artistic condition in *Gertrud*, it was made symbolically apparent in some of the stories written during 1906–07 that did not form the canon of Gerbersau. One of these was the short story "Wolf," which describes a lonely, hungry, majestic wolf in the French Alps being hounded by insensitive peasants. In the final scene, he roars with his dying breath, his heart's blood reddening the fresh snow around him, lonely and imposing on the top of a mountain as the vicious human crew closed in to finish him off. This story was quite possibly the germ of Hesse's *Steppenwolf* written twenty years later. It suggests a furious identification with the footloose and free and with their hatred of the circumscribed society of shopkeepers and peasants with which, Hesse knew, part of himself was also identified. Only a heroic death could be the honorable outcome of this conflict.

These views were expressed even more directly in the autobiographical sketches that were later collected in *Picture Book,* especially the vignettes about his life on Lake Constance, written at the time. As in "Land of the Philistines," restlessness and nostalgia for lost freedom form the theme that holds these sketches together. In one brief prose piece Hesse read *Ossian* while Maria played Schubert next door. After a while she changed to Chopin, one of Hesse's favorite composers and one who was intimately connected with his youth. Still, he did not stir. After a while his wife went to bed while he stayed behind dreaming of his former untrammeled life.[8] After ten years and newly won fame, the anguish of his being alone at Tübingen had given way to the anguish of not being alone on the shore of Lake Constance. Stability had closed in like a prison, even though it was also the soil on which he had grown.

During this year of simultaneous stability and escape the first of three important novellas, later to become *Knulp*, was composed, and the work as a whole was put on the drawing board. Written mostly during the house-building year, 1907, it developed the figure of the perennial wanderer—literally a sensitive hobo—who could stand out as the vaga-bond *par excellence.* At the same time, he wrote innumerable poems that sounded the theme of the solitary. The figure of the lonely artist remained the counterpoint of a life crowded with jovial people in their recently founded artists' colony of Gaienhofen and with innumerable guests coming to call from far and wide.

This systole and diastole of security and freedom continued during the next two years, which were filled with writing, travel, and eventually getting settled in their new house. It is an uncanny (and revealing) coincidence that the newly built tile stove frequently smoked so badly that Hesse had to escape from his study and leave the house. In March 1908 he reported having just returned from a ten-day trip to Basel.

In May he lectured in Bern. The summer months were spent partly at work and partly on a sickbed. In the fall he went to Vienna, with the usual stopover in Munich. In December he was again on the road, this time attending the wedding of a friend in Darmstadt. Yet all in all it was a year filled more than most with garden and house, with Hesse closed off from his immediate surroundings and open to his friends and readers with whom he communicated more and more voluminously by mail.

II

Hermann Hesse's inner uncertainties did not leave him at rest for long. In 1909, at age thirty-two, the tensions in his life began to take their toll again and led him to a fresh understanding of himself.

The first significant event of that year was the birth of his second son, Heiner, in March. His marriage had led to their first rented homestead and to the birth of Bruno; the building of the house (and the indebtedness to Maria's family it brought with it) led, quite naturally, to another child.

By the summer Hesse's tension had become too great. He faced a severe crisis, both physical and mental, and went to the German health resort of Badenweiler. Here began another of those protracted relationships with doctors and spas that occupied Hesse throughout his life. In a spa he could give himself over passively to another's direction and hence forfeit responsibility for himself. It took him out of place and time. Hesse could leave home yet remain within the bounds of propriety. He could leave wife, young child, and new baby behind him in the care of a maid while being a subject of compassion. In this way, Hesse realized a deeply felt need to take himself out of the everyday into a rarified life where the ailing person is cared for and made the center of attention, the *raison d'être* of his environment. It was, in other words, a way of enacting in life what he constantly created in art: a fictional world in which all tensions could be resolved. Later in his life this world would be a mythic, abstract world—the Magic Theater of *Steppenwolf* and Castalia of *The Glass Bead Game*. Fifteen years later he was to write his famous *A Guest at the Spa* about Baden. At this time he wrote a brief "open letter" to his friends that was published in 1912 also under the title "A Guest at the Spa" in the journal *Jugend (Youth)* in Munich. Writing about his life in "Badenau" (his code name for Badenweiler), where he had stayed from mid-June on, Hesse emphasized his own voluntary abandonment of responsibility: "A very clever and fine physician has relieved me for a while of all responsibility for my nerves, and a wealthy friend . . . is paying my considerable hotel bill. Otherwise I would not be here. . . ."

This was the beginning of a series of visits to "Villa Hedwig" where Hesse was treated by the physician Albert Fraenkel, whose methods of healing Hesse explained, and defended, to his father as "a way of reducing all disturbances of one's emotional life (insofar as they do not have recognizable physical causes) to unharmonious conditions and experiences of the soul."[9] A clever, thoughtful, and experienced physician, he explained, seeks to gain a complete picture of his patient, partly through direct questioning, partly through observation. He may then compare the "picture of the illness" with others in his experience and finally lead the patient to attack his dislocated psyche of objectifying his feelings and then regarding the image of himself with some detachment.

It is not difficult to see in this description Hesse's own way of projecting the psyche into many of his stories and novels, even though he conceded that for artists and poets this task is especially difficult, since such people are unique. In many ways, his relationship with Dr. Fraenkel anticipates psychoanalysis; it certainly prepared Hesse for becoming one of the first major writers to be psychoanalyzed. But it also provided him with a new society—he often had dinner with his doctor and otherwise enjoyed the amenities of the place, the baths, and the back rubbings—and a paradigm for his work. The anxieties of his life, ranging from his personal concern for his family to his general discontent with imperial Germany, appeared momentarily resolved. He learned to view the contradiction within him between home and freedom as a "harmonious image of the psyche" to be viewed with detachment. "Villa Hedwig" in Badenweiler, where Hesse was to spend many months during the next few years under the care of Dr. Fraenkel and his disciples, became indeed the "House of Peace" he described in a brief vignette in 1910.

The rest of the summer continued to reflect the old ups and downs. In a letter written early in August he told his sister Adele, whom he had long since called Adis,* of a few pleasant events, notably that a plaque of his likeness was being produced by a Viennese sculptor. He enjoyed his garden and even regretted that he was not able to take Mia with him more often. The new baby had tied her down so much that he had been able to go on only one excursion with her. Late in August he appealed to his sister to stay with him in September because he was not feeling well. Mia and the baby had gone to her family in Basel while Bruno and the maid had remained with his father on Lake Constance. Little

* Henceforth Adele will be usually referred to by her more familiar nickname "Adis." Maria will be called by her nickname, "Mia."

rapport with the boy emerges from Hesse's letter; only the need for his sister to come and fill the void. That emptiness was soon papered over: in October he went on a lengthy lecture tour of Northern Germany. He avoided the pressures of Berlin and the Prussian atmosphere that depressed him, remaining in the western part of the country, and visiting beautiful old cities like Hildesheim, Goslar, Bremen, Hannover, and finally Braunschweig, where he paid his respects to the aging writer Wilhelm Raabe. This was more than a journey of eyes and mind, even more than a lecture tour of reading his poems and stories. It became a new departure into illness.

On November 7, 1909, Hesse wrote a mysterious letter to his father from Frankfurt, almost at the door of his Swabian homeland. The letter began, ironically, with an exhortation for his father to undergo surgery for his intestinal trouble and the offer to foot the bill. Then, almost in passing, he mentioned that he was in some pain himself and that his doctor would decide the next day whether an operation, possibly for appendicitis, would be necessary. The sojourn at "Villa Hedwig" must have had some physical as well as mental implications. In any event, Hesse descended into anesthetic and operation, emerging in pain and querulous until Mia rushed up from Lake Constance to be at his side. By the end of the month he had improved enough to "visit a real men's pissoir" instead of the damned bottle (as he reported to Finckh) and was able to be transported to the home of his friends the Rosengarts, where he had been staying when he fell ill, until he could be given permission to travel home. The summary of the experience is crystallized in a note to Wilhelm Raabe which he dispatched on November 16:

> [Here in Frankfurt] my appendix was removed, and on the second day after my operation when for the first time I awakened with some clarity from that vapor of misery and chloroform, it was noon and I heard with some astonishment that all the bells of the city of Frankfurt were ringing in unison.

But the bells were not ringing for Hesse's awakening after all. It was Schiller's Memorial Day. Hesse used the occasion to pay Raabe a handsome compliment by linking up this image with all kinds of characters from Raabe's work. The poignancy of the awakening remains, however. He had, so it seemed, returned to life, and the bells around him were celebrating that moment.[10]

On this note the year passed and flowed into 1910 and the beginning of the end of Hesse's idyll. It started with an excursion with his wife to Alpenzell, followed by a lecture tour, to St. Gallen by himself. Meanwhile plans for a big trip were beginning to ripen, and Hesse's restlessness could at least work itself out in imaginary dreams and projects. In April he got a helper for house and garden. He was a "volunteer" from Vienna named Herr Rappaport who had become tired of business and wanted to assist him in his outdoor work. But not long after his arrival an enormous fire broke out in the village. Rappaport worked furiously to help put out the blaze and promptly fell ill, which did not help the gardening. By May Hesse was again in Badenweiler, occupying his usual room at the Villa Hedwig, hoping to find a cure for his headaches, eyeaches, and rheumatism. He saw little of Dr. Fraenkel himself upon this occasion, but felt equally safe in the hands of his various younger assistants.

In the meantime, *Gertrud*, which had been originally scheduled for the fall of 1909, was finally slated to appear with the publisher Albert Langen in Munich, the man who was behind the journal *März* on which Hesse continued to expend a great deal of energy. In renewing his standing contract with his publisher, S. Fischer, in 1908, Hesse had specifically exempted one of his next four novels to give it to Langen. There was some protest by Samuel Fischer, but Hesse remained adamant. Actually it took until late 1910 before the book finally emerged between covers.

The work on *März* had become more and more absorbing. Ever since 1907, when he became a contributing editor, he had tried to define his place in it and the anti-Wilhelminian position that collaboration on that journal entailed. On this level, too, he felt conflict and tension. He agreed with the journal's editorial policy at the time of its founding, its attempt to join Baden, Bavaria, Austria, and northern Switzerland into a South German cultural sphere as a protest against Prussian domination. Thanks to Albert Langen's Parisian connections, some bridges were established with France and they featured stories by Anatole France and other French writers. Although in its original conception the point of *März,* as distinct from *Simplizissimus*, had been to be constructive rather than satiric, rapier thrusts occurred. At one point Hesse found himself in the midst of a controversy about the insulting suggestion that Basel might be a citadel of unthinking provincialism. But generally during the eight years of its intense life, *März* provided a springboard for many important as well as beginning writers of the day, from Maxim Gorki and Selma Lagerlöf to Stefan Zweig. It was by Hesse's fine contribution that he was able to establish excellent ties with many writers on the European scene.

Yet Hesse's need to maintain some political distance remained. He continued to call himself "unpolitical," and though he focused much of his unhappiness on the political aggressiveness of Wilhelm's empire, he also kept aloof. His very work on *März* once again illustrates an internal conflict. As Hesse made clear, he entered a political arena when Langen, Thoma, and the others persuaded him to contribute regularly to *Simplizissimus,* which led to the work on *März*. His very activity made his prominent participation a political act. At the same time he sought cover under the mask of being "only" the literary editor. He sent stories and poems roughly typed on the back of business letters with carefully read and discussed literary contributions. In 1910, when his eyes hurt, he complained of the endless reading work for *März*; but his prominence, his intensity, his social participation in the editorial group (he was regularly Langen's houseguest when he was in Munich) kept him involved. When some years later he chastised both *Simplizissimus* and *März* for supporting the German war effort, and eventually left both publications for that reason, it had become clear that beneath the "unpolitical" self there remained a heart politically, if ambiguously, opting for peace. It was indeed the underlying issue of pacifism that increasingly involved Hesse in attacks against him, and it was this same issue that was to become the focus of many of his difficulties.

In the late fall of 1910 Albert Langen finally brought out *Gertrud* and for the first time the critical response was not very favorable. In a letter to Theodor Heuss (the future president of West Germany), with whom he was to work three years later on *März*, Hesse defended himself against the charge that he appeared no longer as strong and powerful as in the earlier novels like *Peter Camenzind*. Hesse agreed: "I am not really as fresh as I was eight years ago when I wrote *Camenzind,* and I would be stupid if I acted as if I were. I have six years behind me which to a large extent dissolved into nervous trouble and eyeaches; surgery was in there too—such matters don't make one any livelier and I got back on an uphill path only a short time ago."[11] On the other hand, he thought his new use of language was effective, that he had made a conscious decision to abandon the effusiveness of *Camenzind* for sparser rhetoric. This point he clarified further in a second letter to Heuss written four days later, on November 21, in which he warded off the compliment that he should strive to be a modern Swabian Flaubert. True, he wrote, the problematic core of his new book was the simultaneous love of and flight from the world, which he saw as the artist's fate. But Hesse insisted he could not be like Flaubert because he did not want to reflect big themes. Rather, "as a secret lyricist the wish for a pure melody was perhaps higher on my scale of values than the assimilation of large subjects. . . ."[12]

For all that brave talk, however, Hesse felt let down by the negative reviews, which he thought were carping, and some of which he attributed to the "literary Jews of Berlin." A week after the letters to Heuss, on November 28, he wrote his lawyer and friend Conrad Haussmann that *Gertrud* was eliciting peculiar responses from the critics. "Side by side with uncritical praise" he found more and more instances where the press took revenge for its own exaggerated praise of the past. It has "touted an author as a genius for so long that it has become tired of it and now declares him to be a cretin."[13] Although *Gertrud* was up to then Hesse's most mature work, the negative comments left him no rest. At the same time, this man who above all wanted to be loved began to receive hate letters from his readers—threats and denunciations (mostly for his political associations). This was a burden he was to bear for the rest of his life, but at this time he still dismissed it as "the other side of fame."

Before these events had darkened the year, Hesse had again gone to Italy, his second home. Writing to Adis from Mantua in October, he told his sister wistfully that he now experienced summer for the first time that year. "I must show you a piece of Italy some time." He enjoyed the sunshine and the long walks in the country. But the poor reception of *Gertrud* cast these moments of relief into darkness. When he returned, plunging from the Italian sun into the German winter, his depression was fed by the criticism he encountered. His gloom even extended to *März*, whose editor he called dry and lifeless in a long letter to Ludwig Thoma. Their political writers lacked vitality, he thought, even his friend and attorney Conrad Haussmann, who was a frequent contributor, and he dredged up names to provide livelier alternatives. A "shrewd expert" on Russia and East Asia was needed, for example, and others should be drawn in, he advised.[14]

All these carpings and complaints about poor reviews were, as usual, both symptoms and causes of a new depression. At Christmas 1910 Hesse wrote his younger sister Marulla: "The condition of deep depression, of alienation, and lack of self-confidence have become so well known to me over the past few years that I would prefer just about anything—even pain." It seemed that nothing could forestall the threat of an oncoming crisis—not his new house, his children, his often neglected but much loved garden, his friends, his walking tours in Italy, nor even his writing, lecturing, and diverse journalistic tasks. Instead, Hesse attempted to deal with it by taking a trip to the spiritual home of his parents and grandparents, which he had planned for over a year. He went to India.

III

The year 1911 was perhaps the most crucial in Hesse's second new life, for it brought to an end that period as an "immoralist" that had kept him and his marriage together during those years of consolidation and prosperity. The repressed vagabond asserted himself intermittently in wanderings and cures, as well as in his writings, but his intermittent presence also allowed Hesse to cement his domestic life. Not coincidentally, perhaps, Mia was again pregnant with a third child, who was expected that summer. Despite the pregnancy and Hesse's obvious concern, despite even the plans of a very long trip to India to be undertaken later in the year, he went on his usual hiking trip to Italy in April in the company of two close friends, the composer Othmar Schoeck and the composer-director Fritz Brun.

They were based in Florence, then started south together toward Bologna and beyond, by train, by horse cart, but mostly on foot. Two postcards to Mia (the only correspondence that survived the 1942 fire that destroyed all of Hesse's mail to her) attest to the warmth he allowed himself to feel for her and the children alongside the "vagabondage" he acted out with his friends. "Dearest," he wrote in a note from Orvieto on April 26: "Under a wonderful starry sky I am going to bed in a beautiful room in Orvieto, paved with stone. Below the window, a silent dead alley, a little well, and a garden. I would love to show all that to you and Buzzi. Sing my Song of Torero to little Heiner and take many many regards from your Hermann." From nearby Spoleto, two days later, he even proposed to bring Mia and the children to this place for a couple of months. The town was "the most beautiful discovery I have ever made in Italy." They might even earn good money together, combining her photographs with his feuilleton essays about the region and its wealth of "hardly known beauties, mountains, valleys, bridges, oak forests, monasteries, waterfalls, etc."[15] But when late in May he sent a note to Fritz Brun after their return, the old problem reemerged in all its starkness:

> I would give my left hand if I could again be a poor happy bachelor and own nothing but twenty books, a second pair of boots, and a box full of secretly composed poems. Now, however, I am a family father, homeowner, and only too favorite author, and since I have little talent for and confidence in pathos, I try to accept this lightly and perhaps become after a while a fair humorist. . . .[16]

Hesse's wandering during the year of his third child's birth, his profound restlessness culminating in a long voyage abroad at the very time of Mia's pregnancy, was clearly part of his profound problem and style. His correspondence of that summer of his thirty-fourth birthday reveals his partial awareness of that duality. Responding to Conrad Haussmann a week after his birthday in July, he wrote: "My wife expects a baby at the end of the month, and if all goes well I shall disappear from this region and will be beyond reach."[17] Whereupon he sketched out the details of his projected journey.

On July 27, 1911, on a Wednesday morning, the third child, Martin, arrived, and Hesse's immediate conduct did not differ from that of any other new father. He appeared proud and happy. Perhaps the only unusual aspect of his behavior was the language in which he announced his new son to his family. He had prepared himself for his trip to India by learning English. He promptly composed the birth announcement to his father in the rediscovered idiom that Adis had tried to teach him laboriously, and unsuccessfully, in Calw at the age of eighteen. "As I have written on a postcard," it began, "we have got a little boy the day before yesterday. The little fellow is in good health and likewise is his mother." And he ended: "Now my english acquirements are exhausted. I am, with kindest regards, yours H." Along with passport, shirts, socks, and various tropical garments, Hesse tried to pack some English as a passport to freedom. This fact also indicates how long he had planned the journey. Yet when he wrote his family in Calw on August 15, a bare three weeks before his departure, he suggested it had all been recently planned. He had mentioned it to Adis and others for a year, though in referring to his forthcoming journey to Genoa where they were to take the boat, he said: "Strange that I am making that journey again. This past spring I was also in Milan and Genoa without any notion that a few months later I would return as a voyager to Sumatra."[18]

Hesse did not travel alone, but in the company of a friend, the painter Hans Sturzenegger. He went, so he claimed "out of sheer inner need."[19] As stability solidified beneath him and his house had closed even more completely around him, the motive for the trip became clear. It also explains not only Hesse's state of mind at the time of his departure but also the effect of his Indian journey as a whole. It was an interior voyage following an inner need, projected upon a real world. After two days' travel in the heat of late summer through Switzerland and Lombardy, they arrived in Genoa on September 6 and boarded their ship the next day. They sailed at noon, and for a brief moment Hesse breathed easier. He had cut his bonds not only with his family in Gaienhofen and Calw, but with all of Europe and its quibbling critics, its questioning journalists, its narrow politics and life. For a while it seemed as though he and Sturzenegger had truly escaped.

Actually Hesse had made his get-away after much haggling with Samuel Fischer and had received a round sum to support his travel without any commitments to early and even definite publication. He was free in every respect—from family and house, from pressure to write for a deadline, from his social and journalistic entanglements, and even from immediate financial worry. As the coast of Italy, and with it that of Europe, dropped away and they turned into the sumptuous dining room for their first dinner at sea, Hesse felt, momentarily, like a new man.

The trip was conventional from the beginning. There were the usual shipboard acquaintances and long hours of reading and leisure on deck chairs while the planks trembled slightly with the hum of the engines. They stood by the railing, watching the banks of the straight and narrow Suez Canal pass by—a new sight at the time—against the background of a monotonous landscape. But freedom did not increase as the ship left all vestiges of Europe behind when it emerged into the Persian Gulf. It is another element in Hesse's paradoxical inner life that despite his family's involvement with the East, despite all their talk of India and the various mementos, the physical experience of India was to depress rather than release him. It was, as he wrote later, only through the *ideas*—not through the reality—of that world that he could assimilate that part of his own and his family's past. The actual trip to India—and it was really more to Sumatra, Borneo, and Burma than to the India of his parents and grandparents that he traveled—was in fact a disappointment. Although he delivered several passages describing various landscapes with some feeling in his notebooks and diaries, his notes did not ring wholly true. His feelings for landscapes and people remained tied to the southwestern corner of the German-speaking world that, for a moment, he had been so glad to escape. In Asia he was oppressed by the noise, the beggars, the dirt. Surprising in a writer who was to compose *Siddhartha*, he did not like Indians, and treated them and their society with typical European prejudices. He hated the heat, the smell, the dangerously lush landscapes, the pretensions of the Europeans, although he singled out the Chinese as more cultured and controlled. "The way to India and China," he wrote later, "did not go by way of railroads and ships. I had to find the magic bridges myself."[20]

Hesse and Sturzenegger arrived in Singapore weary from the heat of the Indian Ocean, then took a small Dutch steamer to southern Sumatra. Finally they went up the Batan-Hari River in a small Chinese riverboat with gigantic wheels until they arrived in Palembang, whereupon Hesse's patience came to an end. The original plan had been much more ambitious. He did accept the invitation of Sturzenegger's brother, whom they joined in the city of Kuala Lumpur. Actually, their brief visit to

Ceylon was truncated and their plan to visit the family's field of activity, Malabar, was aborted. However, Hesse took a great many notes and composed poems and even some fiction. He also presented at least one illuminating dream, which suggested that the interior journey went on while the exterior journey had lost itself in disenchantment.

Both Hesse's external and internal observations were to be combined in a small book, *From India*, which Fischer published in 1913, and which, in retrospect, is far more interesting and substantial than it seemed at the time. His physical descriptions give a fine sense of Hesse's method of observation, his accurate eye modifying his sharp judgment. At the same time, the interior voyage is reflected in brief poetic sketches and diary entries, to be fully contained in the long story "Robert Aghion," and similar narratives, rendering an artistic reflection of his sense of defeat by that world from which he had hoped release.

Hesse's impression of Sumatra, which combined the external and internal perceptions most clearly, is contained in a piece he wrote in 1916, on the occasion of an exhibition of Hans Sturzenegger's paintings:

> On a damp, hot, glorious evening in Penang, for the first time the surging life of an Asiatic city burst upon us; for the first time we saw the Indian Ocean glittering between innumerable coral islands, and we stared with astonishment at the many-colored spectacle of street life in the Hindu city, the Chinese city, the Malayan city. A wild, colorful human swarm in the ever-crowded alleys, at night a sea of candles, motionless cocoanut palms reflected in the sea, shy naked children, dark fishermen rowing antediluvian boats![21]

These perceptions of port cities, as well as of jungles and primeval forests, created images (or "pictures") "until everyone of us had found India, his own Asia, and carried it within him." This relationship between the inner and outer journey, probably colored in retrospect by the psychoanalysis he was undergoing in 1916, had not been nearly as present to him five years earlier when Hesse experienced the East. The broader description of their first Asian stopover, Penang, which was reprinted in *From India,* is less vivacious, less colorful, and again stresses the differences between the measured knowledgeable Chinese and the supposedly overexcited Malayans. Visits first to a Chinese, then to a Malayan theater seemed to reinforce that impression. The former was thoughtful, allegorical, displaying a mannered style, "each movement prescribed and full of meaning, studied and led by expressive music"; the latter was wild, with crazy scenery, "a parody of all the excesses of European art, stupidly droll and hopeless." Hesse thereupon indulged in some rather superficial speculations about the "poor Malayans," who were like dear, weak children, hopelessly lost to the most evil of European influences.[22]

Despite all this moralizing, more of the later Hesse's oriental imagery can be discerned in these notes than appears on the surface. His impressions of Singapore were projected in two ways, first as a straight travelogue, recording the sights of the city as seen from a ricksha: the blue and black colors of the ocean, the white of the buildings, the evenly laid out streets and well-formed squares of the Chinese city contrasting with the arrogantly enormous buildings of the Europeans. But this sketch, "On Going on a Ride," is followed by another, "A Feast for Eyes," in which a similar journey turns inward, and becomes a faintly humorous, touching vignette in which Hesse imagines he is on a journey through the city in the company of the Chinese girl to whom he had just given a dollar. Leading the reader from one kind of bazaar to another—Chinese, Japanese, Javanese, etc.—this sketch also sought to develop an understanding of the meaning of that world as a dream. Everything that costs money, he wrote, may be dubious—from bed to food to service and the exchange of money—but "around it shimmers inexhaustibly the wealth and the art of Asia," raped and weakened, and perhaps already in a struggle unto death, "but still richer and more varied than we could ever dream about it in the West."[23] Again, to underscore the conflict, he appeared to sympathize with the Indians, Malayans, and Chinese around him while his actual feelings produced horror and relief at being able to retire to his European hotel.

There is no question that here as elsewhere Hesse's divided self burdened him more than he had hoped. In a very poignant scene, caught in the sketch "Hanswurst" (or "Clown"), he described the menial task a woman of evident brilliance and style had to perform in a Malayan play where she was made to act as a silly and ugly fool. Indeed, he compared her to the Fool in Shakespeare's *Lear*. When she was inadvertently stirred by a movement of one of her fellow actors, "she rose, life flowing through her entire being," and parodied that movement with devastating exaggeration. "But this brilliant woman," he concluded, "was only a clown; she was not allowed to sing Italian arias like her colleagues."[24] For a moment Hesse projected his sense of the artist ignored by society, even in that colonial world, as he allied himself with the brilliantly misunderstood.

The bright colors of the continent on which Hesse moved emerged everywhere in these passages. True, his reflections about the simple "natives" who could "teach" the aging, overly ripe and sophisticated European remain condescending. They also contrasted sharply with his other image of the "native" struggling against social and cultural extinction. But he successfully described both the conflict that prevented his relief from depression at the time and the inner vision that was to find its fulfillment in *Siddhartha*. One of the most interesting sketches that revealed both the problem and the vision was his famous "Dream in Singapore." This memoir displays Hesse's state of anxiety succinctly in a setting of an Eastern but also European city.

The account opens with a brief summary of a stroll the author had taken. It describes how he had hunted butterflies among well-kept gardens before returning to the city on foot in the heat of the day. Dinner in the hotel was served in style and comfort by Chinese waiters, however, and the writer had a chance to recover. Bright flashes of light caught in the ice cubes of his scotch and soda accentuated the strange contradictions in his current life. After dinner his friends decided to go to the movies and, though he felt tired from the day's excursion, he finally agreed to join them. They were barely seated in their privileged seats at the theater, looking above rows upon rows of Chinese heads at the small illuminated square of the screen on which ghostly figures moved crazily, when Hesse dozed off. When he reopened his eyes in the dream he found himself on the deck of a ship at dusk. A few oil lanterns were burning, and, in their dim wavering light, Hesse recognized his father. When he inquired where they were going, his father answered simply, "to Asia." They spoke Malayalam mixed with English. It was a mélange of languages his parents had spoken when he was a child if they wanted to keep secrets from the children. Now, the dream-Hesse remembered it well. But this Asia was no real continent; it was "a very specific place, somewhere between India and China."

With the distance of hindsight, the dream easily yields the elements of the vision that was the true message Hesse tried to read in Asia. The figure of his father became identical with that of a smiling Buddha. "I do not teach you," his father said kindly in his dream, "I merely remind you." And his smile was like that of the Savior before he disappeared. When Hesse next looked for his father, another elderly man, disguised as a British ship's officer, told him that his father was everywhere—within and outside him. After involved scenes featuring a beautiful Miss Annie Wells from America as well as friend Sturzenegger, he came upon a missionary and finally an Indian guru. When he woke up at last after witnessing various transformations of his dream figures, he felt he had seen the true, symbolic India he had wanted to discover, the world in which all things were one, a place that had little to do with actual streets, jungles, and heat-filled cinemas:

I rose [still in the dream] and opened my eyes. They were all around me, my father, my friend, the Englishman, the guru, and all human faces I had ever seen in my life. They looked straight ahead, with moved, beautiful glances, and I too looked and before us a thousand-year-old grove opened up, eternity rustled from the heights of treetops that reached to the heavens and deep in the night of holy shadows gleamed, golden, an ancient gate of the temple.

These lines sound almost like the later Hesse and reflect his realization that the actual India he had rejected still gave him the strength to entertain a vision he had to create himself, as it was based on inner rather than outer perception. The dream ended (just before he awoke to find himself back in the Malayan cinema):

Thereupon we all fell on our knees; our longing was satisfied and our journey was at an end. We closed our eyes and bowed down deep, and beat the earth with our foreheads, once again and again in rhythmic devotion.

In fact, Hesse had actually been beating his forehead rhythmically on the wooden railing before him; but the vision remained of unity at the end of his interior journey.[25]

After Singapore the two friends boarded the Dutch steamer, crossed the equator, and landed in southern Sumatra. Naturally he was traveling first-class—always the disenchanted European who needed the security of his world without being able to shed his need to understand "the natives" on their own terms. Vivid descriptions of the Sumatran landscape with its junglelike entangling lianas and tree trunks, heat-shimmering primeval forests and naked "natives" also conveyed Hesse's sense of being caught —green lianas around his legs and arms, enmeshed in a hopelessly bottomless world. Sleeping in a jungle hut in inland Bata-Hari, he felt threatened by the "wild lustful" jungle and viewed with anger the colonial white masters whom he nevertheless recognized as the true conquerors. Finally, he found himself blinded by a terrifying thunderstorm that broke upon them with vengeful violence. At their last stop in Palembang, Hesse felt as though all these disenchantments had come together. He was embarrassed at the strutting white colonialists and their destruction of nature; he suffered from the heat, the dirt, the insects, and the "primitive" people he saw as childlike "natives."

Toward the end Hesse's interior vision—his mythic sense—prevailed, even if it had to involve him in some self-deception. They had reached Kandy, the capital of Ceylon's central province, which contains the "Dalada Maligawa," a sacred Buddhist shrine. Several memorable images are captured in his description of their visit to the ancient temple; a blind old man stepped from a ferry and was led to the shore of the sacred river—a striking image that seems to provide a setting for Siddhartha and Vasudeveda, his ferryman friend, written a decade later. In this atmosphere of lush nature and the darkened grotto within the mysterious shadows of rocklike temple walls, Hesse was more at home than either in the jungle or in the smelly, teeming cities. A priest showed him the inner sanctum, and as their eyes grew accustomed to the dark he saw, gradually revealing itself, the reclining head of an enormous Buddha. The statue filled the cave with its enormous body; the rock raised on the left shoulder: "If [the Buddha] would rise, the entire mountain would collapse upon us."[26]

Similarly, in a "diary page from Kandy," Hesse reported other excursions to the sacred places of Buddhism, including the great temple where Buddha's holy tooth, supposedly brought there twenty-five centuries before, was treasured. Pontificating, he contrasted the naive understanding of Buddha's teaching by "mere" native idolaters celebrating him in pictures with the equally incapacitated colonial whites who, he thought, were closer to the source of Buddha's revelation.[27]

Whatever Hesse's feelings about Buddha may have been, Kandy was the place where their journey found its somewhat premature end. Unhappy, plagued by dysentery, living on "red wine and opium," Hesse could hardly find the strength to visit the holy places of Kandy. The friends decided to cut the visit short, and Hesse never visited his mother's birthplace or his grandfather Gundert's mission in Malabar. As one of his last gestures—his dysentery finally under control—he climbed the mountain of Pedrotallagalla, which overlooked a large part of Ceylon and controlled the region. The event is unimportant in itself; climber Hermann Hesse obviously had to try a high mountain before leaving Asia. He found the climb invigorating, but not very challenging by Alpine standards. He was about to give vent to his disenchantment— another of those myriad disappointments that had plagued him during his Indian journey—when he envisioned the majestically towering mountaintops in an ice-cold, crystalline atmosphere:

> This primeval landscape spoke to me more strongly than anything I had seen elsewhere in India. The palms and birds of paradise, the rice fields and the temples of the rich coastal cities, the valleys in the tropical lowlands steaming with fruitfulness, all this and the primeval forest itself were beautiful and enchanting, but they were always strange and extraordinary to me, never quite close or quite my own. Only up here in the

cold air and the seething clouds of the raw heights did it become fully clear to me how completely our being and our northern culture are rooted in raw, impoverished lands.[28]

It is an interesting passage, because it illuminates Hess'e paradoxical position sharply, if not grotesquely. This is the voice of the measured European—northern, Swabian, and Swiss—the bringer of order as he braved the inclement weather and bracing winds. He found "culture rooted in raw, impoverished lands" as against the screaming colors, the lascivious scents and noises of the overheated jungles. It was precisely those noises, those scents that had persistently drawn him away from his Gaienhofen idyll, not just on this abortive journey to India, but constantly to the south, to Italy. He reiterated the same conflict in different terms. Much later, when Hesse had left his solid life, he moved to Italian Switzerland outside the compass of his northern and German-speaking homelands. The man who held up northern rigor as opposed to the "simple, unpretentious and childlike people" of the lush valleys of Ceylon was also the man who was inspired to paint when in the twenties he settled amid the bright colors and heat-shimmering walls of the Italian south. Whenever the systole had taken him toward abandon, the diastole brought him back to the closed-in "home."

However depressing the Indian journey had turned out, one meaningful result cannot be overlooked. Although Hesse found himself disliking Indians, Malays, and all other nonwhites except Chinese, whom he called pitiful remnants of paradisical peoples, he carried home with him an awareness of unity above the differences imposed by life as a genuine spiritual experience. The final paragraph of his notes returns to this recognition:

My ship steams on and on. The day before yesterday the untamed sun of Asia burned upon our deck. We sat airily in thin white clothes and drank ice-cooled liquids. Now we are already close to the European winter, which greeted us with cool temperatures and rain showers immediately after we left Port Said. Now the hot shores of the eastern islands and the glowing noons of Singapore will assume splendor in our memories; but all this will never be as dear and worthwhile to me as the strong sense of unity and close kinship of all human beings which I had gained among Indians, Malays, Chinese, and Japanese.[29]

In Hesse's contradictory mind, the details may not fit, but the image of unity remains as an abiding motif that cast luster upon his life. During the war he was to gain an even stronger sense of this worldwide community. In commemorating Hans Sturzenegger's painting about their Indian journey in 1916, he stressed this sense of unity with a renewed emphasis, for during the war, he had recalled this encompassing brotherhood to counter the divisions of Europe. He made clear that the idea of this universal fraternity, a specific result of their trip, extended to all the people they had met on their journey; pity for the oppressed and contempt for the oppressor were present in one world. Even in this later political context, a deeper, spiritual recognition of unity emerges:

> It is only from this point of view, from the recognition of brotherhood and inner equality, that what is strange and dissimilar, the colorfulness of nations and of peoples, attains its profoundest charm and enchantment.[30]

In his outward relations to people and places in India, Indonesia, and Ceylon, Hesse never managed to overcome his Western attitudes. But he had gained some understanding in an interior vision, a "magic" that this encounter with people other than himself had provided.

IV

When Hesse arrived home at the end of November after two months' absence, he found that the problems that had troubled him had not been solved. Already on the homeward voyage, writing from the deck of the steamer *York*, he dispatched an angry note to Haussmann, breaking his ties with *März*. The two editors in chief, Haussmann and Ludwig Thoma, had decided henceforth not to accept fees and asked Hesse to do the same, since their journal was in trouble. His response was querulous and negative. The same crisis in their relationship was to continue throughout the next few years until Hesse finally severed his connections with the journal in 1915. At this point, however, the grounds on which Hesse refused his friends' request were primarily economic, based on the fact that he could not donate free time because he had a household with three small children to support. Hesse's relationship to money was always problematic. He had driven an extraordinarily hard bargain with Fischer before his trip to India and had been able to finance a good part of the journey with the proceeds.[31] He was also still earning well, even if *Gertrud* did not sell as extravagantly as the other books. Hesse was only cautiously generous about money, as his continuous haggling over his contribution to Theo Isenberg's pharmacy indicates. But it is understandable that at this point in his life, when he did not know what to do after this depressing abortive journey, he needed the security of his income.

Upon his return, the "raw cold" winter on Lake Constance did not revive his spirits any more than the hot shores of East Asia. His restless spirit could not find solace in garden and house. On Christmas Day he wrote his physician and therapist in Badenweiler, Dr. Albert Fraenkel, that he was suffering the consequences of his unforgivable stupidity by returning from the beautiful sunshine of the tropics to their "inhospitable desert" with a bad cold and sore throat.[32] He would have loved to visit him at once, but the season was not suitable and his wife would not have liked it. Already at this point an inner decision had been made to move. He was ready to sell his house: buildings, garden, and meadow altogether for 30,000 marks. The time of Gaienhofen, with its small circle of friends, its growing colony of artists, and his own important place had come to an end after little more than seven years, though only four years had passed in the new house that had been built to their specifications.

If the journey to India had been one attempt to restore Hesse's balance —an attempt that had failed—his decision to leave Gaienhofen was another. Clearly, life with Mia was not the most congenial, and the presence of a new infant did not help. It is difficult to say who of this strange couple was the more emotionally burdened. Both had long histories of mental anguish; both fell victims to depressions, rheumatism, and headaches. But Hesse was gregarious a good part of the time, while Mia was constantly withdrawn. His many absences could not have helped her condition; she fell into frequent fits of melancholia. The illness of their first months of marriage had become a frequent occurrence. At the same time, these states of withdrawal drove her husband away and increased his need to assert his freedom. At this point there was not yet any suggestion of separation, but dismantling the citadel of his bourgeois success was clearly a first, even if unconsciously taken, step.

Soon after the New Year, Hesse went on an extensive lecture tour that took him to Vienna, Prague, and Dresden; he then considered their move in earnest. Although they thought of various possibilities, Mia's voice seemed to count most, for they agreed that with Hesse's constant absences it was too hard for her to live with three children in such an isolated locale —difficult even without her melancholia. As for the choice of a new place of residence, Hesse rejected Conrad Haussmann's suggestion that they move to Swabia and Mia wanted to get back to her own country, Switzerland, for she preferred to see her boys grow up Swiss. Hesse felt that he did not perform a real function for his family except to provide them with the necessities of life. He therefore deferred to her wishes.

A house fell unexpectedly vacant near Bern. A friend, the painter Albert Welti, and his wife had both died during recent months and the

Hesses were therefore able to rent the empty house for a reasonable sum. In September 1912, having rented their own Gaienhofen place in turn to two young painters, they moved into the beautiful mansion in the suburb of Ostermündigen. Hesse had arrived on Lake Constance as a conquering author. He had settled and built a life while undermining it through his questioning and his restless wandering. Now they were leaving the homestead that they had founded. But the immediate depression had been served. For Hesse at least the flight to Bern was successful. Author and immoralist combined to create a healing novel.

5

From Crisis to War

I

The place we now wanted to move to after eight years in Gaienhofen
was Bern. Of course we did not want to live in the city itself, that
would have been a betrayal of our ideals, but we wanted a quiet country
house in the vicinity of Bern, perhaps one like the marvelous old estate
my friend Albert Welti, the painter, had been living in for some years.

But when we actually decided to leave Lake Constance for Bern,
everything had become quite different.

—From "On Moving Into a New House"

THE WELTI HOUSE was indeed a beautiful place. A good walk from
the last stop of the streetcar line from Bern, it had survived in a setting of
fields and woods. This last monument to the death of the Hesses' marriage possessed all the qualities he and Mia had sought in an "ideal
house for our kind of people." The address, Melchenbühlweg 26, suggested a far more urban setting than was actually the case. Their street
led directly through open country up to the ancient patrician house that
stood decorously among large old elms.

Hesse described the place well in his sketch "Upon Moving Into a New
House," and in his fragment "The House of Dreams." The latter especially
indicated much of their motivation behind the move and the way they
had directed their search. It reflected art, music, solidity near Switzerland's capital, yet it retained for them the dream of simple country life
that had been witness to their marriage. Being part of an estate, the
property contained some farmland that was worked by a tenant who
supplied the family with milk and gardener Hesse with manure. Indeed,
it was the garden that embellished the dream. With fruit trees and a
small grove on a hilltop, it spread out under ancient trees south of the
mansion overlooking the landscape below. As Hesse described it, a
stone well stood behind the house and the large veranda on the south
side was open to a marvelous view. Beyond the treetops and the wooded
hills they could see in the distance the great Jura mountains with the
Jungfrau constellation in their midst.

159

The inside of the mansion was stately and elegant. The large rooms were decorated with ancient mirrors of greenish glass. In addition to old-fashioned tiled stoves there was also a huge marble fireplace where Hesse lit a fire on early autumn evenings. It did not seem to matter, at first, that the house lacked most modern conveniences, including electric light, and they had to manage their cooking on a wood-fire stove.[1]

As Hesse made clear in "On Moving Into a New House," however, they were acutely aware of the tensions hidden beneath this pleasant façade. If it was a fresh start, it was a "derailed" fresh start. The Welti house was after all the legacy of an old friend, and of his wife, who had both died during the previous year. At first the Hesses had been reluctant to rent the house under these ghoulish circumstances: "It smelled too much of death." But their choice had been limited, for nothing else that was suitable for their family turned up in the vicinity of Bern. They had to take the Welti house and for a while Hesse was actually rather pleased with it. They took over house, furniture, and garden—even the Weltis' Alsatian dog—yet they also felt tainted by these artifacts the dead couple had left behind. From the moment they moved in, Hesse kept himself apart. His depression gradually returned, and as his new novel, *Rosshalde*, began to take shape, it did not at first provide the usual relief. At the same time, Mia sank back into her old melancholia and blamed the place. The house oppressed her and filled her with fear.

The weird circumstances of their occupation of the Weltis' stately mansion, however, were hardly the main reason for their problematic life. The tensions of Gaienhofen renewed themselves in Bern. Outwardly all went well. Their life appeared more even to their observing friends and acquaintances. They seemed to enjoy their splendid view of the mountains, their fine fruit trees in the garden, and the proximity of the old city where they had good friends and could enjoy good music. Hesse reported of this time that he still sat down occasionally to listen quietly while Mia was playing the piano, but that it happened more and more rarely. Soon his absences again began to take on the ominous quality of their last years in Gaienhofen. Again sudden business engagements took him unexpectedly to Zurich and Munich while Mia withdrew more and more into herself.

In one large compartment of his life, Hesse remained a lonely man and relished the role. In a loving sketch of this period, "Old Music" (1913), he described a Sunday night's outing to the city where he went alone to listen to a concert in the Münster, Bern's cathedral.[2] As Hesse reported the trip, his eyes ached from overwork and illness as he got ready to leave. The children were asleep. Mia had withdrawn to her room. He picked up the concert ticket from the sideboard, chained the dog, and walked out into the gray, drizzling rain—down the country road past fields and forest to the end of the streetcar line. Eventually the warm, brightly lit trolley car stopped and took him in. Soon the great church was upon him, and he entered in slow paces, taking in the peace he felt as he allowed himself to sink into the large deep chair. The sonorous sounds of the organ swelled and filled the huge expanse of the old church—a piece for the organ by a French master (he could not recall the name), an old Italian violin sonata (by Veracini, Nardini, Tartini, who knew?), then a prelude and fugue by Bach. The music filled the space around him like thunder from Heaven. Hesse reflected, contrasting the rising body of sound with the pettiness and miserable incompetence of daily life. When it was over, he walked out again without speaking to anyone. Slowly he passed through the large nave, hesitated for a moment at the door to notice that the rain had stopped. Then he began to walk all the way home—through the sleepy square, past the long rows of street lamps, across the high river bridge and out into the country. As he got closer to home, gentle winds stirred the oak trees by the country road. Finally, he climbed the last hill and entered his sleeping house.[2]

It was not just nostalgia, or even self-pity, that presented the past to Hesse in this way: it was also profoundly part of his life, his continuous, self-monitoring existence in which he constantly compared the great moments of experience—of nature and art—with his own often irritable reactions. But the stance of the lonely sufferer was a favorite pose—deeply rooted in him yet functioning as a convenient mask—and it went along quite peaceably with a good deal of social activity as well. Switzerland is a small country, and by moving across the border to Bern he had moved closer to many of his friends, like the composers Othmar Schoeck and Fritz Brun, the painter Ernst Morgenthaler, and many others. He also retained his ties with Germany, especially with his friend in Munich, Reinhold Geheeb of *Simplizissimus*, as well as with *März* on whose masthead he continued to appear. In fact, his work on *März* constituted one of Hesse's few overtly political acts, despite his disclaimer, yet he felt always uncomfortable and touchy about it. By December 1912, when he began his visits to the Münster, he had started to remove himself again. This drama of hesitations was captured in a series of exchanges published in Hesse's *Collected Letters* (1973). It began with a letter to Reinhold Geheeb in December which made it clear that he was miffed by the recent behavior of an editor at *März* who had neglected to print some of his contributions and had unduly delayed others. He therefore announced that he was removing his name from the masthead, a statement he repeated two weeks later in a polite formal note to Ludwig

Thoma. But within six months he had retreated from this extreme position. In a letter to Theodor Heuss in June he offered to resume his contributions to *März* and wished the journal well, provided the remiss editor would finally print the contributions he had withheld.

The Welti house was the last station on the line of his dissolving marriage and the scene for changing and rechanneling many of his past relationships as he gradually distilled a new form of existence. It was the last point of departure still poised on the edge of a bourgeois life, and it therefore naturally became the center and theme of his last conventional novel, *Rosshalde*. All the strands of Gaienhofen and his marriage came together in this book—his final book on art and artists in a time of peace—and projected for the last time a poetically realistic picture of his conflict. Physically, the Rosshalde estate of his latest novel was neither like the house he had built on Lake Constance nor like the Welti house he had chosen in Bern, but symbolically it appeared as a fusion of both. Its majestic expanse, its lake and wood, suggested a dreamlike expansion of his Gaienhofen home. The interiors, the studio, and the paraphernalia of a painter's life indicated the lingering presence of the late Albert Welti.

Rosshalde contained some of those prophesies of a writer's personal life that come true because they are based on his anxious self-perception. It presented the *persona*, the painter Johannes Veraguth viewed both from within and from the angle of his doppelgänger, the visiting friend Otto Burkhardt. The friend finds that the painter and his wife already live practically apart. They hardly communicate, their sole remaining bond the child Pierre. The first prophesy was self-fulfilling; the incredible strain of the marriage—which expressed itself in the familiar tension between the artist's need for freedom and his desire for control—was bound to lead to the painter's emotional collapse. Moreover, it is no coincidence that a novel about the author's *persona* as a painter follows *Gertrud* in which he was a great composer and performer of music. In fact, though music had been Mia's métier it had also been Hesse's own love. Borrowing from Nietzsche, he self-consciously saw it as the Dionysian or passionate element of the self. If the great composer Muoth broke down in that earlier novel, it was because he had been seized by a mysterious yet uncontrollable passion. Painting, by the same token, was Apollonian, or formally limited and graceful. It set physical boundaries and urged restraint. But the restraint remained the other side of Hesse's precarious dialectic and his painter *persona* Veraguth had to break down as well.

The despair and depression that had culminated in the attempt to escape to India (Veraguth was about to take the trip his creator, Hesse, had just completed) are provided a literary form in the novel. Another far more amazing prophesy was the illness and death of the young boy Pierre, for it anticipates little Martin's severe struggle with meningitis only a few months after the completion of the book. In the novel, the child's death acts to liberate the hero effectively from the bondage of his suffocating marriage, after which Veraguth can find his independence. The entire book reflects the ambience of the Hesse household in 1912–13, but it was to take several more years before the prophesy contained in its ending would finally be fulfilled. That it was about his own marriage and his decision to change his life is beyond doubt, as it is also beyond question that Frau Veraguth—one of the few credible women Hesse created—appears as an idealized yet realistic version of Mia.

At Christmastime, when Hesse was still at work on *Rosshalde*, he again seemed weary. They had been in Bern since September and he felt worn out by an inexplicable illness and depression. He waited impatiently for Christmas to be over—for the children's gifts and festivities to be part of the old year—before he could go off to Grindelwald. He had intended to go skiing as far as the St. Gotthard Pass, but ended up in a spot closer by where the weather was good, the wine passable, and the snow nonexistent. The New Year ushered in an easier time and the next few months were not too disturbing. By January 11, Hesse was able to report to his friend the painter Otto Blümel that *Rosshalde* was finally finished and that he was busy with corrections.[3] He had now turned to his vagabond story *Knulp* and was revising the journals and sketches he had drawn up during his journey to India in preparation for the publication later that year of his travelogue *From India*. And as usual he lectured, moving restlessly on his circuit to Baden, Zurich, and other cities.

Finally, at the end of March 1913 Hesse was ready for his regular Italian journey, which he undertook in the company of the painter Fritz Widmann, who had joined him in 1906 and 1910, and his old friend Othmar Schoeck. They traveled together through northern Italy—from Como and Bergamo to Verona and back to Milan—enjoying, despite the lingering frost, the magic of the Italian landscape and the beauty of its art. In the lecturing manner he always used in writing to his family, Hesse explained to his father and Marulla in Calw that he now enjoyed sculpture more than painting and that he had been awed by Padua, which had been visited by the spirit of Dante and Giotto. He sounded happy and enthusiastic.

In June Adis visited the Hesses in Bern. Hermann picked her up in Interlaken and toured the Bernese mountains with her before arriving at Melchenbühlweg the next day. It was a fairly good summer filled with children, lectures, and manuscripts, yet the contradictions in Hesse's behavior persisted. In September, he wrote his friend Erwin Ackerknecht, the city librarian in Baltic Stettin, that he was again in a depression not unlike the one he had been in when he wrote him last: "I wished I could write to you today in a happier vein, but for some weeks I've been in the same vale of misery that my physical and psychic nature gets me into each year."[4] He also reported good work, an introduction to Goethe's *Wilhelm Meister*, and continued labors of love on German romantic poets. In October he took Mia on a trip. He had been asked to lecture in Salzburg and decided to combine the Austrian journey with stopovers in Vienna and Munich. They spent five pleasant days seeing friends, enjoying Vienna and its music. The trip did Mia "a world of good," as he reported to Adis, including the sojourn in Vienna. They enjoyed especially the stopover in Munich where they spent a fine evening with a painter in a handsome house overlooking Lake Chiem. Hesse felt invigorated and ready for an autumn of new labors.

Yet contradictions continued. If he took Mia on one journey, he left her behind on the next three. When he was home he closeted himself in his study. All along, as a sad counterpoint to all his work, he wrote pages of intensely personal and sentimental poems, which were printed as *The Solitary's Music* during the following year:

> How hard are the days!
> There is no fire to warm me
> No sun to laugh at me any longer;
> Everything empty
> Everything cold and pitiless,
> And even the dear clear
> Stars look at me disconsolately,
> Since my heart has learned
> That love can die.[5]

It was in this spirit, along with his occasional working moods, that he turned to the new year 1914: busy, strained, without a major project in mind, and full of worries.

In March of that year, their youngest son Martin fell seriously ill. He woke screaming at night, jumped out of bed, and suffered violent anxiety attacks. The pediatrician diagnosed the illness as a nervous disease, ordered that the child be isolated and given constant care. Five-year-old Heiner was sent to friends, the Schädelins, and though Bruno, then a third-grader, could stay home, he was not allowed to see his little brother. Mia, whose nerves had shown great strain since they had moved to Bern, was now wholly absorbed in the child's illness. "Mia camps totally in the bedroom with the little one, behind half-darkened windows, and hardly gets away even for a moment. She also eats there most of the time. . . . And that is supposed to go on for weeks."[6] In a letter to his father, Hesse unfolds the same tale—how Mia's entire being was absorbed by the small child's illness, how she was unable to get away from his bedside for even a quarter of an hour. "In the evenings we read to each other, that is, if the child falls asleep, which, despite bromide is not always the case." But the same letter, which creates the image of a close couple facing the severe illness of a child, also contains comments on *Rosshalde*, which had just been published.

On March 16, 1914, Hesse wrote to his father:

Today my new book has come out. The novel created a great deal of difficulty for me and represents for me, at least for a while, a farewell to the hardest problem which has occupied me. For the unhappy marriage with which this book deals does not rest only on a wrong choice, but, more deeply, on the problem of marriage for an artist altogether. It raises the question whether an artist or thinker—that is, a man who not only wants to live life instinctively but also wants to represent it as objectively as possible—whether such a person is even capable of marriage.[7]

Focusing on the problem of the book rather than on the life that produced it, Hesse professed to have no answer, but in life he soon removed himself from the scene of the family illness. In an undated letter to his father that spring, Hesse described the itinerary of his journey later that month, to Lake Constance (also to see his old dentist), then to Italy for two or three weeks, especially to the vicinity of Florence. On April 4, he sent Adis fond greetings from Bergamo. Later in the summer he expected to take Mia and the children to the mountains.

The uncertainties of the child and schoolboy, those counterpoints of his written work, were soon put to their severest test as the war, which began that summer, engulfed Hesse along with the entire world. When the "guns of August" sounded in 1914, Hesse's feelings were already attuned to the disaster.

II

Then came the summer of 1914, and suddenly everything looked different, inwardly and outwardly. It became evident that our former well-being had rested on insecure foundations, and accordingly there now began a period of misery, the great education. The so-called time of testing had come, and I cannot say that it found me better prepared, worthier, or superior to anyone else. What distinguished me from others at that time was only that I lacked the great compensation so many others possessed: enthusiasm.[8]

At the age of thirty-seven, an artist who loved peace, yet who was deeply concerned about his role as a citizen and writer, Hesse found that the war subjected his indecisiveness to its severest test. His repugnance at the slaughter was genuine. In "Life Story Briefly Told," which was written years later, in 1925, he emphasized his lack of enthusiasm and described, with ironic contempt, how the life of an enthusiastic old lady had been given meaning by the war—caring for the wounded.[9] But he also applied to the German embassy as a volunteer, only to be told to wait for his age group to be called to the colors. He did not, then, place himself beyond the pale of the German establishment as real antiwar refugees like Leonhard Frank or his close friend of the twenties Hugo Ball had done, who were then gathering in Zurich and Bern. Rather, Hesse took both steps at once, denouncing the war with one stroke of his pen and supporting it, however reluctantly, with the other. As he had done when he was a schoolboy, he made a point of his subversive convictions, but at the same time he wanted to be accepted by those in authority, whether they were parents, or school, or the government. There was always the misdeed and the need for forgiveness, for the saving goodnight kiss.

His first gesture—mild perhaps but outspoken in the atmosphere of the war hysteria—was taken in a brief feuilleton piece published in the *Neue Zürcher Zeitung* on November 3, 1914, which was promptly picked up by about twenty German newspapers. "O Friends, Not These Tones" ("O Freunde nicht diese Töne") was actually a rather diffident complaint addressed to journalists on both sides of the war. The title was taken from Schiller's "Ode to Joy," which forms the final chorus of Beethoven's Ninth Symphony, but the message was an appeal to all scribblers to mute their voices. Hesse asked them to consider the obvious bond that transcends belligerency: a common humanity formed by Shakespeare, French poetry, and German music. The sentiment was not only mild and diffidently expressed; it was also nonactivist, indeed, nonpolitical, for whatever pacifist sentiments were voiced were channeled into comments about literature and art.[10] And yet the reaction, especially in Germany, was surprisingly strong. Newspapers were indignant, and old friends, as Hesse said wryly in his "Life Story Briefly Told," decided that they had "nurtured a viper in their breasts."[11] He was deluged with angry anonymous letters, an experience that was then relatively new to him, but which was to repeat itself in ever increasing volume for the rest of his life.

Yet the ambivalence remained. The same pen that had written the feuilleton for the *Neue Zürcher Zeitung* had written very differently to his father two months earlier. Although Hesse deplored the slaughter, he hoped, now that it had started, that there would be a revolution in India or sudden disaster for the British fleet, for "if that happens, and Austria manages to survive, Germany would have the principal voice at the peace conference, and, as a result, there would be some hope for the survival of life and culture for the immediate future." Otherwise, "England would be on top and then Europe would be left in the hands of those moneybags and the illiterate Russians."[12] In short, European culture would have to be practiced in secret. These feelings about the need for a German victory, now that war had started, did not necessarily contradict a dislike for the war as such, but they suggest that his appraisal of the international situation in 1914 was not too different from the view Thomas Mann expressed in his notorious *Reflections of a Non-Political Man*. They were standard rationalizations for those who believed in the official German position that the Central Powers were fighting a war of survival not only for themselves but for European culture as a whole.

It is easy to see how both sentiments—antiwar and patriotically German—could exist side by side in the mind of a man who was torn by a conflict between critique and acceptance of authority. Hesse continued his childhood practice of wanting to be iconoclastic and approved at the same time. Again, a passage in "Life Story Briefly Told" illuminates this uncertainty. In commenting on the fact that his antiwar feuilleton had been misunderstood, Hesse linked it with a crucial moment in his adolescence; he called the anger and misunderstanding he aroused in the winter of 1914 the "second great transformation" of his life. "The first transformation," he wrote, ". . . took place at the instant when I recognized my determination to become a poet. The hitherto model pupil Hesse became a bad pupil, he was punished, expelled . . . he caused himself and his parents one worry after another—all because he saw no possibility of reconciliation between the world as it happens to be or seems to be and the voice of his own heart." All this, he continued, repeated itself during the war years: he was again "in conflict with a world with which [he] had until then lived in complete contentment."[13] If one glances back over the last two years in Bern and, earlier, to the journey to India, or to Hesse's state of mind in Gaienhofen that had prompted him to take the trip and to move to Bern in the first place, one senses the oncoming weight of his real and imagined isolation. But his words expressed a greater fear. Total rejection and full acceptance were both at stake at a moment when a crisis in the world was reflected as a crisis within.

Letters to friends during the first war year gave a good indication of his divided feelings. Good friends like the painter Otto Blümel and others had by then been inducted into the army. Hesse wrote them long letters, congratulating them on their decorations, making them feel that their service was worthwhile and admirable. He himself had to undertake another trip to the border town of Lörrach to present himself for service in the *Landsturm* (as second-line units composed of men in their thirties were called), only to be again rejected for reasons of health. He acted properly as a German citizen abroad and, on the surface at least, did not use his permanent residence in neutral Switzerland as a way of protesting the war or refusing service.[14]

His correspondence, like his actions, reflected Hesse's divided position. A few days after the feuilleton had appeared, he wrote a close friend, the Swiss cigarette manufacturer Emil Molt, that he "felt wholly with Germany" and comprehended the overpowering spirit of nationalism fully, although he could not quite share it. For since he lived abroad he felt distant from the great psychosis. Although he agreed that this rage and psychosis were necessary for Germany to fight the war, he could not find it splendid or the harbinger of a golden future. Expressing his international sentiment—based on his father's origin as a German living in Baltic Russia, his maternal grandmother's origin in French Switzerland, and his own life divided almost equally between a Swabian and a Swiss home—Hesse sought to strike a fair balance between the German patriotism he felt was required of him as a citizen and his antiwar feelings.[15]

Hesse could also sound a different note. In a letter to a Swiss friend, the composer and conductor Volkmar Andreä, he seemed to attribute to the war an ethical, almost a metaphysical, value, which one might have found in the writings of a cultured Junker. Andreä had been serving a tour of duty as a Swiss officer when the war broke out. Hesse wrote at length about the feelings he and other civilians shared that summer when the guns first opened up, an experience Andreä had passed up in the isolation of his army camp. Now he had to sense it anew. But what was this sense? "German as I am, and feel that I am," Hesse wrote, "nationalism has always also signified a certain education for the ideal of humanity." Hence, the modern state with its laws of conscription, "has become one of those points of crisis when sense becomes nonsense and acts fatally." Yet, he said also: "I esteem the moral values of war on the whole rather highly. To be torn out of a dull capitalistic peace was good for many Germans and it seems to me that a genuine artist would find greater value in a nation of men who have faced death and who know the immediacy and freshness of camp life."[16] Although little of value would flow from war directly, he felt certain that, as a whole, culture would not be destroyed by it.

In this divided state of mind, Hesse entered the new year 1915, skiing with Mia in Gstaad. Unfortunately she had a bad fall and hurt her knee, which left her in some pain for several months. Meanwhile, Hesse's problematic stand affected his life and his ability to work. Early in January he wrote angrily to Theodor Heuss that he would not interfere with the editorial policies of *März*, whose antiwar stand had been softened in response to current war hysteria, as long as they agreed to place some of his reviews so that "something will be audible above the din and the sabre-rattling." Similarly, he also attacked the change of policy of his beloved humor magazine *Simplizissimus*, which Ludwig Thoma had led into the prowar camp as well. He could no longer take it seriously, he wrote, and, if this cultural nonsense continued, he might decide to become a Swiss citizen. Hesse's conflicting loyalties were in suspense.[17] For while he often fluctuated in response to the war, he also underwent a gradual development, which started out with the recognition that for him the outer crisis of the world and the inner crisis of the self were intertwined. "Before long I found myself obliged to seek the cause of my sufferings not outside but inside myself," he wrote in "Life Story Briefly Told."[18]

If Hesse suffered from the violent condemnation he received from the German press following his feuilleton about the war, he was also rewarded with the discovery of a new friend. Two months later he received an enthusiastic letter from the pacifist French writer Romain Rolland, who was then living in Geneva. "Your essay in the *Neue Zürcher Zeitung* came to my attention," Rolland wrote in French in February 1915, "and I shake your hand cordially. I have wanted to do this for a long time, ever since I started to read your books, but especially since I heard spoken once more, above all this torment, those words that dissipate the clouds of hate, the words of Beethoven Redeemed." While he agreed that they could do nothing to stop the "furor of the nations," he felt that therefore it was even more necessary for those who have "undertaken the guardianship of the European spirit" to reaffirm their ties with one another and to reject the "bestial folly of the war." And in a postscript he asked whether Hesse had any connections with the antiwar periodical *Weisse Blätter*.[19]

This letter, as Hesse has often written, was the single kind word spoken in a chorus of hatred and contempt. Although he continued to have many friends with whom he remained in contact, official rejection was uniformly depressing. The sales of his books in Germany dropped dramatically as booksellers began to refuse to display them. For all these reasons, it was a relief to have found a "companion on the road," someone who, like himself, "had been sensitive to the bloody nonsense of the war and its war psychosis and had stood up against it."[20] Yet Hesse also distanced himself from involvement in a pacifist cause. His response to Rolland on February 28, 1915—in German—treated his inquiry about *Weisse Blätter* with caution. He wrote that he had no personal connection with that journal but that he told the editor of Rolland's interest, "There is much raw youth there, but also good-willed noble youth." He also mentioned that an international review for the exchange of ideas and mutual understanding among intellectuals divided by the war was being planned. His comments are interesting, for they show his way of removing himself from active involvement: "I was offered the editorship of this journal," Hesse wrote, "and there was some hope among the editors to win your collaboration, too. [But] *I am a quiet lyricist who is not activist enough for this sort of thing*." Hesse's place was taken by a Swiss-German professor named Hans Haeberlin, but the venture never got off the ground.[21]

By the summer of 1915, while Hesse was still a civilian in Switzerland, he had already made a place for himself to help in the emergency in a manner consonant with his uncertain attitude toward the war. Uppermost in his mind was some service that might be rendered to German war prisoners in France. This "service" was soon to blossom into a mail order library for prisoners of all ranks who were supplied with books and reading material originating from an office in Bern that had collected this material from donors all over the German-speaking world. A letter sent to his lawyer and friend Conrad Haussmann in July 1915 evidently formed the beginning of this project, which may perhaps have already had the blessings of the German government. A gentleman from Paris would be by chance in Switzerland on a certain date, and Hesse wondered whether Haussmann would care to come over at the same time to discuss the possibility of the prisoner service.[22]

Meanwhile, Hesse's relationship with Rolland grew into an important experience. They shared similar interests and a sense of working together for similar ends. Nor was this relationship one-sided. Rolland wrote in his memoirs of these years, *Au dessus de la mêlée (Above the Struggle)*, that of all German writers Hesse was practically the only one who "maintained a truly Goethean attitude during this demonic war."[23] And when they finally met in August, the cordiality of their face-to-face encounter reflected that bond. Rolland, who was then staying in Thun, announced his desire to visit on August 9. Hesse answered the next day and invited him to supper with great warmth. Several people interested in peace wanted to see Rolland, Hesse said, but he wanted him for himself. Some reluctance to be involved crept into even this note: "For myself, I am quite unpolitical and am attached to an Asian passivity."[24] Rolland agreed that he was not inclined to meet political people. He, too, was surfeited with political life. "For several weeks and months," he answered, "I have retreated into art. I have to regroup my forces in that realm and breathe pure air."[25]

The visit came off well. Mia entertained the two men with tea and supper, and they conversed deeply despite their language difficulties. A short while later, Rolland decided to leave Switzerland, but he made clear that the evening at the Hesses was among his finest memories. "The hours I spent at the Melchenbühlweg are a dear memory. I shall see you often in my thought. I press your hand affectionately . . . when one thinks that the barbaric law of nations will make enemies out of us."[26] This pleasure at their meeting is echoed in the privacy of Rolland's diary that August. Their letters had crossed, however, for on the same day, August 24, 1915, Hesse had dispatched a note to his correspondent in which he told him that his age group had finally been called up.[27]

Meanwhile Hesse had firmed up his relationship with the German embassy. He was put in touch with a zoologist, Dr. Richard Woltereck, who had been running a zoological testing station in Positano, Italy, as an expert in reptiles. Now Woltereck moved to Bern and soon became a frequent visitor at Melchenbühlweg where the two men mapped out their plans. Aided by the International Red Cross, their office designed to supply German war prisoners with literature was made an extra-territorial section of the embassy, at first with some independence. Woltereck handled organization and politics, but much of the actual work was done by Hesse, who wrote to his friends and acquaintances throughout Germany, Austria, and Switzerland requesting gifts of books, grammars, dictionaries, and other material that he then sent on to imprisoned soldiers.

It became a momentous task. Book lists were carefully drawn up and separated according to recipients' education and class. They collected books suitable for workers, businessmen, students, even scholars and scientists. Later that year Hesse also began to publish a biweekly newspaper, the *Sunday Messenger for German Prisoners*, and later on started his own small publishing venture, *Library for Prisoners*, which produced cheaply printed and bound books on various subjects to be sent to individual prisoners who asked for them as well as to libraries in French prison camps. There were also additional tasks to perform. In a chatty letter written early in August, he told Adis that rather than being inducted into the army or working as a war correspondent, he would be "used here politically." Partly it would be within an organization for the care of prisoners of war, but it would also include something else (he added mysteriously) about which he had to be silent. Hesse's lack of involvement, therefore, did not quite extend to the German authorities. He did not turn himself into an exile, but rather entered into the ambiguous life of a German civilian functionary in a neutral capital.

Early in September the call-up date arrived. Hesse had taken Mia on a "last" trip into the mountains before he again took the train to Lörrach to present himself for service. On the ninth, he wrote his friend Emil Molt: "Not inducted!"[28] He had failed the test for reasons of health and had been given a furlough until mid-November as well as permission to return to Switzerland. Thus freed, he joined Woltereck on a business trip to Germany to make further arrangements for the *Center for the Care of Prisoners* in Bern. They traveled through Baden and Württemberg and Hesse was able to stop off in Stuttgart to see some of his friends and relatives and to meet with officials in Munich.

They returned before the end of the month and soon Hesse delivered himself of an essay about his impressions. Called "Back in Germany," it was published in the *Neue Zürcher Zeitung* on October 10, 1915. On the whole the article was a very innocuous piece of writing, in the well-wrought lyrical style that was Hesse's trademark at the time, that conveyed a rather noble impression of wartime Germany. "Everything has become different after all; it is more serious, heavier, more thoughtful and yet at the same time simpler, more self-understood. . . . One sees how serious people have generally become as they go their way, resigned and thoughtful." Country girls, who came to visit their uniformed lovers or brothers in the city, were not lively or flirtatious, but serious, sometimes in tears, silent without the usual excited gestures. "In short, I found from the first hour that the stories told to me by so many have been confirmed: Germany has become different, Germany is more silent, more dignified, more serious, and more mature. And that does not seem oppressive, as one might fear, but beautiful, even noble."

Hesse appeared mostly approving and deeply sympathetic. True, he allowed himself a few asides about the silly practice of expunging French names and words from street signs, buildings, or people's speech, and there were a few other remarks that might have been considered faintly critical. But these were very minor points in a most understanding essay about his country at war. Hesse sought to convey to the German-speaking readers of that influential Swiss newspaper a sense of a large nation seriously occupied with a common national tragedy and held together by a common national bond. Yet the outcry this essay unleashed rivaled and indeed surpassed in intensity the outcry in response to his article about the wartime press the year before.[29]

The abuse heaped on Hesse, on this as on the previous occasion, was, paradoxically, the result of his uncertainty. Had he been a real exile, an émigré writing subversively against the war, a deserter from the service, his words would have been dismissed as treason and trash. But Hesse was a force to be reckoned with, a man who held a position of some import-ance as a well-known writer, who was well connected by marriage with Swiss society, and who had maintained his ties with the German military and political leadership as well. His position as *Auslandsdeutscher*—a German abroad—set him as apart from jingoism as from its opposite. As he put it to Adis in August, he therefore pleased no one in Germany. However sympathetic his view of the German world at war may have been, his article did not conceal its emphasis on the suffering, on the national tragedy, on the warmth of togetherness among people struck by an identical fate. It did not celebrate the heroism of battle. He treated the war as a disaster that brought out the noblest instincts, but not as an opportunity for martial enthusiasm.

This sensible point of view was buttressed by the ending of the essay. Here the departing son of wartime Germany stepped across the border into neutral Switzerland feeling genuine relief. Evidently this remark, and the opening paragraph suggesting a preference for peace over war, ignited the indignation of the German public.

The article began:

> I had not been back in Germany for a long time. At first external forces held me back, then as the war went on and I approached the age of those eligible for service I had to fear that I would not be allowed back after a visit over there. When finally the induction notice came I had long since undertaken a piece of work in the service of war prisoners in con-junction with various Swiss organizations and was no longer required to exchange this more beautiful and peaceful task for a warlike one.[30]

The expressions "fear" (of not being allowed back) and the "more beautiful and peaceful task" in preference to a warlike one did not escape the notice of German editors who were particularly displeased because the article had appeared in the *Neue Zürcher Zeitung*—a paper con-sidered hostile to the German cause. Within two weeks an angry article appeared in the *Kölner Tageblatt*, which seized on this introductory paragraph to accuse Hesse of draft dodging. After quoting Hesse's own first paragraph (italicizing "damaging" words) the Cologne paper de-clared:

> Thus no one less than the well-known writer *Hermann Hesse*, the much praised author of *Peter Camenzind*, begins an essay on his impressions while traveling in Germany in the *Neue Zürcher Zeitung*. Every honest German must blush with shame, when he hears that in the time of his

nation's greatest need—a time when older German poets like Dehmel, Bloem, Löns stand up for their fatherland weapons in hand and joyfully give their blood for its cause—a heretofore celebrated German "knight of the spirit," can actually boast of *shirking* [his duty] and of his *sly cowardice* and can actually make fun of his success in hoodwinking his country and its laws during this great time. . . .

The article focused entirely on this introductory statement and ignored Hesse's sensitive description of wartime Germany. It made that ill-considered introduction into an accusation and then included other utterances by Hesse in which he declared that he could not adjust to the war and that he hoped Germany would be as successful in its spirit as it had been with its arms. With venom and anti-Semitic overtones, the editor's diatribe culminated in these words:

Not like a knight of German spiritual nobility, like Ewald von Kleist, Körner, or Löns, but like the *knight of the mournful countenance* of a d'Annunzio-Rappaport, thus the shirker Hermann Hesse wanders along, a fellow without a country who has long since shaken the dust of his homeland's earth from his shoes.[31]

This outburst had two distinct implications for Hesse's life and for his later work. One was the surprising echo this article found in Germany, which once more shocked and amazed him. Respectable journals, even in his native Swabia, reprinted the article in full, and it added to the damage done by the feuilleton "O Freunde nicht diese Töne" of the previous year. Already for some time past Hesse had had to defend his position toward the war in important German newspapers like the *Frankfurter Zeitung* without expressing a decisively pacifist point of view. His stand toward the war—even though he remained correct in his dealings with the German government and his obedience to military laws—was clearly unconventional and at least questionably "patriotic." But though his defense of martial virtues had been revised, he retained a real sense of identity with the German cause. This sense of identity as a German, and as a German writer, which he preserved even after he settled permanently in Switzerland and became a Swiss citizen in the twenties, made Hesse henceforth particularly vulnerable to attack, for it implied that to some extent at least he felt that he had to share the values of those who reviled him. The second implication concerned Hesse himself and his own response to the attack made upon him.

Hesse responded to the "outrage" of the attacks in the German press by mobilizing his friends. It became a *cause célèbre*. If he had rested his case upon his pronouncement alone, if he had pointed out only that he had viewed the war in tragic terms and had not entered into the controversy about his draft dodging, he would have been, in a sense, invulnerable. As it turned out, however, he felt forced to enter into his opponents' arguments with lengthy denials of the charge that he had evaded service. His friends wrote articles in his defense in various newspapers—Theodor Heuss in the Heilbronn *Neckar-Zeitung* on November 1; Conrad Heussmann the next day in the Stuttgart *Beobachter*. Both pointed out the "quiet nobility" of Hesse's perception of wartime Germany, but they also laid heavy stress on his devotion to the prisoners and on the correctness of his dealings with the army. They tried to prove that Hesse was not a "fellow without a country," but that, on the contrary, he was an active member of the German community.[32] Hesse's own reply in the *Neue Zürcher Zeitung* on November 1 branded the attack as "slanderous," and indeed the whole episode has since entered the annals of Hesse's history as the "Cologne calumny."[33]

Hesse's view of this affair was succinctly expressed in a postcard he wrote to Adis on November 2 in which he announced yet another trip to Germany. "Please don't be frightened," he urged, "by the stupid slanderous article that is circulating at present. A full defense that will compel a retraction of all allegations is under way. The authorities, headed by the German minister here, protect me fully and I have just received a declaration of their complete confidence."[34] Citing the fact that he had volunteered for service at the outbreak of the war, he declared that it was vile enough to make him grow gray hair but not vile enough to shake him or to interfere with his work. He asked that this message be conveyed to their father, whom he hoped to visit briefly on his forthcoming trip. He also asked that the slander be refuted and that the denial be brought to the attention of any friends or acquaintances who had heard of it. Actually, Hesse received the supportive statement from the German ambassador the next day. It certified that he had volunteered for service and had responded to each call-up punctiliously. Finally, the ambassador declared over his personal signature that Hesse was doing excellent service for the German prisoners in France and was even publishing a newspaper for them along with other meritorious work.[35]

This incident, which looms larger than it deserves because of the war hysteria of the time and Hesse's own exaggerated reaction, documents the uncertainty that weighed down his actions and decisions. Whether after the formality of volunteering (and being promptly rejected) in 1914 his continued civilian status was entirely due to his bad eyes or at least partly to his Swiss connections may be a matter of debate, but it does not enter into the article that had aroused the Cologne editor's ire. Hesse simply expressed pleasure at being occupied with the welfare of prisoners in neutral Switzerland rather than with guns on the western front. One might call this preference dodging service or one might view it as a higher service to his country. The nationalistic editor had evidently taken the first point of view, but given his bias and the evidence of Hesse's text, there was nothing slanderous in his allegation. It was only nasty.

Hesse confronted a choice. If he had wished to firm up his position by defying these German attacks, his introductory paragraph would have been quite in order and the predictable consequences just one more cross to be borne. But if that interpretation concerned him, as the excitement generated by the "Cologne calumny" proved, he should have revised the paragraph. These apparent quibbles about an unimportant text gain serious significance for an understanding of Hesse's manner of living and writing. He complained of being misunderstood and blamed it on people's inability to comprehend a middle-of-the-road position. Yet there were many people—not the least his new friend Romain Rolland—who fathomed that point of view and supported it. Hesse was inordinately concerned about what "people" said about him, but he suffered especially when he was reviled by those who were his rightful opponents. He wanted their tacit acceptance, or at least admiration, as well.

The uproar about the "Cologne calumny" foreshadows another "slander" thirty years later when Hesse's wartime silence during the Second World War came under attack from the other side of the political spectrum, from anti-Nazi German émigrés, and his response as an old man was equally frantic and severe. Both incidents relate to a great need to live, and to be accepted, in contradictory worlds. In the Second World War as in the First, Hesse was concerned with maintaining a neutral position, opposed to any kind of organized action; in both cases (whether the attack came from the left or the right) he had been deeply intent upon maintaining a firm or at least neutral relationship with established authority despite his deviating views. His ties with the German government and embassy during the first war led him to fight the editor's "slander." During the Second World War, his lack of active involvement in the opposition to Germany saved his books from condemnation for a long time but also rendered him vulnerable later on.

Another controversy, which occurred during the same month of November, underlines Hesse's need to shore up his defenses in every direction and therefore to draw fire from every quarter as well. Having offended the "patriots," he felt the need to prove that he was not subversive. Whether by coincidence or design, he composed an article hostile to the pacifists that appeared on November 7 in the Viennese daily *Die Zeit*, just at the time his slanderers in Germany were making their official retractions. This article was as ambiguous in one direction as the article that had offended the Cologne editor had been in the other. Part of the time Hesse dwelt on his convictions about the ideal of peace, about which he was as lyrical as he had been about Germany's wartime spirit in the earlier article. But he also attacked Pacifist organizations frontally for not living in "a real world," for giving money, writing pamphlets, and delivering speeches, while there was real suffering everywhere.

This riposte could be explained as another instance of Hesse's active dislike for any organization, but his praise of the war, and its spirit of sacrifice, his expression of regret for not being able to do justice to the war spirit as a civilian, went considerably further. Though war was terrible, he wrote, it had its place as a means to an end. It would be easy as well to dismiss this response merely as further evidence that he could not coherently hold a point of view offensive to his father, family, and the authority of the state he still served. It may also be that he genuinely felt both the great spirit of peace and international brotherhood he conveyed to Rolland and the front line soldier's suffering, his derisive view of pacifists as international do-gooders with which he also did not like to be identified.[36]

Hesse's private correspondence with his family and with friends like Stefan Zweig and Romain Rolland continued to be filled with assertions about the wastefulness and terror of guns, bombs, and torpedoes. At the same time his service to the prisoners could never have been as effective if he had lacked empathy with the life of German soldiers in the field—men who were after all his contemporaries, and their younger brothers, who were now facing death, wounds, or imprisonment. An open Christmas letter to the troops of Württemberg, published in the *Stuttgarter Neue Tagblatt* on December 25, 1915, suggests the pendulum swinging in his mind between a rejection of the war and an awareness of its implications of heroic suffering. Toward the end of the article, after suggesting that those at home had now come to understand the soldiers' life more fully, he wrote:

Everything has now become a little different for all those of us who take our fatherland and its future seriously. We think of you no differently; in fact, we are even more grateful and understand the value of your holding out far more deeply. And we ourselves, who at first were just private people who had remained without specific tasks, have also been gradually mobilized, each from within himself in accordance with his powers and his passion. We have recognized duties and have taken them over; we no longer live for ourselves, for our advantage and our comfort, but for the community—for that which you are defending at the front with your arms.[37]

These words are not those of a skeptic. Indeed, the mere fact that Hesse had decided to write this "open letter" to the troops suggests that he felt moved—from guilt as well as from caution—to expunge even the possibility of being identified as an opponent of the war or as an insensitive shirker of wartime duties from the consciousness of his public. He gained a full sense of the war's uselessness only after further suffering.

At this point, on the threshold of 1916, Hesse felt alone and reviled wherever he turned, but he was also sufficiently acclaimed to be asked to write open letters to soldiers in the field and to be sought out for advice. In the midst of these contrary currents he felt isolated yet strangely "pure." In a revealing passage about his wartime activities in "Life Story Briefly Told" he related that his very suffering and his obsession with isolation acted as a shield against the outside world. Politics, bribery, espionage from all sides went on around him, directed at him even without his knowledge, a fact he discovered only after the war. The preservation of "purity" among the informers, diplomats, political agents, spies, journalists, war profiteers, and crooks with whom Hesse had to deal in wartime Bern reflects his constant desire to uphold that "pure self" as the neutral ground absorbing contradictory currents and passions to re-create them in a new consciousness or imagination. On a more practical level, it also gives an inkling of the complexity of Hesse's mind and of the diverse roles he sought to perform.

Working for "his" prisoners was one way of dealing with his own difficult life. The work was most suitable to his needs, for it reflected the contrast between his opinions expressed to Romain Rolland and his indignant response to the "Cologne calumny" and the pacifists in Vienna. But the vituperative German zealots did not cease their attacks, nor were they appeased, for they brooked no questioning. Hesse continued to suffer. At the same time, his personal life became more difficult. His child's illness, which had been a source of distress before the war, was never fully cured even after the crisis had passed. Mia's depressions grew more severe, as the war years in the Welti house passed slowly and she was very much alone, burdened with the children, while her husband was shut away with his war work. During the early months of 1916 the crisis about both the war and his domestic life, which had been building up gradually during the past two years, seemed to become more severe. "For months," he wrote Romain Rolland in January, "I've had no private life." He had suffered more than his share of hostility since they had seen each other the previous summer, and he had now lost himself completely in his work. "I am supplying German prisoners with reading matter and have had to learn all manner of work I've never had to do before. My home has become an office and I no longer even know my garden."[38]

This sense of being overworked and at bay communicated itself to Hesse in headaches and eyestrain. He was also always concerned about army service. At the end of January he reported to the painter Otto Blümel that in addition to all kinds of aches and pains in head, stomach, and intestines, he had again just returned from Lörrach where he had undergone another physical examination and had been asked to report back in March.[39] In addition to this uncertainty about his future, his job changed significantly. The German government evidently decided to exercise tighter control, for on March 1, 1916, he reported to Erwin Ackerknecht that the Book Center had now become directly connected with the German embassy and the German War Ministry, though he and Woltereck would continue to run it. He thanked Ackerknecht for books received and expressed the hope that there would be more. But one week later, a severe shock broke into this routine. On March 8 his father was dead.

Plagued by headaches, almost blind, the sixty-nine-year-old Johannes Hesse had been living in Kornthal with his unmarried daughter Marulla since leaving their home in Calw shortly before the war. This small Swabian town, where Marie Hesse had gone to school and where she had met her first husband, Charles Isenberg, was situated in a valley at the foot of the Black Forest mountains. Hesse visited him frequently during those years after his move to Bern in 1912—as often as he could find time to come to Germany—and they continued to correspond as regularly as they had done during Hesse's years in Gaienhofen. Although Johannes could barely see, his mind was sharp, and he told his son a great deal of his early life as a missionary, which enhanced their closeness.

In many respects, father and son had become more and more alike. Physically, the old man's white flowing beard covering his thin frame made him appear rather different from his son, but his incessant headaches, eye troubles, insomnia, and insatiable curiosity about everything around him reinforced the urgent style in which they talked. At least this is the way Hermann Hesse remembered his father when he heard the news of his death. They had last seen one another in January, he remembered, when his father had tried to teach him a game with Latin phrases to get over his insomnia. Now all the son could feel was guilt. Only the week before he had written his father a careless postcard, complaining of overwork and promising a "good letter" soon. Remembering this note became for him more than a triviality. It became symbolic of that which was irretrievable, never to be recaptured. The pacifist dilemma, still unsolved, turned into a personal crisis.

III

Bern, March 19, 1916

Dear Herr Dr. Ackerknecht,

. . . Your package with grammars and dictionaries were waiting for me upon my return. My very best thanks.

My father's sudden death, overwork for some time, a bad cold, the arduous trip back across the frontier, made me feel very run down so that I have worries. . . .

The crisis had come unexpectedly. On March 8, 1916 Hermann Hesse was standing on the station platform in Basel. As he told it in his brief memoir, "In Remembrance," Hesse was about to get on a train when a friend approached him and asked him not to leave.[40] For a moment Hesse was puzzled and demurred, but the friend put his arm around his shoulder and led him back into the station. He had just received a wire from Mia in Bern (which Hermann had left just that morning) asking him to intercept her husband before he took the train to Zurich. The telegram announcing that Johannes Hesse had died had arrived at Hesse's home shortly after he had left.

Numb, Hesse thought only of the details to be taken care of before he could get back to Württemberg inside that country at war. He had to go back to Bern quickly to transact the necessary formalities for a renewed border crossing. Did he have an adequate black suit? When was the next train he could take? But in the midst of these mechanical thoughts, while he was already in the train that was taking him back to Bern, his thoughts groped toward an awareness that Hesse later caught in an image:

Now and then a half-awakened consciousness of my loss rose oppressively and took my breath away and hurt inside my head, behind my eyes. Then I tried to pull myself together and with intense concentration sought to reproduce a picture of the deceased within myself. But it never appeared bright and true. The only good feeling that breathed within me for moments with any purity and consolation was this: he is well off; he has his rest; he is where he longed to be. Then I recalled times When I had known my father ill—ill and tormented by endless pain, and suddenly I did see his picture distinctly, too sharply, with his dear moving, pain-filled gesture, as breathing deeply he pushed his long hair from his temples while his eyes rested upon me, still and sadly, as if coming from foreign shores. And now I sensed, again, at least, his being within me, purely and distinctly, and I said to myself: "They have never understood him. Nobody. Not even all his friends. Only I understand him fully, for I am just like him, alone and understood by no one."[41]

Back in Bern, he took the streetcar for Ostermündigen, the suburb where they lived, keeping himself aloof and staring at the darkened window to watch his reflection. When he got to the end of the line, he found that Mia had walked across the fields to meet him and silently they returned together to the house. A brief glance at the mail, at the telegram on the hall table. . . . Then, after a long restless night, he spent an endless morning in various offices: at the German legation for his passport and permission to return, in Swiss government offices for return visas and similar formalities. The hours of waiting in the dusty, stuffy offices seemed interminable. Finally he was ready to leave. It was now early afternoon and his two older sons, eleven-year-old Bruno and seven-year-old Heiner, had just gotten out of school. He was able to say goodbye to them hastily before he had to return the same way he had come the night before. This time, however, he traveled to Germany. In Friedrichshafen, on Lake Constance, he got off, for there was no connection north that night. He spent the evening walking around the town, recalling his earlier years on the lake when he had tried to establish a stable life. Only when he sat down to eat his fish and to drink his wine did the sense of his immediate loss invade him again.

After a day spent mostly on trains winding through Black Forest valleys and another stopover, Hesse eventually reached Kornthal. Adis and Hans were at the station. They embraced, then walked together up the hill and entered the small house where Marulla was waiting. For a while, they sat together quietly, then Hermann went into the next room where their father's body was laid out among flowers. He sat down at the bedside and placed his hand where he had been often asked to place it—on his father's forehead. The sensation, as Hesse recalled it in his later memoir, produced a host of recognitions:

When, weeping, I kissed his hands and placed my own hands, warm with life, upon his stony forehead, I remembered how, in my boyhood days, when one of us came home with cold hands in the winter, he used to ask us to lay our hands on his forehead, just a little, for he was often afflicted with severe headaches that lasted for days. Now my restless warm hands were placed on his forehead, seeking coolness from him.

And all that was chivalrous and all that was superior and noble in his being was written in his face with exaggerated clarity and dignified like a silent snowcapped mountain. O Father, Father!

Hesse's account of this scene elaborates this image of coolness and perfection. The next day he was again alone with his father: "He still seemed to listen to the great peace, fervently, and a little surprised." His son became "wholly one with it" and "again cooled forehead and hands on this sacred fountain." Hesse found that "whatever hurt him was nothing compared to that great coolness." If he had been a bad son, and unworthy of his father, his soul would still be calmed and his restless pulse cooled. And he concluded: "If no other consolation could be found in the midst of all this suffering, it would always be this: my forehead, too, would be so filled with coolness and my senses, too, would thus flow into that which is essential."[42] The father's cold forehead, absorbing the pain and contradiction of life, yet separating them from ordinary existence through its crystalline detachment, became a significant counterpoint of stability for the restless, wandering impulse that haunted Hesse. It was an image that was to occur again and again— from the frozen body of dead Hermine in *Steppenwolf* to the detached smiling Music Master of *The Glass Bead Game*. Here, however, tone and imagery approach those of *Demian* and the fairy tales that were to take form from this simple memorial.

The intensity of Hesse's feelings cannot be measured by the sentimental pathos of his words. The very fact that the memoir was written, that he felt moved to take the arduous trip across the border and to sit, devotedly, at his dead father's bedside, is in itself significant, especially in view of his refusal, fourteen years earlier, to travel to his mother's funeral under far easier circumstances. His awareness of his father's significance after many years of anger, contempt, and a growing sense of his own importance became deeply intertwined with his sense of rootedness, of home. Hesse's need for his father after the failure of the Gaienhofen years did more than confirm the rapprochement they were able to achieve.

His father had become his route to stability, to the settled existence that had always eluded Hesse in the past. Now, separated from his German roots by the war, he held his father's wedding ring in his hand, which his brothers and sisters had given him. It seemed to him a symbol, a memorial of those roots that tied him not so much to Germany as a country as to his missionary family that had once been unified under the aegis of the Mission Institute in Basel. The ring had been originally given by Marie Hesse to her first husband, Charles Isenberg, and was then passed on to Johannes. Now it served as a bond between these families. In fact, in his memorial Hesse viewed it as an embodiment of a "secret knighthood" which he and his brothers and sisters held in common. It was like an order or *Bund* from which none of them could resign and which imposed on them a common duty of service.

Hesse's emotions at his father's deathbed in March 1916 were deeply connected with his sense of home and homelessness. Partly because of this feeling, partly too because of his self-appointed role as a prophet, which led his brothers and sisters to regard him as their leader, it was difficult for him to conceive of himself as stepping into his father's shoes. Hesse articulated this sense in concluding the memorial to his father with yet another image that recurred explicitly in *Demian*—that of the bird breaking out of its cage. While struggling against the thought, he also felt he had to accept rootlessness as part of the conflict of life. The fluctuations between a striving for home and the striving for freedom became hopelessly enmeshed with his awareness that at first his country, then his father, and eventually his wife and sons were being removed from him. The counterpoint of home to the freedom he sought became weak and indeterminate. Freedom was now equated with death:

Whosoever has set out on the road to maturity, cannot lose, only gain— until, some time, for him, too, the hour will come and he will find the cage open and with a last pounding of the heart will leave the land of the inadequate.

If one of our kind would search in the Bible and other books for a good proverb and slogan that says all and wants to say all, but that will still catch its most gracious glow in a mirror—such a one would find no better proverb anywhere than the verse of the psalm: "The rope is torn. The bird is free."[43]

An exhausted Hermann Hesse, wracked by coughs and headaches, returned home across the borders set up by the war. As he told an acquaintance on March 19, he had a difficult time getting back. One border, at Singen, had been closed, and it took him forty devastating hours to get across the frontier at Lörrach.[44]

Meanwhile, Hesse was again moving closer to a "crisis of nerves." Mia's gradual collapse, which was to lead eventually to her confinement in an institution, was only one of the more explicit ways in which the bonds of home were to be loosened. One side of the picture seemed to be hopelessly askew, and a sense of inner terror often engulfed him. He left on various trips and cures. Soon after his return from his father's funeral he went on a walking tour in Italian Switzerland. In a rather relieved letter to Adis he described how he was lying high on a rock in the mountains. Rucksacks were stuffed with food, which he and his friends shared that sunny day. But nothing really helped. The insecurity of his life, his wife's and child's sicknesses, and his father's death plunged him into a depression, and he had to look for a more drastic cure. On April 18 he wrote Erwin Ackerknecht that he had spent three weeks in Locarno and Brunnen searching for a cure and that he was now supposed to go to a private clinic. "My work goes on, of course. Only I had to let go of some of the mechanical work, something I should have done sooner." A short time later, Hermann Hesse entered a private clinic near Lucerne.

In most respects the "Kurhaus Sonnmatt" was no different from many of the other places where Hesse had been treated for his various inner and outer ailments. It was a large building, functioning as a hotel and a hospital with well-scrubbed white walls, strong dark beams, and balconies running around the building in the manner of Alpine architecture. It was perhaps too urban to be a Magic Mountain, but it was set aside in a splendid park, bathed, weather permitting, in sunlight that left its bright pools in the meadows and gardens around it. In these partly suburban, partly rural surroundings, Hesse was subjected to mild electric shocks, massaged, sunbathed, and protected. Reflecting on what he called his "crisis of nerves," he wrote a friend: "A crisis is coming on in which the physical is only of peripheral although symbolic significance."[45] Hesse felt reduced to a state of helplessness for the fourth time since adolescence: in his twenties in Basel; at thirty in 1907 when he was just moving into his house in Gaienhofen; in India when he was unable to face himself in an alien world; and now, following the death of his father, it was threatening again. Still, this time his malaise seemed more incisive and hopeless, for there was no stable situation that he could build and fortify—no house as in Gaienhofen in 1907; no family to return to as he still had after his failure in India in 1911. His home may have still been physically intact, but it appeared to be more and more insecure in its foundations.

The great change in this experience, which allowed Sonnmatt to become crucial in Hesse's life, was psychoanalysis. It was a revolutionizing encounter. This transformation, which produced the different texture of *Demian* and the books that followed it, came to Hesse in the person of an odd, heavyset young man who became his doctor. His name was Josef B. Lang, a student of Carl Gustav Jung, who was delighted to meet, and to attempt to heal, the well-known writer Hermann Hesse. Psychoanalysis was still very uncommon, and for Dr. Lang, this meeting must have appeared as a great opportunity. They were about the same age: Lang was thirty-three to Hesse's thirty-eight. He was withdrawn and physically overpowering, his large head resting on wide shoulders. Yet he reached out to Hesse with great intensity and with an apparent success that belied his hesitant exterior.

While Hesse was at Sonnmatt between the end of April and the end of May, with a return visit in early June, he had twelve analytic sessions with Dr. Lang, though later he visited his therapist in his Lucerne apartment where they met fifty more times. These early therapeutic meetings sometimes lasted up to three hours. They helped Hesse, though perhaps less because of the new psychoanalytic doctrine per se than because of the salutary presence of a friend who shared his inner life intimately and entered into his dream world. Feeling homeless, cut off, Hesse allowed himself to be guided into another world.

Dr. Lang's appeal to Hesse was very personal, as the quotations preserved from his diary, which refer to later stages of his therapy, have shown. But Hesse's condition, while difficult, did not entirely disrupt his life and work. He wrote letters to his sisters and friends, carried on his work partly by returning now and then to Bern, and altogether managed to combine his cure with continued activity. By July he was again fully at work, while he traveled to Dr. Lang in Lucerne on his psychoanalytic quest. "So far," he wrote Erwin Ackerknecht in a lengthy postcard, "I have unfortunately overcome nothing. Rather, I am still mostly stuck in my critical time, which began three months ago. By the way, I'm in treatment with a physician." But if the inner "revolution"—which by his testimony began during these months and continued into the following year—was not determined by the intellectual content of psychoanalysis but rather by his personal relationship with Josef Lang, his thought was nonetheless deeply affected by psychoanalytic theories which turned his work in fresh directions.

Hesse by then had read Freud, Stekel, Bleuler, and most notably Jung, whom he had also met at the time. Actually Jung's myths and archetypes led Hesse to reassess his past, his bonds with his father, mother, and grandparents, and their missionary work in the East as well as their connections with the Baltic. It linked his own search for symbols of his change—found in Persian and Indian gods and goddesses to whom he was led by Lang, and by his own researches inspired by him—to the conceptual framework of Jungian psychoanalysis, which gave him a rationale for his personal and social insights. It provided him with an intellectual home to replace the actual home he had lost and which he would soon leave. While his outward life became more and more difficult, Hesse's inner life gained in resilience and strength.

The great change was at least as much intellectual as it was personal. Hesse became more and more convinced that he must leave Mia and a life mired in contradictions. It is hard to fathom the degree to which he felt imprisoned and caught in those mental absences that left him helpless, yet pinned him down in the echoing halls of the Welti house. He needed an escape. At first this need was visible primarily in his work. Nature, art, and friendship, the major themes in most of his writings from *Hermann Lauscher* to *Knulp*, had exhausted themselves and could no longer help him in building a "home" in fresh surroundings. Something new was required that would nevertheless allow him to retain his ties with the past. "We shall try," Hesse wrote in his revealing postcard to Ackerknecht, "to overcome this time." By seeking his roots in the Asian "home" of his family, which he could accept emotionally even as he had to reject it physically, Hesse hoped to rediscover his new destiny. In the end it was to be only partially effective, but this turn of mind led him to a greater use of Eastern themes. The "bird was out of its cage" and Jungian psychoanalysis had helped him open it.

Although Hesse had been concerned with things Asiatic before, it was not until his "revolutionary" year of 1916–17 that he used the East intellectually to any large extent to break out of his romantic mold. There had been a few hints in *Gertrud*. The fairy tale "The Poet," which is about a Chinese sage, had been written as early as 1914. But basically the shift can be traced to the year of crisis that burst into the open with his father's death in March 1916. Most of his family who had been connected with India were now gone, but with the help of his analysis, Hesse built a new bridge by approaching it through his thought and his imagination. Moreover he retained an important link with the missionary Gunderts: his cousin, Dr. Wilhelm Gundert, who lived in Japan and was to give Hesse some crucial advice with *Siddhartha*. In 1916, however, the war was still very much with him and the need to reflect it on a larger canvas led him to utilize symbols of the East. *Demian* was the result.

While Hesse's personal life did not change at once, this was not true of his art. The "rules" had been altered and his outlook had become substantially different as he absorbed his psychoanalytic recognitions and linked them with symbols of his family's past. The successor of nature poets of his parents' generation, like Nikolaus Lenau or Hermann Löns, had turned in a fresh direction. Stefan Zweig pointed to this in his appreciation of Hesse in 1923 when he wrote of the "astonishing and important metamorphosis and deepening of [Hesse's] poetic nature." A real transformation had indeed taken place. At Christmastime he wrote to his Indian companion Hans Sturzenegger that he had been introduced to one further ingredient in his outlook and style. Thanking his friend for a painting of the beach of Penang, a scene he recalled from their unhappy journey, Hesse revealed he had also started to paint:

Do come to Bern some time. And when there is peace I will come to you and will frighten you by showing you some of my own pastel pictures. Since I no longer have time for writing and thinking, I have started to paint during my brief moments of free time and have picked up carbon and paintbrush for the first time in forty years. I won't be competition for you, for I don't paint anything in nature—only dreams.[46]

Later, in 1919 and 1920, Hesse took up landscape painting in earnest but at this point he mostly enjoyed drawing dreams, putting into practice some of the insights he had gained from Dr. Lang's Jungian therapy. All these elements combined in the fairy tales that he began in 1916. While it is difficult to say how much was imitation—how much, for example, he owed to expressionistic experiments that also began to be produced in increasing numbers at that time—there is little question that Hesse had made an internal decision to "paint his dreams" as part of his search for emotional salvation. This turn was the first concrete indication that Hesse looked toward a new style in his life and work. Before taking up paintbrush and canvas more completely three years later, however, he had to translate his dream "pictures" into his own medium, words.

Dr. Josef Lang's influence on Hesse during the year 1916–17 was considerable. They remained friends for life, and Lang functioned as Hesse's therapist many more times, although gradually their relationship was reversed and the analyst took on more and more the role of his patient's disciple. Intense feelings both separated and brought them together. These were expressed in Dr. Lang's diary, recorded after his sessions with his famous and difficult patient. Unfortunately, only a few entries have survived the zeal of Josef Lang's daughter, who destroyed all of his notebooks after her father's death in 1945. Even these fragments survived only because Hugo Ball had been allowed to quote a few excerpts from those notebooks. They are entries made four days in late October 1917 when Hesse was about to finish *Demian*.

Biblical in tone, Dr. Lang wrote on October 23: "You will hear the voice that calls out from the primordial depths of the earth" to proclaim the "Laws of the Dead" who shall be the harbingers of the New Era. Two days later, he rhetorically asked his patient: "Where are you today?" and then projected an image of himself, the therapist, as a laborer within Hesse's psyche, hammering to break the crust that prevents him from penetrating the ice of his patient's soul. "I seek to approach you in order to touch," ends this strange entry—a new means of breaking down the barriers between men. The third entry, of October 26, 1917, contains the most vivid and significant image. Dr. Lang refers to the psyche as a mine shaft: "I hammer within my mine shaft that encloses me and gives me no light that I do not radiate myself. You hear my hammering in the roaring within your ear. Your heartbeat is the hammering of my arms that long to be freed." In the final entry cited by Ball, of October 28, 1917, Dr. Lang hammered in his patient's mine shaft: "Some time you will understand and chisel out the rocks of your soul, the primordial signature of men which you must teach them: the tablets of the Law of what is to come."[47]

The therapist identified with the patient, the friend with the friend: their souls were compared to mine shafts in which they worked separately but through which they could meet if they managed to break down with gigantic hammers the walls that separated them. This strikingly physical way of portraying a mental state owes a good deal of its power to psychoanalytic energy and imagination. It is the type of imagery that began to filter into Hesse's work as he sought to portray inner experience in pictorial and dramatic terms.

In choosing just these entries for his book, Ball was suggesting a decisive change in Hesse's style. Hesse had told Hans Sturzenegger that he did not only wish to describe and report dreams, as he had done in all of his work since the 1890s, but to represent them. The romantic seer of external nature became the seer of an inner world as his eyes were turned inward. Realism, even poetic realism, was gone. Nature and art were not to be subjects but merely the techniques with which he would unlock an inner world. *Demian* and the fairy tales were the products of this new inward turn of hammering within the mine shaft of his soul.[48]

This new bent in Hesse's art was neither wholly new nor was it entirely without its external stimulus and influence. In many ways, he seemed to return to the symbolic imagery of *One Hour Behind Midnight* and the dream figures in *Hermann Lauscher*, as well as to the fairy tale motifs which he thought he had left behind in his novels of poetic realism that cemented his successful career of his second new life. Now that he was about to embark on his third new life, new winds of fashion were blowing, too. It was, after all, the beginning of the new avant-garde, the time of Dada and the Café Voltaire in nearby Zurich, and surrealism and expressionism were in the air. Dreams were becoming once more *de rigueur*, and symbolism in place of realism was coming back to the fore, as the reality of the war drawing to its denouement virtually called for its imaginative antithesis. It was Hesse's uncanny ability to perceive the new directions that were about to open up without ever wholly losing touch with the main body of taste, without becoming outré or prematurely embracing an avant-garde. The step from *Knulp* to *Demian* was not so large as it may have seemed. Instead of perceiving nature, the wanderer perceived hallucinations and dreams.

From late 1916 until the end of the following year transformations of great weight and importance occurred in Hesse's life that helped shape his new book. His personal suffering and the pressures of politics and war finally fashioned his work. "Dear Herr Rolland," he wrote his "fellow traveler" on August 4, 1917, "Your kind greetings have given me great pleasure. I have been constantly ill . . . and have sunk into loneliness." Indeed, in spite of the ministrations of Dr. Lang, his own condition seemed to have hardly improved. On one level his problems continued to be political. Hesse was changing in his attitudes toward the war, and although he continued to work for the prisoners, he felt more and more opposed to it. Moreover, his disillusionment not only with the war itself but with the inability of people like Rolland and himself to make themselves heard oppressed him. "The attempt," he wrote his friend, "to apply love to matters political has failed." Wherever possible he longed to transcend the actualities of the fleeting present and to reach toward the timeless. For even a concept of "Europe" transcending individual borders in a new family of the spirit had ceased to be an ideal: "As long as men kill each other under Europe's leadership, any classification of people must be suspicious." Again he looked for a solution outside the reality of his life. He projected a vision of Asia, which did not share Europe's common guilt: "I do not believe in Europe. I believe in humanity, only in the empire of the soul on earth in which all nations may share, an empire whose noblest embodiment we owe to Asia."[49]

Following this shift toward a more determined opposition to the war, Hesse's politics began to influence his work as well. His creative renewal led him to write polemical articles with an antiwar stand. They appeared under the pseudonym "Sinclair," which was also the name of the protagonist and putative author of *Demian*, and were reprinted in 1922 in the aftermath of the war under the title of *Sinclair's Notebook*. Among these essays can be found many prophetic statements. The short vignette "The European," for example, which suggested the superiority of the Asian over the Western man heralded Hesse's new, revised "romanticism." Written in January 1918, during an intensely productive period, it accompanied his attempt to refashion the form of the fairy tale to represent dreams and the inner life in the terms of his newly found insights based on Freud and Jung. "A Dream Sequence," "The Difficult Road," and especially "Iris"—all written between 1916 and 1917—joined his political commentaries to be set down in *Sinclair's Notebook* as the first harbingers of his third new life.

While Hesse was striving to find solutions in his art, his life in the Welti house steadily continued to deteriorate. His family, his marriage, all the trappings of his outward success began to crumble. It is no coincidence that his finest, most successful fairy tale, "Iris," described Mia tenderly, was dedicated to her, and symbolically presented his departure. The tensions between them became almost unbearable. The household stopped its regular routines, and the children had to be sent to stay more and more often in the households of friends and of Mia's sister Mathilde in Kirchdorf. Hesse's money had begun to dwindle under wartime pressures, while his obligations had increased.[50] Even financial prosperity, the outward sign of success, began to fade. He was impatient for a change, yet his war duties still kept him in Bern.

IV

These were the ingredients of the novel that was to make Hesse famous for the second time. They amounted to a fresh commitment to different perceptions, different forms, and different modes of action. *Demian* was yet another spiritual autobiography. The story of a boy and young man, torn between the need for the security of his home on the one hand and for freedom, sensuality, even crime outside the home on the other, had been Hesse's perennial theme. It also happened to be the theme he shared with most concerned adolescents, especially at that time near the end of the war. With an uncanny sense of identification with those trying to find themselves after the uncertainties of puberty, Hesse created from his life's arduous pilgrimage a symbolic biography that a whole generation in wartime Germany could make its own.

Four ingredients made this thinly disguised autobiography different from all those that had preceded it in Hesse's career. First, it was the turn toward the East as a way of iconically representing an interior world that changed the outward realism into an apparently more obscure but compellingly accurate way of representing the psyche. The awareness of its hero, Emil Sinclair, for example, that Cain rather than Abel was the Elect, the man who can transcend the simple dichotomy of good and evil, or the gnostic Abraxas myth in which good and evil are combined, propel the reader into an internal landscape in which conflicts can be apparently resolved.

The second ingredient is the painting of dreams. Sinclair drew and redrew the picture of his dream woman, Beatrice, until he saw in it his own longing and found strength to be himself. It almost does not matter whether this feminine image corresponds to Annette Kolb for whom he had once almost committed suicide—as the chronology of *Demian* as autobiography might indicate—or whether she is still, or once again, tinged by the memory of Elizabeth Laroche, who had been the "Beatrice" of his Basel days. She furnished, in any event, the imagery of his mind by which a sense of himself could be distilled as a painting.[51] This way of presenting an interior reality was intertwined with the third ingredient: psychoanalytic insights. Josef Lang appeared in the person of Sinclair's teacher Pistorius, who unlocked the secrets of the self. Given the role of a distracted but brilliant organist, this ultimate teacher hammers within the mine shaft of his pupil's soul. Pistorius leads Sinclair to those ancient yet living religions that presupposed Nietzsche's recommended leap to deeper insights across the boundaries between good and evil.

The final ingredient was the war and Hesse's changing attitude toward it. In the novel, his uncertainty served him well, because it was precisely his dual portrait of the war that contributed to the book's success. He was able to identify with his readers—both with their spiritual needs and commitments and their sense of betrayal and loss to paint a collective portrait of a wartime generation of the educated young born around 1900 who were still on the verge of adulthood in 1916–17. Hesse, of course, was not young, nor had he been a direct participant in the war, but his understanding of that generation was so deep that his readers thought of him as one of their own.

The forms Hesse used were not iconoclastic. The very progression of events in *Demian* from the childhood home, divided between light and dark, to the hallucinatory apotheosis in the midst of shellfire suggested the novel of education— the *Bildungsroman*. Emil Sinclair learned how to overcome the guilt and shame of his childhood and to achieve with the help of his school friend Demian (the daemon), the therapist (ostensibly the organist) Pistorius, and ultimately Demian's mother, Frau Eva, a new vision of himself transcending inner divisiveness, outer hostility, and war. He had become the "bird that had broken out of its shell." Engaged in a pilgrimage toward a "grail" of salvation, Sinclair suffered an almost fatal wound just when he had a concrete vision of all men being drawn into a large cave that turned out to be the womb of Mother Eve. He was finally saved in the hospital where a dying Demian bestowed on him his mother's saving kiss.[52]

Sinclair's efforts were rewarded, because his pilgrimage toward a new level of self-awareness was a quest that had succeeded. He *had* the expected vision. Both the novel of education and the quest were basic forms in Hesse's German tradition, but in this novel he gave them an inward turn. These forms did not just describe or portray a dream journey: they were a dream journey. They did not refer to hallucinatory visions: they literally painted these visions in words. They did not just refer to religious emblems and symbols that were precisely the opposite of Christian meanings of these same symbols and forms: they lived in them and acted them out in the texture of the book.

It was no small achievement for Hesse to have converted a simple, adolescent story into a serious novel about an interior pilgrimage toward salvation in a civilization of discontents. His power of empathy with the wartime generation was so great that he was able to show how the breakdown of one could be symptomatic of them all, and how the great collapse and renewal, in the perspective of 1917, was the collapse and renewal of an entire European generation. His own crisis at Sonnmatt in the spring of 1916 had given him the means of achieving this transformation. Since the pilgrimage was interior, this novel required a succinct memory of his own childhood and adolescence—from his striving for the circle of light of his family to those drunken days of Cannstatt—and his sense of identification with those who were now of the same age. It also required his new knowledge of psychoanalysis, the recognition that psychoanalysis itself is both a quest and an education for interior, symbolic goals. This recognition of the identity of the two quests, that of his novel and that of the psychoanalytic process, lent his experiences during the First World War a special weight. He did not have to have served as a front-line soldier to know the trauma of death, since that was the universal recognition shared by all during this time. He only had to have the sense of visualizing that recognition in concrete terms. Psychoanalysis had given him that ability, and for this reason his crisis of 1916 created a new method. Its effect on him was far more radical than any of his earlier episodes.

Demian was also written at a time when Hesse evidently renewed some of his contacts with the "guru" Gustav Gräser. This man and his commune had by then drawn the fire of the authorities not only in Germany but in neutral Switzerland for their active involvement in antiwar activities. Perhaps at this point, when his decisions had ripened and his stand had become clear to him, Hesse no longer minded that the connection between him and the group might be known to some; most letters that have been preserved are dated from 1917 onward. Clearly, Hesse, looking everywhere for assistance, would have found in Gräser and his group welcome support. One need not accept the view that Gräser represents Demian or that his wife Elizabeth was the model of Mother Eve. But something of the strangely tense bond between Sinclair and his guiding daemon probably relates to that episode.[53]

Nearly three years later, in 1919, *Demian* finally appeared in print under the name of its hero, Emil Sinclair. Hesse used a pseudonym partly to make clear to himself that he had embarked on a new life, partly to dissociate himself from the war controversy in which he figured. The choice of the name had been inspired by that of Isaac von Sinclair, a friend of the German romantic poet Friedrich Hölderlin. For one year the name held good. Hesse received the Fontane Prize as the writer of a "first novel" and even luminaries like Thomas Mann, who professed great excitement when the book appeared, did not know his identity. He could find out nothing about Sinclair, Mann wrote a friend, for their publisher Samuel Fischer claimed only that he had received the manuscript through Hesse. He was supposed to be a young, sick poet living in Switzerland.

In 1920, the truth was uncovered by a journalist, Eduard Korrodi. In response, Hesse owned up officially in *Vivos voco*, the journal he then edited with his wartime friend Richard Woltereck, and returned the prize.[54] Meanwhile, however, the power of *Demian* had taken hold just as Thomas Mann described it in 1947 in his preface to the American edition:

> The electrifying influence exercised on a whole generation just after the First World War by *Demian*, from the pen of a certain mysterious Sinclair, is unforgettable. With uncanny accuracy, this poetic work struck the nerve of the times and called forth grateful rapture from a whole youthful generation who believed that an interpreter of their innermost life had risen from their own midst—whereas it was a man already 42 years old who gave them what they sought.[55]

Hesse himself was fully aware of this effect. "What will come is unthinkable," he wrote about the world that Demian sought to clarify. "The soul of Europe is a beast that has been chained too long. . . . [Yet] deep down something [is] in the process of becoming, something like a new humanity."[56]

V

With the completion of *Demian*, Hesse's personal life propelled itself into the final year and a half of the war. His marriage, despite Mia's episodes and his own bouts with depression, limped along as he firmed up his own resolve to strike out on his own. Work for the prisoners became more and more arduous. He still collected money and even took a brief holiday in Ticino in the early summer of 1918. His reports about the children to friends and family were those of a proud father. Adis was subjected to painstaking copies of nine-year-old Heiner's poems. Bruno, he reported, had gone on a long hiking trip, also following in his father's footsteps. At the same time, Hesse needed money, for himself and his prisoners. Consequently, he tried to promote special sales of some of his manuscripts to be donated to the Schiller Museum in Swabian Marbach (which was to house most of his material). In August, Mia celebrated her fiftieth birthday, just after Hesse and his office were moved out of the embassy into a suburb of Bern, and there was a brief respite in the tension between them. So it was not until October that his family life really fell apart. Ironically, that change manifested itself simultaneously in a wedding and a separation.

The wedding was that of his younger brother Hans; the separation, of course, was his own. The precariousness of Hesse's life on a personal and political level finds in *Demian* a symbolic resolution. But the exposed nature of his psyche was nowhere better illustrated than by the depressing contrast between himself and Hans, who had settled in Switzerland since 1911, working as a corresponding secretary for the Brown Bovery arms factory. The town was Baden in Aargau, a Swiss manufacturing and resort town, the same place that was to receive Hesse at least once a year for extended cures from 1923 on. At this time, however, it was chiefly associated in Hesse's mind with his younger brother, who had failed in everything he had tried. Still, when Hans decided to get married early in October 1918, Hesse decided to attend the wedding. He did so with some reluctance, but since, with the war still on, none of the other German relatives would be able to cross the border to attend, he felt he could not decline. In his vignette "Remembrance of Hans," Hesse recalled how difficult it had been for him to go, not only because of the war but also because of his own "psychological crises." He had become a shy person who just managed by drowning himself in meaningless tasks, but too lethargic to join in a celebration. Clearly, the contrast between a marriage just entered into and his own marital life disturbed him most. Although the actual break with Mia did not occur until later, it was already evident to Hesse that his "own marital happiness had just been finally shattered." He felt it would have been a thousand times better if he had never married, and he recalled the inner resistance with which he had celebrated his own marriage fourteen years earlier. Hesse seemed to relate this recognition to a failure in himself. Despite psychoanalysis, he felt that he shared the common fate of the entire family. His presence at his brother's wedding could bring the groom no luck, for

> nothing can come of it when the likes of us get married and play bourgeois. We weren't made for that. We were made to be hermits, scholars or artists, saints in the desert . . . but not husbands and fathers. When we were children, great pains were taken "to break our wills," as

pious pedagogues called it in those days, and indeed all kinds of things were broken in us, but precisely not that will, not that unique quality which has been born with us, not that spark which has made us into outsiders and cranks.[57]

Almost seven years later, in March 1925, when Adis asked him to attend the silver wedding of their half brother Karl Isenberg, Hesse recalled this scene in his note of refusal. Family celebrations, he told Adis, were not digestible for a "Steppenwolf." "The most difficult celebration," he wrote, ". . . was the wedding of our good Hans in Baden. That was just at the time when my first marriage came apart and when Mia, already half mentally ill, made my life in Bern into a living hell."

At the time of the event, it must have been, at least in part, a welcome escape from his increasingly tense life. At least his report to Adis on October 14, 1918, was not very sad. Clad in festive black, he had attended the church ceremony, then had ridden with the party in two carriages to the nearby village of Ehrendingen for the wedding dinner. Hesse was impressed by the charming, still, and serious bride Frida and the sober in-laws. It turned, Hesse confessed in his essay, into the first pleasure he had known in a long time—the fun of being in a healthy country atmosphere far removed from revolutions and war. They walked back together—Hesse, the minister, and the bridal couple—through the vineyards just being harvested in a misty autumnal dusk.

Even in his rather cheerful letter to Adis of October 14, threatening dangers made themselves felt. Referring to the ravages of influenza, of which everyone was then afraid, Hesse mentioned that the schools were closed for a week and that Mia had gone to Ascona with Martin to stay with a doctor of their acquaintance for a few days. Only two weeks later, Hesse reported that the final disaster had actually occurred:

During the fourteen years of my marriage I have suffered much that no one knows. The last few months were the hardest—for Mia and for myself. For a while I thought I now knew what suffering means and that the goblet has been emptied. But we have not yet come to that end. A great suffering [has occurred] (not totally unexpected but one that has come true, confirming all fears). Mia who was in Ticino with Brüdi [the youngest child, Martin] for the past three weeks has been overtaken by a heavy psychosis and had to be sent to a sanatorium in the greatest confusion and disturbance. She is in Küsnacht near Zurich.

The rest of the letter was devoted to domestic details. Friends were helping him out. The children were in good spirits after being told that their mother was in a hospital and would simply be gone for a while until she was better. He would eventually send the children out for boarding and keep the house up with the maid. While there is a hint of the actual trauma in the letter to his sister (how he had to hunt for the sick woman's luggage), it was not fully revealed to her. By contrast, Hesse was amazingly frank with a friend, Mathilde Schwarzenbach, who shared this time with him. Fräulein Schwarzenbach was a middle-aged spinster living in Zurich whom Hesse had befriended for some years. She was of sufficient means to have been a benefactress for Hesse's prisoners. But on this occasion she was more than that: she helped Hesse personally through a difficult episode.

As can be reconstructed from the correspondence with Mathilde Schwarzenbach in October and November 1918, Mia, having promised the seven-year-old Martin that they would return home from Ticino at last, suffered a total nervous collapse en route. Hesse rushed to meet them in Lucerne to rescue the child, on whom, in her confusion, Mia had heaped verbal and physical abuse, and to take care of her in her disturbed state of mind. In Lucerne he got in touch with Mathidle Schwarzenbach in a desperate state. She in turn put him in touch with a friend in Lucerne, a Frau Dr. Brun, and with her help Hesse managed to get on top of the situation in an agonized day and night. The luggage seemed lost. Some of it was found as far back as the Ticino station of Bellinzona. Other suitcases, packages, bags, and similar containers were picked up on various stations on the journey north, which took Mia two days until she finally reached Lucerne. Many of her things, including her watch, had been simply thrown away, and an economical Hesse still tried to retrieve them. But his concern for the child was greatest. Apparently there had been many altercations, and Hesse made immediate inquiries that might lead him to people who had witnessed at least some of these scenes. In the meantime he secured a place for Mia with a Dr. Brunner in an institution in Küsnacht and tried to calm the child who had been subjected to the scenes. The scattered baggage began to arrive from various stations while he and the maid found substitute clothing for Mia to send to Zurich the moment he had returned to Bern. As Hesse put it in a letter to his friend Emil Molt on November 3: "For a week now my wife has been in an institution near Zurich. There are prospects she will be cured but how long it will take nobody knows. At best I foresee running a house all alone with three children." He was, as he told all his friends at the time, thinking only in practical terms.

Fall and winter continued dismal without much change in Hesse's pattern of life. The end of the war in November did not immediately lessen the pressures at the office. It rather increased them for a while, because now the prisoners were impatient and communication was becoming easier; hence a greater volume of traffic kept them hard at work.

Mia improved enough to ask to see at least one of her children at Christmas, a request that was supported by her physician, and Hesse sent nine-and-a-half-year-old Heiner with the maid to Zurich where they were taken care of by their friend Fräulein Schwarzenbach. Basically, the two younger children continued to live in Kirchdorf with their aunt. After New Year's, which he had spent mostly in Zurich, Hesse was almost reluctant to return to the "cold empty house" on Melchenbühlweg, which he now inhabited alone with the maid. The great advantage the house had held for Hesse six years earlier—its seclusion—now made it intolerable. Since there was no electricity, and the kerosene supply ran out frequently, Hesse spent long evenings, deep into his insomnia-filled nights, sitting alone in the dark. In January 1919 he was at least able to install some electric light, which made the nights a little more bearable, but his life still appeared as a weight he could not quite cast off.[58]

As the winter wore on, it also became increasingly clear that Mia would return within a foreseeable future. Her improvement in the clinic was steady and reports about her progress remained optimistic; hence decisions had to be faced. In the midst of Hesse's concern for his defeated country, while writing many empathic letters to his friends across the frontier, Hesse continually worried about Mia's health and his personal future. He began to retreat from the hard line of rejection that he had established before and during her breakdown. In a letter to Mathilde Schwarzenbach in February, he explained that he thought Mia quite touching in many of her ways and that he had often done her an injustice because of his own inhibitions. She possessed, he declared, "a better character than I" as well as a good and strong constitution. In any event, he hoped that with the help of the physician, whom she had found particularly helpful, she would soon get back on her feet, although Hesse thought that she should probably stay somewhat longer in Küsnacht to make the best use of him. That there is no inkling in this account of a long-standing resolution on Hesse's part to be free may seem strange, but he probably fluctuated and had to conquer his own ambivalence. It was also premature to reveal that plan to a devoted but relatively distant friend like Mathilde Schwarzenbach. That busy spinster, however, had a very clear appreciation of Hesse's needs. She offered to take in one of his boys permanently, and though he refused, the thought suggests that she was not far from understanding his desire to be free.

That spring Hesse traveled in his usual way, visiting Volkmar Andreä in Zurich to keep him company while his family was away. Meanwhile he also worked again in the garden of the Welti house, tying up the trees tossed and broken by the storm, and still enjoying the view beckoning from the Jungfrau. At last, the relative barrenness of the last war year gave way to fresh creativity early in 1919 when calm once more seemed to return to his life. During the first few months of peace since 1914 Hesse wrote feverishly. In January, despite the heavy work load with the prisoners and the impending decisions about his family life, he composed the novella "A Child's Soul," really a spin-off of *Demian*, which elaborated the theme of the "two worlds" within and beyond the parental home. In three intense days and nights he completed the Nietzschean parable for the First World War, "Zarathustra's Return," in which the great sage castigates the Germans for finding fault with their fate rather than with their hubris of elevating war, and their enthusiasm for war, to a higher level. It still had to be published anonymously. Hesse also wrote the first act of a play that he published the following year in his and Woltereck's journal *Vivos voco*—a political drama about "Homecoming."

VI

Hesse's final months in Bern until April 1919 were filled with a sense of creativity, of dedicated writing, with the success of *Demian*, which brightened the first year of peace for him, but they also led him to define at last his political stand against the war. Now that the coercion of government and service was over, he could clarify, without ambiguity, a position he had reached during the past two years: war was not essentially a political act but a human tragedy that required no political stand or allegiance, only a human impulse to reject. Such views did not earn him undivided support. Although "Zarathustra's Return" was published anonymously at first, Hesse revealed his authorship a year later and he was again amazed by the vehemence of the attacks against him. By then the issue had been joined. In *Sinclair's Notebook*, which contained many of these nonfictional writings of the final years of the war, Hesse told why the name Sinclair had become important to him. The importance of Hölderlin's patron and friend during that romantic age was not just an idiosyncrasy on Hesse's part. Rather it reflected an entire vision of Hölderlin's world, which Hesse equated with his own:

> And under the sign of "Sinclair" I still sense today that burning epoch, that death of a beautiful, irretrievable world, that awakening—painful at first, then deeply affirmative—to a new understanding of world and reality. It is that flash of insight into unity under the aegis of polarity, the coincidence of opposites which the Chinese masters of Zen tried to unite in magic formulae a thousand years ago.[59]

As Hesse prepared to begin anew—to leave Bern, Mia, and the children for a fresh start—his life was in tune with the beginning of the new era he hoped to find in the outside world as well. Although, as he reported in his "Diary of 1920," "My external life was most harried, full of misfortune and need," although his separation from his family took place in April ("everything filled with worries without and within," as he told Erwin Ackerknecht), a new spirit allowed him to replace the crisis of the war outside himself as well as the crisis within to usher in the most productive time of his life. Rejection of war, politics, family, even illness and depression, moved into a background from which they forever haunted his life. Into the foreground he placed, so he told himself, a new and fervent creativity. As he wrote in "On Moving Into a New House":

> It had become clear that from now on there was morally only one possibility of existence for me: to put my literary work ahead of everything, to live only for it and no longer to take seriously money troubles or any other consideration.[60]

The Sign of Sinclair was Hesse's own. With *Demian*, and its radiating effect, he entered another New Life.

6

The Third New Life: Vagabond of the Imagination

I

Beside the dark opening in the cliff at the entrance to the gorge I stood hesitating, and turned to look back.

The sun was shining in that pleasant green world, above the meadows brownish grass blossoms waved and flickered. It was good to be out there in warmth and well-loved ease, out where one's soul hummed deep and satisfied like a hairy bumblebee in the heavy fragrance and light; perhaps I was a fool to leave all this and climb into the mountain range.

—From "The Hard Passage"

THE POSTURE IN this brief scene is remarkable: it is that of the seer, the poet, looking back before turning toward an uncertain future, and it is that of the painter who takes in the landscape he is about to leave with a final photographic glance. And both of them use *eyes*: those forever sore and tortured organs of sense that were Hesse's instruments, and burdens, throughout his life.

The poet-painter shades his eyes and looks back at the world he is about to leave: the world of normalcy. For Hermann Hesse, this was the world of middle-class comfort, of marriage, of a secure social position extending from the last decaying years in Bern, to Gaienhofen, to Basel, and ultimately back to the Swabia of his childhood and adolescence. The landscape viewed by the departing eye encompassed it all. But the moment is also fraught with the suffering of his recent crisis, for the fairy tale "The Hard Passage," of which these are the opening lines, had been produced under the impact of his breakdown in 1916. It was the year his departure had been emotionally decided, and this brief symbolic sketch, imbued, like *Demian*, with the pressures and elation of his psychoanalysis, prophesied his new beginning. Now, three years later, it could be put into practice.

The departure, when it came in the spring of 1919, was hurried and complete. Hesse's war work was practically done five months after the armistice, and it did not take him too long to close down his side of the operations. Spurred on by his recognitions, it did not take him too long to unravel, at least temporarily, the complexities of his personal life. Early in March, Hesse had written Erwin Ackerknecht that Mia was expected home soon from the clinic and that the time had come to make decisions. By March 26 he was busy dismantling his library, trying to reduce it to half its size before leaving. His children he arranged for with the help of devoted friends and relatives and by April he was on the train, leaving Bern and the Welti house, which had become both his prison and the symbol of his disintegrating life.[1]

Hermann Hesse was heading south: self-consciously following the trek of Nietzsche, of Richard Wagner, of Goethe, of the German emperors of the Middle Ages. It implied for the German historical sense both exile and cultural regeneration, and Hesse continued to gaze into the mirrors of cultural history. The mountain through which the "hard passage" led him at the age of forty-two was the St. Gotthard Pass, a pass he often described as a forbidding place, swept by ice-cold winds. For the first time, he was leaving the German-speaking region of Swabia and northern Switzerland with an expectation of permanence to find refuge in Italian-speaking Ticino, that broad, pointed triangle that pushes the Swiss border to the gates of Milan. As the train sped toward its goal, the landscape changed to take on a hue of strangeness. The novella "Klein and Wagner," the immediate product of his exile, describes this change graphically, as "The Hard Passage" had presented it symbolically. Author and hero speed past lakes, mountains, and waterfalls, "through numbing tunnels and over gently swaying bridges." The foreignness of the new world seemed to him like "pictures from schoolbooks and postcards." Somehow, everything was dipped in strange, psychologically tinctured colors, for the journey itself Hesse (unlike his hero) had undertaken many times in the past. But this time it was different. Hesse, like his hero, knew that there was "no returning home," and it was this knowledge that gave those portraits of his new pilgrimage their distinctive tone.[2]

He had a discerning eye. In his sketchbook, *Wandering*, published in 1920, he lovingly described the last German-style farmhouse, which he viewed with nostalgia before he plunged through the pass into the Italian-speaking world to the south.[3] Here he wrote about the joy of crossing frontiers, of overcoming the impulse to be settled and turning into a prophet of movement toward the future. The conflict between wanting to be settled and wanting to seek fresh exiles Hesse now caught in visual pictures. In the novella, he and his alter ego Klein saw "grape-vines on green terraces, golden brown walls half in ruins, as in old

engravings, and rosy, blossoming trees. A small station rushed by with
an Italian name, something with *ogno* or *ogna*." The train ride that
takes up a large part of the novella caught the sense of movement and
its psychological complications with the vividness of a first impression.

Both Hesse and Klein left guiltily. The transparent biographical
analogy was papered over by manufactured circumstances, but these,
too, betrayed the conflict. Klein ("small" in German) was the settled
part of himself yearning for release. By describing his hero as a minor
bank official in flight with embezzled money in his pocket he made himself even smaller, but by linking the man on the run with a fearless
"Wagner" (the false name Klein assumed in his flight), he made himself larger as well. His fictional companion was associated with Richard
Wagner, the artist par excellence, and at the same time with a notorious
schoolteacher named Ernst Wagner who had murdered his wife and
children to escape from a suffocating routine.

These analogous reasons behind Hesse's and Klein's flights tinged the
landscapes both of them observed through the window of the speeding
train. "Yes, it was so," his character suddenly observed, "it had happened
because of his wife. Solely because of his wife." And the sights merged
with an inward vision, perceived from "a high tower of awareness," in
which life and time are described with the imagery of Knulp, the
wanderer, that was to dominate the first year of Hesse's exile. The sights
turned within, and the emerging dream was the perennial dream of his
life: the grandiose vision of the amoral, free, and sensuous artist super-
imposed upon the compulsive fantasy of murdering his bourgeois past.
Klein-Hesse perceived them both as the interior landscape turned into a
long, arduous road: "He looked back over the great long line, his whole
marriage, and the distance he had traversed seemed to him a weary,
dreary road in which a man toils through the dust, bearing heavy burdens
on his back."[5] Somewhere at the beginning of that road lay the bright
landscape of his youth that he now sought to regain—the domain of the
artist. With a new name(like his own "Sinclair," which Hesse still used
at the time) and with a refurbished self, he would face an alien world.
But Klein's end was suicide in the water of Lake Lugano. Hesse began
his new life as a vagabond of the imagination.

When the train stopped in Lugano, Hesse's exile began—at least for
the time being. He was full of plans and tried to execute them at once
while looking for a permanent place to live. He first stayed in a farmhouse in the village of Minusio up on a mountainside at the outskirts of
town, overlooking valley and lake below. He dropped his things to
begin work on "Klein and Wagner," filled with his impressions. If the
sketches in *Wandering* are any indication, he immediately began to

explore the countryside: south toward Agnuzzo, east up the mountain toward the church and cemetery of S. Abbondio, deeper into the country following the winding road toward the village of Montagnola, which was to become his permanent home, and up steep footpaths toward the old church of Madonna dell'Ongero—all landmarks-to-be for the rest of his life. Wherever Hesse turned he faced the broad cap of Mt. S. Salvatore in the north, which he was to climb time and again during the next forty years. Although none of these places were truly unfamiliar, he evidently perceived them with a fresh eye, the eye of the exile, of the actually footloose wanderer looking for a point of departure. Writing, keeping up old acquaintances with many of his artist friends who lived in the region, Hesse also tried to relive his old dream of the sensual artist. As a sketch from *Wandering* tells it, he celebrated his new freedom by striking out into the new Italian landscape, a bottle of *vino* in his hand, a woman on his arm, to greet the artist's life with the erotic upsurge that, he felt, shapes all wanderlust.[6]

The old paradox remained that made of Klein-Wagner such an apt biographical figure. For the very moment of abandonment, of being free at last to find his new way as the wandering Knulp, was accompanied by an intense search for a permanent home. Anxiously he inquired among his friends where such a place could be found. After a month in his farmhouse he moved on to Sorengo, another village a short distance away, and he was most relieved when Volkmar Andreä turned up a pleasant apartment for him in nearby Montagnola. The place was appropriate for many reasons. It combined creature comforts with a sense of quaintness and apartness, of openness to a world in which he could roam yet feel permanently settled. The small apartment, whose balcony looked out onto a magnificent landscape, opened on the other side to the narrow alleys of Montagnola whose Italian-style houses virtually hugged the entrance to his building. It was the Casa Camuzzi, a bad nineteenth century imitation of a baroque hunting castle, but it combined the warmth of being close to an intimate world with the grandiose distance from the world of men that the view from the balcony provided. For the next twelve years this building furnished him with his permanent residence in the midst of all his frantic moves. The village remained his home for the rest of his life.

If Hesse's departure was viewed as a physical event, so was his arrival. The palazzo that contained the apartment was a feast for eyes. It was, to use his own words, a "monstrous" place. With its weird lines, its diverse styles done up in a crazy-quilt pattern, it fulfilled all the expectations of a visual, sentimental, and yet also ironic imagination. On one side it strutted, acting the part of a medieval castle. On the other side, the aloofness was reversed. The very smell of cookery from the neighboring houses permeated each room. This peculiar place Hesse described again and again in loving detail—in his letters, in sketches of *Picture Book,* and in his rambling essay "Upon Moving Into a New House"—always dwelling on its grotesqueness, its incipient wildness: a house half solemn, half comical, with many wings and huge portals.[7] The garden, which plunged downhill abruptly, beyond the first terrace on the open side of the building, seemed to burst with vegetation—the very opposite of the groomed garden a settled Hermann Hesse had planted in Gaienhofen twelve years earlier. It was a veritable jungle through which a path wound downhill, connecting several terraces on different levels until it lost itself in impenetrable thickets. And halfway down the slope there was a small grotto in which a thin stream of water silently trickled, where Hesse was to write and meet his friends for many years. It was a whole world composing a romantic daydream that he constantly re-created for himself.

Again it was the first sensual impression recreated through a fictional *eye* that conveyed the meaning of the place. This time it was the eye of the painter Klingsor, the hero of the second of the large novellas written during that creative summer of 1919. This somewhat frenzied figure, partly van Gogh, partly Gauguin, and mostly Hesse himself, inhabited his own four-room apartment in the Casa Camuzzi. And, like Hesse, he looked down from his balcony to view the cacophony of the senses below:

> Just back home after a night walk, Klingsor stood on the narrow stone balcony of his studio. Below him, dizzyingly precipitate, the old terrace gardens dropped away, a densely shadowed tangle of treetops, palms, cedars, chestnuts, judas trees, red beech and eucalyptus, intertwined with climbing plants, lianas, wisterias. Above the blackness of the trees the large glossy leaves of the summer magnolias gleamed pallidly, the huge, snow-white blossoms half shut among them, large as human heads, pale as moon and ivory. From the massed leafage, penetrating and rousing, a tartly sweet smell of lemons drifted toward him. From some indefinite distance languorous music winged its way toward him, perhaps a guitar, perhaps a piano; there was no saying. . . . Starlight flowed through the wooded valley. High and deserted, a white chapel, enchanted and old, peered out of the endless forest. In the distance, lake, mountains, and sky flowed together.[8]

This view is substantiated by a flood of observations Hesse recorded in his own person. In one of the sketches in *Picture Book* he described the identical experience, or vision, as the artist Hesse returns from a long excursion from the country. Here, too, sight and sound, painting and music, become one at the point of infinity where the eye can no longer follow. The same impressions are conveyed: the magnolias, the scent of lemons. "The night wind rustled in the trees below my window. Moonlight falls on the flagstones."[9]

It had to be "home." Hesse sent for his things in Bern, but he actually brought little to his new retreat except most of his books and the large desk he had already used in the first farmhouse in Gaienhofen. These he installed in the little study off the balcony in his small apartment. Somehow the place seemed to provide the underpinnings he needed for his vagrant self. Although he now lived only with rented furniture, although he was "no longer master of the house" with children and servants and a dog to whistle for and a garden to tend, the wild garden and the "lovely, marvelous house" sustained and revived him.

The life he had chosen was clearly less secure. If he now lived in the most original and most "beautiful" house he had ever lived in, he was also "a little, penniless, literary man, a threadbare and rather dubious stranger who lived on milk and rice and macaroni, who wore his old suits till they were threadbare and in the fall brought home his supper of chestnuts from the forest." This monastic sense of self-imposed poverty and isolation was also part of the romantic image of himself that brought the Gräser cult closer to home: being a footloose stranger with holes in his pants might be the last step before wearing Indian garb. Hesse never tired of painting himself in these sentimental colors, but while his financial precariousness was real, his isolation was largely fictional. He kept up his interminable correspondence (which he always cursed and always missed when it seemed to abate) and maintained his contact with the literary centers in the cities. He wrote newspaper articles (usually under his pen name Sinclair) and joined Richard Woltereck in starting and running *Vivos voco*—so named because it called upon the living in testimony of the dead to help create a new postwar culture. The social and cultural ties with the past remained, in fact, largely unbroken. Hesse was no longer affluent; his wife and family remained a constant drain on his resources. For the present, he needed contributions from well-meaning friends to supplement his income. Clearly, he missed being the gentleman of Melchenbühlweg while reveling in the image of the hermit's life.

The visual wealth around him compensated, in part, for the lack of money and possessions. It soon was to stimulate his desire to paint, but it also kindled an ecstatic rush of writing. During an amazingly short time that late spring and summer he wrote his two best novellas, "Klein and Wagner" and "Klingsor's Last Summer," in which he sought to define the nature and difficulties of his third new life. Indeed, this rush of creativity, capitalizing on his departure, was the most important change in Hesse's condition since the completion of *Demian* in 1917. "I had pulled myself together again. I was still capable of work, of concentration: the war years had not, as I had half feared, done me in intellectually." This sense of productivity was a source of great elation. "It was like waking from a nightmare that had lasted for years, I inhaled freedom, the air, the sun, I had solitude and my work."[10] "Klein and Wagner" described the anxiety, guilt, and hesitant joy of his departure. "Klingsor's Last Summer" dramatized the elation of his arrival—its productive result—in colorful language. It expressed the view that the artist must portray his sensuous self. Klingsor was the magician of art. His name alludes to all the magical images of creativity from *Parsifal* to Goethe to the poet-teacher in Novalis's allegorical novel, *Heinrich von Ofterdingen*. But in Hesse's story the magician-artist becomes a painter who rendered a likeness of himself that turned into a likeness of the entire world, an echo of Hesse's earlier attempts to "paint his dreams," which he had mentioned to Sturzenegger while he was still in Bern. He had become the man with the eye that sees both the outer world and the inner self and renders them as "magic."

In his daily routine, the fictional Klingsor seems to reflect Hesse's own life from the moment he stepped out on the balcony to view his favorite garden. Like his counterpart in life, he was never really much alone, although he talked about it a great deal. His "last summer" was filled with people as much as was Hesse's first. He supposedly slept with a few women and drank and talked with friends whom he gave Chinese names and other epithets. And he found time for all this drinking, talking, and lovemaking, just as Hesse, writing rapidly, seems to have found time for many of these activities.

Names in the story are thinly disguised names of real friends, and events (if one consults Hesse's letters) seem to have been very much borrowed from that first summer in Ticino. Whether he actually had all the encounters that occur in the story is beside the point. For example, a love scene with a peasant woman reflects a wish dream which often recurs in Hesse's books rather than a believable episode. A sturdy farm wife allows the great painter to work in her yard; he asks for a drink of water; they fix each other with a hard look; later she follows him into the mountains; her approaching footsteps are heavy with sensuous meaning. Their language is only of the body as he beds her under the pine trees. This scene, by no means unusual in Hesse, not only portrays an expressionistic cliché of the time, but also the entire romantic ambience surrounding the sexual myths by which his admirers of the Youth Movement lived. Hesse himself began his new life with a girl on his arm and he

wrote of various amorous encounters—*Liebschaften* as he called them—
although he soon became involved with the woman who was to become
his second wife. More important than correspondence to fact, however,
is the atmosphere reflected in the novella. Its events portray an inner and
outer life during those busy first months in Ticino with unmistakable
precision.

These correspondences are especially clear in the general picture of
social life the novella intermittently draws. Friends come and go in
Klingsor's place as they came and went in Hesse's Casa Camuzzi. His
lifelong friend, the French-Swiss painter Louis Moillet appears in the
novella as "Louis the Cruel" who "dropped out of the sky." "[The]
traveller, the unaccountable friend who lived in railway cars and whose
studio was his rucksack." They painted together, sunbathed in the nude,
and talked about art and the purpose of life. The fictional Louis is made
to express the exuberant, sensual side of Hesse, which he was then trying
to act out in his life:

> "Who knows if all this painting has any value?" asked Louis. . . . "If
> you always had a girl that pleases you on your knees and the bowl of
> soup you want for the day, you wouldn't trouble yourself with this
> child's play."[11]

This bit of sentimental wisdom, playing with the old romantic theme of
sensuality and art, suggests Hesse's involvement at the time with the
question of sublimation.

During his last year in Bern, Hesse had written an interesting small
essay, "Artist and Psychoanalysis," about the relationship between the
conscious self-monitoring artist and the unconscious grounds of fantasy
and imagination from which he worked.[12] Warning against overly facile
attempts to apply psychoanalytic thinking to the understanding of artists
and art, Hesse admitted that Freud's new method provided a key for
artists to understand themselves. Three ways exist, however, in which
artists have found themselves confirmed by psychoanalysis. The first was
the general emphasis by all psychoanalysis on the unconscious and
therefore on the artist's precious ground of the imagination. "Analysis,"
Hesse wrote perceptively, "confirms the artist to himself." His raison
d'être was always founded in unconscious activity. But while this recognition could be of use to anyone who might know psychoanalysis only
intellectually, from the outside, the other two points could only be understood by those who were more deeply acquainted with the psychoanalytic
way of approaching human experience.

The first of these benefits is the artist's new intimacy with his own
unconscious: "Whoever has gone seriously even a short distance along

the way of analysis, its search for origins within the soul from the depth
of recollections, dreams, and associations, retains as his lasting profit,
that which one can only call a close relationship to one's own unconscious"—a warm, fruitful, passionate experience of the back and
forth between his conscious and unconscious life that allows him to bring
out into the light of day what usually occurs only beneath the threshold
of awareness. The second benefit was ethical, the requirement to be
true to oneself. Psychoanalysis teaches the artist to acknowledge what he
has repressed—indeed, what generations before him had repressed.
"Already in the first steps one takes in one's analysis, this is a powerful,
indeed, an immense experience, a shock down to one's roots." Such a
person finds himself more and more isolated as he proceeds along the
road to self-knowledge, while at the same time he gradually perceives an
image of truth and nature:

> Beyond father and mother, beyond peasant and nomad, beyond ape and
> fish, origin, belonging, and hope of man have been experienced nowhere
> as seriously and devastatingly as in committed psychoanalysis. What is
> learned becomes visible, what is known becomes heartbeat, and what-
> ever anxieties, uncertainties, and repressions come to light, the sig-
> nificance of life and of the human personality arises in a purer and more
> demanding state.[13]

By sublimating, by submitting the unconscious to the conscious idea,
Hesse suggests, the artist fulfills this role. Throughout the twenties he
argued these points with himself, with his friends, with Josef Lang, and
even in an exchange of letters with C. G. Jung in which he defended
this more classically Freudian point of view.

The dialogues with Louis and the other friends give a vivid impression
of Hesse's mood at the time, his alternations between anxiety and withdrawal on the one hand and his need for communication on the other.
As one point, Klingsor poured out his troubles to Louis:

> Often he suffered from anxiety, from melancholia; often he lay bound
> and gagged in the dungeon of darkness. . . . Then it did him good to
> see Luigi's face.
>   But Louis did not like to see these weaknesses. They pained him, they
> demanded sympathy. Klingsor made it a practice to reveal his heart to
> his friend, and realized too late that in so doing he was losing him.[14]

In the story, Louis had to disappear. They ate well together and
emptied a bottle of wine. Then his friend jumped on his bicycle and
vanished in the dusk.

These episodes in the novella illuminate the feeling of Hesse's life
both present and past. The troubles Klingsor communicated, for example,

were actually Hesse's own, for they still dealt with the problem of reconciling his present freedom with his guilt about the past. The resulting ambivalence emerges in the alternating pictures of light and dark: incidents of carousing, of walking tours with friends, of amorous episodes contrasting with visions of death and despair. These images, moreover, are sensually induced: Klingsor *hears* the "music of doom," and after an intense drinking bout with friends he *views* the ancient Figure of Death in the dusty highway. Even the way Klingsor worked (having sublimated his senses in his artistic vision) is a faithful reproduction of Hesse's own way of life: work done in feverish haste through long days and nights without letup capsuled within many more days of drinking, talking, and worrying. Except for the medium of their work Hesse and Klingsor were brother magicians. Their inner and outer eyes took in fresh landscapes and converted them into "art."

Despite his dedication to art, to a solitary existence, to close one-to-one friendships, Hesse constantly maintained a veritable court of friends and acquaintances, and his new life in Ticino, mirrored in his novella, proved to be no exception. In addition to Louis Moillet, his old friend the architect Josef Englert belonged to the population of "Klingsor." Hesse worked faithfully with Woltereck on *Vivos voco* until the magazine's demise in 1923. Even his old friend Ludwig Finckh, who had become an arch-conservative, did not wholly disappear from sight.[15] Othmar Schoeck, Ilona Durigo, and many others with whom Hesse had been intimate in Gaienhofen and Bern remained in his life. And his friendship with Fritz and Alice Leuthold, his "Siamese" friends with whom he had renewed and intensified his intimate connection since 1916, was constantly reinforced, even during this supposedly solitary summer with long letters and visits. Along with these old friends, new faces appeared. During his last year in Bern, Hesse had met the wealthy manufacturer Max Wassmer. With his second wife Tilly, this patron of the arts held court in the picturesque castle of Bremgarten near Bern where in later years Hesse often found refuge. A mere enumeration of these names draws a picture of Hesse's life that finds its visual correlative in "Klingsor." Even in this new life, as in all his past lives in Basel, Gaienhofen, and Bern, the image of the solitary was constantly counterpointed by the image of a man whose very existence was defined by unceasing contacts with people who entered, exited, and returned to the stage of his self.

"Klingsor's Last Summer" also records Hesse's first meeting with the young singing student Ruth Wenger who was to become his second wife. She spent her summers in Carona, a village across the lake from Montagnola, where her parents maintained a summer home. In the novella, this house becomes an enchanted palace and the girl is converted into a "Queen of the Mountain." She appears as a lovely young lady dressed in bright red, dwelling in her castle—actually a pleasant, Italian-style house and courtyard with yellow stucco walls and whitewash. The fictional scene provides a partial insight into the ambience of her life. When Klingsor and his friends called on her on one of their walking tours, they heard her singing her scales, tuning her piano. In fact, "The Day in Kareno," as the episode is called in the story, was filled with a mixture of actual visual impressions and highly imaginative flights of fancy into worlds of childhood and dream. "The house seemed to lack an entrance; there was only the yellow wall with two balconies and above them a bit of painting in the stucco of the gable: blue and red flowers and a parrot. There should have been a painted door here and if you knocked three times and pronounced Open Sesame the painted door would fly open. . . ." But instead of veils, slave girls, and the Queen of the Mountain sitting on a high dais, Klingsor and his friends had to content themselves with a slightly different reception: "A large black dog came rushing, a small blonde lion after him." And "in the background the piano sang the same tone eleven times."[16]

The dogs, the cat, the constant scales were to become the bane of Hesse's existence in later years, but at this point at least the fictional Klingsor found them charming. Her impression on Klingsor, the painter, was probably much more highly charged than her impression had been on Hesse, the incipient lover. Yet the response in fiction is resonant with a romantic intensity that subverts a visual picture into an interior "poetic" impression. In the bright, exaggerated diction then in vogue, Klingsor exclaimed to himself:

Suddenly the Queen of the Mountain stood there, a slender lissome flower, body straight and pliant, all in red, burning flames, image of youth. Before Klingsor's eyes a hundred beloved pictures scattered away and the new picture radiantly took their place. He knew at once that he would paint her, not realistically, but the ray within her that had struck him, the poem, the tart lovely tone: Youth, Redness, Blondness, Amazon. . . .

The reticence that follows this outburst describes the usual dimension of darkness—the negatives, the doubts—that Hesse felt about every experience:

For a second the feeling darted through him: "If only I were ten years younger, ten brief years, this girl could have me, capture me, wind me around her finger. Now, you are too young, little red queen, too young for the old wizard Klingsor! . . ."[17]

Pictures of the actual Ruth Wenger, whom Hesse soon mentioned in his private correspondence, show how much the Queen of the Mountain had been embellished by the magic of poetry, and how, undoubtedly, she had drawn to herself a whole accumulation of images of other people. In a photograph taken some years later at a family picnic she is seen as subdued, almost depressed, pitifully holding a little white lapdog as she sits on the ground beside her towering mother, the Swiss writer Lisa Wenger. She looks shy and withdrawn. Her father appears as a solemn patriarch, though actually he was weak and interminably ill. Into this family Hesse soon allowed himself to drift to replace the marriage he had left behind in his flight from Bern. When he became "footloose" he at once sought a permanent place, a "home"; when he freed himself from one set of ties he paradoxically sought another.

At the time of their meeting, however, these were still moot questions, but the image Hesse began to form of her remained nonetheless crucial. The discrepancy between Klingsor's vision of the Red Queen and the actual person is deeply suggestive of Hesse's artistry and his picture of women. For *woman*—when she was not an older, maternal guide— remained the sensual image the artist absorbs, takes in, and converts into his "art." But this disparity between the "real" and the "imaginative" visions is also indicative of Hesse's new program as an artist. The picture was not to be realistic. It was to render a poetry of experience.

Hesse felt he had revolutionized both his life and his work. In August 1919, he wrote to Erwin Ackerknecht: "Even as a poet I confront all kinds of revolutions. Of the old Hesse nothing is left." During the same month he wrote Samuel Fischer that he had "changed in recent years" and had "shed his skin." His entire course had been rechanneled since the war—actually "since 1915." He begged Fischer to continue to protect his pseudonym as the author of *Demian*, because that novel and some of the fairy tales had been his "first attempts at liberation," which he now considered "almost complete." Now, since his arrival in Ticino, he had done new work that represented his most significant point of departure, "Klein and Wagner" and "Klingsor's Last Summer," which he wanted to add to an earlier piece done in Bern, "A Child's Soul," to make up a new volume. Especially these two recent novellas were the immediate product of his new life—"my latest revolutionary work." And he added, oddly at this presumed height of his happiness, that if anything should happen to him Fischer was to bring out this most significant body of his work at all cost. It will be "my most important book, that and *Demian*. . . ." He was not sure how far he would go "in the direction of the expressionists," but he felt he had made a clear break with the past.[18]

The "revolution" Hesse had in mind in his remarks to Ackerknecht,

Fischer, and others consisted of a deliberate departure from the "poetic realism" that had marked most of his published writings up to that time. This presumed change was also evident in another decision, his choice to turn seriously to another artistic medium, painting, which accompanied his selection of the painter Klingsor as the hero of his second large novella. In taking up the craft, he did not depict the substances of dreams, as he had told Sturzenegger earlier, but rather sought to portray his new surroundings in soft, hazy watercolors, which he identified with his new persona. These pictures which he continued to produce for many years were done around the Casa Camuzzi and on various solitary outings. They were usually gentle impressions of lake, mountain, and gardens, which sought to catch the ambience of the southern countryside in often pale yet suggestively lush pastel shades. He also sketched the façades of Italian houses, straighter, less embroidered, yet somehow gentler than the farm houses of the Black Forest and northern Switzerland that had been his home. He seldom depicted figures and faces; rather, he projected his feelings into the objects that peopled the world in which he tried to live.

Hesse's turn to painting as an avocation reinforced his sense of himself as a man who experiences life through his eyes and transmutes it, in the process of seeing, into an inner awareness. He also coupled it with his turn toward "revolutionary" writing. "And then, behold, one day I discovered an entirely new joy," he wrote in his "Life Story Briefly Told." "Suddenly, at the age of forty, I began to paint. Not that I considered myself a painter or intended to become one. But painting is marvelous. . . ."[19] Unlike the monotony of having inky black fingers after writing, he suggested, there is variety in painting, for one ends up with red and blue fingers. These remarks, which he made over and over and which have been quoted time and again, were both a polemic about his new ideas and another example of his need to advertise his "new" way of life.

In his small sketch "Life Story Briefly Told" composed in 1925, Hesse reflected on his feelings at this time. He cited a list of reproaches by his unidentified "friends" that focused on the fact of his "change." They had refused to allow him to change his "face": "But my face refuses; it wants to change often. That is its need." And he at once identified this need for change with his own decision to turn away from realism as a writer: "They tell me I have no sense of reality. The writings I produce and the pictures I paint do not correspond to reality." But reality, he added, "is an accident, a bit of life's debris." This, indeed, is the source of his "revolution," to which Stefan Zweig also referred. Life and nature were no longer to be embellished in the old romantic way but to be replaced by a new reality that would be of his own creation:

In my writings people often miss the customary respect for reality, and when I paint, the trees have faces and the houses laugh or dance or weep, but whether the tree is a pear or a chestnut, that for the most part cannot be determined. I must accept this reproach. I admit that my own life frequently appears to me exactly like a legend. I often see and feel the outer world connected and in harmony with my inner world in a way I can only call magical.[20]

It is part of Hesse's interior physiognomy that in the greater part of this passage he pronounced as a new discovery ideas that could be found in every communication of the expressionists. Although the movement itself was as old as the century, Hesse had significantly ignored it while it was outré. But it had been on the rise especially since 1916, the year of his own conversion, and in the postwar ferment it had become positively fashionable. Moreover, Hesse's manner of enlivening objects by projecting into them aspects of the artist's imaginative self conformed precisely to the dominant vision of this segment of the German avant-garde. Hesse, however, had never been an avant-garde writer. The people to whom he addressed himself, where they did not belong to the established audience that had enjoyed *Gertrud* and *Rosshalde*, were young idealists who were disillusioned with things as they were and therefore shared Hesse's distaste for the war and the postwar scene, but who still sought their salvation in magical worlds of nature, fairy tales, and dreams.

Hesse had an unerring sense for cultural change. By being both advanced and conservative, he could make his "revolution" acceptable without leaving the moorings of his familiar world. In the latter part of his statement, then, the expressionistic phraseology gives way to the "old Hesse" whom everyone could recognize. Here he refers to his life as a legend, of the harmony of the inner and the outer, and of the "magic" that binds them together. These are all notions familiar from romantic poets like Jean Paul and Novalis, carried over from Hesse's earlier years. Although he was to embellish these ideas with Indian and Chinese motifs that were then beginning to take firmer root in his work, they provided the mythical subsoil he and his readers shared.

This double sense of continuity and change in the style of his work is portrayed in Hesse's very description of the style of his life. The sketches in *Picture Book*, though published in 1926, reveal his posture at the time. In one such sketch, "Summer's Day, 1919," he takes his reader through an entire day of rambling and working. "Carefree . . . the sun rises each morning and the birds begin to sing in the enormous chestnut trees." He puts a piece of bread, a book, and a pair of swim trunks in his pockets and leaves the village "to become the guest of forest and lake for a whole long day." Everything is visual: the chestnut trees have just ceased to bloom and small prickly fruit is now hanging from their branches. Huckleberries have given way to blueberries. He finds a lonely spot to read and to draw. Toward evening he has a bowl of rice or macaroni in a nearby village, for this is the time when he is a vegetarian. Finally, he walks home in the dark through forest and mountain trails, past the villas of the rich from Milan "where many hydrangea bushes appear magically in their pale, gracious colors." Back near home, at around midnight, he scents the lemon flavor of the magnolias and sees the lights of the village glittering by the lake.[21]

The sense of self-imposed poverty, of nearness to nature, and of creative work conveyed by this sketch is by no means only a pose, for it conforms closely to Hesse's image of the artist and reflects many of the pictures of himself he had drawn in his fiction and in his personal memoirs. There is no reason to believe that a good part of the time he did not live that way. But clearly if this was his life-style during his first summer in Ticino, and intermittently thereafter, it was also a self-conscious style. The idyllic existence related in "Summer's Day, 1919" is "explained" in a concluding passage. Here Hesse steps out of character to deliver an appeal to his "friends" in Germany still involved in less salutary pursuits:

> Friends at home: what are *you* doing? Are you holding flowers or hand grenades in your hands? Are you still alive? Are you writing me nice letters or again libelous articles? Dear friends: do what you like, but remember now and then, just for a moment, how short life is.[22]

Feeling misunderstood and despised by the world was, of course, a perennial theme in Hesse's life. During this period, however, it was still reinforced by the reality of his wartime activities for peace and his continuing stand that did not express undivided sympathy for his defeated country. The attacks made upon him, especially by right-wing students, were to become even stronger after he admitted his authorship of "Zarathustra's Return" in *Vivos voco*. This sense of insulation from the world, of apartness, also supported his view of himself as the solitary artist, the hermit, who in his isolated and honest way hammers away at the building of a new culture. His new life was by no means only pretense: it was a necessary condition of his continuity as a writer. When close friends tried to persuade him to abandon the rustic life and move to a cultural center like Munich or Berlin, he refused. "The wind of World and Fate passes through here, too," he wrote Fischer, "even in Montagnola, even in my study overlooking the old garden. Berlin would change nothing for me."[23]

He wanted to grow roots where he was while seeking change in voyages of the imagination. When his first summer of freedom was nearing its end, he felt ready to embark on the next and most important of these voyages: his first imaginative Journey to the East to supplant that dismal actual journey to India he had undertaken before the war. He began work on *Siddhartha*.

II

Hesse's double vision of rootedness and "revolutionary change" expressed itself in two events that marked the later months of 1919: the first, *Siddhartha*, was essentially artistic; the second was personal and social. *Siddhartha*, which began to take concrete shape late that summer, proved to be one of the Rubicons of his life that he almost failed to cross.[24] The other, the personal event that in effect helped him cross that river in the end, was his meeting with his future biographer Hugo Ball and his common-law wife, the poet Emmy Hennings, and their rapidly growing friendship that was to provide a thread of stability during the ensuing months of depression and despair.

Unquestionably, the substance of *Siddhartha* was deeply rooted in Hesse's life, and the late date of its conception is surprising. For it seems strange that as a child of two generations of Indian missionaries, raised in a home permeated by the spirit of India, with an actual trip to the Indian subcontinent behind him, he should have waited until he was over forty before he was to work seriously and coherently on an Indian theme. India was present everywhere in his memories: its books, its languages, its *objets d'art*. Gradually, it came back to him early in the century, following his mother's death and the outward solidity in his personal life. He became intermittently engrossed in Indian studies and Eastern thought, and although he responded, in part, to a growing literary fashion, he also began to face up to his difficult theme, to recapture his past.

Hesse's physical "homecoming" to India in 1911 had been a crushing personal failure, and the sketches he collected in the Indian book of 1913 had been done hastily during and after his trip. Still, these notebook entries—fiction, poetry, and other jottings—began to form a substance from which he was to draw for his later novel. It was the crisis of the war, however, in its personal and social dimensions, that brought Hesse back to his family's spiritual homeland. By the time the war had engulfed him, and had left him isolated, he had begun to reach back toward his father. On his various visits to Johannes Hesse in Germany during the early war years he began to talk to him about India, to draw him out, and learn from his father's tracts.[24]

Hesse's real engagement in an Indian theme was made inevitable by his "conversion" to a new life and art after his own breakdown in 1916. His father's death that year had been an unexpectedly severe blow, for at that time of personal instability he was shocked by the recognition that the vast gulf that had separated them through much of their lives had been his failure as well. His breakdown had been the signal, and the mythological symbols that his friend and doctor Josef Lang conveyed to him had released a series of reactions that turned Hesse toward the entire spectrum of Eastern thought. Starting with the Abraxas motif of *Demian*, a direct reflection of Jung, he came to focus more and more on a non-Western response to personal as well as cultural crises. Soon he came to feel, with Romain Rolland, that the East would provide a true counter-culture as an alternative to the decline of the West. Like many of his readers and some of his models, he sought a mystical aura, and his occasional contacts with Gusto Gräser suggest how much he had been attracted by this subterranean spirit. His road had to lead him back to India. It had to take him back to the worlds of his family, to the memories of his childhood.

On every level, Hesse's return to the East was problematic, for it involved both cultural decisions and stratagems as a writer, and the entire weight of his personal history. His recollections of his grandfather and mother, and of their connections with India, were rarely set down with as much loving care as Hesse was finally able to do during the years immediately after the task of *Siddhartha* had been mastered and overcome. "Life Story Briefly Told" and especially "Childhood of the Magician" both betray his intense involvement in that "maternal" Indian world. These brief pieces may have been fragmentary, and the references to India short and scattered, but they express what Hesse had finally come to feel about his mother and his grandfather, their conversations in English and various Indian tongues, the folk songs, and the strange visitors from another continent. They helped him weave a poetic texture in his memory. It was at this point that Hesse recalled that his father did not fit their pattern, that he could not "sing."

This strange aside about his father, reiterated at a time when the book's task was well behind Hesse, suggests the depth of his conflict. There is no question that he had learned much of what he knew from his father's influence and work. Hugo Ball, in his authorized biography of Hesse, first called attention to the importance for Hesse of his father's missionary writings, speculating that *Siddhartha* was made possible by Hesse's inward reconciliation with his father.[25]

The missionary spirit of Johannes Hesse's tracts were not to prove useful to his son. While his father had created a veritable library of pamphlets brought out by the Calwer Verlagsverein, they were essentially designed as material for missionaries in the field. Along with similar titles produced by old Hermann Gundert, Hesse could find a brochure on "Three Buddhist Priests Who Became Christian," written in 1894, a treatise on the "Conversion of Three Women in India" from 1896, and many others. A study called "Lao-Tse as a Pre-Christian Witness to the Truth" had been published as late as 1914, two years before his father's death. If these pamphlets could not have served as "literary" models in the usual sense, they were bound to affect his struggle for identity, for the issues of Confucianism and Buddhism, in which he became increasingly engaged, intersected with his father's positions.

It was this sense of his father's presence that emerges in another, later section of "Life Story Briefly Told." Significantly, in this passage he did not describe childhood memories but his actual experience of the hard year 1919–20. In a humorous note he recalls that his friends had begun to call him a Buddist. This, he countered, is far from the truth, but they were not wholly wrong. On the one hand, he could not be a Buddhist, for if he had been free to choose his own religion, he would have chosen a "conservative" religion like Confucianism or Brahmanism or Roman Catholicism. But on the other hand, this would not have been an undivided choice. "I should have done this, however, out of a longing for my polar opposite . . . for it was not by accident alone that I was born the son of pious Protestants."[26]

His father's tracts and the memory of his "maternal" past seemed to exist side by side in Hesse's imagination as he settled into his Indian book during that gradually waning year in Montagnola. There is no way of knowing how far these different impulses represented a crippling conflict. Given Hesse's personal history, this return to the myths of his family, while strongly desired, could not have been an easy homecoming. Still, the beginning was propitious, for despite the oriental trappings the story did not seem too far removed from his experience.[27] The style of his life, after all, was that of a Samana in twentieth century Switzerland. It recalled the exercises in self-deprivation on Monte Verità during the early 1900s, which he had described in the essay "In the Rocks" and which seemed to have been a particular preparation for meditative renunciation.[28] As he continued to eat chestnuts, to live on rice, milk, and macaroni, and to wear patched clothes as he went on his walks in the Ticino landscape, he assumed that contempt for the world that pervades the early sections of *Siddhartha*.

In an amusing letter to his "Friends in Berlin," included in *Picture*

Book, Hesse describes his life that winter as he tried to catch the last remnants of outdoor warmth while reading, writing, and painting. At one point, he allowed himself to be lured to a lunch in one of the great hotels in Lugano where he had been asked in his old incarnation as the well-known writer. He thought of his hosts as war profiteers, which many of them undoubtedly were, and identified himself with the poor, slugging German foot soldier (though he had been a rather elevated civilian official in Bern). From this vantage point, he looked down on his hosts and their guests, aware of his down-at-heels but apparently more moral existence. With his blue patch on his knee in a glittering world of elegant food and choice wines, he disdained the rich as profiteers and crooks.[29]

This spirit of the Samanas had survived his father's death, psycho-analysis, and the move to Ticino. It was also contained in bulky notes that had accompanied Hesse on his train ride in April. Yet he could not take up the idea seriously until Klingsor's vision had been created. For the figure of that inspired painter had developed from Hesse's immediate conflict, from his dissolved marriage and his new program as a writer. Siddhartha's pilgrimage, on the other hand, had emerged from Hesse's family history and from much earlier conflicts in his life. Finally released from his novellas early that fall, he was at last free to devote his energies to *Siddhartha* and his Indian past. After some preparation, he began to write fast, in his usual manner, and was able to complete the first part that winter. The figures of Siddhartha and Govinda among the Samanas emerged swiftly as they mirrored his actual and imaginary life in the usual legendary disguises. As the distant Orient could still be portrayed as a legend, the picture required only an exotic halo to be cast over the romantic vagrant, not substantially different from many such halos Hesse had cast over his tales. He had not yet reached the point where he had to become crucially engaged.

The first part was printed during the following summer in two install-ments of the *Neue Zürcher Zeitung* (August 6 and 7, 1920). One year later, in March 1921, it was brought out in Fischer's *Neue Rundschau*. Dedicated to Romain Rolland, it bore witness to Hesse's political inspiration on this first sustained Journey to the East. But soon after he had gotten into the second part, Hesse seemed to lack the will or the vision to continue. It had happened, he said with at least a partial aware-ness of his problem, because he had to "catch up with the ascetic and meditative life" so that the "world of the Indian spirit (which had been . . . close to me since my youth) could truly become a home for me again."[30] These words have been often cited as an explanation of Hesse's block, but in the "Diary of 1920" he gave a fuller account of him-self that partly contradicts, and surely expands, this cryptic remark.

"For many months," Hesse wrote in 1920, "my Indian poetry, my falcon, my sunflower, the hero Siddhartha lies fallow." The book had begun beautifully; it had flourished straight and clear, and then, suddenly, it was over. There was, of course, a simple explanation: as long as he could write of his own experience, the meditative life, and recapture the mood of a young Brahman searching for wisdom, he felt safe. But when he had to pass from the ascetic to the "victorious" Siddhartha, he could not manage. He could not make his hero's further progress credible without leaving his own self-enclosed world.[31] For he had to create a person who had achieved what he had not—a sense of fulfillment—and he had to place him into a world he could not yet fully imagine even as a "legend," a concrete world in which his parents and grandparents had been at home. The task proved too formidable. A new depression came over him that was to last for more than a year.

It was during this time of creation and sudden awareness of failure that Hesse met Hugo Ball, whose biography was to illuminate him even to himself. On the surface, it would seem that Ball and his temperamental wife might fortify the "revolutionary" side of Hesse's spirit, for they had spent their lives in theater, cabarets, antiwar action, and the avant-garde —all activities Hesse had anxiously avoided while regarding them with a curious longing. By the time they arrived in Agnuzzo, a few kilometers from Hesse's Montagnola, they were writing as Catholic intellectuals, filled with a moral conservativism without abandoning their footloose way of life. They became Hesse's "polar" opposites, questioning his trust in psychoanalysis, "diagnosing" many of his ailments, his eyeaches and headaches and gout, as plain hypochondria. They assailed his various disenchantments. They also represented in life what *Siddhartha* suggested in art, a fusion of inner division, of restless wandering with a stable vision, with rest.

The three of them met when they were all at a crossroads, at a moment, in 1919–20, when they were all in flight yet had reached a point of rest. The Balls' vagrancy was rooted in both their lives, but the phase that had ended with their arrival in Agnuzzo had begun just before the war.[32] At that time Hugo Ball had worked as a director in the Munich Repertory Playhouse, while Emmy Hennings had been a singer in a cabaret called *Simplizissimus* (named after the famous humor magazine). Originally a Protestant from North Germany, she had recently converted to Catholicism. Abandoned by her husband after a brief marriage, she began to support herself and her small daughter. This took on various forms, because Emmy had discovered she was a poet and even received the first signs of recognition just at the time she began to live with Hugo Ball. At the outbreak of the war, the brief stability she had achieved through her work and her liaison was shattered. Emmy was arrested by the German authorities, evidently because she had been involved in anti-war activity, and, after her release, she fled to Zurich with her Steffgen (as Hugo Ball was affectionately called by his friends) and her daughter Annemarie. At first the Balls supported themselves by working in variety shows, Emmy as a performer, Hugo as a pianist, but in February 1916 they were able to rent premises in the Spiegelgasse where they established the famous Café Voltaire. The place soon became the center of an intellectual underground of Dadaist artists and activists against the war. Ball was soon catapulted into fame as a major proponent of dadaism, but he was also surrounded by a large group of like-minded friends. People now well known, like Jean Arp, René Schickele, and Tristan Tzara were part of this group that viewed itself as a core of a cultural and political resistance.

During this period of their parallel histories Hesse and the Balls were unable to meet, although they all lived in Switzerland and held similar views about the war. For the Balls belonged to a circle of an anti-imperial underground which Hesse studiously avoided. He had retained, after all, his ties with the German establishment, was a German functionary in neutral Switzerland during wartime, and activists were people from whom he stayed aloof. Moreover, the Dadaist movement, with its cultural iconoclasm, was not to his liking. A year after the war the situation was different. The Balls had become different persons. They had returned briefly to northern Germany, to Emmy Hennings's home, only to find themselves repelled. In a scathing statement from Hamburg in July, 1920, Hugo Ball condemned the unreconstructed German spirit even during the early heady days of the Weimar republic. Now, in Agnuzzo, they tried to start a fresh life, and at this point a meeting with Hermann Hesse became possible.[33]

All three people reported their first encounter in glowing terms: Hesse in several letters as well as in his later memoir of his friend. Hugo Ball in a brief notice in his book, *Flight from Time*. Soon after the Balls' arrival Hesse had appeared at their door at noon, looking younger than they had expected. Hugo Ball wrote undoubtedly from hindsight when he said that his visitor's sharp features "wore the expression of a man who was suffering."[34] But since this was the beginning of Hesse's long depression, his agony may have been evident. Ball was then a tall, thin man, his elongated face austere beneath dark hair cut short, almost like a soldier's, while Emmy looked blowsy yet also surprisingly mannish. Her round head framed by the short hairstyle of the twenties sometimes appeared almost severe. There was a quality of warmth, of immediate communication among the three, as the Balls welcomed their unexpected guest.

The long afternoon spent talking during this first encounter ushered in a period of close contact. Hesse's "genius for friendship" once more asserted itself. He came often to visit, and soon he and Ball began to spend long hours in conversation either in Agnuzzo or in the Casa Camuzzi. They went on walks or sat in the grotto below Hesse's house, talking and drinking wine. Beneath the avant-garde exterior of his recent past, Hugo Ball revealed very close affinities with Hesse's way of thinking. Later, after Ball's untimely death, Hesse recalled that they responded to an entire substratum of similar cultural and intellectual pasts. Their talk moved from Goethe and Nietzsche to German poetry and theology to Italian paintings and architecture and landscapes, but it also moved deeper and became quickly intimate. It soon seemed as if their lives had become closely enmeshed, and the intensity of their rapport seemed to suit them well at this juncture of their lives.[35] Hesse needed a sounding board, a younger disciple, a Govinda for his own Siddhartha. Ball was not much younger—he was born in 1886—but the nine years that separated them gave him the aura of a younger companion. Emmy was a year older than her husband, but in her slightly distracted ways she always acted toward Hesse the part of a willful, dependent daughter, gifted yet filled with those feminine uncertainties that fitted in well with his picture of women. To both people he could be a parental guide. His stature as an established writer placed him, despite his psychological agonies, in a secure position from which he could help his penniless, rootless friends. At the same time, he constantly depended on them for intellectual nourishment and filial criticism. With all their contradictions, the Balls brought some stability into his life just as he was facing the difficulties of *Siddhartha*. They made the transition to 1920 and 1921 bearable and perhaps even possible.

Change constantly desired, change constantly resisted—this pattern in Hesse's life remained unaltered, and the Balls helped him maintain it. A good part of the time he lived with the trappings of the Samana as he continued his outings and shut himself off. Part of the time, too, he maintained many of his old and new acquaintances, added even the fresh intimacy with the Balls, enjoyed (despite disclaimers) his vast correspondence, and began lecturing again. All the while he faced the core of his artistic and personal self, which had become enshrined in the undone task of *Siddhartha*. Only a great deal of work, a great deal of pain and barrenness, a great many disappointments and ultimately even renewed psychoanalysis could finally allow him to bridge that painful interregnum of 1920–21. His crisis had once more become acute.

III

The year 1920 was, according to Hesse, the most "unproductive year of my life" and therefore the saddest. "For a year and a half," he wrote in his diary, "I now live like a snake, slowly, and economically." The artist's self, such a bright figure in "Klingsor" despite intermittent shadows, had begun to fade: it "had run out," was "finished"; it had "blown its top and burned out."[36] These remarks, while undoubtedly hyperbolic, bear out the image of Hesse, who had indeed "burned himself out" during that summer of fresh liberation when he had written, painted, and drunk with his friends.

While it is true that Hesse was suffering from his inability to finish a major work, in many other respects it was a time not wholly without value, nor was it as substantially different from other periods. Crisis had always been the theme of Hesse's life, and it was from the substance of crisis that many of his writings emerged. The years 1919–20 were also years during which his reputation was refurbished. *Demian* had appeared in 1919, and though he had at first concealed himself in his pseudonym, its great commercial success was of some help to him as well. By December he had received accolades from many initiates, including a most complimentary letter from C. G. Jung, who had been told of the author's identity.[37] And when Hesse revealed his authorship of *Demian* and *Zarathustra's Return* in 1920, the flood of mixed enthusiasm and anger began to reach him personally.[38] But the most substantive gain during this critical time was his discovery of Jung, which may have been more crucial than he allowed himself to admit.

In one sense, Hesse's barrenness was real. He could not go on with *Siddhartha* and did little imaginative writing. He marked time by occupying himself with other things—painting, lecturing, doing those many small reviews with which he earned his daily bread—while waiting for his moment of light during these dark months of depression. But his involvement in cultural and personal crisis, for which *Siddhartha* was to supply the key, continued to occupy his thoughts. In 1919 he was able to deliver two important lectures on Dostoevsky, which he included one year later in his volume *Gazing into Chaos*. He presented a familiar image: Dostoevsky's "sickness" or "hysteria" as a "barometer of the soul" is projected onto the landscape of the East, of Russia, then still torn by its revolution. It was a landscape marked by a frightful abyss along the edges of which a drunken Dmitry Karamazov reeled in prophetic exaltation. This vision frightened the burgher while the Seer and Saint viewed it with tears in his eyes.[39]

Hesse sidestepped India. He focused instead on the psychic "chaos" from which the transcendent vision was to emerge. And so he used in *Gazing into Chaos* the familiar image of Dostoevsky as the Mad Novelist, which was then in vogue, to fortify his own sense of the identity between crisis in the world and crisis within the self. It is easy to magnify the importance of these essays, for at the time they were surely a minor effort. But they remain important, because they are way stations in Hesse's evolution. While the tone of these lectures does not conform to the spirit of *Siddhartha*, their substance anticipates the vision he eventually achieved: the search for unity within the self.

This vision, which Hesse had nurtured for many years, he now explored in its direct psychological implications. Illness intervened late that year in Montagnola, and when he recovered he moved back into familiar territory—not just to psychology but also to the old traditions that had made him into the person he still essentially was: that Swabian, Swiss-German writer who had grown up with the books of Goethe and Gottfried Keller. The themes that he sought to distill in *Siddhartha* as images of meditation he now reviewed in his own familiar setting. He entered into contracts with publishers to edit the masters and spent much time selecting and commenting upon the writers who had been with him in his grandfather's library in Calw, in Tübingen, and in Basel: poets like Friedrich Hölderlin and Novalis, romantic storytellers like Jean Paul. He avoided the crossroads of *Siddhartha*, the confrontation with his material, by occupying himself with writers who expressed for him similar thoughts in less disturbing ways.

Hesse displaced his problem. He backed away from the material of his family and childhood, from the Indian "world of images." Moreover, the full life he led along with his supposedly solitary existence took him back to his immediate past. This was the time when *Vivos voco* had finally become a reality. Its first issues appeared and took a welcome toll of Hesse's energy. This journal devoted to "the moral reconstruction of Europe" was to have been a new response to postwar cultural decline. It was also an attempt to perpetuate the spirit of those war years when he and Woltereck had worked closely together to ensure its survival, with all its caring, in the uncaring twenties.

In the pages of *Vivos voco* Hesse acknowledged his authorship of *Demian* and "Zarathustra's Return" and opened the door to the floods of invective that disturbed and sustained him throughout his life. His letters of the time, the conversations he held with his friends, the long disputations with the Balls, all suggest that his view, described in the "Diary of 1920," was not mistaken: the involvement in cultural politics, the battles, real and imagined, with his right-wing antagonists, the sense of being an "outsider" at bay, all contributed to a mystique through which he could cover his temporary retreat from *Siddhartha*. At the same time, most of his lectures and casual writings of the time, his editings and his discussions, suggest a continued preoccupation with his novel's theme. He refined the ideas of *Siddhartha*, but he did so on safer ground.

By early in 1921, Hesse's depression had lasted long enough to move him to seek a solution. The previous year had already been filled with travel. More and more frequently he had forsaken his idyllic palazzo, the Casa Camuzzi, and had gone on lecture tours and visited friends. He was a frequent guest in the Wassmers' Castle Bremgarten near Bern and often visited other friends like the Leutholds in Zurich, taking in music, feeling, as he wrote on one occasion, "the spirit of Demian everywhere." His relationship with Josef Lang, reinforced by visits in Lucerne and conversations with him in Ticino, continued as a prolonged and highly personal therapy. But early in 1921 he turned to Jung himself. When he had first come to Zurich in January, it had been planned as merely another visit—to see the Leutholds and other friends and to spend a little time with Ruth Wenger, the young woman he was to marry, who was then taking singing lessons in Zurich. He had intended to return to his southern retreat after only a short stay, for he was very much attached to his home in Montagnola and to the friends he had left behind in Agnuzzo. What seems to have held him in the city, partly against his will, was his decision to undergo a series of analytic sessions with C. G. Jung.

Except for various statements to friends about the extreme difficulty of his analysis (and the hope that Jung would not charge him a fee), Hesse has left few clues about the content of these sessions.[40] But it is known that he was in Zurich, at least intermittently, between mid-January and June and the tone of the letters that mention the real purpose of his stay suggests that it was not haphazard. He lived in pleasant surroundings, in the forest near the Zürichberg, tried to work and at the same time come to terms with his analysis. In a letter to the Balls he was quite explicit about his life and its difficulties:

> I'm up and down. City and work are very tiring, but I live in a very beautiful spot high up near the forest on the Zürichberg, and occasionally I see dear people. But my psychoanalysis is giving me a great deal of trouble, and often Klingsor feels old and incorrigible. The summer is no longer his.
> I shall stay here still longer, the fruit I have bitten into has to be eaten to the full. Dr. Jung impresses me very much.

Although the exact length of his stay is uncertain, it is clear that it was arduous and that Hesse had at least temporarily settled into a routine. It is a long way from the Zürichberg to Jung's home in Küsnacht, yet his son Heiner (who was then twelve years old) recalls that his father walked each day to his regular sessions. It was a self-imposed ordeal that took a great deal of energy. Some sense of the intensity of this experience can be gained from another letter he sent to the Balls. This letter, on black-bordered writing paper still left over from his father's death, contains a strong defense of his analysis against friends who, as Catholics, were most skeptical about its benefits as a secular form of confession. In this letter, written from Zurich in the middle of June, Hesse wrote:

> About psychoanalysis I do not wish to enter into any discussion. The support a man finds especially in hard times cannot be a subject of debate for him, so much less so when he, like myself, does not feel qualified to judge dogma and correct forms of belief. I too feel sorry that we know no more about the methods and techniques of the early monks, but that they deviate very far from the recognitions of other religions I do not really believe. I do not believe in an essential difference between Catholic humanity and the rest of it. And so today's psychoanalysis . . . can have at bottom hardly any other goal but to create a space within ourselves in which God's voice can be heard.

The clue in this defense of psychoanalysis is, of course, the Jungian formulation that analysis creates a space within the self in which "God's voice can be heard." At this time in Hesse's life, however, it also suggests an important image that finds its reflection, as Jung himself was to recognize, in both his major works of the next few years. For in both *Siddhartha* and *Steppenwolf* Hesse used the idea of interior space in which temporal strife is displaced by a transcendent vision. If in his earlier books ailing eyesight is transformed into a healing vision, in most of his new books this entire process is placed within the psyche. The actual eye is replaced by an inner eye that no longer feeds on external nature. Perhaps it is this sense of "vision" Hesse had fought to gain during his barren months of struggle for *Siddhartha*. The experience, however, was also intensely painful. A private message to the Balls concludes the didactic note: "Meanwhile, my analysis has become a fire for me which I must pass through but which hurts very much." And he added: "Already duties and danger have emerged from it for me which I can as yet barely think of."[41]

Hesse was getting closer to the core of his personal problem. His work still kept him from writing fiction but it did take him to a new interest in publicizing his personal, in fact, his psychological biography. The "Diary of 1920" evolved into a literary work and passages were garnered from large numbers of notebooks to make up the *Diary of a Derailed Man*, which was published in *Simplizissimus* in 1922–23. All this self-involved activity suggests Hesse's usual habit of exploiting publicly a carefully edited picture of himself as the artist defined by his private agonies. For this Jung chided him with the Olympian irony of the analyst. In a brief note written late in January 1922, ostensibly to thank Hesse for the poems he had sent him, he marked that he had noticed a rather unfavorable review in the *Neue Zürcher Zeitung:* "As I notice in the newspapers, you have sent terror into the hearts of the Hottingen literary brethren with your autobiography, which seemed to stray into boundless space."[42] He was referring to a reading of the "Diary of 1920" earlier that month to the Hottingen literary club in Zurich. Yet these acts, however uncomfortable for their audiences or however tasteless in the mind of the analyst, indicate how Hesse had begun to concern himself with his problems. He used his actual life—"ten notebooks of my diary"—rather than a symbolic transformation of it. It was a practice that reached beyond the conclusion of *Siddhartha* and informed most of his work during the 1920s.

If the association with Jung had been partly responsible for an increase in Hesse's direct preoccupation with himself during the remainder of 1921, it may have also extended to his gradual recognitions about the limitations of his work. For the "displacement" of his task from the images of *Siddhartha* to the images he knew so well from his German models was surely in itself a technical barrier that kept him from his book. An incident that occurred in 1921 suggests that he had become aware of these barriers. Samuel Fischer had asked him to write a preface to his *Selected Works*, which he thought of issuing on the occasion of Hesse's forty-fifth birthday in July 1922. At first he was pleased and flattered. Delightedly he wrote Adis that he had apparently become sufficiently fossilized to merit this conventional enshrinement. But when he sat down to write the preface to his *Works*, he found himself, and the project, to be inadequate.

In the brief essay based on this request, Hesse sought to explain his barrenness on literary grounds. His place as a novelist, he wrote, was not among the greater or lesser bearers of traditions in world literature, but rather among the German romantic lyricists who used the novel to "make music" and who used storytelling as a pretext for creating an image of "self and world."[43] He therefore prevented the publication of the projected *Works*. Such aesthetic modesty involved a more personal recognition: an awareness that he was still unable to see others outside himself. It was not just German romanticism in which he was caught but an entire perspective on his life and his person, which is articulated equally in the diaries of this time. Isolation had always been one of the proverbial conditions of the artist that Hesse liked to sentimentalize. The magic of the unconscious, the magic of art, was destined to release him in his work.

Hesse tried simultaneously to escape from the "core of the self" and to wrap himself around it in self-imposed isolation. External social life was both needed as nourishment and deplored as a drain on his energies. That summer of 1921 he could still enjoy the company of the Balls and establish himself more fully in his relationship with Ruth Wenger and her family, who were occupying a summer house in nearby Carona. Again, this double life that imposed sociability on his programmatic seclusion was not without tension. At the Wengers he had to cope with the father's opposition, for Herr Wenger seemed far less enthusiastic than his wife and daughter about Ruth's growing intimacy with a family man in his forties.[44] And he was less impressed than they by his credentials as a famous writer. But mother and daughter made up for the father's reticence by courting Hesse assiduously. Indeed, Hesse began to develop a close relationship with the mother, Lisa Wenger that lasted much longer than his brief marriage to her daughter. For Ruth's mother was not only a fellow writer with whom he could talk about their craft but also the older guide he usually sought in women.[45]

While Hesse became a frequent visitor at the Wengers and himself received constant visits from his sons, sisters, and friends, he also retained his persistent desire to withdraw. In August he wrote a postcard to Emmy Ball asking her to drop in on the Wengers. Two of his sons were coming, and, after they had left, he would have to go to Ascona to confer with Mia. It was Hesse's characteristic way of begging off an obligation that even then seemed burdensome. But the postcard concludes with an illuminating note: "I need a few days alone. Everything looks dark and hostile."

Jung's help initiated earlier did not bear immediate results, and the feeling of creative void that had been present during the past year continued through the summer. By now even Montagnola was no longer a haven; even there he did not feel happy. In September he went on his first major lecture tour to his native Swabia since the war, but even that experience was far from satisfactory. He was unable to sleep. By the time he reached Stuttgart he was ready to come home. And the depression that he also projected onto the outside world seemed more impenetrable than ever. "Germany today," he wrote Erwin Ackerknecht in his gloom, yet not without sharp insight, "is a kind of America. One has to swim and bustle around in it to keep from drowning. If one can do that one is all right." The trip ended pleasantly enough. A wealthy friend drove him to Zurich by car, and motoring through the Black Forest gave him pleasure. Back in Switzerland he spent some time with

Ruth Wenger, who had returned to Zurich for her singing lessons, took in some music, and lapped up sympathy and friendship before returning to Montagnola early in November.

Permanence and change, self and other, these perennial themes provided the motifs for Hesse's motion-filled life while the unfinished novel, *Siddhartha*, remained like an irremovable rock: he could neither write it nor ignore it. Meanwhile, he received another jolt when unexpectedly, during his absence, the Balls decided to pull up stakes and move to Munich. Their sudden disappearance was a real blow for Hesse, although he tried to help them get established in their new home. He wrote to the brothers Geheeb, his friends at *Simplizissimus*. He sent money and helped the Balls make connections in the city. But their absence affected him profoundly. Temporarily at least, Ticino had become empty for him. When he got back from his journey and found them gone he felt lost. It took him a week before he could bring himself to go near their abandoned house in Agnuzzo. He walked around it sadly, feeling deserted, watching the sun shining on the empty cottage and garden.

Unable to stand the solitude he valued so highly, Hesse was off again within two weeks after his return. Partly, of course, his movements can be explained by his need to earn money. He had to be constantly on the road, lecturing in Olten or Bern or Zurich, because in addition to book reviews, public lecturing supplied him with regular sustenance. But it was also symptomatic of his restlessness, his inability during this time of low spirits to be content anywhere. When he was in Montagnola it was too cold: an icy wind was blowing from the St. Gotthard. When he was in northern Switzerland he regretted the cold days and nights: not a single sunny day in this dreary country. After a few weeks at home during the first part of November he was off again, making the usual rounds to the Wassmers in Bern, to Ruth Wenger and other friends like Volkmar Andreä and the Leutholds in Zurich. He did not get back until early in December, yet when he accepted an invitation to spend Christmas with the Wengers in their home in Délémont, he was able to say that he welcomed the "interruption of my hermit's life in Montagnola."

Hesse's relationship with the Wenger family had become closer since the summer, for he required a permanent involvement, especially after the Balls' departure. By Christmas, he was busy helping them decorate their tree. It was a magical beginning of a magical year that was to bring at last the completion of *Siddhartha*. When Emmy Hennings sent him a new book of hers, which reached him in Délémont just in time for Christmas, he was able to write that "the fairy tale of life is enacted everywhere," even in Munich. It was a chance remark made to a friend who was having her troubles in the new city, but it suggested a new direction, a return to seeing life as a "legend" and "fairy tale" and as a "theater of the mind," which was to help him unlock the door that barred him from the completion of his book.

On the surface, the new year 1922 was to be no less mobile than any other year of Hesse's recent past. He assured his friends and colleagues, and even himself, that he lived the withdrawn life of a hermit, yet no sooner had he gotten back from his holiday with the Wengers when he was off again on a lecture tour. This time he went to St. Gallen to lecture on the Indian spirit, and while the subject made clear that he had finally returned to his book, this return had to be acted out literally on the run. On the same trip he stopped off in Basel to read some more from his works and accepted an invitation to lecture in Zurich, which he used to visit Ruth and his friends. While this was clearly the time when he reapproached his Indian subject, the dominant theme of these early weeks in 1922 continued to be his restlessness. When he got back to Montagnola after three weeks' absence, he complained of snow, of a frozen well, of the stark loneliness of winter in the country. He also told Hugo Ball that he needed rest. "I'm tired," he wrote, "of constantly being a guest in other people's houses."

Hesse's life was a continuous dialectic. When he was temporarily settled, as in his early weeks in Montagnola, he converted his restlessness into work that expressed him as a vagrant of the imagination: Klein-Wagner, Klingsor, the early *Siddhartha*. At times of physical mobility, his work remained a beacon for him as well, a *fata morgana* that constantly eluded him but that, when caught at last, expressed the firm vision he sought, a reflection of his peripatetic wandering in the serenity of art. This was true of the final passages of *Siddhartha*, which came to him at last in the spring of 1922. The actual work had been sandwiched between episodes of visiting and receiving visitors. After his many trips in January he was off again in the middle of February to visit Ruth in Zurich and to lecture in Winterthur and to meet his son Heiner. The material of his novel, then, must have been literally refined on the road while he was preparing his lectures.

One break which Hesse credited with much of the help in his final success was provided by an important visit early in February. His cousin Wilhelm Gundert, his "Japanese cousin," stopped by briefly. This professor and missionary from Tokyo stayed much too briefly to have been of decisive help, yet by dedicating the second part of *Siddhartha* to him Hesse signaled his indebtedness. Gundert had been in Europe for only a short time and was on his way back to his post in Tokyo without his family. His wife had accompanied him as far as Lugano and Hesse was able to see him for a few days in his nearby Montagnola. Nothing more illuminates Hesse's way of working than his claim that this short visit (enriched, of course, by their earlier correspondence) should have lent him the support he needed to finish his book. With Gundert, he wrote the Balls, "I can live wholly in Indian thoughts and ideas. He lives in them as fully as I do, and it was good to taste all that again."

The speed with which the book was finally completed at the time of constant wandering suggests how thoroughly *Siddhartha* had been a figure of the imagination fashioned by attitudes Hesse had absorbed during a lifetime of personal struggle with his Indian theme and by the general vogue of a century. Suddenly he felt psychologically released. A few weeks after Wilhelm Gundert's departure he told Hugo Ball that he was "now entirely stuck in Ancient India." All of his lectures now had to do with "Brahman and Atman, also with Buddha."

In his lectures that preceded the breakthrough, Hesse drew a dialectical picture of Indian art and religion reminiscent of Nietzsche's division between the Dionysian and Apollonian spirits, which had fascinated him since his early years in Basel. Two contrasting ideas of India existed side by side: the India of idols and temples; images of gods with many breasts, two heads, heads of elephants and monkeys, a jungle of forms, "chaotic, splendid, barbaric" and the gentle India with its image of the all-knowing, all-compassionate Buddha, with monks and saints deeply sunk in meditation. His family had not opened him to this knowledge, for as missionaries they viewed both forms of expression through the crusading Christian's eye. Still, there was much in their traditions to build on, and the romantic view of an India steeped in its contradictory past coincided with his own.[46] The Samana in twentieth century Switzerland sensed that the divisions he discerned in the Indian spirit expressed his own paradoxical condition of being both free and confined, in motion and at rest. He had arrived within. He had crossed the Rubicon of his life by defining himself and achieving the insight that allowed him once more to view his "life as a legend." He had received help from every quarter: Hugo and Emmy Ball, Doctors Lang and Jung, and his many friends scattered in the cities and towns of northern Switzerland. For the moment at least he had regained his strength: the vault of *Siddhartha* had been reopened.

IV

Hardly more than six weeks had passed in Montagnola between Wilhelm Gundert's visit and the last hurried trip north, and a fresh journey undertaken in May, but it was during these few weeks that

Siddhartha was finished. It remained an agony, for creation, as he told Emmy Ball, was a torture, a "process of life, no less than a birth, and often the two can be mistaken for one another." He had finally found the "inward way" not as an abstraction but as a personal, indeed a psychological, reality.

The fruit of Hesse's long depression had been a new sense of himself that allowed him finally to view the inward way concretely as an interior landscape. This was the new vision he brought to the completion of *Siddhartha*, a vision that cast his probings of *Gazing into Chaos*, his diaries, his dabbling in German romantic poetry, in a palpable perspective. Jung's hand had seemed more evident in this recognition than anyone else's, for Hesse had found at last a way to create that space within the self in which "God's voice can be heard." Although he had always been naturally inclined to view outer in terms of inner experience, at this time it had become a specific idea involving personal and artistic insight that expressed itself in a new kind of imagery. The body, the living self, had become an instrument played on by the mind, which provides the only true reality.

This idea, which made it easier for him to recall an "Indian world of images" as "images of the soul," was accompanied by a psychological way of thinking that provided him with fresh images. When he heard in April, for example, that his younger sister Marulla might suffer from tuberculosis, Hesse wrote to his confidante Adis with surprising harshness that "it is not really the lung." Rather, he suggested that Marulla was resisting a move to Munich then under discussion. What is interesting about the note is not the rather commonplace psychological interpretation, especially commonplace in a man who had been in analysis for many years, but the images used to describe it. He called Marulla's hesitation "a theater of conscience," an image he made clearer in a second letter to Adis for which he seems to have found time in the midst of his work on *Siddhartha*. Responding favorably to Marulla's decision to make the move after all, Hesse wrote:

> As you know, I look at everything from the perspective of the soul, or from an emotional center of life, and I consider lungs only as the keys of the piano we play on. And so I believe that Marulla has only displaced her irresolution and anxiety to her lungs—I don't mean that her lung ailment is imaginary, but it represents an attempt to escape. . . . Up to our final illness, the illness we die from, we always play on our few piano keys, and make "theater" of them, each of us in his own way.

If as a concept these remarks are no more than a psychoanalytic cliché, as an image they provide some insight into the inward way portrayed in Hesse's books of the twenties. Beginning with *Siddhartha* and culminating in the Magic Theater of *Steppenwolf*, the notion that events portrayed in a novel are really images in an interior space (a theater of the mind) is articulated more and more fully in Hesse's work. In *Siddhartha*, it is interwoven with an imaginary Indian landscape and a mystical view of private experience.

Hesse's lectures delivered to various audiences at this time—to young students in Zurich, to patients in sanatoriums, to ladies' groups and literary circles—began to reveal more and more of the reshaped content that marked this theme with the imprint of his own sensibility. The material he presented was rather commonplace, partly so because of the popular nature of many of these lectures, but it nonetheless reflects the final shape of *Siddhartha* as an expression of the psyche. Hesse spoke of the Brahman ascent from magic and ritual to a clarified vision, to saint-hood. He also spoke of Buddha's recognition that the self is a mere receptacle, that the saved soul must struggle away from the error of individuation and become one with universal harmony, an image Hesse captured in Siddhartha's final vision. Such ideas grew out of more than general observations about Indian religion: they were created by a new awareness. Siddhartha's pilgrimage may exhibit his ascent from the various stages of Brahmanism to Buddhist serenity, but it does so in conjunction with the psychological perceptions with which Hesse sought to come to terms during the years of his silence. The conclusion of *Siddhartha*, which had eluded Hesse so long, depended on a particular inner vision that sketched a unique interior landscape.[47] The tension in Hesse's life between constant arrivals and departures, and the illusion of his isolated, solitary, and unchanging existence, provided a bio-graphical clue to the mystical ending of the book. A combination of the Indian world of his imagination and the psychological recognitions of his daily life allowed him at last to find the magic key to his work.[48]

The restless man sought stability in a momentary vision of stillness. "It was the Self, the character and nature of which I wished to learn," Hesse's Siddhartha said at the end of the first part of the book. "I wanted to rid myself of the Self, to conquer it, but I could not conquer it. I could only deceive it, could only fly from it, could only hide it."[49] Hesse's unsettled psyche, never at home with himself and therefore nowhere else while always striving to be wholly at rest, was caught in this image of the wandering Siddhartha. For his life, like his author's, was always one of departures: Siddhartha leaving his father's house; Sid-dhartha leaving the Samanas; Siddhartha leaving Govinda and the disciples of Buddha; Siddhartha turning his back on the worldly life. But the image Hesse created in that difficult second part becomes a counterpoint to all these leave-takings. At the moment of fulfillment, Siddhartha himself is left by the ferryman Vaseduveda who had been his guide through the "narrow passage" of his life. At this point, a new serenity and wisdom prevailed. As Hesse wrote slyly to Emmy Ball: "My Siddhartha does not, in the end, learn true wisdom from any teacher, but from a river that roars in a funny way and from a kindly old fool who always smiles and who is secretly a saint."[50]

The vision of the unity of things, which Siddhartha discerns in the flux of the flowing river, in the motions and sounds of the river that "roars in a funny way," emerges as the novel's finale. It is both a visual image and a musical chord that brings all of life's contradictory movements together: an image caught by eye and ear, yet turned inward. The river crossing of a blind old man, which Hesse had described lovingly in an Indian sketch written a decade earlier, suggests similarly an inward projection of an external setting. Knowing the river and the opposite bank, the old man's unseeing yet farsighted eyes lead him firmly up the steep bank on the other side. But in this later version of the episode, placed in the context of a novel, the fact of physical blindness disappears as the entire outer landscape is absorbed by the mind. The river has become part of Siddhartha's mind; the serenity he discerns in the flux of motion and sound is mirrored in his features. This image appears as a response to all the departures in the novel, as the missing link sought during those agonized eighteen months of Hesse's block. He had known it theoretically all along, but it took an inward recognition to portray it successfully: the sense of inner space in which he could exist at peace with himself and his past. Momentarily at least, during a brief moment between departures, Hesse was able to perceive, inwardly, the image his psychoanalysis had taught him to attain.

V

"Buddha's Way to Salvation," Hesse said in one of his lectures, "has been often criticized and doubted, because it is thought to be wholly grounded in cognition. True, but it's not just intellectual cognition, not just learning and knowing, but spiritual experience that can be earned only through strict discipline in a selfless life."[51] This was the message of *Siddhartha*, which earned him his success. However commonplace these thoughts may appear at a time when they were well publicized by Count Hermann Keyserling and Lafcadio Hearn, they reached deeply into a consciousness of a generation that longed for regeneration, for a discipline of the spirit. Hesse's words affected them as they had done before, in *Peter Camenzind* or *Demian,* expressing a feeling that was given fresh substance through his simple and direct yet highly charged language.

Siddhartha was put to a test even while the book was still in the printing shops of S. Fischer in Berlin. On August 7, 1922, Romain Rolland invited Hesse to an international conference in Lugano where such luminaries as Bertrand Russell and Georges Duhamel were to congregate. As a further inducement, Rolland mentioned that a young Indian scholar would be present, a professor of history from Calcutta. Hesse had just returned from lecturing in Zurich and was not eager to attend the conference. He was such a hermit, he wrote Romain Rolland (while barely unpacking his bags) that he had not even been in nearby Lugano for a year.[52] But he finally consented and, in fact, actually performed. In place of a lecture he read the ending of *Siddhartha,* in which the hero perceives the unity of all things. Few, he reported, understood what he was reading. Duhamel complimented him on his language. Bertrand Russell's reaction remains unreported. But the young Indian historian, Kalidas Nag, felt instantly drawn to him.

The responsive chord Hesse struck in the young scholar is prophetic of the fortunes of *Siddhartha,* for Kalidas Nag's reaction was intensely personal. They talked for a time at a party given by Romain Rolland's sister.[53] And a note Hesse sent his admirer was met with an overwhelmingly adulatory letter in English: "Your profound sketch of the history of our first mutual discovery," the letter began, "created such an impression on me that I dropped all my work and came to you for that solemn communion. It is so easy to come to you." This was familiar language. But that an Indian scholar should have felt moved to address him in this way is a tribute to Hesse's ability to transcend distances between people if he felt a positive resonance. The time he had spent with Hesse, Kalidas Nag continued, had been a time of communion. They had been bound together by a wordless language. Debate or discussion was useless because in their "eloquent silences" the whole of reality presented itself to them in a "flash of personal revelation." An echo indeed of the final images of *Siddhartha!* "It is a book," the letter concludes, "which should be translated in all the European languages, for here we face for the first time the real East presented to the West."

How "real" the East was that Hesse presented in *Siddhartha* has continued to be a nagging question. In a peculiar way, the interior vision of *Siddhartha,* portraying in a language beyond words the unity of "self and world," echoes the Pietism of Hesse's own family within the same Indian context in which that tradition had functioned for his parents and grandparents. It was also a feeling that communicated itself only to those who by virtue of their youth or their mystical sensibility were ready to share in it. For this reason, perhaps, Kalidas Nag's hope for universal translation was not immediately fulfilled. Early hopes that the book might gain many readers outside the German-speaking countries remained unfulfilled. In 1923, Hesse wrote happily to Adis that a translation of *Siddhartha* into English was in progress, but actually no official version of the novel appeared in English until the 1950s, when various translations in several Western (and Indian) languages were also published. The slow progress of the novel in gaining a wide international audience was linked to its particular emotional appeal. To many readers outside the German tradition it seemed a slight, sentimental tale that reduced complex religious issues to the simplest terms. But the simplicity and sentiment were precisely the sources of the novel's strength. Kalidas Nag's idolizing language and exaggerated claims were symptomatic of a vast response. Many of Hesse's readers agreed with him, and few of them were Indian. It was Hesse—not any of the more established authorities like Count Keyserling—who spoke meaningfully to German youth. The reason for this appeal can be found in the intimately personal projection of a writer who had again managed to write a spiritual autobiography, a romantic legend in the form of an Indian poem. It is in these intimate terms—the authenticity of a soul baring itself in its search for a new vision—that the East was communicated to the West. It had its own psychological authenticity.

Hesse's novel described his interior dialectic. All of the contrasting poles of his life were sharply etched: the restless departures and the search for the stillness of home; the diversity of experience and the harmony of a unifying spirit; the security of religious dogma and the anxiety of freedom. In this way he was himself and not himself. In the novel he retained for his hero many of Buddha's qualities and ideas, including even the name of Siddhartha, yet Buddha and Siddhartha remained separate figures. The ambivalences Hesse displayed in his life become counterpoints of a book that is about Buddha while it is not about Buddha. This dialectic of his life, of being both himself and not himself, of desiring to be contained by precept and home and being free, was also the dialectic of the lives of his readers, which he rendered as a legend in highly lyrical terms.

The writer who plays two different roles also reflects his own inner tensions in a tale structurally simple and at the same time most complex in its psychological texture. It clearly bears the earmarks of Hesse's attempt to transform himself into another person while preserving the essential core of his being. This theme, which would occupy Hesse more and more during the ensuing years, enabled him to view the culture of a distant continent both as the man he was and as the man he assumed the creature of that other culture to be. Like the Chinese Elder Brother, whom he created in *The Glass Bead Game*, his Siddhartha wore Eastern dress while displaying his own features. The enthusiasm with which Indian intellectuals like Kalidas Nag received the book was created in part by the freedom with which Hesse could assimilate their culture without condescension while making it his own. But the intensity of the book's appeal to Hesse's young countrymen can be explained by his highly personal, loving transposition of Eastern ideas into his Western context—by his dual physiognomy.

A missionary in the best sense, Hesse could approach another world, another identity, and make it his own while also maintaining his Christian and Western self. This was possible only in fiction. If he exhibited the usual European bias on his actual trip to India, on his journey of the imagination this bias disappeared. Here he continued to act as his dual self, both German and romantic and Taoist and Buddhist, living simultaneously in two seemingly opposite interior worlds. But while this ability lent him strength and appeal, it was also his weakness, for it entailed great difficulty in maintaining a single attitude. Soon he was to characterize himself as the Protestant Steppenwolf. At this point, he was the Protestant Siddhartha.

VI

Hermann Hesse's Indian work, as it was completed in the spring of 1922, fashioned the inner self-portrait of the imaginative vagrant who remained the wayfarer of the romantic tale and became his projection into an imaginative East. It was one of his greatest successes. For this legend, along with the fairy tales, with *Knulp*, *Demian*, and "Klingsor", established a coherent body of literature on which the German Youth Movement relied as texts for a new culture. He was once again considered one of the important writers of his time, a serious novelist for his contemporaries and the creator of a canon for a generation younger than himself. Hesse was deeply aware of this role. In July 1922, just after his forty-fifth birthday, he had been invited to a lecture in Zurich. This time he was not very eager to go, because it was midsummer and he disliked traveling in extreme weather. But he felt compelled to accept, because "I must not miss any opportunity to spend an evening speaking to receptive young people." In their company he was comfortable and felt wholly accepted. Like Kalidas Nag, they thought it was "easy to come to him." This kind of communication was his greatest reward after the agonies of writing *Siddhartha*. The imaginary hermit spoke to his actual followers and responded to their needs.

Hesse's life continued to be precarious. He was anxious and depressed. He leaned heavily on his friends. He was pursued by eyeaches and headaches. But his life as a spiritual leader of the young took on a particular tone in the early twenties. It turned into a mystique: the arrival at the station in Zurich or Basel or St. Gallen or Bern; or in Stuttgart and other South German towns; the hurried walk or ride to the lecture hall; the warmth with which his listeners responded to him and overwhelmed him with questions and pleas for personal advice. Then there was usually an evening with friends, an overnight stay, and he would be off again— home or to some other place and some other reading or lecture.

When Hesse had first arrived in Montagnola, he had turned his sore eyes into the instruments of the painter Klingsor, who reproduced on his canvas a self-portrait that was also a vision of "self and world." Three years later, after the agonies of self-doubt and analysis, he recreated that portrait as a spiritual vision, an inner space that offered his readers a legendary alternative to the actual world. He was successful because, in rendering it, he could be both young and middle-aged as he could be the Brahman Siddhartha and at the same time the Swiss-Swabian writer Hermann Hesse, the son of Pietest missionaries.

Clearly, with this conception enshrined in *Siddhartha*, Hesse had confirmed his reputation as a teacher. He had captured the imagination of a large portion of those who had lived through the war as adolescents and young men and women and who rejected, as he did, a postwar civilization that seemed as irretrievably corrupt as the civilization that had produced the war. With him, they sought a transcendent state, that inner space in which all things could be unified and simply understood. If Duhamel and Bertrand Russell did not understand him, this generation was filled with his longing. More and more bothered by his aches and pains, never wholly at home in his body or at peace in his mind, Hesse gained strength from their acclaim, from his voluminous correspondence, from his reputation as their teacher. The vagrant of the imagination had again found resonance among the wayfarers of German youth.

7

The Ailing Traveler

I

This is my dilemma and problem. Much can be said about it, but it cannot be solved. To force the two poles of life together, to transcribe the dual voices in life's melody will never be possible for me. And yet I will follow the dark command within me and will be compelled again and again to make the attempt. This is the mainspring that drives my little clock.

—From *A Guest at the Spa*

SIDDHARTHA HAD AT LAST become part of Hesse's personal history. While the sense of satisfaction in having completed the small Indian book sustained and revived him, the relief that attended his accomplishment did not find lasting resonance in his daily life. His suffering and his need to feel isolated were too intense to allow him a long reprieve. The physical pain in his eyes and legs, and his times of despair, were real enough, and no amount of psychologizing could whisk them away. He was also always plagued by a need for money, a sense of poverty induced partly by the role he had assigned to himself but partly also real. His obligation toward Mia and his sons took up a good part of his earnings, and although he tried to lead the life of an ascetic hermit, he had other needs: for travel, for a social life, and, at least intermittently, for personal comfort. He allowed himself to be haunted by deadlines for those many reviews with which he supplemented his living, and to enter into contracts with publishers for anthologies and editions of greater and lesser authors, which involved long hours of painstaking reading that only increased his eyestrain.

Hesse's active work did not cease immediately after he finished *Siddhartha*. Late in May he was still able to write his accomplished fairy tale "Piktor's Metamorphoses," a story that was clearly the outgrowth of his latest book, which he carried with him for two years and read at public lectures before he finally allowed it to be published, in a limited edition, in 1925. In this story he could be more direct and succinct than he had been in *Siddhartha*. In a few days of feverish writing, still carried by the momentum of his novel, Hesse had clarified the implications of his larger work in the more familiar idiom of the German romantic fairy tale. His hero, who turns into a stone and a tree while maintaining himself, reflects not only Hesse's feeling for the identity of physical and spiritual levels, but also his sense that each person comprises several existences at once: self and other, material and immaterial, the one and the many.

By coincidence, Hesse was working on this story when T. S. Eliot followed up his gracious note in French written two months earlier and called on him in Montagnola. Much has been made of this visit by various biographers who have seized on this meeting as evidence of Hesse's international stature at the time, but what little is known of their encounter does not support this importance. Eliot's knowledge of Hesse remained largely confined to the contents of *Gazing into Chaos*, which had caused his enthusiasm, and he published one of its essays, "On Recent German Poetry," in *Criterion* in October 1922. His memory of the visit to Montagnola remained vague. Hesse, in turn, never wrote anything on Eliot, although the latter's poems were translated into German and Hesse wrote on writers and poets far and wide. But especially at this time, after *Siddhartha* and "Piktor's Metamorphoses" their conversation (such as it was with their linguistic barriers) could have no more than underscored their differences.

Eliot had sought out a "sage" in the Swiss mountains who had written that essay on Dostoevsky's *The Brothers Karamazov* from which he had quoted in *The Wasteland*. Hesse's ideas of the meaning of chaos and the possibilities for salvation were very different, and his view could never have appealed to Eliot's orthodoxy. Their talk probably never got down to these issues, but their paths, in any event, moved in divergent directions: Eliot's toward the *Four Quartets*, Hesse's toward *Steppenwolf*.

After "Piktor's Metamorphoses," his active creation was over, for the time being at least. For weeks Hesse labored over made work, his suffocatingly numerous reviews and feuilletons. He went on lecture tours, hiked, painted, received visitors, and nursed his pain. Friends and children called frequently at the Casa Camuzzi during the summer of 1922, and Hesse spent long and often happy hours in garden and grotto. Ruth Wenger was back, too, staying in her parents' house in Carona, tending her garden and even a goat. They saw each other often in both their houses and went on walking tours together along the trails radiating outward from Montagnola, or up the steep paths of Mt. San Salvatore. Hesse carried the painting things, Ruth a picnic basket, and they would settle down at picturesque places to paint, eat, and bask in the sun. Often they were joined by others. His sons Bruno and Heiner stayed

for a few days each, usually individually, and he would receive visits
from Adis, Karl Isenberg, and friends like Othmar Schoeck and Josef
Englert. Many times, however, Hesse went painting alone, usually at
dawn, to take in the bright early light. At noon he would sunbathe,
sometimes for one or two hours, in the belief that this would help
his gout and ease his pain. The doctor had made clear that it would not
do anything for his ailments, but the sun had been Hesse's mystical link
with health for decades and he could not give it up, especially as he felt
the burden of his physical condition.

On his birthday Hesse usually demanded special attention. It was an
unusually meaningful occasion for him, and his forty-fifth this July 2 was
no exception. In the morning mail he had received letters from both
Balls and a miniature Indian picture from their small daughter Annemie
as she was affectionately called. Bruno, a painter, had sent a self-portrait
in oil. Ruth arrived later in the morning to convey her congratulations
and spend the day. Yet when he wrote the Balls three days later to thank
them for their attention he made clear that he felt neglected. Except for
the Balls, only his sisters had written to congratulate him on this great
occasion, and he mused that being thus forgotten by all his other friends
was proof that he had become a hermit. "That's how it goes when one no
longer lives in the world."

These feelings found a convenient resonance in the Wenger house on
the other side of the valley. It seemed like a ready-made if painfully dis-
torting mirror. Herr Wenger's fevers and pains, which made him absent
so much of the time, appeared as an ironic reflection of his own struggle
with his aching body. On the one hand, he judged that Ruth's father was
"sliding downhill," yet on the other he regarded those complaints and
withdrawals with that sidelong glance at the possibility of hypochondria
that he resented so much when his friends applied it to himself. Herr
Wenger's birthday happened to be on the next day, July 3, and now it
was Hesse's turn to repay the attention of the daughter. He went to
Carona early and helped Ruth and her mother decorate the dining room
with foliage and flowers, but the results were disappointing. Herr Wenger
had to take morphine and was not at all well, and Hesse felt affected as
if by a brooding depression.

It was during this summer that Hesse's relationship with Ruth
became fixed on the course that ended in its early consummation and
demise. There is little question that he needed the Wengers at this time,
in spite of his hesitations and withdrawals. His various remarks to the
Balls (to whom he confided more fully than to most of his friends at the
time) suggest how much being with Ruth's family reminded him of his

own childhood and adolescence. He never warmed to Ruth's father, with those many ailments, and he disliked the older man's impotent show of authority. Still, he had joined a family. Ruth's mother remained an enigma. Hesse liked her as an intuitive, creative woman, but he disliked her aggressiveness and her overpowering hold on her daughter. In fact, it seemed to him as though mother and daughter connived, in a very old-fashioned way, in capturing his middle-aged body and spirit. Despite these contradictory feelings, Hesse was deeply involved in the Wenger ménage and their various activities that summer.

Yet Hesse was lonely. After his lecture trip to Zurich in mid-July (to speak to "receptive young people") he settled back into his routine of painting, walking, doing his literary chores, and receiving visitors, while continuing to participate vicariously in the Wengers' life. When his future in-laws proposed to invite Hugo Ball, then in Munich, to visit them in Carona, he was enthusiastic. His letter to Ball gives a full measure of his loneliness, his need for a close friend:

> How I understand your longing for the South and your desire to get away from Munich. I can only agree with you and to wish from the bottom of my heart that you will soon succeed. And then we'll see each other! If you stay in Carona for a while I can show you the many many pages of my sketchbook which I have filled with paintings this summer. And to look into your eyes again, and, altogether, it's grand that you're coming!

This urgent, indeed fervent letter, persuading his friend to accept, suggests how his need for close communication remained unfulfilled that summer in Montagnola, despite the involvement in his courtship and in the affairs of his fiancée's family—and also in spite of his other friends, acquaintances, and fellow artists who sought him out.

In August, while the region around Lugano became thickly populated with tourists, he kept to himself. While waiting impatiently for the actual publication of *Siddhartha*, which Fischer managed to produce by October, two months sooner than they had originally planned, he again busied himself with his various small tasks. Among other projects he completed an introduction to an edition of the writings of the Swiss-German poet Salomon Gessner—another quirk suggesting his contradictory and yet complementary involvements. For Gessner, an eighteenth century poet of pastoral idylls, was also a painter and engraver of landscapes. In a modest return from the merging vision of unity, of the multiplicity of selves in *Siddhartha* and "Piktor," he now occupied himself painstakingly with the miniature writings and drawings of a kindred spirit close to his own kind—in origin as well as in sensibility. The idyllic countryside he loved to paint on the trails and by the banks of the lake seemed to be amply reflected in the work of this other poet and painter. It was another reflection of yet another part of himself. The small edition of Gessner was brought out in Leipzig as part of a series on the role of Switzerland in German intellectual life, and Hesse's introduction also appeared separately in periodicals in Leipzig and Bern.

The work on Gessner was but a sample of the large amount of labor Hesse expended on his various editorial projects, some of them abortive. It was labor he resented because it cost him eyesight, but it also served to keep him busy and financially afloat with honoraria and advances while he was renewing himself for the possibility of new work. In September 1922, Karl Isenberg stopped by for a visit. Hesse's mood was not high. He went for a walk with him and Ruth, but both his guests felt tired, and he ended up doing a color drawing of Carona. This fatigue was symptomatic of Hesse's state of mind, which was relieved for a spell by the bright moment of the Balls' arrival. His friends had finally decided not just to come for a visit but to forsake Munich and to return to Ticino for good. Hesse's pleasure at their decision clearly made the balance of September into a time of relief and repose. Although this bright moment could not remove his physical pain, or wholly dispel his depressions, it filled him with fresh hope.

Yet no particular event could provide lasting repose. By the beginning of October, Hesse was ready for a cure. His eyeaches had continued unabated, and, as his doctor had predicted, the sun baths had done nothing for his gout. Moreover, after a brief respite, his financial worries increased and contributed a great deal to his illness. The German inflation, which was then assuming outlandish proportions, ate up most of the German earnings on which he depended. The proceeds from those innumerable reviews and laborious editions had to be quickly converted into francs to be of any value at all, and often the speed was not fast enough to cover the losses. It was like living on quicksand, a condition that heightened Hesse's feeling of being unproductive again. "[For] literary work I have no stomach at all," he complained to Adis early in October, "and paper is worth more blank than written on these days." To underscore this sense of failure, he received, just at that time, the balance of the sales price for his Gaienhofen house. It was 15,000 marks, at that point exactly 37 Swiss francs—not enough for a month's salary for his housekeeper. "And for that," he mourned, "I gave away house and garden in those days. It's laughable."

At the same time, Hesse continued to suffer his various ailments, but he also remembered that his troubles were really within. Just as he had interpreted Marulla's ailment as a symptom of the soul, so he felt that his own aches and pains were basically expressions of his psyche. In view of the old age he was to reach, and his sustained creativity for more than twenty years, this recognition, which he shared with no one, probably contained a grain of truth. However, he also attacked his problem physically, preparing himself for the sanatorium of Degersheim near St. Gallen to take a cure, as he ironically told Adis, "for gout and old age." Again, the usual uncertainty plagued him. He did not like physical cures—baths, electric therapy, etc.—since the essential part of a cure should be emotional. On the other hand, he saw no other way. In this spirit, he reported in November that he exercised strenuously in the cold at seven o'clock in the morning and allowed himself to be dragged through baths and massages in the hope that along with everything else he would also secrete the gout.

If he confided to Adis that his physical ailments lay partly within, he left no such opening in his letters to his friends. Here he dwelt only on his physical debility and resented any suggestion that his ailments might be the product of his mind. He told the Balls, for example, that he felt ninety years old and could not even walk sixty steps from his bath to his bed without taking a rest in between. He felt run-down, exhausted from the cure, his weight reduced to 108 pounds. He had been living only on raw vegetables and fruit and even that diet was interrupted by frequent fast days. Finally, he was made to do gymnastics at dawn in the bitter cold. "So it goes with your old forest owl from Montagnola," he wrote the Balls, and concluded with a feeble joke: when the nurse told him that after his cure he would feel younger by the same number of years that he now felt older, he replied that he would have to get himself a baby carriage.

The contradictory reports he sent out from Degersheim in the fall of 1922 can already be considered the basis of his book *A Guest at the Spa*, his funniest and in some ways the most penetrating of his various fictional and semifictional autobiographies. Although this book is about a cure in Baden one year later, it is in every sense a product of this entire time as it is of Hesse's character as a whole. We witness the same hesitations: the need to remain and the need to depart. The life he had established for himself underlined these needs. He was the hermit who never left his den and also the "guru" in constant motion. This is the "double melody" of Hesse's life, which, as he pointed out at the end of his book, he wished to catch in his own music, in words.

II

The year 1923 can be thought of as the time when the foundation for three important books was laid. *A Guest at the Spa, Journey to Nuremberg*, and, finally, *Steppenwolf* (a synthesis of the two preceding works) had all evolved from the two events that came to fruition that year: his routine visits to Baden and his marriage to Ruth, which was celebrated during the first days of 1924. Both events furnished the blood and marrow of these three important works of the twenties.

The truth of Baden can be easily pieced together from Hesse's letters and published writings. Here we have another example of the itinerant Hesse turning immobile precisely as the immobile Hesse turned itinerant. From his first visit in the spring of 1923 on Baden became a second home for a lifetime—more of a home than any place except Montagnola. Baden housed both large hotels and facilities for bathing and drinking from health-giving waters and large factories with high chimneys which produced tools and small arms. It was in this latter part of town, already familiar to Hermann from his brother's wedding, that Hans Hesse lived and worked until his suicide in 1935. For Hesse, however, the town became a fairyland, where his needs were automatically anticipated even as he groused and complained. Here he felt revered as well as taken care of, happy as well as protected. And yet, though he returned again and again, there was always a querulous note to his caring, always a questioning inflection in his voice, disguised as self-criticism, which made palatable to his own uncertain sense of himself the usual critique of his time.

Hesse described Baden with satiric relish in his *Psychologia Balnearia*, the immediate product of his jottings on his first visit in 1923 that became *A Guest at the Spa* later on. Even the scene of the arrival with all the sciatics ("colleagues and brothers") carefully descending from the railway carriages with their anxiously contracted behinds and their vivid facial drama transformed the anguish of his body into vivid comedy.[1] The lengthy descriptions of the baths, the process of rising early, sinking himself luxuriously into hot sulphur water, of the exhaustion afterwards and finally the diversions of life as a suffering yet well-heeled patient—all of these are presented in the most loving detail. His first letter to the Balls in May 1923 suggests most of these elements, which soon became part of his privately printed brochure about the psychology of the man seeking a cure and the process of continuing one's "decrepit" existence as a way of life. "Dear Friends," he wrote:

How are you? Is it hot? Are you swimming in the lake? Here it is terribly cool and dreary, and so it's good that one is being heated up each day with baths, electrical gadgets, etc. Every morning around six I fall out to take my bath in mineral water . . . which lasts for half an hour. Before and afterwards I drink a glass of sulphur water right at the spring, which by the way tastes rather good. The doctor told me at once right after the examination: I could get well but have to stay here five weeks *and* return to Baden once more for another cure in the fall.

He then continued with a brief description of Baden, only part of which found its way into print:

Baden is a little town in the narrow valley of the Limmat. The old part of the town is nicely Gothic, medieval. People walk very slowly in the streets, on canes, limping a lot, although everyone tries very hard to conceal his sciatica. I too act in public as though I were a gentleman traveling through, who is looking at Baden merely for his own pleasure, and so everywhere there [dominates] an artificial gaiety and graciousness while secretly the baths give us horrible pains and the hotel bills even more. At noon and in the evenings, following an old custom of spas, we eat extremely lavishly, course upon course, and in between people relate their entire biographies while I remain a silent listener, for I live here as much as a hermit as I do in Ticino. . . .

That's life here. In addition to the modern and romantic Baden there is also another Baden which our friend Dr. B. has created, where at noon and night streams of workers pour out of factories and down the narrow streets of the suburbs. And when one wishes to strain one's rheumatic legs just a little, one can put all of Baden behind one in a brief half hour and disappear in the mountains, in the forests. With cordial greetings. Your. . . .

The book *A Guest at the Spa* is more generous than the letter, replete with humorous asides in the manner of Jean Paul's romantic tour de force, *Dr. Katzenbach's Journey to the Baths*, which had served as his literary model, as well as with references to the bathing rituals among the Brahman and other Indian religions, which still lingered in Hesse's mind one year after the completion of *Siddhartha*.[2] Most striking is the scene in which the insomniac author sought to subdue a noisy neighbor who kept him awake with an act of imagination and will. This scene, which relates to a disagreeable Dutchman next door, bears an uncanny resemblance to Herr Christaller in his noisy boots loudly reciting Arabic overhead during Hesse's Tübingen boyhood. The baths are particularly sumptuous, and Hesse spares no nuances of detail to communicate the ritual of ease, the passive surrender to all these bodily ministrations. Similarly, the humorous way in which eating also becomes part of a regimen that dominates the patient reminds the reader, as it did Thomas Mann, of the grand dinners in *The Magic Mountain*, which had appeared a year later, in 1924. Contrasting, yet complementary as well, are the amenities of a twentieth century hotel along with sentimental greeting cards, gambling, and teatime concerts.

One of the more interesting aspects of this satire is its manner of mirroring the patient Hermann Hesse, who needed his cure, in the eyes and perspective of the recording artist who wrote the book. As an observer, Hesse sees himself going through all the rituals of the typical *Kurgast*. But as the object of this observer's attention he is also visibly transformed into a character of fiction gradually succumbing to the sumptuous ease and hygienic rigors of the place—the "magic of Baden"—while at the same time telling the reader what he is doing. A moment at dinner —which, next to the baths, is the most typical scene of the Baden show— may be a case in point. It is a paradoxically generous meal for people with digestive ailments, which is turned by Hesse into a serious confrontation of the two selves:

> I sat down in the high bright dining room at my lonesome little round table, and at the same time I saw how I was sitting down, how I was straightening the chair under me and biting my lip a little because it hurt to sit down, then how I mechanically picked up the vase of flowers and moved it a little closer, how I slowly and indecisively took my napkin out of the ring.

Hesse as sciatica patient was the object of Hesse as observer. He looked at himself as "with a disciplined but profoundly bored expression," he poured water and broke bread without any intention of consuming either, while he as object, in turn, watched the busy headwaiter and his horde of pretty waitresses in black dresses and white aprons moving about against a backdrop of large walls adorned with landscape paintings. Throughout the scene, the two "eyes" remain juxtaposed:

> Now the one who was keeping watch on me . . . was not the guest and sciatic Hesse but rather the old somewhat antisocial hermit and lone wolf Hesse, the old wanderer and poet, the friend of butterflies and lizards, of old books and religions. . . . This old Hesse, this "I" that recently had become somewhat alien and lost, was back again now and observing us.

He was his own secret audience aware of the amusing spectacle of the entire proceedings, including his pain. He also produced an intricate pattern of mirroring that placed the "old Hesse," that nature lover and mystic, in the perspective of the modern hotel world in which he remained the outsider playing a game with the possibility of his cure.[3]

In the concluding passage, Hesse related this dual mirroring to the search for harmony as a cure for illness, which, in turn, he considered in an analogy to music where a single harmony can contain counterpoints. The writer's sensibility works in the same way as music whose chords combine dissonances in a fresh, harmonious creation.[4] Moreover, Hesse's model, Jean Paul, had also assigned a similar function to humor, which he viewed as a magic bridge from "reality" to the "ideal." This slight autobiographical tale serves as a link, with all its experimentation with new techniques, between the harmonious vision of *Siddhartha* and the cacophonous refractions of *Steppenwolf*. Finally, Baden became yet another home where each time he was cured and magically transformed. Like Maulbronn and the Casa Camuzzi, like the farmhouse in Gaienhofen, and the Welti house in Bern, the Hotel Verenahof in Baden became a Magic Theater of Hesse's imagination.

III

The contribution of Hesse's involvement with Ruth Wenger to his crisis of the early 1920s and to the evolution of *Steppenwolf* reflects his strain on a personal level. The tensions of this relationship made themselves felt early on and contributed to his bad physical state in 1922 and 1923. Clearly he did not want to be caught and yet found no way to escape. There were moments of sweetness. In *A Guest at the Spa* he alluded to her several times as his "beloved" and especially to her ear lobes, yet it is curious that at the time this book was written, in 1923, there was so little direct sexuality in his descriptions. Ruth was young and reasonably attractive, but these were not the qualities in a woman to which Hesse usually responded. Clearly, it was the attraction of a father of three sons to a daughter that dominated this relationship (as well as a lasting attachment for Ruth's mother). Be this as it may, sexuality was to seek its way to the surface at a later time, after courting, marriage, and the brief married life were over, during those difficult years between 1924 and 1927. But at this point it was not overwhelmingly present, for Ruth was neither the wise teacher-woman nor the courtesan Kamala, the types that usually filled Hesse's repertoire of sex.

Writing from Baden as early as June, however, Hesse asked his faithful sister Adis whether she would not perhaps see Ruth, for since "Ruth (though you must tell no one) [will] soon be my wife, and since I am not really able to travel, it would be a family thing to do, eh?" This theme now constantly appeared in Hesse's correspondence, rivaling only talk about his lack of physical fitness and his need to return to Baden in the fall. While he felt uncomfortable about the relationship as a whole, Hesse was also extremely sensitive to amenities. If Adis, for example, could not meet Ruth in Montagnola that summer, he wrote in another note from Baden, she must visit her in Basel later on.

The summer in Montagnola between the two Baden cures was mostly devoted to seeing Ruth, who again lived in nearby Carona. It was once again a hot Italian summer. Adis came for a time and Hesse enjoyed the visit. As he wrote her in September (once more from Baden): "It was so beautiful that you were here and you must come back next year. Even if we get old and never drink full cups again, life still brings us its riches again and again, and its 100-colored surprises—and so it was in Carona with you and Ruth and Carlo. . . ." Along with the usual plethora of visitors, his close friends, and his constant traffic with the Wengers in the neighboring village, his life proceeded well, though it remained marred by his anxious anticipation of a marriage he did not really want.

During September Hesse was again in Baden, busy on his "psychology of baths," which became his major work of the year. But the immediate future continued to occupy his mind. "I've been back from Baden for a week now," he wrote Emmy Ball in October, "and am now busy with a literary work I started there. On this work I've been busy, sitting at the typewriter eight hours each day and longer, and am more or less finished with it. It consists of psychological jottings from Baden and my experiences there." In the same letter he also wrote about his impending marriage to Ruth and expressed his doubts in concealed ways. He complained of bureaucracy and expressed his anxieties about his imminent move to Basel.

The final months of 1923, following his return from Baden, became sheer terror for Hesse, because he evidently saw himself heading for disaster. While he was busy every day with his notes for his book about the cure, Hesse could not shake his preoccupation with the oncoming marriage. Within two weeks of returning from Baden, he already wrote Adis that he would soon go to Basel and that his address there would be the Hotel Krafft (where Ruth Wenger also lived), a small residence hotel in a narrow street, whose rear view overlooked the Rhine as its front faced a narrow sidewalk opposite his favorite wineshop. Hesse's letters were full of concern about the future. At one point he wrote that he would like to marry Ruth within the next few days, since his divorce from Mia had become final. On another, he claimed that he was thwarted everywhere by officialdom, notably by German officialdom, and that he might have to become a Swiss citizen in order to be able to marry. He was fidgety, unhappy, barely able to keep his head above water in anticipation of the event. In the midst of this pressure, which was surely fanned by Ruth and especially by her mother, the necessary involvement in annoying details about papers and officials and government offices connected with the divorce were almost a welcome way of working out a disagreeable decision.

With all these thoughts in mind, Hesse once more packed his bags and said farewell to Montagnola. The weather was gray and dull as he climbed on the train in Lugano and rode those familiar tracks to Basel through the pass of St. Gotthard and the majestic mountains. A letter from Ruth, urgent and full of forebodings, had propelled him north more quickly than he had expected. The *Psychologia Balnearia* manuscript was still in his pocket, not quite finished, and he had hoped to meet Hugo Ball. But all that had to be cancelled abruptly. A note had to be dispatched to Ball with the message that Ruth wanted to see him urgently, that she could not travel, and that her father was near death.

Hesse got off the train in Basel, cross and unhappy, and made his way to the Hotel Krafft where Ruth had reserved a room for him. His depression deepened; it was to last for the rest of that winter. "I have acclimatized myself badly in Basel," he wrote his sister just ten days after his arrival. "The entire situation is still oppressive and disgusting; my health is only moderate, but I hope to pull through." It was not only the relationship with Ruth, her father's gradual and grudging death, or the impending marriage from which he saw no escape—his own past, indeed his entire life, was in the forefront of his thought. His continuous involvement with Mia, her illnesses, and her intermittent helplessness interfered with his concentration on the future. Now, deep in the fall, he faced the prospect of what to do with his young son Heiner, then sixteen years old, whose school would be over in April and who had no idea what he wanted to do. If he joined his mother in Ascona, as Mia wished, Hesse feared he would not learn anything. At the same time, the prospect of his new marriage worried him more and more. Some of the language in his letters, in fact, suggested the same kind of reservations before the fact as he had felt on the occasion of his first marriage in 1904.

By early December Hesse was busy making final arrangements for his wedding. He continued to feel burdened by paperwork in preparation for it, but thought he could see the light "by about early or mid-January." He felt ill at ease, physically as well as psychologically. In a note from Basel to go along with a watercolor he was sending to Romain Rolland, he expressed his hopelessness:

Basel, Hotel Krafft, Dec. 7, 1923

Dear Romain Rolland:

For some time I had wanted to send you one of my watercolors. Today I'll finally do it. It is a Ticino sketch, from Montagnola. But I am sending it from Basel, for I have been here for several weeks, in order, for the first time in five years, to spend a winter in the city.

He then went on to give a very clear picture of his feelings:

> With most of the attractions of the city I really don't know what to do;
> above all I treasure my warm room and the masseur who treats my
> sciatica. But now and then I hear music, too; for example, tomorrow
> I'm going to hear Haydn's *Creation* and am looking forward to it. The
> way back to socialization, however, I don't find here either, not even
> through my decision to marry again in the near future.

And he added cryptically: "In my heart I am a Samana and belong into
the forest."[5]

Hesse escaped into music, which he could share with Ruth. In Basel
they heard *The Creation* in the cathedral (reminiscent of his musical
events in Bern ten years earlier) and he took Ruth to several good per-
formances of Beethoven and Mozart, especially *Fidelio* and *The Marriage of Figaro*. But basically his mood was grim. "Dear Adis," he wrote
on December 14: "I thank you for your dear sermon. I know how kindly
you think of us. Our difficulties, of course, have not disappeared, but
we're working them out. It's just that I feel too old to marry, and too
sick, and too accustomed to loneliness and quiet work. But all of this
must somehow be lived through and adjusted to." The strain under which
Hesse suffered at this time is expressed in a touching note on which this
last premarital letter to Adis ends. It is touching, because Ruth's
childish fondness for animals was always a great source of discomfort
to him. "Ruth's little white dog, the faithful Zilla, died the other day,
much to Ruth's distress. Little Muschi is sometimes in my place or ac-
companies me on a walk. In addition to him, there is also that large gray
cat which you already met in Carona. . . ."

Christmas 1923 was spent at the Wengers' home in Délémont from
where Hesse wrote several moving notes to his friends, almost like unanswerable cries for help. A letter to Rolland, written on the second day
of Christmas from the home of his future parents-in-law, sounds almost
like a farewell to old friendships:

Delsberg [Délémont], Dec. 26, 1923

Dear Romain Rolland:

> During the Christmas holidays I am staying with the parents of my
> bride (on whose gift table the ten volumes of *Jean Christophe* have been
> placed). So from here I am expressing my thanks for your dear beautiful
> letter, which gave me so much pleasure, and for your piece on Gandhi,
> in which I took particular pleasure in seeing that you too, parallel with
> me, are taking an Indian route. Your presentation of "Gandhiism" is
> indeed European, but it has to be so, and it far transcends in the clarity
> of its formulation anything I have read about it elsewhere. And most

of all I love, beneath your clarity, intelligence, and precision, the love and heartfelt warmth with which you, too, now embrace that distant world which has been close to me for an unthinkable time.

After some business notes about a projected French edition of *Knulp* and an announcement of his *Psychologia Balnearia* to be published that fall, he concluded: "For the new year I wish you and your sister all the best and myself the preservation of your friendship."[6] The next day, he told Rolland, his address would again be at the Hotel Krafft in Basel, and it is from there that the last notes before the wedding were sent. In a postcard, forwarded through friends in Stuttgart, he reported early in January that he was very ill—40½ degrees C. now down to 38 C. It sounded like a last S.O.S. from a sinking steamer, and it is in this mood "after six days of bad illness and high temperatures" that he presented himself for his wedding.

The wedding, which Hesse described in various letters, is as ludicrous as the preceding three years had been nightmarish. He was depressed, smothered by illness and high fever. Yet Mama Wenger seemed doggedly determined to make the wedding work. A week before she "made the mistake" of telling him she wanted to invite his friends the Balls, who were then living in Rome, but since he did not want to make anything of the occasion he refused. As he confessed to Ball later that month, if Mama Wenger had kept it a surprise he would have been overjoyed.

It could not have been the pristine wedding of a young man, since Hesse was in his late forties, burdened by family obligations and guilt, nor was it what a young girl in her twenties could have hoped for. They were married on January 11. Hesse's laconic account to his sister describes at least part of his mood:

> The day before yesterday was our wedding, or at least the rather stupid comedy of a civil wedding. Circumstances were not too noble, for after six days of severe illness and high fever I could get up only with an effort and go along. But since we never promised ourselves anything elevating, we thought it better to get done with it as soon as possible. . . .

He at once told Adis about family worries. What would become of Heiner? Would he lose him as he had lost Martin, who was living in Kirchdorf with Mia's sister? Despite his worries, his description of the wedding to Hugo Ball admitted some moments of pleasure, at least at the banquet.

Hesse's friend and therapist Josef Lang had been invited; so were his "Siamese" friends the Leutholds, who had been his most steadfast supporters during the years, and the architect Josef Englert, who had been a friend since 1919. The singer Ilona Durigo, with whom Hesse had been friends since his prewar Bern and even Gaienhofen days, was not only present but also sang a great deal. At the banquet, Josef Englert was especially entertaining, "and young like a real best man." Another friend was sufficiently inebriated after midnight to try to break some of the laurel trees that graced the banquet room in colorful pots. "Durigo sang beautifully and Ruth was in green velvet. Too bad it's over." These are, at any rate, among the last positive statements not only about the marriage but about this relationship—a relationship about which Hesse felt so reticent that he asked Ball not to mention it in his biography. Between these descriptions of the wedding one paragraph stands out in its misery. He told Hugo Ball:

> Shall we meet again in the spring? In any case, I'm looking forward to it, to you and the flowers and the lake. Life in Basel has not tasted well, and physically I haven't been this bad in years. Add to that the marriage, the formalities, the damned offices with which I have to go on working, for now I have to work on my naturalization. You may laugh, but I cry sometimes.

The next two and a half months—like the next two and a half years, in which *Steppenwolf* was to be experienced and formed—turned into a steadily darkening nightmare from which there seemed to be no escape. Hesse tried to square his continuing deep involvement with Mia and his sons with the difficulties of his new marriage. All of these motifs are suggested in a postcard written on February 8, less than a month after the wedding:

> Within the next few days I'll have to have my son Heiner and my former wife here to discuss Heiner's school and future. In between I sit in the doctor's office. Ruth is very busy with her music and makes progress, and now and then Mama Wenger shows up for a day or two. . . .

On February 14 he wrote Adis that the meeting had taken place. Mia had been there for a few days, and it had been rather uncomfortable. Although Mia's meeting with Ruth, which he wanted to take place naturally, went rather well, the whole thing still left him with stomachaches. Now Ruth had gone off to Délémont to visit her parents, to whom she remained extraordinarily attached, but she was expected back the following day. One pleasurable note: Samuel Fischer, whom he had not seen for a decade, was to visit him the next day, a door at last out of the family.

It is perhaps significant to record the dates of Hesse's mishaps during the next few weeks, because they provide a sense of the tapestry of his mind from which, in his usual way of ultimately curing himself through his writing, the novel *Steppenwolf* was to emerge as a document of his suffering and as a fresh artistic vision. The suffering was indeed intense and led to illnesses in himself and those around him inextricably involving both his physical and mental energies.

The crisis of the new marriage came very quickly, for it confirmed all of Hesse's fears about returning to a conjugal way of life. He felt again hemmed in, literally caught. In a long letter to Hugo Ball, written as early as February 24, he suggested that his silence may well have been due to silent suffering. During the winter he had barely been able to belong to himself and to live in his way and at his pace. Instead, he had to grapple with problems too numerous and complicated to load on his friends. He then clarified his problem in a way that suggests, in embryo, the "outsider" motif of *Steppenwolf*—the novel in which all these agonies were to find their artistic reflection:

> Being married, which I'm now supposed to learn again, doesn't turn out too well. I tend toward running away, toward living some place alone and concentrating on some intellectual work or on the salvation of my soul. And only now and then do I recognize how egoistic that is after all. It is truly harder for a poet and thinker who is used to going his own way, and who knows how to play his own lonely games, than it is for other people to surrender himself and to forget his own little ego a little.[7]

Although he firmly believed that it was Ruth who made living together difficult, he also managed to recognize his own inability to reach out to her. Actually, Hesse soon yearned for the spring in Montagnola and for a decent way of removing himself there alone. "What will become of my marriage," he wrote less than two months after the wedding, "is difficult to say." Perhaps Ruth might spend the summer at her parents' house in Carona while he could retire in solitude to the Casa Camuzzi. These plans—and the hidden import they had for their lives—remained largely unspoken, and Hesse left the future to take care of itself.

Still, they tried to make it all appear right. On March 1, Hesse wrote a postcard to Emmy Ball, who had just returned to Ticino. Congratulating the Balls on their arrival, he reported flu and fever "twice this winter" and a good deal of pain, but he also sounded a happier note:

> I'm very pleased you're back, you self-willed wanderer, and to wish you a big hello. Ruth has a lot of work to do, especially at the moment when she has me down sick again. She will write you surely soon. She is very dear and her singing gets better all the time . . . and now she has a black poodle.

The early letters to his sisters are somewhat more mixed. He repeated that he now had no fever, less pain, but told them he was very tired. He also reported another visit from Lisa Wenger (she "happened" to be in Basel), and, finally, he broke the hardly welcome news that the Wengers were planning to move to Basel in the fall. "Ruth spends much time with me," he added. "Also, she now has, in addition to the dwarf Muschi, a big black poodle whom I gave the name Ponto, for there is a poodle by that name in Hoffmann's *Kater Murr*."

A professional undercurrent remained. Hesse was able to read the German translation of Romain Rolland's *Annette et Sylvia* and to comment on it intelligently and to deal with endless complications about the translation of *Knulp* into French, for which apparently he had given permission to two different people. But the final lines in a note to Rolland (dated March 3) again suggest his malaise and his longing: "And now I lie sick again, as so often this winter, and I long very much for Montagnola. May all go well with you, and may you often glance into life with those eyes of love as you do in your splendid book."[8]

The first break apparently occurred sometime before March 10, less than two months after the wedding. A sick, blacked-out Hermann Hesse woke up one fine afternoon and found himself in a strange room in a different part of town. It was a hospital. On the same day, March 10, he was also able to write to Adis and to Romain Rolland. He told Adis that he was now in a room overlooking the corner where forty years ago she had once prayed at *Fastnacht* time. He had awakened a few days ago in a strange bed and had noticed a poplar under his window. They had taken him to a clinic, but things were better now. Forty years ago, he wrote, they had been scared of the big boys and their masks at just this place, and he concluded that whatever frightened them since had not been much more important than that. Similarly, Hesse mentioned to Romain Rolland that just after his letter had arrived he had awakened in a totally strange room with a poplar under the window. He was able to respond to Rolland's request for a good title for his latest book, *L'Ame Enchantée*, which had just been translated into German: *Verzauberte Seele*, Hesse insisted with utter lucidity, and called upon Rolland to ignore the translator's protestations. "That title," Hesse wrote, "saying everything, concealing everything, belongs to your most beautiful music. God bless you for it."[9] But in a letter to Hugo Ball, he revealed the full depth of his sense of degradation, his sickness and despair.

That letter, dated only "Basel, Tuesday," written from the hospital, repeats the same story: how, the previous week when he was doing especially badly, the doctor had him taken to a clinic where he was about to be released soon. For suddenly he had awakened in a room in a strange part of town and there he was now lying, very tired, and very reluctant to decide to start life over again (a motif repeated later in the *Steppenwolf* poems and novel). Responding to Ball's report of his concern for Emmy, who seemed to have been in a distraught state, he clearly sensed they were in trouble together. "I have your letter in mind next to my own drama. . . ." It seems, he concluded, that he was quite ill and glad that none of his friends could see him lying with his gray stubble beard and shaking his head in response to everything. Now he had been shaved again and could eat a little, and had a great longing for the yellow and blue flowers of Ticino, though he knew it would be a while before he would be able to pack his suitcase and get away from there. Evidently, he had been forbidden to see his mail except for the newspaper in which he read that the Caliph of Egypt had been deposed. "I too felt like a Caliph," he wrote, "like a deposed though great historical figure."

It is not difficult to read between the lines that the illness that sent him to the clinic was more than just successions of flu and sciatica, or even a mere intestinal problem, though it was probably all of these. The gradual return from withdrawal to which the letter to Hugo Ball poignantly alludes is very suggestive. Between the lines describing his past illness and present return, his friend could read that Hesse understood Ruth's role. Comparing his own with his Ball's marital troubles, he wrote with a rare touch of humor:

> It is really funny. You have a wife who is in love with poverty and adventure. And I, friend of loneliness and monasteries, have, as an old fellow, taken on a wife who would only be too glad to give away a few ideals for a pair of nice shoes and a pretty dog.

And he added:

> Still, we're both getting after all what's coming to us, and if we don't go this way to Heaven, none other will lead us there. May I succeed in following the way of love since I have after all left the way of loneliness.

The poem to his sister, however, which he attached to this letter, speaks a more severe language:

TO MY SISTER

(When I was very ill)

Now I stand confused
And alien at every place
Now far have I lost my way
From my home.

You flowers which I knew
Mountains heavy and blue
You people and you lands
I know you no longer.

Soon into his garden
Will fetch me into dusk
Where father and mother are waiting
The good gardener Death.[10]

The premonition of death and the blue flowers of Ticino were to be
the twin motifs that suggested his salvation and ultimately became that
universal mirror of the immortals in which the Steppenwolf's dissolving
image was to be caught. Clearly, the concept and motif, the entire problematic situation of the novel and its surrounding canon began to grow
during this time, and as early as a year later, in March 1925, he could
refer to himself confidently as Steppenwolf in private correspondence.
And so it was Ticino he sought, without Ruth, after his release from the
clinic, and his first letter to Adis from his old hunting ground of
Montagnola sounded overjoyed with the pleasure, despite the rain, of
being back at last, of being reunited with the Balls, of seeing his old maid-
servant Natalina again. His private printing of what was to be *A Guest
at the Spa* was not doing very well in Switzerland, but he felt free.
Heiner's school problem was solved. Ruth had gone back to her parents
in Délémont for a while, for, so he could explain to those who needed to
be protected from the idea of his fresh separation, her teacher had gone
on a concert tour.

Life seemed easier again. The sun was shining. That spring and summer were still difficult, but Hesse felt less exposed. There was a good
deal of coming and going around his Montagnola retreat. Ruth visited
for ten days in June with her brother, but it was a visit, not a conjugal
reunion. When she left, Martin arrived. Later, Ilona Durigo came to call,
and finally his eldest son Bruno stayed for a week. Meanwhile, there
were toothaches, trips to the dentist in Lugano, and wine drinking in the
grotto with the Balls. He felt better than he had for a long time, though
complaints naturally continued. In August, he wrote Adis that he was
having a restless summer with unusually many visitors, while his constant
trips to the dentist in Lugano cut into his time. Also, the relationship with
the Wengers in Carona remained far too lively for his liking. Ruth and a
girlfriend visited together, to practice their singing, and they came to see
him a few times. He also reported that the Wenger house in Carona had
been so filled with visitors that Ruth had to stay with him for two days, a
fact he evidently deplored.

There were also good reports—no severe crisis that winter—and welcome visitors. One such visitor, evidently brought by *Siddhartha*, was a young Hindu, "a noble, beautiful young Bengali, schooled in the Vedas." He conveyed the rumor that Mahatma Gandhi was in Switzerland, but when Hesse checked it out with Romain Rolland it proved to have been ill-founded. Still, he was happy to be with his Hindu friend and "to hear the Indian accent again." Also at this time the first attempt was made to translate *Siddhartha* into English, and Hesse sent a sample to Adis. Other happy events occurred: a most successful visit from Martin Buber late in August and a quick trip to Zurich to see Samuel Fischer. By early September he announced a new trip to Baden for a month's stay and the more immediate project of attending the festival for the three hundredth anniversary of the church of the Madonna dell'Ongero nearby, where he went with the Balls and Samuel Fischer.[11] In fact, his love and longing for his rural Ticino home, to which he faithfully returned in the summer, were very genuine emotions. They expressed his sense of belonging, of identification with the poor small farmers, with the girls and boys who came to festivals for the Madonna, and the warm, colorful landscape that appeared again and again in his drawings. It was not all bad (not everything was in psychological turmoil) and when Samuel Fischer thought he had become "sufficiently ossified" (as Hesse reported not without tender self-deprecation) to consider issuing his *Collected Works* again this time he was hardly displeased. The summer ended on a not too dissatisfied note:

> Today the Wengers are leaving; I was still over there yesterday. In a week at the latest I'm going to Baden and will stay there again 3–4 weeks at the Hotel Verenahof. Before that I hope I'm successful in getting a stove installed in my place. Until yesterday we had sunshine; now it is raining and it is becoming fall. . . .

The cure in Baden, which lasted through October, seemed to serve as a bridge between a reasonably good summer and at least one more unfortunate attempt to spend another winter in Basel. Ruth had visited him during his cure while he was once more "stuck in hot sulphur water, going the old ways of the *Kurgast*." Jean Arp had come by for an afternoon to report that his poems had just appeared and had set people to puzzling. He also went on his usual forays to nearby Zurich to visit close friends, especially the Leutholds. So it is difficult to say how Hesse's mood changed.

He returned to Montagnola early in November to pack up for the winter. A much needed stove had been installed in his study during his absence, and he mused in a letter to the Balls, who were again in Rome, about the perversity of leaving, after freezing through many winters, at the very time he had finally obtained a stove. Generally his mood was sentimental rather than bitter: the farewell to Montagnola without the Balls in Agnuzzo was not too difficult. Before he left he had one more visit: "The other day a quiet, almost shy young man appeared at my door." It was the well-known Communist writer and dramatist, Ernst Toller. "He was very dear and I kept him with me for several hours. What he told of his life in prison was very bad and sad." Soon thereafter he locked his door and went north. Within days he was in Basel, ensconced in a room in an apartment on Lothringerstrasse 7 near the Johannisthor. Ruth too had returned to the city, but she was staying in their residence of the previous winter, the Hotel Krafft. Hesse felt better, he confessed to various friends, than he had the year before. He planned to go to Germany that December to lecture in Freiburg and Stuttgart. It would be the first time in years that he would be back there and the last time he would be traveling with a German passport. His naturalization was at last almost complete. It was not to be entirely the last time, but that problem at least was nearing its solution.

Hesse's decision to spend yet another winter in Basel was well motivated—a last attempt to make the dead marriage work—but it soon turned into another disaster. December went reasonably well. They were together in the same city but did not live as husband and wife. When Hesse planned a family get-together in nearby Ludwigsburg on the occasion of his lecture in Stuttgart, and decided to let Ruth accompany him, he made elaborate preparations not to have them put up in the same room. The trip went smoothly, and the reunion with Adis, who had a fondness for her brother's young second wife, came off well. Christmas Eve he celebrated alone with Ruth, who had prepared a small tree in her hotel room overlooking the Rhine, and on Christmas Day they went together to the Wengers in Délémont. But having done his duty for the holidays, Hesse soon fled, leaving Ruth behind for a few more days. Mia had appeared on her way through Basel with Martin, and Heiner followed soon. Hesse tried to brace himself for the New Year.

The year 1925 burst upon him with the recognition that the life to which he had felt committed was intolerable. This insight included not only his marriage, but especially the barren months laden with unproductive labor—reviewing books and working out contracts with publishers for various bibliographical enterprises. For months during the summer and fall of 1924 he had worked on an anthology of "forgotten" German prose, an "eye-destroying labor," only to find, early in 1925, that the publisher was about to renege on his commitment. The shock proved traumatic and was papered over only by various travels and frenzied activity: a lecture in Lucerne, a trip to a conference with a professor in Freiburg, a lecture in the German spa of Baden-Baden, conferences in Basel with the publisher about his unhappy project.

In the midst of these activities Hesse nonetheless felt very homesick for Montagnola. He constantly fretted about his marriage, which he combined in his mind with the publisher's cancellation of his contract as yet another example of treachery. He confessed to Ball, who tried to keep him from leaving Ruth, that his life had not changed by his marriage. To achieve such a change Ruth would have had to be stronger. He added: "Since I am now as before a one-horse cart and lead the life of a lonely somewhat odd elderly gentleman, it would be better for me to remain in my rooms in Montagnola than in my narrow room in Basel."

Actually, Hesse liked his quarters in Basel that year rather well. He enjoyed his landlady, Fräulein Martha Ringier, without whose quiet and friendly manner he might not have been able to survive in the city for so long. But he also continued to isolate himself. Although later he believed that Ruth had left him rather than the other way round, he clearly constructed a relationship in which she could not be comfortable, in which she remained outside. He often had dinner or lunch with her in her hotel, but his evenings were spent alone in his old wineshop, which he had known when he lived in Basel as a young man. There he sat, sipping his wine with "stupid devotion" like all the other quiet regulars, a "wine philistine." In a note to Emmy Ball, who was then in Rome, he put it even more poignantly:

> I don't know if my life in Basel is any more fantastic than yours in Rome. It is very lonely. Only in the evening I sit occasionally in a little wineshop and drink a little wine and watch other people sitting at other tables, drinking wine, too. That is clearly my fault in life: I remain always alone and can never penetrate the great void that separates me from other people. With the parrot—with him I have the most in common.

He reported to his friends that Ruth was making good progress in her singing, but he also elaborated upon her small menagerie. She had ordered a terrier, which had not yet arrived; a whippet named Amoretta, the tomcat Figaro, and her parrot Coco all lived with her in her little room. Hesse thought he would be dispensable and could therefore escape to his haunt in Montagnola.[12] At that point his pains returned. "With my legs it is so-so," he wrote to Hugo Ball. "Sometimes I seem to be perfect and I can climb on a streetcar without effort. On other days I limp about, a bit sad. I am often in pain, but the pain in my legs doesn't bother me so much for it doesn't interfere with my work, while my eyeaches dis-

turb and torture me much more than should be the case." He could not
wait to leave.

Before he was able to return to Ticino, however, Hesse's life changed.
In January, Ruth had come down with a fever, the first stage in a chain
of illnesses that was to color Hesse's life during the twenties. Just as he
was beginning to make plans for his separation from Ruth this illness
turned out to be serious. Her indisposition in mid-January did not improve. After four weeks in bed her heart was found to be weak and her
doctor decided to take her to his clinic. Relieved momentarily from the
responsibility for her illness, Hesse took himself off to Baden to relieve
his own pain. Meanwhile, he plunged into routine work that could serve
as an anesthetic. But all these activities were mere diversions. Hesse's
life, as he suggested to Emmy Ball, was like a burst paper bag: he had
neither a satisfying personal life nor a satisfactory new project as a
writer. He trotted like an animal in his old circle and was tired out.
Unable to endure the narrowness of life in Basel, he escaped twice
despite Ruth's illness, once to Zurich and Baden, and on another
occasion to Bern where he visited with old friends. But he always had to
return.

By March the Wengers had installed themselves in their Basel house.
Hesse was not displeased. Since he had long since separated from Ruth,
her parents' presence in the same city was no longer irksome. In fact, he
felt pleased that she would have a real home with her mother nearby,
which would make him less indispensable and tied to Basel. Now, early
in March, Ruth seemed better. After six weeks of illness she was weak
but able to give singing lessons, which satisfied her. Hesse was free to
leave.

The first letters from Montagnola give a grim retrospect of the Basel
months. Comparing the impending breakup of his marriage to Ruth with
his first divorce, Hesse wrote to Adis on March 23:

> Now it isn't as bad as it was in those days. But if I now get back into my
> old cell after these dreadful months in Basel, still dead tired from pack-
> ing and all that, after months of looking for my food twice a day in
> another restaurant and ruining stomach and intestines because of it, then
> I don't imagine myself as being so successful.

And, perhaps again to please his conventional sister, the minister's wife,
he added:

> In any case I hope to preserve Ruth and a little piece of my marriage,
> but so far these attempts have not been very encouraging.

He was more pleased with some domesticity—rather than with a supposed wife wholly occupied with her dogs, cats, parrot, and illness. His

housekeeper Natalina had taken over: "Now I am pleased to have at least something like domesticity and someone to sew on all the buttons that tore off in Basel."

The winter in Basel had been an attempt to recreate for one final time the semblance of a life together. It is not altogether clear how much Hesse had been rejected by Ruth and, finally, by her illness and how thoroughly he had rejected her. "I've been home again in Ticino for the past two weeks," he wrote the Balls on April 1, 1925, "after my attempt to reestablish a life in Basel had become a fiasco. Now I sit again, as I did three years ago [when he experienced his loneliness sharply], only richer by a severe disappointment and a new great responsibility." In response to Emmy Ball's suggestion that it was good for Ruth to have her parents with her, he was able to answer that this might indeed be good for Ruth but perhaps not for him. Again he reiterated how strongly he had attempted to make the relationship work: "Well, that is all fine and comfortable for Ruth, and relieves me too, but my attempt, made not without sacrifice, to make a temporary life together work, foundered precisely on the discovery that she does not need me, that she has her parents, and that I don't know what to do with parents and family. . . ." All of this seems very much like a battle with windmills, a subtle game with various rationalizations. He knew Ruth insisted she loved him, but he had no answer for her. There is no doubt of the final sentences in this letter, no doubt of their authenticity and seriousness, despite their self-mockery, and no doubt of the growing motif in his life that was to culminate in his *Steppenwolf*:

> The meadows are full of flowers, but I see little of that. I am mostly prone since my legs are bad. Every step is painful and a walk to the end of the village is an accomplishment, which for the past two weeks I've tried to achieve only twice. For a while I was rather desperate and didn't want to live any longer. But then I found a way out. I decided that on my fiftieth birthday two years from now, I will have the right to hang myself if I then still desire it—and now everything that seemed hard has assumed a slightly different face, for at worst it can only last two more years.[13]

Except for the method of possibly dispatching himself (Harry Haller of the *Steppenwolf* wants to use a revolver rather than a rope), this is exactly the promise with which his first large novel after these episodes begins.

Hesse's letter to Adis the next day reiterated his plight, but it was calmer and contained concrete proposals. He asked his sister not to reveal any of his doubts to Ruth, who might be harmed by that knowledge since she was sick again in her mother's house in Basel with a low temperature. Again, his feelings were ambivalent: he resented Lisa Wenger as a rival and was relieved by her help. He also hoped, more practically, for Ruth's speedy recovery, and thought she might come up to visit him in Ticino for a few weeks so they could thrash out their problem, presumably without the proximity of her parents.

But events were stronger than hopes, and by May and June all decisions were made for him. For one thing, Ruth's health did not really improve after all, and by May she had again been ill for nearly three months with pleurisy and fever. Nothing more definite could be established. She was not even allowed to get up and go to the hospital for X rays, but continued to lie in her mother's house in the expectation of being sent away for a cure soon. Clearly, tuberculosis must have been on everybody's mind, but that diagnosis took a few more weeks to become definite. Meanwhile, for a brief spell Hesse's life in Montagnola turned more placid. After the Easter rush of tourists it became quiet again. Natalina brought him hot chocolate twice a day. In the evenings, he lit his fire, smoked, and drank a bit, reading as much as his eyes would allow. His true life turned into fantasy. To the Balls he mused:

> There should be a boat from Lugano going directly to you in Salerno. I'd get on it tomorrow, take along my paint things, a couple of shirts, a bottle of wine, and a volume of Jean Paul and drift slowly down to your equatorial region without counting the days and latitudes. Then a beautiful sunny beach would emerge and you would stand there with your kindly faces and you would laugh and shout Ciao and drag me to Albori on a donkey . . . and we would invite the entire village to a joyful drinking bout. . . .

It was a slight and pleasant fantasy in keeping with "Piktor's Metamorphoses," then still on his mind, and with the imaginary transformation of the Magic Theater of *Steppenwolf*, which he was to write the following year. But fantasy by itself was not enough to reestablish Hesse in his professional life. His personal life, determined by the need to care for two failing wives and three young sons, allowed him no peace.

In May Ruth's symptoms were definitely diagnosed as tuberculosis, and in mid-June she moved to Carona, taking a small flat of her own in order not to live with her family. From half past nine in the morning until about the same time at night she lay stretched out on her lawn chair in the garden. A servant brought her food on a tray. Her parrot was perched on a pole behind her and the little dog Tilla sat by her side, defending her against would-be intruders. Thus she lay during the long summer days—carried out in the morning, carried back at night—

unable to walk or sing. With a rigid cure the doctors hoped to restore her to health within a year. Already before she moved to Carona, Hesse had felt threatened in his Montagnola retreat. He would be tied down, and there could be no serious work. In late May he invited Adis to visit him—sending her the fare—in the hope that it might lighten his burden to share it with his sister. In this letter, sardonically, he pinned down Ruth's illness as an unconscious act, as two years earlier he had diagnosed his younger sister Marulla's lung ailment as a "theater of the mind." "It is really funny," he wrote Adis, "that Ruth's passivity toward me at the very moment I was about to go on strike against it takes on the form of this illness so that now she has been relieved at last of any responsibility for caring for me a little." Considering Hesse's impatient flight from her the previous year this was an odd conclusion, but it underlined his awareness that he was hopelessly caught in responsibilities he could not control.

As in a piece of music, the Ruth motif was soon followed by a similar motif in his life—Mia. On June 8 he was summoned urgently to Ascona, where she lived, to discover a disaster in that part of the family. Mia's older brother had committed suicide, and her other brother took the occasion to lose his reason. Mia consequently had a breakdown too, the episodes of her nervous disorder suddenly flaring into the open again and seeming worse than ever. Her younger brother was committed to an institution in Basel. He had been the administrator of Mia's financial affairs, and with his going all worries about her livelihood fell back on Hermann Hesse. But it was Mia's state of mind that was most troublesome. During that long month of June, while Hesse's second wife, Ruth, was an invalid in her garden in Carona, his first wife, Mia, was being taken care of by a nurse in Ascona until she had to be committed to a nearby clinic in Mendrisio.

In the meantime, Hesse picked up his son Martin, then almost fourteen, and placed him in the home of Mia's sister in Kirchdorf. He also made sure that there were things to do for his older sons. Bruno, then twenty, lived with friends near Bern and was waiting to fulfill his military obligation. But the status of sixteen-year-old Heiner was problematic, and it was only after some difficulty that his father found a place for him with friends near Zurich. Throughout all these weeks of excitement, Hesse said or wrote little about the trauma of his children, especially of Heiner and Martin, who were close to their mother. They were part of the terror of Hesse's existence, the illnesses that ran through his life coming together to jar his nerves with cacophonous sounds that drowned out the harmonies he required for his work. As he put it in one of his most dispirited letters to Adis:

The days in Ascona were bad, but worse still was the homecoming to Montagnola, into the emptiness and senselessness of my present life. If that publisher hadn't cheated me, I'd have at least the chance to find some anesthesia in mechanical work, although I couldn't go very far in that either with my eyestrain. Life has never appeared to me so stupid. If the Balls were here, or some other friend, but I have nothing but my many books and in the evening my wine bottle. . . .

The third motif, illness in himself, became the inevitable counterpoint to these upheavals. Reporting to Ball on the events of the past few weeks, Hesse wrote as much about his own mental and physical troubles as about Ruth, Mia, and the boys. He began:

For a long time I have been living in such a hell that I couldn't think of writing letters. The situation is, of course, internally grounded and adds up to a constantly increasing, paralyzing, and almost unbearable listlessness and melancholia, accompanied by almost constant pain, especially in my eyes and head.

The tone of these letters, as well as others he sent to intimates like Alice Leuthold, suggests an almost equal balance of disasters: Ruth's illness; the excitement, telegrams, arrangements about Mia and her family (and the renewed involvement with her); and the comparatively paltry blow of the publisher's decision to renege on the contract of the edition of "forgotten authors." Throughout, Hesse's psychoanalytically attuned consciousness made him experience the entire complex of events as scenes in the theater of his mind, a huge play lodged within a tortured yet struggling self, which he gradually shaped into the Magic Theater of his next novel. It was at this point that the "outsider" theme of the marriage was joined with the death and suicide themes of those weeks of despair. He focused sharply on both for his future novel, for they seemed to be equally involved in the texture of events that life had woven for him. In response to a concerned letter from Emmy Ball, he wrote in July:

In your dear letter you made a strange request: that I should not die. Yes, I truly believe that after a few weeks of this sadness I will not die but will continue to muddle along. But surely this does not correspond to my real desires. I don't like to continue along this dusty, arduous, and (for me most disagreeably) useless road. . . .

Although Hesse added that he could believe as little in the value of his literary efforts as in the value of any of his other activities, the final sense of this important letter suggested the opposite. He viewed his caring for Ruth, Mia, and the children as a hindrance to his work that had become an insurmountable obstacle. Clearly he did not do these tasks because he felt personally compelled. Rather, it was one way to justify his existence in the absence of fresh work. Mia, who probably knew him best, seemed to be aware of his stratagems. "With the sharpness of the mentally ill," he wrote in the same letter to Emmy, "my first wife senses this distinctly and takes none of my actions seriously." Hesse agreed. He was coping mostly because that was the only way to give meaning to his present life. He required a new, more impersonal purpose to make him whole and stronger, more fully aware of the need to combat his flirtation with death. His physical ailments, however, prevented him from realizing himself. He had, he wrote Emmy, suffered less from Ruth's illness, Mia's madness, and his concern for the children than he had from his own eyeaches. If he could have one wish that would be magically fulfilled, he would spend it not on Ruth, Mia, or the boys: he would use it to relieve himself of his eyeaches for just a few days to enable him to do a little work.

Events distorted Hesse's perspective as the pain of sciatica and gout plagued his legs. There seemed to be no letup in this strange regression in himself and in his surroundings to the days of ten years before. Mia, still committed in Mendrisio, began to write letters again as though nothing had changed, and the sequences of breakdown, remission, and renewed attack once more communicated themselves with the unbearable impatience and irritation that had seized him after 1916. In the midst of these confusions and regressions, Hesse still searched for the meaning that would sustain him, which he communicated to Hugo Ball in a long letter written at the end of July. He responded at that point to his friends' concern that he might commit suicide:

> I didn't mean to say that our sufferings are senseless. When I use the word "senseless" I am expressing my mood on all these days when I don't succeed in finding meaning in the things I go through: in my eyeaches, in my disgust with life, in my disgust with my own profession, in my marriage misery, etc. On those days I experience all this as senseless and myself and my life as a failure and thrown away. And such days were far more frequent during the past three months than other (more meaningful) days. In between I do see the childishness of my attitude and see, like a faint premonition, some meaning, but never for very long.[14]

Once more, as in the barren days of *Siddhartha*, Hesse looked for a way to validate his search for meaning in the work of his imagination. *A Guest at the Spa*, with its insights before his new marriage, had been the first step. The inchoate traumas of 1925, following upon his flight from marriage and his sense of being caught after all by both his wives, provided the means of reaching the second step. It took one further distancing act, and a prolonged engagement with suicide threats and despair, before his new creation could actually take place.

IV

In the autumn of 1925, Hermann Hesse was looking for escape—for a break from all those troubles that had poisoned his spring and summer and had condemned him to inactivity as a writer. Just forty-eight years of age that previous July, he began to chart a way for himself, not yet in sustained work, nor yet in any Magic Theater, but by taking cures and traveling and visiting his friends, his lifelong remedies. As he had done during the months when he struggled to finish *Siddhartha*, he replaced the wandering of his imagination with restless physical travel. Again he started to move. Late in August he decided to go to Zurich for a few days to visit the Leutholds. He disliked living alone when he could neither work nor have a good time. And in September and October he planned an extended trip to Southern Germany, with several lecture stops in important German cities. These two trips Hesse later combined in his partly fictional travelogue *Journey to Nuremberg*, which became a sequel to his imaginative journal of the suffering patient in *A Guest at the Spa* and another vestibule to the Magic Theater of *Steppenwolf*. One was the Magic Cure, the other the Sentimental Journey. Together they were designed to heal his soul, as the Magic Theater in *Steppenwolf* was intended to heal the soul of Hesse's protagonist, Harry Haller.

Zurich was almost his Paradise at this time of stress.[15] The Leutholds, with whom he stayed, were well acquainted with Hesse's traumatic year and tried their best to help him. They opened their doors to him with warm hospitality as they had always done in the past. The Asiatic flavor of the decor in their house made him feel at home in a symbolic sense as well. He was enveloped by the scent of rice and curry. A golden cabinet of a Siamese temple and a bronze statue of Buddha, which his hosts had brought with them, conveyed the exotic atmosphere of a journey of the imagination. At the same time, he felt released enough to enjoy the city—a premonition of another aspect of *Steppenwolf*.

Emerging from the sanctuary at the Leutholds, leaving their "exotic cavern," Hesse found pleasure in sauntering into town, into the modern, playful, elegant world of art exhibitions, theaters, and movies. He enjoyed the city, including even its modern paraphernalia like automobiles and bright lights, acting like an innocent from the country and peering into each store window to read the advertisements. Finally, he ended up in a small wineshop in a side street, watching maids, butlers, chauffeurs, and truck drivers. He saw films, not large historical movies, which he disliked because "they try to teach you something," but comedies like Charlie Chaplin's, which he thought less objectionable. He joined his friends at art exhibitions and listened to gossip in cafés. At one point he was struck by the reconstruction and exhibition of an entire Senegalese village with the same European naiveté he had shown during his journey to India before the war. But from each of these excursions—as he noted in his book *Journey to Nuremberg*—he returned to "Siam," content to sit under the Buddha, between the Chinese bowls, enjoying the warmth of being the guest of good friends, the pleasure of laughing, of talking seriously, of clinking glasses—the pleasure of being taken care of rather than being alone weighed down by needy dependents asking for his caring.

The Leutholds tried to make his stay pleasant, as they did on every occasion he visited them, not only by taking care of his creature comforts but also by arranging for a social life. In a letter to Adis, Hesse mentioned much coming and going of visitors. He saw Ernst Toller again ("that Communist who spent five years in prison"). Josef Englert arrived from nearby Zug, and his old companion Dr. Josef Lang came from Lucerne. They rented a boat to watch fireworks on the lake and, among others, Hesse asked his old friend Ilona Durigo. The next day he went to a performance of *The Magic Flute*. But the dark clouds of his personal life were never far away. Heiner came down to visit him from nearby Frauenfeld, where Hesse had placed him earlier in the summer, and their meeting was strained. Hesse was too impatient with his waywardness, the lack of responsibility he thought he sensed in his younger son, and Heiner felt oppressed by a partly imperious and at the same time absent father. Altercations ensued about plans for school and the sixteen-year-old's immediate career—all played against the background of Mia's collapse.

Hesse disliked the confrontations with Heiner. He also continued to worry about Ruth and what would happen to her once she was driven out of her flat in Carona by the winter weather. Yet when he got back to Montagnola, he was able to enjoy the brief stay of Carlo Isenberg, his half brother Karl's son, who had stopped by on his way home from a tour in Italy. He was as run-down as an adventurous young man would be after a busy summer of hiking, with stomach trouble that kept him constantly in the bathroom, so much so that the old housekeeper Natalina began to fear for his life. He was, however, full of vigor, and his good constitution allowed him to get over his problem. His presence brightened the few days after Hesse's return. When Hesse visited Ruth in Carona he heard that she had decided to move to a hotel in Arosa for a further cure, a decision that eased his mind. With these improvements in his situation he prepared himself for a big "journey to Nuremberg," with a return to his Swabian homeland as his primary goal.

A Guest at the Spa had been written during the crises of 1923 to describe the agonies of illness in a universal perspective, sentimentally and seriously, humorously and playfully. Similarly, Hesse's *Journey to Nuremberg*, based on his trip of the autumn of 1925, was composed to overcome the malaise of his personal and social life. Hesse made his case clear in the early pages of the book:

> This was the situation with my trip: summer had come, the melody of my life at the moment had not become any sweeter, cares from outside beset me, and my old favorite comforts and pleasures, painting and reading, had lost much of their charm, for I was suffering from a continuous pain in my eyes, something that I had, to be sure, known in the past, but which was new in the degree of its severity and persistence. I felt clearly that I was once more at the sorry end of a wish fulfillment and that my life must shortly come under some new sign in order to achieve meaning again.[16]

He had, so he continued in his book, created for himself a hermitage in which he could hide and devote himself to his "games and sins, thought and fantasy, reading, painting, wine bibbing, writing," hidden from the world and alone. And now that this idyllic life began to lose its potential for happiness, as his eyeaches and pains again undermined his lonely paradisical life, a new condition had to emerge, a "new incarnation" such as he "had undergone before." He went on a pilgrimage to his origins—South Germany and especially Swabia—and yet also into a fairyland, following in the tracks of his literary model, young Heinrich von Ofterdingen of Novalis's romantic novel, who searched for the "blue flower" of poetry by returning to Nuremberg and, through that magical city, entering a fairyland.

The public rationalizations for his trip were in keeping with Hesse's familiar posture: that of the man hidden in his small isolated world in Montagnola, its study and balcony, its luscious garden, rather than the man who had just spent restless winters in Basel and had undergone a traumatic summer involving two women who depended on him in their illnesses. The pose suppressed the travels, the peripatetic wanderings, and the great need for company, even as he proclaimed his need for isolation. But as usual, these prounouncements served a purpose, for they clarified Hesse's continuous dialectic. The *Journey to Nuremberg* functioned as a counterpoint to the mythic hermitage in Montagnola. Disguised as a travelogue, it continued the theme of the pilgrimage that in some form underlies many of Hesse's literary productions. Of course, the author was aware that the grail or blue flower might never be found. If the trip would do nothing, he shrugged, it would at least provide some change, fresh images and scenes, and new people. By the end of the summer, as he still struggled with the agonies of Mia and Ruth, his plans had been made, the lectures had been lined up, and he was ready to leave on his adventure.

Hesse's first stop was to have been Baden, but actually he started his trip in nearby Locarno. The reason for his decision claimed in the book was the presence of friends and the fact that he could begin his journey gingerly in a locale close by, but actually he had some unfinished family business to do. He may have loved the Ticino landscape in the fall, but he also had to confront Mia and Heiner. He arrived in the city at the time of the international conference that resulted in the famous Locarno agreement between Germany and her former enemies. The city was bedecked with flags and decorations, and Hesse enjoyed the festive atmosphere. At the same time, the family meeting reminded him sharply of his personal difficulties. Mia's health was much improved, but her brother's continuing confinement in a mental institution in Basel had revealed what Hesse had secretly suspected: the man who had administered Mia's small estate had used up most of it, leaving Hesse once more to worry about his first wife's livelihood. As he wrote his sister: "So everything I've done for years has gone into a hole that was never filled."

Baden, where he was finally able to escape, helped Hesse a great deal, despite continuing eyeaches and intestinal troubles. When he arrived there on October 2 his brother Hans greeted him with flowers. They enjoyed a cordial, though somewhat shy and formal relationship, as it would have to be between two brothers, one unsuccessfully struggling as an office clerk in an arms factory, the other a famous author. Hesse tried to refrain from being condescending toward his younger brother, but the effort only resulted in greater reticence. For while he spent several months a year in the luxury of the Verenahof, enjoying the life of the *Kurgast* in the comfort of the large hotel, his brother was one of hundreds streaming through the factory gate in downtown Baden.

Hesse described in his memoir of Hans how he would wait for him at the gate and spot him among the gray mass of workers and clerks, how they would then repair to a wineshop or to his hotel or to Hans's house. This visit was no different, and they spent several evenings together in their usual awkward way struggling to rekindle and sustain some warmth between them. Others visited him, too, as Hesse usually held court when his sojourn in Baden took him to northern Switzerland, where most of his friends lived. Dr. Lang joined him, a fact he alluded to lightly in the *Journey to Nuremberg*—"My friend Pistorius . . . resurfaced"—[17] but in his letter to Adis, written ten days after his arrival in Baden, he made clear that he had been not merely a casual well-wisher. This time, he told his sister, he was not content to treat his ailments only with physical therapy. He wanted to go to the root of his troubles: "We're doing a bit of psychoanalysis," which he found difficult and taxing. All in all, his stay in Baden that October seemed to have been most successful. He was buoyed by his analyst and by all his other friends and fellow guests at the spa, as he allowed himself to be served and feted. Eventually the stay in Baden came to an end: his "work" was about to begin.

In the *Journey to Nuremberg*, Hesse records an interesting interlude that sheds further light on his uncertainty. His original plan had been to leave Baden on a morning train and to make an early connection in Zurich for the journey to Germany. The train was to leave at eight o'clock in the morning. Hesse's suitcase was not large enough and he had to pack the black suit he needed for his public readings in a cardboard box. But at the last minute he could find no string for it. This very fact seemed to give him the idea to abandon the trip altogether. For nights, so he reported, he had been sleepless, dreading the ordeal of reading in public, wishing he could remain in his sulphur bath in Baden. Why should he "sing his songs" to all those "masses of unknown and unknowable faces"? He decided to go to Zurich, put up at the Leutholds, and then wire all those lecture committees in Ulm, Augsburg, and Nuremberg that the "dear tenor" was unfortunately too indisposed "to sing." But Alice Leuthold, meeting the distraught author in the station restaurant in Zurich sipping a glass of Macon wine while the overflowing cardboard box and the bloated suitcase lay at his feet, was able to dissuade him. She took him home for the night. "Scornfully the great Buddha looked down on me. . . ." After a good supper, wine, and a sleeping pill, he started out the next day at the "civilized" hour of noon.[18]

The trip became a sentimental journey, especially during the few days before he reached Ulm, the first place where he was to appear in public. In Singen near Lake Constance he met several friends whom he had known when he lived in the region during his Gaienhofen days, and then traveled on to the Swabian town of Tuttlingen. After dinner in the strange town he went sightseeing in the dusk and dark before turning in for the night. As he recorded his impressions in his travelogue, he tried to establish himself as the romantic wanderer who joins perceptual images with memories, observed objects with allegorical motifs from fairy tales and myths, personal with historical experience. His life, traumatic and sentimental alike, was projected in a larger perspective—in a "magic mirror." The language of *Steppenwolf*, especially of its Treatise, came more and more to be heard. Reflecting on his Swabian experience he mused:

> It was Hölderlin in that moment under the gabled houses of Tuttlingen, it was Mörike with the lovely Lau, I had also felt the influence of Arnim and the Guardians of the Crown, it was the builders of all the altars, all the choir stalls, the headstones, and the magnificent edifices. And just as on this trip, always and everywhere the dead have been around me—rather, the immortals. And these long-dead men, whose words have been alive for me, whose thoughts have educated me, whose works have made the dull world beautiful and poetic, were they not all strange too, sick, suffering, difficult men, creators out of need, not out of happiness, master builders from disgust at reality, not out of acceptance of it?[19]

Elsewhere he used the consonance of the medieval town and a poem by Hölderlin to suggest a similar magic mirroring of life. The sense of being in the presence of immortal art counteracts pain, despair, and disgust with a sacred moment; a sublime form can offer an affirmative response to the conflicts of everyday reality.

It is this romantic vision that brings together *A Guest at the Spa*, composed in 1923, *Journey to Nuremberg*, composed in 1925, and *Steppenwolf*, chiefly written in 1926, as a sequence in which mortal illness is diagnosed and an immortal cure within the perspective of the magic mirrors of art is suggested. It also sheds light on the development of Hesse's mind during the first half of the twenties and established a canon of his work. In *Demian* and in "Klingsor's Last Summer," Hesse's way to portray life's fluidity—its pain, anxieties, depressions, and other horrors—had been to represent it in pictures. Emil Sinclair drew himself in numberless shapes and finally composed the painting of "Beatrice" in which much of his inner vision was contained. At that time, we recall, Hesse reported to his friend Sturzenegger that he had learned to paint his dreams. Klingsor realized himself in his last summer by painting a comprehensive self-portrait, which included myth, imagination, and dream, as well as everyday reality.

In *Siddhartha*, however, a shift had occurred. As the image of the fluid mirror of the river, in which time itself is caught, indicates, direct visual self-representation was gradually replaced by the refracting mirror in which different segments or parts of the self were separated and exposed. As Hesse gradually remolded and eventually overcame his psychoanalytic point of view, the idea of the aesthetic mirror reflecting the image of a divided, tortured self "under the aspect of eternity" became more and more prominent. It dramatized, and rendered concrete, the encounter between self and "other" as yet another aspect of the self's activity. It also made visually apparent Hesse's restless motions—his inner divisions, his personal ambivalence. The use of the spiritual mirror of art as the reconciling instrument became Hesse's way of replacing self-portraiture with self-encounter.

In *Journey to Nuremberg*, Hesse continued to explore the theme of the "double melody of life"—the opposition of point and counterpoint —which he had begun to sound in *A Guest at the Spa*. The "two poles" within the self that had formed the thematic spine of the earlier book were realized as concrete images. In this later travelogue, however, they portray an encounter between the living "mortal" self and the "immortal" self, the self perceiving its mortal antics within the magic mirror of its artistic consciousness. Consequently, in choosing the style for his transitional book, Hesse fell back on very traditional forms, the journal and the "sentimental journey" associated with eighteenth century writers like Lawrence Sterne and Jean Paul Richter, to re-create the relationship between the perceiving, feeling self and its mirror. These stratagems, which he tried out especially in his *Journey to Nuremberg*, established his book as the final stepping stone to *Steppenwolf*, the novel he wrote the following year.

On his way to Ulm, Hesse stayed two days in the small Swabian town of Blaubeuren, where he enjoyed meeting old friends and rediscovering his childhood through familiar landmarks and the sound of Swabian speech. But when, in Ulm at last and facing his audience for the first time, he had to perform, Hesse became again intensely aware of his dual self:

> Well, then: A poet who has the profoundest doubts about himself and the worth of his poetic efforts stands before a hall full of listeners, who for their part have not the slightest inkling of the tangled processes in the soul of the respected performer. Now what is it that makes it possible for this poet to read his poems aloud instead of running away and hanging himself? What makes it possible is, first of all, the poet's vanity. Even if he can take neither himself nor his audience seriously, he is nevertheless vain, for everyone is vain, even the ascetic, even the self-doubter.[20]

In this way, Hesse analyzed himself and his own vanity as though he were an object, much as the impersonal voice of the Treatise of *Steppenwolf* analyzed the hero, Harry Haller. Moreover, in addition to explaining why his vanity saved him, Hesse also explained how the magic eye of the poet must refashion reality to make life bearable. In fact, he suggests that the poet must remold the everyday in accordance with his will, just as in *A*

Guest at the Spa the insomniac Hesse was able to overcome the Dutchman next door with an act of his mind. Similarly, at his reading the audience must be forced to be silent and to listen to him while he saved himself by singling out one seemingly sympathetic person on whom he could focus with his love. All these reflections are interesting not because any of the ideas could conceivably be new to Hesse (his livelihood had depended on public readings and lectures for decades), but because he used this German lecture tour as a vehicle to express his sense of self and society in relation to art, which was to become the principal theme of *Steppenwolf*.

Hesse could go through with his readings because he could force himself to be indifferent to his audience and their reaction to him. On a personal level this judgment might seem dubious, for few men were more sensitive to outside reactions than Hesse, but on the level of his literary creation, the personal myth that is the *Journey to Nuremberg*, it opens yet another door to the Magic Theater. "Reality" and its horrors can be overcome by reflecting the self in the "immortal" or "eternal" self of the artistic consciousness. He labored this point distinctly and concretely. If everyday existence were "correct," he reasoned, if only a mortal self existed, if the discontented were merely neurotic, if it were better and more correct to be just a bourgeois, a family father, a regular taxpayer; better to just make business deals and beget children; if factory, automobile, and office were really the normal, true, and meaningful contents of human life, then why do we create art at all? Art—true art, not the journalistic claptrap produced by a busy literary establishment—functions precisely as the universalizing mirror, the Eternal Self. "I know," Hesse wrote, "better than anyone that condition in which the Eternal Self in us watches the Mortal Self and judges its bouncing and grimacing, full of pity, full of mockery, full of neutrality."[21]

This relationship in which mortal life is reflected in the immortal mirror of the Eternal Self makes it possible for the poet to view both himself as a human being and the external world inhabited and refashioned by other human beings with some understanding. As the "bard" Hesse went from Ulm to Augsburg, he could cover up his chagrin at the bustle of big-city life by viewing it within the aspect of the Eternal Self. And so he discerned yet another dimension of the universalizing mirror that also became significant in *Steppenwolf*: humor as an instrument of art.

> And once more I felt the lightning flashes between the opposite poles, over the abyss between reality and the ideal, between reality and beauty, felt the swaying of that airy bridge: humor.

Hesse found his usual traditional label for a seemingly subversive idea: the famous definition of humor as a bridge to the infinite rendered by his model Jean Paul. For with humor, Hesse continued, "everything is bearable, even the railroad stations, even the military barracks, even the literary lectures."[22] In his description of his stay in Augsburg, his meetings with old friends to make the public appearance more palatable, he sounded an ironic if not precious note in describing himself, his own antics, and those of his friends as though all of them were viewed from a higher perspective: the Eternal Self of souls like Goethe with a twinkle in his eye. For he could view himself for what he was—part of the entire "intellectual industry" he despised, the "performing bard" constantly looking for an exit to fresh air—and yet he also wanted to see himself and that world in an ironic mirror that would provide the magical or universalizing perspective.

Following his performance in Augsburg, Hesse had a few days to himself before he had to read in Nuremberg. This interval he decided to spend in Munich where he stayed with the Geheebs, caught up with news of *Simplizissimus*, and especially with his mail, which (though he always complained of its volume) he missed desperately when he was away from his desk too long. Soon he had to leave again for the final engagement in Nuremberg, which he found especially distasteful since the seemingly chaotic state of the city appeared to mirror his own continuing depression. In spite of the beauty of the old town, the birthplace of Albrecht Dürer, he saw mostly the modern city: barren, loveless, crowded with clanging streetcars and roaring automobiles, signifying a pace that could not tolerate graciously decorated wells in shady courtyards or small flower gardens. These sentiments, which form the paradoxical climax of that "magic" *Journey to Nuremberg*, Hesse expressed even more clearly, after his return to Munich in mid-November, in a letter to Emmy Ball, who was then living near Salerno. Reporting on the strange and "partly fantastic journey" that lay behind him, he wrote:

I made a few stopovers in Tuttlingen, Blaubeuren, Ulm, Augsburg, Nuremberg, and Munich and have seen many strange and beautiful things on the way. The strangest experience was Nuremberg, which I had not known. Never have I had such a violent impression of the curse of our time and of the irretrievable nature of all beautiful things of the past as I did in Nuremberg. Here is an unusually beautiful, well-preserved old town with enchanting churches and old merchants' homes, drowned out by the noise of overheated modern traffic and industry in a fantastic way. One has the feeling as though just today all the ancient splendor that trembles among the trucks will cave in. I'm pleased to withdraw from this uncomfortable world.

25. *(top)* Carona, in Ticino (Italian Switzerland), where Hesse's second wife, Ruth Wenger, and her parents had their summer home, 1921

26. *(center)* Carona, with his friends the Wassmers and Moillets

27. *(right)* Hesse with Ruth Wenger, 1925

28. Casa Camuzzi, panorama from window, 1927

29. Casa Camuzzi, the little "palazzo" in the village of Montagnola, where Hesse
    had an apartment between 1919 and 1931

30. *Trees, Houses, Mountain,* watercolor by Hesse, 1928
(*From* Hermann Hesse als Maler, *Suhrkamp Verlag*)

31. *Bay with Mt. Caslano,* watercolor by Hesse, 1924 (*From*
Hermann Hesse als Maler, *Suhrkamp Verlag*)

32. *(above)* Hermann Hesse, at the time of the composition of *Siddhartha*, 1921

33. *(right)* Hermann Hesse, at the time of the composition of *Steppenwolf*, 1926 *(Photo by Gret Widmann)*

34. Dr. Josef B. Lang, Hesse's therapist in 1916 and lifelong friend, June 1942

35. Hesse's friends Hugo and Emmy Ball, a few months before Hugo's death, July 1927

36. *Left to right:* Lisa Wenger, child, Ruth, Hugo Ball, Papa Wenger

37. *(left)* Hesse resting in his garden at Casa Bodmer *(Photo by Martin Hesse)*

38. *(below)* View of Casa Bodmer in Montagnola with garden shed in foreground *(Photo by Martin Hesse)*

39. *(top)* Hesse and friends, September 1929. *From left to right:* Fritz Leuthold, Ninon, Hermann, Alice Leuthold, and unknown friend

40. *(center)* Hermann and his third wife, Ninon, July 1933 *(Photo by E. Keller)*

41. *(left)* Hesse and Ninon, at the beginning of their courtship, S. Maria d'Agno, 1927

42. Hans Hesse, shortly before his death in 1935

43. Hesse with son Bruno in Baden, 1935 *(Photo by Martin Hesse)*

44. Hesse with his sons on his 60th birthday, July 2, 1937
From left to right: Martin, Bruno, Hermann, Heiner

Deutfche
Kriegsgefangenen-Fürforge
Abt. Bücherzentrale
BERN
Thunſtraße 23

Tel. { 4459
      { 5479

Ausg. Nr. ....

Büro III
Literariſche Abteilung
(In der Antwort anzugeben)

Bern, den

3. Nov. 18

Lieber Freund Molt!

    *Vor einigen Tagen erhielt ich wieder
das Monatliche von deiner Zürcher Firma.Das
ist mir immer sehr lieb,und jetzt doppelt,da
ich zur Zeit in sehr schweren Sorgen fast unter-
sinke,die freilich nur zum kleinsten Teil ökonomi-
sche sind.*

    *Wegen des Schwabenbuches wollte ich sagen,daß jener Redakt-
eur Jäger schon ein Genie von Schwindler ist.Die Sache läuft
jetzt seit April,zu machen war das Buch,wenn jemand irgend
sich Mühe gab,in drei,vier Wochen - und bis heut hat er nichts
getan.Telegramme der Gesandtschaft,auch dringende mit bezahlter
Antwort,läßt er ruhig unbeantwortet.*

    *Auch von dem Steinerbüchlein für die Gefangenen ist noch
immer nichts angekommen!Wo stecken denn die?*

Aus der Literatur.

„Demian".

    Von vielen Seiten werde ich aufgefordert, mich darüber zu erklären, warum ich die Dichtung „Demian" nicht unter meinem eigenen Namen herausgegeben habe, und warum ich gerade das Pseudonym Sinclair dafür wählte.

    Nachdem einige Journaliſten meine Autorſchaft feſtgeſtellt und mein kleines Geheimnis zerſtört haben, bekenne ich mich denn zu dieſer Verfaſſerſchaft. Die Anſprüche auf Enthüllungen und pſychologiſche Erklärungen über die Entſtehung des Demian und die Gründe für ſeine Pſeudonymität kann ich jedoch nicht erfüllen, auch nicht anerkennen. Die Kritik hat das Recht, den Dichter zu analyſieren, ſoweit ſie es vermag, ſie hat auch das Recht, das, was ihm wichtig und heilig iſt, für Dummheiten zu erklären und ans Licht öffentlicher Diskuſſion zu ziehen. Damit jedoch ſind ihre Rechte erſchöpft. An den Geheimniſſen, zu welchen die Kritik nicht vordringt, bleibt dem Dichter nach wie vor ſein ſtilles Recht, von dem nur er weiß, ſein kleines, behütetes Geheimnis.

    Ich habe, da nun einmal leider der Schleier zerriſſen wurde, den Fontanepreis, der dem Demian erteilt wurde, zurückgegeben, und meinen Verleger beauftragt, künftige Neudrucke des Buches mit meinem Autornamen zu verſehen. Ich halte meine Pflichten damit für erfüllt. Und für ein künftiges Mal weiß ich nun, durch Erfahrung klug, einen guten, einen vollkommen ſicheren Weg, im Schatten zu bleiben, falls ich nochmals im Leben ein mir heiliges Geheimnis haben ſollte. Ich werde ihn aber niemand verraten.

                                          Hermann Heſſe.

45. *(top)* Letter to Emil Molt from Bern, November 1918

46. *(center)* Statement in *Vivos voco* (1920) declaring Hesse's authorship of *Demian*

47. *(right)* Postcard Hesse sent to Adele in February 1945, with premonition of their separation after the end of the war

48. At work in Casa Bodmer, 1937

49. Hesse with Wassmer, 1943

50. Adele *(left)* and Marulla, 1940s

51. Hesse with son Heiner, 1957

52. Hermann Hesse, 1960 *(Photo by Martin Hesse)*

For all his grousing about Nuremberg, Hesse's reading was well received. But the city pursued him and he responded angrily. The hotel room was unbearably hot. He could not shut off the steaming radiator or open the window because of the street noise that persisted all night. The infernal telephone rang shrilly early in the morning, jolting him out of heavy, hard-earned sleep, which he had just caught after an insomniac's night with raging pain in head and eyes. It was in Nuremberg, he concluded, that he felt "ninety years old and on the point of death." And so he appeared to himself as he returned to Munich: with a destroyed brain, burning eyes, and bent knees. This image, of course, represents the other side of the literary *persona*—it is that of the suffering outsider who must be drawn into the magic mirror—but it also expressed part of his conflict. Where to withdraw? he asked in his letter to Emmy. He was wholly undecided, more suspended in air than he had been in years, but he would probably spend the winter in Zurich rather than living in isolation in Montagnola. Yet in the travelogue he was neither undecided nor contradictory about the goal of his fantastic journey: he envisioned the magic mirror of humor and art he was to create fully in *Steppenwolf*.

The final weeks in Munich were not too uncomfortable. He felt guilty that he could not meet all his friends and unhappy that his sister Marulla had fallen ill again and was recuperating in the country. He had a difficult evening in the house of Thomas Mann, to whom he was then tied in a problematic relationship of admiration, rejection, and tenuous dependency. During the twenties they were often thought of as twin stars in the German literary firmament. Yet Mann, while fond of Hesse as a person, had great difficulty taking his romanticism seriously. Later in life they would be closer to each other, but at this point their relationship was awkward and detached. Hesse's brief reference to the evening indicates these difficulties, especially since they occur in the public context of his book. He appreciated Mann, because he performed his work so conscientiously, in such a workmanlike way, yet he continued to be aware of the questionings and the despair of their common profession. "I sat at his table till late at night and he conducted the occasion handsomely and stylishly, in good humor, with a touch of cordiality and a touch of mockery, defended by his beautiful house, defended by his cleverness and good form."[23]

In Munich, in the suburb of Nymphenberg, Hesse allowed himself to be pampered and spoiled by his friends. He spent the day cooling his eyes and walking among the old trees. But the artistic mirrors he had created soon after the end of his journey did not relieve his physical pain or his strained psyche. Watching the falling leaves drift before the wind as he sauntered among the large trees during the last days of his journey, he sensed that in life, as in art, more was needed than the musings he had so far provided. He still felt like an itinerant, still felt adrift:

> Often I looked at [the leaves] in sadness, often I looked at them and laughed. Like them, I am whirled along today to Munich, tomorrow to Zurich, then back again, searching, impelled to flee pain, impelled to postpone death a little longer. Why does one struggle so hard? I laughed: because that is the game of life.[24]

The laughter, the magic mirror, the artistic conscience, none of these were yet enough to provide Hesse with the relief that would allow him to lose himself in his work. At this moment in November 1925, his second marriage a failure, his personal life again in shambles, he had attempted a homecoming, as he had tried once before when he traveled to his family's "home" in India in 1911. Once again he had failed.

8

Symbolic City:
The Self's Inferno

I

Sometimes I'm sorry I embarked on this
Steppenwolf life so late. It might,
If I had only started sooner,
Have been a source of infinite delight.

       *   *   *

Soon I shall die,
Already I'm coming unstuck.
My bones will lie
With other bones in the muck.
Hesse, the famous poet, is gone,
Though my publisher's profits will go right on.

      —From *Crisis: Pages of a Diary*

THESE LINES from different poems describe the two poles of Hesse's mood as he looked toward the new year of 1926. The poems are part of the *Steppenwolf* canon, expressing his need and fear directly and personally as an unadorned outpouring of himself. Hesse's inner landscape had become the arena of his life, the stage on which his anxieties were directly exposed. He molded a form that he thought commensurate with this condition and found an adequate symbol in the modern city.

Steppenwolf was the first and actually the only work by Hesse in which the entire action takes place in a contemporary metropolis. In almost all of his other work the scene was nature or the Middle Ages or a symbolic Orient. For this choice of the city he was to be attacked by many of his followers, but it agreed with his experience. The combination of Zurich and Basel that he used to develop his symbolic city was designed to expose the individual and collective neuroses Hesse viewed as symptomatic of his time. Its dehumanized mass culture he had already condemned in his travelogue *Journey to Nuremberg* of the previous fall in which he had assailed the degradation of ancient Nuremberg by commerce and industry. The tone of the city is set by the *Musik des Unter-*

gangs, the "music of doom." Among its tenements, in its boulevards lit up by electric lights, its automobiles and clanging streetcars, its modish shops and bars, Hesse sensed the temptation to which sensual man is subject, as well as the premonition of his anonymous death.

Personally, of course, Hesse enjoyed cities even while complaining of them. He spent at least as much time in Zurich as he did in Montagnola, and he loved Munich—but he also rebelled against them. By the time *Steppenwolf* had grown in his mind, he associated cities with drinking, hallucination, and sexual abandon. From within this hell (which was not always unattractive), corresponding to the hell of the inner self, a new spiritual recognition was to emerge: a magic theater. Seeking to display man's schizophrenia openly, divided as he is into flesh and spirit, as part of the schizophrenia of the time, he produced the Symbolic City, as in *Siddhartha* he had produced the Symbolic River, to display ultimate harmony. The city, then, was not just a scene or a locale. In fact, in his novel it was mostly suggested and rarely described. Rather, it functioned as the showcase in which man's social and psychological entrails were displayed.

The two poems just cited express the two poles that were to be joined in the city landscape, the landscape of Hesse's mind. They suggest despair, depression, and suicide on the one hand, and, on the other, a sense of orgiastic pleasure from which a universalizing mirror was to be developed. The "Protestant Steppenwolf," as he called himself, was to be seen in the mirror of art—the mirror of the immortals—that would make a reconciliation possible.

Hesse's double melody—despair and the search for pleasure—began to be sounded at once after his return to Montagnola. On December 3, 1925, he told Adis that he wanted to do a larger essay on his Nuremberg trip, but that his eyes hurt. And he reported that the following week he was about to leave for Zurich. The Leutholds had found a place for him in the home of a family named Ullmann, on Schanzengraben 31, an address he was to retain for many winters to come. Meanwhile his personal life continued to be complicated. Ruth had made good progress in her cure in Arosa. Hesse had encouraged her to spend Christmas with her family in Basel and to join him in Zurich for New Year's Eve. The other motif of his music was also heard. Mia was now fully restored and declared her intention to return to Ascona. Hesse sounded the leitmotif for 1926 in a letter to Adis in which he described his circumstances:

Funny. Everywhere I have a wife sitting around and neither one knows what to do and each is alone, and most of their worries fall upon me.

Writing to Hugo Ball the next day, Hesse reinforced this sense of isolation. He had been home from the Nuremberg journey only two weeks (the letter was composed on December 8), but his isolation was complete.

Before he could escape to Zurich, another event occurred, another motif of death and its transcendence that was to become his theme for the following year. Alice Leuthold's brother, who lived in Lugano, suddenly died of a heart attack. Since the Leutholds were not only his dearest friends but also his loving patrons, he could not refuse when Alice asked him to go to Lugano. He spent twenty-four hectic hours in town, in severe cold, seeing to it that the dead man found his coffin and was sent off to Zurich to be cremated. Hesse's arrival in the city, then, was clouded. He attended the funeral, then went off to Baden for a few days to keep from being underfoot in the household of his mourning friends.

Christmas was spent in Baden, where Hesse arrived on Christmas Eve to celebrate the holiday under the tree of his physician, Dr. Josef Markwalder, the brother of the owner of the Verenahof to whom he had dedicated his *A Guest at the Spa*. On Christmas Day Franz Markwalder, the owner, invited him to his family dinner. The next day, however, he moved into the strange new home that the Leutholds had provided for him. He described it in a letter to Adis:

> In Zurich I live in very odd circumstances in an old part of town next to a canal in the house of two Jewish dwarfs who are grown up and work in offices but are not taller than small boys. On the doorpost of my room there is a small Torah scroll, and in the bathroom a little children's bench has been installed for the smaller of the dwarfs, quite low, close to the floor where he has his small cake of soap and his little sponge. The household is kept by a small but approximately normal-sized aunt. It is sometimes annoying that the dwarfs play the piano together until 10 o'clock at night, but all in all it's all right.[1]

Except for breakfast, he ate mostly in restaurants and spent almost every evening with Josef Lang, who now lived in Zurich.

New Year's Eve with Ruth came off as planned and did not seem at all unpleasant. In fact, it was so successful that they met once more when she passed through Zurich on her way back to Arosa. Ruth had been busy making plans for her impending release from the sanatorium. Consequently she had rented a small apartment in Basel and intended to give singing lessons. "She breathes visible sighs of relief," Hesse wrote Adis in January, "since she knows that I am no longer making any demands on her." In any event, since they were more distant from each other, things were more pleasant. "That I had to pay for these nice hours in very expensive coin," he wrote, "with divorce, remarriage, etc., etc., all that I just have to try to forget." And he added philosophically: "Sometimes it occurs to me how funny and oddly mendacious and involved all relationships among people are, and how one can only laugh about them." He posed a final, albeit naive, question, which epitomizes the dual feeling that pervades *Steppenwolf*: "Is it a pleasure to have been born human?"

This question Hesse attempted to answer in his life and in his book. In the tortured autobiographical poems and in letters to his family and friends he projected the dual image of intense suffering and an equally intense desire to find a release that might lead to another new life. "For months," he wrote Hugo Ball on February 17, "I have walked almost every hour past the abyss and did not believe that I would get off free. The coffin had already been ordered."[2] But at the same time he entered into the spirit of the *Fastnacht* season, which was then about to begin and which became for him the antithesis to his suicidal life. On February 15 he had called at Jean Arp's place to order a ticket for a masked ball for which Arp had made the decorations.

He found himself surprised at the thought of still being alive. He even answered an advertisement in a newspaper and took lessons in ballroom dancing (a pastime he had so far disdained) and seemed to force himself to an appreciation of jazz. And so he could write to Ball: "I am still around and shall go to a masked ball and though I don't know yet what will happen to me in the future, I haven't hanged myself yet." In a letter to Romain Rolland, mailed January 30, 1926, which is chiefly devoted to a discussion of the attacks made against Rolland for his wartime pacifism and to the fact that the French translation of *Siddhartha*, just out, had omitted Hesse's dedication to Rolland, one small paragraph suggests once more the duality of Hesse's effort to conquer his condition: "I am going through hard times and start life anew each day only with repugnance. But in between I laugh again and at brief moments possess wisdom and humor."[3] As he reported to Ball: "It didn't work, though, without a great deal of alcohol, and, in consequence, my gout is back. But since a short while ago I gained the feeling that it will somehow go on and life will be possible again."

During this difficult winter Hesse tried to surmount his crisis with alcohol, often in the company of women, in order to gain a fresh perspective. His marriage to Ruth he considered at an end despite its ambiguities. When after a slight relapse she returned to Basel early in March, he was pleased that she was settled in her flat and actually giving singing lessons. In *Steppenwolf* she appears briefly as Erika, who implores Hesse's double, Harry Haller, to return to her. But in his life, as in his fiction, he turned to the pleasures of the city. Rather, pleasure was not quite the word to describe his feelings, just as Zurich, where many of these events occurred, is hardly a pleasure capital of Europe. In fact, Hesse was motivated by a desperate desire to recapture life, as he had done during his boyhood escapades in Cannstatt, which he related in *Demian*.

As "Klingsor", "Klein and Wagner," even *Siddhartha* had shown, Hesse usually viewed sense involvement as a means toward salvation, a necessary station on the way to a purified level of existence. It was therefore a rather forced, problematical, in fact, puritanical pleasure he involved himself in. But as Hesse pointed out in his postface to *Krisis,* the Steppenwolf poems published in 1928, this occasion was the first time that direct sensual involvement was the main substance of his work as it had temporarily become that of his life. The imagined sin capital of Zurich and the imagined artist were to join in a death dance of sensuality not unlike that of the plague, which he was to describe in his next book, *Narcissus and Goldmund*.

II

Hermann Hesse's life during the winter of 1925–26 and his novel *Steppenwolf* evolved together toward an inevitable climax. He lived in his small flat with the dwarfs on Schanzengraben next to the canal, guarded by the "Torah scrolls" on his door. He spent most of his days drinking, his evenings in bars, and his insomnia-filled nights writing poems such as the following:

> Every night the same old story:
> Dancing, laughing, drinking; dead
> Tired returning to my room,
> Falling into my cold bed;
> Waking after fitful slumbers,
> Scribbling verses, God knows why,
> Rubbing bloodshot eyes, uncertain
> Whether I should laugh or cry.
> In a mound of rumpled bedclothes
> And of shattered dreams I lie,
> Aching in my heart and bones,

> Pouring whisky down my gullet,
> While my stifled spirit moans.
> Morning from the depth of Hades
> Creeps at last into my room,
> And upon my sins the daylight
> Stares with eyes of bitter gloom.[4]

These poems, and many more like them, written during the winter and spring of 1926, represent Hesse's original notion of the "Steppenwolf," of the outsider who howls on the fringes of society, as a lonely wolf howls on the edge of a village. They were initially published under the title "Steppenwolf: a Piece of Diary in Verse," in *Die Neue Rundschau*, but they finally appeared in book form under the title *Krisis* in 1928. During the early months, before the so-called prose *Steppenwolf* had matured, it was this collection of poems Hesse primarily thought of when the word "Steppenwolf" came to mind. For example, in one poem he described his feelings while reading part of his "Steppenwolf" to some well-meaning friends who left him with the sense that they were not particularly enthralled, and on that occasion he clearly referred to the verse. Other poems deplored his miserable life away from his wife and children, as well as illness, drunkenness, fever, and violent death. In yet another poem he even described the unfortunate evening in the house of the nationalistic professor who figures prominently in the novel. Accompanying their literary purpose, these poems describe Hesse's life with some accuracy: his sense of being blocked in his work (despite his attempts to start a new novel), his drinking, his pain in eyes, head, arms, and legs, his insomnia, his depression, his half-hearted but also more passionate if thwarted forays into a world in which he felt anything but secure.

The immediate material on hand for Hesse's new novel was evidently this collection of poems that had been accumulated during those insomnia-filled nights in Zurich. Most of them were sent off to Fischer early in June, which suggests that somehow they represented a closed period for him. But it also indicates that the foundation had been laid and that more difficult work (for which he felt as yet unequipped) lay ahead. The prospect of "a renewed beginning in Montagnola," about which he voiced such need and fear in his correspondence, was focused on this task. At first there were only the poems and he was fearful about them. Knowing his sister's scruples, he warned her away from them: "I have not shown them to you yet [the poems he had just sent off], because once you see them, you will dislike them. But that, too, will have to be said and be lived through at one time or other. I am thinking of having them printed and of sending them to my friends when they congratulate me upon my fiftieth birthday." When they finally appeared, in November 1926, Fischer still refused to publish them as a book and he continued to deny Hesse's wish to publish them along with the novel after the work was completed. Their content, and especially their quality, made his publisher hesitate. His sister and friends were repelled by them as well, and others, too, seemed to have responded negatively. Fischer's judgment was sustained.

Hesse must have had some sense of the inadequacy of his Steppenwolf poems even before their publication, and this sense could not have improved his spirits. But, gradually in his letters, a new notion began to emerge that was still largely absent in his poems. While individual scenes of the germinal novel already existed in the poems, he now unified them by focusing them in the mind of the Steppenwolf—a construct denoting the outsider, which can be traced to the short story about the dying wolf that Hesse wrote in 1907. For over a year he had thought about this idea of a metaphoric wolf of the steppes concealed in the unconscious of a very human, in fact, humane and cultured writer. When he returned to Montagnola that summer, he faced this idea in all seriousness and found it to be an appropriate mask for the themes of crisis and sensuality that he had first developed in his autobiographical poems.

The "Steppenwolf" poems, however sentimental and self-pitying they may be, portray at least an important aspect of Hesse's state of mind. They also define the state of mind he was to attribute to his protagonist Harry Haller in *Steppenwolf*. They dramatize his psychological condition as well as the protagonist's attempts to learn how to break through the repressions they shared. Many themes in the poems are documented by corresponding events in Hesse's life during that long winter in Zurich. They also emerge, in an artistically refurbished state, in Hesse's new novel: in Harry Haller's dancing lessons, his visits to cafés and bars, his reputed love affair. It was at this point, in February 1926, that the idea for the novel took concrete shape even as the events that make up the novel's plot actually occurred. By that time, too, the idea of the outsider, which had grown to fruition during the previous year, was linked with the idea of the novel. This outsider was a literary Steppenwolf, but he was also a frustrated, middle-aged, bourgeois writer who was trying to recapture what was left of a sense-giving nature. Instead of looking for it in the mountains of Ticino or in the valleys of the Black Forest, as Hesse had done in the past, he now looked for it in bars. The transition from despair to pleasure, which in the novel is accomplished through a Magic Theater, occurred in a Zurich night spot, as the following poem relates:

GAY NIGHT

It's dismal to lie awake with your feathers drooping,
Lonely, dejected, your bloodstream half congealed.
It's pleasant to lie awake when your heart is loop-the-looping
With love, and all the springs of longing are unsealed.

Alone I'd sat at the bar, for hours on end benighted.
I paid for my whisky and shuffled out. But then
Halfway down the stairs I stopped, delighted,
Ready to start the evening all over again.

The trotting "wolf" is intercepted by two girls:

There was Fanny and there was Adelaide.
Meanwhile the band had struck up an entrancing
One-step. How fast, how liltingly they played!
And how we all soon throbbed and burned with the dancing!

And he reflects on his rescue at dawn:

Now as I lie abed the dawn is breaking.
That shimmy keeps running through my brain.
Fondly I think of those girls, tired but aching
To start this beautiful night all over again.[5]

It is, of course, easy to exaggerate Hesse's activities during this time
by focusing exclusively on these poems. He was busy in many other
ways, still trying to get together that anthology of forgotten German
authors, corresponding widely, and writing his reviews. But he was
clearly worried and engaged in a search. Gradually, as he pursued the
nightlife many of the poems record, his actions and feelings, his poems
and letters gave rise to the "Prose Steppenwolf" in which his life could
be contained—the first major work since the completion of *Siddhartha*
four years earlier. He started drafting the book on the back of old
business letters when his spirits seemed at their lowest ebb. Constantly on
the verge of an emotional collapse, enveloped by liquor, wine, and self-
pity, he nonetheless sought a way out of his straits—in his life as in his
art. His personal dissolution he tried to halt with the help of Dr. Lang,
whom he saw almost daily for those long conversations that were
partly intimate talks between friends and partly analytic sessions.[6] But
the question also extended to his work. It was how to find specific means
of distancing himself from his troubles, of resolving them as an artist by
finding a viable literary form.

It is from this dual need to represent the sufferer's state of mind in a
mirror of those immortals who were above Person and Time that the

idea of the structure, plot, and theme of Hesse's novel developed. He introduced a protagonist, Harry Haller—the author himself—and established a particular perspective of this outsider by first introducing him through the eye of a very limited nephew of his landlady in a place, smelling of floor wax and cleanliness, closely resembling a combination of Fräulein Ringier's place at Lothringerstrasse 7 in Basel and the Ullmanns' place on Schanzengraben 31 in Zurich. From this safe harbor of bourgeois respectability, Hesse developed the *inner* escapades of his outsider-hero whose unconscious longing and impulsive actions suggest that beneath the shy, studious exterior of the writer lurked a bloodthirsty wolf of the steppes. This inner world is revealed to the narrator when he finds some notebooks left behind after the mysterious roomer's disappearance, and the reader then shares the narrator's eye as he joins him in a voyeuristic foray into the departed man's unconscious. It reworks the obvious autobiographical detail and presents it as an artistic image.

In the first stages of the fantasy that forms the core of *Steppenwolf*, Haller seeks solace from despair. He meets three illusory characters—Hermine, a spiritual guide who is also his sister, even an aspect of the author whose name (a feminine version of Hesse's own first name) suggests that she functions as a feminine version of himself; Maria, who becomes Haller's physical mistress, whose name alludes curiously not only to the Virgin Mary but also to Hesse's first wife Mia; and Pablo, a mysterious Mexican saxophone player who turns out to be a master magician and eventually Mozart, the artist par excellence. From these figures Haller learns the art of shedding his inhibitions. In the latter stages, he meets himself in a Magic Theater over which Pablo presides and where he is tested, tried, and eventually transformed. That sequence begins with a gigantic ballroom scene and ends in various peepshows in which parts of his personality are acted out in pantomimes. It was in these final scenes that the denouement of the novel is enacted: Hesse's *persona* Haller sees Hermine, whom he had desired all along, in Pablo's arms in the heavy sleep of satisfied love and, in a fit of jealousy, kills her (who was no longer real but was merely a mirrored image) with a mirrored knife. This was his transgression, for the point of magic had been that it was merely illusion and play. He had "soiled the magic stage with the blood of reality." Pablo is revealed as Mozart, and, in a final Kafkaesque scene, Haller is condemned to death for this transgression while Pablo-Mozart picks up Hermine (who had now shrunk to the size of a small figurine) and puts her in his pocket. Haller realized that he would have to traverse the road through the "hell of himself" again before he can accept the detached "magic" of the immortals, before he can be saved.

An accompanying element of this novel is the argument that runs

through the entire work and is only ultimately dissolved by the fluid encounters of the Magic Theater. This argument, which derives much
significance from Hesse's thought at the time, and from his exchanges
with C. G. Jung, functioned on two levels. The first level concerns the
unity of the self as an entity. Feeling personally threatened by a dissolution of himself—filled with the sense that the bourgeois "insider" has
no trouble believing in a unitary self, capable of undivided action—he
sought to prove that virtue lies precisely in the acceptance of inner
division. From the recognition that this tame intellectual could be both
man and wolf, Hesse rose to the point of viewing man's soul as composed of multiple elements, male and female, young and old, present and
past. The second level concerns the relationship between the psychological fears and insights that gave rise to the novel and the literary reflection that would cast these personal crises in a universal perspective.
On this level, Hesse created the authoritative chorus of the immortals
whose visible proponents in the novel are Goethe and Mozart. These
immortals are the great voices of art, and of humanistic culture, under
whose aegis a personal struggle to accept oneself in all one's agonies and
inner divisions could rise to an ascent toward an ideal. The Magic
Theater—however deliberately deranged its conception may have been—
became the instrument for this ascent, which turned a psychological plot
of the twenties into a humanistic novel of education.

This is the aspect of the novel that was misunderstood by those of
Hesse's readers in the twenties who felt that he had abandoned the lofty
standards of *Siddhartha* and had descended into the gutter, as well as by
those of his readers in the sixties and seventies who thought that the entire
work was a journey into hallucination. For Hesse's construction was not
haphazard, as in psychological association or undirected dream, but
composed as in music and abstract painting. His ideas were directed by
the specific humanistic assumptions that he associated with his principal
metaphoric figures, Goethe and Mozart. A novel of psychoanalytic
education—of a person's attempt to resolve his difficulties through insight—becomes an ascent to the values of order and education held by
these immortal artists. It becomes a humanistic *Bildungsroman*. In this
way, the relationship between the person's crisis and the corresponding
protagonist's reconstructed symbolic world (which includes the world of
humanistic education) provides the tension and peculiar fascination of
the book.[7]

On both these levels, Hesse used the image of the mirror or mirroring,
for unlike the picture, which had been Hesse's chief instrument up to the
early twenties, the mirror could function as a prism for multiple elements
of the self and also as a means of receiving, reflecting, and reconstituting

on a fresh level the antics of the individual self in life as he is caught in the prisms of art. *Steppenwolf* is full of mirrors. The novel sets out with the reflection of lights on wet asphalt streets and enters into more and more complicated worlds in which physical mirrors take a prominent place. Haller's "sister" Hermine looks in a pocket mirror and the entire action culminates in the Magic Theater, which is also described as Pablo's Cabinet of Mirrors.

Even the characters are intricate mirrors for one another. Haller's entry into the inner sanctum of the Magic Theater is preceded by a reflection of himself in a full-length mirror that then breaks, its individual shards still bearing the reflections of parts of himself, which are then reconstituted in various playful combinations by the theater's manager. In fact, even Hermine was a mirrored reflection, and the knife with which the illusory murder was committed had been itself composed of shards that had contained pictured parts of Haller's image.

The most interesting application of the mirror, however, is verbal. Part of the argument of the book is conducted in expository language in a so-called Treatise. This document, which in the original German editions was printed on different paper, in old-fashioned script, bound within the regular volume between two yellow sheets, had been supposedly handed to Haller by a strange man in the street just before his departure from the everyday world had begun, and which he had then taken to his room to read. Its language and ideas applied only to Haller, and it turned into a verbal reflection of himself. For in rather high-handed, satiric tones, the unknown "authors" of the Treatise drew a picture of Haller's innermost being. With the voice of a mysterious authority these authors pitilessly compared his ideal self with his inadequate self-in-the-world. In fact, the scene in which Haller sits down at his desk and reads about himself recalls a crucial scene in the German romantic novel *Heinrich von Ofterdingen* by Novalis in which the hero reads a novel in a hermit's cave where he finds pictures from his own past and present and blurred suggestions of the future.[8]

This way of viewing ideas and feelings, intellectual and psychological struggles, within actual and metaphoric mirrors constitutes Hesse's solution to his problem of transforming crises of life into crises of art. It explains the importance he attached to the poems that had preceded the novel and his misguided insistence that the novel must not be published without them. The entire book reveals itself as an intricate network of mirrored images converting moments of Hesse's life into motifs of his art. In one of his most self-pitying poems, for example, Hesse viewed his own anguish as a reflection in a mirror, which then finds its further echo in the novel. In this sentimental litany, called "After an Evening at the

'Stag,' " the middle-aged poet finds himself sleeping, a little drunk, leaning against the scented white neck, fur, and black hair of a young lady in a bar where he had joined a group of youthful people. Suddenly realizing he did not belong in this company, he took his hat to go back to "Aquarius and Pisces/Home to my accustomed misery." Calling himself a clown and a fool, he trotted home toward the canal whose surface mirrored tired stars. An unknown cur at the door left him quickly after sniffing at him. Upstairs, where he dragged himself on tired feet, he looked in the mirror:

> I looked into the glass and saw red eyelids,
> Withered gray hair, an ugly coated tongue.

And upon seeing this apparition of himself, a reflection of his personal decay, his thoughts return to the dog that had left him:

> If only that dog had bitten me, eaten me up![9]

This poem describes its author's condition, but it also contains some of the artistic elements that went into the making of his novel: the mirror in which the disturbed psyche is not only reflected but revealed; the dog that runs away from the man as the man had run away from his friends. The first image prefigures the mirror images of *Steppenwolf*. The second image, in which the animal shuns the man as the man had shunned his friends, suggests the reversal of "man and wolf," the inverse mirroring of the two figures, which Hesse had used in the sequence he called "Steppenwolf Training" in his novel. The self-pitying stance, the sad surroundings, the glance into the mirror to disclose a rotten self-image, and the split between man and dog in the end—they all seem to be "life studies" for the fully deformed self-portrait provided in the Magic Theater of *Steppenwolf*.

This relationship between the anguish of life and its remolded artistic counterpart appears also in many of the letters Hesse wrote to his friends and family at the time. For example, one of the anxieties suffered by Harry Haller was the approach of his fiftieth birthday with nothing to show for it. He had made a pact with himself to feel free to kill himself on that day if he wished, and the Magic Theater, its curious crew working under the watchful eyes of the immortals, enacts and resolves this choice in the realm of play.

Hesse's painful letter from Montagnola, written in the spring of 1925 when he was down with bad legs and depression, contained a similar resolution. He told the Balls that he had decided he would have the right to hang himself on his fiftieth birthday two years hence, and that at the very moment he had made that decision, everything seemed less difficult.

In the novel, these words are contained in that part of Haller's psyche that was reserved for the immortals. They are spoken in the impersonal language of the Treatise. Replacing the personal anguish of sciatica and gout with a general anxiety about contemporary culture, the "chronicler" of the Treatise writes:

> Finally, when he was about forty-seven years old, [Harry] had a happy not entirely humorless thought. He set the date of his fiftieth birthday as that day on which he could allow himself to commit suicide. On that day, he agreed with himself, he would be free to use or not to use that emergency exit. . . .[10]

From then on, continues the Treatise, whatever had tortured him in the past was now no longer difficult to bear. The theoretical, psychologizing passage that precedes these statements is equally interesting. In a man disposed toward suicide, the Treatise suggests, the temptation to cast off his life can be converted into a very serviceable philosophy of life. The mere knowledge that such an "emergency exit" exists can give a man so inclined strength to bear his pain. Moreover, it enables him to be a detached onlooker who can observe the antics of his suffering self with grim *Schadenfreude*. "I am curious to see," the suicidal person might muse, "how much a man can actually bear! If I have reached the limits of the bearable, I need only open the door and escape."[11]

These passages from the Treatise are not only expansions of Hesse's own thoughts, which he tried out in notes to several friends. They also represent an effort to render feelings as ideas within an intellectual framework. Since this odd pact with the devil of suicide is reported in the Treatise, its partly flippant, partly real resolution of crisis is no longer part of Hesse's own analysis, nor even quite that of his protagonist, who might have introduced it immediately in his own notebooks. It essentially concerns the "Steppenwolf" construct: a purely theoretical, literary being. Playing person and protagonist against each other, the Treatise mirrors this motif several times: it views Haller's psychological antics in its own perspective and even suggests how a humorously detached Haller may look on as the anguished Haller goes through his paces, much as the author Hesse in *A Guest at the Spa* had observed the *Kurgast* Hesse trying to eat his dinner. Since this interplay of mirrors reflects an author who conceived of this pact in the first place, it functions as a dramatic structure through which Hesse detached himself from his own psyche and rendered it, artistically, as play.

One of the trademarks of Hermann Hesse's work, which in part accounts for his various waves of great popularity, is the reciprocal relationship between his personal life and his art. More directly than most writers, he used his work as a means of managing his psychological crises and used the crises as the subject and form of the work in order to overcome them. *Steppenwolf* was a most prominent example of this strategy: the immortals were introduced to provide stability to his fluid existence. Yet the very passage to these immortals was found in the midst of his ambiguously dissolute life. The masked balls Hesse decided to attend during the *Fastnacht* season of 1926 became part of his cure just as he thought of building his own crisis into the intellectual structure he was beginning to put together in his mind. On March 2, 1926, after complaining to Adis about his usual eyeaches, he told her that he had attended a series of masked balls for the first time in his life and that he had found them to be a marvelous way of anesthetizing himself, of counteracting his depression "with dancing, with wine, with this and that."

Hesse remained uncertain: joy was always also his misery. In one *Fastnacht* experience, which was transmuted fully into the final scenes of *Steppenwolf*, he appeared full of pleasure in public, yet full of misery when relating the same events in his poems and letters. The occasion is a masked ball on March 16 to which he was taken by the sculptor Hermann Hubacher. It was a particularly important occasion, for the masked ball was a *Künstlerfest*, a ball specifically designed by and for artists. Hesse was bound to find many artists at the dance, friends like Louis Moillet and Othmar Schoeck who were his intimates, and patrons of the arts like Max Wassmer who had by then become one of Hesse's principal benefactors. Hubacher picked him up at the Ullmanns' on Schanzengraben and brought him to the Hotel Baur au Lac, which was to become Pablo's Dance Hall and Magic Theater in the novel. Hubacher's description gives an especially vivid picture of the decor, with lights and reflecting mirrors illuminating the turning couples, creating many of the effects caught in the grand dance that ushers in the final sequence of the Magic Theater.

When Hubacher arrived with Hesse, the party was already in full swing and they were greeted noisily by their friends. Hubacher relates:

> Hesse watched the hubbub with a somewhat sweetly sour face, rather quizzically, until suddenly a charming Pierrette recognized him and, with élan, sat down on his knees. And, see here, our friend was "partu pour la gloire."

As he described the dance, Hubacher approached the parallel scene in *Steppenwolf* even more clearly:

The great dance hall was dark and in the midst of it, floating above, turned a huge illuminated globe bedecked with small mirrors which cast its lights, like small flashes of lightning, over the dancing couples. The bands played the latest hit tunes. Everyone hummed along, and now and then one could discover familiar faces in the half-dark. It was wild. Paper streamers sent their colorful signals from table to table, from couple to couple. . . .[12]

In the novel, this scene appears as a more rarified image, filtered through Hesse's imagination. It also alludes to Novalis's description of a gigantic ball in *Heinrich von Ofterdingen*, which precedes Heinrich's entry into the magic world of Klingsor, his teacher of the mysteries of poesy. In Hesse's life the consequences were more mundane and in his art more ambiguous, but the parallelism is clearly discernible. In *Steppenwolf*, the dance is seen as a swaying union of many combined into a single rhythmic whole:

> . . . the exultation of a festive communion, the secret of a person's submergence in the mass, the *unio mystica* of pleasure. . . . I was no longer I, my personality was dissolved in the intoxication of the festival as salt is dissolved in water. . . . [All] women belonged to me and I belonged to them all. We all took part of each other. And also the men were part of it; in them, too, I existed . . . their smiles were mine, their wooing mine, my wooing theirs. . . .[13]

The dance as a union of multiple elements, divided among many people, combined in a *unio mystica*, mirrors in Hesse, as in Novalis, sexual union as well. In fact, Haller had learned in bed with his mistress that their union was mirrored at least threefold: Maria was not only his lover but Hermine's as well, and both of them were lovers of the musical magician Pablo. "[And] I thought," he mused, "of the thousand souls of the *Steppenwolf* Treatise."[14]

Hesse's behavior at the party, like Haller's behavior in the Magic Theater, was full of contradictions. Outwardly he seemed to have a great time. Hubacher lost sight of him, and it was almost dawn when Hesse emerged again "in the most genial mood" at a time when the rest of them were drooping with drink and fatigue. Yet he was more sprightly than any of them, "leaping on top of the table and dancing a one-step for us so that the glasses were clattering." He then wrote some verses on the starched shirtfronts of his friends; Othmar Schoeck, his composer friend, added a few musical notes. "Never before," concluded Hubacher, "have I borne my breast home more proudly."[15] However reliable this account may be—and Hubacher included it among his personal reminiscences published in 1965, long after *Steppenwolf* had appeared—there is enough in this description to show that at least his friends at the table thought that Hesse was in a glorious mood. But his subsequent responses to the occasion were oddly contradictory. The next day, Hubacher received a thank-you note in which Hesse complained jokingly that his friends had allowed him to live for decades without acquainting him with the joys of *Fastnächte* and then asked for the name of the pretty girl he had met at the bar.[16] Implied in this humorous admonition is the querulous complaint his protagonist Haller had uttered just before he submerged himself in the dance: "An experience . . . unknown to me in fifty years . . . every adolescent girl and every student finds it familiar."[17] At the same time, he also experienced a negative reaction to the party. In one of his poems about the subject, he expressed a bitter sense of betrayal:

POOR DEVIL ON THE MORNING AFTER THE MASKED BALL

I'm just unlucky. It began so well.
She sat on my lap so lovingly. But then
She ran off with that miserable Pierrot,
And I in my rage began to drink again.

After a while I knocked some tables over
And somehow got this rotten dent in my knee.
My money's gone, my glasses smashed to pieces.
That's right, you little minx, you've ruined me. . . .[18]

In another poem about the "morning after" a masked ball, Hesse was even more explicit about feeling betrayed. It has been assumed that the subject of his passion was Frau Julia Laubl-Honegger, who is pictured as a "muse" of the artists' ball in a postcard photograph that has been preserved. A note Hesse sent her in June from Montagnola suggests intimate memories as well as disappointment. In the poem he wrote:

MORNING AFTER THE MASKED BALL

How wildly your lips sucked themselves to mine!
How desperately the words of passion poured!
And now you've driven off and left me,
A docile female with her rightful lord.
Cheated, I stand here in the early light.
Oh, well. In a certain sense you're right. . . .[19]

As they take off in their "Fiat car," the poet wishes them a quick demise with a dog sniffing at their remains. He continued to be the outsider.

These poems are striking, because they suggest the dark side of Hesse's "sensual play"—betrayal. The masked ball was most helpful to his imagination, but it had not done the same for his actual psyche. It ultimately conveyed a striking image of his mood of betrayal and reversal, as discrepancies between public utterances and private feelings to be caught and reconciled in the imagery of his autobiographical novel.

Hesse's personal crisis was caught in the mirror of his novel as his conflicts were translated into literary devices, and reversals were arranged as counterpoints portraying the author's ambivalence. For example, in Hubacher's description, Hesse's sour mien suddenly brightened; in the novel, both moods were rendered in rapid alternations. In the poem "Gay Night," Hesse was about to leave a bar—"disappointed, alone" —only to be dragged back to dance by two persuasive girls. He was "ready to start the night over again." In the novel, a similar reversal occurs when Haller receives his invitation to join the Magic Theater just as he is about to leave the masked ball in disgust. But the invitation (mysteriously inscribed on his hat-check) turns him around. He is released to dance that great dance with all men and women, which narrows to Maria, and ultimately to Hermine. True, in the novel reversals are produced by a kind of supernatural machinery that can only exist in dreams or in the fantasy of artists. The mysterious invitation mirrors the earlier invitation to the Magic Theater flashed on the deserted wall. But, though these mysteries are accounted for by the game of masks that the occasion of the *Fastnacht* requires, partly they indicate the transformation of life into art, the manner in which personal ambivalence is turned into contrapuntal images and motifs. Hesse's sense of reaching out to an alluringly sensual world, and of feeling both wanted and rejected, becomes Haller's pilgrimage among alternating motifs: those depicting pleasure, a unified vision, humor, or transcendence, contrasted with others that depict isolation, failure, betrayal, and despair.

Ambivalence transmuted into art is most dramatically shown in the teasing charade of masks that resolves Haller's relationship with Hermine —a resolution, however contradictory, about which the novelist had aroused the reader's curiosity since early in the book. A gradual descent from joy begins as soon as Haller perceives Hermine (for the second time) under the mask of the Pierrette that Hubacher had observed in life. Hesse's friends had still seen her most happily poised on his knees, but they were unaware of the contradictions that were to be made part of Haller's magical quest.

The playful resolution of Haller's love for Hermine echoes the same contradictions: the mystical union of the grand ballroom turns into defeat along the corridors of Pablo's Cabinet of Mirrors when the hero "kills" his lady and soils the "magic stage" with the "blood of reality," the mirrored knife in his hand forged of fragments of his own soul. Real emotion, real jealousy, and a real sense of betrayal, suggested in the poem, are refracted in an array of masks. Conversely, as Haller sits by the rigid body of the "dead" Hermine (herself a mask, a mirrored image), contemplating her ice-cold form, the author's description suggests a parallel scene in his life when, ten years earlier, he had sat by the rigid body of his dead father and had placed his hand on the cold forehead.[20] In the novel, all these relationships are extended further by the literary use of the mask. The dance hall in the Hotel Baur au Lac with its mirrors and lights, its upper and lower regions, is masked by various allusions—not only to Novalis but to Dante as well. At Haller's wake with the deadened part of himself, personal feelings and literary traditions combine. *Unio mystica* as a step beyond transcendence in the spirit of Novalis finds its counterpoint in the ice-cold damnation of Dante's *Inferno*.

A writer's personal crisis is significant to his readers to the degree that it finds its distillation in his book or in the further refinement of the tools of his trade. In Hesse's *Steppenwolf* we discover a unique new work that combines highly traditional allusions and forms with experimental tricks and techniques that surprise the reader. The device of notebooks left behind by a mysterious stranger, which are then edited by an obtuse narrator, is very old. So are the various literary allusions that still betray the depth of Hesse's involvement in romanticism. But his use of fluid associations in hallucinations and dreams within a controlled scheme that by Hesse's own testimony was modeled on the most rigorous musical form, the sonata, suggests further experimental deftness. It reinforces the paradox implicit in the book of rendering psychic breakup directly, yet placing it within a rigorous form that substitutes the formality of artistic discourse for the objectivity of the external world.

Hesse's most original invention to display this paradox was that of the Treatise, around which, as Hesse put it in one of his letters, the entire work was to be "tautly stretched."[21] An expository insert that dissects the protagonist's mind from the lofty height of the immortals, it states the point of the book by extolling the divided psyche as a higher form of consciousness. We have seen how the Treatise mirrors both theme and plot of the book as Haller "acts it out" on the "magical" stage, but since it exists as part of the notebooks, and hence as part of Haller's mind as well, it can also be viewed as an aspect of his psyche (like a Freudian superego), a mirrored image reflected by another part of his mind—in both psychological and literary terms. The mirror is Hesse's most significant explicit device and, in the way he used it, also his most original invention. It connects him with his formal *persona* in the novel. The distinction between this form of mirroring and self-portraiture—

which had been prominent in all his work, but especially in *Demian* and "Klingsor"—already emerged in his travelogue *Journey to Nuremberg*. But as *Steppenwolf* developed, Hesse came to use the motif of the mirror dynamically: its surface resembled painting, while the rhythmic motions it reflected and dissolved suggested music. In this way, it came to function as these two art forms functioned in Nietzsche's *Birth of Tragedy*, where the tragic vision is compounded of the Apollonian and the Dionysian spirits. As Hesse's novel grew, and he became more and more aware of the discrepancy between himself as a source of his consciousness and as a viewer of himself, which he had already explored in *A Guest at the Spa* and *Journey to Nuremberg*, the mirror obtained an even larger significance. It caught an interior as well as an exterior vision of the self, a representation of spatially confined features as well as of the fluid unconscious underneath, of the entity we appear to be and the multiplicity we actually represent. The mirror expanded from a physical object to a manner of viewing oneself from within and so turned into an instrument of the Symbolic City.

III

The crisis mirrored in *Steppenwolf* was at its height during the last few months in Zurich in the spring of 1926, when the novel had not yet been written. During that time at the Schanzengraben, Hesse tried almost experimentally to connect himself with a world that was distant from him in age, experience, and inclination. Artists always constituted the atmosphere and milieu in which alone he could function socially with any ease, and he was also often an elder teacher or guide for young people. But during that winter and spring when he felt caught by a deepening personal crisis, he tried to be part of a world—a jazz, bar, and café world—that was outside his normal range of experience. The Pierrette, Lolo, who ran off with her husband after fiery kisses at the masked ball, suggests the passion which Hesse may have felt at the time for Julia. Individual instances, however, hardly matter. What is significant is that Hesse continued to live on the fringes of a society of artists, many of them young, and, like the outsider in his novel, Harry Haller, tried to overcome his shyness and be accepted in their life.

At the same time Hesse looked, as usual, for an anchor of stability, and seeking it usually in a woman, found it in a twenty-nine-year-old art historian who had been an admirer of his work since her childhood. She was Ninon Dolbin, née Auslander, the divorced wife of a Viennese painter and caricaturist. Then living in Vienna herself, though of

Rumanian origin, she was especially interested in Greek classical art. Their friendship soon turned into intimacy.

When they met in 1926, however, Hesse was still very much married to Ruth, not only legally but also in an unending, exasperating involvement. She was not yet ready to sever with him, and received much support from Hesse's own family and friends. In an angry letter written in March, he chided the Balls for sermonizing about his duties toward Ruth. His tone echoed the mood of the *Steppenwolf* poems. The Balls' devout optimism, he wrote them, did not serve him:

> You and Emmy always write how much Ruth loves me, while in reality it is she who left me, and how well the Madonna protects me, and how easily she could cure my eyeaches, etc. For a man facing despair every day, such consolation, if you forgive me, is nothing edible but just hot air. And since man, when he suffers, is particularly egoistic, it has been no longer possible for me to write you of late.

But after some further information about Ruth (her improvement and move into a Basel apartment) he added that she required a person (her niece) to live with her because "she has a need to be something for some human being." When he spoke about his immediate and his long-range plans, he expressed more fully his sense of himself:

> I shall probably stay on here in Zurich for the greater part of April, although I can scarcely bear it any more. What happens after that I don't know yet. Perhaps I shall be able to work again in Montagnola, for in the end that is still the best anesthesia for an old workhorse. Here I can't do it, and anesthesia must be forced night after night with alcohol.

Still, as usual there was another side to Hesse's complaints. On April 20 he wrote Adis that he had been to a great party from which he still suffered a hangover. They had watched a long procession, lasting for hours, featuring figures and scenes from Gottfried Keller and Conrad Ferdinand Meyer. Afterwards he had spent the whole night drinking and dancing with friends. In fact, if he had walked as long as he had spent doing dance steps that night, he might have gotten as far north as Karlsruhe. He announced himself for a visit to Stuttgart, for some reading, for the middle of May, and hoped to see Adis there. He was uncertain whether he would stay in Zurich until that time or stop by Montagnola in between. But in fact, he remained in Zurich until mid-June, unable to move.

The trip came off in May, but it did not seem to have been too happy. He was able to see Adis in Karl Isenberg's house in Ludwigsburg, but the readings in Stuttgart, Blaubeuren, Ulm—all way stations of the

Nuremberg Journey, which was then appearing in *Die Neue Rundschau* —were unusually trying. The weather was bad and a disgruntled Hesse rushed back to Zurich with a toothache. It turned out to be a root infection, and from then on he was in the constant care of a dentist, wracked by pain in his mouth in addition to all his other aches and pains for weeks, which forced him to postpone the return to Ticino again. But his family troubles began to abate. Mia had been to Baden for a cure of her own, then went on to Basel and Kirchdorf to visit their son Martin before returning to her home in Ascona—the episode finally done with. Ruth came up to visit Hesse in Zurich for half a day, evidently in good spirits. But although his outer life began to look up for him in that late spring and early summer, his inner malaise continued. The constant rain, the constant depression and toothache got him down. He loathed having to postpone his departure and yet he also had the insecure sense that beginning all over again in Montagnola would not be successful either. And so, with visits to the dentist and the sense of work undone, he dragged himself from one day to the next in agony. His novel was still to be written.

In the meantime his collection *Picture Book* finally appeared. This volume contained many sketches, vignettes, and passages from intimate journals dating from his Gaienhofen years to the summer of 1924. The title, *Picture Book*, suggested a sketchbook as well as a children's picture book, full of mood images of Hesse's life. The stories were also mirror images of their author's outer and inner biography. Especially the account of his first marriage—those years as the respected bourgeois author with his villa, family, and dog—was retold from an underground perspective that had remained mostly concealed from his public.

More and more Hesse came to see life as though it were refracted and filtered through a looking glass. While still in Zurich he wrote Adis a rather moving letter in commemoration of their father's death on March 8 ten years before, in which he complained that beauty had been looked down upon in their home as "*only* beauty and *only* art," that their parents did not rate it nearly as highly "as morality, character, will, ethics." These teachings had ruined his life and, despite the peace he had made with their father, he had to reassess constantly not only the pleasures of his teaching but also the permanence of the injury he had received at his father's hand. When at last he arrived in Montagnola on June 18—after shedding toothaches and other discomforts—he was again touched strongly by the memory of his father because his father's birthday had just been on June 14 and birthdays were always of great importance for the Hesses. Whereupon he dreamed a "mirroring dream." He was again at his father's funeral. Johannes lay in the coffin as an object to be buried, but he was also present among the mourners. Startled by this double image, the son awoke and faced a blue day in Ticino and the novel, *Steppenwolf*, which he was then beginning to take up again seriously and in which precisely this layering of different aspects of consciousness was to be the main focus.

When Hesse finally started to write his novel in Montagnola, his life seemed happier. Ninon was with him part of the time, although Ruth also came in early July and stayed with her family in nearby Carona. Hesse managed to avoid a meeting between the two women. He enjoyed being back in Montagnola, where he felt calmer than he had in Zurich. In spite of rain and thunderstorms, the tooth still hurting, though bearably, life seemed to hold some pleasures as well. His oldest son Bruno, a tall, tanned twenty-one-year-old serving his year in the Swiss army, visited him for a few days. But in July he had a special pleasure of a different sort. Several watercolors by Hesse were included in a collection to be shown in Berlin and Dresden, and he professed to be more pleased about that than about his success as a writer. He visited friends, roamed with them in the country along the mountainous footpaths around Lugano and swam in the lake. He invited Adis, again sending her the fare so they could spend her birthday, August 15, together. Heiner and Martin came and went, while he held court and wrote, snatching a few moments to lie in the sun. The gout was back, he wrote at one point, especially in his hands, but something was happening to him. Here Zurich and its agonies seemed to fall into place; perspective was restored as he drank wine in the grotto with his friends rather than whiskey in bars. In this "oasis in Paradise," as one of them called it, he tried to recover. He was beginning to see the self-tortures of the *Steppenwolf* poems in the mirror of his prose.

IV

The irony of Hesse's life achieved its highest form of mirroring that summer as he and his friend Hugo Ball came to play an almost uncanny double role. The occasion was largely promoted by Hesse himself. It reinforced the mirroring of *Steppenwolf* and formed its ingenious companion, almost like the secondary theme in the musical composition Hesse had conceived his novel to be. Hugo Ball had been one of his most intimate personal friends, though perhaps not the most artistic and surely not the most successful among his friends at this time. As Hesse's eulogy after Ball's premature death in 1927 indicates, he saw him as his foil and image, and their relationship was not unlike that of the twin figures

Narcissus and Goldmund of Hesse's next novel. Their long separations did not interrupt their friendship; their vivid correspondence seldom ceased. When they were together they spent long hours discussing the miseries and corruptions of the postwar world, and Hesse felt a great cultural affinity. From the same roots in Christianity, they both sought to oppose the corrosion of Western culture: Ball with his return to the Middle Ages, his revival of sainthood; Hesse with his interest in myth and psyche, his renewed discovery of India and especially China. They disagreed a great deal, but their values, as Hesse made clear, remained almost identical. In 1926, as Hesse's indispensable ally and confidant, Ball epitomized the relationship between the self and its identical yet opposite image and so fitted into the mirroring structure of the novel that was then forming in Hesse's mind. His significance to *Steppenwolf* became even more poignant during those months of recovery in Montagnola.

It was the summer of Hesse's forty-ninth birthday on July 2, 1926—a year before the age that he had set as a target date for making the decision whether to hang himself or not—when the idea came up to celebrate his fiftieth birthday with an authorized biography. Samuel Fischer was interested and agreed with Hesse's proposal to commission Hugo Ball. Hesse's recommendation was partly motivated by his wish to help his friend, who was always in need of money, and to secure a sympathetic voice. But in large part, too, he was compelled by a sense of their closeness, the contiguity he knew to exist in their manner of thinking. As it turned out, the biography was to be laudatory but not exclusively so. It is still one of the best portraits of Hesse, despite a few factual errors, and has remained a classic to this day.

Formalities with the publisher proceeded fairly smoothly and, along with the gradual evolution of the prose *Steppenwolf* in Hesse's mind, the biography took up a good deal of his thinking. The two books evolved side by side. Ball was the faster writer, for a postcard Hesse wrote him in September already indicated that some work had been done: "Dear Herr Ball, Would you come for a visit Thursday evening? We'll eat supper at my house or go to the grotto. Do bring your MS along." And he informed his friend that he was expecting Dr. Lang, the psychoanalyst, whom he should get to know. A while later Hesse mailed him his three earliest publications, the book of verse *Romantic Songs*, the prose poetry of *One Hour Behind Midnight*, and the first novel, *Hermann Lauscher*. He thought they would be important for him, and since they were all out of print at the time and hard to get, he gave him *Lauscher* and lent him the other two for use in the biography. "The 'Midnight' book is very impersonal," he wrote, "and without content but important as an experiment in style. 'Lauscher' is significant because of its content. It is the only one of my early books which is still dear to me." With these comments, Hesse sought to send his friend in directions he considered appropriate.

Meanwhile, *Steppenwolf* was still slow in coming to fruition. In late October Hesse went off to Baden for his usual cure and then stayed in Zurich while Ball remained behind in Agnuzzo. But while he worked on his novel in his northern hideout, Hesse continued to spend much time and energy supplying Ball with material. Fischer had agreed to pay his biographer's fare to visit him in Baden for a conference. A note written early in October enclosed samples of letters from adoring readers to supplement hate letters from nationalistic students that were already in Ball's possession. The extent to which Hesse was involved in the project of his biography is indicated by his letter of instructions concerning topics to be discussed at their forthcoming meeting: "Let us discuss, in addition to any questions you want to ask, sundry biographical matters, and, in addition, the history of my relationship to India and Asia, then also my position during the war." There were also admonitions about what not to include: "My first marriage is sufficiently far in the past to be pointed out briefly, if necessary. My second marriage, by contrast, cannot yet be discussed." Hesse entered into all of the aspects of Ball's project in great detail. Should there be a separate chapter reserved for Hesse the literary critic? Perhaps not. He had never been one of those to dabble in general cultural critiques. "Perhaps some instinct and psychological economy warned me away," he wrote Ball, "and kept me from entering too fully into purely intellectual statements so as not to dry up the soil on which literature grows." Yet *Steppenwolf*, still largely unwritten, should find a place in Ball's book at least through its verse: "My most recent, only half accomplished incarnation as Steppenwolf can still be included. For last winter's poems, entitled 'Steppenwolf' will still appear before your book is out."[22]

Of all these sundry instructions and prohibitions with which Hesse sought to help his friend along, one comment throws his great concern with the biography, and its relevance to the novel *Steppenwolf*, into sharp relief. Early in his letter he wrote: "As far as my biography has any meaning at all it is probably that the personal, incurable, though scantily mastered neurosis of an intellectual is at the same time a symptom for the soul of our time."[23] In the novel's "Preface" he wrote in 1940 that it had been an attempt to "overcome the great illness of [Haller's] time not through circumventions and embellishments of the truth but through the effort to make the illness itself the subject of his presentation."[24] More generally, this was indeed the theme of his novel and the aim of its intricate mirroring—to portray the identity of the hero's anguish with the anguish of his time. Hesse's conception of the biography appeared to be a perfect image of its author's features.

The meeting of subject and biographer finally came off in November in Hesse's Zurich apartment, and, among further instructions and admonitions, Ball apparently received the reassurance that he felt he needed that his work would not be in vain. Apparently Fischer was worried whether the project was economically viable, but Hesse felt he could assure his friend that while his publisher was more conservative than most, he kept his promises. Ball stayed with him for a few days, receiving instructions, addresses of family members and friends to get in touch with, and was especially told of Adis and her knowledge about the Hesse family. After he left, Hesse began to work again seriously on his own book, which until then had existed mostly in his head, on innumerable sketches, false starts on the backs of business letters, and various drafts of chapters. But he was now determined to follow up last year's *Steppenwolf* poems with this year's *Steppenwolf* novel. There was one more interruption. In late November he went off again, lecturing in Stuttgart and meeting Adis once again at the Isenbergs' in nearby Ludwigsburg. In addition to this usual Swabian circuit he went on to Darmstadt, Marburg, and Frankfurt, and visited Count Keyserling as well as the translator of the *I Ching*, Richard Wilhelm. By early December he was back in Zurich and at work on his novel at last.

The mirroring of *Steppenwolf*, however, the sense of betrayal that is echoed in its concluding sections that seemed closely tied in with Ruth, had made itself felt during these same fall months and seemed to place further emphasis on his composition. While he was still in Baden, Hesse was informed that he had been elected to the Berlin Academy, an event on the surface wholly at odds with his posture of the outsider and an honor more nearly suitable for the Hesse of Gaienhofen days than for the sage of Montagnola. He was to resign that honor later on, but when at this point his estranged wife Ruth refused to acknowledge it, he felt hurt. He had written Ruth, he complained to Adis, and had told her about the academy. He had even sent her a new poem, but there had been no sound from her. These remarks reveal a sense of the betrayal he often expected of women. But they also herald a new anxiety, for soon thereafter he was to be involved in his second divorce, which Ruth was to initiate. But, though he felt querulous and rejected, he had the strength to continue his work on his novel.

The prose *Steppenwolf*, begun seriously and coherently in November before his German trip, was finally written in December in Hesse's usual haste. The weeks of its feverish composition were also filled with cor-

respondence about Hugo Ball's project—where to find the black notebooks in which Adis had written down the main facts about their
paternal family's history, how to discover parts of his mother's diary in
his Montagnola apartment (in the drawer of a table in front of the green
sofa in his study), or a portrait of grandfather Hesse ("above my bed on
the right side of the big picture of Ruth"). Before Christmas, now addressing his friend in the familiar "du," Hesse registered pleasure that his sister
had helped him so much. At the same time he was now able to report
news about the other side of the mirrored image, the *Steppenwolf*. He
had completed the first version. "I have something to report. The first
draft of the prose *Steppenwolf* is done. There will still be months of work
before proofs are ready. But what is important is done." He regretted
not to be able to read it to Ball yet, for "showing it for the first time to
close friends is actually the only really enjoyable part in so long a work."
He had dear friends in Zurich, such as the Leutholds, but "none with
the sensibility for the nuances of so odd a composition."

As novel and biography moved toward their completion along parallel
tracks, Hesse's winter in Zurich resulted in a great improvement. The
tone of his letters appeared quite different, despite continuing aches and
pains, from that of the previous Christmas seasons in Basel and Zurich.
Hesse's sense of accomplishment kept him aloft. In a quick postcard to
Ball, for example, he told his friend that both Dr. Lang and the Leutholds were down with the flu and that "the Steppenwolf cannot, at this
moment, dazzle with green leaves" (a peculiarly mixed image), but
that he had spent a good evening giving a friend a fine send-off on a
trip to America with lots of cognac. The tone of the postcard was
buoyant. This was true, even though disagreeable events had occurred
as well. Hesse again dealt inadequately with Heiner's plans, who was
as rebellious about formal education as his father had been at the same
age (he was then just seventeen). At that moment ("although she knew
about Heiner," as he insisted to Adis), Ruth demanded her divorce. That
this should have occurred after all these years should not have been
amazing, but Hesse was nonetheless taken by surprise. He was indignant
to find that she had already turned the matter over to a lawyer. Day after
day he now sat down at his typewriter answering his large correspondence
and dealing with Ruth's lawyer. Yet though he felt frustrated by this
turn, through which the further drafts of the novel were slightly delayed,
not even this event derailed him. The twin projects of Ball's biography
and his own *Steppenwolf* continued to receive equal attention.

Gradually, however, both the composition of *Steppenwolf* and the
writing of Ball's biography were drawing to a close. A month after his
Christmas announcement to Ball that the first draft of the prose *Steppen-*

wolf was done, on January 21, 1927, he could write to Adis about the agony of having completed a major work and feeling great anxiety that he would never do anything further in the future:

> Meanwhile, I've been working like mad, day and night, and have finished the prose *Steppenwolf*. And now that it's over I more or less caved in. I am suddenly aware of the overwork, the sleeplessness, etc., and at the same time I am sad, for now the pleasure of creation which temporarily gives some sort of meaning and pleasure to my life, is once again behind me and it may take years before I will experience this once more if it comes to that at all.[25]

The anxiety was heightened by the fact that the same letter had to contain the news of Ruth's imminent divorce action.

In February, the first reactions to both works set in as *Steppenwolf* reached Samuel Fischer's desk and the biography, which was not to be completed until the end of March, caused more concern in his offices. At their meeting in Zurich early in February, for which Hesse had interrupted his Baden cure, Fischer had to be reassured that Ball's work would be marketable to a wider audience, that it was not so academic as he feared. But about the prose *Steppenwolf* Fischer was enthusiastic. He had read it quickly on the train on his way to meet Hesse and was very moved, although uneasy as well. About the poems he continued to be adamant. Hesse had insisted, with his odd misjudgment of his talent, that they were at least as important as the prose and that the two parts be published together—just as late in his life the poems and poetic biographies of Josef Knecht were published along with the main text of his magnum opus, *The Glass Bead Game*. It must have taken all of Samuel Fischer's persuasiveness and diplomacy to convince this cantankerous though lucrative author to let go of the poems as part of the *Steppenwolf* volume. In a compromise, he agreed to schedule them as a separate publication for the following winter. While the novel was freed from being hitched to the poems, Hesse continued to worry about the fate of both works. On February 9 he wrote Adis from Zurich after his meeting with Fischer:

> With the Steppenwolf you inquired about it is like this: There is the novel Steppenwolf, in prose, which I finished a short time ago. It is now with the publisher and will appear as soon as possible. Fischer who still read the manuscript en route gave me his verdict yesterday. In 25 years I have never heard him speak about a new book so shaken, so enthusiastic, but also so uncertain. The book will cause quite a stir, but not only in a good sense. For the enemies, especially in the political camp, will stir—perhaps even the prosecutor's office. But you must not mention this to anyone.

Then, turning to the poems:

> In addition to the novel, there are also the poems. Some of them you
> got to know and where horrified, as were several other friends. Part of
> that collection was printed in the *Rundschau* and it is to them that [your
> friend] Frau Kommerell's remark referred.[26]

Hesse's anxieties were not altogether misplaced. Fischer kept his
promise, as Hesse had told Ball he would, and the poems appeared in
an enlarged version, though in a cautiously limited edition, early in
1928. Entitled *Krisis: A Piece of Diary in Verse*, they had a limited
appeal. Since the book had been immunized from the novel (even the
designation "Steppenwolf" had disappeared from the title), it could be
viewed more or less the way it was advertised, as a special contribution
by the author to thank his well-wishers on his fiftieth birthday. Samuel
Fischer's sense of the disparity in value and interest between the two
"parts" of *Steppenwolf* was fully vindicated. For example, Thomas
Mann, who usually treated Hesse with great respect, could not suppress considerable irony when he thanked him for an advance copy of
Krisis in January 1928. The poems, Mann noted, reflected an atmosphere that "may not be to everyone's taste." He continued: "The
endearing quality of your hypochondria and the fundamentally youthful
longing for 'dissolution' have, as so often in your work, touched me
deeply. One is getting more and more disgruntled and choosy about one's
reading and can't digest most of it. Your *Steppenwolf* [the novel] has
taught me once again what reading can be like."[27] With this high praise
for the novel taking the sting out of the irony, Mann pointed his finger
at the discrepancy between the two works. But actually enough of the
spirit of the poems had survived in the novel; the fate of both works remained intertwined.

Hesse's most extensive comment of his position is contained in his
postface to *Krisis* when it appeared early the following year. He wrote:

> Yet the problem of growing old, the familiar tragicomedy of the man of
> fifty, is by no means the sole content of these poems. They deal not only
> with the flaring up of the life-drive in an aging man but still more with
> one of those phases when the spirit grows tired of itself and abdicates,
> making way for nature, chaos, and animal instinct.

Hesse then responded to those readers who were wondering why the
author of *Siddhartha* should have written a work like *Steppenwolf*. Still
referring to the poems, but clearly suggesting a wider relevance, Hesse
added: "Throughout my life, periods of intense sublimation, of asceti-
cism aimed at enhanced spirituality, have alternated with periods of

abandonment to naïve sensuality, to childlike folly and the dangers of madness."[28] This explanation was intended to fend off criticism about the verse, but Hesse found that it applied to his novel as well. He was to offend the admirers of *Demian* and *Siddhartha*, who saw in poems and novel alike a betrayal by their author, a surrender to a mass culture for which the intricate modernistic structure served only as a mask.

In the winter and spring of 1927, however, these responses were as yet unknown, and much of Hesse's time was taken up by the promotion of *Steppenwolf*. Despite the complaints and pains that had long since become routine in Hesse's life, that spring was a reasonably happy, productive time. The fear of barrenness that he had communicated to Adis that winter did not prove justified. Quickly he went on to another novel, *Narcissus and Goldmund*, which he began that spring. In February, he had still complained to Hugo Ball that he felt sickly—he had been down with the flu and had gone to Baden, then interrupted his cure for that conference with Samuel Fischer in Zurich—and again used that odd image of the Steppenwolf's wilting leaves ("but the leaves of the Steppenwolf are no longer green. I can barely stand up; my ears are wilting"). He was also able to enjoy himself. Later that month he read from his novel at C. G. Jung's psychoanalytic club, then (recalling the season of the previous year) showed up at another masked ball. It was almost midnight when he arrived. He had a headache and some pain in his heart left over from the flu earlier that month. But he warmed once more to the sight of the women around him and, though he had to sit down more often than he liked to catch his breath, he went on dancing and kissing until the chairs were piled on the tables and the streetcars began running in the gray dawn outside.[29]

With this renewed flickering of his Steppenwolf behavior, Hesse launched his novel and waited for its mixed reaction. On one level, it seemed most promising. Colleagues who received advance copies were impressed and praised the novel for the deftness of its composition as a fine example of a new experimental style. The writer Oskar Loerke, for example, responded to the galleys of the novel and typescript of the Treatise with a genuine awareness of Hesse's delicate balance between individual and social consciousness in his delineation of his work:

> Now you point up in all clarity the tendency toward the Steppenwolf as a fate and show, without pressing it too hard or using force, how human and wolflike natures dwell together and how these natures have to care more for the world than the world cares for them. . . . I find it extraordinary how in all the twistings and turnings time always flows into Harry Haller's soul and how he has to come to terms with the

whole even as he comes to terms with himself. . . . Your story is so
beautiful, so touching and liberating, precisely because you have not
overburdened it with plots.[30]

Hesse responded almost at once with a note thanking Loerke for his
comments. But an additional purpose of his letters sheds some light on
Hesse's anxiety about his unconventional image. He asked his colleague
to cancel his membership in the Berlin Academy, which he had chided
Ruth for not congratulating him about. Clearly, the invitation must have
been a psychological balm for his frail ego. But now he also sensed that
he could lose by being a member, for belonging to an institute like the
academy might eventually align him with suspect spirits as well as
disturb the Steppenwolf image as Hesse sought to present it.[31] It was not
until later in the summer, after the book had officially appeared, that he
realized that it had cost him, at least temporarily, the unquestioning
allegiance of his most loyal audience, although he was praised by others
who were stirred by the evidence they perceived of an avant-gardist
technique and spirit.

At the same time Hesse also involved himself more and more in the
final stages of the "mirrored image—the biography." "I am looking
forward to your work," he wrote Ball. "It will be odd to glance into this
mirror." And in March, still writing from Zurich, he corrected various
errors in dates and locations in Ball's manuscript, principally making
clear that *Siddhartha* was begun in Montagnola during the winter of
1919 and not, as Ball thought, before Hesse had left Bern. Although he
felt stuck in Zurich, as he did every year when the spring was drawing
to a close and Montagnola was beckoning, and although Ruth's divorce
action pursued him like a "devil . . . threatening to suffocate me,"
basically the time was less devastating than it had been in the past.

On March 29, 1927, Hesse was able to write to his friend:

And now you have reached the end of your piece on the Protestant
Steppenwolf. For this I congratulate you most cordially. The best that
we gain from our work is experiencing that moment after its completion
when we can feel: now I have once again accomplished something and
have put it behind me.

This mutual pleasure lasted through the month of April. Students in
Zurich invited Ball to lecture for them at Hesse's suggestion. The "Steppenwolf" "guzzled" in Zurich and hoped that his mirror image could keep
up. And he looked forward to seeing his friend in Ticino. But when he got
there, old pains and disappointments again made themselves felt. Hesse
had hoped to join Ball on an automobile trip, but they missed each

other, and, gout-ridden, he returned to the Casa Camuzzi without seeing him. He again felt intense physical pain, despite his new rush of writing. He hoped to escape the discomfort by going on another trip (the usual palliative of the peripatetic wanderer), although he had just arrived in Ticino. But as he learned that his mirror image Ball was now also feeling pain, he could not help but make a point of their parallel conditions and remind him of the Balls' constant habit of berating him for his hypochondria. He could tell his friend:

> And perhaps now that you're ill yourself you can see that being ill is no pleasure and that pain is pain and that nature has its limits. Only when other people are in pain and can't manage any more, the psychologists smile ironically. . . .

Emmy was traveling in Italy that late spring and early summer. Hesse had aches and pains, which he had all his long life. Hugo Ball was developing an intestinal tumor.

The curves for Hermann Hesse and his *Doppelgänger* Hugo Ball moved in opposite directions. While Ball's illness was beginning to plague him more and more, Hesse's life began to achieve a level of quiet resolution. He had started to work on *Narcissus and Goldmund* toward the end of April and in May was able to view the first parts of *Steppenwolf* in print. The Treatise was printed separately in Fischer's *Neue Rundschau* and Hesse promoted the book by reading from the manuscript to various audiences. In May, too, the divorce from Ruth became final, thus ending an agonizing relationship extending over eight years, although they had lived together for less than two months. For some time Hesse continued to be very touchy and defensive about this protracted episode, but the cause of that sore had been finally treated.

For the great day in July, Hesse's oncoming fiftieth birthday, friends and publisher, admirers everywhere, began to plan a series of festivities in his honor. It was the day when he had promised, in life and in art, to decide whether to do away with himself, but though he naturally complained of aches and pains and wanted to be rescued from the vale of tears even during that reasonably calm spring, the date came and went without a suicide. A reprieve from life was not to be granted to Hesse for another thirty-five years. But the festivities were also not to his liking.

Steppenwolf and Hugo Ball's biography were published together in June to celebrate the oncoming occasion, and Hesse was besieged with invitations to take part in many of them by speaking, reading, giving interviews, or just making an appearance. His pose as a hermit demanded that he look upon all these requests with a jaundiced eye. He had not yet settled down fully to work on *Narcissus and Goldmund* and he suffered a lingering trauma of separation. At one point he even wished that he had suppressed both *Steppenwolf* and Ball's book. Ten different publishers now wanted to get into the act. A composer wanted to write music for his poems. Painters wanted to paint him. Editors wanted to know the dates of his biography. And the mayor of Constance—the city nearest to his prewar residence in Gaienhofen—wanted to celebrate his birthday with a festival and requested his presence. But by late spring and early summer when the time came nearer, the occasion clearly required a mask. The Steppenwolf manner demanded that he endure these requests with resignation; they were necessary gestures for the promotion of both books.

June came, gray and rainy. Hesse's limbs were aching and the weather kept him from painting. But the appearance of *Steppenwolf* and Ball's biography gave him pleasure. Of course, he professed to be too shy to see himself as a center of discussion, yet he sent copies of the book to all kinds of people and praised Ball highly. He thought that Hugo Ball had written not just the outward story but the *legend* of his life for which his friend had discovered the correct "magical formulae." In fact Hesse felt that Ball had taught him something new about himself. He mentioned especially the close relationship between two of his early works, *Hermann Lauscher* and *Peter Camenzind*, of which he himself had been unaware. Comparing his book with Ball's previous work on Byzantine saints, he wrote to him that the biography was his second-best work, and second only because the dignity of its subject could not compare with that of the Byzantines.[32]

Two images occur in this important letter—the last that Ball was to receive from him in at least bearable health—and both point toward the mirror. In one image, toward the end of his letter, Hesse praised Ball's biography as the work of a "master of true poetry," who had proven himself by finding "hieroglyphs and ideograms." And he added that it made him feel happy to be understood just in this matter by one of the few to whom he felt related like a brother. The more important image, early in the letter, relates to a dream in which the mirror image explicitly occurs:

> Last night I had a dream in connection with your book: I dreamed of seeing myself sitting, not as in a mirror but as myself, as a second living figure, more alive than I was. Some inner prohibition forbade me to look at my self closely, that would have been a sin. So I twinkled for a moment through the slit of my eyes and I saw the living Hesse sitting there.[33]

Hesse's caveat, denying that he viewed himself in a mirror, is insignificant—he merely wished to point out that the reproduction of himself was not two-dimensional. What the dream did indicate (like that similar dream about his father's funeral) was his self-conscious awareness of mirroring. The parallelism between seeing himself reflected in the mirror of his friend's eye and in his own eye gazing at himself easily recalls the mirror images of *Steppenwolf*—in which Harry Haller encounters himself—outside and within.

Reciprocal mirroring between novel and biography continued that June despite the growing seriousness of Ball's illness. The last pages of the biography contained a very lucid if hasty analysis of a novel its author had read in typescript and galleys. It reflected both Hesse's own view and the peculiar perspective of his younger friend—an understanding of the *persona* of the artist and a perception of twentieth century man combined in the figure of Harry Haller. It also viewed that figure as part of a romantic tradition, and with a romantic intensity Hesse himself had often rejected. Despite its hasty composition, Ball's comment on *Steppenwolf* remains a formidable statement, with a keen awareness of the concealed intention of the book: "The problem of tragic genius has occupied this poet again and again in recent years; this as well as magic as an art to maintain oneself and as an art to dissolve oneself."[34] Therefore, in the midst of the urban crises of the twentieth century, Ball continued to see Hesse as a last romantic—a spirit who not only holds onto the heritage of German romanticism but also seeks to live it even within the pathological consciousness of a postwar outsider.

As Ball concluded his image of Hesse, seen through the prism of his own critical eye, Hesse continued to express his delight at Ball's work. By mid-June Ninon had joined him once more in Montagnola, and her presence, despite his usual discomforts, seemed to act like a tonic. Meanwhile, Ball's health slipped noticeably. After he had been in pain for weeks, unable to eat, Emmy finally came back from Italy and on June 29 took him to Zurich for an operation. The intestinal tumor turned out to be cancer: Hesse's and Ball's physical discomforts were not really comparable after all. The combined publication date had been adhered to, but the birthday festivities had to be subdued.

Hesse's fiftieth birthday—anticipated and dreaded—came and went while Hugo Ball began his painful journey toward death. In a hurried postcard to his sisters, Hesse told them that Hugo's operation had taken place on July 2, the very day of his birthday. He was now lying seriously ill in the Red Cross Hospital in Zurich. Emmy Ball was staying in Hesse's Schanzengraben apartment. Meanwhile, a muted but pleasant birthday celebration took place in Ticino. The Wassmers arrived from their Castle Bremgarten near Bern. Dr. Lang, Josef Englert, and a few others joined him and Ninon for a festive supper and a bottle of good wine in a restaurant.

Ball received another compassionate letter from Hesse while he was trying to recuperate from his operation. Hesse once more struck the note of their fraternity. Reviews were coming out in which Ball's and Hesse's books were treated side by side, and he informed his friend that he had sent a letter by an old acquaintance, a forester, for Emmy to deliver. He could gather from it how much his book was appreciated "even by those who could hardly understand its deepest roots and tendencies." He also reported that Steppenwolf was doing rather well that summer of its first publication. He demurred that it was "no pleasure to find that suddenly every smooth journalist and every society dame with intellectual pretensions discovers the Steppenwolf in him- or herself and slaps me on the back as a colleague and fellow creature." But this remark also implies satisfaction with the way both novel and biography were being received. And by the usual standards of publishing—reviews, discussions in newspapers and on the radio, requests for lectures, and debate pro and con—it was well launched and promised to be lucrative. The biography, too, received much critical praise, and Hesse was pleased for his friend not only because it might distract Ball from his illness but also because the combined success of the two books seemed to vindicate their mutual ideological position: "All this praise [of the biography] gives me a lot of pleasure and I hope it pleases you a bit, too, dear friend and comrade on the Don Quixote ride against materialism and its priests." And he ended this letter by saying that the two of them were again named together on this occasion.

There was another touching note that brought them together in the same way. Just two days before Hugo Ball's operation, on June 30, Emmy sent Hesse a note from Zurich:

Just a little postscript. Below here, along with soft and wildly colored silks Steppenwolf is being bought, very much, the sale is lively—it touches me very much as just then I was buying a few sheets of paper to write you. Our Steffgen [Hugo Ball] wanted to give his doctor a copy of your biography—we do have Steppenwolf in our suitcase just now—and so I suddenly, on impulse, bought the last copy [of the biography] that was lying there, but suddenly I cried a little, although I had actually nothing to do with my tears. The little salesgirl asked whether I was crying about the book before even reading it. Yes, I said, it seems so. The two names dearest to me are on the cover. . . .[35]

Emmy Ball gives a touching account of her husband's struggle for life during these last few weeks of the summer of 1927. Hesse, though he remained naturally involved, himself felt better since Ninon was with him. They went mountain climbing together, and ate their lunch on the top of Mt. San Salvatore while Hesse was doing some painting again. But he continued to worry about Ball, who had been moved back to Ticino near Hesse's house and whom he now visited regularly every other day. "Things are going badly with Ball. The last few days were again full of worries," he wrote Adis on August 6. And on August 21 he reported: "Things don't go well with Ball. He is done for. Emmy is completely exhausted and eaten away," and then added a strangely self-involved note: "Most recently Ball does not want to see anyone. So far he has always wanted to see me, but now he wants to be even spared by me, so for the past five days I haven't been there."

Ball finally died on September 14 in his Ticino home. A brief postcard to Adis stated the fact: "On Friday morning we buried friend Ball in San Abbondio. Your Hermann." It was a small funeral. Their mutual friends Josef Englert and Dr. Lang followed the coffin, which was preceded by long thick burning candles. It was raining. They listened to the mass and then took him to the cemetery behind the large cypresses.

Emmy Ball-Hennings and her daughter Annemarie went to Hesse's house that evening so they would not be alone on their first night without husband and father. Emmy described their feelings in her note of thanks:

> San Abbondio, Sunday morning,
> Sept. 18, 1927

> Dear good friend Hesse, it was so good to come to you Friday night, although the road was as dark as never before. It stormed, rained, and there was lightning, and our Hugo lay in the earth alone for the first night and no longer in my arms as on the last night of his life. We walked past the cemetery but the gate was closed. Only through the fence the bright stones could be seen shimmering a little, and they are so cold and immovable. I had to think and strain my longing where Hugo actually is. We have words and say Heaven and we speak of the Spirit that lives on, and that can be a consolation, sometimes. But for me something was missing and is still missing, something I cannot name and it is a homesick[ness] quite different from the usual.

And she continued:

> O, it was very dear of you to have taken us in, just during this night and that you have nourished us so well and that you read to us of

Narcissus and Goldmund and of the chestnut tree, and for this growing book and for you, dear Herr Hesse, for me one and the same, I have wished much blessing which will not stay away—that I know from the past. . . .[36]

Narcissus and Goldmund, that next mirroring pair developed just at the time *Steppenwolf* was out in the world and the biography was done.

Ball's death moved Hesse deeply. In his letters to his family and friends he constantly emphasized not only the nature of his own loss, but especially the waste of a man whose brilliance had always been misunderstood and who had died destitute only to be discovered by the critics and journalists when it was too late. When Ninon, who gave him strength and courage, left him to return to Vienna for a while, his spirits sagged once more. On October 11 he wrote his friend Erwin Ackerknecht: "After Ball's death I fell pretty much apart. Tomorrow I am leaving for a while without an address. . . ."

The nonexistent address, of course, was Baden, where he again tried to cure his various discomforts. Later in the month he wrote Emmy from Montagnola that he was again down with an intestinal flu: "Thus the Steppenwolf spends the autumn of his life." And in another postcard to her he reported from Montagnola that the gout had rendered his left hand unusable. Nor was his trip to Zurich much of an improvement. All his friends—the Leutholds, Lang, and so forth—had left him alone on his sickbed. He was, he wrote, "the thinnest Steppenwolf," but not even the flu could kill him. Yet something had changed, and the change was more permanent than similar turns of mind had been in the past. The litany of illnesses and the myth of loneliness and the desire to die or the disgust of life—all these continued. But if during the years before *Steppenwolf* these feelings actually defined the content of his personal life, now they seemed to take on a different role. Ninon now and then visited him in Zurich. When she was present he could rest his eyes, because she read to him (which, by his testimony, she enjoyed); they could go to concerts together; he felt anchored once more.

The glare and noise of the symbolic city that Hesse had revealed in his latest novel and poems was once again transformed and removed to a medieval idyll. In Baden, at his familiar desk in the Verenahof, in his Montagnola study, that new novel took shape as he nursed himself back to life. True, he still complained when he was alone and when his eye-aches bothered him or when the gout came back. But for the moment at least some of his crises seemed to resolve themselves. The city, Zurich, where it had happened, and Basel and Stuttgart and even Cannstatt and all the other places of his life where he allowed himself to be open to "dissolution"—all of them once more resumed the status of mere places to live rather than sources and receptacles of metaphysical evil or metaphysical joy.

In 1928, when the appearance of *Krisis*, the Steppenwolf poems, once more led him to reassess his life, Hesse thought of it soberly and with some detachment. He confided to Adis:

> These were the two greatest disappointments and recognitions of my life: the break of confidence between myself and Mia, with whom I was not happy but whom I liked a great deal and whom I regarded very highly, and the War, which showed me that even in a large context, even among nations, matters are such that people can be had for everything, for the stupidest and the worst before they could be had for everything noble and good. Until then I still harbored some secret idealism and belief within myself, the belief in something like nobility in people. Well, that does happen but how rarely, and when it happens the morality of the world today calls him wrong.

This letter describes, after almost a decade, the nature and the seriousness of Hesse's great break after World War I. It shows that this break never healed, that he had never gone "home" again. From then on, he seriously sought to restructure his universe. The Magic Theater had been a magnified version of the divided psyche viewed as a spiritual ideal. When he awakened in 1928 and found that despite success many of his favorite readers had rejected that solution, he reached toward new and firmer ground. The Way Within turned in a fresh direction.

9

The Fourth New Life:
From Sense to Spirit

I

For two years Goldmund labored over his work. . . . Within the carved stairwell he created a small paradise, like a poem: with lusty pleasure he formed a gracious wilderness of trees, foliage, and weeds with birds sitting in the branches amidst the bodies and heads of animals peering up to them. In the midst of this peacefully sprouting primordial garden, he carved several scenes from the lives of the patriarchs.

 . . . . On rare occasions a day would come when he found it impossible to work, when he was driven away from his creation by restlessness or disgust. Then he assigned his apprentice a small task and escaped into the country on foot or on horseback, breathed the open air in the forest and gained from it an admonishing scent of freedom and vagrancy. Now and then he sought out a farmer's daughter, or he went hunting, or lay in the green fields for hours, staring at the treetops above, vaulting like the heavens, and into the confused wilderness of fern and heather below.

—From *Narcissus and Goldmund*

THESE IMAGES ILLUMINATE the spirit in which Hermann Hesse reentered the world after having emerged from the inferno of the symbolic city. Now the setting had shifted from the hallucinatory stage with its urban props to a fancied version of the Middle Ages, while the divided hero of the new novel, *Narcissus and Goldmund*, was actually split up into two separate characters each of whom bore one part of the Steppenwolf message. One is Narcissus, representing intellect and spirit. The reader first meets him as a young monk in the monastery of Mariabronn and then observes him as he rises to prominence in his church through the exercise of discipline and intellectual control. The other is the artist Goldmund—or Golden Mouth—who begins as a novice under Narcissus's tutelage, then breaks away to fulfill his "sensual self." Goldmund spends much of the novel roaming through the world, taking in the pleasures and the colorful textures provided by the senses and transforming them into works of art before returning to Narcissus to create his masterpiece—a magnificent carving of the Madonna—within the walls of the monastery before his death. The relationship between these two figures, who complement one another as sense and spirit, weaves the tissue of the novel and makes this book one of the most revealing but also one of the most beautiful novels Hesse wrote.

These images, however, do not merely mirror the novel that contains them. They reflect the conflicts of a lifetime—of a childhood in Basel and Calw; of marriage in Gaienhofen; of the many journeys in Swabia, Switzerland, and Italy; always counterpointed by the devout ascetic in his garden or by the settled citizen on his homestead. They recall that sketch "In the Land of the Philistines," written just after his arrival in Gaienhofen, which describes how in profound discomfort with a settled life he had just begun, Hesse had taken his hat and had walked out into the storm-tossed forest just to feel for a moment like a vagabond again before returning to house, lamp, cat, and sleeping wife. In this way, that rich passage from *Narcissus and Goldmund* provides a texture woven of all the adolescent dreams Hesse had portrayed: from the encounters of Gerbersau to Klingsor's erotic visions, to the showcases in Pablo's Hall of Mirrors of *Steppenwolf*. Indeed, like the entire story of *Narcissus and Goldmund*, this passage appears as a Magic Theater unraveled. The fantasies displayed in the earlier novel against the backdrop of the modern city were now detached from their setting and placed in the landscapes of the Middle Ages. No wonder those of Hesse's readers who had thought they had been let down by Harry Haller and his crew felt their old Hesse had returned to them. Gerbersau, Klingsor, even Siddhartha, were revisited in this sentimentally constructed medieval allegory.

The most triumphant achievement in this novel, however, was Hesse's success in projecting the two impulses that had directed his life: the impulse to be accepted by authority, to remain in place and rise in prominence, and the desire to move from place to place, to defy authority, to run away and fashion new forms with the artist's golden mouth. Although he had succumbed again to his depressions during the *Steppenwolf* months, the task of forming nature and sensibility into art occupied him constantly. At the same time he was always aware of its conflict with social and political authority and his own ambition to be welcomed in their world. Now, having returned to his citadel in Montagnola from the northern cities, moderately secure in a new relationship, he could face this duality once more from a different perspective. He found it in the characters of Narcissus and Goldmund and in "the story of a friendship," which details their intimate connection.

The themes of Hesse's new novel, however, did not just mirror his life. *Narcissus and Goldmund* is also replete with literary allusions to his own books. It is almost a *summa* of his labors. The most obvious parallel is

Beneath the Wheel. The monastery providing the citadel of stability is named Mariabronn. Teaching and learning go on there. The book is about two friends who represent opposite aspects of a divided self. Its theme is escape and the prodigal's return. It is easy to see in this work of Hesse's middle age the contours of Maulbronn, the business of education, the characters of Giebenrath and Heilner. One can also discern the more focused setting devised by an older man who converts suicide and escape into the more profound conflict between controlling thought and artistic creation. But the novel also contains resonances of many other books Hesse had written during the last quarter of a century. Its structure, based on the itinerant seeker and his ultimate vision of salvation, is reminiscent of *Demian.* Goldmund's growth, like Sinclair's, is traced through successive pictures, which culminate in comprehensive visions: Frau Eva's in the earlier novel, the Madonna in *Narcissus and Goldmund.* Portraiture also suggests "Klingsor's Last Summer," for Goldmund, like Klingsor, is an artist par excellence and achieves a perfect representation at the point of his death. In the earlier work we faced the artist's universal self-portrait; in the later novel this is replaced by the all-encompassing statue of the Virgin, which Goldmund creates at his peril upon returning to Narcissus and the monastery.

Sense patterns are rich indeed in this new novel of Hesse's fifties: colors pleasing to the eye, and fields and woods in which women blossom like flowers. Goldmund, we read in our passage, now and then sought out a farmer's daughter. He used her as an image through which he could replenish his vision. Beginning with the gypsy girl Lise before the monastery gate at the start of the novel, to the last foray into the garden of the senses in the end, Goldmund uses women as the artist's receptacles, as chalices. The chorus of female figures—as representative as Hermine, Maria, and the androgynous Pablo had been in *Steppenwolf*—ranges from Lise to the proud Lydia to dark-eyed Rebecca, until they become indifferent and nameless. They are as necessary to Goldmund as spiritual texts are to Narcissus. Encounters with them are not deeply felt, nor are they supposed to be. Rather, they represent rich, pleasurable, or searingly painful involvements of mind and feeling to be joined by the sins of adultery and murder, by the Black Death and its desert of misery. They reflect the fruits of the Fall endemic to man's biological condition, on which the artist's vision depends. But it was Goldmund's death as lover and artist, which coincides with the creation of his masterpiece, that projects the same resolution Hesse had evoked with different techniques in *Steppenwolf.*

Using women as two-dimensional figures had always been an important feature in Hesse's romantic repertoire. We may only recall

Kamala in *Siddhartha,* or the taciturn farm wife who followed Klingsor to make love upon his merest signal, or Maria's miraculous appearance in Haller's bed. In this novel this practice is turned into one of the two central motifs. One such high point is the scene when Goldmund finds himself sharing the same bed in a castle with two girls, "a blonde and a dark one." Unlike Mallarmé's famous faun, Goldmund did not quite fail to make his choice. And even the aging artist, as our passage shows, had to make forays into the world to seek out a farm girl to reassure himself of his creative power.

Narcissus, the stern part of the artist's self and Goldmund's metaphoric brother, had no such needs. If Jung's *anima* supplies creativity, his *animus* conveys masculine control and spiritual independence. In the course of the novel Goldmund is supported by one further male figure who functions as Goldmund's teacher in a different, though complementary, sense. He is Master Niklaus, the master of the art of woodcarving who teaches Goldmund the craft that enables him to realize his genius in concrete works of art. He not only provides technical guidance; he also takes Goldmund into his family and surrounds him with the pleasures and limitations of bourgeois society. The artist-vagabond who had escaped the monastery is caught for a time in a walled-in small town. He becomes the meticulous yet limited craftsman who labors in many pages of Hesse's early novels and stories before the temperament of the brilliant artist beckons him out into the world once more—the world of love and death by sword and plague.[1]

II

It seems surprising, in retrospect, that this important novel was begun in the spring of 1927, after a period of great emotional tension. *Steppenwolf* was being produced by S. Fischer in Berlin, and Hesse still lived through the agonies of growth toward a fresh recovery. Hugo Ball became ill at that time and soon lay dying. How much "the story of a friendship"—the subtitle Hesse had chosen for *Narcissus and Goldmund*—reflects that relationship is uncertain, but that there was a connection is highly probable. Although Hesse functioned as the caring older brother, Ball was the ascetic Catholic. Although the Balls were almost always footloose, Hesse's roaming spirit was anchored in the Casa Camuzzi to which both he, and Ball, could return. As we know, the newly widowed Emmy Ball stayed at Hesse's house with her daughter after the funeral, and Hesse read to them from the manuscript of his new novel. At the same time, the book was inspired by the need to rewrite the results of

Steppenwolf in the less disturbed spirit of its aftermath, to view the Magic Theater in the old context of nature and romance. But perhaps the greatest impulse for the new burst of creativity in the spring and summer of that dismal year was the new relationship with Ninon.

They had known one another for a long time. They had exchanged letters as early as 1909 when Ninon was barely fourteen, and later when she was counted among his admirers during the *Demian* years. But soon after they met properly during the hectic days of *Steppenwolf* she came to fill an important need. Obituaries after her death in 1966 suggest that she supplied some features to Hermine in the final version of the novel. As even her photographs show, she was a perfect embodiment of Hesse's antipodes: male and female, Occident and Orient. Her almond eyes and sensuous mouth in the earlier pictures contrast with the almost mannish severity of her later photographs—and both elements were clearly present in the more mature woman with whom Hesse had now allied himself. Moreover, these same contrasts permeated the new novel, *Narcissus and Goldmund*, in which she was far more pervasively present, for by then she had become indispensable to Hesse. As the year went on, and his eyes hurt as usual, Ninon began to read to him regularly and shared much of his work. As early as the summer of 1927, Hesse reported to Adis that his "friend from Vienna" was with him, even as he described Hugo Ball's illness in great detail. When Hesse reemerged, therefore, from his latest bout with aches, pains, and depression, he focused on a new "home," which he again viewed in terms of feminine ties.

The year 1928 was filled with great business and creativity as well as with a real sense of pleasure. Although Hesse's restlessness had not been stayed, he appeared happy for the first time in his life, despite the perennial routine of physical discomforts. After his usual stay in Baden that fall, he met Samuel Fischer in Zurich late in November. Hesse was still feverish with a violent flu, which made negotiations about the new book difficult, but they came to the usual favorable agreement. His correspondence indicated that he had a real sense of progress. In a letter to Adis he was full of plans, which included another Swabian journey to be undertaken the following spring. In fact, Hesse's life resumed a pace to which he used to be accustomed but which he had not been able to maintain during the previous year. After the bout of intestinal flu, with the usual eyeaches, while Ninon was with him to look after him and to read, he headed with her for two months in Arosa—a place that was to serve as another annual retreat for a while.

A fourth new life was beginning to take shape as a highly organized affair, in many ways contradicting Hesse's earlier carefree pace. Between headaches, painful arms and legs, and intestinal and eye troubles he rechanneled his depressions and managed to fit his work into well-marked rubrics. The year now began with two months in Arosa (later to be replaced by St. Moritz). The spring was spent in the north (in Germany or Zurich); summer and early fall in Montagnola; October to early December once more in Baden before he returned to Ticino for Christmas and the start of the new cycle with yet another sojourn in Arosa or St. Moritz. By late February Hesse was working in Zurich in his Schanzengraben apartment while trying to help Heiner, then nineteen, get settled in an apprenticeship as an interior designer and artist. But while the pattern of Hesse's life was more peaceful, he continued to be plagued by doubts. In a letter to Emmy Ball later that month he referred to his restlessness as well as to his longing for stability. He was homesick for Montagnola, he told her from Zurich, though he was also afraid of it—afraid of those piles of books that had collected by then and of those swarms of "grasshoppers" (Berlin tourists trying to see him) who would leave him no rest until fall. "In S. Abbondio, next to Steffgen," he concluded, "would be the best place. But that one is waiting for us and doesn't run away." At the end of his letter Hesse used the theme of wandering even more conspicuously, again linking home and rest with death. "We run around on this earth, always on the move, and we often wave our hats and call out greetings when the other wanderer has just disappeared in the valley and has become invisible, perhaps even altogether engulfed by darkness." A strange way indeed to describe himself at one of the happiest times of his life.

Partly, of course, this letter was a familiar aspect of the posing novelist's projection into his correspondent's state of mind. Emmy Ball was still steeped in the memory of Hugo's death while Hesse had begun to remove himself, reliving the pain mainly in retrospect. But even granted the pose, it was a significant image. Similarly revealing of his state of mind was the work on which he was then engaged. For that February he was not busy with *Narcissus and Goldmund* but with a selection of his poems that were to appear the following year. Ninon helped him sift wheat from chaff, but although he often deferred to her negative comments, he basically followed his own instincts in making the selection. The collection was to be called *Consolation of Night* and although the poems had been written during the previous fourteen years (Hesse had not published a volume of poems since *The Solitary's Music* during the first year of the war), the title strikes a familiar note, which is also reflected in many of the poems. The "consolation of night" is a "consolation of philosophy" fused with the spirit of Hesse's model Novalis. It suggests that "home" and "night" (the "darkness" in the letter to Emmy) had become death's responses to the fluidity of life.

The Swabian journey—the first with Ninon—turned out to be most successful. It also extended far beyond the boundaries of Württemberg. After the lecture in Heilbronn, he and Ninon went to Ludwigsburg where they met Hesse's sisters. Precisely what kind of an impression they made on each other is not immediately recorded, but Adis usually went along with her brother's choices (though she continued to have tender feelings for Ruth), and Ninon soon wrote her lover's favorite sister cordial and even affectionate notes. After the meeting Hesse took his new friend to Claw to show her the places of his childhood, and even to Maulbronn, before their ways parted. Ninon then went on to Paris while Hesse continued his trip through southern and central Germany, stopping in Würzburg and Goethe's Weimar, until he reached Berlin where he expected to be feted by Samuel Fischer and his friends. How much feting took place, however, is uncertain, for Hesse soon fell ill and flew back to Stuttgart the moment he was in a condition to travel, then took the train to Zurich. These tours still followed the model of the *Journey to Nuremberg*: they began on a high note of optimism that was soon deflated. When he returned to Montagnola in May, Ninon joined him again and he could face new crises with equanimity.

The first crisis did not turn out to be as explosive as Hesse had expected. The Steppenwolf poems—now entitled *Krisis*—did not seem to shock nearly as much as he had feared or anticipated when they appeared that spring. Although Adis had to be mollified once more, and a few others raised eyebrows, the event passed without too much excitement. More problematic for Hesse was the publication of a study of his works by Hans Rudolf Schmid in the series "Switzerland in German Intellectual Life." From the perspective of half a century this small book appears to be a harmless, somewhat limited, and unnecessarily "psychological" work, in no way weighty enough to cause the outrage it unleashed. Hesse called it an "evil and unclean work," inexact, unobjective, and poorly written. Yet he thought the reason why the entire Swiss press praised this "worthless volume" was that they were only too pleased to find someone who was telling Hesse "a bit of truth." In a note to Adis from Baden, where he was suffering from an unusually severe attack of sciatica, he wrote that the book was directed against "Hesse from the bourgeois-moralistic side of the fence," which would be welcomed by everyone, especially by "those literature professors in Zurich." Rudolf Schmid had been one of Hesse's early admirers, but when he was received by the object of his adulation at a time when his work was still in its early stages, he had been disappointed. Hesse claimed he had perceived at once that Schmid's view of his work had been superficial, and so he had talked to him in a friendly, correct, but rather cool manner.

As happens to many rejected lovers, Hesse felt, Schmid's love had turned to hate. The whole petty affair suggests that even at this time of relative calm Hesse continued to see himself at bay, fighting off adversaries on the left and right.

During the winter of 1928–29, which turned into an especially vulnerable time, the tender story of *Narcissus and Goldmund* was gradually completed. Hesse's feelings and his need for Ninon were remarkably strong, yet, though they lived together part of the time, she was as restless as he. A touching note to Adis in December suggests how deeply dependent he had become on their relationship: "Nothing new to report, or rather, there is something after all: for now at last the girl Ninon has returned—from Vienna, Cracow, Czernowitz, Breslau, and Berlin and, because of it, my life, which has so far consisted of twenty hours of eye-aches a day, has become lighter and more beautiful." This note was written from Baden where he had gone for his usual pre-Christmas cure at a time when he was still deeply enmeshed in the affairs of both his former wives. He was furious at Ruth Wenger for still calling herself Ruth Hesse despite their recent divorce, and since she appeared this way on concert programs he suggested to Adis that she had married him in the first place only to use his famous name to advance her career. True or not (and his loyal sister demurred at the thought), it was nothing compared to his fear for Mia and her precarious health, especially as it affected his sons. In fact, while Ninon was still in Cracow, Hesse received news from Mia that she was planning to spend the winter close to their youngest son Martin, who was then just seventeen years old, after having "caused confusion" in Heiner's life just the year before. "I can't prevent it," he wrote his sister in despair, "there are no means. . . . Of course, I can understand Mia's wild egoism very well, but the whole thing again hangs over me like a sword dangling from a thin thread."

Still, these struggles remained part of his daily life, as it had been since 1917, and finally did not deflect him from his work on *Narcissus and Goldmund*. Just before Christmas, while he was hard at work on his manuscript in Baden and Zurich, he sent Emmy Ball (along with best holiday wishes from Ninon, the Leutholds, Schoeck, etc.) a detailed description of his work schedule. He was then staying in the Schanzengraben apartment while Ninon had a room in a nearby hostel. He slept late. His dinner was brought to him in the early afternoon. Then, after a long visit from Ninon who read to him, he would withdraw to work deep into the night. Hesse even noted the point he had reached in his narrative: "Goldmund is now returning to the monastery of his youth, pretty much run ragged by life but by no means conquered."

By the end of the year Hesse had finished a large portion of his manuscript and sent it off to Emmy for her comments. She responded glowingly, almost by return mail. "That you find my Goldmund lovelier than I do myself," Hesse replied from Zurich, "I readily believe. You know only the raisins, but I know all those many dull passages without life or verve." A short time later Hesse and Ninon were off to Arosa where he continued to work on his book. "Wish me luck with my Goldmund," he wrote Emmy, "he needs it." His correspondence with Emmy, which was to last for decades, was at that time especially alive, as in her loneliness he tried to support her as her mentor. She wrote beautiful letters, but also deeply personal ones. Along with vivid portrayals of her daily life he became the recipient of intimate dreams. "You have dreamed such a colorful, many-sided dream," he wrote her on January 22, "and you have written it down so beautifully and tenderly," so he could benefit from it as well. And he responded with a drawing of a nearby mountain and a lively description of his skiing with the wind whistling about his ears. But Goldmund had now fully taken over and controlled his mind, as his image had encompassed the entire book. For at this creative time, Hesse's shorthand title for his novel was always *Goldmund*. Narcissus appeared to be subsidiary; it was now Goldmund's work, that deeply colorful dream world for the problematic artist, which he had shared with Emmy. But while his friend's distraught and gifted widow had become, temporarily at least, his responsibility and charge, she did not pose the moral alternatives to the artist's life that had been the burden of Goldmund's women and, usually, Hesse's. The ghosts of Ruth and Mia, which still surrounded him, appeared to undercut his work, while Ninon represented support.

In a strange way the women Hesse used enhanced his name in one way or another, but his relationship with his sisters (especially with Adis, who remained closest to him) was quite different. For he ruled over his sisters as their *pater familias*, a role he had denied himself in relation to his wives. An analogous situation existed in his friendships with men. He was known for his "genius for friendship," and was praised as a man with great gifts for providing warmth, for taking care of needy friends like the Balls, and being taken care of in turn by friends like Leuthold, Wassmer, or Bodmer. But with his sons, and with his younger brother Hans, his attitudes were paradoxically distant. Hans, as he sensed again and again, was Hermann Hesse manqué. He still worked for an arms factory in Baden as a clerk, but despite Hesse's frequent sojourns at the spa, they saw each other more rarely than one might expect. But that fall and winter of 1928–29 Hans had unusual difficulties. His wife Frida, sturdy though she was, suffered from that old Swiss disease, tuberculosis. Hans shared the Hesses' propensity for depression and was unhappy on the job, feeling left out, moving from pillar to post. He was filled with gloom and thoughts of suicide. Hermann labored hard to allay his brother's fears during his stay in Baden as well as in letters from the ski resort. But the burden of Hans was not the only shadow on their Arosa vacation. Ninon reported that soon after their arrival Hesse hurt his foot skiing and had to spend some time lying on a deck chair in complete rest. Fortunately, he had a room with a veranda and so he could at least enjoy the sunshine, but he complained bitterly not only to Ninon but to any of his friends willing to lend an ear. In a note to Erwin Ackerknecht he groused as though the accident had been inflicted on him by an adversary, along with the sour note that neither his *Piktor* nor his *Life Story Briefly Told* would be republished. Eventually, his spirits lifted as his foot improved, and with it the opportunity to return to skiing as well as to his manuscript.

By the beginning of March, Hesse was back in Zurich—with a new eye problem. The inflammation of the tear ducts that had plagued him back in 1903–04 while he was at work on *Peter Camenzind* had returned. At the time, as he reminded Adis in a brief letter written in Zurich on March 5, he had to cover his eyes continuously with hot compresses. It was, he felt, one of the most discomfiting ailments, and it recurred several times until at one point, in Munich, he was subjected to very painful treatment, and, at another time, he was operated upon evidently without permanent success. He had gone back to the oculist he had seen during his Gaienhofen years—now a very old man—who again put him to bed with hot compresses, regretting that he had ever favored an operation, until he could probe the tear duct with an instrument and clear out the infection. And so Hesse spent his days in the Schanzengraben apartment, lying in a darkened room, suffering through sleepless nights and being cared for by Ninon, who read to him from Dickens's *The Old Curiosity Shop*. By April, however, he was well enough to visit Geheeb in Munich, taking Ninon along, before settling down to a summer in Montagnola for more work on *Narcissus and Goldmund*.

It was an uneventful and busy summer: heat in Ticino, the usual flocks of summer tourists, and welcome as well as unwelcome visitors calling at the Casa Camuzzi. Yet these interruptions, which both annoyed and pleased Hesse, did not alter materially his pace on the novel, which had been close to completion before the summer began. When September arrived with the first yellowing leaves he was ready for the usual trip north: to take his annual Baden cure and to enjoy the amenities of city life in Zurich. Ninon went with him, staying with their friends the Bodmers, who were beginning to assume greater importance in Hesse's life. A year later they were to become his benefactors, for they financed the building of his now famous house in Montagnola, but already at this point he mentioned them in one of those brief informal notes he regularly sent to Adis, (along with the Leutholds) as his most intimate friends— the only people he really wanted to see after his cure. In fact, visiting these two couples who were so dear to him would be his main purpose in staying in Zurich, since he had already heard that concerts would not be good that month, and all he expected to do, so he told his sister, in addition to visiting, was to see a single performance of *Figaro*.

At the same time he was planning a lecture tour and family reunion in his native Swabia for November as well. In fact, near the end of his cure these plans took precedence over anything he might have wanted to do in Zurich. In a very loving note to Emmy on October 25 he confided that the prospect of leaving Baden and going to Zurich was not a happy one. He planned to stay just long enough to repack before taking off on his Swabian tour, which was to include lecturing, radio talks, and family reunions. Ordinarily on these occasions he would find everyone gathered in Karl Isenberg's house in Ludwigsburg, and it is not sure from Hesse's letters and notes at the time whether he liked the idea. In fact, it is difficult to know how Hesse really felt during those weeks as his new novel was approaching its completion. On the one hand he felt confident of a renewal of his energies with his new book. But in his letter to Emmy he also presented himself as an old man, sliding visibly toward death: "One dies so damnably slowly, piece by piece: each tooth, each muscle and bone says its special farewells, as though one had a particularly good relationship with it, and then the eyes and everything." And he ended on the note of rain drumming on the windowpanes: after having spent most of the day in bed he had been up just for a few hours in the evening and was about to return to bed with a sleeping draft—"still the best powder the Germans have invented."

This malaise and reference to death on the installment plan appears odd in a man still in his fifties (especially if we consider the fact that he was to live another thirty-three years), but the sense of aging, of being in the process of decay, had obsessed Hesse even as a young man. This feeling was clearly nurtured by the incessant eyeaches that had pursued him since the beginning of the century and which certainly did nothing to alleviate his tendency toward depression. It was present again at this point and affected the entire tenor of his northern journey.

A miserable Hermann Hesse set out from Zurich on the gray morning of November 2. He almost felt as though there had been no Baden cure at all as he complained of intestinal pains and the usual sleepless nights. Still, it did not turn out too bad. He established his main base in Stuttgart, where he lectured and even gave two radio talks. Then he went on various forays into the familiar Swabian country. In the company of his sixteen-year-old niece, the daughter of his favorite cousin Wilhelm Gundert, "the Japanese cousin," who had just arrived from Tokyo, he went on a nostalgic pilgrimage. Since he had some lecturing to do in Tübingen as well, he called at Heckenhauer's bookshop, visited with Herr Sonnewald who, thirty-four years later, treated his former apprentice with great deference as the famous writer he had become. Another excursion took him to the small town of Marbach, where Schiller had been born. In another note to Emmy he mentioned that he visited both Schiller's birthplace and a former schoolmate's furniture factory. Although the chairs were more comfortable in the factory, he wrote, he much preferred the "Schiller House" in all other respects as he looked upon the steep, cobbled alleys and the benign old buildings that surrounded it. In his final foray from Stuttgart, on Sunday, November 10, he took an automobile trip to his older sister's cottage in Hopfau where he visited with Adis for a few hours before returning to the city. In a few brief words to Emmy, written a week later after his return to Zurich, he recaptured the entire feeling of this return to times past. Of his car trip he noted: "I saw the Black Forest again and the old valley of my homeland while traveling past; on the places where I spied for weasels and adders as a little boy, teams in red and black were now busy playing football. And the old Hirsau monastery still stood where it always was, and from its ruins still grew that high elm tree that had been almost as high at the time of my childhood."

The next day, a drizzling Monday, he started out from Stuttgart on another circuitous trip home by way of various places where he was expected to lecture. Again, as in that literary journey to Nuremberg four years before, he stopped at the town of Blaubeuren where he lectured and met friends, then moved on to Ulm where he made his headquarters for the rest of the week. Again, in that informative little letter he sent Emmy Ball, he chatted about the pleasant time he had in Ulm. Present in the city at the time was the famous humorist Joachim Ringelnatz, a mutual friend, whom he also heard lecturing, not without some envy. His presence, however, had created yet another bond between present and past: "Last night I stayed up till midnight with whiskey and soda," he wrote Emmy, "and with whom? With Joachim the Mariner, with our Ringelnatz, and there was much talk of Emmy and ship's captains and Hamburg and St. Pauli," alluding to Emmy Ball-Hennings's origin in the north German city and the Balls' intermittent ties to it. It was a vigorous attempt to introduce a cheerful note.

The next morning, a gray Monday, Hesse left for Zurich by way of Lake Constance, again retracing the old route of his life. He took with

him some warmth, some cheer, some pleasure in the past after all. But
he was also glad to go—physical ailments of the usual sorts (eyeaches,
headaches, and sleeplessness, as well as intestinal pains) underscored his
depression. He called off further lectures in Lucerne and other Swiss
cities and headed directly for his Schanzengraben apartment. He had
not felt well when he left, and despite the nostagic search for the past,
which after all informed his entire life and the work he created from it,
he always felt spent after one of these binges. Seeing Heckenhauer's in
Tübingen, talking with Herr Sonnewald, and especially seeing his
half brother and sisters always appeared as a weight that, seeming to lift
itself from his chest, settled upon it more heavily after all. Those cheerful
remarks to Emmy about Ulm and Ringelnatz were preceded by a sour
note of recognition:

> So I went playacting again [he wrote about his lecture tour as a whole];
> it was a somewhat melancholy journey not just because I felt ill and
> could neither eat nor sleep but because everyone had become so old. In
> these reunions with my brothers and sisters, etc., everyone is just a bit
> mellow, because the things that interest us all as a group lie far behind
> us in the previous century. And so, in saying our good-byes, everybody,
> myself included, acted so goddamn gingerly, saying nothing and patting
> each other on the back, while everyone thought: will we see each other
> again?

The rest of his German stay, visiting with his various friends, attending
some concerts after all, and working on his book, brought no great improvement for his health or his mood. December turned out to be a
grueling month. He was plagued by the fiercest eyeaches, and had to lie
in a darkened room, with reduced ability to read and hence greater de-
pendence on Ninon as his reader. But then the pendulum swung in the
opposite direction. Hesse experienced a semblance of peace. In fact, 1930
brought with it more happiness than Hesse had enjoyed in a very long
time. He wrote a new book. It was the beginning of his *Journey to the
East*.

III

Hermann Hesse's life flowed on evenly during the two years immediately following his completion of *Narcissus and Goldmund*: the span
during which his *Journey to the East* was lived through, written, and
eventually published. The usual systoles and diastoles of movement and
rest now seemed less disorderly: his life was channeled into a routine
for which, in part, Ninon's ordering hand was responsible. When the

time came for the usual skiing trip after the New Year they decided to replace the annual sojourn in Arosa with winter sports high in the mountains above St. Moritz. The place was Chanterella, a large and expensive hotel that turned out to be exactly the anonymous place they were looking for. As Hesse told his sister apologetically, it was indeed a place for profiteers and capitalists from Berlin, as well as for the international set, a place where only money and title counted: one either had to consume champagne every day or be a nobleman. They had to live high on the hog for as much as thirty francs per person per day. Yet precisely because this was a world where only titles and money counted, no one knew of Hermann Hesse or was the least bit interested in him. Hence, he argued, it was perfect for them: they remained secluded and anonymous in the midst of all those lavish goings-on. Besides, the food was superb.

Whatever their reasons or rationalizations for choosing a luxury hotel —to which they were to return for many seasons—Hesse and Ninon felt comfortable. When they arrived for the first time on January 10, 1930, Josef Englert picked them up at the station and immediately brought them up to that high point on the mountain where the hotel was situated. Hesse noted with some faint satisfaction that all the while their friends, publisher Samuel Fischer included, had remained in the town below. Yet it is not surprising that the very letter that contains this and other descriptions of a peaceful and prosperous time also contains a painful sentence that continues to express Hesse's exaggerated awareness of his failing powers: "The feeling of growing old, of not being able to make it any more, which had reached its peak last November on my Tübingen trip, has this year become even stronger for me, and of course those innumerable visits to the eye doctor haven't improved it." Again he also veered in the opposite direction: skiing was *real*, he suggested; it gave him a sense of being *present* on this earth. It required *strength*. And indeed during these weeks Hesse dealt with that odd feeling of "coming apart" by the most vigorous skiing.

This revealing letter to Adis, written on January 30, three weeks after their arrival, testifies to Hesse's uncertainty by producing several vivid pictures of their daily life on the mountain. One of these vignettes described a picnic with Louis Moillet, who lived conveniently nearby, and although the account is full of that didactic and narrative tone Hesse had used in his correspondence with his family since high school, it is sufficiently broad in its illustrative sweep to be of value. Hesse and Ninon had met the Moillets—Louis, his wife, and their two children— for their picnic lunch high in the mountains above Chanterella. Together they sat in front of the cabin basking in the Alpine sun. A maid pulling a sled that bore their feast arrived with rich food and wine. Children and the Moillets' dachshund romped in the snow. When the sun began to slant in the later afternoon the women set out to walk down the steep path while the two men and the Moillets' older boy skied down the steep glide. But when farther below they crossed a footpath crowded with tourists they met another caravan—two dogs, a familiar couple, and their four children—the Englert family. They stood about chatting until the two women, maid, child, and dachshund had caught up with them, then ended the day by having tea at the Englerts' ("he must be terribly rich"). Only later, as night fell around them, did they return to Chanterella: below, they could see the shimmering lights of St. Moritz.

What is interesting about this episode is not its rather quotidian ordinariness—two middle-aged men and their families and friends enjoying themselves in the Alps—but Hesse's inability to accept any enjoyment wholeheartedly. The same letter that describes these simple happenings contains after all those statements about aging and the impending loss of health, those perennial complaints about headaches and eyeaches. In a postscript Ninon referred to the hard times they were going through: those long hours of reading to Hesse while he was resting on a deck chair, the sad story of his limbs and eyes. What made these complaints difficult was that they were grounded in truly burdensome fact. His increasingly bothersome eyes created those depressed moods that cast shadows over his work, his daily life, and, sometimes over his relationship with Ninon.

Still, for any outsider Hesse's life was one of steady improvement. He actually traveled more, although he now fitted his journeys into an organized pattern. The rhythm of his life became even more controlled. In addition to alternating lecture tours, cures at Baden, and winters in Zurich with months of rest in Montagnola, Hesse now undertook those spring journeys to Germany more regularly, extending them beyond Swabia and even Munich to include points farther north, especially Berlin. In April 1930 he met Samuel Fischer in Tübingen to sign the contract for *Journey to the East* and to celebrate the official appearance of *Narcissus and Goldmund*. The public's verdict, when it came, was positive: the novel was evidently less problematic than *Steppenwolf* had been, and Hesse found himself being praised for having returned to simpler forms. Some of his readers still identified the sexual emphasis of *Steppenwolf* with that of the new novel, even thought both books pornographic and attacked them with the severity of the radical right.[2] Later, in 1932, Hesse was to report to Adis that one woman complained that *Camenzind* had been so beautiful and "German" but that both *Steppenwolf* and *Goldmund* were now so "Jewish" and ugly and dealt only with obscenities. (Hesse added that only when he got to the words "German" and "Jewish" did he recognize Hitler's melody).[3] But basically, especially at the time of its first publication *Narcissus and Goldmund* was viewed as a considerably less controversial, more acceptable work than its predecessor, which in Germany had been appreciated only by some intellectuals on the radical left—politically as well as intellectually. As Hesse wrote to his friend Erwin Ackerknecht in November, 1930:

> Goldmund delights people. It is, of course, in no way better than Steppenwolf, which defines its theme even more clearly and has been built in the form of the composition of a sonata, but in reading Goldmund the German reader can smoke his pipe and think of the Middle Ages and fine life so beautiful and sentimental, and need not think of himself and his [own] life, and his business transactions, his wars, his culture, and other such things.[4]

Judgments elevating the new novel above *Steppenwolf* were evidently so frequent—and in Hesse's view unjust—that he selected a comparatively large number of letters for his first very sparse publication of his letters which were devoted to the defense of *Steppenwolf*. He constantly reiterated that the musical structure (usually a sonata, sometimes a fugue and even a round) was at least as terse and finished in the earlier novel as it was in the more recent book.[5] Similarly, the remark to Ackerknecht about the medieval theme allowing the German burgher a far more comfortable escape was also frequently repeated.[6] As Hesse told Adis soon after the new book's appearance early in May: "The Berliners are now buying and reading my Goldmund; he is being metamorphosed into money by my publisher—that is the relatively nicest form in which Berlin manages to handle poetic literature."

As usual, the joys attendant upon Hesse's latest success were undermined by his constant sense of emotional and physical deprivation. Ninon had left him to himself while he was in Zurich that spring. She had gone on one of her frequent journeys, and Hesse felt lonely, blaming his friends like the Schoecks for leaving him "in the lurch" and lamenting the fact that Alice Leuthold, though making great efforts, could not really devote herself to him because her mother had been in the hospital for many weeks and required a great deal of attention. Though he suffered uninterruptedly from burning and itching eyes, he pulled up stakes during the second week of May to attend a Mozart festival in Basel. It was a good way to use up the last week before Ninon's return from her three-week trip. He stayed at the comfortable Hotel Bauernhof and went to all the operas, including *Così fan tutte*, which he had not seen before, and a great many of the concerts. Warmed by his enjoyment of the music, Hesse returned south to Montagnola to await Ninon's return at the Casa Camuzzi. On May 20 she arrived, full of stories about Berlin. As her letters had already suggested, she had found the literary industry rather ridiculous. Hesse was sure, too, that she had been fascinated nonetheless by the entire ambience of life in the capital. He was glad to have her back.

The summer went by in its usual way: professional visitors like Max Brod in June alternating with sons, daughters-in-law, and personal friends. Flattering tourists, on the other hand, were inwardly welcomed but outwardly rejected. They were not allowed to enter his presence. In the meantime, Hesse's new book *Journey to the East* was nearing its completion. It became one of the most affirmative works he had written. Composed during the last year before his third marriage, it celebrates his new life with marvelous enthusiasm, turning inward and becoming oppressed only in the final section. The early pages are filled with a sense of joy. Its style and "magic" may remind the reader of famous German romantic poets like Novalis, Eichendorff, and E. T. A. Hoffmann, but the book is also vibrant with a love of life and friends seldom duplicated in Hesse's books. Its pages mirror his many days with the Wassmers in Castle Bremgarten and his lifelong attachment to Basel, whose streets and alleys form part of the decor. They also portray his relationships with his closest friends. Louis Moillet appears for the second time since *Klingsor* and Othmar Schoeck and Josef Englert are made part of the company. But a negative note asserts itself in the end. If Hesse's letters countered each positive moment with references to illness, depression, or pain, so the celebrations in this little book also had to suffer their counterpoints.

The pair of friends—or the two aspects of the divided self who had been the emblem and *persona* of the previous novel—are now a reversible pair of master and servant. They are the hero H. H. (Hermann Hesse abbreviated in the manner of Kafka's K) and his alter ego, the servant Leo. As in *Narcissus and Goldmund*, the separations and reunions of this pair make up the plot. But in addition to these two selves, the first part of the novel is populated by a large company of pilgrims— the *Bund der Morgenlandfahrer*, as Hesse called them in a new turn of his familiar imagination—"the League of the Pilgrims to the Orient," a "magic theater" in motion. Projected into a future following the "next" war, this small book makes the juxtaposition of actuality and illusion the subject of its dramatic tensions, the tissue of its plot. The pilgrims are at first a joyous company living always at least partially in a world of dream and carrying out a romantic image in which the boundaries of the "real" become blurred. In their trek toward that mythical East, past and present, fantasy and daily life exist in a single realm where all the figures of fact and fancy ride together: Parsifal and Sancho Panza, the romantic poet Clement Brentano as well as Hesse's own Klingsor and Gold-

mund, characters from romantic novels and stories like that seeker after
the blue flower of poesy, Novalis's Heinrich von Ofterdingen, and Ludwig
Tieck's fanciful Puss'n Boots. Among the pleasant masks of Hesse's
friends, the reader also meets Ninon. H. H. "met and loved Ninon,
known as the 'foreigner' " who "was jealous of the Fatima of his dreams
though she was probably identical with her without [his] knowing it."
The epithet *Ausländerin*—foreigner—alludes playfully to Ninon's maiden
name, Ausländer. Even the celebration that ushers in the collective quest
is partly literary, partly "real." It appears as a magical mix of one of
Wassmer's great parties at Castle Bremgarten and the grand ball in that
old novel *Heinrich von Ofterdingen*, which then as now precedes the
hero's departure in quest of an ideal—poesy and the East.[7]

The reversal comes soon enough: anxiety must reassert itself. The
company comes to grief when the Servant Leo vanishes inexplicably in
the gorge of Morbio Inferiore. Now H. H.'s journey turns once more into
the Way Within as he must find Leo to be whole again and to remain in
the League. If the fairyland world and celebratory tone of the beginning
may remind readers of Hesse's first romantic incarnation, Hermann
Lauscher, the increasingly hallucinatory world and tone of the second
part bring back the image of the Steppenwolf in an increasingly Kafkaesque environment. H. H.'s journey takes him to a town composed
partly of Basel, partly of Calw—the places of Hesse's childhood. His discovery of Leo, magically, in a great hall of records—Basel's Town Hall,
which thirty years earlier had been redesigned by his wayward friend
Heinrich Jennen—coincides with the discovery of his own identity. And
the appearance of Leo first as his judge, then as a statue to which H. H.
is joined back to back, compounds the mosaic of romantic illusion and
Kafkaesque distortion that fashions the book. During the depressed days
of *A Guest at the Spa* and *Journey to Nuremberg*, in 1925, Hesse had
written a favorable review of *The Trial*. Now the dark, interior journey
that serves as a contrast to the brighter romantic pilgrimage of the book's
beginning is tinted by lights and shadows from Kafka's world.

Unlike Kafka, however, and unlike the usual Hesse up to this point,
is the near absence of *anima*—of female *eros*. Kafka's erotic scenes may
be colored by his sexual *chiar'oscuro* of need and recoil, but they retain a
strong sense of the presence of women. They are ultimately unable to
help K in his distress only because he usually responds to them as sexual
beings. Such responses had the opposite effect in Hesse's *Narcissus and
Goldmund*: women—however two-dimensional—had helped the artist
by virtue of their sexuality. Their erotic functioning had made the
creation of the Madonna possible. But at this ostensibly optimistic time
in Hesse's life, at the threshold of a new marriage, the erotic element had

begun to fade. True, Ninon was briefly mentioned: she whisked across the stage, almost indistinguishable from the image of "Fatima" of H. H.'s dream, but little else remained. *Journey to the East* had become a counterpoint to Goldmund. It contained only Narcissus.

Yet Hesse's need for Ninon was extraordinary. Like his two previous wives, she was to be his symbol and staff of stability to protect him from his wanderlust. Hesse resented not only her travels; he became restless at her slightest absence. The same hesitations, doubts, and moments of despair accompanied the approach of this marriage, as they had accompanied the previous two. As before, impending marriage had to be sealed by a new structure that would mold the notion of stability concretely. Gaienhofen had to be refashioned in Montagnola: Hesse thought again of building a house. The old dialectic that had informed his life continued to move his actions: the fourth new life was sealed by a house as a firm haven of stability, which Ninon helped to provide. Actually Hesse had hoped to build a house in Ticino for some time to provide him with a better-lit study to protect his eyesight and to give him a sense of ownership he had not had since he had left Gaienhofen. He also wanted to resume gardening intensively; yet even with his literary successes such a property had seemed financially difficult to acquire. But suddenly, in the spring of 1930, the dream came closer to reality. Hans and Elsie Bodmer, that wealthy manufacturer and his wife who had already become his close and admiring friends, approached him with the proposal to build a house for him and his bride-to-be. They offered to purchase the land and pay for the building of the house in Montagnola. It would be Hesse's and, after him, Ninon's as long as either of them lived. After both their deaths, however, it would revert to the Bodmer family. Hesse accepted enthusiastically.

By June a lot overlooking the valley had already been purchased. He described it eagerly to Adis on June 14: purchase of the land was already in full swing; they had picked the terrain and an attorney was negotiating the terms. It was a very large lot—about three acres—on a steep slope with meadows and vine, including even the edge of a small grove. Located just south of the village off the main street, the lot seemed sufficiently isolated (no direct road had yet been built to it) to give them privacy, and the absence of many neighboring buildings allowed them a magnificent view of all those mountains Hesse loved to climb. A negative counterpoint was also noted: "Whether there will be fewer worries in the new house, I have no idea. I have confidence in Ninon, but a house requires servants, and I think the problem of servants in always difficult." The isolation, the privacy, the lonely view are now seen negatively: "In a house so far away from the village, a quarter of an hour on a dirt road for each errand and purchase, dark and at night—for that one doesn't get maids who stay." But he concluded that it will probably be done and they would just have to try it to work it out.

These events—the cementing of his need for Ninon and the building of the house—were as crucial to Hesse's work in the direction of stability as the breakup of his first marriage and the dissolution of his house in Bern had been in the opposite direction. *Journey to the East* was a landmark of this new sea change in Hesse's life: the point of intersection between past restlessness and future rootedness. His attachment to Ninon was substantially different from his relationship with Mia, and, as a result, home building, too, took on a different aspect. In one sense, history seemed to repeat itself, for Mia, too, had at first been his manager, scouring the region of Lake Constance in search of their first home while Hesse had remained in Calw working on *Beneath the Wheel*. Older than he, she at first played an authoritative role. But that had been a quarter of a century earlier—in 1905—and their roles were soon to be reversed. As Mia's withdrawals and breakdowns became more and more frequent and lasting, Hesse had to take over the direction of the household, of their children, of her as well as of himself. But his steadfast refusal to play this traditional role of the *pater familias*—as Hermann Gundert had been and Johannes Hesse constantly attempted to be—reinforced all his attitudes. Hesse's life conformed to his art: his protagonist was very rarely the father.

Ninon, however, soon took over as *pater familias*.[8] Her early appeal to him could not have been untinged by sensuality, for the sexual imagery of *Narcissus and Goldmund*, written during the early stages of their relationship, suggests that fact. Unlike Mia, she was younger—she was only thirty-one to his fifty when they began living together. Her relative youth never took on the kittenish quality of Ruth Wenger's dependency —the only time it was required of Hesse to represent the *pater familias* unambiguously to a woman. Rather, Ninon's often stern personality came to express Hesse's new way of life: the discipline of stability. Where Mia had been blowsy, artistic, relaxed in her good moments, Ninon was contained. But it was her tendency to judge, to appear like Leo at the court of law, as well as her managerial competence that lent a distinct coloration and purpose to their relationship.

As Ninon started to manage their life, the quality of Hesse's work also began to change. It became a shift as "revolutionary" as his break of 1916 had been when a new style had emerged from despair and psychoanalysis. Similarly, *Narcissus and Goldmund* had been the last book of his second new life of his forties and early fifties, while *Journey to the East* had come to reflect his new situation. Hesse not only reverted to that vaguely allegorical form with learned allusions that many of his readers had disliked in *Steppenwolf*: he actually pushed it further. Unlike Haller's quest, that of H. H. had become specific: the immortals were implicated in a crusade to the East—the Land of Poesy—and they join the reader in observing his journey with romantic eyes. Allusions to romantic ideas, sifted from thinkers like Friedrich Schlegel and Novalis, who had accompanied Hesse since his adolescent years in Tübingen, are much more obvious in this new book than they had been in *Steppenwolf*, despite the more pronounced invocation of the Orient. They consist of actual quotations of passages and themes from these and similar writers, yet they are viewed in the light of the newly refurbished concept of the symbolic wayfarer to the East.

It seemed, then, as Hesse was channeling his energies in a new direction, that the *persona* H. H. representing him was not just another voyager toward the Grail, as Sinclair, Siddhartha, Haller, and many others had been in Hesse's books, but that Hesse was carrying out an important decision he had made more than twenty years earlier after his journey to India. He then recognized that the physical journey to the Orient had been disappointing and depressing, but that it had to be a voyage of the mind—allegorical, symbolic, certainly internal—through which he could recapture the *ideal* of the Orient as he saw it. Indeed, it was the identification of the Grail with the East—the *Morgenland* of German lore going back to the crusaders—that lent this short novel a special dimension. It also forms the beginning of further, more intensive studies of Eastern philosophy, literature, and religion—with a marked turn from India to China—which were absorbed more and more into the patterns of Hesse's late work.

In *Die Morgenlandfahrt*—its German title alluding to that ancient German trauma of the crusades and turning it into a mystique—the East still signifies an otherworldly, mystical realm in which resolutions to earthly conflict can be found. Wholly internal and symbolic, it had now become part of a game—and "game" indeed was the hallmark of the new Hesse. "Servant" and "Master" (Leo at the beginning and end of the story), everyday life and the "transcendent" East playing reversible roles, are not mere dream images; they are clearly defined motifs manipulated by the author, who holds the strings. They anticipate a more serious game —the Glass Bead Game—which Hesse began to develop in 1931, the year of house and marriage and the completion of *Journey to the East*. Neither of these allegorical, abstract, yet sedentary works could have been accomplished without the new direction in Hesse's life. Partly, this change was prompted by chronological age, for the twelve years of composition of his *magnum opus* were to span his life from the age of fifty-four to sixty-six. Partly, too, it was connected with the politics of the time, for the years of composition encompassed the Nazi years in Germany to their apotheosis in World War II. In the deepest sense, however, the altered direction discernible in these last two books of his career can be perceived as embedded in his fourth new life. In his daily life as in his books, picaresque wanderings for their own sake became increasingly rarer. Although he still traveled north—most often of course to Baden but also to his friends in Bern and Zurich—the pendulum of his travels prescribed shorter and shorter arcs. He finally became indeed the hermit of Montagnola, with a forbidding sign at the gate of his new villa, which, in his later years, warned visitors not to disturb him. He withdrew into himself.

As Hesse's relationship with Ninon became settled and his relations with his friends were subtly altered, Hesse's treatment of his material underwent similar changes. Though actual physical wandering diminished significantly, the impulse toward wandering remained, and it is one of the most important features of *The Glass Bead Game*. If the figure of the sensualist Goldmund harks back to Hesse's previous work, the figure of Narcissus dominates the last two important books of the fourth new life: Leo and the Magister Ludi, Josef Knecht. At the same time, the sense of being judged, which was always present, becomes part of the protagonists' makeup: it is their passport to the ideal world these cerebral heroes always seek to attain. Here we meet not only with the stern admonishments of Narcissus but also with Hesse's final scene in *Steppenwolf*, in which Haller is judged and found wanting. Like that middle-aged hero par excellence, all the protagonists of Hesse's late creations had again and again to traverse the infernos of themselves recreated as *games* akin to the chess game Pablo played with the shards of a shattered personality in the final scenes of his Cabinet of Mirrors.

The new novel, *Journey to the East*, looks back to themes of the past precisely as it projects itself into an as yet undetermined future. We discern Narcissus and the judgmental ending of *Steppenwolf*. If in addition to romantic poets like Novalis, Kafka's hand is unmistakable in the endings of both *Steppenwolf* and the latest book, the question remains why he once more reverted to this route in the first new novel of his fourth new life. Kafka's vision at the projected conclusion of *The Trial* (the moment of execution) is literally portrayed as an interior event in *Steppenwolf* and rendered as a stylized image capping a trial scene—the statue that joins Leo and H. H. back to back—at the ending of *Journey to the East*. Yet the spiritual judge (embodied in the immortals, Leo and the pilgrims to the East, and the authorities of mythical Castalia in *The Glass Bead*

Game) became the formal focus of his fiction, an outwardly visible sign. In the same way, all action was displaced from the author's and hero's consciousness to an unreal, allegorical, abstract universe, which related to the perceived world as point relates to counterpoint. As stability closed in, Hesse's personal ambivalences were caught in his prose: not only in the moves and countermoves of the characters in his various narrative plots, but also in various symbolic patterns that found their most original form in the dialectical figures of the Glass Bead Game, its spiral and circle. This shift leads, in most cases, to a suppression of imagery accessible to sense and psyche, still evident in *Narcissus and Goldmund* and in the first part of *Journey to the East*, and its displacement by musical and geometrical design.

Hesse was most aware—indeed, self-conscious—about this change in his work, though perhaps not so aware of it as an extension of the transformations in his life. His new stability was to a large extent a crust and an outwardly visible veneer capping the same difficult inner life that had dominated him since childhood. But as Ninon took over, she soon helped him conceal these upheavals of depression, illness, and anxiety that had always been in plain view. With her help, Hesse could withdraw more and more successfully from the uncertainties implicit in the sensual tapestry of his life, although, as many of his stories and large sections of *The Glass Bead Game* show, he could still evoke them artistically as counterpoints.

As his fortunes improved, however, Hesse's health deteriorated. While the Balls had been right in suspecting that many of his complaints about his health had been hypochondriacal, his eye problem had always been real, and many of his other complaints, like his constant headaches, were clearly connected with it. The old inflammation of the tear duct, which his old doctor had cleared out for him once more as recently as 1928, began to bother him again, only now it was more and more often accompanied by a keen sense of failing eyesight. Beginning in October 1930, Hesse and Ninon began to visit a famous eye specialist, Count Wiser, who lived in Lindau on Lake Constance, not far from Hesse's old home in Gaienhofen. The treatment altered Hesse's life as decisively as marriage and house. He was given new glasses, which lessened his pain but reduced his vision. The mere experience of weakening sight naturally reinforced one of the major anxieties of Hesse's life. His deteriorating eyesight and fear of going blind contributed to a change of vision in his books, and a gradual change in his language and imagery. A more abstract eye sought to convert color and shape—the visible textures of life itself—into musical and mathematical formulae. At the same time, as he maintained that familiar counterpoint of sensuous imagery in "fictional" biographies and a "symbolic end" of the next novel, the main weight rested on the austere, two-dimensional world of his *Glass Bead Game,* which even then began to take shape. The main composition of 1931 (eleven years before the completion of the book) was the chronicler's painstaking exposition of the nature and history of that futuristic yet medieval educational province that was to become the context and setting for his last great work. Here it can be seen how sight is reduced to dialectical tension, geometric design, and musical harmonies (abstractly conceived), and how all of these devices find their expression and form (but not their color) in the ingeniously devised Glass Bead Game and its two-dimensional players.

The summer of 1931, which was devoted to the composition of the earliest sections of *The Glass Bead Game,* was clearly the great summer of consolidation. In July, his "Japanese" cousin Gundert paid a brief visit along with other members of his family who helped him celebrate his fifty-fourth birthday. The new house was expected to be ready for occupancy in August. Ninon had spent days from early morning until late in the evening at the construction site. As an art historian, and even more as the new manager, she felt completely involved in the work. The building that emerged was indeed pleasant: a villa with bright white walls and large windows overlooking the valley with the lights of Lugano in the distance and the mountain passes beyond.

They moved in during July, a ceremony that brought together the Bodmers, the Leutholds, and many other friends in this singular celebration.[9] In November, despite, no doubt, his usual hesitation and anguish, Hesse and Ninon were married in a simple ceremony. On the occasion of his two previous marriages the wedding had marked a noticeable break with the past; in this third marriage this was no longer the case. Partly by choice, mostly by circumstance, their life together had already been established for some years. Still, the occasion confirmed the creation of a stable life and ushered in three rich decades for Hesse in his specific role of the "Sage of Montagnola."

In the winter of that year, while he was still occupied with the foreword to *The Glass Bead Game,* Hesse underwent his treatment with Count Wiser again, which again left him shaken. But New Year's Eve carried him into 1932 on the wings of Mozart's *Magic Flute* and comforted him with a relaxed party in the Leutholds' "Siamese" apartment in Zurich. The comfort was needed, for in his highly sensitized spirit, Hesse knew that psychologically as well as politically the world was coming apart at the seams. Still, with house and wife firmly in place, he had secured the refuge of the spirit that might insulate him against those ravages of history to come.

IV

"Morgen in die Berge!" ("Off to the mountains tomorrow!"), Hesse announced to Adis early in 1932, and they were off indeed. It was in January of that year that Hermann and Ninon Hesse met the writers Jakob Wassermann and Thomas Mann, as well as publisher Samuel Fischer, in their usual retreat near St. Moritz. It was this meeting that produced a famous photograph in which Hesse, Mann, and Wassermann look earnest about their skiing. Hesse and Mann appear as sportsmen to the core, while Wassermann seems more alien in the snowbound surroundings of Chanterella. In another picture, which includes Ninon, she looks severe and forbidding. That mountain—a truly "magic mountain" with its three masters—represented everything Switzerland and the citadel against history would come to mean to Hesse during the ensuing years. The picture was taken exactly one year before the Nazi takeover in 1933, a time when each of them in his own way would become a victim and an outsider. Jakob Wassermann was one of the foremost Jewish writers of the time. Thomas Mann was to become an outspoken critic of Nazism and was to spend most of the thirties and the war years in Switzerland and America. Although for a time Hesse was to remain more acceptable in Germany, he continued to be regarded with suspicion, an outsider who was finally cast out during the last year of the war. The mountain, Switzerland, momentarily contained them, but it was Hesse who chose that route in his personal life and in the work that became its symbol, *The Glass Bead Game*.

That sunny winter in the grand hotel of Chanterella also displayed less professionally weighty friendships. Just before they had to leave their idyll in March, Hesse described a splendid Easter ski trip with his old friend Louis Moillet which conveyed a real sense of his joy in mountains, snow, and sunshine. This letter to Adis, dated in March, shows his continuing closeness to "Louis the Cruel" as they slid down mountain slopes, at one point on the seats of their pants, in a sudden rush to get Louis to the station in time for his train. That same letter to his sister, however, contained the sad announcement that Ninon was packing their bags for the trip to Zurich where they were finally moving out of that old Schanzengraben apartment. Hesse had still holed up in it during part of the previous winter, working on the foreword to his *Glass Bead Game*, but now the time had come to part from it permanently. Surrendering that old refuge was genuinely difficult for him, but he told his sister bravely: ". . . if old gentlemen still build houses, get married, etc., they have to change course, give up old habits, take up new ones, etc., etc."

Contracting his life in Montagnola was only an outward symbol of more far-reaching transformations. The shadow cast by the oncoming changes around him pursued Hesse in 1932 as it darkened the lives of everyone.[10] In his usual way, he sought in literature and art the countervailing force. During that centennial year of Goethe's death he wrote a small volume of tribute not in the satiric vein of *Steppenwolf*, but as a serious appreciation and criticism, entitled *Thanks to Goethe*. It was the appearance of *Journey to the East*, however, that projected itself most prominently into the fateful fourth decade of the twentieth century, signifying a cultural reorientation that became political as well. Hesse's two works of these crucial years—*Journey to the East* composed in 1930 and *The Glass Bead Game*, written between 1931 and 1942—were deeply political books in a sense quite different from the previous novels.

Once Hesse's life had been rechanneled by house and marriage, his routine remained largely unchanged. He was ill again later in the spring, but soon recovered. During the summer, in his new house, he received colleagues like Hans Carossa, Indian scholars, and sons and friends. At the same time he continued to honor the many commitments with which he earned his daily bread, writing many reviews, as well as those very feuilleton articles that he had decried since *Steppenwolf* as symbols of decadence.

The response to *Journey to the East* was naturally divided; the great success of *Narcissus and Goldmund*—a work once again meeting most of his readers' expectations—could not be sustained. But Hesse had caught something else, a new spirit that was to help the little book with the public. A rather unfortunately penned poem by an admirer states the point clearly:

> Dear Poet. Have thanks.
> Prophet of our souls' homeland.
> The League that thou prophesiest
> Is the brightest cell of consolation in our need.
> Though only few live to be in this Circle
> Our goal, for that, will remain ever purer.

When Hesse conceived of this mystical East, it contained all the connotations of his previous work in addition to the allusion the *Morgenland* must carry for German readers—that of the crusaders. Moreover, when he referred to the wayfarers or pilgrims as a holy company—existing partly in dreams, partly in literature, and partly in life—he found a new symbol for the immortals who had played such an important role in *Steppenwolf*. But when in a book composed in 1930 he used the word

Bund or "league" to describe the company of the elect, wayfaring toward the *Morgenland*, he touched a symbolic nerve that had to react politically as well. As Hesse's versifying correspondent had rightly perceived, it expressed the ambience of the time. The word *Bund*—time-honored in many literary manifestations and forms—could not be used in Germany or even in other German-speaking countries at that time without assuming definite connotations.[11]

The Youth Movement, a monolithic organization before the First World War, had now fallen apart into many groups and splinters, some politically oriented throughout the spectrum from right to left, others eschewing politics altogether. Among them, however, were smaller *Bünde* whose primary purpose was not to encompass large numbers of members but rather to gather the elect. It was to this group, in part, that Hesse's small novel appealed and to whom in effect it was dedicated. If he found wife and house in 1931, both were prefigured by the elect— a symbolic *Bund* reflecting an authoritarian spirit. To understand Hesse's extension of his personal uncertainty to the political sphere, one must understand that there was an elitist ingredient—that of a communion of the elect—in both Nazi and Fascist ideology. In addition to the search for safety and the striving for identity that form the main theme of *Journey to the East*, Hesse also used the vehicle of that strange little book to project alternatives to the vulgar squabbles of the present by turning to a *Bund* of the Elect.

Clearly, Hesse's readers of *Journey to the East*, when it appeared in 1932, were as torn as their poet was to be during the ensuing years. On the one hand, many were put off or at least disaffected by the modernistic style of the novel's ending. At first they were seduced by the scenery, then alienated in the second part when the action no longer took place under the aegis of poetic realism and fantasy but turned directly to a dissection of consciousness and the distortion it implied. Others, on the other hand, were caught in a spirit that appealed to their needs: beyond strife and possible war in their own time they envisioned the *Bund* through which the terrors of the time could be dissolved in a transcendence of the spirit. This identification with a league of the elect to counteract the confusions and vulgarities of the dying Weimar Republic, which Hesse supported on different grounds, was to become an important motive for many who aligned themselves with the National Socialist revolution during the following year. Hesse tapped that impulse in his book as it tapped the strength of his own feelings. The league of the elect had become for him a symbol not only for his personal life, and its fortifying decisions, but also for the kind of regeneration many wished for during that final transitional year.

The movement from sense to spirit, from the dissolutions of *Steppenwolf* to the ascetic spirits of Leo and of Josef Knecht, was accompanied and fortified during five crucial years by a new relationship and marriage, by a new house, by a strong desire to build a bulwark of the spirit that could withstand the encroachments of a world of sense in which history displayed its ugliest features. Fashioned by an urgent austerity, the *Bund* of wayfarers to the Orient and the spiritual province of Castalia lend substance and tone to Hesse's last evolution.

10

Citadel Against History

I

[In] the final analysis every important cultural gesture comes down to a morality, a model for human behavior concentrated into a gesture. . . . The human attitude of which classical music is the expression is always the same. . . . Classical music as gesture signifies knowledge of the tragedy of the human condition, affirmation of human destiny, courage, cheerful serenity. The grace of a minuet by Handel . . . the tranquil composed readiness for death in Bach—always there may be heard in these works a defiance, a death-defying intrepidity, a gallantry, and a note of superhuman laughter, of immortal gay serenity. Let that same note also sound in our Glass Bead Game, and in our whole lives, acts and sufferings.

—Josef Knecht in the introduction to *The Glass Bead Game*

ON JANUARY 28, 1933, two days before Hitler and his party took power in Germany, Hermann Hesse wrote a revealing letter to his publisher, Gottfried Bermann, Samuel Fischer's son-in-law, with whom he had established a close, almost fraternal friendship. The subject was Hesse's writing block. *The Glass Bead Game*, beautifully conceived and well launched, had stopped in its tracks. As he reflected on his listlessness, he clearly connected his psychological condition with a public or political one: "I am caught in my anxieties and inhibitions, and my psychological training is sufficient to bear them but not to overcome them, for since 1914 I have become most skeptical about all overcoming and winning out and all that glorification of will and energy."[1]

Two days later their lives were changed when those elements in German life came to power which were bent precisely on glorifying energy and will in a shallow echo of Nietzsche. This aggressive striving Hesse viewed as a European condition, diametrically opposed to Chinese wisdom, which he preferred but felt inadequate: "And so there has grown up between me and my work a certain lack of interest, a knowledge of the valuelessness of all doing and writing." All this would be well and good, he added, if he could be content, like Lao Tse, with all that lack of activity, but he was a "hungry and egoistic European"

342

who longed for the naive happiness of creating, fathering, producing. What these lines implied, and could not state, was that "doing and writing," which would have moved his book along, was now tied up with the political will to power and the energized striving he rejected.

In drawing a detailed picture of his projected novel, Hesse showed even more fully how that final effort of his life was as implicated in the historical changes of his own time as Thomas Mann's *Doktor Faustus* was to be of the nineteen forties. Referring to the Preface that he had written the previous year, Hesse told his publisher and friend:

> I can tell you nothing about what is meant by the Glass Bead Game that you haven't already gathered from the Foreword, except this: I have in mind to write simply the biography of a Magister Ludi. His name is Knecht and he lives at approximately the time the Foreword ends. The creation of a purified atmosphere was essential to me. I did not, this time, turn to the past or the timeless world of the fairy tale, but built up the fiction of a precisely dated future. The worldly culture of that time will be the same as today. By contrast, there will be an intellectual culture in which it pays to live and to serve. That is the wishful image that I want to paint.[2]

Both the utopian image and the projection of the need for cultural change created fresh barriers at this time of uncertainty. Although he was superstitious that this summary might nip his great project in the bud, he did want to communicate with Bermann to reassure him that despite his unproductive life something at least was stirring behind the scenes.

Two days earlier, on January 26, 1933, Hesse had written a rather vitriolic letter to his old friend Reinhold Geheeb in Munich, in which he complained about the latter's admonishments that he was not sufficiently alert to financial matters. Geheeb had chided him for some of his monetary doings—small earnings on the one hand and, on the other, the desire to shift the weight of his publishing to Switzerland. Hesse responded that he had always anticipated a loss from *Journey to the East*, since it was a book destined only for the few and not for a mass audience. It was a professional decision he had made as a writer. But when it came to the possibility that he might publish only in Switzerland in order to escape exorbitant German taxes (since he was after all a Swiss citizen), Hesse became quite clear about his political self-consciousness:

> As soon as the thought emerges that I might . . . publish in Switzerland, which is my homeland and where I am a citizen, you suddenly admonish Hesse and remind him of his ideal duties and discover that a soap manufacturer might do these things but not a Hesse. I do not particularly like this double morality and don't take it seriously. It has led you into the

World War and will lead you into the next one, in which I will not participate even if the world makes me kick the bucket for it.

The current of thought that led him to politics was a non sequitur; it had little to do with money and publishing in Switzerland. A new phase began to open up in his life, which brought to the fore some of his struggles of the twenties—the hate letters from right-wing students and intellectuals, as well as his anguished and angry responses that led him to reaffirm his attitudes of the First World War. Now, in the very disavowal of political involvement, a new era of political self-consciousness began. The sentence concluding his remarks about double standards signaled the attitudes that would describe his life and work for the next twelve years. "I will not participate even if the world makes me kick the bucket for it." It expressed the politics of nonpolitics that he was to pursue during the years ahead.

In this spirit Hesse received the news of the events that took place in Germany on January 30, 1933. The change broke upon them at once and transformed their lives. During the following few months a good number of refugees were to cross the Swiss border, and many of them sought temporary shelter in the Casa Bodmer in Montagnola. Some were in flight because they were Jewish, but most during those early days were fleeing because of their political convictions and associations. The first emigrant to arrive in March was a writer, Heinrich Wiegand, who, among other things, had worked as a cultural organizer for the Labor Movement in Leipzig. His work at the time had consisted in arranging concerts and plays for the workers and participating in a Workers Educational Institute, which, of course, had been immediately dissolved. In addition, he had edited a newspaper that had been forbidden. Both Thomas Mann and Hesse had known him previously as a contributor to *Die Neue Rundschau* who had written an important essay about them both. He was evidently an agreeable guest. Both Ninon and Hesse took a liking to him while he and his wife stayed with them before they continued their flight to Italy. Wiegand was soon followed by Thomas Mann himself, who did not stay at the Hesses but paid extensive visits.

Not all his visitors were refugees, however. In April, Gottfried Bermann and his wife Tutti (Samuel Fischer's daughter) showed up at the Casa Bodmer to discuss the problems Hesse had outlined in his letter about the original draft of *The Glass Bead Game*, a visit pleasant but not overly helpful in reopening the doors that had kept him from his work. Perhaps most decisive for Hesse's life during these late years was the appearance that spring of a young man from Dresden, Günther Böhmer, a painter and printmaker. He was not a refugee but a pilgrim. Like the

Wayfarers to the East, he had traced his Master's steps throughout the Swabian landscape, traveling on foot by way of Maulbronn, Calw, Hirsau, and Basel. He had bought books by Johannes Hesse in the Basel Mission Store and had proceeded to study them. And he had made fine drawings in Calw, which he brought with him. Hermann and Ninon Hesse received him warmly as he put down his roots in the Casa Camuzzi, Hesse's previous residence in Montagnola. "A dear, gifted, fine, tender person," he wrote enthusiastically to his sister, "musical and only twenty-one years old." Eventually Böhmer settled in Montagnola for good, much to the Hesses' delight.

Already, on the occasion of Hesse's fifty-sixth birthday that year, young Böhmer acted as part of the family. Joining Ninon, the distant sons, and old Natalina, Böhmer brought his gifts of drawings and wine on the celebrated July 2. For the present, his friendship was one of the few bright lights of a sad period during which old loyalties were tested and too often compromised. It was Hesse's own position in particular that was constantly at issue. Not a day went by, especially during the early months of the regime, when it was not required or at least expected of him to take a stand. Many refugees had already fled to Paris where they were establishing an opposition camp not unlike the antiwar group in Zurich during the First World War. At the other end, still inside Germany, were conservative friends like Emil Strauss and Ludwig Finckh, a multitude of devoted readers, and nonpolitical but accommodating friends like Reinhold Geheeb.

Hesse's own values were clearer than he has often been given credit for. He naturally despised violence, warlike spirits, book burning, and racism. What clouded his attitudes was a deep sense of obligation to his readers and to his own role as a German writer who experienced the same kinship with his German friends and readers as he had felt during the First World War with the veterans he had celebrated even while rejecting the cause they fought for. For this reason, while he recognized the barbarism implicit in the public burning of books, he was not wholly displeased that his own were not among them. "My role in Germany and in the literary industry over there," he wrote Thomas Mann in July, "is this time, for the moment at least far more agreeable than yours. Officially I have not been bothered." He was cited neither among writers supporting the regime nor among the "asphalt littérateurs" whom strident appeals to the Hitler Youth and other Nazi organizations had condemned.[3] Unlike Thomas Mann, who had an international following, his own work was known mostly in the German-speaking world. And since he had based his livelihood since 1904 exclusively on his writing, he needed to retain his "market." Thus, while his correspondence of that time showed that he was horrified by the savagery of the regime's first year of consolidation, when thousands were killed, tortured, and imprisoned, he refused to speak out publicly, sign manifestos, or take an official stand.

Hesse had chosen his exile in Montagnola. The man of fifty-six, who was expelled from his family at the age of six, found true exile intolerable. On the deepest level, he also remained in contact with certain cultural sources that were condemned by the regime. A Jewish wife and many exiled or persecuted friends also commanded his loyalty. But there was a countercurrent, an intellectual and emotional light that radiated toward him from his audience, from those many people who continued to inundate him with their letters. Some of the mail was vituperative and written in anger, but a great deal was also approving, looking to him for support. Much of this mail came from people who responded with fervor to the new Reich. Hesse disliked their politics, but he felt called to still their spiritual hunger.

In many letters Hesse wrote during the 1930s and the war years he displayed a sense of a common language of heroism and sacrifice, even when he assigned it a negative value. And he showed understanding for his two old pre–World War I friends, Emil Strauss and Ludwig Finckh, who had both become National Socialists. In his diary soon after the coup Hesse wrote in detail both about his own reaction to the changes in Germany and of his two friends, using the "language of nobility," with its evocations of home and *Heimat* to emphasize his points.[4] Actually, he sensed the reason why both Finckh and Strauss (his old neighbor in Gaienhofen) had been converted, and he admitted to himself that by and large they had been moved by the best of motives. Their conversion implied, he felt, an ability to love, to give oneself to a greater cause, to an impersonal collective higher than one's own self. The ability to serve and to sacrifice oneself for an ideal above "person and time," which became after all the leitmotif of his new novel, was seen here as the ideal that his friends had embraced because they had not understood that the so-called New Germany would deceive them.

His relations with both friends underwent a severe crisis, however. To some extent they had to reject Hesse, for his position vis-à-vis the National Socialist government was always subject to doubt. Of the two, the break with Finckh became the most painful. They had already drifted apart in the twenties, because Hesse had continued to be outspoken in his rejection of the war, while Finckh had displayed a persistent nostalgia for kaiser and fatherland. The appeals to the Hitler Youth had been manufactured by Finckh, who had risen to a position of some responsibility: "Now, in the Reich of loudspeakers," Hesse wrote his friend Otto Hartmann, "[Finckh] has suddenly betrayed me. He has just released an appeal to the Hitler Youth of Baden concerning German poets, in which he advises his charges to follow simply the instincts of their own feelings and hearts in choosing their poets, yet presents them with a list of sheep and goats. And (what would have been unthinkable the day before yesterday) . . . he omits his old friend Hesse." He added that the omission was barely conscious but that Finckh sensed danger and so remained silent.[5] It pained Hesse to see his old friend as a Nazi functionary, even though he had known him to be on the right side of the political spectrum for years. At this point Finckh had become a symbol of his disenchantment. On several occasions in his diary that summer, while trying to account for his depression and writing block, Hesse was inordinately concerned about Finckh's defection—in empathy as well as in anger. The rift between them was not to be healed until sometime after the war.

As a Swiss citizen, Hesse felt he could ride out the storm, retain his readers, and even uphold most of his values, as long as he refrained from public declarations. At first this course of action seemed to work fairly well. He still meant a great deal to young people in Germany, who visited him each year on foot and on bicycles to seek his advice. He wanted to help those who did not "dissolve" easily into a mass by putting on uniforms and entering the huge organizations set up for them by the regime. If he had broken publicly with the new government, any contact with these young people would have been impossible and he would then have betrayed them. The way he phrased it, he could function best not by joining the regime or by "senseless opposition" but by sabotaging the entire business of power and politics "to form islands of humanity and love" in the midst of the killing and the satanism.[6] To reach into that world, to continue to speak the language of those who were caught in it, and to call on them to sabotage power through love—this possibility still tied him to Germany and gave him the inner justification for maintaining his ties. He continued, to some degree at least, to hold on to that bond throughout those twelve difficult years of National Socialism, and, though he remained suspect, German soldiers were allowed to carry his books with them into battle during the Second World War. Yet as he confessed to Thomas Mann, he was not nearly as involved in the German debacle as he had been in 1914. He had distanced himself: he was not again to be caught. In spirit as in physical fact he had created his bulwark against history and time.

II

The tensions of the early months of the New Germany directly contributed to Hesse's most barren time since *Siddhartha*, but ultimately it led to the formation of his *Glass Bead Game* during the next few years. Josef Knecht, his main protagonist, became more and more a representative German of that time: until his conversion in the end, he was the embodiment of his institution. The educational province of Castalia, which provided a setting for the novel, came to resemble Hesse's childhood Swabia physically while assuming more and more the function of his adopted home, neutral Switzerland, which in turn embodied his own antidote to the crises of his time. It became the "island of love" or at least an island of the spirit.

While Hesse was outwardly engaged in many activities—writing reviews, worrying about wife, house, and Mia's recurring illnesses, as well as endlessly justifying his silence to his publishers—in his art he created an almost motionless universe, a symbolic representation of the stability he thought he had found in his life. As part of the rethinking of his entire project, Hesse began to study once more the works and biographies of eighteenth century Pietists like Johann Albrecht Bengel and Friedrich Christoph Oetinger.[7] He also did some further writing. He expanded the Chronicler's Introduction by adding a description of the origin of the Glass Bead Game and finished "The Rainmaker," one of Knecht's so-called fictional biographies. Both were printed in the *Neue Rundschau* in 1934. That journal, which had been an extension and outlet of Samuel Fischer's publishing house, had been taken over by Peter Suhrkamp, who later assumed ownership of the entire firm.

It was apparent that Hesse considered his new novel a contribution to a cultural and political critique, yet he was careful to retain its symbolic alienation from contemporary fact. His alternative to the present state of affairs, which he had to accept while refusing to come to terms with it inwardly, was a utopian civilization. Using many of the themes and places of his childhood—the hierarchy of the Basel mission; the monastery of Maulbronn; a gallery of friends, relatives, and acquaintances often only thinly disguised—he invented his own "system" to supplant a disintegrating culture. It was his answer to the question he had hoped in vain psychoanalysis would solve for him since 1916, and he gave it on a personal as well as social and cultural plane. By no means without irony, Hesse rendered a tableau of ingeniously devised intellectual relationships. It is both the strength and the weakness of this novel that ambivalence itself was now represented by a wholly intellectual picture whose chief symbol was that of the spiral. As fiction, the novel remained thin. Nothing much happens, and human relationships are too often supplanted by musical or mathematical constellations. It also appears as a rewriting of *Narcissus and Goldmund*, this time almost entirely from the point of view of Narcissus—now secularly canonized as Josef Knecht. Finally, Castalia is a flawed paradise. Its hierarchies indicate the lines whereby each person can attain to a pure, impersonal condition, and the various figures, described in elaborate gestures, take the place of human relationships, which are reasserted only in the end.

The Glass Bead Game, itself is, however the cleverest and most original invention of the book. This idea was gradually distilled from Hesse's various involvements during the years of his growing stability. Conceived four years earlier, while he was still at work on *Narcissus and Goldmund*, the virtue of the game is that it is plausible even though it can never really be described. Hesse conveys much of its genesis and function. The nearest analogy is chess, but figures and moves are given various complex meanings—unlike chess or symbolic logic they do not stand for themselves—which ultimately amount to a lingua franca that encompasses all human knowledge. It therefore simulates the activity of the mind in the process of cognition itself, yet, being a game, it is objectified. In describing the game, Hesse brought up many antecedents and analogies: the Pythagorean "music of the spheres"; scholastic systems of philosophy; eighteenth century concepts of universal language; and especially music itself. Indeed, in the hierarchy of Castalia music is only one step below the Bead Game in the order of things and the Old Music Master one of his most touching figures. As Hesse created the three focal points of his novel, the reader becomes aware of an intricate pattern of mirroring. The protagonist Knecht, the province of Castalia that is his realm, and the Bead Game as the symbolic instrument reflect each other. Each is subject to hierarchies, each is designed to bring together disparate elements, each must arrange them in a pattern that reflects the image of the human mind in an objective setting.[8]

Outside Castalia lies the world. Outside Lugano and Montagnola and Baden lay a civilization more sensuous perhaps and with greater color than Castalia could display, but dedicated to its own destruction. Castalia, like Hesse, resisted the incursion of history, the European disaster, by creating its utopian antithesis. A counterpoint of "life" is retained. The utopia, as an "island," required the outside world as its opposite. Knecht had to write those "spiritual autobiographies" that would account for his historical heritage (Hesse wrote four for him, although only three were finally incorporated in the book while one remained a fragment in four different versions). And in a strange ending (which for the Castalian had to remain a "legend") Knecht became a renegade who exiled himself from that utopian "island" he himself had administered brilliantly, entered the actual world by becoming the tutor of his best friend's son, and died in an ice-cold mountain lake. He had returned to "life" itself—Jung's *anima* in contrast with the purely masculine Castalia. While this ending may give a different turn to his argument, its main emphasis remains on Castalia. In place of a historical process, Hesse had drawn an abstract design.

The contradictions and uncertainties of Hesse's life were at least potentially resolved in his magnum opus. Contemplation, the secrets of the Chinese *I Ching*, and Western mathematics and music fashioned the perennial conflicts of his life into a unifying design. Hesse had formerly presented himself primarily as a man of feeling, yet in his old age he constructed a citadel of the intellect which contradicted this image. Nowhere was this more fully the case than in the dialectical intricacies of *The Glass Bead Game*'s antiseptically spiritual construct.

This dual state of mind is particularly evident in Hesse's relationship with Eastern literature and thought. As Adrian Hsia has observed in his important study of Hesse and China, he had singled out the Chinese as the truly harmonious counterpart to the Indians (or rather, the Indonesians) he encountered on his trip "to India" in 1911; and it is no coincidence that the most satisfying part of that abortive trip had taken place in Buddhist Ceylon. This awareness accompanied Hesse into the work of his middle and old age. The Indian story *Siddhartha* turns toward Taoism in the end, and *The Glass Bead Game* clearly shows a pervasive influx of Chinese thought. In fact, Hesse's turn from Indian puritanism to the acceptance of polarities conceived within a concept of unity was the result of long and detailed studies of Chinese literature and thought in translation. He asserted that Richard Wilhelm's famous translation of the *I Ching* had given him a "spiritual" answer to the problem of crisis and to his tendency to relate to different sides of a question at once.

When observed both through the telescope of Hesse's psyche and the imagery in his books, a final "order" emerges in which the psyche is presented as a system of mathematically related symbols that define the unity of the spirit. The serenity Hesse found in his old age, with the help of Bach and Lao Tse and the Chinese thinker Chuang-Chsi, among others, was therefore more than merely a bulwark against the incursions of history; it was also an attempt to find a nonsensual and hence unifying formula for precisely those antitheses in his thinking, writing, and conduct for which he has been both lauded and condemned. It was his attempt to show that crises can be successfully placed on artistic coordinates which will present the violence, the passion, and the apostasy of life as a grand geometrical figure.

III

While Hesse transformed and slowly enlarged *The Glass Bead Game*, political life in Europe became more and more polarized, leaving him partly enclosed in his Casa Bodmer on the quiet Swiss "island" of Montagnola. He became less and less restless. Part of his routine continued. He still went on annual journeys to Baden and occasional lecture tours to Germany, until the onset of the war made that difficult if not impossible. The house he and Ninon had built with the Bodmers' help had become a more lasting and permanent haven than most places in his life. There he lived, repeating some aspects of his early life with Mia in Gaienhofen that he had tried hard to reject. He now had a garden for his full use once more. And old Natalina, who had served him since the early days at the Casa Camuzzi, now cared for him more steadily since he was more frequently at home. Ninon was more peripatetic than he: continuing her work as an art historian she took off on her various missions for Vienna, Berlin, Paris, and Athens. As Hesse traveled less, he was able to enjoy people's visits more than he had been able to in the past. For years his stay in Montagnola had been no more than an extended summer from May to October. Now he was there most of the year and as a result he felt less pushed and crowded.

As time went on and the New Germany became established, injustice and even terror became part of the daily news. The excitement had worn off, and though Hesse disliked the constant confrontations he had to undergo—the regular frequency with which he was required to take a stand when his stand was not to take one—he was nonetheless able to integrate these moments with the rest of his life. Early in 1934 he traveled once more to Tegernsee, a lake in Bavaria, where he visited his eye specialist Count Wiser and met with his friends Reinhold Geheeb and Annette Kolb in Munich. As he reported at length in a letter to Adis in February, their stay was interrupted by the sad news that Wiegand, whom he had sheltered during the first weeks of his exile during the previous year, had suddenly died in Italy. Despite eyeaches and headaches, they traveled back to Montagnola to receive Wiegand's widow, who stayed with them until March.[9]

Some work was done after this sad beginning. Hesse wrote a few poems and composed part of Josef Knecht's fourth fictional autobiography, which dealt with south German Pietism in the eighteenth century and which he discarded later in the year. He also made a selection of his poems called *The Tree of Life* for the publishing house Insel Verlag, a fact that was resented by Reinhold Geheeb who felt he had greater claims. In response, Hesse observed drily that he had already discerned that a kind of low-grade anger was the order of the day in the "germanized" empire to the north. The summer developed pleasantly, however. His nephew Carlo Isenberg (immortalized in *The Glass Bead Game* as Carlo Ferromonte) stayed with him for a while and helped him out with various theoretical subtleties about music that Hesse wanted to use for his novel. In August, to his pleasant surprise, he received the Gottfried Keller Prize in his adopted Switzerland, which served as a good antidote to the official rejection he now correctly perceived in his former country.

Still, while fragments and pieces of *The Glass Bead Game* developed and fitted together, there was remarkably little movement in the work as a whole. The "block," written about and discussed for at least a year, continued, and it was not helped by the oppressive atmosphere of Central Europe during the thirties, which penerated even to Montagnola. It is no coincidence that during the fall of 1934 Hesse should have involved himself in a now famous exchange with C. G. Jung on the controversial question of sublimation. It began with "On Several Books," a review written early that year for the *Neue Rundschau*, which included a brief discussion of Jung's essay "Sigmund Freud in His Historical Setting." Hesse was quite pointed in his initial remarks, chiding Jung for his ironic dismissal of Freud's important concept and suggesting instead that far from being an empty word, "sublimation" is a key to all important rituals and transformations endured by saints and artists alike.[10] Jung responded in September, first by denying he had criticized Freud on this issue merely out of resentment, then by upholding the view that sublimation, as Freud sees it, was merely repression, an avoidance of difficulties. "*Sublimatio*," wrote Jung, "is part of the royal art where the true gold is made. Of this Freud knows nothing. . . ." Conscious channeling of "instinct into an inauthentic field of application," such as Freud proposes, must be sharply distinguished from an "alchemical transformation."[11]

Hesse's response, which came quickly that same month, was more circumspect than his initial review had been. It turned out, as he developed his ideas in a long letter, that he did not really disagree with Jung, or even that he fully agreed with Freud, but rather that he wanted to propose a third alternative. His alternative turns on the familiar fear that psychoanalysis might destroy the artist if the main impulse that created the art in the first place is neurotic. "Just for that reason is psychoanalysis so difficult and dangerous for artists, for it can prohibit those who take it most seriously all their artistry for their entire lives." In the case of dilettantes this may be all to the good, but it might have deprived posterity of Handel or Bach. His main statement, however, concerned his own present condition. Distinguishing between the pretense of sublimation and true sublimation (a metamorphosis in Jung's sense), Hesse concluded that "within our category, within art itself, we artists practice genuine sublimation, and not voluntarily or from ambition, but because of a state of grace—only, naturally, I don't mean just the 'artist' as the populace or the dilettante thinks of him, but the servant . . . the victim."[12]

A brief note from a mollified Jung, on October 1, 1934, still drew a line between them, insisting that art itself is a "primary instinct" that so pervades the artist's entire self that all other instincts are "in abeyance." Alchemical transformation, or metamorphosis, is produced by a special gift deeply embedded in the artist's mind.[13] For Hesse, to whom suffering both physical and mental continued to be justified as the matrix of his work, this response would have been only small consolation. Jung remained deeply complimentary about his function as an artist, but did not allow him the benefit of all his aches and pains. It provided little light for the tunnel of his incapacities.

That October Hesse went on his trip to Baden, but when he arrived there on October 15 he heard that his lifelong mentor and publisher Samuel Fischer had died in Berlin. His reaction was complex. Hesse owed Fischer the start of his career as well as his continued prosperity, but their business relations had been marked by hard bargaining and Hesse was not an easy author. In the main their relationship had been positive. It was fraught with the meaning Hesse projected into any lasting relationship with anyone who had been like a father to him and toward whom he therefore felt a mixture of affection and antagonism. His memorial, hastily written for Fischer in Basel for publication that following December, suggested these feelings only in the peculiarly muted tone of its rhetoric. He wrote almost entirely of the probity and reliability of his business dealings and the relationship of trust and respect which could therefore be the result. Only toward the end, he allowed himself a touch of intimacy. Referring to the smile of his somewhat deaf mentor he ended: "With this smile Father Fischer will remain in my memory."[14]

In a different context, however, Hesse found himself able to defend Fischer and his firm vigorously. A note on the literary page of the Basel *Nationalzeitung* of January 13, 1935 accused Fischer's publishing house, in a paltry matter of opportunism in relation to the National Socialists. In a letter to the editor of the paper just four days later Hesse delivered a ringing defense. The Verlag Fischer and its journal, *Die Neue Rundschau* represented one of the few places where reason and human manners still found some refuge in the midst of chaos. The "Jewish" house Fischer was taking enormous risks (its publications were the only ones where Hesse could place articles and reviews about Jewish or Catholic authors), and was criticized for the omission of a footnote friendly to Jews as an index of its opportunism, while other publishing houses, like the non-Jewish house Reclam, which ran much smaller risks, behaved far more opportunistically.[15] This latter reference referred to a demand by Reclam that he delete all Jewish authors from his *Library of World Literature*, a booklet listing his favorite authors since the *Epic of Gilgamesh* which he had published with them some years before.[16]

Nevertheless, Hesse had complicated feelings about Jews. On the one hand, Ninon was Jewish as was naturally her sister who visited them often. He was a great admirer of Martin Buber. At the same time he shared certain clichés about Jews that had already entered the language of the time. The word "Aryan" crept into his personal letters; Buber's Christian wife is referred to as German in contrast to her husband's Jewishness—significant in the context of those years. Especially revealing was a letter to his friend Josef Englert, written in 1933, in which Hesse wrote at length about the "cowardice" of the German Jews (which exempted Rumanian Ninon and her family), echoing the German Jewish prejudices against Eastern Jews in allowing himself a phrase like, "One might almost say that it serves them right if that were not too cruel under the circumstances." His lack of prejudice, by his lights, was underscored by the further remark that "Jews, like Germans, include next to their rough, stupid, and cowardly majority, a fine, wise, brave minority." And he praised Buber for not having given in "either to the German or to the cowardly German-Jewish kind."[17] Whatever his sentiments, these remarks suggest that he had absorbed, at least to some extent, the racist language of the day. They also anticipate an unfortunate tendency (born perhaps out of his need for aloofness) to equate the virtues and faults of aggressors and victims. In his relations with the German-Jewish house of S. Fischer, his cordial friendship with Gottfried Bermann, Tutti Bermann-Fischer, and indeed the patriarch Samuel Fischer remained undiminished until, during the following year, his loyalties became divided.

A letter to Adis early in 1935 contained a note of complaint that described the times. It was written on stationery drawn by Günther Böhmer showing Hesse at the typewriter in his spacious studio, and he complained that it had taken two weeks to get the package of stationery through Swiss customs. This was, he felt, a typical event that showed they were already half at war. Worse still for Hesse, Germany did not release most of his royalties. Eventually he placed these funds at the disposal of his two sisters, who could use them in Germany. It was the beginning of a very bad year for Hesse.

With German funds no longer reaching him, Hesse had to rely more heavily than in the past on the additional income from feuilletons and reviews. He began to contribute regularly to *Carona*, about which he wrote Adis in some detail, but that income was also not enough. Since it had become more difficult to publish book reviews in Germany (and since he could not transfer most of the funds earned in Germany to Switzerland), he accepted an offer to become a regular reviewer for a Swedish literary magazine, *Bonniers Litterära Magasin*, principally on the subject of modern German letters. The contract was signed in January; Hesse's first review appeared in March. After meeting with Gottfried Bermann in Zurich, he spent the late spring and summer in Montagnola where he wrote the long poem *Hours in the Garden*, which contains a full description of his daily routine in well-modulated hexameter verse. Ninon had gone to Lugano. Natalina was in the house. With his straw hat, blinking in the sunlight, he indeed saw himself in the image of the Chinese Elder Brother who appears in *The Glass Bead Game*.

In September, his Second Literary Report appeared in *Bonniers*, containing a discussion of Thomas Mann's recently published collection of essays and some reflections on Mann's status as a contemporary bourgeois writer. Several weeks later he and Ninon went to Baden for his annual cure. Then the Third Report appeared, followed by a bombshell as disagreeable as a similar episode had been in 1915. Constantly careful not to offend, Hesse nonetheless had inadvertently opened the door to the very episode he had strenuously sought to avoid. The devastating salvo came from the German periodical *The New Literature*, which attacked Hesse in language reminiscent of that earlier occasion in 1915 when he was called a traitor to his country. The articles were written by a Nazi polemicist named Will Vespers who disapproved of Hesse's discussions not only of Thomas Mann but also of figures like Freud, Stefan Zweig, and the young Marxist Ernst Bloch.[18] Vespers's polemic used the cruel cant of the day:

> Thus speaks the German poet, Hermann Hesse. . . . He acts as though Germany, the New Germany, contained no poets, as though all of the new German literature were produced by modish quacks. He betrays contemporary German literature to the enemies of Germany and to the Jews. Here one can see clearly how deep one can sink when one eats off the table of the Jews. The German poet Hermann Hesse takes on the treasonous role of yesterday's Jewish critics. Helping the Jews and the cultural Bolsheviks, he helps in spreading false ideas abroad, which are damaging to his country.[19]

Hesse answered this article on December 3, but, just as he had done twenty years earlier, he gave a weak response. It lacked substance or political content. Besides being outraged by Vespers's tone, he made two points, neither of them central to the issue. The first was that he was taking German literature seriously enough to stand up for it even in a hostile foreign milieu, presumably in a liberal journal in Sweden. He did not enter into the question of whether it was right or wrong to consider Bloch, Freud, or Mann part of German literature.

More revealing was the prominence Hesse accorded his Swiss citizenship. "The worst part of your article," he wrote the editors of *New Literature*, "is not just the total misreading of my intentions and the actual service that I render German literature with these reports. The worst is that your reviewer represents the situation as though I were a German from the Reich and therefore a traitor to my people. In response to these assertions, I wish to declare that I am not a German national but Swiss and have lived in Switzerland uninterruptedly for a full twenty-three years."[20] Consciously opposed to the vulgarities of Will Vespers and his New Culture, Hesse nonetheless had an ear for their language. As both his publisher and his lawyer were soon to point out, the mere fact that Hesse deigned to answer this attack fanned the fires. Vespers was an opportunist; he had been Hesse's predecessor at *Bonniers*, a job from which he had been fired. To the extent that this man had allowed himself to become a mere instrument of the German Ministry of Propaganda, Hesse was powerless in any event. To the extent, however, that he could have damaged his reputation abroad, Vespers was powerless, indeed ridiculous. But Hesse was unable to sustain indifference: he was desperately afraid that his work would be banned in Germany, and he therefore felt that he had to convince his opponent of his correct intentions.

The results were predictable. Hesse's response did not bring vindication. A biographical sketch, composed by a relative, Aegidas Hunnius, was printed specially for the purpose in April 1936. It showed that Hesse had been born in Germany and had achieved his first reputation there.[21] It also documented the fact that Will Vespers had indeed been Hesse's predecessor at *Bonniers*, though as early as 1932. It was a draw. Vespers was right in saying that Hesse was essentially a German writer: who could deny that, in view of his rich life in Gaienhofen and his Swabian childhood and homeland? And Hesse was right in making clear that his antagonist was an opportunist who had once worked for the same journal. The reason why this confrontation turned into such a farce, however, must be found in Hesse's own uncertainties. If there had been no resonance, if there had been only disdain, if there had been no hurt, the matter would never have come to public attention outside the strained atmosphere of Germany in 1935–36.[22]

The crisis of the mid-thirties indeed reveals part of Hesse's refusal to face the issues that separated him from his enemies. He spent as much ink on this "calumny"—and stirred up as many legal threats—as he had done in the Cologne affair during the First World War. Yet another crisis erupted from the opposite direction, which underscored his ambivalence even more. Just as twenty years earlier his concern about the Cologne calumny had been matched by a strong statement against pacifism, so in this case the tempest surrounding Will Vespers and his *New Literature* was accompanied by an equally disagreeable series of attacks from the left—the circles of emigrants in Paris.

In the émigré journal *The New Daily Record (Das Neue Tagebuch)*, which appeared in Paris, his publisher Gottfried Bermann, though himself a Jew, had been bitterly attacked. The author, a man named Leopold Schwarzschild, had called Bermann "a Jew under the protection of the National Socialist publishing industry" and had viewed him as a silent partner of the Propaganda Ministry in Berlin.[23] A few days later, on January 19, 1936 a journalist named Georg Bernhard wrote in the emigrant paper *Paris Daily (Pariser Tageblatt)* that both Hesse and Annette Kolb had been guilty of contributing to the *Frankfurter Zeitung*, which he called, not without justice, "the fig leaf of the Third Reich," designed, through a show of respectability, to deceive the outside world about Germany's true nature.[24] Hesse felt the sting of double persecution sharply. As he wrote Hubacher at that time: "I am being shot at from two sides: from my colleagues in Germany who denounce me ever more violently and recommend to the authorities that they should finally forbid me because I think Jews and emigrants are human, too, and occasionally recommend their books. And now they shoot or rather spit from the other side—those very same emigrants who are, in part, a pack of pigs and who try to wring my neck."[25] In response, Hesse gave up his work for *Bonniers* after the third contribution. Since he had conceived of it as a way of writing about authors who were forbidden in Germany, and since the ingrates obviously did not deserve the sacrifice, there was no point in going on.[26]

Again it was a tempest in a teapot, yet it continued to have serious repercussions and elicited various revealing responses. In this case, Hesse was moved to sign a protest along with colleagues like Annette Kolb and Thomas Mann (despite his allergic reaction against signing any documents), but Schwarzschild's accusations were directed, unjustly they thought, against their publisher Gottfried Bermann.[27] On the whole, it is difficult to say which of the two sides—the persecutors in their seats of power or the victims footloose in their Parisian cafés—Hesse found more repulsive. But one issue led to another and Hesse was forced to take yet another stand. The question was raised whether Hesse was an emigré writer. Schwarzschild had asserted that most of German literature was being produced by emigrants, and he included Hesse in their ranks. This raised a difficult issue for Hesse, since just before, in his response to Vespers, he had publicly denied that he was a German writer. Schwarz-schild was vigorously opposed in his assertion in an article in the *Neue Zürcher Zeitung* by Ernst Korrodi, the Swiss journalist who fifteen years earlier had blown the cover of Hesse's pseudonym as the author of *Demian*. In his article, which was colored by his right-wing and anti-Semitic politics, Korrodi identified himself with the official German point of view and suggested angrily that if Schwarzschild were right all German literature would have to be substantially Jewish. This would leave out important German writers—Gerhart Hauptmann and Ricarda Huch among them. Hesse responded, but in doing so he once more missed the point. Instead of questioning the issue Korrodi had raised, he mainly declared that he was not an emigrant but a Swiss citizen.[28]

Hesse felt hurt by these attacks from emigrants with whose camp he at least partly had to sympathize. Moreover, in his way of viewing matters in 1935, his entire relationship to the so-called New Culture created by the Third Reich seemed to be focused on Jewish affairs. He was the only one in Germany, he declared, who had dared to recommend Jewish books, and, in writing for *Bonniers,* he had "supported the emigrants simply because I felt sorry for them." For their sake he had risked his position in Germany only to be spattered ungratefully with mud.[29] While he denied anti-Semitic feelings, he again revealed, in his language, some echo or resonance of it. Although he had never been an anti-Semite, he wrote, he had occasionally entertained "Aryan feelings against Jewish traits." And he added that if his Parisian adversaries were disgusting, the same thing could be said of Aryans like the notorious Julius Streicher or Will Vespers without conceding any importance to blood.[30] The choice of words can be explained by the times. The word Aryan can be used innocently. Still, it is surprising to note the emphasis on race even if the sentiments point in the opposite direction.

In the midst of these petty arguments it still seems difficult to under-stand why Hesse was unable to see the emigrant culture as the hopeless, doomed society it was, and why he could not see that by attributing so much power to these impotent intellectuals he was merely echoing pre-vailing propaganda. At the same time, the other side continued to heap abuse on his head, just as nationalistic students, writers, publicists, and readers had done since the twenties. One extreme example is this excerpt from a letter he received during that year: "Of course, you've never had any feeling of shame. The contempt of the entire world may burn in your soul. You are the excrement of a badly suffering nation. You are a dog—a cursed dog!" This bit of prose was naturally connected with the *Bonniers* affair and may explain Hesse's impatience with those emigrants (whom by and large he always regarded with suspicion) for whose sake he had become the victim of such missives.[31]

Of all the years of Hesse's later life, following the consolidation of marriage and house, the year 1935–36 was probably the hardest. In addition to the moral and political crisis of that time, he went through the personal crisis of his brother's suicide, which again exacted a moral stand. It occurred during that same autumn in Baden when the storm over Will Vespers broke loose and countered that political farce with a real tragedy. Hans Hesse chose the time of his famous brother's annual visit to the town to take his life. Hermann and Ninon had arrived only two weeks earlier. Their relationship had always been clouded, and Hans accepted the existence of a vast class difference between them, which had been created by his inability to rise above the status of a clerk. From those early days on, when he had failed at the Mission House in Basel, Hans had always been in difficulty, though after his marriage to Frida his life had appeared calmer. Working in the arms factory as a bookkeeper in the very town where his brother was a celebrated visitor each year could not have been easy.

The suicide had been caused by great anxiety. Hans was afraid of losing his job. Just ten days before the tragedy, Hesse had invited his brother to the hotel. They had supper together, and though Hans first talked wildly about being surrounded by intrigue, he became calmer when Hermann offered to help him find a new job. They ended the evening amiably, and Hesse noticed that his brother became agitated only when the office was mentioned. The precise event is recorded in great detail in two letters to his sisters (Adis and Marulla were then staying together in Adis's house) as well as in the affectionate essay "Remembrance of Hans."[32] On Wednesday, November 27, a Parson Preiswerk called on Hesse in his hotel and told him his brother had disappeared, that he had left the house a few minutes earlier than usual but had never arrived at the office. At first they merely feared that Hans was especially disturbed and was drifting about the countryside, but as time went on that hope faded. Frida finally notified the police. Hesse remained with her until after midnight, when he returned to his hotel. The distraught wife kept the lights on through the night in the hope Hans would return, but that hope was in vain. In a postcard to Adis and Marulla on Thursday evening, Hesse reported the final news: "I'm just coming from Frida's and both her sisters are now with her. Well, they found our poor Hans. He has it behind him." He added that he had been pushed all day and that, with Emmy Ball being their guest in the hotel, he had not had time to take it all in.

Hans had been found at noon on Thursday. The police had discovered his body in the fields. He had used his pocketknife. Many aspects of the disappearance and death of this middle-aged man recalled young Hermann Hesse's adventure in Maulbronn. Equally reminiscent of that earlier event were the well-concealed anxieties that broke out at last as the disturbed had walked into the fields in the driving snow.

The funeral erased some of the terror of the suicide and the image of Hans as a driven, anxious man. It was raining, but though it was a good half-hour's walk to the cemetery, a large crowd of friends from Baden and nearby villages followed the coffin to the grave. "That half hour on this less than beautiful rain-drenched cemetery was very fine, solemn, and consoling," Hesse wrote his sisters. It reminded him of that other occasion during the First World War when he had attended Hans's wedding. While he felt touched deeply by his brother's tragedy, even in the eloquent pages of his essay in Hans's honor, one finds little awareness of a *moral* stand. Could he have helped Hans at that supper ten days earlier if he had done anything specific about the search for a new job or offered to help him get a physician's assistance? It is difficult to say whether and how much Hesse could have helped. In any event, he could not but identify with the suicide, which had been an important motif in his own life and work, and which now reasserted itself with fresh poignancy.

During this year, too, Ninon became ill rather often. The tables were turned on these occasions and Hesse had to take care of her with Natalina's help. Their travels became even more restricted. Their main journey was to Baden, with only a brief stay in Zurich thereafter. They went to Germany once more in 1936, but even these trips, which involved some lectures, became ever rarer. Hermann Hesse withdrew more and more completely into the citadel in Montagnola.

IV

Hesse was not the only person for whom 1935 was a critical year. It included the reconstitution of the German army, the reoccupation of the Rhineland, and, during the Nazi Party Congress in Nuremberg that year, the promulgation of the racial laws. Hesse now confronted a major moral choice that turned out to be the most crucial decision he had to make in the peculiar political context of the 1930s.

The Nazi government's practice of "Aryanizing" Jewish-owned businesses through forced sales to non-Jews reached the firm of S. Fischer late in the year 1935. At that time, Dr. Goebbels's Propaganda Ministry requested that the Fischer family separate themselves from the firm. Ironically, the request arrived just as Gottfried Bermann had been accused of collaborating with the enemy. The sensitive partner in this situation was Peter Suhrkamp, who was to become one of Hesse's close friends.[33] He had been appointed editor of the *Neue Rundschau* as early as 1933 and appeared to be a most suitable buyer of the firm. Prodded by both the Propaganda Ministry and the Commerce Department the sale was quickly concluded. As early as November 21, Hesse noted on a postcard to his sister that he had read in the papers that S. Fischer had been sold. According to the deal officially completed early in 1936, the Fischer family was paid large sums of money and, as Suhrkamp was to insist defensively, had even received additional funds for resettlement.[34] It was the arrangement about authors, however, that affected Hesse most vitally.

Bermann had at first tried to reestablish himself in Zurich, and if he had succeeded in doing so, Hesse's relations with his firm might have taken a wholly different turn. However, the Bermann Fischer Verlag, as it was soon to be called, was not permitted to settle in Switzerland despite strong and active support from Thomas Mann because of the vocal opposition of the conservative Swiss Publishers Guild with the rightist journalist Korrodi in the forefront.[35] He therefore relocated his truncated firm in Vienna. By arrangement with Suhrkamp he was able to take with him those authors who were already forbidden in Germany. Consequently, writers like Stefan Zweig and Thomas Mann went with the old firm as it resettled, at least for the two years remaining before the German takeover of Austria. Others, including Hesse, who were not forbidden or considered hostile to the government, were told that they must remain in Berlin under the new management.[36] Bermann, then still confident that the firm would be eventually allowed to settle in Zurich, informed Hesse of this decision early in January, 1936. He would be, so he told his author, among those whom he could not "pry loose" and Hesse was therefore advised to sit tight, observe the scene, and wait for the first opportunity to break away. Bermann, of course, fully expected that Hesse would merely wait for the chance to leave the old firm now tainted by having been nazified.[37] But this expectation turned out to be false: Hesse remained with the Berlin Fischer Verlag under Suhrkamp's direction to the end.

The moment of decision was to arrive in 1938. Meanwhile, Hesse's life had not been easy. Ninon's illness had resulted in a serious operation in Vienna early in 1937, and that Easter his half brother Karl Isenberg died. Although he had written some poems and a little more prose, including "The Confessor," his *Glass Bead Game* was still stuck in the morass of his inhibitions. Moreover, his angry impatience with the constant requirement to make moral choices he did not care to make took its toll of his general health. Now he experienced a further blow, which extended from a public tragedy to a personal sorrow. The Germans occupied Ninon's Vienna, and their lives were changed once more.

It was a moment of real choice for Hesse, because this was the time when a writer would do well to rescue his property abroad. Since he was a Swiss citizen he was in a particularly favorable position, a fact that makes his failure to do so even more poignant. Bermann meanwhile was puzzled when Hesse made no move to join his old friends who were with him in Austria and were now preparing to make a further move. In June Hesse replied that what held him in Germany (as far as publication of his books was concerned) was a contract with a firm with which he had been connected all his life and "which up to this day has made the greatest effort to please me."[38] This response was not wholly disingenuous, since it identified the "aryanized" Fischer Verlag with the original house whose legitimate successor was now striving to maintain it abroad. It was particularly unfortunate because it came at a time, after the German occupation of Austria, when Bermann-Fischer had to pack its crates and move once again. This time they relocated in Sweden, where the authors on their list were published during the remainder of the thirties and throughout the Second World War. But since their books were printed and distributed in a non-German-speaking country they were therefore perceived as being outside the mainstream of the literature in their language and were clearly marked as émigrés.

The main reason for Hesse's choice concerned his audience. He wrote Gottfried Bermann:

> In addition to the contract which, as you know, runs to the end of 1939, I must also consider my audience. Outside Germany I have few readers and a book like "Josef Knecht" will be understood without a residue of puzzlement by some ten thousand people in today's gagged Germany, whereas in all of America there are not three persons to whom this book could mean anything. . . .[39]

However wrong he was about not being understood abroad, especially in America, his sense that he and his readers were bound together by an identical tradition, and therefore had to stand together, had been his personal credo for a long time. As never before, Hesse felt bound to his readers by their common language. He therefore remained with S. Fischer, Berlin, and his intimacy with Gottfried Bermann passed on to a similar intimacy with Peter Suhrkamp.

Hesse maintained his options. At one point he actually threatened Peter Suhrkamp that he might sell future books abroad, but essentially his decision had been made. He was as unable in 1938 as he had been in 1914 to break his ties with his German friends and admirers and with the politicians and arbiters of taste in Germany, no matter how he may have despised them. His need to be accepted and at the same time to break away was as strong in the man in his sixties as it had been for the adolescent and child. This pattern reinforced his need for a dialectic that would reconcile conflicting impulses and transpose them onto a plane where they could be abstractly perceived. This was done in his final novel, *The Glass Bead Game*, and in view of his need to act out these conflicts in his life one can easily see why it took him so long to write it.

In 1938 and 1939 *The Glass Bead Game* moved forward once more. The important chapter "The Calling," in which Knecht envisions his position as Magister Ludi, was completed that year, and with it the first section of the book. Although this was the year of political upheavals—the Czech crises and eventually the crisis over Poland and the actual beginning of the war—Hesse began to work remarkably well. In fact, for the first time since beginning his novel seven years earlier it grew steadily chapter by chapter. This was in itself an extraordinary feat, for as he entered his sixties Hesse's haphazard writing habits were beginning to work against him. He had always written feverishly for several days and nights with barren stretches in between. Most of his books were actually written in relatively short periods of time, and *The Glass Bead Game* was no exception to this pattern. The crucial difference between the composition of this last great novel and that of his earlier work was that he could no longer rely on the final push to bring him close to the end. Partly, of course, the longer time had to do with the great amount of research he had to do, and partly because it grew with him while he lived out some of its problems. But to a large extent the book took so long to write because the stretches of barrenness between moments of activity became longer and longer and because the intensity of his work had to be reduced. At this moment, however, the longest hiatus since *Siddhartha* was coming to an end, and though it would still be some time before he finished the book, he was now moving steadily ahead.

By early 1939 a good part of *The Glass Bead Game* was done, and as the war outside his retreat became more and more imminent, his imagined Castalian island became purer. It remained the island of "humanity and love" that Hesse had promised his readers as a response to the harsh nationalism and militarism they were expected to serve. When the war actually broke out in September, he faced it with composure. He went to Baden the following month for his usual cure while

Ninon took a vacation of her own. Worn out once more by his eye- and headaches, Hesse expressed his sour disenchantment to Adis:

> The world looks a bit dim. Nothing surprises me, of course, not even the increasing signs of greater crudity in German political life. As long as one doesn't suffer from it one observes it quietly, but now we all feel the nonsense of what's loose in the world (by no means only in Germany) on our own skins.

This letter, written in October, accurately expressed not only Hesse's judgment of the new European war but also his own detachment. As dangers increased outside their Ticino citadel, the Hesses consolidated their intellectual and physical lives within. In 1940, he and Ninon built a new addition to their house to provide him with more room for his study and greater space for houseguests. When the war began in earnest that year, Hesse seldom left Montagnola except for his annual Baden cure. However, the intensified war brought a few benefits as well: fewer tourists from the Reich, or from anywhere else, flocked into Ticino to disturb their retreat during the summer, and Hesse was left alone to pursue his gardening. Whatever terror had occurred and was about to happen, a centripetal force pulled Hesse into his actual and metaphoric retreat. The citadel against history was fortified.

Suffering and pain, of course, were by no means absent. As the war continued, many friends and close members of their family were drawn into the fighting, just as they had been in 1914. Carlo Isenberg, the beloved nephew who had helped Hesse with his musicology for *The Glass Bead Game*, was sent to the Eastern front. But there were also troubles on Ninon's side. After a subdued birthday on July 2, 1940, with Dr. Lang and Günther Böhmer in attendance, they heard bad news about Ninon's relatives, who were at that time in the midst of the battle zone in the Balkans and were reported in flight. And Emmy Ball's daughter Annemarie Schütt drifted about the Italian peninsula with husband and child, intermittently lost and rediscovered.

Despite all these anxieties, their personal life continued with its usual fluctuations. After a trip to the Engadin in the summer Ninon returned not too well restored. Hesse expressed his concern to Adis in the middle of August: she seemed extremely tired and nervous. His own pains in his legs became worse than ever, and Dr. Lang began to give him injections. Yet, for all that, they were able to go on a few good hikes. Even some work was done. Hesse reported being busy with the clean copy of yet another chapter of "Knecht" he was finishing, but he regretted that now he could do only two pages a day when before he could do twenty. The main concern in September, however, was not about his ailments, which would soon send him to Baden, nor about Alice Leuthold's fiftieth birthday, but mostly about Ninon.

On September 2, 1940 Hesse mentioned to Adis that Ninon had invited a young philologist to stay with them, a girl of twenty-five who was teaching her Aeschylus in exchange for room and board. Evidently Ninon was very happy to have that help and stimulation, but just the tone in which Hesse reported that visit then and later did not suggest total approval. "Ninon is happy," he wrote in that first notice of the event, along with the further news that the house was full of workmen, as they were converting to electric heat. In a postcard later that month he mentioned that her "philologist is still around" in addition to the news that another section of "Josef Knecht" would soon appear in the *Neue Rundschau*. And in a note of that same month to the publicist Rudolf J. Humm, he said nonchalantly that "Ninon is happy." "She has her long-desired philologist with her for a few weeks. With her she reads Greek for two hours each day, so far Agamemnon by Aeschylus."[40] He was probably quite pleased to find her happy because this was a time of great tension for Ninon, but he also always felt unhappy when her attention wandered away from him for too long—whether it was to her *Griechin*, her Greek lady, as he would later refer to her, or to her own occasional journeys to Greece.

Another matter of concern during that first real war year of 1940 was the problem of evacuation. In a lengthy correspondence with his friends the Humms, who lived in Zurich, Hesse discussed in great detail the role they might be expected to play—and were not ready to play—in case an evacuation plan would have to be put into practice. At issue, of course, was the possibility that in the event of air raids or a German attack, the great Swiss cities in the north and west—Zurich, Basel, Bern, Lucerne, Geneva, etc.—would have to be evacuated and inhabitants of the Ticino region and other rural and mountainous areas of the country's interior had to be ready to receive these potential refugees. Hesse was greatly concerned that his peace might be demolished and that, if the inevitable should happen, they would at least be able to take in friends or acquaintances or others whom they knew by reputation.[41]

These personal worries, ranging from petty details to tragic circumstances, continued to invade Montagnola and formed a steady undercurrent to *The Glass Bead Game*. Not all these happenings were connected with the war. In 1941, he lost his last male sibling, his half brother Theo, and he felt oddly alone with only his two sisters—Adis and Marulla—as the surviving pillars of the family of Pietist missionaries. At the same

time, Ninon began to suffer more and more visibly from the uncertainty about her relatives who continued to be in a war zone.[42]
That fall they went to Zurich and Baden. A tired, distracted Ninon
buried herself in the public library in Zurich for three to four hours
each day, then took the train to visit her husband in Baden in the
afternoons. But when they returned to Montagnola after Christmas,
Hesse did not feel much better. He told Adis that he now slept late in
order to escape the cold and to conserve his eyesight, but that even when
he was up he had to limp about. Later that spring he mentioned in detail
how his joints ached, how little he could get around, and how he had to
drag himself once or twice a week by bus to the masseur in Lugano,
but to little avail. Ninon's concern, meanwhile, increased, especially
about her sister Lilly, to whom she was close. After a long lapse she
finally heard from her and could breathe more easily. But *die Sorge
bleibt*—the worry remains—was a symbolic motto for those difficult
years.

Hesse was also concerned about his new friend and publisher Peter
Suhrkamp, who after years of overwork now appeared to be seriously ill.
This personal concern expressed as well as masked a very sturdy professional relationship.[43] Despite the war, Hesse was able to continue
publishing in Germany for some time, and he was greatly helped in this
by Suhrkamp. He had assessed the situation shrewdly and correctly. If
he had followed Gottfried Bermann into literary exile, he would have
long since been branded a "forbidden author." Of course, gradually, as
the war progressed, it came to be his turn as well to be excluded from
the officially approved literary scene. For the longest time, however, he
remained protected by his enormous German reputation, although (as
Finckh had correctly perceived in 1933) it had always been a little risky
to be involved with Hesse. Yet he was an important writer, not wholly
unacceptable to the regime and protected by his Swiss citizenship. Since
he had deliberately refrained from taking a public stand and had not
published subversive material or joined anti-German causes, he had
been left largely alone. And whenever difficult questions arose, Peter
Suhrkamp and his associates stood up for him.

Daily routine continued to leave its mark on the slow progress of *The
Glass Bead Game* for yet another year. Late in 1941 his old servant
Natalina became mortally ill (after taking her to the doctor Ninon re-
ported cancer of the stomach), while on the other side of life's spectrum
Heiner visited that Christmas with his wife Isa, who was then expecting
a child. In January, Ninon's *Griechin* came back as poor Natalina was
dying, and Hesse became the grandfather of a little boy. Reports of
Ninon's Siamese cat became more frequent (a sick tom named Archi

finally died) and Hesse clarified the significance of the event: "[Ninon] is very sad; except for me, it was Natalina and Archi whom she loved here."

Above these details of daily life hovered the complex novel that, exactly as Hesse had described it to Jung eight years earlier, transmuted the anxieties and small human pleasures of that difficult time into a strangely different medium. The result was the static tale of Josef Knecht and his Bead Game, whose environment contained no dying Natalina, no dying cat solicitously cared for, no aches and sore joints and newly arrived grandson, but an arid, intellectual world whose harmonies remained theoretical and whose characters were puppets. If a deliberate attempt is made to supply a dialectical counterweight to the theoretical space by stylized "biographies," a "legendary" conclusion in the natural surroundings of a mountain lake, all of these stratagems only underscored that highly cerebral artificial world of nonfictional narrative masquerading as a fictional presentation of life. Hesse's many daily doings were indeed subjected to sublimation, to alchemical metamorphoses as history was flattened into a geometric design. In this way, it was done at last. A postcard was dispatched to his sister:

April 30, 1942

Dear Adis,

Yesterday I wrote the last lines of Josef Knecht.

My best regards to you!

Your

Hermann

They soon went to Baden and, in addition to assisting on a book of his poems, Ninon helped Hesse put the finishing touches on the last part of the manuscript before sending it off. In late July they visited Bern, where they met Hesse's two older sons with their wives and children and spent some time with the Wassmers in Castle Bremgarten. But during that summer one of the old motifs of Hesse's life was sounded once more: Mia had a new breakdown and was confined to a hospital near Lugano. "She is much better," he wrote in August, "though this time it takes very long and causes a great many worries."

A few months later, during Mia's absence in November, her house, which continued to be inhabited by tenants, burned to the ground. All three sons were in the service at the time, but Martin, who had been closest to his mother, received sufficient leave to straighten out the various practical problems. Hesse wrote his sister an exasperatingly detailed account of the affair, about the loss of a valuable piano and violin, antique furniture, all clothes and linens, not to mention a bureau full of Hesse's letters, drawings, and other mementos. He also mentioned Martin's efforts in rearranging his mother's life. Hesse's attention was riveted especially on the peculiar priorities he sensed in Mia and her family. He was concerned about her and her brother's mental difficulties, while these "sturdy folk" were already talking of building a smaller house with the proceeds of the fire insurance and were musing about the type of roof they would like to choose. It seemed to him incredible. As all these events took place, both sections of *The Glass Bead Game* lingered in Berlin. They had been lying there since May.

If Hesse had become less acceptable to German officialdom as the war wore on, many German soldiers who fought in it continued to admire him. As early as 1940, Hesse mentioned a story to Robert Humm in which a young soldier, badly wounded in Belgium, had been left behind close to the enemy lines with a shattered leg. He feared he was lost, but he remembered a few lines of poetry by Hesse that inspired him to crawl back to his own troops under heavy fire, feverish and bleeding, through two kilometers of thick clover.[44] Hesse liked these stories and he cited them often as evidence that he was still loved in Germany despite official frowns. Inevitably, however, he was eventually declared an "undesirable author" after all. There was clearly too much in his past that made him suspect. This not altogether dishonorable appellation meant that while his books could still be bought and read, they were not looked upon with favor. In a wartime economy, when paper is scarce, the allotment of print and paper is crucial to a book, and neither was made available to Hesse. Finally, the worst blow during these difficult years, his German earnings, which he had not been able to transfer to Switzerland in any significant amounts for some time in any event, were now confiscated outright.

When, after working on final corrections of the manuscript of *The Glass Bead Game* with Ninon in Baden that spring, Hesse sent the second half of his book to Suhrkamp in May, he still firmly expected it to be published. He was mistaken. Although some further chapters were allowed to appear in the *Neue Rundschau*, the manuscript itself remained untouched for seven months as the publisher waited for government sanction to proceed. During the remainder of 1942 and early in 1943, however, the political situation sharpened considerably. To Hesse's amazement and shock, his novel was actually turned down. Peter Suhrkamp personally traveled to Montagnola to return the manuscript of *The Glass Bead Game* to its author at the Casa Bodmer and to convey his apologies. At that point, Hesse made arrangements for Swiss publication. By a mutual argreement, Suhrkamp returned all foreign rights to Hesse and, as a result, the firm of Fetz and Wasmuth in Zurich could publish all of his books (including a series of his Collected Works).[45] *The Glass Bead Game* was speedily produced by them during the fall of 1943. Despite his caution, Hesse was ultimately unable to escape the regime's disapproval. In 1943 and 1944, when the dictatorship assumed its most insane proportions, the full, dreaded event became a reality: Hesse's books were actually prohibited. Now reading him inside Germany had become a crime.

V

The sharpening atmosphere to which Hesse and *The Glass Bead Game* had been sacrificed was a sign of the times. Not that it had been bearable before, especially for the victims in Russia and the occupied territories, but as defeat became a possibility, German life contracted even more into an ever icier, crueller aggressiveness. With the invasions across the Mediterranean that began in the fall of 1943 and led to the occupation of all of France, the reversal of the victorious trend in Russia after the defeat at Stalingrad, and especially after the heavy raids had started over Germany, the political atmosphere in the Reich became increasingly tenser. This change communicated itself to each person and spread even as far as the Hesses' retreat in southern Switzerland.

When Hesse wrote Adis in August 1943 about the raids on Hamburg, he appeared to comment on this change, but did so in a strangely muted, self-concerned way: "In Hamburg I, too, lost a thing or two. It was the city from which I received most of my letters for years. In the past not a week went by without a letter from Hamburg." There was also a Frau Spir in that city, a former assistant of Hesse's "Japanese" cousin, Wilhelm Gundert, who had copied hundreds of his poems for him. He then went on to discuss his dried-up vegetable garden, the small tomatoes, and lack of water in the summer heat as though he had commented on a very ordinary happening. And so it was. Throughout that year and the next, his comments continued to be almost casual, yet they occurred again and again. "No news from Suhrkamp or Munich" since the last raids (May 1944); concerned about the attacks on Stuttgart (in July). Ninon's sister Lilly and her other relatives in Eastern Europe were no longer heard from, and, despite his illness, Peter Suhrkamp was arrested in April by the Gestapo.

Deaths and illnesses, quite apart from the war, took their toll from among the friends of Hesse's own generation. Among his elders, the opera singer Ilona Durigo, a friend of Hesse's since his Gaienhofen days, died late in 1943 at age ninety-five. Closer to home, however, was Hans Sturzenegger's death early in January—the painter who had been his companion to India twenty-two years earlier and whose brother they had visited at the time. Sturzenegger had appeared now and then in Hesse's correspondence over the years, most recently during the late thirties when Hesse described him as old, blind, and of failing health. Of greater impact on his personal life was a stroke suffered by Dr. Lang, his close friend and therapist since 1916, in January 1944. But the greatest loss of that year was clearly due to the war. Although he was not to know for sure until almost a year after the war's end, his favorite nephew, Carlo Isenberg, fell in Russia in 1944 at the age of forty-three.

Financially, too, his situation became tighter. With the prohibition of all his books in Germany, all German royalties stopped. They had in effect ceased earlier, because currency regulations made their transfer to Switzerland difficult, but the money was held for him in special German accounts and he could send some of it to his sisters or use for German expenses. Now all that was over, and, as he complained in a note to Adis, his Swiss earnings (even with the beginning of sales from *The Glass Bead Game*) was mere "pocket money." He again found his sponsor, however. The rich cigar manufacturer Emil Molt, who had helped him out financially during Mia's breakdown and the dissolution of their marriage after the First World War, once more came to the rescue in the closing year of the Second. He told Hesse that he would make some "transitional credit" (*Uberbrückungskredit*) available to him to ease him over the difficult time until his earnings could again be his own. In the meantime, his life continued in its usual quiet, withdrawn way. The first reviews of *The Glass Bead Game* started to appear in the spring of 1944. Hesse heartily approved of his sisters' comment that he had created an interior Reich for them in the rarified Castalian atmosphere. Less understanding were more official reviews in the various Swiss newspapers. It was generally found too difficult. One of the more typical misreadings of the novel was quite unofficial. It was reported by his friend Humm in a letter in November 1944. A hairdresser of his acquaintance in Zurich, who had recently read at least parts of the *Bead Game*, waxed most enthusiastic about the book: "*The Glass Bead Game* by Hermann Hesse: that's some book! Admittedly difficult to read: he could manage only five to six pages at a time, and afterwards he just put the book aside and thought about these pages. But all of those fine reflections, about history, for example, about Catholic monasteries." He had been brought up a Catholic, mused that reader, and he knew monastic life very well, and to read about it was a pleasure. "He could feel so completely how it was for Hermann Hesse in Castalia."[46]

After a summer in Bremgarten in 1944 to rest his eyes, Hesse was pleased to see Martin and his new wife. He mused on Mia's birthday (she had just turned seventy-six) and on the death of her brother Fritz who had spent years in and out of mental hospitals and had lived with Mia in Bern and Ascona after the fire. In the fall they went again to Baden, oppressed by the war news, the failed attempt on Hitler's life, and the resultant political crisis that led to further horror, as Hesse ploddingly wrote day-to-day letters about his ordinary doings to his sisters in Germany. Ninon fell ill more and more often and was herself depressed, mostly by her concern for her family, with whom all but the most tenuous contact had been lost. Following the Baden cure they went to Zurich to spend Christmas with the Leutholds and faced the new year of 1945, its deep winter snow, its news of the disintegration of life north of their border, with more than the usual degree of anxiety and trepidation.

When in May 1945 peace was finally declared, it was Hesse's voice speaking his "Poem on Peace" over Radio Basel that announced it to his Castalian world. The audience of that radio station had become accustomed to that voice—there had been several Hesse hours in the past—but this time it reassured them that culture had survived the war. Hesse had emerged like those gnarled old trees he liked to write about, especially as he grew older, for despite all the changes around them, the Hesses' life could continue barely altered. They had worried about Adis, Marulla, and the bombing of Stuttgart and about Ninon's relatives in the Balkans. They were concerned about lost friends like Peter Suhrkamp and lost relatives like Carlo. They were concerned about the whole cultural complex that had passed through war a second time during the past half century. Yet when the war ended that spring, and as Hesse read his poem, their villa, their garden, their *Glass Bead Game* resurfaced, unchanged as though landmarks, temporarily covered by a stormy sea, were now returning to view, their familiar features intact. It was in this spirit, his masterpiece published, his life in place, that Hermann Hesse looked with equanimity toward his final new life.

11

The Final New Life

I

We think of you very much. For it may be possible that mail service may cease for a while. Then we must think of one another with double strength—of each other, of our parents, and of old times. It is strange to think that you will already be seventy years old. You will often be tired and feel as though you have had enough. But we all still need you very much. You must stay here for a long time and perhaps life will still bring you some beauty. From all my heart I send my love to you and all of you. Your Hermann

THIS POSTCARD, which Hermann Hesse sent to his sister Adis early in February 1945, typifies the deep-seated upheaval of the last months of the war and the early months of the postwar era. It is a moving postcard that combines the fear of aging and dying—the stringent desire to remain close to the source of life in their memory of parents and childhood—with the fear and dying of an entire generation. The disrupted mail service became a symbol of the approaching end, expressed with the cautious circumlocution that came from years of evading the censor. Nonetheless, Hesse managed to convey to his sister, with the economy of the artist, a weariness of life at a time when the air raids on Stuttgart were particularly heavy, when it was clear that the entire German structure was about to collapse, and when the dictatorship, in response, assumed features so monstrous that it affected even these two elderly correspondents, the withdrawn writer in his Swiss retreat and the country parson's wife in rural Swabia. Here is resignation, sadness, fear of the future as well as an outstretched hand—a weapon against separation.

The months before that moment of peace was announced on Radio Basel were filled with the anticipation of death. In March, while Hesse was completing the final manuscript of his novel fragment *Berthold*, written long before, the signs of dissolution multiplied. It was in some respects a replay of 1918–19, not just in the obvious sense of two parallel defeats but also in the personal sense of inner and outer dissolution. "Herr Maurach," he wrote Adis in March, referring to an acquaintance, "just wrote that since he had resettled from the Baltics he had moved his people and goods to Poznan. Now all his possessions are gone, including his library, and his people are in flight. He, too, will start on his journey at once in order to help them as much as possible. Desperation and misery everywhere. I think of you each day." The increase in interest in their father's family in Estonia at this point had been motivated by the fact that all the German communities along the Baltic coast had been on the move and their Baltic relatives and friends had made contact with the Hesses in Switzerland. Similarly, Ackerknecht had left Rostock in Northeastern Germany and eventually turned up in Swabian Ludwigsburg. Everyone still alive seemed to be on the move.

In an uncanny way, however, a sense of dissolution also affected the personal lives of some of the *dramatis personae* of 1919 in a way not directly connected with the war. In March, Mia had finally bought a house in Bern with Martin, who was still in the army, to replace the house that had burned down in 1942. But at the same time she had yet another attack of the emotional disorder from which she recovered in April in a private sanatorium—just as she had done during those earlier years.

Losses everywhere. At that time Carlo was still thought missing and they were waiting anxiously for a word from or about him. Peter Suhr-kamp also had not been heard from, while Ninon feared her sister and family were lost in the East. Still, Hesse's situation and attitude were quite different from those he displayed in 1919: it was a different music. As a counterpoint to his awareness of the German defeat there emerged a sense of stability that kept him at least partly aloof. The music, then, was not in the least cacophonous. It was that of the Old Music Master rather than the music of doom that first sounded in "Klingsor's Last Summer." Although Hesse with one part of himself rejected the suggestion that Castalia was a refuge from political, social, and eventually psychological instability—a bulwark against history and change—with another he knew that this was to be the role of his creation. But he almost broke with Humm when his friend insisted on this interpretation.[1] As late as 1970 Siegfried Unseld, a Hesse scholar of note as well as his present publisher, asserted that the history of *The Glass Bead Game* is inseparable from the political history of the Nazi era and the Second World War.[2] Humm's critique was no less valid than similar remonstrances about Hesse's "hypochondria" had been, which had angered him so much in the Balls during the twenties.

If in 1919 Hesse deliberately destroyed a secure life, dismantled his home, left his wife in the care of doctors, relatives, and friends, and scattered his children, in 1945 he enjoyed the citadel of his Casa Bodmer and channeled those inner and outer fears into a subterranean life of the word. His friend the painter Ernst Morgenthaler moved in as early as May and stayed with them through much of the summer while he painted a portrait of Hesse for Ninon's fiftieth birthday later that year. During the summer, Carlo's death was finally confirmed, as was Peter Suhrkamp's survival.[3] He had been released with broken health. The usual birthday celebration took place on July 2; Morgenthaler was still with them, as indeed was his wife, who had joined them for the occasion. And Günther Böhmer, who had married two months earlier, came to celebrate with his new wife. It was a memorable day during an equally memorable year.

A few weeks later, the Hesses packed their bags to go on vacation. They chose Rigi-Kaltbad, a mountain resort south of Lucerne, to regain some sense of order and proportion. For Hesse, the place became a symbol of the polemics he was about to enter into during that crucial first year of peace.

II

We have been here up on the Rigi for almost a fortnight, 1600 meters high, in a rather desolate Grand Hotel and will remain at least another week.

It had been a dreadful summer, Hesse wrote in this letter, congratulating Adis on her seventieth birthday: two months of incredible heat and drought. With the exception of a few flowers the entire garden was burned out. And, to top it all off, Ninon had intestinal flu. It had been an awful time. They deserved a vacation.

It was this vacation which gave rise to a few pages that are still haunting, for they connect his present consciousness with that of his young manhood, his present with the past. In August, probably just as this letter to Adis was being written, he wrote in his now famous *Rigi Diary*:

From dried-out, burned-out Ticino, from our dried-out and burned-out garden, we have fled to Rigi-Kaltbad for a while where we were still granted a few summer days with the brightest view reaching far into the distance.

One could, if one cared, take pleasure in identifying or recognizing those many peaks, or, while resting, one may simply surrender to the constantly changing flow of colors, light, and shadow—the bizarre geometry of a gigantic panorama.

Hesse likened the "alternations of rock and snow, sun-drenched ledges and dark abysses" to the rhythms and caesuras of poetry. The ascetic strength of the mountain was described in the images of geometry and poetry. He also opposed them to the water of the lake at Vitznau where he once "wrote the diary of Lauscher and the first studies for *Camenzind* forty-five years ago."[4] Moreover, not surprising in this dialectical writer, the end of his *Glass Bead Game* had combined precisely these elements—the ice-cold watery grave in which Josef Knecht had died, momentarily joined in the same element with the young disciple, and the height of the mountain, far removed from the struggles of daily life, even though lake and mountain were situated outside the Castalian realm.

If present and past were joined symbolically in his descriptions of their landscape in the Rigi Mountain, Hesse brought them together in more specific political terms toward the end of his *Rigi Diary*. If in describing the relationship between mountain and lake, the present and the past, Hesse projected an opposition of "masculine" order and "feminine" dissolutions in history and life, in the final section of the *Rigi Diary* he contrasted the disorders of 1919 with those of 1945. He also repeated salient themes of the *Bead Game*. In this well-known portion he dealt with the situation as it existed in Germany, and as he perceived it, immediately after the end of the war. "Mail sometimes brings surprises. So it was yesterday," Hesse began his reflections. "Letters from Germany!"[5] These letters were not by former adherents of the Hitler regime but by people who had been opposed to it and had suffered throughout the years of the National Socialist regime and the Second World War. They were liberal democrats, Catholics, most of them former Socialists, who had kept their reservations to themselves in a "silent emigration" but had been suspect nonetheless, just as Hesse had been. These sufferers were especially exposed, Hesse wrote, for unlike Poles and Russians, or even Jews, they had to suffer individually and in silence. There had been no camaraderie, not even a community of sufferers, to alleviate their solitary pain.[6] No wonder, then, that they resented the admonitions of the Allies and the concept of "collective guilt" that Karl Jaspers and even C. G. Jung had espoused.

On the one hand, Hesse did not support this notion. He was too much aware of his own safety while his Swabian relatives and friends had been in danger. "How can a person who sits in a house that has not been destroyed and who has enough to eat every day, who had annoyances and worries during the past ten years but had to suffer no harm to his person . . . how could such a person have anything to say to those of you who have suffered so much?" On one point, however, he could not defend his friends and on that point he was an expert. Since the First World War Hesse had discerned and fought nationalism. In the same way his friends in Germany could deal with that evil better than either victors or neutrals. The momentary opening afforded by the German collapse allowed them to experience an unfolding, an opportunity to become adult. "You could see through that delusion of nationalism, which you already hate deeply, and liberate yourselves from it." If they have really been cleansed from this nationalistic delusion, Hesse suggested, they could withstand the attacks made upon them about their "collective guilt."

On this note the excerpt from the *Rigi Diary* ends, but the reflections of the concluding passage became a prelude to an intense period of political utterances that continued for three more years similar to a parallel period before and after the First World War. Political statements, reflections, and essays became Hesse's way of filling up the last fully productive years of his life in place of another major imaginative work and perhaps compensated for an inability to create one. They represented a new challenge, as he was one of the spiritual giants of German culture who had lived through the anguish of National Socialism and had rescued prewar ideals for the postwar world. But they surely indicated also his awareness that for the foreseeable future no major work was likely to develop.

Contrasts as well as similarities mark the two postwar responses in Hesse's career. The time of his strong emotional involvement in the politics of peace and antinationalism runs parallel to his preoccupations of 1919. But for Hesse at the threshold of the 1920s, this involvement was also associated with a veritable renaissance—a "revolution," as he called it—in his literary productions, while the years following the *Bead Game* were essentially occupied with reissuing, rearranging, and re-editing old work. *The Glass Bead Game*, with its imposing structure of scholarship in Western and Chinese thought, had been a *summa* of his efforts in both art and life. Hesse's postwar writings continued to be under the sign of that contrast between Castalia and the "world," an attempt to move out of that Castalian redoubt at last and to respond to the ringing claim of living history that had been sounded in his novel by Father Jakobus, the figure representing Jakob Burckhardt.

While the war had still been in progress, the claim of history had remained confined to literature. After the war, however, both personal and historical events in the world at large had led Hesse to evoke the same principles in his life. As he collected his political essays of World War I and added some of the writings he had composed after World War II, he put a book together that he hoped could stand up as his political testimony. Published hastily in 1946 with the by no means modest title *War and Peace*, the little book sought to allay two difficulties at once: the charge in some quarters that he had once more been a safe bystander in Switzerland, that he had withdrawn from the fray, and, on the other hand, the charge that he might have lent too much support, however tacit, to the Nazi government and the war. In a foreword to the book, written during the early postwar months, Hesse invoked Burkhardt's guiding spirit. Noting that three influences had fashioned him, he enumerated them as his Pietist Christian home with its international spirit, the wisdom of the great Chinese thinkers, and "the one historian to whom I have ever been devoted in confidence, veneration, and grateful emulation: Jakob Burkhardt."[7]

In this spirit 1945 moved into its final quarter. Mail service with Germany had not yet been reopened and Hesse had to employ all kinds of stratagems to stay in touch with his sisters, mostly by using official and diplomatic connections. At one point he reported that the vice consul who had forwarded mail for him had been transferred and that therefore he had to find another route—which he evidently did. Actually, it did not take too long for regular mail service to be restored just a few months later, but indirect communication had been in operation for him for some time. His letters to Adis were often as chatty about minutiae as they had been in old times.

Hesse reported at length about their celebration of Ninon's fiftieth birthday. He had gathered a large bunch of flowers for her—the finest roses, zinnias, dahlias, and anemones—and had presented them to her in the morning. His main present, however, had not yet arrived. It was the best of five portraits of Hesse that Ernst Morgenthaler had painted that late spring and summer. It was not yet available for presentation because it was still being shown in an exhibition. However, Martin, who, like his mother, was a professional photographer, had done five nearly life-size photographs of the original canvases and displayed them in a large portfolio on the gift table. These details were, of course, carefully selected to entertain his sister, who was interested in such things, but they also illustrate the extent to which their lives flowed on at an even pace.

Like a thunderbolt out of a clear sky, however, a small incident that fall gave rise to a conflagration in October. It came as a violent counterstatement to that continuing exchange in which Hesse had been engaged for the past thirty years, since the beginning of the First World War, between his unpolitical stance, his refusal to be drawn into political action, and his antiwar, individualistic, and antichauvinist values. Clearly, the last section of the *Rigi Diary* had been a response to pleas from German friends who had wanted him to speak out against the Allies and the concept of "collective guilt." Now another voice was heard—from one of those former émigrés who had already annoyed him during the thirties. In a fit of pettiness perhaps attributed to his age, Hesse com-

mitted an error of judgment. This lapse, however, expressed his personality completely, as indeed it agreed with his strangely involved
detachment from most events on the European scene.

It began innocently enough. As Hesse describes it, Swabian friends
told him that a newspaper in Stuttgart, edited by the American Army of
Occupation, had reprinted his poem "On Toward Peace" from the Swiss
journal *Die Weltwoche*. The two final lines, so Hesse's version goes,
had been omitted, which distorted the meaning of the poem. He thereupon sent a note to the editor of that paper, protesting against the un-
authorized publication of the poem and against its mutilation by several
German papers published by the American Army of Occupation.

Actually, Hesse was most annoyed. To begin with, it had been printed
without his permission, and he had always felt that copyright infringe-
ments belonged to the greater sins society can inflict on authors whose
livelihood was derived from their writings, and he refused to make an
exception in 1945. But the misplaced comma and the omitted lines that
he claimed to have perceived made it worse. The indignant letter to the
American authorities evidently contained the word "barbarism" to indicate that lapse—a rather unfortunate choice of a noun in a writer who
was usually so sensitive to words. It was made worse by the fact that the
American captain in charge of these publications was one of those
former émigrés who had been an annoyance to Hesse in the past. The
officer concerned was Hans Habe, an Austrian refugee, himself a fairly
well-known writer in civilian life.

Habe's response was as virtriolic (and as impolitic) as Hesse's inter-
vention had been foolish. Writing from Bad Nauheim, headquarters of
the 12th U.S. Army Group, on October 8, Habe began by stating
sardonically that the poem had been cleared for reprinting during a week
he had not been at his desk. If he had been on duty it would not have
been reprinted—but not for the reasons Hesse had in mind. Habe made
clear that armies of occupation are beyond the copyright law. "Protection
of the author is an important matter; an even more important matter is
to contribute to the work the American Army has accomplished in
Germany and is still accomplishing in its effort to prevent a Third World
War." He then turned to the word "barbarism" and made the expected
observation: "I know precisely how painful it can be for an author to see
only a word misprinted, a comma misplaced. But we who have not observed the events of this world from the sunny perspective of Ticino, we
still believe that barbarism in our century does not mean the rape of a
comma." And he naturally mentioned the horrors of Belsen and
Auschwitz, the conquest of Czechoslovakia, Poland, and Holland, the
deportation of slave laborers from France and Belgium and the gassing

of Jews, the People's Courts and concentration camps for dissident Germans, before making clear that he would have prevented the publication of Hesse's poem in his papers for ideological, not grammatical, reasons. In a ringing voice, not unlike Zola's famous "J'Accuse" of the Dreyful case, Habe declared:

> While the best German minds raised their voices from exile against the barbarism of concentration camps and book burnings, while Thomas Mann, Stefan Zweig, Franz Werfel, Fritz von Unruh shouted their accusations against barbarism into the ether, you sat in Ticino in elegant retirement, for which we don't envy you in the least—an observer of the uncertain outcome. While other German poets, like Ernst Wiechert —to name only one—undertook the heroic, hopeless attempt to fight that very barbarism, so well understood, within Germany, your friends, colleagues, and admirers inside and outside Germany waited in vain for a voice from Switzerland. But that voice was busy battling the barbarism of punctuation.

And he ended with the unkindest cut of all—which Hesse never forgave:

> If you, honored Herr Hesse, believe that you have any claim to an honorarium from our papers, we will be glad to oblige. But in a justification for Hermann Hesse ever to speak in Germany, we do not believe. For that reason—and not because of that comma—your poem would never have appeared in our newspapers if I would have had the opportunity to prevent it.

Hesse was deeply wounded. He sent copies of this letter to many of his friends and colleagues, including Thomas Mann, and again considered legal action. He was in touch with the same lawyer and friend who helped him before—Conrad Haussmann in Constance. In general, Hesse reacted precisely as he had done in 1915 in the matter of the "Cologne calumny" and again in 1936 in the matter of Will Vespers. And once more he indulged in irrelevancies. There would have been much to criticize in Habe's intemperate statement, which clearly continued the feud Hesse had been engaged in since the thirties. Clearly, this was not the time to indulge in subtleties. As an emissary of allied propaganda, Habe was not required to recognize ambiguities and ambivalences. But Hesse, a serious writer, was not required on his part to recognize one-sided propaganda. Once again he could have either ignored the attack or answered its substance.

Instead, Hesse moved with surprising speed, focusing on mere personal counterallegations. Typical is a note to Erwin Ackerknecht. Hesse was in rather frequent correspondence with him at the time. Ackerknecht's son lived in New York (working at the Museum of Natural History), and

Hesse served as an intermediary for their correspondence, since it was still easier to get mail through to Germany from Switzerland than directly from the United States. Though he treated it with studied lightness, the subject of Habe could not be repressed. Hesse enclosed the offending letter as early as October and added: "Just for fun, I'm adding another letter, from an American captain and press officer who wants to banish me from German literature. Funny people." Having confirmed that Habe's original name was Bekessy, moreover, Hesse proceeded to point out: "The father of that Bekessy was that famous Viennese Bekessy whom Karl Kraus [a writer and dramatist who had died in the thirties] had exposed as impossible and chased out of Vienna after a wild career as blackmailer and revolver journalist. What monkeyshines!"

The irrelevance of Habe's parentage was as ridiculous as the stir Habe had created in response to a simple letter of complaint. However, there was some substance for Hesse to worry about. Habe's threat to prohibit him from speaking in Germany suggested that his work might be forbidden by the American army as it had been previously forbidden by the Nazis. Yet this constant reiteration of the story about Habe's forebear—those alleged misdeeds of that lamented father, which he repeated to Thomas Mann as well as to his family and friends—did not address itself to the point.[8] Hesse was still worried as late as December when he wrote Adis: "The matter of the alleged American prohibition of my writings is only half as bad as it looks. First of all, it affects only newspapers run by America, and I'm not in the least interested in that collaboration. Secondly, it was not a consequence of systematic action but only of the action of a single individual who had fun dressing me down. I have not answered him." He ended by suggesting he had powerful support: "You can gather how we look at it from the letter by Thomas Mann that I sent you." But while he tried to give the whole matter an air of relative unimportance, it actually had become his *cause célèbre* of the 1940s.

Eventually, Hesse felt he had to reply. With the assistance of powerful friends like Mann, his complaints were sent as high up as President Truman, and apparently a reprimand of sorts was sent down the political ladder to Captain Habe. Thomas Mann interceded vigorously, if somewhat ironically, in Hesse's behalf, and so did many others.[9] Meanwhile, the wide distribution of Habe's letter among Hesse's friends did not escape the attention of the Swiss press, who, contrary to Hesse's usual expectations, came sharply to his defense. For this incident surrounding a prominent writer who was a Swiss citizen was beginning to assume international proportions.[10] Consequently, Habe wrote once more in January. He had not yet dropped his hostility (he was to modify his stance some time later), but rather reprimanded Hesse for having stirred up a campaign against him through the press in Switzerland. In a sense—if perhaps not in a technical sense—this was undoubtedly true. It may have even been justified, given Hesse's need to "clear his name" in an inevitably paranoid time. But Hesse's response was to deny his role altogether.

In replying to Habe's second letter Hesse composed three answers, two of which he did not send but kept carefully on file. The first unsent letter, written immediately after he had received Habe's, was written in the third person and was evidently intended for American authorities. It made clear that Hesse was not a German emigrant, but that he had been a resident of Switzerland for thirty-four years and was a Swiss citizen, a statement he had made lamely ten years earlier in his abortive defense against Will Vespers. As the subject of a neutral country, moreover, he could not speak out in wartime, though this statement neglects that he had not been very outspoken during the prewar thirties either. However, Hesse also made some valid points. His Jewish wife had lost almost all her relatives during the years of terror, and he could not have been immune to that tragedy. Close friends had languished in the camps and prisons of the Gestapo, and any provocation might have been their death sentence. On the other hand, Herr Habe knew nothing of Hesse's many years of working for the emigrants' cause, nor did he consider his literary work, which had been in itself a protest against Hitler. Be that as it may, Hesse insisted that the threats of the Swiss press to boycott and blacklist his opponent had not been of his making. On the contrary, he had made every effort to suppress them.

The letter Hesse finally dispatched in January was more official, colder, and more cautious. It rejected the attack of October simply by stating that his adversary could have found out the truth about him, had he cared. Since he did not, Hesse also did not care to work for publications run by the Americans. The response in the Swiss press, about which Habe had complained, had been caused by rumors that had penetrated to the public from his innermost circle of friends. Hesse claimed he had been as surprised and outraged as his opponent and had telephoned several newspapers, including the offending *Neue Zürcher Zeitung*. He had also lodged a complaint with the Swiss Writers' Union for having in its turn complained to the American Embassy. Why Hesse felt the need for all these denials is not altogether clear, for he also could not help but feel buoyed by these moves to sustain him.[11]

This incident deserves attention primarily because it sheds further light on Hesse's ambivalence, even in his old age, which inevitably found its reflection in his politics. In a strange way, both he and his assailant had been right. They had only exaggerated. But this and similar affairs after the end of the war were at least partly responsible for Hesse's renewed interest in politics, and for his revival of the spirit and attitudes of 1919 when he had also resolved an ambivalent position after years of uncertainty. This episode, and episodes like it, contributed to the final gap in Hesse's long career, for the world was never offered another major work after *The Glass Bead Game*, although he lived for twenty more years after its completion. The 1940s, when he still could have written a sustained work, were filled with his need to redeem himself. He gave this last productive span to collections and essays, many of a political nature, and to endless, self-justifying correspondence. Until 1950, when he was seventy-three, his views of matters German, of war and peace, of chauvinism versus individual worth, remained his main preoccupations and concerns. Finally, these attacks on his political integrity connected Hesse with the past, with his one *real* emigration to Ticino in 1919 when he had literally changed his life and started anew on the way within. In 1946, it served to strengthen the Castalian security of Montagnola and to supply it with suitable fortifications.

Hesse was plagued by his political readjustment, for his sympathies were truly in the middle. He had never been in any way even mildly understanding of the Nazi regime and had always found it to be anathema to everything he stood for. Yet he had remained aloof. Habe was not wrong when he criticized Hesse for having remained in his "elegant retirement" in Ticino. As a political writer, Hesse upheld antinationalistic, antiwar sentiments, yet we saw how he turned on Humm, a friend of many years' standing, for even suggesting that the creation of Castalia had been a political act of noninvolvement during the war years. At the same time, he was overjoyed when he heard reports of German recruits during the war having spent nights copying his *Tree of Life*. The only member of that squad who survived the war showed the notebook to Hesse. It gave him great pleasure.

If Hesse seemed to be in the middle of postwar controversies, he nonetheless meted out harsh judgment to those who claimed to have been opposed to the regime yet who had benefited from it greatly. His old friend "Ugel" Finckh had survived intact. Although he had been a Nazi official, nothing untoward had happened to him. Hesse pretended great admiration for his ability to write at length about his children and grandchildren without ever even alluding to his political involvements of the past. He wrote him several times, calling his past to his former friend's attention, especially a long letter of reconciliation in 1947 in which he tried to fix Finckh's responsibility for his past actions. But by far the greatest effort in his political writings of the time went into clarifying his own position. Two letters written in 1946, which were made part of his collection of political essays, were especially instrumental as statements of belief. One of these was a long letter to Adis, the other to a "young German."[12] Both letters were actually articles on a by then familiar theme: although Germans had suffered a great deal from the effects of the war, they had also suffered morally because they had supported a blind and corrupt nationalism. Worse still, they now denied their own complicity, without which the regime could not have functioned. The only way that fateful acquiescence could be turned to better advantage in the postwar world was to assert a common humanity above nationalistic divisions.

Late in 1946, the book of essays entitled *War and Peace: Reflections on War and Politics Since 1914* was published by Fetz and Wasmuth in Zurich (to be reissued in Berlin in 1949 with various additions). As time went on, however, the urgencies of the war began to fade and life in Montagnola returned to normal. Hesse once more discovered his pains and commented on Ninon's ailments as well. If he once more headed for trouble, he also approached the greatest honors of his life.

III

Whatever may have been the lingering consequences of that tempest in a teapot surrounding Hans Habe, it was soon dwarfed by the news that Hesse had received the Nobel Prize for Literature for his *Glass Bead Game*. Thomas Mann had recommended and supported him. It was a singular honor not only for him personally but also for the institution of German literature to which, despite all the arguments about his Swiss citizenship, he naturally belonged. It was, in fact, a liberating event for many Germans to see a German writer honored so soon after the end of the war.

Hesse did not travel to Stockholm, but he sent the usual, though in his case rather truncated, message. It was a very brief statement, less than two pages, that he sent for the Nobel celebrations on the occasion of Alfred Nobel's birthday on December 10. His apologies were linked to a statement about his sacrifice to National Socialism. He could not attend, because his always fragile health had been totally ruined by the heavy stress he had to suffer since 1933, which had ruined his entire life's work in Germany, and had burdened him with ever heavier duties. He then took the opportunity to stress international understanding and culture while at the same time expressing his gratitude that a poet and a work in the German language had been chosen for the honor as an evident gesture of reconciliation after the war. Finally, he praised his Swedish

hosts, and Sweden as a country, for its international spirit and its individual culture that would not infringe upon the wealth of differentiation
in human culture as a whole.[13]

These words were read at the celebration. But although neither Hermann nor Ninon Hesse went to Stockholm to receive the honor, a celebration took place on December 10. Since the end of October Hesse had been
in a new therapeutic setting, for it was actually true, as he suggested in
his brief message to the Nobel Prize committee, that he had suffered a
physical and emotional decline since the end of the war and in the face
of the constant need to justify himself. They decided on a place called
Marin near Neuchâtel in the French-speaking section of Switzerland.
They traveled to Bern on October 26, saw Martin for coffee, then were
taken by Max Wassmer to the health resort near Neuchâtel by car. He
was to be under the care of Dr. Riggenbach, who had been recommended for Hesse's various ailments. Ninon stayed with him a couple of
days, then went on to Montagnola to close the house and dismiss the
maid before going on a trip of her own. In mid-November Hesse spent
some time in Baden for a renewed attack of sciatica, but early in
December he was back in Marin.

A surprise party took place in any event, although Hesse had not
wanted it at first. Ninon had insisted on staying with him on the day the
Prize was conferred and they had invited Dr. Riggenbach and his wife
for a festive meal in the country. The restaurant celebration, however,
was unexpectedly cancelled and the Hesses were invited instead to spend
the evening at the doctor's house, where the surprise occurred. Hesse
described the festivities to Adis with obvious relish. A huge fire was lit in
the fireplace. The Hesses were asked to be seated on a small sofa,
whereupon Mrs. Riggenbach disappeared. For a moment they were
alone in the large room; then a door opened and a small choir of five
women and girls and three men (the doctor among them) appeared
to serenade him. Hesse was a little embarrassed, but then he rose
and thanked them all. But no sooner had they sat down again when
a red-cheeked, blonde little girl of four emerged from one of the old
high doors of the grand room, followed by a series of children each
taller and older than the last, until the procession was concluded with
the doctor's own teen-aged children. Each gave him a present and
spoke a verse composed by the doctor's wife. After that they ate a festive
meal (most of the children and serenaders who did not belong to the
family having said their farewells). A banquet was held in the large dining room around a table bedecked with beautiful old china and flowers:
trout, roast chicken, and special wines. The old servant arrived with a
tray full of telegrams, but they had all been manufactured by the doctor's

wife. One wire was from Gustavus Adolphus of Sweden; another one was from Heaven signed "Knulp"; a third one from Noah's Ark; and a fourth directly from Mount Sinai. The moment almost made him forget the aching legs he had come to cure.

Earlier that year Hesse had also received the Goethe Prize from the West German government, which Ninon accepted for him. He wrote a somewhat longer appreciative speech than he had composed for the Nobel Prize. He began by mentioning his hesitation about accepting the prize, since it might imply that he had made peace with official Germany, which had deprived him of his life's work during the war. Then, however, he had changed his mind because he wanted to warn those very officials who had bestowed the prize, as well as German posterity, against the twin evils he held responsible for the terrible condition in which they all found themselves: the hubris of technology and that of nationalism. It was, so he held in his written statement, to call for battle against these two diseases in the spirit of Goethe that he had consented to accept the prize. In this spirit he ended his statement on a positive note:

> And so our Europe, mortally ill, having renounced its leading, active role, may perhaps become again a concept freighted with high value, a quiet reservoir, a treasure of the noblest recollections. It may become thus a refuge of souls in the sense perhaps in which until now my friends have used the magic word of the "East."[14]

Literary efforts continued, but except for occasional stories, essays, and poems, most of Hesse's late publications were new editions of past work. He brought out a fine collection of fairy tales, short stories, and sketches he had done since the twenties in a new volume entitled *Dream Trail*. He also began to collect poems for further volumes. But he was also concerned about his health.

It was not Hesse's way to accept stability lightly, no matter how much he sought to attain it in house and marriage, politics and work. He suffered a collapse in 1947, of which the stay in Marin during the previous year had been a harbinger, which he partly attributed to a new wave of petty annoyances. As he confided to Erwin Ackerknecht, he now felt abused by German publishers. During the Nazi years he had been suspect in spite of his caution and they were then reticent to work with him. But now, since he had received those prestigious prizes, they had begun to publish work without his permission. "How much the attitude of German publishers toward me during the past two years has contributed to my collapse I cannot say," he wrote his friend, for even as he was feted on his seventieth birthday with singular honors he felt pursued by neglect. His German friends never cared for him and his countrymen—despite all the Swiss sacrifices—to help them in their defeat. No one "has ever taken the smallest step in my behalf." He continued to chide the Germans who sent dozens of letters every day "quite in the old German tone," assuring him of German innocence and asking him and his Swiss countrymen to turn their criticism on the Allies. He ended a particularly strong statement with the remark that in a few days he would allow himself "or what is still left of me" to be taken to a clinic "for lengthy examinations and similar tortures."

The destination was Lausanne, where he was taken by car. His ailment was diagnosed as "polyarthritis," which was to be cured by injections. But it is quite possible that this was already the time when his severe illness was discovered. In her eulogy in 1962 Ninon revealed he had died of leukemia, which was never acute except for the last few months, but which, so she wrote, had been with him in a latent state for many years.[15] The strange doings at Lausanne—the high hopes followed by an announcement of failure—may have been an early encounter with that disease, which, in retrospect, places many of Hesse's complaints in a new perspective.

A long letter to Adis from Bremgarten at Whitsun described an outing in Wassmer's car. They managed to visit his sons Martin and Bruno and the latter's wife Kläri in nearby Oschwand. They also allowed themselves to be fed coffee, cake, and wine by the wife of the painter Amiet, whom they visited unannounced. Plans for the seventieth birthday celebration were still afoot. It was to take place in Bremgarten, for Hesse was slated to receive an honorary doctor's degree from the University of Bern, although he was unwilling to subject himself to public ceremonies. In fact, the birthday was properly celebrated on July 2. Family and friends appeared, and much attention was paid him on the occasion, but a typical aside to Adis suggests that he was still alert to slights. The timing of that honorary degree from the university seemed to him rather late. He had discovered that he had been expected to receive this honor ten years earlier but had been blackballed. This reflection, in turn, gave rise to the thought that he had also been nominated for the Nobel Prize time and again, but that the German ambassador in Stockholm had prevented it each time.[16]

In the fall Adis joined him for a while in Montagnola to nurse him while Ninon was often ill and on journeys mostly in Hesse's behalf. He had been well enough for the ceremonial birthday, which Suhrkamp had made specially attractive by presenting him with a handsome new edition of his collected works, but his health was always precarious. Nonetheless, the context in which his final new life took shape was firm and well ordered. He was in place in Montagnola interrupted only by various trips to cure his aches and pains both physical and spiritual. During the last decades of his life, when he received many tributes, he appeared increasingly placid to the public eye, while actually his painful loss of eyesight seriously troubled him more and more and his sciatica became an impediment.

Gradually, prosperity came to the Hesses as German money finally began its flow and his sales increased with the resurgence of his popularity during the late forties. The Hesses enlarged their house, and in 1948 they made a purchase that would have been a sin in *Steppenwolf* days: Ninon acquired a car. This entailed laborious driving lessons and impromptu trips into the country to give her a chance to practice. It also involved the building of a garage. Friends came and went in their new, solid world surrounding house and garden. The Manns arrived several times and were put up in the Hotel Bellevue near the center of the village, where the Hesses often went to eat. At the same time, Hesse's correspondence remained voluminous and he even did some new writing, mostly of verse. During those final years Hesse published two volumes of new poetry as late as 1953 and dictated a sufficient number of poems to Ninon for her to put together a posthumous volume for him in 1963.

During the fifties, Hesse drew further into himself, into that garden he had associated with the Chinese Elder Brother, into the study where Ninon read to him and received his dictation. He put up a sign at the gate of the Casa Bodmer asking visitors not to disturb him. As the crises within and around him began to lose their bite, he truly became the hermit he always wanted to be.

At last some of the questions that had pursued him began to be resolved, though life and controversy still touched him. The person who was closest to him, his sister Adis, died in 1949: she had survived his admonishing letter of 1945 by just four years. In 1950 he embroiled himself in two angry exchanges. One concerned a bizarre and protracted affair involving an archivist, Erich Weiss, who had founded a Hesse collection in the Rhineland, which was later moved to Marbach and formed the nucleus of the archives at the Schiller National Museum, where they are still on deposit. He branded Weiss a confidence man in numerous circular letters because he had gone about soliciting manuscripts and letters. The affair was vastly exaggerated, but it engaged the old man in a way that made him feel alive and sense the old furies. More serious was the continuing problem involving the Suhrkamp and Fischer settlements. Peter Suhrkamp was sued, and Hesse was asked once more to take sides by both members to the dispute, Peter Suhrkamp and

Gottfried Bermann, both former and present friends.[17] He found the Suhrkamps "tired old people" who had never recovered from the war and their legal battles, but their correspondence suggests the strong ties between them. In the argument with Fischer, Hesse remained firmly with Suhrkamp.

Marulla, the last of his siblings, died in 1953, and Hesse entered into complicated procedures to save her estate, because her literary possessions involved many of his letters, which he wanted to preserve. On that occasion he wrote to Ackerknecht, who was now working as a librarian in the Schiller Museum's library in Marbach: "Whether [his papers in Marulla's estate] will interest posterity, whether [there] will even be a posterity for our world, yours or mine, we need not discuss. Where we now stand we must act as though we can answer that question in the affirmative." The same words could have been spoken about all his letters, for his correspondence remains the richest documentation of his life.

Honors continued to come to him. In 1955 he received the Peace Prize of the German Book Trade. Ninon traveled to Frankfurt to accept it for him in the presence of Hesse's old friend of the days of *März*, Theodor Heuss, who had become president of the Federal Republic. More significant were the accolades he received two years later on his eightieth birthday. Peter Suhrkamp presented him with yet another new edition of his works, and Martin Buber spoke in his honor. That speech, "Hermann Hesse in the Service of the Spirit," describes the new direction of Hesse's works after the First World War: "In 1917, after a number of books that took pleasure in their own narrative virtuosity and that were happily received as such, Hesse entered the service of the spirit." And after a pointed discussion of his major narratives from *Demian* to *The Glass Bead Game* Buber concluded: "Hermann Hesse, in his capacity as writer, has served the spirit by telling of the conflict between spirit and life and of the struggle of the spirit against itself. Thereby he has rendered more tangible the obstacle-ridden road that can lead to a new wholeness and unity." Noting that as a human being Hesse had always taken a stand for the wholeness and unity of the human condition, he ended: "It is not just the Journeyers to the East and the Players of the Bead Game all over the world who salute you today, Hermann Hesse. All those who serve the spirit, throughout the entire world, unite in a great greeting of love. Wherever the spirit is served, you are loved."[18] Clearly for Buber the spiritual message of Hermann Hesse's later narratives had absorbed and recreated that difficult psyche to produce a new cultural vision.

Gradually the Hesses' lives began to conform more and more to an old man's pace, although he continued to enjoy his garden and his outdoor walks. Ninon still needed her journeys to Greece which she took as long as she felt she could leave her ailing husband in another's care. In the spring of 1954 she went on a "scholarly tour guided by trained archeologists" and returned "exhausted but most satisfied." Meanwhile, death continued to take his friends all around him. Peter Suhrkamp died in 1959 and many others among his contemporaries died during the 1950s. Two statements to Erwin Ackerknecht, to whom he wrote more and more often in his old age, may typify what he felt as he established the counterpoint of pain to his long life of honors. In May 1954 he wrote about his eyes, which now began to interfere even with his main relaxation, gardening. His eyes were affected so strongly "that I sit around for days with tearing, painful eyes which are good for nothing. When I think of death, the idea that it will mean a cessation of this small private hell of mine makes it most agreeable. Half my life has been dimmed by it." And during the following year, in 1955, he sent Ackerknecht a photograph of himself, visibly aged, his hands clasped in his lap. In the caption, he wrote: "Dear Dr. Ackerknecht: Ja, this is how we sit around when our sack has gone to pot. With warmest regards, your H.H."

As early as 1950, Hesse had already given voice to the feeling that had been with him since his early manhood, but which now, in old age, began to assume a different kind of reality:

Sliding down into old age and weakness has made great progress during this year. How good that our life has its limits, that one is certain of the end. It is the only security in a human life which in other respects the existentialists don't understand very well.

In 1956, announcing another spring journey to Greece by Ninon, he wrote: "Spring is again giving me a great deal of pain. It is a torment until one gets through that final narrow pass."

Their last years until 1962 turned on a more and more quiet life for the aging man, with Ninon taking on some of the relationships and some of the hasty movements from place to place that had marked Hermann Hesse's life. She read to him and continued to take his dictation. She sorted out and presented his correspondence to him as his eyesight failed him more and more. Their friendship with Karl Kerenyi and his wife Magda, which had begun during the 1940s, was by then carried mostly by Ninon, who used Kerenyi's approach for her own Greek studies, corresponded with them, visited with them, and attended the Eranos-Jung lectures in Ascona with punctilious regularity each year.[19] Hesse was beginning to be more and more a consumer of news and ideas she brought to him.

The "narrow pass" was crossed at last six years after he had written those words. According to Ninon, in an open letter to the Suhrkamp Verlag in the fall after his death, Hesse's latent leukemia had flared into an acute stage only in December 1961 as the result of a bout of influenza. At his eighty-fifth birthday on July 2, the celebration was as generous as as ever. More than nine hundred presents, letters, flowers, and telegrams had been received by the end of three days of celebrations (including, among other things, a colorful reproduction of a large bird by an artist, Yargo de Lucca, whom they had not known). The intimate birthday party took place in a restaurant in a village near the St. Gotthard Pass, attended by the closest family and hosted by Max Wassmer. But there were also official fetes. On Saturday night the local "filaminia liberale" serenaded him, and on Sunday Hermann Hesse, an official citizen of Bern, was proclaimed honorary citizen of Montagnola. He responded with a few words in Italian, a language he rarely spoke, although he had lived in their midst half his life. He received an ovation: he was their most famous citizen.[20]

Five weeks later he died, during the night of August 9, 1962, of a brain hemorrhage. In the long open letter to Dr. Siegfried Unseld published in a memorial volume, Ninon described the evening and night of his death in great detail. She also tried to place the events of her husband's last days in a larger perspective. He continued to enjoy the country—walks in woods and mountains—though the effort of walking itself tired him easily. On his last day they went for a walk in a small wood near their property where he enjoyed gathering twigs of firewood for his garden; one twig was still too tough and alive to be broken off. During the afternoon, he conversed about French literature with a woman who had translated *Gertrud* into French, though this may have been the grieving wife's fond memory. But without doubt they listened to a piano sonata by Mozart over the radio, and he wrote a poem about the branch that refused to die. It has now been reproduced in many forms as the last work of Hermann Hesse, which ends, as Ninon ends her account: "The branch in the wood still holds."[21]

On August 11, 1962, Hermann Hesse was buried in the cemetery of S. Abbondio where thirty-five years earlier he had buried his friend Hugo Ball. He had chosen the site carefully in his lifetime. Ninon was led by Max Wassmer. His sons carried the coffin. Like so much in Hesse's life, and now in his death, the ceremony was sanctified in a special publication.

House and garden were now without their master. Ninon lived on and served his memory, attending to his affairs and to the letters which still flowed into the Casa Bodmer. By a strange stroke of fate this woman who was so much younger than he died in 1966 at the age of only seventy-one. The Casa Bodmer has now reverted to the Bodmers' heirs. It did not become a shrine or museum in Hesse's memory, but is occupied by a businessman from Milan. Hermann Hesse's life in Montagnola had come to an end except for a quiet, beautifully designed grave in S. Abbondio. As crisis had come to its rest, that life was already a myth.

EPILOGUE
Pilgrim of Crisis

I

He who in autumn recalls a troublesome
But by no means hapless life,
Who, smiling at his youth, recalls
Those old roads and pilgrimages
Whose common goal had always been hidden
By other goals nearer by,
For him the thought of feasts and festivities
Is far distant as is also the
Pleasure in glory and in honoring applause.
For him, seeking quietude is the more immediate task
To extinguish one self and go out into the woods
Like that Indian King,
To confront, in simplicity and reverence,
The Laws of the Gods.

> —From "Backward Glance—A Fragment
> of ca. 1937"

THESE OPENING LINES from a long fragmentary poem Hesse wrote when he was sixty have often been quoted. In its entirety, the poem was yet another attempt at a "Life Story Briefly Told," an accounting of his creative and personal acts by means of an autobiographical statement. The essence of this statement, written at a time of great crisis—with his tournament with Goebbels's press and his brother's attempted suicide less than two years behind him—called for contemplation. As in *The Glass Bead Game*, on which he was then intermittently at work, Hesse suggests that the confusion of the world of the senses, overcast by the "veil of Maya," had to be countered in concentrated visions directed toward the "center," the seat of all understanding in personal and in universal life. The "old roads and pilgrimages," once his means of overcoming the confused crises of his youth, were now relinquished in favor of an inward route, that old way within now entirely transformed into a contemplative perspective.

393

Throughout the many decades of his life, Hesse had lived as a self-conscious artist who viewed his function as that of a painter not of mores but of the inward features of man whose glory and suffering were beyond time. This inner face was sharply etched as it pictured modern man's alienation from his feelings. The uncertainty with which Hesse has often been charged was, in fact, a sign of his humanity, of his need for and his success in reflecting the inner visions of those around him. In *The Glass Bead Game* Hesse mirrored himself and his time in delicate intellectual imagery. In his art at least, though not in his life, he was thus able to replace the multivarious perception of colorful nature and its built-in conflicts with a spiritual vision in which these conflicts were ultimately reconciled.

II

Hesse's goal could not remain removed to the end of his infinite pilgrimage. The dialectical turn that constitutes the ending of his final large work makes it clear that, however rarefied, the ideal of harmony must be reconciled with life on earth. Like the figures in his novel, Hesse had come full circle to accept life's crises even as he contemplated them with detachment on a loftier plane.

The myth of Hermann Hesse, then, is that of a Pilgrim of Crisis. He gathered his followers and led them from the early days of *Peter Camenzind*, at the beginning of the century, to *The Glass Bead Game*, composed during one of the Western world's most disastrous wars. Each generation of Hesse's admirers had a different reason for its enthusiasm, yet they shared a longing for simplicity, for the conquest of the spirit to which Hesse gave voice and which remained a counterpoint to his life-long conflicts.

The crisis that marked Hesse as a man, and the inconclusive yearning that formed it, bears the stamp of several generations. Above all his antitheses, he always maintained a single theme—an unwavering belief in the ultimate value of the individual—even when it ran counter to the social values around him. He stood aloof as much as was possible in order to preserve himself, but he sensed in the inner divisions that marked his life the dynamic which was to create the images on which all his work was constructed. In trying to realize himself, he had to realize his conflicts—a fact that reflected both his and his readers' crises, and thereby created his appeal. Whenever he was at home, he wanted to be abroad; whenever he wandered, he wanted to stand still. Whenever he sought an ascetic spirituality, he looked for the fluidity of the senses.

Yet these were not merely banal oppositions that may have engaged his young readers. They were, in fact, the elements that determined the crisis of the culture he had portrayed as a poet of the West.

Hesse's message to his readers was elitist and disdainful of the masses, yet throughout the world vast numbers of young people (and many not so young) have read and continue to read his work. The "Hesse phenomenon" has its roots in that immediate response to personal and social crises, which Hesse mirrored within himself—a response in which choices become impossible but where a new symbolic perspective may project a fresh insight, confronting, like that Indian king of the poem, "the Laws of the Gods" in simplicity and reverence.

Hesse's strength lies in his double and often triple vision. Gifted with words, he gave voice to that exile which had left him outside at the age of six. Separated from his home, he strove back to the light where his family sat. The need to be independent and yet to be at home remains a need to which young people respond when turning to Hesse during times of crises. Whatever the wider import of the symbols he used and developed, the solutions conveyed to many of his readers were plain and neat. Obscuring his elitism, his conventionality, the contradictory attitudes that lie behind his work—obscuring even the simplistic thought that mars many of his books—these symbols, in presenting Hesse as a mythic *persona*, a pilgrim whose voice reads as a sacred script, have rendered him a powerful influence on several generations.

Hesse's message of wholeness that can never be whole, of exile that strives toward but can never reach home, emerges fragmentarily from his many novels, stories, and poems. But Hermann Hesse delivered this message most powerfully in his life, which he committed to paper in the rich correspondence that began in his childhood. It is this life that lends coherence to his struggle, and it is to this life that this book has been dedicated. In this critique of a driven yet deeply understanding man lies the love that every biographer must feel for his subject.

Notes

Prologue: A Perspective

1. Peter de Mendelssohn observed the same quality in an incisive essay, "Repräsentanz des Aussenseiters," *Über Hermann Hesse*, ed. Volker Michels (Frankfurt: Suhrkamp Verlag, 1977), II, 140–48. Some of the above passages have been adapted from my essay, "*Person* and *Persona*: The Magic Mirrors of *Steppenwolf*," *Hesse: A Collection of Critical Essays*, ed. Theodore Ziolkowski (Englewood Cliffs, N.J.: Prentice Hall, 1973), pp. 153–79.

2. See Ralph Freedman, "Hermann Hesse im Wandel der Krisen," Symposium Essay in Honor of Hermann Hesse's 100th Birthday. Marbach, Germany, April 1977. Note especially the Foreword and pp. 1–7, 27–28.

3. Hesse himself almost uncannily referred to his capacity of serving as a mirror for his readers. In a letter "to a reader seeking advice," dated ca. 1930–31, he wrote: "But this Hesse [whom you address] is your mirror, and what you call out to him, you should call out to your own self, the good as well as the bad." Clearly, Hesse here refused to be a mirror for his correspondent, but his very use of this image is instructive. It should be noted that unlike other, more extensive collections of Hesse's correspondence, this small book of letters was selected by Hesse himself. *Briefe*, 2d ed. (Frankfurt: Suhrkamp Verlag, 1965), pp. 46–47.

4. Detailed information about Hesse's reception in America is contained in Theodore Ziolkowski's essay, "Hermann Hesse in den U.S.A.," Symposium Essay in Honor of Hermann Hesse's 100th Birthday. Marbach, Germany, April 1977. Further by Ziolkowski: "Saint Hesse Among the Hippies," *American-German Review* XXXV (1969): 18–23; and "Hesse's Sudden Popularity with Today's Students," *University: A Princeton Quarterly* XLV (1970): 19–25. For a comparative assessment of German and American reactions to Hesse, see also Egon Schwarz, "Hermann Hesse, the American Youth Movement, and Problems of Literary Evaluation," *PMLA* LXXXV (1970): 977–87. See also Volker Michels, "Hermann Hesse: Perennial Author of the Young Generation. The Writer's Renaissance and Its Causes," tr. Patricia Crampton, supplement to *Hermann Hesse: A Pictorial Biography* (New York: Farrar, Straus & Giroux, 1975).

A history of Hesse's reception from the point of view of the American counterculture is traced in Fred Haines, "Hermann Hesse und die amerikanische Subkultur," tr. into German by Ursula Michels-Wenz, *Materialien zu Hermann Hesses "Der Steppenwolf"* (Frankfurt: Suhrkamp Verlag, 1972), pp. 388–400. A negative evaluation, especially in relation to Hesse's impact on the so-called "hippie culture" can be found in George Steiner, "Eastward Ho," *The New Yorker*, 1969, pp. 87–97. Another negative assessment, directed more toward American college students, was made by Jeffrey L. Sammons, "Hermann Hesse and the Over-Thirty Germanist," *Hesse: A Collection of Critical Essays*, pp. 112–33. Finally, a good summary of Hesse's American reception, including statistical data, can be found in Rudolf Koester, "U.S.A.," *Hermann Hesses Weltweite Wirkung*, ed. Martin Pfeifer (Frankfurt: Suhrkamp Verlag, 1977), pp. 155–71.

5. Haines, "Hermann Hesse und die amerikanische Subkultur," p. 391.

6. Timothy Leary and Ralph Metzner, "Hermann Hesse: Poet of the Interior Journey," *Psychedelic Review* 1 (1963): 167–82.

7. Essays on Hesse's reputation in various European and Asian countries (though not in South America) are contained in *Hesses Weltweite Wirkung*. Fred Haines directs attention to the discrepancy between Hesse's established reputation in his own country and the subterranean role he has played in America. "I believe we were all rather surprised when years later we discovered that in his native country Hermann Hesse was in no way considered an underground writer." Haines also dealt with the argument that the American appreciation of Hesse was detached from Hesse's own literary and cultural tradition and commented, after an approving analysis of Timothy Leary's description: "As erroneous as Leary's and Metzner's theory may have been from a *literary point of view*, its *social effect* was of *immense importance*, because it moved Hesse into the foreground as precisely the poet who articulated the goals and ideals of the American counterculture most precisely." "Hermann Hesse und die amerikanische Subkultur," pp. 389, 399. [Italics mine.]

8. Ziolkowski, "Hermann Hesse in den U.S.A.," pp. 19f.

Chapter 1: Childhood and Its Discontents

1. Hugo Ball, *Hermann Hesse: Sein Leben und Werk* (Frankfurt: Suhrkamp Verlag, 1956), p. 21. (Special edition in Hugo Ball's honor. The first edition was published by S. Fischer Verlag, Berlin, in 1927).

2. Material for the background of Hermann Hesse's family was gathered from Ninon Hesse, "Nachwort," *Kindheit und Jugend vor Neunzehnhundert: Hermann Hesse in Briefen und Lebenszeugnissen, 1877–1895* (Frankfurt: Suhrkamp Verlag, 1966); Adele Gundert, *Marie Hesse: Ein Lebensbild in Briefen und Tagebüchern* (Stuttgart: Gundert Verlag, n.d.); various published biographies, as well as some hand-written manuscripts cited in the text and the notes. Unpublished manuscripts are on deposit in the Hesse Archives, Deutches Literaturarchiv, Schiller Nationalmuseum, Marbach, Germany, and are reprinted by permission of Suhrkamp Verlag, who hold the copyright.

3. Gundert, *Marie Hesse*, p. 6.

4. Ibid., p. 8.

5. Ibid., p. 11.

6. Ibid., pp. 57–58.

7. Ibid., p. 67.

8. Ibid., pp. 143–49.

9. Cited in N. Hesse, *Kindheit und Jugend*, p. 529.

10. To Adele Gundert, December 13, 1944. Unpublished letters from the Depositum of the Schiller Nationalmuseum in Marbach, Germany, will usually *not* be footnoted. Dates and correspondents will be noted in the text.

11. N. Hesse, *Kindheit und Jugend*, pp. 526–27.

12. Ibid., pp. 549–50.

13. Gundert, *Marie Hesse*, pp. 157–58.

14. Ibid., pp. 157–58.

15. *Hermann Lauscher, Gesammelte Werke* [Hereafter referred to as *Werkausgabe*.] (Frankfurt: Suhrkamp Verlag, 1970), I, 218–19.

16. *Eine Stunde Hinter Mitternacht, Werkausgabe*, I, 202.

17. N. Hesse, *Kindheit und Jugend*, pp. 9–10.

18. See Bernhard Zeller, *Hermann Hesse in Selbstzeugnissen und Bild-Dokumenten* (Hamburg: Rowohlt Taschenbuch, 1963), p. 14. Cf. Bernhard Zeller *Portrait of Hesse: An Illustrated Biography*, tr. Mark Hollebone (New York: Herder and Herder, 1971), pp. 15–16.

19. The following letter by Marie to her husband on August 2, 1881, is illuminating: "Herzensjohnny: . . . Pray with me for Hermännle, and pray for me that I may have the strength to bring him up. I feel as though my physical strength were insufficient; the boy possesses a vitality, a gigantic strength, a powerful will, and truly a sort of astonishing intelligence for his four years. Where is it going? It literally eats away at me—this inner battle with his high tyrannic spirit. . . . God must begin to work on this proud sensibility, then something noble and splendid may become of him, but I shudder at the thought of what could become of this passionate person with a false or weak upbringing." Gundert, *Marie Hesse*, p. 208.

20. N. Hesse, *Kindheit und Jugend*, pp. 12–13; Gundert, *Marie Hesse*, pp. 230–31.

21. N. Hesse, *Kindheit und Jugend*, p. 14.

22. Ibid., p. 13. See also Adele Gundert's notation that in the Sunday School Hesse remained a model pupil. Gundert, *Marie Hesse*, p. 231.

23. N. Hesse, *Kindheit und Jugend*, pp. 14–15.

24. The pamphlets were published by the Calwer Verlagsverein, Calw, under the directorship of Dr. Hermann Gundert and his successor, Johannes Hesse. They are now available at the Basel Mission Institute and in the library of Basel University.

25. N. Hesse, *Kindheit und Jugend*, pp. 15–16; Gundert, *Marie Hesse*, p. 238.

26. "Kurzgefasster Lebenslauf," *Werkausgabe*, VI, 403–04. "Life Story Briefly Told," *Autobiographical Writings*, ed. Theodore Ziolkowski, tr. Denver Lindley (New York: Farrar, Straus & Giroux, 1973), p. 55.

27. "Kindheit des Zauberers," *Werkausgabe*, VI, 374–78. "Childhood of the Magician," *Autobiographical Writings*, pp. 6–9. See also "Grossväterliches," *Werkausgabe*, X, 302–11. In translation: "About Grandfather," *Autobiographical Writings*, pp. 34–43.

28. N. Hesse, *Kindheit und Jugend*, p. 22.

29. Ibid., pp. 30–31.

30. See long letter by Marie about Hesse's school situation to her son Karl Isenberg in which she shows herself quite optimistic about Hermann's chances in the school. Reprinted in Gundert, *Marie Hesse*, pp. 244–45.

31. N. Hesse, *Kindheit und Jugend*, pp. 117–18.

32. *Werkausgabe*, II, 107–08; *Beneath the Wheel* tr. Michael Roloff (New York: Bantam Books, 1970), p. 125.

33. H. Hesse, "Kurzgefasster Lebenslauf," *Werkausgabe*, VI, 394–95. "Life Story Briefly Told," *Autobiographical Writings*, pp. 46–47.

34. Gundert, *Marie Hesse*, pp. 249–51; N. Hesse, *Kindheit und Jugend*, pp. 180–82.

35. Letter from Marie to Karl Isenberg, March 13, 1892. Gundert, *Marie Hesse*, pp. 249–51.

36. N. Hesse, *Kindheit und Jugend*, pp. 233–34. Joseph Mileck indicates that several decades later Hesse made Eugenie Kolb the model of his Beatrice in *Demian*. See *Hermann Hesse: Life and Art* (Berkeley: University of California Press, 1977), p. 91.

37. Ibid., pp. 265–66. The entire letter, pp. 257–66.

38. Ibid., p. 268.

39. Ibid., p. 278.

40. Ibid., p. 323–25. This is the entire letter, comprising the quotations from p. 82 on.

41. From Marie's diary, cited in N. Hesse, *Kindheit und Jugend*, pp. 325–26.

42. See Gundert, *Marie Hesse*, pp. 254–55; N. Hesse, *Kindheit und Jugend*, pp. 356–57.

43. In addition to references in the correspondence reprinted in N. Hesse, *Kindheit und Jugend*, compare Hesse's fictional presentation of this episode in *Beneath the Wheel*: *Werkausgabe*, II, 158ff.

44. Reprinted in N. Hesse, *Kindheit und Jugend*, p. 511.

Chapter 2: The First New Life—
From Bookseller to Author

1. Hermann Hesse was preceded to Tübingen by his sister Marulla. A chatty letter to Hermann on his birthday, written on June 30, 1895, to Calw, describes her participation in a service at the Wurmlinger Chapel as well as her plans to come home within the next few weeks. She soon moved to Stuttgart to begin training as a teacher. For Marulla's letter, see *Kindheit und Jugend*, pp. 495–97.

Quotations from unpublished manuscripts are not footnoted; dates, recipients of letters, etc., are cited in the text. All manuscripts are on deposit in the Hesse Archives, Schiller Nationalmuseum in Marbach, Germany, and are quoted by permission. Some of these materials have been subsequently published in the second volume of *Kindheit und Jugend, 1895–1900.*

2. See the extensive letters Hesse wrote to Ernst Kapff before and after his move to Tübingen. Letters from Calw are reprinted in N. Hesse, *Kindheit und Jugend*, pp. 464–69, 487–93. Letters from Tübingen are contained in *Gesammelte Briefe*, eds. Ursula Michels, Volker Michels, and Heiner Hesse (Frankfurt: Suhrkamp Verlag, 1973), I (1895–1921), 12–17, 19–20.

3. Two long letters to his parents on his studies are of interest as further examples. *Gesammelte Briefe*, I, 17–18, 21–22.

4. See Gundert, *Marie Hesse*, pp. 258–79.

5. *Hermann Lauscher, Werkausgabe*, I, 222–25.

6. *Werkausgabe*, I, 11.

7. Ibid., p. 14.

8. Reprinted in *Hermann Hesse–Helene Voigt-Diederichs: Zwei Autorenporträts in Briefen, 1897–1900* (Diederichs, 1971), pp. 1–5.

9. Ibid., pp. 36–41.

10. *Die Gedichte*, I, 30.

11. Rainer Maria Rilke, *Gesammelte Schriften* (Leipzig: Insel-Verlag, 1930), VII, 462. Cited and discussed in Eike Middell, *Hermann Hesse: Die Bilderwelt seines Lebens* (Leipzig: Philipp Reclam, 1972), p. 52. Cf. Zeller, *Hermann Hesse*, p. 38; Zeller, *Portrait of Hesse*, p. 42; etc.

12. Cf. Bernhard Zeller, "Einleitung," *Briefe: Hesse–Voigt-Diederichs*, p. xii.

13. *Werkausgabe*, I, 240–52.

14. Ibid., p. 261.

15. Ibid., p. 269.

16. To Julie Hellmann, Calw, August 26, 1899, reprinted in *Gesammelte Briefe*, I, 60–63.

17. To Julie Hellmann, Basel, November 28, 1899, ibid., pp. 66–67.

18. Ludwig Finckh, " 'It's from Hesse . . .': A Small Adventure about the Distant Friend in Montagnola" ["Es ist von Hesse: Kleines Erlebnis um den Fernen in Montagnola"], written in 1946, published *Schwäbischer Merkur*, October 18, 1955.

19. *Gesammelte Briefe*, I, 74–75.

20. "Basler Erinnerungen," quoted by Zeller, *Hermann Hesse*, pp. 39–40; Zeller, *Portrait of Hesse*, pp. 43–44.

21. *Werkausgabe*, VI, 396; *Autobiographical Writings*, pp. 47–48.

22. "Beim Einzug in ein Neues Haus," *Werkausgabe*, X, 138; *Autobiographical Writings*, pp. 231–32.

23. Cited by Zeller, *Hermann Hesse*, p. 40; Zeller, *Portrait of Hesse*, pp. 44–45.

24. This relationship is discussed in detail in an unpublished letter to Hesse's parents on October 22, 1899. See also the letter to Helene Voigt-Diederichs, *Briefe, 1897–1900*, p. 109 and in *Gesammelte Briefe*, I, 68–69. Cf. ibid., p. 69n. for a description of the joyful excursions as described in "Basler Erinnerungen."

25. To parents, March 10, 1900, reprinted in *Gesammelte Briefe*, I, 71–73.

26. Ball, *Hermann Hesse*, p. 87.
27. *Werkausgabe*, I, 314.
28. *Werkausgabe*, VI, 198.
29. Reprinted in *Gesammelte Briefe*, I, 88–89.
30. Gundert, *Marie Hesse*, p. 280.

Chapter 3: The Second New Life— The Author and His Household

1. To Cesco Como, May 7, 1902, *Gesammelte Briefe*, I, 89.
2. October 19, 1902, ibid., pp. 90–92.
3. Cf. ibid. p. 93n.
4. February 5, 1903, ibid., pp. 94–96.
5. *Werkausgabe*, XI, 25.
6. Cited by Ball, *Hermann Hesse*, p. 99.
7. The entire exchange is reprinted in *Gesammelte Briefe*, I, 496–97.
8. Ball, *Hermann Hesse*, p. 99.
9. Ibid., p. 103.
10. *Werkausgabe*, XI, 25–26.
11. *Werkausgabe*, VI, 396–97; *Autobiographical Writings*, p. 48.
12. *Werkausgabe*, I, 373–74.
13. An excellent account of inversions and parallels in sexual relations in *Peter Camenzind*, though with a different emphasis, was given in Mark Boulby's study *Hermann Hesse: His Mind and Art* (Ithaca, N.Y.: Cornell University Press, 1967), p. 24 et passim. "In all Hesse's major novels . . . the friendship theme is an introit —or else is played in counterpoint—to the theme of heterosexual love." (p. 24)
14. To the family, April 8, 1903, reprinted in *Gesammelte Briefe*, I, 100.
15. To Cesco Como, June 4, 1903, *Gesammelte Briefe*, I, 104.
16. Ibid.
17. To Cesco Como, June 21, 1903, ibid., pp. 105–07.
18. In addition to the letter to his father of June 24, 1903, cited in the text, which is quoted from the manuscript, Hesse wrote another long letter to his father, dated simply "June 1903," excerpts of which are quoted in *Gesammelte Briefe*, I, 105.
19. To Cesco Como, October 26, 1903, ibid., pp. 109–10.
20. *Werkausgabe*, VI, 117. *Strange News From Another Star*, tr. Denver Lindley (New York: Farrar, Straus & Giroux, 1972), pp. 131–32.
21. Ball, *Hermann Hesse*, p. 104.
22. To Franz Karl Ginzkey, October 27, 1903, *Gesammelte Briefe*, I, 110–11.
23. November 19, 1903, ibid., 113–14.
24. June 3, 1904, ibid., pp. 120–21.
25. June 26, 1904, ibid., pp. 121–22.
26. "Beim Einzug in Ein Neues Haus," *Werkausgabe*, X, 139–40. "On Moving into a New House," *Autobiographical Writings*, pp. 232–33. See letter to Franz Karl Ginzkey, August 12, 1904, *Gesammelte Briefe*, I, 123.
27. September 11, 1904, ibid., pp. 124–26.
28. September 2, 1904, ibid., p. 124.
29. *Werkausgabe*, X, 141–48; *Autobiographical Writings*, pp. 234–40.
30. To Helene Voigt-Diederichs, October 25, 1904, *Gesammelte Briefe*, I, 128.
31. To Hans Bethge, December 26, 1904, ibid., pp. 132–33.
32. January 3, 1905, ibid., p. 133.
33. Ball, *Hermann Hesse*, pp. 117–22.
34. "Im Philisterland," *Werkausgabe*, VI, 175–80.

35. "Der Weg Hermann Hesses," originally published in *Freie Presse* (Vienna, February 9, 1923), reprinted in *Materialien zu Hermann Hesses Siddhartha*, ed. Volker Michels (Frankfurt: Suhrkamp Verlag, 1974), pp. 26–32.

36. Boulby, *Mind and Art of Hermann Hesse*, pp. 39–49.

Chapter 4: The Idyll Unraveled

1. May 6, 1906. *Gesammelte Briefe*, I, 498–501. Fritz Böttger, a Marxist biographer-critic from East Germany, made the point succinctly: "For six years, until December 1912, Hesse was an official collaborator of the magazine. . . . Yet he never wrote political articles or commentaries like Ludwig Thoma, Hermann Bahr [etc.] . . . nor did he have to be responsible for them. And he never got into conflict with the government or with public opinion." *Hermann Hesse: Leben, Werk, Zeit* (Berlin: Verlag der Nation, 1974), pp. 119–20.

2. A book on the subject by Hermann Müller, *Der Dichter und Sein Guru: Hermann Hesse—Gusto Gräser* (Schelkingen: Neuland Verlag, 1977) has proved unobtainable. The above information is partly derived from promotional excerpts and includes some oral confirmation by Hesse's son, Heiner, who edits the biographical material. In a history of the Monte Verità Commune, in which both Gustav and his brother Karl Gräser are prominently discussed, Hesse's presence in 1906 is briefly mentioned. "Hermann Hesse, who also enjoyed a good drop of the grape in quantity, drew yet another conclusion. . . . In 1906 he gave himself into the care of the Sanatorium Monte Verità [which Gräser distinguished sharply from the Commune]; conforming to its natural life style, he submitted to an antialcoholic cure which restored his undermined health." Robert Landmann, *Monte Verita. Ascona. Die Geschichte eines Berges*, 3rd ed. (Ascona: Pascaldi Verlag, 1934), p. 99.

3. In addition to references in unpublished letters to his father, the house is described in "Beim Einzug in ein Neues Haus," *Werkausgabe*, X, 143–47; "On Moving into a New House," *Autobiographical Writings*, pp. 237–40.

4. See Chapter 3, Note 33.

5. E.g., *Werkausgabe*, X, 142–43; *Autobiographical Writings*, pp. 235–36.

6. "In den Felsen: Notizen Eines Naturmenschens," reprinted in *Materialien zu Hermann Hesses Siddhartha*, II, 339–47.

7. To Josef Victor Widmann, July 31, 1907, *Gesammelte Briefe*, I, 140.

8. "Wenn es Abend Wird" [When Evening Comes], *Werkausgabe*, VI, 180–86 (dated 1904).

9. "Kurgast" [A Guest at the Spa]; open letter, later printed in *Jugend* (Munich, 1912), reproduced in *Gesammelte Briefe*, I, 154–58.

10. November 16, 1909, *Gesammelte Briefe*, I, 162.

11. November 17, 1910, ibid., pp. 183–84.

12. Ibid., p. 186.

13. Ibid., pp. 189–90.

14. December 1910, ibid., p. 190.

15. April 26 and 28, 1911, ibid., p. 193.

16. Ibid., p. 194.

17. Ibid., pp. 194–95.

18. To the family, reprinted in *Gesammelte Briefe*, I, 200.

19. Cited by Ball, *Hermann Hesse*, p. 123.

20. "Besuch aus Indien" [Visit from India] (1922), *Materialien zu Hermann Hesses Siddhartha*, I, 317–18.

21. "Erinnerung an Indien," 1916, *Werkausgabe*, VI, 289; "Remembrance of India," *Autobiographical Writings*, pp. 63–64.

22. *Aus Indien* (Berlin: S. Fischer, 1913), pp. 17–19. All quotations of this material are from this collection, although they are also contained in the various editions of Hesse's collected works. They are cited from this original edition because it most fully preserves the unity of these diverse items.

23. "Augenlust" [Feast for Eyes], *Aus Indien*, pp. 31–32.

24. "Der Hanswurst" [The Clown], ibid., pp. 33–34.

25. "Singapur-Traum" [Singapore Dream], ibid., pp. 40–49.

26. "Spaziergang in Kandy" [Stroll in Kandy], ibid., pp. 98–100.

27. "Tagebuchblatt von Kandy" [Diary Page from Kandy], ibid., pp. 102–07.

28. "Pedrotallagalla," ibid., p. 111; *Autobiographical Writings*, p. 71.

29. "Rückreise" [The Voyage Home], *Aus Indien*, p. 118.

30. *Werkausgabe*, VI, 293; *Autobiographical Writings*, p. 68.

31. Peter de Mendelssohn, *S. Fischer und Sein Verlag* (Frankfurt: S. Fischer, 1970), p. 577ff. These passages were reprinted in *Gesammelte Briefe*, I, 509–11.

32. Ibid., pp. 203–04.

Chapter 5: From Crisis to War

1. *Werkausgabe*, X, 148–50; *Autobiographical Writings*, pp. 241–44.

2. "Alte Musik," *Werkausgabe*, X, 15–20; "Old Music," *My Belief*, tr. Denver Lindley, ed. T. Ziolkowski (New York: Farrar, Straus & Giroux, 1974), pp. 177–181.

3. *Gesammelte Briefe*, I, 218–19.

4. Ibid., pp. 231–32.

5. "Wie sind die Tage schwer," *Musik des Einsamen* (Heilbronn: Eugen Salzer, 1915), p. 11.

6. March 1914, *Gesammelte Briefe*, I, 240–42.

7. March 16, 1914, ibid., pp. 242–43.

8. *Werkausgabe*, X, 397; *Autobiographical Writings*, p. 49.

9. *Werkausgabe*, X, 397–98; *Autobiographical Writings*, pp. 49–50.

10. *Krieg und Frieden: Betrachtungen zu Krieg und Politik seit dem Jahr 1914* (Zurich: Fretz & Wasmuth, 1946), pp. 17–26; *If the War Goes On* (New York: Farrar, Straus & Giroux, 1973), pp. 9–14. Translation mine.

11. *Werkausgabe*, VI, 399; *Autobiographical Writings*, p. 50. Hesse mentions the date 1915, telescoping this event in late 1914 with a later event which occurred during the following year.

12. September 9, 1914, *Gesammelte Briefe*, I, 244–47.

13. *Werkausgabe*, VI, 399; *Autobiographical Writings*, p. 51.

14. December 4, 1914, *Gesammelte Briefe*, I, 252–54.

15. To Alfred Schlenker, November 10, 1914, ibid., pp. 248–50.

16. December 26, 1914, ibid., pp. 255–57.

17. January 4, 1915, ibid., pp. 257–58.

18. *Werkausgabe*, VI, 400; *Autobiographical Writings*, p. 51.

19. *Hermann Hesse–Romain Rolland: Briefe* (Zurich: Fretz & Wasmuth, 1954), p. 9.

20. "Geleitwort," *Krieg und Frieden*, pp. 9–11; Foreword, *If the War Goes On*, pp. 3–7. Translation mine.

21. *Hesse–Rolland*, pp. 11–12. [Italics mine.]

22. July 1, 1915, *Gesammelte Briefe*, I, 258–59.

23. Romain Rolland, *Au dessus de la mêlée* (Paris: Librairie Ollendorff, 1915), p. 128.

24. *Hesse–Rolland*, p. 17.

25. August 10, 1915, ibid., p. 18.

26. August 24, 1915, ibid., p. 23.

27. Ibid., p. 22.

28. Unpublished postcard. See also one month later, October 10, 1915, *Gesammelte Briefe*, I, 287–88.

29. The material concerning the so-called Cologne calumny is collected in the newspaper and periodical section of the Hesse Archives in Marbach and has been reprinted in *Gesammelte Briefe*, I, 532–39. In 1972 this material was used extensively in a broadcast over the West German Radio's Third Program by Volker Michels, an editor of Hesse's biographical estate, and Hans Daiber, entitled "The Distanced German: Hermann Hesse and the Fatherland." See also letter to Conrad Haussmann, *Gesammelte Briefe*, I, 290.

30. Ibid., p. 532.

31. Ibid., pp. 537–38.

32. Ibid., pp. 539–45.

33. "In Eigener Sache" [In My Own Defense], published in *Neue Zürcher Zeitung*, November 2, 1915. *Gesammelte Briefe*, I, 304–06.

34. Reprinted in ibid., pp. 303–04, as a telegram, though the actual document was a postcard.

35. November 3, 1915. Reprinted from the literary estate in *Gesammelte Briefe*, I, 545.

36. Ibid., pp. 308–09, 548–54. This material was also used in the West German Radio broadcast noted above, as it was designed to underscore the fact that on the one hand Hesse did not betray Germany and undermine the suffering of German soldiers in the field, yet, on the other hand, also remained an opponent of the war, as his followers saw him.

37. December 25, 1915, ibid., p. 316.

38. *Hesse–Rolland*, pp. 24–25.

39. *Gesammelte Briefe*, I, 318–19.

40. The following account is adapted from Hesse's own narrative of his father's death and funeral, "Zum Gedächtnis," *Werkausgabe*, X, 121–33.

41. Ibid., p. 123.

42. Ibid., pp. 129–30.

43. Ibid., pp. 132–33.

44. See *Gesammelte Briefe*, I, 321.

45. See letter to Helene Welti from Lucerne, May 18, 1916, and letters to Walter Schädelin, Lucerne, May 18 and 21, 1916, ibid., pp. 322–25.

46. *Briefe*, pp. 10–11.

47. Ball, *Hermann Hesse*, pp. 142–45.

48. Cf. above letter to Schädelin, May 18, 1916, *Gesammelte Briefe*, I, 323.

49. *Hesse–Rolland*, p. 28.

50. In an unpublished letter to his friend Emil Molt, the owner of the Waldorf-Astoria Cigarette Company in Zurich, Hesse wrote on May 29, 1916: "I take in at most ¼ to ⅓ of my regular needs and I won't resume writing for money as a matter of principle. At the moment I still have some savings left over from better days, but they are tied up in German papers inside Germany and by eating into those I'll lose almost a third in the transaction."

51. See Ralph Freedman, *The Lyrical Novel* (Princeton, N.J.: Princeton University Press, 1963), pp. 70–72.

52. A classic on the role of *Demian* as a daemon is Oskar Seidlin's essay, "Hermann Hesse: The Exorcism of the Demon," *Hesse: A Collection of Critical Essays* (Englewood Cliffs, N.J.: Prentice-Hall, 1973), pp. 51–75 (originally published in *Symposium*, 1950). Theodore Ziolkowski analyzed *Demian* as a pilgrimage toward a Grail. Originally published in the *Germanic Review* (1973), it was reprinted in ibid., pp. 134–52. Cf. also Ziolkowski's earlier analysis of the novel in *The Novels of Hermann Hesse* (Princeton, N.J.: Princeton University Press, 1965).

53. See Chapter 4, Note 2, p. 44ff.

54. The entire correspondence, including the article that "blew" the cover, has been reprinted in *Gesammelte Briefe*, I, 564–70.

55. "Introduction," *Demian* (New York: Bantam, 1970), p. ix.

56. *Werkausgabe*, XI, 35–36.

57. "Erinnerung an Hans," *Werkausgabe*, X, 227–29.

58. "Beim Einzug in ein Neues Haus," *Werkausgabe*, X, 151f; "On Moving into a New House," *Autobiographical Writings*, pp. 243–44.

59. *Werkausgabe*, XI, 33.

60. *Werkausgabe*, X, 151–52; *Autobiographical Writings*, p. 244.

Chapter 6: The Third New Life—
Vagabond of the Imagination

1. See, among others, Hesse's brief account in "On Moving into a New House," *Werkausgabe*, X, 150–53; *Autobiographical Writings*, pp. 244–45. Also compare the extensive letter to Walter Schädelin of August 16, 1919, reprinted in *Gesammelte Briefe*, I, 411–13.

2. *Werkausgabe*, V, 204; *Klingsor's Last Summer*, tr. Richard Winston and Clara Winston (New York: Farrar, Straus & Giroux, 1970), p. 45.

3. *Werkausgabe*, VI, 134–36; *Wandering*, tr. James Wright (New York: Farrar, Straus & Giroux, 1972), pp. 5–7.

4. *Werkausgabe*, V, 210; *Klingsor's Last Summer*, p. 51.

5. *Werkausgabe*, V, 209; *Klingsor's Last Summer*, p. 51.

6. "Dorf," in *Wanderung, Werkausgabe*, VI, 139–40; "Small Town," *Wandering*, pp. 19–26.

7. *Werkausgabe*, X, 153–54; *Autobiographical Writings*, pp. 245–47.

8. *Werkausgabe*, V, 294; *Klingsor's Last Summer*, pp. 149–50.

9. *Werkausgabe*, VI, 303.

10. *Werkausgabe*, X, 152–53; *Autobiographical Writings*, pp. 244–45.

11. See also letter to Georg Reinhart, August 31, 1919, in which Hesse wrote of the "blessing" of his new life in terms of concentration and creative energy, a height unreachable in times of well being. *Gesammelte Briefe*, I, 417.

12. "Künstler und Psychoanalyse," *Werkausgabe*, X, 47–53; "Artists and Psychoanalysis," *My Belief: Essays on Life and Art*, ed. Theodore Ziolkowski, tr. David Lindley (New York: Farrar, Straus & Giroux, 1974), pp. 46–51.

13. *Werkausgabe*, X, 51; *My Belief*, pp. 49–50. Translation mine.

14. *Werkausgabe*, V, 305; *Klingsor's Last Summer*, p. 162.

15. See, for example, the intimate letters to Finckh during the summer of 1919 and early in 1920 reprinted in *Gesammelte Briefe*, I, 413, 436, 439.

16. *Werkausgabe*, V, 315ff; *Klingsor's Last Summer*, p. 174ff.

17. *Werkausgabe*, V, 316–17; *Klingsor's Last Summer*, pp. 174–75. The first letters to Ruth Wenger date from August 1919.

18. *Briefe*, pp. 13–15.

19. *Werkausgabe*, VI, 405; *Autobiographical Writings*, p. 56.

20. *Werkausgabe*, VI, 405; *Autobiographical Writings*, p. 56. Translation partially mine.

21. *Werkausgabe*, VI, 300–303.

22. Ibid.

23. *Briefe*, p. 15.

24. The following discussions of *Siddhartha* have appeared, in part, in a previously published essay. Ralph Freedman, "Peripetie und Vision: Bemerkungen zur Entstehungsgeschichte des *Siddhartha*," tr. Ursula Michels-Wenz, *Materialien zu "Siddhartha,"* II, 206–16.

25. Ball, *Hermann Hesse*, pp. 147–49.

26. *Werkausgabe*, VI, 403–04; *Autobiographical Writings*, p. 55.

27. Ball associated the first part with the ambience of *Märchen* [Fairy Tales] of 1916. Ball, *Hermann Hesse*, p. 147.

28. *Materialien zu "Siddhartha,"* II, 339–47.

29. "Brief aus dem Süden" [Letter from the South], *Werkausgabe*, X, 303–07.

30. Cited in Zeller, *Hermann Hesse*, p. 94; Zeller, *Portrait of Hesse*, p. 102. Hugo Ball recognized that the interference, particularly of *Klingsor*, delayed and reshaped the composition of *Siddhartha*, a recognition that remains correct even though Ball was in error about the exact sequence in which these books were composed. Ball, *Hermann Hesse*, p. 151.

31. *Aus einem Tagebuch des Jahres 1920* (Zurich: Verlag der Arche, 1960), pp. 9–10.

32. Hugo Ball, *Die Flucht aus der Zeit* (Berlin: S. Fischer Verlag, 1923) [Edition used published in Lucerne by J. Stockert, 1946]; Emmy Ball-Hennings, *Hugo Ball. Sein Leben in Briefen und Gedichten* (Berlin: S. Fischer Verlag, 1930); Emmy Ball-Hennings, *Briefe an Hermann Hesse*, ed. Annemarie Schütt-Hennings (Frankfurt: Suhrkamp Verlag, 1956).

33. Emmy Ball-Hennings summarized and quoted from Hugo Ball's speech to the Hamburg local of the Peace Society. See her foreword to Ball, *Die Flucht aus der Zeit*, p. xv.

34. Ball, *Die Flucht aus der Zeit*, pp. 276–77. Cited also by Zeller, *Hermann Hesse*, p. 92; Zeller, *Portrait of Hesse*, p. 101.

35. "Nachruf auf Hugo Ball," December 16, 1927; *Werkausgabe*, XII, 398–408. Hesse expressed himself especially on their reactions to the war which, he felt, were similar. See his foreword in Ball-Hennings, *Hugo Ball*, p. 17.

36. *Tagebuch 1920*, pp. 33–34.

37. *C.G. Jung Letters*, ed. Gerhard Adler and Aniela Jaffé (Princeton, N.J.: Princeton University Press, 1973), pp. 573–74.

38. Cf. "Zu 'Zarathustras Wiederkehr' " [On "Zarathustra's Return"], *Eigensinn: Autobiographische Schriften* (Frankfurt: Suhrkamp Verlag, 1972), pp. 114–17. See also "Hassbriefe" [Hate Letters], ibid., pp. 149–56. (In reading the diaries of 1920 and 1921, one finds it remarkable how closely political and literary matters are intertwined. Clearly, this renewed rejection of his politics as a result of "Zarathustra's Return" was a factor in Hesse's block.)

39. "*Die Brüder Karamasow* oder der Untergang Europas," *Werkausgabe*, XII, 320–37; "*The Brothers Karamazov*, or the Decline of Europe," *My Belief*, pp. 70–85.

40. See letters to Lisa Wenger, May 2, 1921, and to Hans Reinhart during the same month. *Materialien zu "Siddhartha,"* I, 122–28, 130.

41. Reprinted in ibid., pp. 130–31.

42. *Jung Letters*, pp. 37–38.

43. "Vorrede eines Dichters zu seinen ausgawählten Werken," 1921, *Werkausgabe*, XI, 7–12; "A Poet's Preface to his Selected Works," *My Belief*, pp. 108–12.

44. A letter to his future father-in-law, Theo Wenger, might serve as an example. Dated June 1921, Hesse's letter suggested that he had known Ruth for almost two years, loved her as best as he could, but that he had no idea what would become of the relationship in the future. In not moving in the direction of marriage, Hesse realized that he violated some codes of bourgeois morality, but he followed a different and no less sacred morality—the voice within himself. *Materalien zu "Siddhartha,"* I, 132–33.

45. Cf. the extensive correspondence with Lisa Wenger reprinted in *Materialien zu "Siddhartha,"* I. For example, in a long letter dated May 2, 1921, he explained both his literary and his personal situation in great detail. Ibid., pp. 122–28 et passim.

46. Lecture in St. Gallen, January 13, 1922, reprinted in *Materialien zu "Siddhartha,"* I, 145–48. See also Hesse's statement in his diary of 1920 in which he explores precisely the relationship between these two Indias that has escaped him before. *Tagebuch 1920*, p. 26.

47. See, for example, the St. Gallen lecture noted above, reprinted in *Materialien zu "Siddhartha,"* I, 145–48. For the concept of *Siddhartha* as a "landscape of the soul," see Ziolkowski, *The Novels of Hermann Hesse*, pp. 146–77.

48. Furthermore, Volker Michels's introduction to the second volume of the *Materialien zu "Siddhartha,"* summarizing the history of *Siddhartha*, emphasizes a shift toward more rigorous Chinese thought in the second half of the novel. *Materialien zu "Siddhartha,"* II, 7–26. See also Adrian Hsia, *Hermann Hesse und China* (Frankfurt: Suhrkamp Verlag, 1974), pp. 240–48.

49. *Werkausgabe*, V, 383–84; *Siddhartha*, tr. Hilda Rosner (New York: New Directions, 1951), p. 31.

50. Reprinted in *Materialien zu "Siddhartha,"* I, 156.

51. Cf. above, note 47.

52. See *Hesse-Rolland*, pp. 38–41, for their exchange concerning the invitation to speak.

53. Hesse to Rolland, August 25, 1922, ibid., pp. 42–43.

Chapter 7: The Ailing Traveler

1. *Werkausgabe*, VII, 10–11; "A Guest at the Spa," *Autobiographical Writings*, pp. 74–75.

2. Mark Boulby has aptly described the ritualistic aspects of the book. *Hermann Hesse: Mind and Art*, p. 166. Boulby quotes Hesse: "On the way to penance, to punishment, to the sanctity of work, through baths and washing, physicians (and) Brahman magic, I tried to achieve what can only be achieved by way of Grace." *Werkausgabe*, VII, 101–02; *Autobiographical Writings*, p. 158.

3. *Werkausgabe*, VII, 89–91; *Autobiographical Writings*, pp. 146–49. Cf. Ralph Freedman, "*Person* and *Persona*," *Hesse: Critical Essays*, pp. 156–57.

4. *Werkausgabe*, VII, 113; *Autobiographical Writings*, p. 169.

5. *Hesse–Rolland*, p. 61.

6. Ibid., pp. 64–65.

7. Partly reprinted in *Materialien zu Hermann Hesses "Der Steppenwolf,"* p. 41.

8. *Hesse–Rolland*, p. 68.

9. Ibid., p. 72.

10. Cf. *Gedichte*, II, 500.

11. See the sketch based on that visit in *Bilderbuch*, *Werkausgabe*, VI, 325–33.

12. To Emmy Ball-Hennings, January 25, 1925, reprinted, in part, in *Materialien zum "Steppenwolf,"* p. 41.

13. To Emmy and Hugo Ball, April, 1, 1925, partly reprinted in *Materialien zum "Steppenwolf,"* p. 43.

14. Ibid., pp. 48–49. See also Hesse's letter to Alice Leuthold, June 7, 1925, ibid., pp. 47–48.

15. Adapted from Hesse's account of Zurich in his *Journey to Nuremberg*, *Werk-ausgabe*, VII, 138ff; *Autobiographical Writings*, p. 188ff.

16. *Werkausgabe*, VII, 127; *Autobiographical Writings*, p. 179.

17. *Werkausgabe*, VII, 141; *Autobiographical Writings*, p. 192.

18. *Werkausgabe*, VII, 143–45; *Autobiographical Writings*, pp. 192–94.

19. *Werkausgabe*, VII, 162; *Autobiographical Writings*, pp. 211–12.

20. *Werkausgabe*, VII, 156; *Autobiographical Writings*, p. 206.

21. *Werkausgabe*, VII, 156–57; *Autobiographical Writings*, p. 206.

22. *Werkausgabe*, VII, 164; *Autobiographical Writings*, pp. 213–14.

23. *Werkausgabe*, VII, 176–77; *Autobiographical Writings*, pp. 224–25.

24. *Werkausgabe*, VII, 177; *Autobiographical Writings*, p. 225.

Chapter **8**: Symbolic City—
The Self's Inferno

1. To Adis, December 25, 1925, reprinted in *Materialien zum "Steppenwolf,"* p. 55.

2. To Hugo and Emmy Ball, February 17, 1926, partly reprinted in *Materialien zum "Steppenwolf,"* p. 63.

3. *Hesse-Rolland*, pp. 78–81.

4. *Krisis: Ein Stück Tagebuch* (Berlin: S. Fischer Verlag, 1928), p. 27; *Crisis: Pages from a Diary*, tr. Ralph Manheim (New York: Farrar, Straus & Giroux, 1975), p. 33.

5. *Krisis*, p. 17; *Crisis*, p. 17.

6. *Krisis* includes a poem entitled "Evening with Dr. Ling," which contains the following lines: "So probably the wisest thing/ That I can do is talk with Dr. Ling—/ One of those long, nocturnal sessions/ Devoted to our respective depressions. . . ." *Krisis*, p. 51; *Crisis*, p. 69.

7. See Freedman, *The Lyrical Novel*, pp. 72–93, for an analysis of *Steppenwolf*.

8. Ibid., pp. 76–77.

9. *Krisis*, pp. 18–19; *Crisis*, p. 19.

10. *Werkausgabe*, VII, 232; *Steppenwolf* (New York: Rinehart, 1957), pp. 49–50. Part of the subsequent discussion was previously published. Freedman, *"Person and Persona," Hesse: Critical Essays*, pp. 165ff.

11. *Werkausgabe*, VII, 231; *Steppenwolf*, pp. 48–49.

12. "Mit Hermann Hesse am Künstlermaskenball" [With Hermann Hesse at the Masked Ball for Artists], *Der Bildhauer Hermann Hubacher* (Zurich, 1965); *Materialien zum "Steppenwolf,"* pp. 65–66.

13. *Werkausgabe*, VII, 459–60; *Steppenwolf*, pp. 168–69.

14. *Werkausgabe*, VII, 337; *Steppenwolf*, pp. 146–47.

15. Hubacher, *Materialien zum "Steppenwolf,"* p. 66.

16. To Hermann Hubacher, March 17, 1926, reprinted in *Materialien zum "Steppenwolf,"* p. 65.

17. *Werkausgabe*, VII, 359; *Steppenwolf*, p. 168.

18. *Krisis*, p. 76; *Crisis*, p. 109.

19. A picture postcard celebrating the masked ball and featuring Julia Laubl-Honneger is reprinted in *Materialien zum "Steppenwolf,"* p. 73. Cf. Hesse's note to her, ibid., pp. 76–77. See Joseph Mileck, *Hermann Hesse: Life and Art*, pp. 179–180. For the poem, see *Krisis*, p. 69; *Crisis*, p. 99.

20. *Werkausgabe*, X, 129–30.

21. Letter to Frau M.W., Zurich, November 13, 1930, *Briefe*, pp. 36–37. Cited also by Ziolkowski, *The Novels of Hermann Hesse*, p. 192.

22. Reprinted in *Materialien zum "Steppenwolf,"* pp. 97–98.

23. Ibid.

24. *Werkausgabe,* VII, 203; *Steppenwolf,* p. 21.

25. Reprinted, in part, in *Materialien zum "Steppenwolf,"* p. 105.

26. Reprinted in ibid., p. 106.

27. From Thomas Mann, January 3, 1928, *Hermann Hesse–Thomas Mann: Briefwechsel,* ed. Anni Carlsson (Frankfurt: Suhrkamp & Fischer, 1968), p. 9.

28. *Krisis,* p. 81; *Crisis,* p. 119.

29. Reprinted in *Materialien zum "Steppenwolf,"* pp. 109–10.

30. March 7, 1927, ibid., pp. 263–64.

31. March 9, 1927, *Briefe,* pp. 16–17. See also Thomas Mann's later unsuccessful plea that Hesse rejoin in the name of a "free culture," September 27, 1931, *Hesse–Mann,* pp. 13–16.

32. Reprinted, in part, in *Materialien zum "Steppenwolf,"* pp. 119–20.

33. Ibid.

34. Ball, *Hermann Hesse,* pp. 206–14.

35. Ball-Hennings, *Briefe an Hesse,* p. 79.

36. Ibid., pp. 83–85.

Chapter **9:** The Third New Life— From Sense to Spirit

1. *Narcissus and Goldmund,* with its pair of intimate friends and its conflict of creative sensuality and intellect, elicited the following response from Hesse to an inquiry by Frau Dr. Engel of Stuttgart in March 1931: "First of all, as far as the friendships Goldmund-Narcissus, Veraguth-Burkhardt, Hesse-Knulp, etc., are concerned, to assume that these friendships are completely free of eroticism just because they are between men, is an error. I am sexually 'normal' and have never had physically erotic relations with men, but to assume for that reason that friendships are totally noneconotic would be a mistake. In the case of Narcissus this is particularly clear. Goldmund represents to Narcissus not only the friend and not only art; he represents for Narcissus also love, the warmth of the senses, the desired and forbidden." *Briefe,* p. 49.

2. In a letter written in 1932—two years after the appearance of *Narcissus and Goldmund*—Hesse reported that he was accused of "wallowing in filth" in both novels. "It was the same with Goldmund: dozens of people wrote indignantly [about obscenity]. A young adherent of Hitler from Swabia wrote that [the book] was merely an expression of the lewd lustfulness of an aging man and that he hoped I would soon kick the bucket." To H. Zwissler, ca. end of May 1932, *Materialien zum "Steppenwolf,"* p. 146.

3. To Adis, end of June 1932, partially reprinted in ibid., p. 147.

4. To Erwin Ackerknecht, November 1930, reprinted in ibid., pp. 142–43.

5. To a reader, July 1930, *Briefe,* pp. 35–36; to "Fräulein E.K., Liebstadt," ibid., pp. 74–75; and many others. A more searching discussion is found in a letter to "P.A. Riebe, Charlottenburg" in which Hesse draws the problematics of Steppenwolf and contrasts them with the less challenging reading of Goldmund. Ibid., pp. 70–71.

6. Ibid. In the letter to Riebe, Hesse writes: "The task of Goldmund is infinitely easier [than that of Steppenwolf] and its reading makes no high demands on the reader's quality. . . . The German reads it, finds it nice, and continues to sabotage his own state. . . ." See also letter to "Frau M.W.," November 13, 1930, from Zurich, ibid., p. 36.

7. *Werkausgabe,* VIII, 336; *Journey to the East,* tr. Hilda Rosner (New York: Farrar, Straus & Giroux, 1963), p. 24.

8. In a later letter to Adis, however, Hesse confessed that he may have burdened Ninon too much during that year.

9. See "Beim Einzug in ein neues Haus," *Werkausgabe*, X, 134–35; "On Moving into a New House," *Autobiographical Writings*, pp. 246–47.

10. In his selected letters Hesse in cluded a strong political letter written to a correspondent ("Frau E.L.") in Stuttgart on the occasion of the German presidential elections of 1932 in which he counseled a rejection of parties and politics and in effect a nonpolitical stance as the most honest position. *Briefe*, pp. 85–86.

11. For a literary discussion of *Bund* novels, see Ziolkowski, *The Novels of Hermann Hesse*, pp. 255–61.

Chapter 10: Citadel Against History

1. Reprinted in *Materialien zu Hermann Hesses "Das Glasperlenspiel,"* (Frankfurt: Suhrkamp Verlag, 1973) I, 60–62.

2. Ibid.

3. To Mann, July 1933, and to Hesse, July 31, 1933, *Hesse–Mann*, pp. 32–35. Hesse concludes with the observation that all letters from the Reich were now being written at a high fever pitch, on the one hand praising the new unity and even freedom, while, on the other hand, cursing Catholic or Socialist swine: a mood for war and pogroms, full of pleasure and drunkenness, as in 1914, with the same possibility of blood and evil without the earlier "naïveté." Hesse added, however, that he was nonetheless touched by "the blue-eyed enthusiasm and readiness for sacrifice which one senses among so many." Mann was clearer on the last point. He wrote in reply that news from Germany filled him with horror, contempt, and disgust. "That 'blue-eyed enthusiasm' you are writing about can no longer touch me either. A dreadful civil war appears to me inevitable."

4. July 1933, reprinted in *Materialien zum "Glasperlenspiel,"* I, 64–74.

5. Ibid., p. 70.

6. To Josef Englert, September 29, 1933, *Briefe*, pp. 109–10.

7. To Thomas Mann (end of 1933). Following an appreciation of Mann's *Stories of Jaacob*, Hesse referred to his own reading and blocked plans, mentioning especially his work in "Pietist biographies of the 18th century." *Hesse–Mann*, pp. 38–40. In a letter to a correspondent in January 1934, Hesse mentioned specifically his reading in Oetinger and Bengel. *Materialien zum "Glasperlenspiel,"* I, 78–79.

8. See Freedman, *The Lyrical Novel*, pp. 94–115.

9. Mann, too, commented on Wiegand, who had contributed essays on both Mann and Hesse to the *Neue Rundschau*. "The news of Wiegand's death hit me very hard. Grief and worry have done quick work. A victim, one of many. And a victim for what? I'll also send a note to the widow." March 11, 1934, *Hesse–Mann*, p. 44.

10. *Werkausgabe*, XII, 432; *My Belief*, pp. 359–60.

11. To Hesse, September 18, 1934, *Jung Letters*, p. 171.

12. To Jung, September 1934, *Briefe*, pp. 126–28.

13. To Hesse, October 1, 1934, *Jung Letters*, pp. 173–74.

14. *Werkausgabe*, XII, pp. 302–04.

15. *Materialien zum "Glasperlenspiel,"* p. 101. Cf. "Zum Antisemitismus," *Werkausgabe*, I, 497ff.

16. To Verlag Philipp Reclam, Jr., December 13, 1934, *Briefe*, pp. 132–34.

17. September 29, 1933, reprinted in *Briefe*, pp. 108–10.

18. As in the case of the Cologne calumny of 1915, newspaper and periodical material concerning these episodes is available in the archives of the Schiller

Nationalmuseum in Marbach. The director of the museum, Professor Bernhard Zeller, has collected Hesse's reviews and reports during his service to the magazine and added an appendix containing the unpublished and published material surrounding the ensuing scandal. Hermann Hesse, *Neue Deutsche Bücher: Literaturberichte für "Bonniers Litterära Magasin" 1935–36*, ed. Bernhard Zeller (Marbach: Schiller Nationalmuseum, 1965). [Hereafter referred to as *Bonniers*.] Additional material has been reprinted in *Materialien zum "Glasperlenspiel,"* I.

19. *Bonniers*, pp. 148–49.

20. Ibid., pp. 150–51. Hesse's answer was reprinted (and glossed) in the January 1936 number of *Neue Literatur*. See also *Materialien zum "Glasperlenspiel,"* pp. 136–38. The Swedish editor also wrote a letter on December 12, and Hesse complained to the Swiss Writers Union. Ibid., pp. 149, 152.

21. *Bonniers*, pp. 151–52; *Materialien zum "Glasperlspiel,"* I, 153–59, for the complete text, including the "Hunnius" biography.

22. As late as 1937, German officialdom suggested that they did not fully agree with Vespers's attitude. Zeller quotes the following "Confidential Information" from the Reich Ministry for Propaganda: "Contrary to different reports, I state unequivocally that in agreement with the Reich Minister for Propaganda [Goebbels]. . . . I represent the following view for special reasons, *i.e.*, that the writer Hermann Hesse must not be exposed to attacks of any kind in the future and that nothing should prevent the dissemination of his works in the Reich." *Bonniers*, p. 153.

23. *Materialien zum "Glasperlenspiel,"* I, 140n.

24. *Bonniers*, pp. 153–54.

25. January 1936. *Materialien zum "Glasperlenspiel,"* I, 139–40. Hesse sent Mann a copy of the accusations. Mann responded philosophically, saying that "old Bernhard" is a fool; Schwarzschild more gifted but therefore also more unscrupulous and dangerous. *Hesse–Mann*, pp. 60–61.

26. The announcement of the magazine notifying its readers of Hesse's withdrawal includes Hesse's own statement, whose core sentences read: "As may have been expected, my neutral and factual reports [have had the result that] I have been attacked from two sides: the Reich-Germans accuse me because I consider Jews and emigrants part of the human race . . . the emigrants, in turn, accuse me of being in league with the National Socialists. It is an old story that a neutral third gets thrashed by both sides." *Bonneirs*, p. 157.

27. *Neue Zürcher Zeitung*, January 18, 1936. A public protest by Mann, Hesse, and Annette Kolb and a special statement by Hesse alone in the same newspaper of January 26, 1936. *Materialien zum "Glasperlenspiel,"* I, 138–39, 143.

28. Thomas Mann, who, by contrast, identified himself with the emigrant culture (which included many important writers who were not Jewish) wrote a long and important open letter to Korrodi declaring his stand in strong terms. Hesse regretted that Mann had taken that step, but Mann assured him in a subsequent letter that he had to speak out. See *Hesse–Mann*, pp. 61–65. Eventually, this letter was used by the German government as part of the evidence in support of Mann's expatriation.

29. To Klaus Kläber, 1936, *Materialien zum "Glasperlenspiel,"* I, 145.

30. To Eduard Korrodi, February 12, 1936, ibid., pp. 146–49.

31. This statement by E. Helmer, which Hesse included in a letter to H. C. Bodmer, was also reprinted in *Materialien zum "Glasperlenspiel,"* I, 162. It was written from Cape Town on February 25, 1936, and Hesse commented that the man had obviously read the calumnies in the German press.

32. *Werkausgabe*, X, 236–49.

33. In a letter dated April 25, 1936, Bermann stressed Suhrkamp's sensitive handling of the difficult situation. *Materialien zum "Glasperlenspiel,"* I, 159–60.

412 Notes

34. The complicated relationship between the subsequent Suhrkamp and the continuing S. Fischer Verlag—as well as the legal struggles and arrangements between Gottfried Bermann and Peter Suhrkamp— are contained in an appendix to the Hesse–Suhrkamp correspondence. *Briefwechsel Hermann Hesse–Peter Suhrkamp 1945–1969,* ed. Siegfried Unseld (Frankfurt: Suhrkamp Verlag, 1969), pp. 444–53.

35. Letters to Hesse, February 16 and March 7, 1936, *Hesse–Mann,* pp. 64–67.

36. See, for example, letter to Fritz Gundert, April 4, 1937, *Materialien zum "Glasperlenspiel,"* I, 179. Hesse's problematic decision is illustrated by an appeal from Thomas Mann for collaboration on a new journel for emigrant culture and politics. To Hesse, February 23, 1937, *Hesse–Mann,* pp. 72–73. Hesse's refusal, based on financial and family grounds, is contained in *Materialien zum "Glasperlenspiel,"* I, 175. This fact did not prevent Mann from writing a handsome appreciation in honor of Hesse's birthday that following July.

37. From Bermann, January 23, 1936, ibid., pp. 140–41.

38. Ibid., pp. 186–87.

39. Ibid.

40. *Hermann Hesse–R. J. Humm: Briefwechsel,* ed. Ursula Michels and Volker Michels (Frankfurt: Suhrkamp Verlag, 1977), p. 118.

41. To Humm, March 26, 1940; April 10, 1940; and April 13, 1940, ibid., pp. 90–91, 101, 103.

42. In addition to frequent references in unpublished letters to his family, Hesse wrote to Humm, among others, referring to a postcard received from Ninon's sister in Czernowicz the day the Russians moved in. It indicated that they had decided to stay on after the Russian takeover.

43. Cf. Suhrkamp's radio address in honor of Hesse's seventieth birthday, reprinted in *Materialien zum "Glasperlenspiel,"* I, 166–70.

44. *Hesse–Humm,* p. 177.

45. *Hesse–Suhrkamp,* p. 411.

46. *Hesse–Humm,* p. 233.

Chapter 11: The Final New Life

1. Humm wrote an extensive essay on Hesse's *Glass Bead Game,* which was published in *Die Weltwoche,* Zurich, on December 10, 1943. In the essay he showed in detail how that book represents a symbolic retreat from contemporary history: "It is the novel of Hesse and his introversion. It renders the picture of his extreme retreat which be began during the epoch of utmost danger. It is the novel of a German writer—of the last of the German classicists!—in an age of advancing National Socialism. To interpret it means to attempt an exegesis of his flight." *Hesse–Humm,* pp. 318–22. Hesse's rather stern reply is printed on p. 228.

2. "Nachbemerkung," *Politische Betrachtungen,* ed. Siegfried Unseld (Frankfurt: Suhrkamp Verlag, 1970), pp. 166–68.

3. A lengthy, moving description of Carlo's death as a medical soldier in the East was composed by Walter Haussmann in 1967, "Carlo Ferromonte in Komorowo," *Materialian zum "Glasperlenspiel,"* I, 262–68.

4. *Werkausgabe,* VIII, 407–08.

5. Ibid., p. 415.

6. Ibid., pp. 415–18.

7. "Geleitwort," *Krieg und Frieden,* pp. 15–16; "Foreword to the 1946 Edition," *If the War Goes On . . . ,* pp. 6–7.

8. See letter to Thomas Mann, November 5, 1945, enclosing a copy of Habe's letter (as he had enclosed it to Dr. Ackerknecht and many other friends). *Hesse–Mann*, pp. 108–09.

9. See Thomas Mann's immediate reply to Hesse, ibid., pp. 110–11.

10. Letter to Thomas Mann, December 15, 1945, *Briefe*, p. 219.

11. As a further sad result of this affair, the break with Humm became final. Hesse was angry because Humm had continued the supposedly official campaign against Habe at a time Hesse was interested in quieting the affair. See exchange of postcards, January 8 and 9, 1946, *Hesse–Humm*, pp. 256–57.

12. *Krieg und Frieden*, pp. 235–66; *If the War Goes On . . .* , pp. 148–67.

13. *Werkausgabe*, X, 102–03.

14. Ibid., pp. 103–07.

15. Letter to Dr. Siegfried Unseld from Ninon Hesse, *Hermann Hesse zum Gedächtnis* (Frankfurt: Suhrkamp Verlag, 1962).

16. The factual basis for this feeling is made clear in a letter from Thomas Mann: "*You* are that Germany to whom the Prize must go if it goes to Germany. . . . My opponent in this case, however, . . . is the German ambassador in Stockholm." September 5, 1934. Urgent letters to the Nobel Prize official Professor Fredrik Bööks of February and July 1934 are reprinted in the appendix. *Hesse–Mann*, pp. 49–51, 215.

17. The struggle concerned Bermann's claim to resumption of his directorship, which he raised late in 1949. As summarized in the appendix to the Hesse–Suhrkamp correspondence, Suhrkamp was forbidden to enter the premises in a legal proceeding. He then counter-sued Bermann, a suit that was adjudicated in Frankfurt in April 1950. In the meantime, Suhrkamp urged his authors to voice their support of him. In July of that year, he founded his own firm, which now exists side by side with S. Fischer. *Hesse-Suhrkamp*, pp. 443, 445–51.

18. Martin Buber, "Hermann Hesse im Dienst des Geistes," *Neue deutsche Hefte*, IV (1957–58), 387–93; "Hermann Hesse in the Service of the Spirit," *A Believing Humanism: My Testament, 1922–1965* (New York: Simon & Schuster, 1967), pp. 70–79. Reprinted, with a new translation by Theodore Ziolkowski, in *Hesse: Critical Essays*, pp. 25–33.

19. Cf. *Hermann Hesse-Karl Kerényi: Briefwechsel aus der Nähe*, ed. Magda Kerényi (Munich: Langen Müller, 1972). The Kerényis lived in Ascona from the time of their emigration from Hungary in 1944 until 1954.

20. Ninon Hesse, letter to Siegfried Unseld et passim. *Hermann Hesse: Zum Gedächtnis.*

21. Ibid.

Index

About the Author

Ralph Freedman was born in Hamburg, Germany, and emigrated to the United States in 1940. After serving in the United States Army during World War II, he graduated from the University of Washington in Seattle. He holds a master's degree in philosophy from Brown University and a doctorate in comparative literature from Yale. Widely recognized as an important Hesse scholar, he has taught at the University of Iowa and, since 1965, at Princeton. He has also been a visiting professor at a number of universities, including the University of Wisconsin, SUNY at Buffalo, and the University of Southern California.

Freedman has studied Hesse's manuscripts on deposit in Germany and Switzerland for several years and has traveled throughout the region of Hesse's homelands. In addition to numerous articles and reviews, he is the author of a novel, *Divided*, and a literary study, *The Lyrical Novel: Studies in Hermann Hesse, André Gide, and Virginia Woolf*. He has also edited and contributed to a volume of essays on Virginia Woolf, which will be published in 1979.